CIRCLING BIRDS

John Hurrell Crook

Title: Circling Birds

Author: John Hurrell Crook

Date: February 2019

Publisher: Redware Research Limited, 32 Welbeck Avenue, Hove BN3 4JL

Web: http://www.johnhurrellcrook.com/circlingbirds

Document: jhcwcf-57.docx

ISBN: 978-0-9556859-1-0

CONTENTS

INTRODUCTION – SIMON CHILD

John Crook's most prominent qualification for his Buddhist teaching was his Transmission in the Chan lineage in 1993, becoming the first Western Dharma Heir of Chan Master Sheng Yen. But he also had a serious interest in Tibetan Buddhism, receiving many teachings and practices and permission to teach some of these. He also explored and took from other forms of Buddhism, particularly Soto Zen following his training with Roshi Jiyu Kennett of Throssel Hole Abbey. His approach was not at all sectarian, and while emphasising the Chan approach he promoted what he called 'Open Buddhism', openness to all traditions. This extended to non-Buddhist traditions, with an interest in Christian mysticism, and also in Krishnamurti with whom he spent time in India in the 1950s.

John also drew from his academic background, bringing to his Buddhist teaching his psychological and anthropological understanding, and related explorations such as his involvement with the encounter group movement in the 1970s. Furthermore he travelled extensively. During the Korean war his army national service took him to Hong Kong where his connection with Chan was established. His research on weaver birds took him all over the world, and his studies on baboons took him to Africa. His later anthropological research took him repeatedly to the Himalayas, to Ladakh and Zanskar, and he also visited Tibet Bhutan and Nepal, taking every opportunity to encounter hermits and to visit monasteries, reinforcing a connection to Tibetan Buddhism which started when he first learned to meditate at Samye Ling, a Tibetan Buddhist monastery in Scotland.

He loved teaching the Dharma and did so in various ways. He regularly led intensive meditation retreats, most often at his own isolated cottage 'Maenllwyd' in mid-Wales but also other venues in UK and in Europe and USA. As well as teaching on retreats he also enjoyed speaking to other groups when opportunities arose. His talks were lively and energetic and included story-telling and poetic imagery interweaved with instruction in meditation and Buddhist theory. He valued and enjoyed individual instruction and dialogue, both in the format of the one-on-one Zen interview with the master and in general conversation.

Most relevant to this volume, he also liked to write and publish, expressing his teaching in a wide range of formats, styles and topics: transcribed Dharma talks; presentation of meditation methods and Buddhist teachings; commentaries on texts; reports of events, meetings and travels; poetry; social comment; book reviews; and more.

Other than his books the journal New Chan Forum, published approximately twice per year, was his primary vehicle for publishing his Buddhist writings. New Chan Forum was founded in 1990 by John with Hilary Richards and Jake Lyne of the Bristol Chan group. The early issues were quite thin pamphlets, but soon John began to provide more and more content and the issues became more substantial. He was not the only contributor, and each issue contained several articles of various types by others, but his was the dominant content for over twenty years.

I became involved in the publishing of New Chan Forum in 1997, which was also when we founded the Western Chan Fellowship to support and continue these teachings. Initially my role was primarily as picture editor but later I took over management of the process of publishing the roughly presented compilation of articles that John would draw together to create an issue. Often it would be the case that I would remind him, or he would comment to me, that it was time to compile another issue of New Chan Forum, but he wasn't sure he had enough submissions. Then, only four or five days later, he would send me a compiled issue, often including three or four long articles which he had written especially, each completely different in content and style.

To the casual reader some of these articles may appear to be pieces of general prose and not specifically 'Buddhist' in content. In these John was often presenting what he referred to as 'Chan attitude' - a response to the world around us informed by his understanding and practice of Chan Buddhism, and his concerns for such issues as social justice and the environment. He was also drawing on his rich and varied background to produce writings which would engage the readers, both Buddhist and non-Buddhist, on many levels.

This is a massive body of work, and not a book that you will read from beginning to end like a novel. Just dip in and read a few articles selected at random. You will sense the breadth and depth of the man and his writing and will return for more. You may even pick up some 'Chan attitude' along the way, which of course was John's intention all along.

Simon Child, Jing-hong Chuan-fa

Dharma Heir of Chan Master Sheng Yen

Successor to John Crook, Jing-di Chuan-deng, as Teacher of the Western Chan Fellowship

NCF I

A NEW BEGINNING

In introducing the NEW CH'AN FORUM to its readers, I hope that they will find in its pages the beginning of a distinctive voice that will help spread a wider understanding of the Dharma. There is a need for a contemporary view point which, whilst based in orthodox and traditional practice, also relates to the modern world.

When Master Sheng Yen came to the Maenllwyd retreat centre in mid-Wales last April, and led a retreat there, I acted as Guestmaster. At the end of our retreat, and much to my surprise for I had not requested or expected it, he gave me an authorisation to run Orthodox Ch'an[1] retreats in Britain as his representative. He also told me to work hard at clarifying my vexations! After the retreat some of the participants - Paul Cone, Tim Paine, Hilary Richards and Jake Lyne de Ver, all inhabitants of the Bristol area, felt they would like to start a Ch'an Group to follow up the initiative which Shih fu[2] had provided. They asked me if I would function as the group's teacher. We now meet regularly and have just held our first full Ch'an retreat.

Our next major initiative is to publish a book based upon Shih fu's teachings given to us in Wales. Michael Mann of Element Press has expressed a positive interest in this[3]. Already tapes of the twenty discourses Shih fu gave have been transcribed, including a profound series on the ancient text "Calming the Mind" by Wang Ming of the Sixth Century A.D. We publish part of this for the first time in this newsletter.

Another initiative is this journal. Broadly modelled on the journal of the Ch'an Center in Elmhurst, New York, we intend to provide articles from Shih fu's teachings, contributions from members of our group, edited versions of some of my talks to the group, and other contemporary discussions.

Ch'an Buddhism is not well known in this country. Its broad eclectic approach has much to offer Westerners, especially lay practitioners. Master Sheng Yen has passed on to us a view of the Dharma, based on his reception of transmissions in both the Lin Chi (Rinzai) and Ts'ao Tung (Soto) lineages. He is a second generation teacher in the lineage of the Great Master Hsu Yun[4] who did so much to restore Ch'an in China in the early years of this century. Master Sheng Yen has also received a doctorate in Buddhist Studies in Japan and is a considerable scholar. He speaks Japanese and has trained within the tradition of the great Harada Roshi, from whom several lineages of American Zen are currently descended. In attempting to transmit the wisdom of the Patriarchs as descended through Master Sheng Yen, we have a vision upon which we can rely.

All of us in the Bristol Ch'an group hope you will enjoy this initial effort. Send us your opinions and advice, and perhaps join us in practice on some future occasion.

John Crook; Kuo Yung

Notes

1 Ch'an is a form of Chinese Buddhism. The word 'Ch'an' comes from the Sanskrit 'Dhyana', which in Japanese is Zen

2 Shih fu or 'Roshi'.

3 Subsequently published as Catching a Feather on a Fan by Element Press (1991) ISBN 1-85230-194-5

4 See Empty Cloud: The Autobiography of the Chinese Master, Hsu Yun, edited by Richard Hunn. Published By Element Books (1988)

NCF II

EVERYTHING IS AS IT IS - THIS IN ITSELF IS REMARKABLE

MEDITATION TALK

If one is attempting to go into Zen deeply, to understand the relationship between one's mind and the universe, then it becomes important to turn over and over again, going backwards and forwards, backwards and forwards, many times over, the same refrain, the same theme. Not with the analytical intellect, nor with the mind of one who seeks explanation, but within the context of zazen, wherein intuitive insight can arise.

We begin with the thought that everything is just as it is, and that this in itself is totally remarkable, completely astounding, a condition of extraordinary improbability. Spring is coming, summer follows. Just now, this morning for the first time, everyone is arriving: the black-caps, the chiff-chaffs, the willow-warblers, the cuckoo. Summer follows and the days grow shorter. Autumn comes and then the season of ice and snow. Once more with the warming of the days, everyone returns.

Think how extraordinary this is. How it depends entirely on the way the planet revolves. This spinning globe, this planet in space turning at a certain rate, determines the timing of the day and night. Darkness and light, facing the sun, facing away from the sun. And each respective season, tilting sunwards and then away from the sun, so that the heat of the sun on the surface of the globe swings now north, now south, bringing the seasons. Bringing everyone north and taking everyone south, winging their way across the deserts. An extraordinary precision of spin and oscillation.

Consider how it might be different. A little faster in revolution and days would change their duration. Spring and Summer would flash past with a faster oscillation. We could have five years in one or five hundred days in one year. Who set the pattern spinning? Inappropriate question! How did it get fixed at this rate? Quite arbitrarily, maybe, or according to the laws which govern the speed of spinning globes spun off from a distant far off sun in ages long past. Everything is just as it is and everything is connected. The unfolding of the universe, and the setting of speeds, the law of interdependent origination and the laws of the universe.

Emptiness taking form, form congealing out of space. Timed, shaped, processing itself through time. Emerging from being. Returning once more to being. Form to emptiness, emptiness to form. The oscillation, the manifestation of the Law, Tao, the ultimate logos, whatever. Everything is as it is - and how extraordinary! Looking at the hillside as the flowers bloom, know this. There is nothing else. The hillside is It. Standing in the silent church looking at the altar, the altar and the atmosphere of the building, the silence, is It. On top of the cliff watching the swirling sea, is It. Futile to look elsewhere, God is not different from That. Buddha-nature is immediately before your eyes; there is no need to go anywhere. There is no need to go anywhere else. Everything is as it is and that is It. Do not seek elsewhere for that which is right now, before your eyes. Go very deeply into this. Penetrate the obscurities of wanting something else. So much of our dilemma lies in seeking elsewhere that which lies within the palms of our hands. So much dissatisfaction. So much wanting. So much seeking. God is always in somebody else's garden. The Buddha-mind is always in some other state of meditation. Paradise is in the heavens which are not here. Always this quest.

It becomes necessary to STOP. To go into it to recognise everything is as it is. Extraordinary! Everything before one's eyes is It. You are in It. Sometimes when the mind is so busy, so preoccupied, when samsara is spinning with the struggle of life, relationships, fear of death, the multitudinous dissatisfactions of industrial society, it is difficult simply to know that everything is as it is. Very difficult to know, because everything seems to be undesirable. What is wanted is the very opposite condition from that which is right in front of one's eyes. You haven't penetrated to the quality which brings out insight. Instead there is just noise and confusion. What to do?

Begin with gratitude. Notice simple things for which you can be thankful, anything. Each person is different. Notice the small things, the smile on a friend's face, a beautiful person walking in the street, birds overhead, flowers blooming, even the energy of roaring traffic in great cities, the pulsation, the force, the drive. Feel, wherever it may be, the gratitude for being there. After all, there might be nothing at all. Absolutely nothing. You might never have been here to witness it. The uniqueness of this moment is extraordinary. If you are not grateful, the opposites have arisen and you are lost. In the quietness of the mind's eye make gasho. Bow down in gratitude for the universe.

> Homage to the Buddhas in all worlds.
>
> Homage to the Bodhisattvas in all worlds.
>
> Homage to the scripture of Great Wisdom.

TWO POEMS BY THE GREAT MASTER HSU YUN

Master Hsu Yun was perhaps the greatest Ch'an master of this century. He may have lived for one hundred and twenty years, dying in 1959. His great work was the restoration of many Chinese temples and monasteries and the rekindling of the Dharma in China after a period of severe decline. He is the immediate Dharma ancestor of several contemporary Ch'an masters. Master Sheng-yen is a second generation descendant in his tradition.

In 1986 I stayed in Hong Kong with my old friend Yiu Yan-nang. We spent an evening translating some of Hsu Yun's poems. Yan-nang provided the basic English and I did my best to put it in poem form. The verses presented here were written near the end of Hsu Yun's life when he was much persecuted by Communists.

In the spring of 1951 Master Hsu Yun was staying at Yun-Men Monastery. He was holding a ceremony of giving precepts when the monastery was attacked by Communist thugs who believed there were arms stored in the buildings. The master was severely beaten up, a serious matter at his advanced age. Although he continued to sit in meditation he was dragged out and trampled upon with heavy boots. For several days he was believed dead. After a slow recovery, he went to Wu Chang and stayed at the temple of the three Buddhas. It was here that he wrote the first poem. The Government investigated the claims, nothing was found and the provincial officials were told to protect the monastery and the master.

The poem is to be found in Charles Luk's translation of Hsu Yun's autobiography[1]. The part of it referring to the decapitated general only provides his name and the place of his enlightenment. We chose to modify this part of the text to make it comprehensible. The poem itself was inscribed below a photograph taken at this time; both photo and poem are illustrated on p 130 of Luk's book. I am not sure where the second poem can be found. It must be from about the same period.

Notes

1 Luk, Charles. 1988. Empty Cloud: The Autobiography of the Chinese Zen master Xu Yun. Shaftesbury. Element Books, (as revised by Richard Hunn)

1

An evil wind blows me to Wu Chang,
my presence here has caused disaster.
For three months, at Sung Fat Monastery,
this sick and ageing body has attracted trouble,
shame and fear for everyone.
Once there was a decapitated general
calling aloud for his head;
"How many heads have you cut off?"
they asked him, at once he was enlightened.
Today, I too lament,
defeated, tortured, I recall unnumbered heads
in other lifetimes I cut off.
Vast is time and I am reconciled.
No more desire for eminence,
simply the wish to find the Buddha,
along with other people.

2

Why should this crazy guy
seek to make a name in Buddhism
when the whole show's on the wane-
indeed at crisis point?
I try to climb the highest peak,
I plumb the depths to catch the fish,
talk a lot-
find no listeners.
Sorry for myself I waste my time.
Unconcerned by dire predicaments
concern for others should be my task.
Moaning without pause;
whatever for - this grumbling?
Why not let everything go-

Life's suffering never ends.
Suddenly, remembering Emptiness, this mind has cleared.
What a laugh it is!

SIMPLY AN ABSENCE

Simply an absence
And suddenly it's all there
Rain on windows -
The wind of time without beginning.

Suddenly an absence
And simply it's all there
The winter cherry
Blooms without leaves.

Simply an absence
And suddenly it's all there
The last rose of Autumn
Looks in through the glass.

Simply an absence
And suddenly it's all there
The winter landscape
Comes in through the walls of my room.

NCF III

SERMONS TO THE STONES AND TREES

Zen talks come in different forms. There is the academic discourse full of history or philosophical analysis. There is the moral tale, the advocacy of a way of being or a meditational practice. And there is the "teisho", the spontaneous outpouring of a teacher's inspiration given in the moment for which it is called. Each type of talk plays its role in the creation of understanding. The "teisho" is however the closest one can come to transmission. In its accurate reception, the essential insight may pass directly from mind to mind. No need for analysis or even thought. There is just the seeing what is meant. But again, maybe not. Even the speaker may not know what he means for sure. There is just the speaking. "Sometimes we raise the eyebrows of old Shakyamuni Buddha, sometimes we do not."

Some years ago, James Crowden asked me to record some talks for a small meditation group he had established at Shaftesbury. In response to his request, I would take a tape recorder and go and meditate in the garden or on a hillside. When I felt ready I just began speaking. The result was a spoken meditation which could then be played subsequently to the group in their own meditation session. Since these talks were delivered out of doors in the presence of the natural world, I came to think of them as "Sermons to the stones and trees". On the original tapes there are background sounds of bird song, wind in a beech tree, a running stream, also passing aircraft and distant sounds of agricultural machinery.

Since some who have heard the tapes have found them to be useful, I will present slightly edited versions of some of them in New Ch'an Forum. It is a practice I intend to continue.

MEDITATION TALK: "OPENING THE TREASURE HOUSE"

"If you do these things for some time the treasure house will open naturally and you will enjoy it fully." These are the concluding words of a Soto Zen ritual. Remember: "The treasure house will open naturally."

In meditation, it is not that one has to work desperately hard to get somewhere. The practice of meditation should be something like breathing, or walking, something natural. If there is too much strain, too much tension, meditation becomes egoistic. It becomes a form of desire, a form of need. That is why the basic element in the practice of meditation involves a deep relaxation; the use of the breath or of repeating a mantra - allowing the mind to cool down. These things are not meditation in itself, they are preliminaries. They are the ways of bringing the mind to a quieter space in which meditation can happen of its own accord.

When one sits down and faces the wall, the first thing to do is to check out where the mind is. Sometimes it is very quiet and you can just listen to the bird song, but more usually the mind is full of stray energy, darting this way and that. As one practitioner put it to me, "The hunting dogs are out, restlessly searching, restlessly chasing." It's not always clear what they are hunting. The wants of the ego in its need for comfort, its need for security, its need for self-validation or validation by another, all generate the chase. We want the support of credentials, the support that comes from others telling us that everything is alright. There is the endless need for a little bit of love. The restlessness of the free-running ego is like a car idling, continually turning out low-toned noise. This is the restlessness of the needy ego - the basic suffering.

When you sit, the first thing to do is to find out where the mind is. Just to recognise it is the thing. Just to notice the irritation of the approaching aeroplane, this unwanted intrusion by some pilot in the sky. Just to recognise the way in which the mind is disturbed, thrown off centre. And in such recognition often comes a realisation. Simply knowing where the mind is will often do it. "Yes" you might say, "Yes, that's where it is. That's what I'm on about." First thing then - check out where the mind is.

The second thing to do is to open the mind to the universe. The universe is right in front of you. Just open yourself to the sounds in the room where you are sitting, to the white wall, to your own body, to the friends with whom you are meditating. All of that is the universe. What else could it be!

All of it is here right now as one experience. Can you relate to it? Can you open the heart so that the experience of yourself as Just Being comes quietly upon you - no big deal?

Dogen, the great Japanese teacher who brought Soto Zen from China to Japan, speaks of the three activities in Zazen: thinking; not thinking; and without either thinking or not thinking. When the mind begins to sit, it rehearses the past or perhaps the hopes for the future. It is a patterning of hopes and fears that constitutes thought. And when you say to yourself " Oh, I should be meditating, I should not be thinking, I should not be worrying or hassling", that is the rejection of thought, the endeavour not to think that sets up its own problem. The practice of just sitting requires the simple allowing of what is on top to bubble forth.

When we sit down in meditation it is like taking the top off a bottle of beer, everything bubbles up and you need to note what the bubbles are saying. "Yes, that is that. Yes, this is this. Yes that's so and so!" And then don't get stuck with it and work with it, let it drop! Let it go, and resume silence until something else comes up of its own accord. Not searching for it; not trying to work; so that if nothing particular comes up, you are just sitting. This practice is called "Without Thinking And Without Not Thinking!" It is just being, naturally. That is the natural way the unhassled mind works. Things crop up and things blow away.

Sitting in zazen requires three rather old fashioned attitudes. The attitude of faith, the attitude of will, and an attitude which allows one to let go of any particular need for success. Faith is derived from knowing people who have found meditation to be of value. Faith is derived from knowing something about scripture, and having trust in the meditation manuals. Faith comes from your knowledge. When sitting facing the wall the mind may be hassling and troubled. At such times remember there have been times, and there will again be times, when the great peace appears.

This faith allows one to have the willpower to sit. It is necessary to have the will to sit in order to counteract the sort of self-indulgence which says "Well, there's a nice television programme on, I'll watch that!" or, "I'll go for a walk in the bluebell wood, I can meditate another time". Will simply means a degree of confrontation with our comfort-seeking self-indulgences. Faith and Will allow one to work without the driving force of great expectations.

It is important to learn that meditation does indeed yield the treasure house; that it opens naturally. You need a reward; you need the benefit of direct knowledge. That is why at first, one should be very simple and "work" hard. You need to experience the Great Peace, because, once the great peace has been even momentarily touched upon, your faith is then confirmed and the point of exerting will-power becomes clear.

I can tell you that when I first began training in meditation at Samye Ling Centre in Scotland, I was doing about five or six hour-long sessions in each day. And these were very agonizing, great mental struggles, a lot of physical discomfort. But it vanished with time. Some sessions were better than others. And then, on about the fifth day, I went for a walk. The wind was simply blowing though my head. The landscape began glowing as if made of green jade. These are mere words. Each of us has to try it out for ourself.

It is important to know that the unborn mind is lying there within you. The hassling mind is simply the movement of waves on the surface of the ocean. When the waves fall still, and the wind drops, the sea becomes clear. The process of meditation is one of allowing the waves to become quiet. The treasure house opens upon deep stillness. In that stillness there is no longer a wanting. There is depth. Nirvana means "Blown out." The mind has blown out all its wants and petty cravings. There is a deep silence as of a moonlit night over a windless ocean. And as you sit there in that great night, the meaning of the opening treasure house arises within you, a peculiar joy begins to appear. And it is that joy which is the beginning of meditation.

Homage to the Buddhas in all worlds.
Homage to the Bodhisattvas in all worlds.
Homage to the Scripture of Great Wisdom.

OLD NO EYE

My name is No-eye
Hole in the skull
Servant of silence
Walking.

Not I, this skull alone,
moves across this dusty plain.
Mountains rise, valleys,
cool winds and waters fall.
Hot rocks glow on the valley floor.

Through this skull the world moves
like rivers from the mountain
snow water from high ice -
nothing in the way.

Zanskar 1986

NCF IV

A SERMON AMONG THE STONES AND TREES

These talks were spoken originally to a tape recorder in open countryside. They were prepared for a Zen group that wished to hear them when I was not personally available. Later it became a habit and I have recorded a number of such meditations.

NO PATH AT ALL!

There comes a moment in Zen training, a moment both shocking and surprising, when one realises intuitively that there is no path at all.

Ho! What then is Zen practice?

Practice is the realisation that there is no path at all, yet one keeps on going, going on, going on beyond, always becoming being.

Listening to a talk on Buddhism on the radio I heard speaker after speaker extolling in his or her own way, the advantages and benefits of Buddhism. Here, it would seem, is a club well worth belonging to! The beginner joins the Buddhists, she finds a new identity, becomes a newly enrolled member. There is a certain relief in belonging.

In a lonely world, clubs have a certain value. Whether it be in a city, a small town or in the countryside there are many reasons for starting a club. Most of all we want some sort of togetherness, some feeling of travelling to a destination that offers some security, some way out of the morass in which our society is stuck, some way beyond the alienation, heartlessness, criminality and carelessness. Some explanation to make it all feel safer.

So we have clubs, lists of members, buy a building, set up a programme, invite speakers, cajole the reluctant, persuade the unbelievers, reject those who come once and never again. We appoint a secretary, president officials and obedentiaries, find ourselves spiritual advisers. Something like a lay monastery gets set up in our midst and we start worrying about membership, payment of subscriptions, the next speaker. Soon some of us begin to wonder whether the spiritual adviser in the town along the way might not be better for us than the one we've got. After all what's s/he doing for us? A year has gone by and I haven't changed! A hint of divisiveness creeps into the air. Democracy and muddle might be better, more modern, than faith and authority: yet which is right for the times? Do we even know enough to judge?

However benevolent we think we are, all clubs are exclusive. Social psychology tells us that even minimalist groups discover adversaries. If you split an encounter group for half an hour you can easily generate factions. Belonging to one's club, one has a distinctive path, a distinctive teacher. Certainly we have a better practice than those along the way who only sit, pray, talk, sing mantras, have intellectual interests, follow a guru, dance all night or sleep with one another - and so on. Otherwise why join this group rather than the other. Anyway I am investing in it. It had better be good.

Krishnamurti told us repeatedly that creating institutions is divisive. Amongst Western Buddhists this remains subtly, even dishonestly, so. We find it hard to get out of our culturally determined emphasis on competition and individualism. Yet even Western Buddhists don't usually throw stones at one another, at least not very accurately. Dharma gossip is the secret vehicle for dissent, disappointment, frustration irritation, thinking oneself important or merely put in one's place. And the more I am a proven party member the more addicted I become and the more divisive are my biased thoughts. Even Krishnamurti could not stop his followers following. What would he have done if he had?

There are dangers here; following the way of the club you may miss the Buddha's message entirely. As he lay dying he said "All component things pass away. Work out your own salvation with diligence." He did not say "Set up churches!" He did not say "Wear robes, dog collars, create ranks and files, make yourself distinctive. Let it be known who is the wise and who is the unwise". He did not say "Argue your case with the Muslims, the Christians, the Marxists." He simply said "All component things pass away. Go work out your salvation with diligence. Find out for yourself!"

The creation of an outer path is easy. Creating our clubs, we need to examine what is happening to us in the heart. What is the quality of our relationships when we meet. Is it beneficial for us all? Do we pass our merit, if any, on to others? Do we share? Do we give as well as take? Do we focus on the faults and peculiarities of our teachers or do we sometimes manage to catch glimpses of what it is they are trying to convey to us. However irritating or adorable, a teacher who has received transmission may well have something to tell us that goes beyond words. Can we catch the hidden meaning?

We, who so naturally form clubs, need to understand our motivation for doing so. We need to know not what we can get but what we can give. Do we persist in participation when we join or do we just have a look around and then run off somewhere else where the tea is stronger or the teacher more sexy? What is our level of understanding in all this? Clubs are only as good as the self awareness of the members.

It is always good to look at what is happening in the heart, to place it there in zazen and wait until one can see it truly. Don't be in a rush.

One evening in 1986 I was standing on the mountain path above the little monastery of Bo-Lam on Lantao Island in Hong Kong. I was looking at the full moon rising over the forested mountains and the distant ocean. As I watched, a monk came down the path returning from his work constructing stone by stone and rock by rock an extension to the mountain track. Smiling I pointed to the moon. He looked at me and gently shook his head. Extending his hand in the air, he seemed to grasp the moon out of the sky and in one movement placed it in his heart. He smiled. I bowed. As he walked on, he shrugged his shoulders.

If one looks to external things, there is only the path of following. Taking the moon and placing it in the heart is the same as taking the atmosphere of a room or temple into oneself, discovering the uniqueness of the presence of the moment. Breathing in the air, the sound and feel, the ambience of the place becomes one with an inner being, the quiet space where there are no judgements.

When the spirit of place simply hangs in the air about you and you go deeply into it, you will find there is no need to move. There is nothing particular to know. There is no need for elaboration. It is as it is. Even if there is something to be done in due course; in that moment of reflection, when the thing is in the heart, there is nothing to be done. Just see it as it is. Maybe you will see it as you have never seen it before. Now it is Soho, now it is SOHO, yet now it is Soho once more. Was it Soho that changed? Can the flag blow the wind?

Out of moments of tranquillity comes all that you need. When the opposites arise, Dogen tells us, the Buddha mind is lost. When you try to create Buddhism on a path that is outside the heart then the Buddha mind gets lost too. Be wary of officious Buddhists or those with opinions. Look more closely. Salvation with diligence is an inner matter which only gradually takes on external expression. This happens naturally without artifice. There is nothing you can do about this. If you become clear, others will notice it. There is nothing for you to proclaim. Take the opposites and place them in the heart, let the molten moon dissolve in the blood stream. The evening air comes naturally in on the breath. There is no path and you will never know an end to it.

Homage to the Buddhas of All Worlds.

Homage to the Bodhisattvas of All Worlds.

Homage to the Scriptures of Great Wisdom.

NCF V

ZEN AND CHRISTIANITY

The Dialogue

Christianity lies at the root and heart of Western culture. Today intellectually rejected because of its failure to relate effectively with science, and sentimentalised by those who seek popularity within a world of adolescent values that last a lifetime, the traditional European religion none the less continues to stir the heart. Perhaps it is the story of Christ himself, rather than the abstractions of theology or the often hypocritical moralism, that touches us so. Every day we are hearing his story - in Tibet, in Bosnia, among the Kurds and Shiites of Iraq and in our own twentieth century well watered slums.

In a recent article for The Sharpham Miscellany I explored some themes that are in common between Buddhism and Christianity and also some differences[1]. The essential linkage lies in the common concern with compassion while the major differences lie in the psycho-philosophical understanding of the place of the human being in the Universe. Christianity has focused particularly on the alleviation of poverty and plays an active role in politics in many countries. Buddhism focuses more on the alleviation of psychological misery among rich as well as poor and has so far played a relatively minor role in world politics, Tibet excluded.

Buddhism's strength lies in the fact that the profound philosophies of the Madhyamika and Cittamatra schools not only found a deep resonance within modern physics and philosophy but may come to occupy spaces in the intellectual world of the West where the meaning of being requires deeper attention. Here, in the vacuum of modern thought, Buddhism's critique of the self allows a reconstruction of values based upon a deconstructive approach resembling that of contemporary French philosophy in particular. In the world of alienation in which we find ourselves today, this provides hope where only regressive and fundamental religion seems to be strong. Furthermore, it is a message which the emerging underclass of modern society might well understand if and when it hears of it.

Yet the deep strength of Christianity lies today in obscure places where the "deep" religion of inner contemplation and quiet asceticism still sustains itself. A visit to the Franciscan friary at Batcombe in Dorset showed me a caring community with a profound spiritual life, practice and liturgical round. This deep Christianity is anchored in values that approach those of Buddhism closely. Emphasised here is the inner life of contemplation married in various ways to action. Teachers of the pseudo-Dionysian tradition, Meister Eckhart and the mystical writings of obscure saints and priests of the medieval times are important here. The Cloud of Unknowing by an unknown spiritual adviser to priests in 14th century England is very close to Zen, as is the little book of the French monk Brother Lawrence on The Presence of God. What we have here is an apophatic approach to God; that is to say an approach that focuses on what God is not rather than what he may be asserted to be. Such a view leaves the essential mystery untouched by definitions and discriminative thought and allows a contemplative openness that only the spiritually adult can attain. It is in regions such as these that Buddhism and Christianity can enter a productive dialogue. This is no longer possible in those regions where pop Christianity and evangelism maintain their unthinking way.

In Buddhism there is no God. But then what thinking priest claims the existence of God as essential to Christianity these days? So is God a problem? The answer is only affirmative for Buddhists if by God, some fixed unmoveable permanent causative entity, a father figure projected into heaven, is proposed. This God is probably truly dead and gone but his shadows are everywhere. But if by God one means the deep mystery at the heart of the cosmos about whom or which nothing can be asserted other than that the process is one of endless change, evolution and return, then the difference with Buddhism becomes minimal. Indeed this is also the reason why Buddhism can retain a good relationship with Hinduism but only a polite one with Islam. If Christianity ceases to be a fundamentalist religion of the Book and re-emerges with the humility of the Desert Fathers the dialogue with Buddhism can deepen.

But can one then relate to this God? Not as the spiritually adolescent might wish to do in a sentimental and emotional elation that can so easily mislead, but certainly so in contemplative thought and meditation. My own Christian heritage sometimes surfaces when within my sitting meditation in zazen the word GOD suddenly appears like a koan demanding resolution. Today this word has ceased to be a puzzle to me, nor any longer does my personal emergence from an adolescent Christianity produce twinges of guilt. Instead the word GOD has become a power word, a mantra that stands for the whole just as well as Buddha Mind, Tathata or any other term. It arises and passes away. It has become empty and therein lies its ancient power. I feel less at ease with Jesus the Christ. Who was he? What kind of a being was he? Why has the Church made such a mess of his message? For me the koan "Tell me what the cross is?" remains a live issue to which

I must return. There is no way one can escape the deep roots of one's own culture. The way through is dialogue.

Many people, puzzled by the alienation and ennui of our times and by the rising wave of valueless materialism and criminal apathy without heart, have been looking into Buddhism because Christianity fails to be enough. Yet such people often retain deep Christian motifs in their psyche that cannot be denied. To work these through in dialogue is essential to our re-emerging spirituality.

Recently Hebe Welbourne, a child health doctor and wife of the late theologian Fred Welbourne (who I remember well from the days of the Bristol Encounter Centre) of Bristol University, became the "resident hermit" in an ancient house of prayer next door to the church of Westbury on Trym. Feeling the need to explore meditative approaches of our time she came to a Western Zen Retreat at Maenllwyd. Her report follows. It is clear to me that in such meetings lies the essence of the dialogue of which I speak. We have had many Quakers on retreats for they find zen close in many ways to their silence in church. I was once asked to lead a retreat for a Christian community but some unclear resistance developed and it never came to fruition. Today, I think that simply to offer an open door at the Maenllwyd is the way forward. Those Christians who have an affinity with contemplation are likely to find their way there and join this inner dialogue. Sometimes, as in the report "What's the trick?" (below), the Ch'an or Western Zen Retreat allows the resolution of a problem that many Christians experience due to the dilemmas of their own tradition in modern times. The door remains open to all[2].

1 Buddhism and Christianity - bridging the gap. In: Sharpham Miscellany; essays in spirituality and ecology. The Sharpham Trust. Totnes. pp 57-70.

2 Two useful books on Zen and Christianity are William Johnstone's Christian Zen (1971) Harper Colophon Books and Silent Music; the science of meditation. (1974) Fontana/Collins.

For additional reading I recommend:

Allchin, A.M. 1983. Solitude and Communion: papers on the hermit life. Fairacres Publication 66. SLG Press Oxford.

Caussade, J-P de. 1977. The Sacrament of the Present Moment. Fount Paperbacks. Collins

Furlong, M. 1985 Merton; a biography. Darton, Longman and Todd. London.

Leigh-Fermor, P. 1982 A Time to Keep Silence. Penguin

Levi, P.1987 The Frontiers of Paradise: a study of monks and monasteries. Collins Harvill

Sophrony, Archimandrite.1973. The Monk of Mount Athos. Mowbrays. London and Oxford

NCF VI

THE PRAJNAPARAMITA HEART SUTRA

Introduction and Background

Edited text of the lecture on this topic given by Dr John Crook to the Bristol Ch'an Group 4th, November 1992.

This is the first lecture of a series and will be continued in future issues.

> When the Bodhisattva Avalokitesvara
> was coursing in the deep Prajnaparamita,
> He perceived that all five skandas are empty,
> thereby transcending all sufferings.
> Sariputra, form is not other than emptiness
> and emptiness not other than form.
> Form is precisely emptiness
> and emptiness precisely form.

The Heart Sutra is perhaps the most important scripture in Zen. It summarises and captures the root notions fundamental to the teaching of Mahayana Buddhism. The original versions are in Sanskrit and there are ancient translations into Chinese, Tibetan and Japanese. It is not a scripture of the Theravadan Canon but belongs to the "second turning" of the wheel of the Dharma dating from the times when the Mahayana or Great Vehicle scriptures were being produced. In fact the Heart Sutra is a summary of an enormous body of literature known as the Prajnaparamita Sutras.

At one time in India there were a tremendous number of scriptures conveying the Great New Idea. This lay at the heart of the Great Vehicle, the Mahayana, namely, the "emptyness" of absolutely everything. This emptyness was not just the absence of self in the person which the Buddha had proclaimed in his earliest sermons but a corresponding emptiness in all things that could be perceived in the entire Cosmos. Few monks were at first able to understand this widened conception of emptiness-which does not mean nothingness. Buddhism has never been nihilistic.

The Prajnaparamita scriptures of varying lengths all explore this pivotal idea. Its fundamental implication is that no apparent thing has a quality of permanent selfhood as an entity; everything is impermanent and dependent upon changing causal factors and conditions. Everything is a flux or flow, a cosmic process of changing states. Nothing in it is graspable but our most serious illusion is that this is so.

The scriptures were collected together by the monks into enormous tomes known as the Scripture of Great Wisdom. They were really a packaging together of numerous repetitions commonly used for chanting. It became progressively incomprehensible and few monks actually understood it. After all, emptiness is tricky idea!

Learned teachers decided that they had to capture the heart of this vast book and present it in a simple form everybody could understand. The Heart Sutra came to be formulated as a summary of the essential issue. Another summary of a similar kind is known as the Diamond Sutra which comes from a different text but is exploring the same issues.

This whole literature, the Prajnaparamita, eventually became the subject of extensive philosophical criticism. There was a school of logic which eventually gave rise to the next phase of philosophical analysis, namely the Madyamaka and Cittamatra schools. These both have their roots in the Prajnaparamita Sutra of which the Heart and Diamond Sutras are the brilliant crystallisations.

But what does the Sutra actually refer to? The versions that we have in Ch'an are very short ones, the Tibetan one is considerably longer. The Tibetan version provides the context of the discourse. The Buddha has gathered all his disciples together on the top of the Vulture Peak Mountain, which is still known as an archaeological site in India today. The gathering consisted not only of ordinary people, but brahmins, warriors, monks, Kings and important people of the time. Also strange spirit-like creatures and mysterious powerful protectors, mythical beings and dragons. They are described in the Tibetan Scriptures in loving detail. All were sitting on the mountain waiting for the Buddha to speak. But the Buddha was in deep, deep contemplation. Throughout the Sutra he says absolutely nothing. A monk called Sariputra, evidently unable to contain his impatience, calls out "Hey! Can anyone tell me how to practise? How can I practise the Great Wisdom Teachings?" (Of course, this is a literary device to produce a textual answer.) The Buddha, however, continues in his profound contemplation and it is left to the Bodhisattva Avalokitesvara to give reply.

We need here to pause a little bit and look in to the background of these writings. The character of this sutra is mythical. In the earlier stories of the Pali school of Southern Buddhism the events are remembered ones, they are historical and probably close to what actually happened. But the Prajnaparamita Sutras were written several hundred years after the death of the Buddha and are reconstructions. In the Heart Sutra, the idea of a great gathering is being used as a device to present the philosophy and the teaching. Furthermore, Avalokitesvara was not a person. He is a projection of a particular quality of Buddhahood, a personification of an aspect of mind.

One of the interesting things that happened over the years after the Buddha's death was the shift from historical remembrance to the personification of Buddha quality. For example, one of the Buddha's qualities is kindliness, so people began to think of a particular Buddha of kindliness. Many Buddhas begin to appear in the literature who are not historical Buddhas at all but represent ideals, such as the Shining One, Resplendent Beauty, Glorious Insight and Great Wisdom. Some of the scriptures of this period refer to gatherings of persons who are really just names referring to psychological qualities. The most important of these are the Bodhisattvas or the Buddha's sons, Wisdom Beings who provide the teachings.

Avalokitesvara is a condensation of the idea of compassion or kindliness. The function of the Bodhisattva is hidden in his name. Isvara is one of the titles of Shiva, it means Great Lord. Avalo is a Sanskrit word meaning the One Who Looks Down. This can be interpreted as the mother who looks down at her nursing child or as one who looks down from a high place and Sees the suffering of the world and the impossibility of saving everyone. Because he has vowed not to become a Buddha until everyone is saved it also means that Avalokitesvara has no hope of ever becoming a Buddha and a tear drops from his eye. In the Tibetan story this tear becomes the feminine Buddha Tara. Such poetic stories are full of a wonderfully rich tapestry of myth making in which deep teaching is embedded.

Up on the Vulture Mountain, Avalokitesvara is sitting in meditation but he hears Sariputra's question and feels compassion for him. Our text starts off with his reply. Even the question is not given in this version of the text. Sariputra had asked "How can we practice?"

Incidentally, this tradition of question and answer still happens today and it happened to me when I was in Hong Kong. On Lan Tao Island there is a Buddhist monastery which I visited about two years ago. At the end of the Retreat I went to see the master. He was a very attractive dynamic old man with a long wispy beard and wearing ancient Chinese robes with very long sleeves. I asked him about method, in other words the same question as Sariputra's.

"Ha!" he cried, "Method!" as if it was a dirty word. Then he pointed to a scripture hung on the wall and said, "That is method". The beautiful calligraphy was then translated to me as "Heart Sutra". I then asked "OK, well how does one do it?" He pointed to another scripture hanging on the opposite wall. This simply said "What is IT?"

The Heart Sutra is IT. How to practice? But, first of all, why, up on that mountain, didn't the Buddha answer? He just provides presence. It is almost as if at this stage in the development of Buddhism the notion is of the Buddha as a Cosmic Being rather than a human mind. By this date nobody actually remembered him as a person. His enlightened mind was felt to be universal.

It is most important to understand what Avalokitesvara was doing when he was asked the question. He was coursing in the deep Prajnaparamita. What is this coursing? This translation is by the scholar Conze and the word coursing suggests something dynamic, coursing like a greyhound, or flying. Roshi Kennet of Throssel Hole reads it with greater precision in translation from the Japanese version, "When one with deepest wisdom of the heart that is beyond discriminative thought, the Holy Lord Great Kanzeon Bosattva knew that the Skandhas five were, as they are in their self-nature, void, unstained and clean". To understand the Heart Sutra we have to understand that the answer we are given is coming from a person undergoing a very particular experience, that of "oneness with the deepest wisdom of the heart which is beyond all discriminative thought".

The word Prajnaparamita itself comes from the Sanskrit. It means "Perfection of Insight", the highest, clearest, most straightforward or most important insight. This word insight does not just refer to an intellectual insight like the solving of a mathematical equation. It is not to do with words. This is explicit in Roshi Kennet's version which says "Deepest wisdom of the heart which is beyond discriminative thought". Prajna means no thought, yet something which is insight. The meaning is supremely important for us who endure endless wandering thoughts while sitting on our cushions.

Avalokitesvara was experiencing this insight. As practitioners we need to capture in ourselves what this implies and what it means. An insight which is beyond discriminative thought is like an "Ah Ha!" experience. One in which you suddenly see something - "Ah, it's SO!"

If you think about it, the moment when this something strikes has no content. If you capture the moment of "Ha!" in that moment there is wordless insight. Of course you then usually go on to think about it and put it into words. But what if you don't? It's like someone saying to you "Do you see that bird over there?" You look and you look in the trees and can't find it. Then suddenly, you do - and it's

"Ah! There it is after all". When you see through the camouflage, it is not discriminative thought, it is recognition.

This insight then has the quality of recognition. But what is being recognised? Well the scripture tells us. "When the Bodhisattva Avalokitesvara was coursing in the deep Prajnaparamita, he perceived that all five skandhas are empty". What is meant by the skandhas? The skandhas have been talked about in Buddhism since the earliest Suttas. They were the Buddha's description of the nature of the mind. He said that the human mind is made up of five parts or collections; Forms, Sensations, Perceptions, Preconceptions (or prejudices) and Consciousness. Form is our awareness of being here as an apparent object, Sensation is like touch. Perception is knowing what you have been touched by. It is a clarification of what something is. For example you perceive that a noise is a cuckoo calling rather than a cuckoo clock. The Preconceptions (samskaras) are the predispositions which make all of us different, our complexes. They the karmic residues of our personal past and give rise to all sorts of wants and desires, positive and negative. Finally Consciousness is what makes us aware of all these processes. These five words are a total description of the nature of the mind, a model of the way the mind works and it was immensely elaborated in a literature called the Abhidharma.

In the early teachings contemplation of the mind was very important. It consisted in seeing that there is no self other than these processes in endless interaction. Avalokitesvara's practice originated the early writings but he has gone further. He sees that not only does he have no self as a contactible entity but that the skandhas too are empty.

Coursing in the deep insight means that in the period before he heard Sariputra's question Avalokitesvara was engaged in a profound meditation on the nature of the mind. He had pressed that meditation to such a point that he had complete insight into it and this had revealed total emptyness. We are talking about a meditational state. The answer comes straight from it without pause.

We now have to try to unfold for ourselves what it is like to be in a profound state of meditation pressed so far that you perceive that your mind is empty. We may try to do that with the aid of one or two simple exercises. In doing this we should not suppose that we can immediately discover what Prajnaparamita actually is, for that requires either exceptional insight or long practice, but we may be able to generate a simulacrum of it.

This approach is a traditional Tibetan teaching. You set up a psychological trick which gives you an insight and makes you think "Ah! I see". But then the Lamas say, "Steady on - you haven't actually seen it, because that takes another fifteen years of practice, but by doing this exercise you can see the direction in which you have to move. It is a signpost."

Here is an exercise which is derived from Douglas Harding's "Headless Way ".[1]

Let's look at something in front of us, here for example the Buddha statue. Just sit comfortably and look at the Buddha. Don't do anything else such as thinking "What is coming next". Just LOOK.

Now ask the question, 'Where is what I am looking at?"

If you ponder you will find that you are inclined to say "Well it's a few yards in front of me", or you may say "Well it must be in my head somewhere". Well - Is it out there? or - Is it in my head? or - Is it neither? Ask "What is my actual experience of where it is?" You will find that your experience of looking at the object is shaped by the constructs you impose upon it.

Stay looking at the Buddha. It appears that there is a something out there. It has got a certain shape and colour and size. You seem to be at the opposite end from what you are looking at. If you were the Buddha who was looking back at you, you would see a face. But when you examine this face, your face which the Buddha is seeing, in actual experience, you will find your face to be no more than a sort of vaguely perceived screen. You are not your face as such. You are looking out from behind your face. It is something behind your face which is looking at the Buddha.

Can you experience that which is behind your face? Go slowly into this. Take your time and then you can ask yourself the question, "That which is the other side of the room has shape, but does that which is behind my face have shape? (Look to see, don't discuss it in your head.) Place your awareness in the place from where you are looking out. Is there anything there which has shape? That which is on the other side of the room has a certain colour. That which is behind your face, does it have any colour?

That which is in front of you has a certain size. That which is behind your face, does it have any size? In fact is there any word at all that you can use to describe that which is behind your face at the locus out of which you are gazing? Indeed, has that locus even got any place at all in actual experience?

Now, if you continue to follow along, what do you find in that place? Are there words? Void? Silence? Spaciousness? Nothing at all-ness? Emptiness?

At this point we have to be very watchful or else we will turn on the language again and find sensation, perception, volition and consciousness. All these concepts do have a meaning within a realm of discourse but in themselves they are only names.

Something very strange happens here when words are seen to be only names. When you look at the place where the names should be, you won't find them as such; you experience their suchness. So when you say the mind is empty you're not saying there is nothing there at all but merely that it is empty of what the names would seem to imply is there. Descriptions are not IT.

Avalokitesvara was sitting and had turned his gaze inward. If he applied his discriminative intellect he would say, "Ah yes, there is some sensation. Ah yes, there is perception too. Ah yes, and some volition. Ah yes, there is consciousness. And also, there is a certain predisposition there too. How interesting! But if I actually look at all this, at that place where all these things manifest, do I find them?

Avalokitesvara has taken up as his practice the method of directly looking into the mind, the Buddha's special method of Vipassana. It can be formulated as a Koan. What is the mind?" A skilled practitioner wouldn't be examining this question with the intellect, he would be looking directly into IT. He would find the suchness which is empty of the particularity the words implied. This is what is meant by "emptyness".

A sensation entered the ear of Avalokitesvara. "Can anyone tell me how to practice Great Wisdom?"

"Form is emptiness and emptiness is form". Instantly came the response.

To be continued...

1. ID. E. Harding. Head Off Stress. pub. Arkana ISBN 0 14 01.92026

SERMONS AMONG STONES AND TREES

Not Noticing: Death and the Sky

This talk is dedicated to the memory of Georgina Marjorie Crook. It was delivered to the assembly of practitioners at the Two Day Retreat in Rickford, October 24th 1992.

Two things are omnipresent in our lives and yet day after day we fail to notice them - death and the sky. Every day people are dying: if they are our dear ones we know and feel it but the fact of everyday dying, next door, in the neighbouring street, all over town, we choose to ignore. I do not mean the accidents, murders and genocides that are the focus of our news bulletins, I mean ordinary everyday death which is as common as birth.

The sky? How often do we raise our eyes to the great blue dome? On a bright day we notice the sunlight, shining clouds and the shifting shadows moving with the clock. Yet we rarely look deliberately up into the azure haze, passing on and out into unimaginable spaces. Some of us never look. Yet there it is above us all the time. At night how often do you look out between the stars and wonder how far you can see? What is it, this endless space, this awesome void?

Death and Space; awesome, needing the reflective moment few of us give time for; they are outside the run of our concern. Big mind rarely comes from small mind. We usually need a shock.

When you sit at the bedside of a dying person or have the privilege of nursing someone whose life is moving to its close, there is a great opportunity. It is like going on a retreat knowing it could be your last. On the one hand there is the tragedy of passing time, the ending of a personal epoch, the severing of identity. On the other there is often a curious tranquillity as the mind accepts the inevitable. Tears and peace come to inform one another. It is vital not to avoid this experience by taking refuge in gossip or the repression of painful feeling. You have to be really there or you learn nothing.

The Tibetans have a meditation on death. In this process you envisage the slow dissolution of personal attributes. The earth element dissolves into water, water evaporates into air, air disappears in space. The dying self traverses each stage at differing speeds depending on circumstance. In these meditations the practitioner visualises these processes, partakes of them emptying the self of attachment and moving with the flow of dissolution. This is natural, the end game of a cycle which is eternal. In the presence of the dying the practitioner goes through this cycle mentally or verbally, assisting the passage of the other through the stages, passing through the intermediate ones to final peace. Sometimes these phases occur rapidly, all at the time of death, in other cases many of them are complete before the final breath is drawn.

When death has come it is good to sit with the dead far into the night with a candle burning, shadows moving on the beloved face. At first, overwhelmed by disbelief, it is as if the other will turn and speak, waking up once more as on so many mornings. But gradually the room resolves itself, the presence of the other slowly leaves, withdrawing into a deeper silence wherein the night sounds come, wind, leaves flying past the window, night bird's call. You say a prayer. You wish all well, God speed. And then you are alone. The room is empty. The other has gone on. Where? How? What is the meaning? What is it? In the silence the candle burns as you turn to your own rest.

Often the mind itself decays long before death. How can one help the one who is dying without awareness, grimly holding on, fighting every moment towards the end. The aim must be to facilitate tranquillity so that the natural dissolution can move peacefully on its way.

At such a time, remember the sky, letting the mind go beyond the visible into the eternity of space itself. Maybe this will be frightening and it reminds us of the need for profound meditation on the emptiness of all things including the great Universe itself. Cycles of life and death are surrounded by the awesome void of space. Yet here too there are constant arisings and fallings, comings to be and goings out of existence, the becoming and ending of stars, galaxies, worlds. We exist within great cycles like huge mandalas, realms within realms. The nature of being has many modes, not all of them conscious. The realms contain each other. At what level is the brain aware? The neuronal level differs from the mental yet the latter could not be without the former. What then are we?

A mind that probes beyond the relative sees the Universe as "perfect". Indeed whatever could it mean to say it was "imperfect"? The Universe is none other than it is and the only word for it must be perfection without an opposite. Since you and I are contained by, pervaded by, born into and of the Universe, we too partake of this perfection. We are quite simply what we are. To wish otherwise is a form of rejection, attachment to illusion, ignorance and assertion of self. And self we know is highly soluble.

Each one of us works out our karma as best we can. In relativity there is pain and distress. God, the fickle bastard, seems cruel, uncaring, rewarding the righteous with injustice. Yet in the transpersonal vision there is an opening space, the unchangeable root of change. Here is the Eternal of which we cannot speak, for to speak is relative. We can however gaze out between the stars letting go into free fall. Goodbye is present at the ending and in the beginning. And miraculously, without comprehension, love appears in a rising light.

How does the river flow? The stream descends as it must, moulding itself in flow around the rocks and boulders finding its natural way. "Going to where the water ends" means the ocean and the sun raised vapours forming again into great clouds, the never ending return. And the sharp rocks, the obstacles, gradually become softly shaped into round stones all fitting the watery bed in natural patterns. Obstacles and water all shape each other reciprocally. There is a lesson here.

How does the river of experience flow? It runs as it must, a never ending stream which, in the freedom of its own nature, shapes all obstacles as its bed. Broken stones become smooth surfaces, each one fitting the next in a pattern of karmic creation. How does the river flow? Interdependently, as it must within the eternal. When you feel this in your life and meditation you have learned to ride the Ox.

BOOK REVIEW - A BUDDHISTIC PHILOSOPHY OF ENVIRONMENT

Published in "Resurgence" Jan. 1993. Permission to present it here kindly granted by the editor, Satish Kumar.MAURICE ASH

THE FABRIC OF THE WORLD

A Resurgence book

Green Books, Hartland £8.95 (1992)

Maurice Ash has written an extraordinarily succinct and compelling account of our philosophical understanding of environment and the manner in which faulty metaphysics have distorted our attitudes. This is not an account of "the" environment we all inhabit but an analysis of the importance of the meanings we attribute to this concept. The significance of his work is focused in the realisation that the idea of environment holds a redeeming possibility in a world besotted with the materialism of our times and the misapplication of science. Yet this vision is itself threatened with betrayal by those who could best promote it; a betrayal based on the absence of an appropriate understanding. The threat comes on the one hand from the sentimentality of New Age idealism and, on the other, from those who see the environmental issues as contained within the old Cartesian paradigm.

The philosophical approach is one to which Maurice Ash has been deeply attracted for some years; the deconstructive examination of meanings as the uses of words in the manner of Wittgenstein. This process of 'deconstruction' has led to the abandonment of almost all metaphysics of the Western world which originated in Greek thought. Traditionally we see ourselves as separate from the world so that we and the environment are two things. Such dualism, which is the basis of scientific observation in traditional experimentation, leads us to suppose that environment is something outside ourselves which we can manipulate to our advantage. Such a view tends however to split up our experiences of the world into numberless dualities each considered separately; the complex web of interconnection is not perceived. Had our forefathers been able to see the multiple consequences of inventing the internal combustion engine it is unlikely that they would have developed it, argues Ash. The same applies to many of our scientific achievements which have let loose the technologies of our time with scant consideration for the interdependence of their numerous consequences.

The pivot of dualism is the assumption that self is the opposite of context. Yet what if this fundamental dualism is questioned? We begin by unravelling our conceptualisation of self and soon discover extraordinary enigmas. We find that the self we think ourselves to be is no more than an attribution; a term in a story that might be otherwise told, a reification of a process that is inherently open, not closed and which lacks other than conceptually created boundaries. And this reification of self reappears in the whole process of supposing that abstract terms can stand for things when in truth they only indicate conceptions. The closer we get to 'self' in critical thought the less clear are its boundaries and hence its separation from 'environment' is called into question. We are in fact in endless open communication with all around us enabling us to say of the Universe, "I am not it, yet it is all of me." As this realisation dawns we are impelled towards a vision of wholeness in which our roles assume a responsibility unsuspected previously. Yet to conceive of a whole in an uncritical holism is to subscribe to an idealism that could become yet another mistaken ideology. This is because a careless view would see the 'whole' as a reification to be manipulated and hence throw us back into the arms of the dualism we have just rejected. The whole is un-measurably open and cannot be idealised. Such an idea is so confronting to traditional Western intelligence that rather than finding ways of moving with it we have fallen into decadent despair.

Ash writes (p4) "....if this bankruptcy is not yet universally recognised - and it isn't - this must surely be because people still suppose the mechanisms for controlling events... can continue to be operated, could we but sort out the levers. And they suppose this because they know nothing but mechanistic thought." Strong words indeed.

Our concern for environment is an expression of how meaningless our lives have become. In an extended discussion Maurice Ash rejects all approaches in which abstractions about 'the' environment could lead back into ideologies based in dualistic thinking. Only that which is immediately apprehended can make sense. So he focuses on the "small is beautiful" approach because only in local issues can people be truly involved without misleading abstraction. There are perhaps dangers in this approach for I feel it is far from clear that the philosophy necessarily implies that some orders of scale are more important than others. When, for example, does 'small' become 'big'? Where are the boundaries? In any case a locality is inevitably interdependent in innumerable ways (ecologically, geographically, economically, socially) with its neighbours and the relations between them crucial to each. While the shortcomings of the nation state are clear so also must be the fact of interdependence of location within a wider sphere. A pond is not necessarily more beautiful than the ocean. Perhaps a pond is comforting for those who find the ocean awesome. Yet so far as beauty or relevance is concerned both have their place in the scheme of things. Indeed it is exactly this problem of the desirable relations between regions and larger units that underlies the discussions of 'subsidiarity' in the context of contemporary European politics. Maurice Ash indeed admits the role of the 'large' to be inescapable but his taking refuge in 'lifeboats' leaves a number of important nettles ungrasped.

Ash is aware that the contemporary philosophy of deconstruction is little more than a rediscovery of a whole of a philosophy of being that marked deeply the whole tradition of Indian thought and feeling. The prime focus of Madhyamaka philosophy in Buddhism was on the 'emptiness' of concepts. Emptiness implies that no self and no thing has an inherent existence as an entity; everything is process, the aspects of which are all interdependent. Ash writes "The encouraging thing is...that Wittgenstein...entirely by his own efforts virtually reconstituted the thinking of Nagarjuna...from nearly two thousand years ago. This is ...a measure of the distance we ourselves have yet to travel" (p31). Indeed in his emphasis on environment as interdependence, Ash comes near to equating the term with Emptiness itself. To do so might have led him to some interesting conclusions for the 'emptiness' of Buddhism is no mere intellectual construct; rather it is a pivot for a whole way of being based on meditative enquiry. Even so Ash's whole project lies within the field I term 'Buddhistics' wherein these ancient concepts are seen to have a vital relevance to our contemporary dilemmas.

The final chapter, buddhistically entitled "Right Livelihood", indeed emphasises this theme. "The fulcrum of that world whose values must...change if catastrophe is to be averted is the metaphysical self. And the agent of this transformation is the notion of environment. Environment, it might be said, is that to which no Self, in its capacity of a detached observer, can belong. Environment annihilates Self, just as it negates the discrete objects that...compose the reality of the world. The world is composed, not of objects...but of forms of life, of being...of relationships: and not of relationships between things, but between relationships in infinite regression, with no ultimate reference. An environment is hence a form of being in which observer and observed are dissolved."

Ash seeks the supercession of our limiting cast of thought and his project is an exploration of possibilities and of ultimate questions which, like koans, cannot perhaps be intellectually resolved within the frame of language. The heart felt intuition of meditation is also needed here. Our Western individualism needs a total reconsideration, says Ash, and the way forward is through the understanding of connections wherever they occur and upon whatever scale. If, as Ash finally implies, we must be mad before we are sane at least endeavours such as this may act as a red ribbon through a minefield.

Maurice Ash is a bold and convincing writer capable of passages of great philosophical insight and beauty. I can see him at his desk working on an idea; an alternative occurs to him and down it goes in parenthesis. For some this will make his text a demanding read. I counsel persistence for there are jewels here that need to be widely appreciated. Ash wants to "offer a gift to whoever will receive it, because I think I have something to impart." He has, and anyone perplexed by the dilemmas of our time would do well to listen.

WINTER BUDDHA

After midnight, when the still streets
drip from the trees audibly soft leaves
and I smile to hear sleepy voices
silenced by a closing window's sound,
I take a match to an incense stick
and set bright the dark candle in my private shrine.

With six slow breaths the pillared flame
sets this brooding throne aglow
where, pivoted upon some silent thought,
the golden face spans inwardly
the space between the symbol and the seen.

Come close, with eyes as camera
trace the perfections of a latent shot,
memory projected on a screen,
moment immortalised perhaps or trapped;
perceive, half hidden under downcast lids,
the open eyes now fixed yet flexible
filling quietened rooms and grateful heart
with the silent quality of the street-
space between windows
treading softly between couchant forms.

October 1969

NCF VII

THE CH'AN RETREAT WITH MASTER SHENG YEN, MAENLLWYD, APRIL 1992

John Crook: A Guestmaster's View

The role of guestmaster at a Chan retreat entails the responsibility for ensuring the comfort of the participants and visiting Master, the availability of necessary supplies and the organisation of affairs to ensure the even flow of the retreat programme. Together with Chief Cook and the Retreat Disciplinarian the work of the Guestmaster maintains the background quality of a retreat.

When I undertook this task with Shifu, I knew that it would not be an easy one. I wanted to ensure that as many applicants as possible would be able to benefit from Shifu's presence in this country, his first visit since his 1989 introduction of orthodox Chan to Britain at the Maenllwyd. Some thirty-two participants were coming, stretching our accommodation and resources to the limits.

The weeks before the retreat saw a detailed checking of equipment, everything from knives and forks to mats, zafus from Throssel Hole, chairs for mealtimes and new floor coverings. There were shopping expeditions, letters sent and parcels received and a considerable financial outlay to bring the quantities up to the required level and on time for the retreat.

The tunnel through the wall connecting the new Chan Hall to the house had to be completed. I was anxious that we could all move easily between the two to avoid repeated taking on and off of shoes to cross the mud of the yard between events. Edward, the builder, pushed the hole through on time, but everything was covered with the fine dust from his hearty demolitions. I went up to Pant-y-dwr a couple of days early to find the job only just completed and spent hours cleaning as well as laying out the rooms.

This needed careful planning. A Chan retreat has a tight schedule and everything must flow together in sequence. For this to happen all blocks need eliminating, so I worked out a scheme to ensure the optimum flow of persons. From Chan hall to dining space and back again and from sleeping areas to exercise yard and so on. Also because of shortage of space, extra tables for meals had to be erected and laid just before each meal and this had to be organised carefully. Finally I visualised each day's proceedings and imagined the various hold ups that could occur. By arranging everything appropriately I thought the retreat would run easily in spite of the pressure of so many people. Only the event itself would prove me right or wrong.

When everyone arrived they gradually occupied their sleeping places. Some discrete arrangements had been called for, the elderly being placed near toilets and the ladies, being displaced from their usual bedroom, given one of the upper floors of the Chan hall. The "toughies" were allocated the large unheated barn across the yard where they could see clouds or stars floating past the holes in the roof. The "toughies" are a special breed of participant many of whom have been coming to the Maenllwyd since the days when such conditions were the accepted norm. Among them are long distance third world travellers, mountaineers, an ex-Antarctic surveyor and those who just like making conditions for themselves as challenging as possible. When Shifu saw my own tent forlornly withstanding a Welsh April shower he was seriously alarmed for my health. I told him I was off to Mount Kailas in a month and needed some training!

Everything seemed to be settling down nicely when Shifu upset it all! I had carefully spaced out the sitting spaces in the Chan hall by using the upper floors as well as the main room. All this had been agreed by postal discussion. Suddenly Shifu said "No, put 'em all together" or the Mandarin to that effect. Hurriedly I reorganised, reflecting on the beauties of the Zen discipline, until everyone was within millimetres of each other, gasping from compression and appearing to meditate. It was a hard first day but then Shifu relented and gradually we spaced out again up into the attics. I think the need for air flow did it.

Shifu himself arrived with a cold and I was greatly concerned about him because, after Taiwan, mid-Wales in April can be dangerously chilling. Guo Yen Hse was also worried about him and we spent some time eliminating drafts and checking the heating. The "air pollution" was worrying them both and I realised they were caught between the Atlantic freshness of the oceanic hill breezes and the stuffiness of paraffin stoves. My explanation that the air was probably the least polluted in Britain did not seem to convince them and I muttered on in my mind remembering the air conditions in New York and Taipai. Shifu began wearing a surgical mask but whether it was from fear of spreading his own cold, the germs of others or the air pollution I was unable to determine.

Unknown to retreatants things came to a crisis on the third day when Guo Yen Hse was seriously worried about Shifu's cold. Shifu said that since I could run retreats as well as he I had better take over. What sort of Zen joke was this, I asked myself.

I assembled all four participant Western doctors and Shifu provided them with a detailed account of his symptoms. Nodding their heads wisely they tut-tuttingly remarked that antibiotics merely made things worse and that it was bound to pass. I prescribed heavy rest until the evening lecture. Shifu, fortified by this encounter, was indomitably back on form by late afternoon. Grinning, he told me he had taken some of his Chinese medicine. Certainly he never looked back, as all participants know.

One thing I never had to worry about was food. The cooks did marvels and Simon's oriental flair was being much appreciated. In spite of great difficulty, meals were faultlessly on time and the Zen of cookery much in evidence. Working with Guo Yen Hse was learningful. In spite of considerable pressure he was sustaining an ease of manner and a kind of light personal discipline that touched me deeply and gave me confidence. When he felt something needed correction he would take me aside gently and politely mention it. I usually managed to put it right. Likewise the strength of mind shown by Paul Kennedy, our interpreter, impressed me greatly. He was having problems sleeping and sitting but never once did this show in his excellent and often witty work for us.

Surprisingly, once the retreat got underway I lost my anxieties. The flow of events and the way in which, in spite of everything, the retreat fell together delighted me. I let the universe take over and applied my method. Some very good sittings followed and my mind calmed. Shifu's teachings were often inspiring and I delighted especially in the method of Direct Meditation. It came naturally to me as I love the contemplation of nature and it had clear affinity with Dzogchen teaching which I had received from some Tibetan teachers. When the retreat was well advanced Shifu called me to him. He was smiling. Good news, he said, one of the participants has attained kensho. I was delighted especially when I learned who it was. I had known this man, a doctor, for some years. He had come to many Western Zen Retreats previously. During his first retreats he had cried a great deal being blessed by this freedom to weep out his suffering. Then on one retreat, as we were chanting, he had suddenly gained a deep insight into the meaning of the Heart Sutra, an insight that left him weeping and laughing at the same time and at intervals thereafter. He had found the insight so beautiful and yet so ordinary that only so could he express it. Having had a comparable experience myself I felt I knew what was happening. On later retreats these experiences had recurred to him with an increasing clarity until in one interview he had given me so profound an insight into the sutra and its meaning that I felt sure he had "seen the nature". I shared this with him but felt I would like his experience to be validated by Shifu. I had not explicitly identified him to Shifu and awaited the result of his retreat this time with interest. His report is presented below.

Shifu told us he does not frequently validate such insights unless he is very sure. He feels that many transmissions given in Japan are rather trivial because of the pressure of the training system of young monks. He would prefer caution, since true "seeing the nature" is often preceded by emotional states that look like it and feel exceptional but lack the clarity of the real thing. He said that his recognition of this participant's attainment should remain confidential during the retreat. He was against public pronouncements like school prize-givings. In any case, he told us, nothing has been attained except an insight into the ground of one's own nature that was already there. To make any kind of announcement would merely block others, setting up targets, imaginings, envy and making people strain for a goal for which they might not be ready. Furthermore, there is nothing for the person involved to be proud about. Yet he may make the mistake of becoming so and then seeking egoistically for more such proofs of his attainment. This would be a sad if understandable error.

Insights such as this come about by the effects of good karma. I would almost use the term "grace" for it. There is nothing one can do to "attain" it except follow the method and train diligently. It may or may not arise, only doing so indeed when the desire for it and the implied self-cherishing entirely vanish. This is a natural event when certain conditions ripen. Because no-one can find it with a desiring ego, training in humility and patience is the only way. It is for this reason too that the goal of Shifu's retreats is not set on such a target. The goal is training in awareness, the realisation of one's own condition and how little one understands it or controls one's behaviour and inner experiences, repentance and the gaining of a Zen attitude through hearing the teachings and practising the methods.

All this meant that nothing was said in public. It was a private matter like the content of all interviews with the Master. The participant asked Shifu how he should speak of the occurrence. Describe what happened without evaluation, was the answer. Shifu has subsequently mentioned this event in his New York journal and I feel that it is now a good thing to tell of it here, for it is only during the retreat itself that such mentioning can most seriously mislead. To talk about it in the terms above is moreover important. Many people have serious miscomprehensions on this subject and give themselves a lot of trouble as a result. The competitive become more so, the jealous - mean, the depressed - mournful and the successful - arrogant. It is important to read the Masters on this subject. In many cases a great Master had only one or two such deep experiences in his whole life which was otherwise devoted to deep training in compassion towards others. Often the first experience is quite trivial and only after many years is deeper insight attained. Some great teachers never "see the nature" and yet make major contributions to human life. Others stand frequently within its transcending yet ordinary presence. The whole matter is part of the expression of the mystical capacity of the human mind which many Buddhists have also experienced with varying degrees of depth and frequency. Shifu says that the significance of the insight within Zen is the confirmation it brings of the accuracy of the teachings.

While writing this I wondered whether there was anything in the participant's report that might be a guide to others. Reading it carefully I note the following points. Firstly this participant was unusually focused and determined. He already knew what he was after but also that egoistic striving would be pointless. He therefore set himself to apply his method to the exclusion of everything else. Taking Shifu's teaching about self-isolation very seriously he cut himself off from all concern with others. He showed a sort of ruthlessness with himself, discounting his physical pain. He resisted wandering thoughts and the temptation to allow reminiscences to flow through his head. The past was irrelevant, only the present counted. He saw that he had to penetrate beyond the aesthetics of beautiful experiences into their nature within his own mind. Finally he saw that his own mentality was a condition of limitation; it was universal and not personal mind that was flowing. In this identification he found truth.

I learnt many things during the retreat and these will doubtless find their way into later presentations to this journal. None the less when it came to my turn to speak on the last evening I felt I was a bit too enthusiastic about the material success of the event. In spite of being a trained public speaker I always find a terrifying shyness overcomes me at such times. I feel I can never assess such a rich experience so close to it - but then it is not really assessment that is being requested.

I was glad Philip was able to pass on his puppies and that no dogs had to die because of us. In London I was blessed by the company of Shifu, Guo Yen Hse and my old friend Yiu Yan Nang as we visited the British Museum and British Library to see the ancient paintings and manuscripts from Tung Huang in a private viewing. It was a privilege to look at them in such company.

At Bristol Parkway we nearly missed our train. A porter held a door open in time but we almost lost some luggage. It was still sitting on the platform. Remembering the consequent rush I had later asked Shifu how he had felt. He said he had looked at the luggage and, feeling the train move, had said to himself "Ah, there it goes!"

THE STATE OF THE NATION

An Editorial from the Ch'an Hall

I find it embarrassing to write to the above title for all of us could easily pontificate on what is wrong with the world. Yet present events can hardly pass without comment among those of us concerned with the quality of human life. As I write two ten year old boys are being held by police for the premeditated abduction and gruesome murder of a toddler. Of course, if these little boys are guilty they will bear the stigma for the rest of their lives. Yet we must ask if any ten year old should bear the whole responsibility for such a terrible crime. A ten year old child cannot do other than reflect the conditions in the society that has bred him or her. In this terrible killing we see our world reflected. As the angry and distressed crowds stand unaccustomedly in the churches how many are wondering about their own involvement in this crime, the gross social negligence that allowed it to happen?

This event is but the sharp point of a general malaise that has been the subject of much recent commentary. Ministers attempt to talk us out of it but a general despondency reflects the levels of unemployment, crime, rape, child abuse, social and marital discord, all running at high levels. It is no comfort to reflect that in this deep recession similar features are found throughout Europe with racism and ethnic cleansing as its worst manifestation. It is in this sort of situation that fascism gains its hold. Recent and justifiable complaints about the uselessness of our present politicians could lead into that sort of attempted answer.

The causes of our distress are undoubtedly many but a few features are clear enough. Our sense of national and regional identity expresses itself in loyalty and dedication to institutions. Recently most of those which have been historically most enduring have shown signs of failure. There is a general breakdown in community feeling correlating with the centralisation of power in Westminster and the under-funding of distributed power outwards into newly structured systems of medical provision and education. The malaise in Universities is especially striking. But the loss of a sense of community is also related to the high mobility of the workforce, the urbanisation of dormitory villages, the collapse of farming communities and the ethos of economic individualism that allows the careless growth of an underclass of youngsters begging in the hearts of our cities. The Thatcherite failure to address social and psychological needs through favouring a focus on material economy and a competitive free for all is linked to the absence of a caring political philosophy and the collapse of socialist ideals.

What does this mean for those who subscribe to this journal? We need to ask ourselves what we really stand for. Do we attend Zen meditation groups simply to reduce our own anxieties, to find a togetherness with a few others who feel the same way, to seek some relief from our social distress? Have we any sense of community in what we are about? Do we care about the elderly in our own group or about the children of our younger members? Do we merely attend our meetings when the whim takes us or we have nothing better to do? Are we seriously committed to training or merely trying to comfort ourselves as we recline in our comfortable middle class armchairs in front of our imitation log fires?

These are matters we should seriously consider for we are citizens of our land and how we are is the state of our nation. In this issue of our journal Shih-fu warns us about the dangers of busying about do-gooding. He points to the need to work on our own personalities and their expression in the world. In the Dharma this need takes pride of place because everything else follows from it. Yet the forces that rule society are also to a degree independent of personal expression. Institutions, economies and social systems run in their own way and are only indirectly responsive to the personalities that are the cogs within their machines. We have to tap the sources of social power and expression as well as those of our personal morality. The difficulty in society arises as much from our institutions as it does from ourselves. It follows that all of us need to be politicians, to argue for the expression of our practice in society at large. This is not done by huge donations of money but rather through the spread of cells that activate at the personal level and so shift the quality of institutions from within. There is a role for the appropriately subversive in our national structure. Our job is to sustain a continuous critique. It will take the Tibetans a long time to regain control of their land. It will take us a long time to re-enchant our own.

INTRODUCING TANTRA TO THE PATH

A new retreat for annual presentation at the Maenllwyd.

In this retreat we begin with methods common to Zen and to Tibetan Buddhism, calming the mind and gaining insight into its nature and then introduce further methods which are known as Tantra.

The purpose of doing this is to allow participants to become aware of the wide range of methods available in Mahayana Buddhism and to fulfil in part the Ch'an vow to "master limitless approaches to Dharma". Such a retreat is rare and participants are invited to make the most of the opportunity.

The main idea in Tantra is to transform the mind through directly envisaging the presence of the Buddha or Bodhisattva. The visualised being may then confer blessings, purification, peace of mind, power or stabilisation of insight depending upon the specific "sadhana" (ritual visualisation) performed. The practitioner, after appropriate training and initiation, may also identify him or herself with the figure, thereby acquiring, for a brief time, the mind of a Buddha. Although this is merely an exercise, the lamas say that such practice gradually transforms the mind through repeated familiarisation with the psychological content of the image. It is of course essential that this content is truly apperceived, for without that the exercise is only fantasy. The only danger is that, instead of insight, illusions of power and ego enhancement may result. Tantric practice needs to be firmly anchored in the humility and compassion of the Bodhisattva vow.

A further Tantric practice is the visualisation of the chakras and energy channels of the body which, in Higher Yogic Tantra, is then combined with 'deity' visualisation as in the Six Yogas of Naropa.

The aim of Tantric practice is Mahamudra, a term equivalent in meaning to the 'mind of insight' in Zen. There is a "path of preparation", in which one purposefully applies the methods. There is also a "path of completion", which is the expression of insight once it is realised. Within the latter there is no intentionality since the "fox is already caught". The adept knows that the path of completion begins only after the ending of preparation. In each sitting session, preparation may lead into completion. However, for the beginner, the methods of preparation will not yet have yielded the essential insight. In the Nyingma practice of "Dzogschen" the practitioner is wholly within the path of completion. Yet even here, a return to preparation is needed whenever insight is lost.

Zen, Mahamudra and Dzogschen each have a similar goal in mind. The richness of the range of methods available will not be found contradictory so long as a firm understanding of the basis is apprehended. This lies in the Prajnaparamita Sutras of the Buddha and teachings closely related to these.

On this retreat, which focuses on practice rather than philosophy, certain basic tantric methods will be taught, including some limited use of chakra visualisation and the practice of a Chenrezi (Avalokitesvara) sadhana. The way in which these can empower sitting meditation and quicken the deepening of insight is the focus of this retreat. Participants should be enabled to develop an effective practice to take home with them. Individual interviews, as in Western Zen Retreats, will monitor each individual's understanding and consider how far Tantric methods are useful for that person. Talks clarifying Tantra in relation to Zen will be given at intervals during the retreat. Depending on progress an initiation enabling participants to practice the Chenrezi Sadhana outside retreat may be given.

I hope that some of the mystification surrounding the subject of Tantra can be dispelled and the great value of its careful use under supervision be made apparent.

THE PRAJNAPARAMITA HEART SUTRA A BRIEF COMMENTARY

Edited and abbreviated text of a lecture on the Sutra given by John Crook to the Bristol Ch'an group on the evening of November 18th 1992. This is the second part of a short series of talks. Beginning in our last issue the Sutra now continues:

> Form is precisely emptiness.
>
> And emptiness precisely form.
>
> So also are sensation, perception, volition and consciousness;
>
> Sariputra, this voidness of all dharmas is not born, not destroyed,
>
> Not impure, not pure, does not increase nor decrease.
>
> In voidness there is no form
>
> And no sensation, perception, volition or consciousness,
>
> No eye, ear, nose, tongue, body, mind,
>
> No sight, sound, smell, taste, touch, thought,
>
> There is no realm of the eye
>
> All the way up to no realm of mental cognition.
>
> There is no ignorance and no ending of ignorance.
>
> There is no ageing and death and no ending of ageing and death.
>
> There is no suffering, no cause of suffering, no cessation of suffering and no path.
>
> There is no wisdom or any attainment.

Here we have the pivotal message of the "Second Turning of the Wheel of the Law", the doctrine of emptiness as the central feature of the Mahayana. Yet when we examine the way the idea is presented we find the language used belongs at first to the older vision, the philosophical doctrine of the Theravada. Scholars who have studied the text carefully suggest that it was assembled from the huge Prajnaparamita literature during a transitional period in the history of Buddhism when a fresh emphasis was gradually extending the ideas of the original view. The difference lies in the wider scope and greater range of perspective. Let us see how this happens.

The main ideas of the early doctrine go right back to the first sermon when the Buddha spoke to his yogin friends in the Deer Park at Benares. The Buddha expressed his new found understanding, his enlightenment, very simply in the Four Noble Truths, that life is suffering, that suffering is due to craving, that craving can end and that the way is eightfold in method.

The word translated as craving means any kind of wanting, either wanting something you have not got, or not wanting something which you have. Either way it is the movement of desire or rejection which is the root of the lack of ease. Clearly the Buddha is speaking primarily about mental suffering, about attitudes we hold which cause us distress. He is not talking about the pain of a broken leg, but rather the attitudes towards a broken leg which can make a great deal of difference to the manner in which we cope with an accident. He speaks of the mental approaches to life and not some magical or idealistic idea which will stop a broken leg from hurting.

If you find that you are suffering the Buddha recommends that you look into your own mind to see what it is doing with the problem. Instead of evoking some state of passionless trance or samadhi the Buddha recommended his own method of Vipassana. This method requires a practitioner to look directly at the processes of his own thought and feeling without denying them. One has to ask the question "What is going on here?" and then explore it fully by letting thought and feeling express itself within an acute awareness of process.

What do you find? Well, you find sensations, ideas, wants and consciousness. You also realise that all this is situated in the form that is your physical presence. These features are known as the five 'skandhas'. All mental phenomena are structured in this way. Whenever you look into your mind you will find them.

Furthermore they are based in the operations of the eye, ear, nose, sense of touch and awareness and the mental corollaries of these physical systems. You also become aware that these systems get old, wear out and die. At the centre of all this activity is your sense of your "own being", your self, ego or I. This is the Buddha's model of the mind described in detail in the scriptures of the Theravada known as Abhidharma.

But the Buddha also said that such processes of knowing, wanting and rejecting, all centred on the presence of a self, are in a special sense quite illusory. These are the terms you come up with when you set out to analyse and describe the way the mind works. Where is the self? Is it the totality of the body? Is it in the body at all? What is its relation to the body? As you read this - try to find it. Paradoxically while you will have little doubt about the fact of your existence, the precise location or mode of being of what you appear to be is very far from obvious. Similarly, if you seek to locate the roots of experience whether of sensation, volition, thought or awareness you again find yourself tumbling into an absence of certainty, into a great doubt. Such processes are easy to name but when you seek to locate or find them, or observe from where they arise, there is more of an absence than a presence. It is as if these words don't refer to things but to merely transient states the objectivity of which is highly illusory.

The Buddha said that all these words simply isolate aspects of a process of interdependent origination ('pratityasamutpada'); where the mind is so are all of they. But where is the mind? It too is in an interdependent relationship of inner and outer, of before and after, of now-ness and then-ness. Nothing in fact can be pinned down. There is at root just a great flowing together. Furthermore, in meditation these processes flow apart in ways that differ from everyday minding. There are alternative ways of seeing things. Indeed what are things? Are they out there or in the mind, part in or part out? Can one actually say?

The Buddha said that all these processes lacked objectivity as things with intrinsic selfhood. They were empty of "inherent existence", rather their being had the nature of flow which only appeared partible through the activity of a discriminatory mind. Self was therefore empty and, since that was so, to be attached to it as if it were a thing was to be in great ignorance. In fact, this was the root of all illusion and suffering. Meditation on this allows one to drop attachment, drop the illusory projection of objectivity and enter a world of revelatory freedom. Words are names and, as modern thinkers might say, we tend to live within our texts and not within truth itself. To let go of the assumptions of the worldly illusion, ('Samsara') is to find the freedom of 'nirvana' where all texts themselves are dropped.

If you are not here what is there to fuss about? Of course the world remains in itself, ineffably so. There is sensation, form and process and it is beautiful. Why do you want more? Or want it to be otherwise? This is how things are. There is no need to crave or reject because there is nothing substantial to crave or want.

The essential feature of this approach is to realise that it is based in meditation. Thought can raise innumerable objections and create endless metaphysical speculation. The Buddha is speaking out of his enlightenment. He is sharing it, transmitting it. To receive it one has to follow the same path. Philosophically the idea of "self' is a "category error". Self is simply not the sort of thing it seems to be. Meditation is essential to realise this existentially. At some point there is an "Ah ha!" experience. "So that's it" you will say. You have dropped a concept and seen a freedom. These are first steps on the path leading to a place where your view of self as entity itself also falls away.

In the "Second Turning of the Wheel of the Law" these ideas were pressed further. In the traditional view, the Buddha himself taught this extension to certain disciples who were ready for it. Some scholars in fact believe there was a minority belief among certain practitioners which always held the new view. Others think there was a gradual revision of the original insight.

The idea of emptiness came to be focused not only on psychological phenomena but applied to all phenomena of any son anywhere. Whereas the Buddha's first approach had been psychological and had shown how the individual could go beyond self-limitation, the notion of everything as empty now expands and expands until everything you can think of, the vast cosmos itself is seen as Vast Emptiness. Vastness unlimited, unbounded spaciousness, timeless presence.

Do you catch the idea? Imagine the space through which the universe has expanded since the Big Bang. Physicists say one cannot really talk of this in terms of space or time at all since neither of these had existence before the primal explosion. There is eternity, an endless present moment; an imagined vastness.

This is the root of the Mahayana. So also, however, is the opposite realisation. If all form is precisely emptiness, emptiness nonetheless appears to us as form. Form is precisely emptiness but emptiness also is precisely form. Samsara and Nirvana are contrasting perspectives on the Unknown Nature that lies behind it all. The vision of the Mahayana is that both are true in a co-emergent mutuality which becomes the focus of meditation itself.

In the older vision the ending of self-cherishing led to the realisation of the Arhat - one who had gone beyond and disappeared without a care. In the new view no-one has disappeared. The market place is still full of the goods and contending merchants. The sadness of the ignorance, the horror of war, abuse, crime and the knot tied by visions of self-importance or fearful insignificance appear again as real; an illusory vision maybe but one that inspires an appropriate compassion. The new idea is the Bodhisattva, one who seeks enlightenment only so as to assist others to enlightenment themselves.

How can others be helped along the path? This is the way of the Bodhisattva. Paradoxically this way has no path as such, no resolution as such, no wisdom inheres within it. Suffering is empty yet never ceases. There is no attainment. There is however the activity of the Bodhisattva functioning within the dual insight that form is emptiness and emptiness is form. In the co-emergent vision the Bodhisattva knows nothing - yet through his being he seeks to transform the world.

How do we comprehend this? What is our starting point here? Take pain. Look into it closely. In meditation place your awareness on your aching knee, the itch on your cheek or your backache. If you can sustain a disinterested awareness it changes its apparent nature. Instead of pain to be rejected or escaped it changes to mere sensation, neutral. If you just feel it to be so the discomfort slowly disappears. Finally it moves on and something else appears. What then did the word 'pain' mean?

Zen masters are not very sympathetic if you have a backache in meditation on retreat. "Put your mind in it!" they may say. Change may take time but mostly you suddenly find yourself free and realise the extent to which your own fear of pain was creating it. (Of course this practice is not appropriate in cases of actual medical problems).

Now look at form. Is your body really here? If so in what manner? Shut your eyes and where is it? All this has to be gone into. "You" may entirely disappear and instead of your body on the cushion there may be a mere awareness of presence. A presence of what?

Now look at the Universe in all its multiplicity. What happens if you persist with the Koan "What is it?"

If we look at volition, our wants and rejections, we find they are structured by ideas which we project upon our world. These projections are called "samskaras". They are the product of our education, relations with parents, karma rolling down through centuries. We conceive things in highly patterned ways in which our presuppositions create only apparent realities. In modern psychotherapies these are the sources of neurosis, fixed attributions the Illusory nature of which we have not seen. You believe you should be seen as famous or beautiful yet you are not so perceived. Trouble for everyone, pride, jealousy and paranoia, fear that one may not be what one has cracked oneself up to be.

It turns out that it is very difficult to think differently, to change these deeply emotionally rooted presuppositions. Some such 'samskaras' have dreadful consequences. They produce prejudice and ethnic cleansing of all sorts be they in Serbia, Tibet under Chinese domination or the paranoid Muslim fear of Salman Rushdie (he might be right and that must never be allowed).

In what sense are these 'samskaras' empty? If you examine your own prejudices and biases in deep meditation you will find out. Just as pain dissolves when examined with a meditative mind so too do the 'samskaras' weaken their hold upon our attitudes. Prejudice dissolves in meditation as the self becomes freed of selfishness. Pre-conceptions drop away. Others are seen just as they are, as deluded as you are. In the same boat. Compassion has a chance to emerge in the mind.

As meditators you need to examine your own 'samskaras' and work with them. Let them appear in full force and do not shrink from them. Then go into them, examine their bases. How can we test that they are empty?

The purpose of the Western Zen Retreat is to allow your personal 'samskaras' to arise in the communication exercise. Working with "Who am I?" your judgemental nature appears undeniably. After multiple evasions and excuses you have to admit who you are. Gradually it all appears less dreadful. As you realise this is just the way you think, so you realise it is possible to think differently.

But something else is going on. In meditation the mind is much calmer and more insightful. You reach the point of realising that your whole self-conception and that of others is a rigmarole of the imagination. You may reach a point where you simply give it up. You drop it. And, as it disappears, you realise your mind is suddenly cool, clear and empty of discrimination that leads to prejudice. You see others just as they are, as you are. And giving up the self you can understand Shih-fu when he says "Let the Universe do it". You are no different from the Universe.

When the mind lets it all go, becoming still and quiet you may find there is no sensation of time, no fixity in space. There is a sort of cosmic reference, no longer walls, boundaries, horizons. The clock ticks but where is the ticking? It no longer advances in time, it goes backwards and forwards. Momentless presence, eternity. Eternity itself never moves. Have you ever moved?

If you have touched the Eternal you will know there is no wisdom, no attainment, no path. There is the fullness you cannot express. Beyond its limitations the mind can only find the ineffable. What began as a mountain is no more a mountain, but then it is simply the mountain again. What was said can no longer be said, but then it is said again. The text is empty but outside of being it is all we have.

The text of the Sutra moves on. "With nothing to attain, the Bodhisattvas relying on insight have no obstruction in their minds. And having no confusion and imaginings they reach ultimate Nirvana". Afterwards the Bodhisattva will go into the kitchen and prepare for you just another cup of tea. Earl Grey or Peppermint perhaps?

MAENLLWYD

Three Poems

Arriving in the yard
I switch off the engine
and gaze at the view,
evening sun on the rolling hills
yellow fields, dark woods.
In the sudden silence
a buzzard mews,
distantly guiding sheep
dogs bark.

Entering the gate
I come home to my hermitage,
welcoming trees brood
and the old door creaks on rusty hinges
falling plaster needs sweeping from the floor,
softly on cold flags moisture gleams.

Lighting the fire
I watch slow smoke rising,
hang in the windless cwm.
The smells of the hills
roll in through opened windows,
thankfully I breath out city air,
inside my room
no sound.

*

The hills lie still, only sheep disturb
this summer evening's equanimity,
over the farmstead yard
the dark soul'd sycamore broods
bunched branches heavily
together hang.

Wide valley, patchwork fields
roof the bedrock of this land,
few travellers, for tourists hug the towns
and roads that cut like knives,
here shady lanes meander yet,
one travels vaguely,
things do not get
so easily done.

Fading light brings deeper silence,
the grey stone soul turns inward to the cwm,
this sycamore now holds its breath
continuously - my eyes roam
yard to landscape far to near,
behind my chair
the small and unlit house
waits like an old friend.

*

Freshly cool the silent room inhales
the fair scent of summer night
candles on the table flutter
an incense mingling breeze.

Retreated from our seared souls' silences,
those zombie spaces where in the cold snake
kills the warm, composed heart opens
to the pains that move yet are not changed.

If I could give you now this other stillness
wherein the night owl cries beyond the barn
two minds' silences would be as one
grateful emptiness of a midnight calm.

And yet heart's silences like secrets
are for the single one alone -
in your universe and far away you move
here candles flutter in hay scented air

July 1975

NCF VIII

CHENREZI COMES TO TOWN.

An Editorial from the Ch'an Hall.

Walking in the hills the other day I was reflecting on the meaning of "Buddha Nature". I found myself asking "Since the Buddha Mind was originally the Buddha's mind what would he be like if he was here now?"

You can find the most immediate accounts of Gautama the man in the Pali Sutras. Ananda's outstanding memory allowed him to recall Gautama as a friend and preserve his talk. Although framed in an archaic form of storytelling, the person of the speaker still shines through.

Gautama was by nature princely, his mind was sharp, creative and highly original, he worked extremely hard establishing a new order of spiritual practitioners, rejecting caste. He was deeply involved in the politics of his time being an adviser and admonisher of kings and ministers. If you had met him you would have found a pair of siding intelligent eyes. If you were a Brahmin he would have skilfully led you into his way by redefining who you were with an irresistible appeal to your common sense and inner morality. He was ascetic, disciplined, totally positive yet deeply sceptical. Where others were idealistic, he saw through idealism to an acceptance of the illusory basis of human life, pride, shame, gain, egoism and the fear of impermanence. He had found a way through in personal experience and there had been no copying of others. It would be a meeting you would never forget. It would also, in spite of the severity of his message, almost certainly have been fun. The man's charisma must have been deeply infectious.

And now Chenrezi suddenly comes to town. A Bodhisattva has been touring Britain, chatting in princely style with senior ministers, high prelates and influential persons, playing croquet at a country hotel and appearing on the largest platforms in the land, speaking to vast audiences drawn from all walks of life, most of them not Buddhists but fellow travellers inspired by his humanity and positivity.

The Dalai Lama, in spite of his fame, titles, political position and Nobel Peace Prize, comes over as exactly what he claims to be - an ordinary Buddhist monk. To see him come on stage, hands clasped before him, with that slightly stooped, almost shy manner and surprised look, as if the occasion was a refreshing revelation to him, is to have the heart touched. Knowing the sad history of his people, the relentless balancing acts in which he is engaged with the obdurate Chinese communists, the awe inspiring solemnity of his high religious office and his deep learning, it is profoundly touching to see at once that here is a man with whom one could sit down to tea and open one's heart. His power of meditation shows. He is after all the current embodiment of Avalokitesvara, the Bodhisattva of Compassion, Chenrezi. He is perhaps the nearest person in our time to show us how the Buddha must have been.

So what did he say? Homely and straightforward, not complex, his was a simple appeal for goodness. His faith is that humans are at root loving, compassionate beings. Pointing out that, unlike Tigers, we have neither fangs nor claws but soft fingers and vegetarian teeth, he argued that our nature was at root peaceful like animals that pasture themselves gently in the world.

Yet, sadly, we are afflicted by karmic ignorance that gives us illusions of ego, creating needs for power, cravings for fame and antagonism to all who appear to threaten us. We forget that everyone is in the same boat on an ocean of mutual fear. Once we recognise that others are just as fearful and confused as ourselves there is a chance that empathy and compassion can arise.

Compassion is often mistaken as pity and tends to focus on those who, to use Mrs Thatcher's expression, are "one of us". That is not compassion, says the Dalai Lama. Compassion involves the recognition of sameness, an empathy for others that comes from a fearless openness of awareness and insight that even one's enemies are frightened too. Compassion is thus in a sense disinterested, impartial. It wishes well. It is also good for you. Indeed, to be compassionate is the best thing one can do for oneself. And why? Because compassion turns one's thoughts away from self onto others. The focus on one's own fears and prejudices is reduced and with that comes a calm of mind that is the root of creative reflection. It is the way to inner peace.

The opposite is hatred and hatred is the product of fear. Fear lashes out and becomes violence. Weapons are sought and arms races begun. The stupidity of it all is so apparent but still it happens. At every level it is essential to control hatred. Anger is sometimes beneficial for there is righteous anger, but generally speaking, anger allied to hate is nothing other than pure destructiveness. And the selfishness that underlies it is eating up our societies, our world community, our environment and ourselves.

The point is so simple - just the recognition that all of us have the same tendencies to fear and hate. Knowing this it becomes essential to try the other path, the way of compassion, hearing the other's viewpoint, talk and more talk, negotiation, permission to empathise. And this at every level, highest to lowest, in and out the marriage bed. It is essential to realise that Compassion is one's root nature from which hatred is a deviation. Down through time we have all been mothers of one another.

His Holiness has often spoken of his compassion for the Chinese. Indeed, the karmic fate for those who are cruel and destructive is severe. The torturers are in deep need of compassion and need also to learn what this word means. Human rights involve the granting of freedoms of self-expression and government that will foster understanding, empathy and compassion, especially between neighbours.

The Dalai Lama sees hope in the world. Not for him some world-ending scenario. He always sees the buds of May sprouting from wintry branches. He interprets the present chaos as the pain of growth towards new political expressions in which human rights will be respected and economic and political realities. He will continue to work towards this end even though his enemies, for whom he manifests such a studied regard, are perhaps the most blinkered in the world.

If this man with all his cares can be so positive can we not follow his example? His infectious chuckle radiates warmth from platform, TV screen and newspaper. We should place that chuckle in our hearts and live towards others from such deep laughter.

Difficult - you say sceptically? Sure sure. That's what the Buddha said.

THE PRAJNAPARAMITA HEART SUTRA- A BRIEF COMMENTARY.

An edited and abbreviated text of the third and last lecture on this topic given to the Bristol Ch'an Group by John Crook on November 25th 1992.

The Sutra ends with the following words:

> With nothing to attain
> Bodhisattvas relying on Prajnaparamita
> have no obstructions in their minds.
> Having no obstructions there is no fear
> and departing far from confusion and imaginings,
> they reach ultimate Nirvana.
> All past, present and future Buddhas
> relying on Prajnaparamita
> attain Anuttara Samyak Sambodhi.
> Therefore, know that the Prajnaparamita
> is the great mantra of power,
> the great mantra of wisdom,
> the supreme mantra,
> the unequalled mantra
> which is able to remove all sufferings.
> It is real not false.
> Therefore recite the mantra of Prajnaparamita:
> Gate Gate Paragate Parasamgate Bodhi Svaha.

An alternative translation is given by Roshi Kennett in her metrical rendition from the Japanese.

> In the mind
> of the Bosatsu who is truly one
> with Wisdom Great there are no obstacles
> and going on beyond this human mind
> he is Nirvana. All the Buddhas True
> of present, past and future, they are all,
> because upon Great Wisdom they rely,

the perfect and most high enlightenment.
The Prajnaparamita one should know
to be the greatest mantra of them all.
The highest and most peerless mantra too.
Allayer of all pain Great Wisdom is.
It is the very truth no falsehood here.
This is the mantra of Great Wisdom, hear!
Buddha, going going going on, going on
beyond, and always going on beyond,
always becoming Buddha. Hail Hail Hail!

In our two preceding talks we have seen that the Sutra expresses the Mahayana vision of ultimate emptiness. Not only are all the attributes of mind perceived as empty but the whole cosmos and all its components, the dharmas, are seen as empty too. The awakening to emptiness is the heartfelt realisation that no thing stands by itself with an inherent existence or solitary independent selfhood. Emptiness means that apparent things are empty of their thingness. Everything is in intimate relationship with everything else. There is a continuous flux of time and space in which all appearances flow in interdependent origination. "Form is precisely emptiness and emptiness is precisely form". This fluidity of process is itself empty and the ultimate process hidden beyond our understanding: it is ineffable, and experientially void. Yet, here the things are, right before our eyes, ears and under our fingers.

The flux of time appears to us as it does because our sense organs are structured to see them as we do. Birds, bees and bats do it differently. Their sense organs represent the objects of awareness to them in other modes than our own. These various interpretations of our universe allow differing sentient beings to find food, companions, objects and experience in their own ways. Emptiness thus is forms; forms are how emptiness is expressed in sentience.

There is then an emergence together of form and emptiness. Both present themselves together to our minds. The great Tibetan Teacher, Tsong kha pa, remarks that this two-sided vision is one of the most difficult realisations a Buddhist practitioner needs to comprehend. Yet, once the insight is seen, liberation from the attachment to things as such more easily arises.

As we deepen this perspective, we begin to see that there can be no separation between ignorance and insight, time and space, ageing and death or cessation of ageing and death and indeed, amazingly, no path, no wisdom or any attainment.

All such words arise from the reifications whereby we dissect out experience into parts and events, creating a thingness of things where insight reveals an uninterrupted flow. When this is perceived one suddenly sees that there can be no attachment because there is actually nothing at all as a thing to be attached to. And with all attainments and paths seen as illusory there can be no loss or gain and therefore no fear, anxiety or worried concern. The mind, normally confused and troubled by such things, thus becomes free of them. There are no obstructions, only a great clarity. This clarity, in which all basis for attachments has been blown away, is called Nirvana.

The realisation requires meditative insight for the words alone can only convince intellectually, if at all. In meditation, a focus on any thing leads to its dissolution. Insight becomes curiously empty, vast spaciousness, vastness itself, unlimited. Names are no longer realities, just names. Namelessly the Universe unfolds.

And in this experience is a joy that comes from a release into freedom and a bliss that arises from gratitude. The three deep experiences of the Buddhist practitioner are emptiness, joy and bliss from which love and compassion arise as s/he contemplates the world in its encaging worldliness, a world to which we all return.

Those who have not had such a realisation should not dismiss its reality nor doubt their own potential. One practitioner at the Maenllywd was working on a koan during a Western Zen Retreat. Suddenly the meaning of the entire Heart Sutra became apparent as a single all-embracing insight. He was overwhelmed in tears of joy. Later his realisation was acknowledged by Shih-fu for he was so blessed as to be able to activate such insight again and again. For most of us such insights are mere glimpses highly tinged with emotion. We quickly become attached to them and want more. A depth of insight into emptiness has not yet materialised and ideas of attainment, path and goal still pester the mind.

We all have predispositions to create complex scenarios of attachment based on early experience. These samskaras arise because from the very beginning we attribute thingness to things and see them as objects for desire or rejection. Maybe the pattern of receiving mother's breast and the denial of it began the setting up structures of desire and satiation. These become more complex as circumstances unroll throughout life, the never ending elaboration of karma.

In Ch'an practice the samskaras make their appearance in the wandering of thought and emotion as we sit upon the cushion. Often we are warned about allowing the elaboration of wandering thought but, actually, once the mind has quietened down, much of it can be simply seen as clouds wandering across a sky.

They come and go, we can learn to detach from them. This is cultivation in practice and it facilitates the possibilities of insight.

One Samskara in particular lies at the root of wanting and this includes the wanting of enlightenment experiences. This is the "thought that confers the I". If you watch your experience closely you will come to see that the emotional tone of your being is greatly determined by whether this "thought conferring I" is present or not.

To take a gross example, you may be having a jolly conversation when someone makes a remark that is a little critical of you. Immediately you feel the sensation we call "hurt". The remark has triggered your "thought which confers an I", your ego, and you respond defensively as if you were a fortress to be guarded. More subtly, you may be gently cruising on your cushion in a state of mild bliss and a seductive voice starts congratulating you. "Ah, this is it! Any moment now and its anuttara samyak sambodhi for me". Oh sad error. As nothing special happens, disillusionment spreads. Do we learn from this? Usually not. The "thought conferring I" is very deeply hidden.

To observe that it is this thought, almost alone of all thoughts, that is one's own deepest enemy requires persistence in self-examination. And also humility, for we are unlikely to dispose of it once and for all merely because of recognition. Yet recognition is the beginning of wisdom. When we set aside this thought, other thoughts are rarely troublesome. In fact, since thought is natural to the moving mind, thoughts can become inspirational and the instruments of wisdom.

The clarity that arises when the "thought that confers an I" is absent is a very precise experience. Once recognised, this clarity is a door to insight (prajna). Indeed it is the raft that takes one to the other side. All Buddhas of past present and future have or will uncover this understanding and it is what Gautama showed his companions in the Deer Park all those centuries ago.

The Sutra ends with what we may call a celebration. Ananda stands in for the experience of Great Wisdom and, once an association is made between the mantra and the experience, the repetition of the mantra becomes a means of cultivating its signification. Usually the mantra is translated as "Gone gone, gone beyond, absolutely gone beyond, Wisdom, Hail". Roshi Kennett stresses the present moment as "Going, always going on beyond". She emphasises the need for perpetual practice, ever present cultivation.

The going beyond the thought that confers the ego is the central feature of the meaning of the mantra. The emptying of the self of its thingness is now perceived as real and with deepening insight the emptiness of all things becomes ever more clear. Roshi Kennett also stresses that the mind that has gone beyond is itself Nirvana. There is no longer a mind or an ego that has Nirvana. Nirvana simply presents itself.

Does all this seem remote and distant? Well, take heart! It is not so far away. For example, try a change in language as a door to a fresh experience. We normally say "I" whenever we use a verb . Thus: "I have a head ache", "I am resentful", "I am cutting carrots", "I am enduring the heat and crush on the underground". Now try to rephrase yourself without the I. Thus: "There is a headache", "Here is a resentment", "There is a carrot cutting", "There is a hot crushed feeling down here". Such a change allows the actuality to be present without the possessiveness, the rejection or the desire of a needy self-attribution. Things are just as they are. Often they may still be troublesome but we can stop giving them an inflated importance as when the illusory me-ness of my feeling is the central pivot to experience. As Shih-fu says so often, "put it down. Let the Universe do it!" When you are out of the way there is no path and no attainment. You are looking directly at the moon and not at its reflection in the bucket. Try it.

IN CHINESE MODE: THINKING OF A FRIEND

This poem, parts of which were written at various times in the 1960's and revised now in 1993, is dedicated to Yiu Yan Nang, JP, now Deputy Commissioner of Labour, Hong Kong.

Reading a book of Chinese translations
I remember my Chinese friend,
bamboo breezes drift though my study,
moonlight on the terraced temple shines again.
Climbing to those high places
sometimes you picked flowers
and in the monastery monks disliked our intrusion,
tried to put us off, speaking of one infected
who'd died last night in the visitor's room.

Before the dawn the wooden clappers clacked
and in the shrine room I recall
the candles flickered along the wall
the golden images splendidly sat
there was no time at all in that
and now that all these years have flown
and after midnight I sit here alone
I see again the silvered lateen sails
that down the fishing moon's track trailed
as silently they put to sea
below the hill that sprouted guns.

Wearily I reflect, modern life
differs little from the time of Li po.
I too seek my mountain cottage,
winter winds strike the oaks and birches
and the rushing stream gurgles past the muddy yard.
Wood fire bums low

and by my candle I read some far-off words.
This is no bamboo mountain
yet here too the natural stillness
creeps from the stones and trees
as in my secret heart I discover
my lone home.

Thinking of you and the passing years
of war and waste, treaties broken
and pledges meaningless,
the rise in prices and the difficulty of travel,
passports and regulations,
I am comforted to know that old officials
in your ancient land also knew
the weariness of worldly noise,
that little changes in a thousand years
is proven true.
Time and space are endless
and only a fool finds a comfortable way.

NCF IX

JOHN BECOMES A DHARMA HEIR

After the seven day intensive Ch'an retreat in New York in May 1993 Master Sheng Yen held a brief ceremony in which he transmitted the Dharma to John Crook making him a holder of the lineage in the Chinese Lin Chi sect of Ch'an Buddhism with the name Ch'uan-Teng Chien-Ti, meaning "Transmitting the Lamp - Seeing the Truth". To some, such an honour may seem strange. To pass the Dharma to a European Westerner, a layman without the training of a monk, a man without rank in the Dharma, living far from either of the Ch'an centres in New York or Taiwan may appear premature, if not unwise. None the less during the ceremony Shi-fu gave a very clear account of his reasons for his radical action and dwelt at some length on the meaning and responsibilities of transmission.

The event was tape recorded and the account we publish here is directly based on this tape. Shi-fu spoke in Mandarin and was interpreted on the spot by Ming Yee Wang. Our text is a slightly edited version of Ming Yee's translation.

Shi-fu speaks to the assembly:

John Crook has studied with me in Ch'an retreat some five times in New York and twice in Britain but prior to that he studied and cultivated his understanding in many traditions for over twenty years. Today I am giving him recognition as my Dharma descendant. This is only the second time that I have recognised a descendant. I am very happy to be passing this Dharma lineage downwards.

So far as John Crook is concerned this is a great honour and also a great responsibility. It is something very important to him, the great responsibility of carrying the task of the Tathagata. So from now on, based in the merit of the lineage of Lin Chi, he is empowered to spread the Buddhadharma, spread the Ch'an teaching, engage in personal practise himself and, to the best of his ability, have concern for others and help them spread the Dharma.

In the past history of the Ch'an sect there were masters and patriarchs who, when they had established a single Dharma descendent, were ready to die. Their task had been done. I have not died yet, but at least I can feel a sense of lessened responsibility, particularly with regard to the West and especially in Europe. There is now somebody else who can take on and relieve me of that part of my responsibility. In this sense John Crook will be representing me while I will continue to represent Sakyamuni Buddha in the teaching.

Years ago when I myself received the lineage of Lin Chi from my own master, only a few people were present; my Shi-fu, his attendant and a friend who had accompanied me to meet this elderly master. What I felt at that time was both joy and happiness. Joy in that my Shi-fu now recognised that I had the ability to teach the Dharma, the Ch'an Dharma, and happiness because the burden of Shakyamuni Buddha was now on my own shoulders. I felt happiness also because now that the burden of Shakyamuni Buddha was on my own shoulders, if I did not do a good job, it would be my own responsibility and I would not be able to face the Buddha nor the historical patriarchs. Today, therefore, I am sharing my own feelings of that time with John.

(Turning to John) Congratulations to you!

John. May I say something?

Shi-fu. Yes, say some words now. Please.

John. I am deeply touched and honoured by what Shi-fu hi has said this morning. My heart is almost too full to express what this event means to me. I always knew that Shi-fu was going to give me a lot of trouble! Certainly this morning he is giving me both trouble and joy. Trouble because, as he has said, this is a great responsibility and one which I do and will take very seriously. Yet it is also a matter of great joy because I find it remarkable that such faith should be placed in myself. I am only too aware of my defects and the negative qualities in my nature. There is plenty of work to be done on my vexations and this I shall continue.

I'm very grateful to Shi-fu for having helped me establish a small group of Ch'an practitioners in England. Indeed I send thanks to that group because without them of course there would be no work. I have a small house in the countryside in Wales where we do regular retreats. Some of these are Ch'an retreats and some are retreats that can be preparatory to undertaking the full Ch'an seven days. When Shi-fu came to this little house he likened it to the pin head upon which the Buddhas dance. In England we often say "Small is beautiful" and in this little centre I hope to work in a small way but with a quality that is very high. We may create a tiny Bodhimandala from which the influence of the Dharma can spread.

Thank you very much, Shi-fu, from the bottom of my heart.

I also thank all you people here who have been with me and helped in the last week, putting up with my streaming cold and cough all through this valuable and important time. Thank you all.

Shih-fu. We should all be very joyful that this morning we had the opportunity to share in the giving of the Dharma lineage to John Crook. We should also be joyful because we can witness that Buddhadharma is something alive. Despite these changing times it is not something that has died, but continues and with vigour. When such Dharma lineage might be passed to any one of us - that nobody knows. As practitioners we do not seek to attain or gain anything. We do not seek to get the affirmation of others.

As for myself, receiving the Dharma lineage took a very long time. When I was 28 years old through the help of my Shih-fu, Master Ling Yuen, I had an experience which he affirmed as "seeing the nature" Yet receiving such affirmation of experience and receiving the Dharma lineage are really two separate things Even if someone has received the affirmation that he or she has "seen the nature" whether or not he or she will receive the Dharma lineage is something completely different.

A lot of conditions are necessary. Firstly, you must have the correct understanding of the principles of the Dharma. Secondly, you must have your own experience of practice. Thirdly, the right conditions must exist in space and time. That is to say that the circumstances must be appropriate. Fourthly, help must be given to all people wishing to learn. Without all of these conditions being fulfilled, then even if the lineage were to be passed on to you, the transmission would not be fruitful.

In the case of John Crook the transmission is not something accidental. I have been to England twice and have seen and worked with groups in the farmhouse he has provided for retreats. I have also experienced his personal abilities; firstly, in terms of Dharma understanding and his own development and, secondly, in the helping of others. Because he meets all the conditions that I outlined earlier, I decided to pass the lineage down to him.

Indeed, John has helped many people. Some of the people in his group are practitioners of high quality. When I was last in Wales I was happy to give one of them the affirmation of his experience. Could he also receive the Dharma lineage? No, not yet, but at the very least he should be well able to assist John in his retreat activities.

And so we now reach the end of the retreat. Some of us may be tired and need rest. After you have completed your morning tasks you are welcome to depart. If you are planning to stay a little while longer, you are most welcome to do so. If you wish to stay to lunch, until the evening, overnight, for a few days or intend to live here for the rest of your days - please let the Centre know!

EVERYDAY JOY

An Editorial from the Chan Hall

In this edition I share with you my joy and trepidation at receiving from Shih-fu the authority of becoming one of his Dharma heirs. This is indeed a great honour and a major responsibility. Part of me wants to disappear into the mountains and keep quiet, taking stock of what has happened. We know from the story of Hui-neng, who was a layman at the time of receiving the robe, that such a compassionate gift is commonly seen by others with jealous or even scornful eyes. What's this? A layman, a European, an Englishman, a Westerner, of dubious morality and uncertain practice! Can't even speak Chinese! What's he got that I haven't? What nonsense! Shih-fu must be out of his mind!

Yet it is also necessary to rejoice in the sheer radicality of Shi-Fu's action, the adventurousness, the probing into cultures not his own, the awareness of the needs of the West, the compassionate acceptance of inadequacies balanced against hope and faith, the risk taking, the courage, and the challenge. My gratitude to Shi-fu is far-reaching for his faith in me can bring out what maybe has been hidden even from myself. Let us see what can be done and honour the gift he has given us.

I say us deliberately because in his speech to the assembly in New York, Shih fu said clearly that without the Bristol Ch'an group, without a body of people working in the Dharma and without a place of retreat the conditions for transmission would not have been fulfilled. His action is therefore one of trust in our work, our practice, our group and by no means just me and mine. This is not said to inflate our group egoism but to give us confidence and joy in where we stand.

Two years ago, when Shi-fu acknowledged my account of certain experiences as "seeing the nature" and allowed me to run orthodox Ch'an retreats, I had some correspondence with him. He told me then that there is nothing to be proud about in such things. There are always great inadequacies and vexations and any pride would constitute a downfall. Furthermore, at any previous period in the history of Ch'an when there were great teachers around and profound practitioners, I would not have received any recognition at all. Only in the present era, when in spite of superficial brilliance, the darkness of mind is so thick, is it possible for those with attainments as thin as my own to be considered valuable and essential as teachers. So we must all see clearly where we stand! Nothing here to shout about and a great deal of work to be done.

But I do thank the Ch'an group for their support. encouragement and patient forbearance of my enthusiasms. Let us all proceed together helping one another.

I have recently completed a short solitary retreat at the Maenllwyd. I learnt much and will repeat the process. While there, I wrote the following which I now offer to you for your reflection.

In the practice of the Dharma it becomes essential to understand that within the everyday lies the Great Joy. It is not that Joy is elsewhere nor that it has to be laboriously worked for. It is not that one is worthless, undeserving, wicked and hence unable to discover it Dharma Joy itself lies within the everyday.

Why then are we so normally cast down, anxious, restless or depressed, entertaining the notion that the practice of Buddhism is either out of reach, requires more than one has to offer or downright incomprehensible?

The answer lies in the fact that we have to wake up to that which underlies our negative preoccupations, doubts and failures. We see the state of the world and want to help, to bring about some positive change. Yet, in these days when there is no prevailing idealism except material advancement on offer, when Marxism and Socialism, the great creeds, have failed, when all external paths are seen as fraudulent, we often do not know in what direction to turn. The multiple alternatives of this age of post-modern relativism all seem relatively cheap, sentimental or superstitious, lacking anchorage in a firm sea-bed.

Abandoning all we might rush off to Somalia, Angola, Sarajevo Calcutta or even Belfast, filled with a zeal for do-gooding. And indeed those who rescue the afflicted in Bosnia or prevent the slaughter of a whale do achieve something. Activism is truly important. Yet afterwards nothing pivotal has changed. It all goes on again. Where next? Are politicians really as powerless and as characterless as they seem? And the junkmail of endless appeals from charities lacking the aid of any official compassion continue to pour through our letter boxes as if we personally were responsible. And indeed, collectively, perhaps we are - because who else can be?

No wonder we are cast down. The problem lies in the fact that all of us are sleepwalking within the materialist ethos and individual isolationism of our time. There are precious few alert enough to awaken us. We have to do it for ourselves.

For the moment then leave the world as it is; its cares as they are. When you are awake you will find out what to do. Only wake up. First things first. The actions of a sleepwalker rarely achieve anything.

What then is this awakening? Words will not do it for you. Direct investigation can.

Dharma Joy lies within our own mind's heart in the extent to which we can set aside wanting something else, something other. We want something else out of a feeling that we are incomplete; like a shadow seeking its substance or a lonely ghost in quest of a companion on an uninhabited planet. In our ghost towns there is nobody there. There is the endless ache for a love that will fill the hole in the centre of being. Yet those who themselves lack the surety of inner love cannot fill the holes in others. Illusory romance only discloses the unsatisfactoriness of a companion which equals one's own for him or her. There is no inner completion, there is the ache after it.

Are you a ghost or a vibrant embodied being, a sentience? Do you feel your presence in the world now, here from moment to moment, a validated reality, a presence - or an absence? Presence in the world is not knowing about the world, having one's mind in the office already as one drives to work, absenting oneself from the Now. Presence in the world begins with presence in the body.

The Buddha himself had to make this discovery and he put it forward as a prime method. Mindfulness of the body as the body, in the direct apprehension of embodiedness as being the body is the start. Mindfulness means investigation not passivity: asking what is my experience of this body now and taking time to go into it, to bring it into a moment by moment continuing presence.

The method of watching the breath takes one into the body and in this practice you go on to investigate the arising of sensations, perceptions, cognitions and the prejudiced attitudes of the mind in just the same way. In the end you investigate consciousness itself and find it tainted by all that has gone before, the sensations, cognitions, prejudices. Consciousness is coloured by what goes on in these processes for we identify it as the basis that sustains them in awareness.

The practise of mindfulness acts by focusing attention on these realms, shifting it away from the anxious split between what you are and what you might be, where you are in life and where you might be, whether you are good or bad, beautiful or ugly, the endless dualities, and brings you to where you quite undeniably are. In the body there is no duality but rather the immediacy of actual unsplit being.

And strangely where you find yourself to be lies within an experiential continuum that has no boundaries because there are no horizons to the space within which the body, the sensations, the cognitions become objects of awareness. The bare consciousness within which you are aware, indeed which is itself awareness, contains all that which is present yet is in itself boundless and untrapped. As you relax your hold on the body, the sensation, or a thought, and slip into this experiential space you find a felt vastness which like a mirror contains all and yet stands itself in a different dimension. Indeed this awareness remains an inference for the mirror cannot know itself except within the conscious act of reflection - for this is indeed all that it is. Yet the basis of mind, this Rigpa of the Tibetans is more than a mirror. This awareness is a dynamic vastness, a depth and not a mere surface. As Hui-neng said, "There is no mirror bright / Upon what can the dust alight?"

Indeed the dust of our thoughts and preoccupations simply float in this inner vastness like clouds in the sky. The essential thing is to place one's sentience in the sky itself and experience the clouds from there -and not the other way about. Being sky-borne the view is vast and clouds evaporate and reform as situations change. The vastness goes on for ever. If you look at a thought from within this vastness the thought evaporates - its apparent thing-ness just disappears, it self-liberates into inner space. As they say in Dzogchen; a thought is like writing on water - as soon as the sign is made it spreads out into nothing. This is self-liberation like evaporating clouds or melting snowmen.

If you let the meditative attention widen to include the presence of the room, the town, the countryside, the sounds of everyday, these too are at first reflected and then self-liberate into vastness. Here then is freedom. The prison cell becomes the liberating cell of the hermit. And because there is freedom from any wanting, all being complete, a joy arises, an untrammelled joyousness which shines like a lamp in one's being.

After meditation you return to the tasks of everyday life, willingly operating dualistically as you and yours in the world of them and theirs. This is the natural mode of samsara, of becoming, the mode whereby needs are met, needs for warmth, food, adequacies of comfort and relationship. It is the mode of activism.

The Ch'an practitioner who trains with persistence can find within this everyday dualism the inner freedom that meditation discloses. It remains then as a basis, a unity, that divides only functionally not essentially. To get things done there is I and mine and you and yours. Outside and inside of that there is the experiential continuum, the vastness, the matrix of self-liberation.

Our pain stems mightily from the illusion that the split mind is natural, that it has no other depth, that it is an inevitable condition of being bound by time and impermanence. This is not so. A mind lost in duality is drugged, ignorant, asleep, unaware of its basic continuum. The task is to awaken again and again to the joyous spaciousness that lies within.

In the habitual dualism of the illusory everyday you may well feel scepticism and doubt. The Buddha understood that and did not make an assertion precluding your consent. Try it for yourself was always his message. And this must be ours too whenever we are quizzed about these goings-on. The uncovering of vastness is in itself enlightening for this is the light of the mind. Do not waste time for the world is waiting.

John Crook Ch'uan-Teng Chien-Ti 2 November 1993

PILGRIMAGE TO PHUGTAL

A walk to a remote monastery in Zangskar, Himalayas

Poem in two voices

James Crowden, John Crook

In the summer of 1993 John Crook with James Crowden led a tour party on trek in the Indian Himalayas, the most recent of several such guided journeys to Ladakh arranged in collaboration with The Open Gate. The purpose of these journeys is to allow participants to share an inner experience of journeying to remote third world locations of spiritual importance. The 1993 journey was especially difficult in that airline strikes forced repeated changes in the itinerary and there was a lot of illness in the party. None the less we won through and trust the experience has proved beneficial. James and John wrote these verses in Kargil on the afternoon of the return from Zangskar and the piece was read to the group that evening. It was also presented at the meeting of the international Association for Ladakh Studies in Leh later that summer.

Early morning beneath Nun Kim
The sound of boys driving sheep and cattle,
The first light hits the mountain.

Acres of flowers,
The stream, the rocks,
Old carvings of ibex
Willow trees beneath steep snow.
The double rainbow
A corona, circling the peaks.

At Rangdom, old dogs,
Prayers for the monks
Chanting above the water's shingle.
Choughs dive,
The sound of a horsebell.
The glacier gaping wide and beckoning
A slow liturgy of ice
Moving forward, downward
Till the sound of water
Careers through the mind.

The smell of yak dung burning in the dusk
Frozen peaks, sharp and hanging
Above the echo of silence.

The shade of poplar trees
The holy monastery at Sani
The blue poppy beside the stream

Blue flowers at the window
Our bus careers into Zangskar
Inside
Improbably juxtaposed
The would-be inner travellers.

Village grove, slight breeze-
Curious
How silently the sunlight
Makes the sparrows chirp.

At Rangdom Gompa
I am glad to see
The monks still sustain

The revolutions of the Universe.

Since I was here
Yeshe Monlam, fine monk. has died.
For me, remembering him, they chant
The aspirations of the blessed
Dust keeps falling from the Buddha's nose.

Tea with an old friend
At Chushigzhal
Sonam Wangchuk, the Karsha Lhonpo
Surrounded by memories

Old paintings, the moon rising
Such friendship,
Such friendship.

The valley spreads out below
Our path steep and narrow.

And in this foreign monastery
hoping to bribe the villagers
They think naive,
Invading Christian zealots handout
The powerful drugs
Of Western decadence.

Without thanks the pills
Are grabbed and stowed away.
Later, some of them sewn into hats.

Next week,
The yogins' turn.

How hot the valley
Heat pounding in the head,
Road blasting in front of Bardan monastery.

Old chortens and dog roses
Mani walls and fresh streams,
Our path forever hanging
Just there - above the river.

Mahakala puja, old masks in the gonkhang[1]
The smell of rancid butter.

Over the valley
Black mountain peers
Am I menaced or protected?
I am not sure.
'Juno Dunlak'.
Oh do not say this name
Something like darkness
Touches my mind.

Khataqs and incense
Offerings to the lha-
Nobody knows
What precautions we took.

Do not ask the Gods
For favours here
Evoking our own powers
Alone we tread this precipice.
With no intentions
The river merely waits.

Have you got what it takes?

Opposite Pipcha
Water swirling, churning, twisting
Gliding, pummelling its way down,
Carving the rock, dividing the mountain,
The valley's pulse, the "Black Breath"
Lungnag, a thin ribbon of silted water
Linking village with village,
The glacier's melt sharpening its wits
On the water's edge, each bridge
Crossing the eye of the water,
The turbulent pull
Shifting this way and that.

The cloud of dust, as horses
Are gathered in the first light
Driven down the mountain
Ready for the day's work.

Again the smell of dung fires
Creeps along the valley
Slowly mingles from both shores
Drifts and hangs
In the mountain's shadow.

Water swirling, churning , twisting
Gliding, pummelling its way down.

Silently communing with the Gods
Roar of water, clarity of space
Air cooled by tumbling rivers
Blesses the desert with emeralds.

Fire dances in a blinding sun
Space cuts out my mind
Only these feet move
Elemental reverie.

Closed tents,
The sick and weary rest.
Outside, the spirits of the mountain
Dance.

Above my steeping bag
The slowly churning stars.
Where the planet's rim turns down
Day begins.

Powered by farts
My morning stroll
In my guts
Disturbing immanence.

At Purne two rivers join
In spate, two colours merge
The Lingti and the Tsarap Chu.
One from the south and one from the north
One way to India, the other to Rupchu and Changtang.

Choughs at Phugtal
Gliding, twisting and turning
Jive and plummet between prayer flags
And lamas' incantations,
The cave hollowed out with emptiness.

A glance from Drepung
The old geshe[2] in his cell
Prayer wheel surrounded
By texts and photographs
His flight from Tibet with His Holiness
Engraved on his memory.

The smile of offering
A deep resonance.
Beneath the juniper tree
The spring of cold dear water.

Water seeps from the cavern's floor
Refreshment for tired travellers
No witchcraft here.
Sky drunk monks hide
In the deep recesses of the hills.

Old geshe with fading mind
Probably no longer
Remembers philosophy.
Beyond his window
Choughs whirl and stall
In distant cells his brother monks
Intone their liturgies.
With lowered eyelids
Over shining eyes

For seventy six years
He's seen it move.

And in the evening down the valley
The songs and laughter, horsemen

From Kuru, Tablay and Kargiakh.

At Purne the wedding house
Waiting on the hill
The warm night crowded with faces
The valley full of chang
Acres of women crammed tightly together
Leaning in their shawls half drunk
Swaying this way and that.
In the half darkness raucous laughter
Keeps pace with the drumming.

From sperm to tsa-tsa[3]
Momentary vision-

Let's hope they enjoyed it

Milarepa
Holds his hand to an ear
What does he hear?
What does he hear?

Great guru with blazing eyes
What does he see?
What does he see?

Sombre scholar with learned gaze
What does he know?
What does he know?

Touching the earth
The Buddha's hand
E-he - Whose fingers?

And then the reluctant return
Each caravan steady in its pace
Like a ship gliding and surging
Through the mountains.
Horses and mules follow one another
Sacks of atta[4] lashed down on wooden saddles
Sullen muleteers thinking of Manali.

And then the festival at Sani
The dance with monastic music
Echoing through the courtyard
Monks clad in silk and black hats
Veiled beneath the snow-laden mountains
Stepping this way and that
Chancing, glancing
Backing and advancing
Twisting and gyrating
The spirit's pulse transferred
The tantric colours circling
In a vortex
Hypnotic and shamanic
The exorcism, the handling of dark forces
The triangle of unwanted energy
Thrown out, thrown out
And the year's evil
Assuaged before the harvest.

Sunfire blazes
Crackling figures circle
Surge like flames
Cymbals crash, drums boom
Black hat wizardry

Kills the dark and evil thing
Pinioned beneath the tall flag.
Bright night of the long knives.
Before harvest, hearts are cleansed.

The blue glitter of perags
And white khatags[5]
The sense of giving
Reaching far into the mountains
The flat pasture laden with horses
The freedom of the steppe.

High above the swirling river
What do they see
One lammergeier
And two eagles?

Dry, dusty dry, fierce Central Asian dry
The wind pummels the valley.

Pulling out, the old bus
Lumbers over ruts and rivulets.
Tired strangers
Wave to smiling villagers.
"One pen- one pen - kaka -Julay!"
What have they learned
These slumped and jerking figures
Dozing on the long way?

Arid the desert's pulse, the raven's beak.
Think of the ibex and the wolf trap
The sound of the conch shell.

Footnotes:

1. The shrine room of the protective deities of the monastery.
2. Doctor of Buddhist philosophy.
3. Moulded figures prepared from the ashes of corpses.
4. Wheat flour.
5. Woman's head-dress and offering scarf.

LIVING OUT THE LIFE

One day this summer, standing in one of the temples of Phugtal Gompa hidden deep in the Zangskar mountains of the Himalaya, I asked my companion, Nathaniel Tarn, American poet and participant on my cultural tour to Ladakh, whether he was a Buddhist. Nathaniel was inspecting the extraordinary 12th century paintings on the walls, paintings he had laboured hard and with difficulties over the hills to see, and said ,"It's the nearest to what I believe to be true. For me it's just a matter of living out the life".

And so I was made to recall this subtle Zen phrase which then hung around, haunting my imagination, for the rest of the summer.

We had major problems on trek this year: many participants were sick, some had come without adequate physical or mental preparation and airline strikes forced us into repeated changes of itinerary. James Crowden and I felt much relieved after we said goodbye to them and then spent two days with the yogins on a short retreat. Our troubles were not over however. It took us three days of early morning journeys to the airport and many attempts at bribery and corruption to get on the plane from Leh to Delhi. In Delhi too more airline trouble meant we had to change flights and do a slow return via Karachi, Cairo, and Paris, missing one more connection and losing our luggage temporarily on the way. What should have taken two days took seven.

Had I been alone, such a journey would have been very testing. I would have felt alone, morose, claustrophobic, neglected and anxious, fussing about details and challenging myself every inch of the way. Having the staunch companionship of James made it almost pleasurable and we saw some interesting things at Karachi, at the worst moments doing a silly Doug and Pete act to maintain our morale. But the point of all this is that the phrase "living out the life" came back to me as a repeated meditative refrain.

Wasting time in offices, having our wait-listed tickets rejected, enduring the total chaos of the Air India reservation system, waiting for our luggage to fail to arrive in Paris; every time I thought "Hey - this is just living out the life. Let it pass." It became a valuable refrain, a mantra refocusing experience into the exact moment, people's faces, the turmoil of ad hoc travelling, the explosive little rows that came and went in office corners. It all passed by, living out the life. Time passed, mini-event followed mini-event, plane trip after plane trip, Homage to Allah on Air Pakistan, hindi music in India, the clipped tones of the BA captain nonchalantly cruising the businessmen into Heathrow on our last leg. I am the same somehow. The same taste, as the yogins say. Just life passing. One thing after another, nothing to get up-tight about, different companions, attitudes, air hostesses, ways of serving soup, no alcohol on Islamic flights, holier than thou, and the lovely French lass who gave us Air France bus tickets to get from Orly to Charles de Gaulle - when she shouldn't have. Un peu mechant, n'est-ce pas?

All the same; the practice of not good, not bad, evenness. Shih fu watching the train move with his luggage still on the platform. It all works through. Life passes, time passes, day follows day. Sometime it will all stop.

There's a melancholy here perhaps. What of the splendours of passionate commitment? The urge to succeed? The vital elan that wins a race? Well, that's part of it too. No one said that living out the life should be done without commitment and passion. Mother Theresa picking up the dying in Calcutta's streets, night after night, living out the life.

There's a secret here. To use Shih-fu's phrase, the mind "goes down" when it becomes self-centered. Sometimes as I watch the days or hours passing I am filled with a sense of fear, life's sands are not unlimited like those of the Ganges. They are few and flowing down the hourglass rapidly. I get a sense of panic, of things not achieved, of nostalgia for past faces, past times. But this is all a referral to self, to my mortality, a self-pity before the face of oncoming death.

Put that aside - instant sunshine, wherever, whenever. The dullest moment becomes alive in its own actuality. Driving back to the Karachi hotel fatigued by traffic noise and fumes, how wonderfully the painted buses glow. At Cairo airport a passenger slept through the stop instead of disembarking. What a joke. What does a two hour additional delay matter? Another opportunity for contemplation.

And it works. You can meditate in a seat on a plane. Just let the mind go. Things go on around one, nothing to do. The breath settles, tranquillity comes. Why worry - you get there sometime, this year, next year, sometime, never. And why not? Is it

OK to end it now? In the silence of the mind, why not? Everything's the same, just living out the life.

How does a Zen master live out his life? In the clarity of sameness he goes his way with helping hands, offering all he has for the well-being of others. In this there need be no time, no nostalgia, no worry about the future. He or she does what must be done in the moment of its arising. The action, coming from the empty heart of clarity and relying totally on a natural insight, just comes into being, goes its course and travels on.

The master is beyond premeditation. His or her mind is attuned to a silent readiness which becomes possible only when it is unclogged by predispositions, prejudice, defences, biases. That is why such action is an expression of the human truth that the root of the mind is undramatic love. Outward looking, seeing the needs in the face before one, living out the life. Nothing special.

When we reflect on such matters we perceive our need for training because the need for it has become clear. Far from the idealisations and false comfort of New Age spirituality we attempt to stand clear of the ego and see the sameness, the unmoving similarity of every moment. From here we can see the pain of others and compassion arises in our offering. Where there are blocks, there must the work be done.

25 September 1993 In Memoriam GMC

NCF X

DISCIPLINES

How about this?

No man gets to heaven
going by the book
Ten days in this temple
have sent me up the wall
Anytime you meet me
you know where to look,
Fish shop, wine shop, brothel
would each be worth a call

These disturbingly Zen sentiments were sent to me by a friend. I do not know where he culled them from, but I recently came across their true origin.

Ikkyu (1394-1481) was known for his combination of irrepressible impertinence to authority, his wild demeanour, riotously brilliant calligraphy and his zen insight. Born the son of a lady in waiting and the Emperor Go-Komatsu (1377-1433) of Japan, he resented deeply the humiliation of his mother when she was ousted from court by a jealous empress. He never respected any authority again. Although given to altercation, his vigorous scenting out of hypocrisy startled many into a realisation of their error-bound ways. Despite being a monk, he increasingly freed himself from social conditioning, his was a free life style that included love for women and a rejection of monkish ways. Once, after marching out in disgust at the formality of a sham Buddhism at the Nyoi-an temple in the Daitokuji complex in Kyoto, where he had been appointed Abbot, he wrote these lines:

Ten days in this temple and my mind is reeling.
Between my legs the red thread[1] stretches and stretches.
If you come some day asking for me
Better look in a fish stall, saki shop or brothel!

This would seem identical to the livelier translation above and probably its true source. Shortly before his death he wrote:

I won't die

I won't go anywhere
but I won't be here.
So don't ask me anything
I won't answer
Dimly, dimly thirty years;
faintly, faintly thirty years;
Dimly, faintly sixty years
I pass my turds
and offer them to Brahma.[2]

This brief anti-puritan reminder is dedicated to the Dharma in the hope of enlightenment for all contemporary reprobates.

Notes

1 Meaning passion

2 Translations adapted from p 56. Stevens, J.1993 'Three Zen Masters". Kodansha International Tokyo

THERE FOR THE TAKING

Introducing Lin Chi

Before we try to understand Lin Chi, from whom our tradition derives, then are some things to be said. Lin Chi seems strange to us; we who are used to cause and consequence and well-drawn argument. We sit and giggle over the delicious way in which the master affronts his questioners. Yet we have no understanding of why he does it. We marvel over the cleverness of a Zen paradox, but we have no insight into what it means. Shame upon us; we who pretend to admire without any understanding. It is time to wake up and penetrate the meaning.

What use is it to sit and goggle at the absurdities of the old monk's statements? What good is it to seek in explanatory texts what the old man means? What point is there in listening to the vaporising of this your teacher when you should yourself be penetrating the root-essence of your own ignorance!

Yet if we attempt nothing and remain puzzled even while we smile, we cannot advance. When we cannot understand why attainment is not what is meant it is still wrong to give up. In truth, these matters are entirely dear. We only need the right eye for the seeing thereof, if you gain the right eye then you can laugh. There is not anything to it.

Ha - we missed even that one. Truly, there isn't anything to it. But if we leave it like that, we will go home just marvelling at the quirkiness of it all. The gateless gates will all remain firmly shut. What then to say? Anything said will be a great mistake yet to say nothing is not enough.

Two things may be helpful. When we read the word "Mind" in Lin Chi's sayings, we are apt to pass it over quickly as if we knew what was meant. In fact at this very point, you must pause and recognise in your own cognition what the subject of discussion really is. In English, "mind" often means all sorts of cognitions all the way from consciousness itself through to memory and the calculations of sums. Yet, in these texts, "mind" is not always so inclusive. At the root of this mind is the ever present evaluator himself or herself for whose benefit, however obscure, the activity is going on. The mood of this subjectivity is quite different from the state of a subject who is freed from this innate habit; who is just present in the world as immediately given by the six senses. In understanding Lin Chi, this difference is important.

It is imperative that we have a personal and direct experience of this contrast. Those of us who have never left the discriminatory mind cannot understand personally what is being said here because our comparative experience is defective. Yet, even so, if you are intelligent, you can see what the words mean and thereby seek to confirm them. Let us try to make it more clear.

You may be sitting in a garden. The clouds are gathering. You begin thinking of how it might rain. How inconvenient that might be. You must clear up the tea things and put them away. You are annoyed because you were expecting to laze an hour away in the sun. In such a state the subject is judging, discriminating, calculating, all in an edgy condition of self-reference. You may even become irritated if someone asks you what the time is!

Compare this with sitting in the garden, in exactly the same condition, but now you merely observe the clouds. They are simply there. Your senses are open to them, their massive height and grandeur, their slow march across the blue. In creative imagination you see them, mile after mile of them, massively blowing in from the ocean. In your mind's eye, you can see that the furthest clouds have not yet reached the coastline. The massive regiments advance yet, you suddenly sense that up there in the heavens they are moving in total silence, a huge, as it were, pensive silence. Even here among the hills there is only the light wafting of the breeze in the ash tree. You realise suddenly that the great stillness you are evoking is inside you. Your mind is still, no thinking, no calculating and no self-reference. The suchness of the moment hangs before you and you are free. A kind of clarity shines forth from everything being just as it is. Going further - that is how is has always been, always is and always will be. The universe is always quietly on the move in its own way. If you flow with it, all remains at peace. Such an insight is there for the taking at any moment, any time. Even in Trafalgar Square with the traffic.

The mind has switched off its perpetual self-referring judgement. Is it good for me? What am I gaining? What is my status? How long before enlightenment? Is all this worth the bother? Such thoughts, however unbidden and resisted, seem so easily to dominate. Whenever we assert anything, a contrary view can arise in opposition.

Again and again in Zen, we encounter the great NO. Bodhidharma's definition of Ch'an, Hui Neng "letting the mind arise but not putting it anywhere", Lin Chi swatting a monk with his fly whisk even before he has finished his question, Master Sheng Yen telling us that if we open our mouth to answer a koan, we are wrong! Always this mind blocking negation, this apophatic assertion. Why?

If you say anything your mind congeals around it. You set in concrete. If someone objects, both of you set in concrete, congealing around your opposed reifications. When nothing is said, there is no opposition, no judgement, no movement of discrimination. So in facing the Koan - What is it? - Pause, wait, resist the rising response. Say nothing but continue gazing into the space the question has cleared before you. Allow the great doubt to arise. Nothing there? Hey, wait a bit. What is it that is there but cannot be said? What is the essence of the NOT SAYING? This eternal moment.

What is it? The clouds go on moving. They reach down to us and take us up. We reach up to them and take them in. The huge immensity of their movement carries us along. We too could let go like the clouds. Put a £100 note in a bag and just take off in the car. Which way would you drive? No decision. Yet, here you are going along the road. Maybe it is raining. Maybe, the sun is there. When it is all the same there is a start to understanding.

Back at home, the phone rings. There is something important to be done. Going with the circumstance you do the necessary. That is all. When I awake, I get up. When I lie down at night, I go to sleep.

So said Lin Chi. Do we understand him?

NCF XI

EDITORIAL FROM THE CHAN HALL

In June this year the Network of Buddhist Organisations (NBO) in Britain is holding a conference on the "Student- teacher Relationship" at Amaravati Monastery. The intention is to explore the many facets of this relationship from the viewpoints of both teachers and students.

A fundamental concern is our understanding of the present state of our own society. Buddhism is new in the West, it is spreading rapidly, diversifying and responding to socio-economic pressures few of us actually understand. Mistakes have been made and continue to be made, yet at the same time a Buddhist voice is developing that can have some influence on affairs directly, or more usually indirectly.

We who practise the Dharma and are concerned in Dharma education need very much to understand the historical process in which we are embedded. It is complex, diversifying and unstable[1]. By contrast, those who are beginners look to the Dharma for simplicity, unity and stability. Unfortunately they cannot have this on a plate. Such an outcome can only arise from the inner work of Dharma practice. Desires for an easily adopted, comforting and simple belief to help shore up an unstable lifestyle are opposed to the need for an actual understanding of self and situation. This opposition between wants to be supplied from outside and the necessity for inner work generates a tension which may impose a threat to Buddhism. Why?

Simplistic "outer" paths are illusorily attractive because the "work" thereon is done by the institutions and the teachers that provide them, rather than by the practitioners. The "practitioner" may have faith, but no serious personal practice. The result is a cult centering on some simplistic version of Buddhism and focused on a charismatic figure - all too familiar elsewhere in the "New Age" world of make-believe religion. Such cults become fixations that enclose the mind of a believer in such a way that severe distortions of the Dharma can result, taking on fundamentalist, exclusivist, even fascist tones. If the Aum cult of Japan has roots in modern Japanese derivatives of Buddhism, we can see the danger.

The failure of American Dharma institutions to provide safeguards that would protect both the centre and the participants from abuse by so called "masters" has been well discussed[2]. There is clearly a need for critical feedback and democratic structuring. This is something that the Eastern models have failed to supply and Western adherents too immature to insist upon. Such feedback and social control was a feature of the original monastic life - certainly so in Tibet, where the "shung", the body of monks governing the institution, elected abbots on a relatively short term basis. The later focus on reincarnating lamas and Zen masters for life has weakened this healthy basis and led to abuses of power.

These Western failures are set in the context of our social condition. The European "Enlightenment" that disposed of medieval superstition and replaced it with clear minded thought, science and social progress, has also led to a breakdown of community in a world dominated by market place economics[3]. The focus on individual rights, personalised fashions, unique identities and private belief systems is an end result of a long process, leading us away from the constraints of communal ethics and towards a personal freedom that can also become an alienation from society itself. Society in the West is now fragmented to an extraordinary degree. This fragmentation is expressed in many ways. For example in Christian disunity and factionalism extending to an almost total neglect of its deeper roots; in the multiplicity of mutually competitive psychotherapies and counselling services and the pages of mostly dotty activities engaged in by New Agers as advertised, for example, in South West Connection.

This deconstruction of community goes along with a freedom of action and expression which for poorly educated persons amounts to a loss of orientation. All guidance is open to doubt, the only control lies in debatable ethics and laws which are often out of date. The result is the creation of fantasy worlds in which identities unconstructed in a community float freely, seeking some sort of anchorage. In this situation the social holding of an individual is so weak almost anything can happen - as events this month in the USA are revealing.

Those with money can survive and thrive in such a world. At best it encourages a style of life that is critical, sceptical, healthy, expressive, open and innovative. At worst it descends to personal ostentation, egoistic idiosyncrasy and the flamboyance of the merely stupid. However, for the underclass or the unemployed the lack of any community ethic, the Thatcherite neglect of the social and the morality of market capitalism can lead to disastrous alienation and an inward turning to cults that are based in the private worlds of the isolated. How does all this apply to the Dharma? The danger is that lost individuals may seek to reconstruct elements of the Dharma to their own convenience. This would be akin to sick persons rearranging their drugs and dosages without recourse to a doctor.

Indeed this may be to some extent already occurring, although most British institutions appear loyal to one or other of the orthodox and traditional modes of Dharma presentation. I do however know of one self-styled "Zen master" who is totally without orthodox training, and one self-proclaimed "Rimpoche" whose original ambition was to be a magician! Both have some following.

One cannot however simply lay down the laws of what is and is not "safe". The Dharma has always evolved into fresh and invigorating forms; Hinayana to Mahayana, Sutra to Tantra, Yogachara to Zen and so on. These changes are creative but all of them, except possibly some of the more extreme Japanese movements, retain a root anchorage in the Sutras and Sastras and the great Mahayana scriptures and commentaries.

I think that the depth of Buddhist psychology matches that of Western psychological understanding and that each can inform one another. The same is true of contemporary philosophy and in discussion about the nature of the cosmos. It follows that positive debate between these polarities can be vastly creative. Such debate however requires the willingness to study, read and think - both in terms of contemporary thought and with respect to the Dharma. For this, only a few have the inclination, time or energy. Those seeking the Dharma simply for personal relevance and security could undermine such debate if their influence produces more cults and sects centred on simplistic versions of Buddhadharma.

We need to be cautious, neither too restrictive so as to limit creativity, nor too indulgent of the personal needs of the alienated who bang upon our doors. I feel this is not an easy path. We need to develop a user friendly Dharma community of which the Network of Buddhist Organisations could be a beginning and within which individuals can find enough support to begin the investigation of self that leads to openness.

References

1. "The Place of the Dharma in Our Time" by John Crook attempts to explore this issue and is included as a supplement to this edition of NCF.
2. See "A Slice of Zen in America" by Stuart Lachs; New Ch'an Forum No 10. Autumn 1994.
3. See "The Zen of Social Action" by Ken Jones in this edition of NCF.

WORDS OF A GURU

Roger Housden was taking a tour party down the river Ganges. Half way they stopped in Lucknow and Roger took the participants to visit one of the truly insightful gurus of modern India, a man of no-nonsense clarity. All but one of his party stayed on. Even the Ganges was forgotten.

Poonja is is a Hindu without a label. Whether derived from Sankaracharya or the Buddha or both his thought is direct, immediate, personal, touching the present. Only in one respect does his insight veer off from Buddhism. On a taped interview he was asked.

'Poonja, who are you?' Quick as a flash, he replied. 'I am THAT!' A Zen master would have said 'I am THIS.' No dualism.

Listening to this taped interview, I was inspired by much of what Poonja had to say. Here is a brief summary for your reflection.

HOWEVER MUCH YOU HAVE PRACTISED, WHETHER FOR FIVE YEARS, FORTY YEARS OR TWO DAYS, WHEN YOU WAKE UP IT TAKES TWO SECONDS.

SO WHAT IS THE USE OF ALL THOSE YEARS OF PRACTISING? WHY NOT WAKE UP IMMEDIATELY?

YOU ARE IN A DREAM, THE DREAM OF LIFE, ALL THESEPREOCCUPATIONS, OCCUPATIONS, RELATIONS, WORK AND PLAY ALL ARE THE DREAM. SUDDENLY YOU TURN OVER AND AWAKE.

WHAT IS THIS MOMENT?

YOU CAN DO IT NOW. WHY WAIT? PRACTICE IS WAITING. NO NEED TO WAIT.

NO NEED FOR SHEPHERDS OR PREACHERS. THE TRUE TEACHER KNOWS EMPTINESS AND, WHEN YOU FALL INTO IT TOGETHER, TWO MINDS ARE ONE MIND AND ONE MIND IS EMPTY. THEN YOU BOTH SEE IT.

THE TEACHER'S MIND IS EMPTY. WHEN HE HEARS THE QUESTIONER THE REPLY COMES FROM EMPTINESS - NOT THE TEACHER. THE TEACHER IS ONLY A VEHICLE OF EMPTINESS.

HOWEVER DEEP THE KARMA OF MANY YEARS STANDING, ON AWAKENING IT IS ALL CLEARED UP. BUT WHAT IF YOU GO TO SLEEP AGAIN?

STAYING AWAKE IS NOT PRACTICE, IT IS CONTINUOUS REALISING. CONTINUOUS REALISING REQUIRES ATTENTION.

WHO IS IT WHO DREAMS THE DREAM OF LIFE? CAN YOU GET TO HIM? WHEN YOU FALL INTO A DOZE AT NIGHT WHAT IS THERE AT

THE MOMENT OF THAT FALLING? WHAT HAPPENS WHEN YOU GIVE IT ALL UP.

WHAT IS THIS GIVING UP? NO NEED TO HOLD ON. NO SUCH NECESSITY. OTHER THAN THE IMPUTED THERE NEVER WAS A REALITY, PAST, PRESENT OR FUTURE, SO WHAT IS IT THAT IS?

REALISATION IS JUST PERCEIVING THAT YOU ARE NOT BOUND. SUCH A FREEDOM IS THE AWAKENING. NOTHING ELSE HAS CHANGED. WHAT YOU THINK -YOU ARE. IF YOU DO NOT THINK THE DREAM THEN YOU ARE AWAKE.

THE PLACE OF THE DHARMA IN OUR TIME

PART I. THE WORLD WE'RE IN

Introduction

To appreciate the role that the Buddha Dharma may come to play in Western culture we need to have an understanding of the way our lives are framed by the world that both shapes us and within which we play a part. So momentous have been the changes in recent years that our suppositions about who and why we are need a constant updating. To appreciate such a history one has to stand back from it and reflect. Fortunately there are those who do this for us and their interpretations are of great value. The reasons for our contemporary concern with ancient Asian ideas lie within the dynamics of Western culture itself.

Explaining history

There are several ways of describing history but here we need only examine two. The first is to prepare an account in terms of the actions of leading personalities, the sequence of emperors, kings, queens or prime ministers, presidents of great powers, generals, statesmen, philosophers, devines or writers. Here we see portrayed the outcome of skill, wisdom or folly as deployed by individuals in their time. Such an approach, focussing on individual singularities, may be called action theory. The second approach is to examine history in the light of changes in economics, social systems, culture, ethics or technology; in terms, in other words, of processes not persons. Many processes relate together and co-determine one another so that such an analysis tends to become increasingly holistic. Examination may uncover underlying or hidden themes or forces often needing a quite abstract analysis. This approach may be termed a "motion" theory[1].

These two approaches are essentially contrasting perspectives for clearly the one need not antagonise the other. Certainly in some periods of history great personalities have stamped their imprint on their times to an outstanding degree whether for good or ill; others have had long term influences long after their lives have come to a premature close, but always the condition of the times, economic and technological, belief systems and psychology have also played critical roles in determining historical outcomes. Since the industrial revolution, however, the complexities of economics and the geography of supply and demand set within regional ideologies have played a particularly predominant role. The individual actors seem more caged and their influence predetermined by circumstance than before. Recent history indeed suggests that the significance of individuals is being steadily eroded by the role of abstractions deriving from machine intelligence and huge multi-national industrial complexes. Even now however the person may emerge as critical in institutional change, Ford in the development of American capitalism, Gorbachov in the last years of the Soviet Union for example.

Anyone who has lived through the last fifty years is aware of accelerating socio-cultural change on a global scale, much of it profoundly unsettling to established values. No longer are the world's regions largely independent from one another, all are increasingly tied together by an ever expanding and ramifying system of finance which, beginning in the West, has spawned powerful interconnected yet competitive variants in other regions. Old stabilities and assumptions are being undermined at an ever increasing rate. Major political shifts involving changes in regional ideologies have tilted the threat to civilisation away from atomic warfare to that of ecological contamination, over-exploitation of non-renewable resources and biological destruction on a planet wide scale. National identity itself becomes increasingly meaningless in a world of regional unifications financed by transnational capital[2]. We must ask whether there is a theoretical position which provides us with some insight, tentative maybe, into the nature of this progressive change, an insight furthermore that may help us understand the more direct subject of this chapter, the reason why Eastern ideas and especially Buddhism are becoming of serious interest to Westerners.

The emergence of postmodernity

A major theme preoccupying a number of contemporary thinkers is the shift from "modern" to "postmodern" culture. The growth of interest in non-western thought has certainly accelerated with postmodernity so that a theory of such culture change may give us a handle on our problem. In what follows I draw particularly on David Harveys' outstanding text of 1990[3].

Harvey roots his analysis in historical materialism and seeks to provide an account of the processes of culture change in terms of underlying economic determinants, a motion theory approach of considerable power and persuasiveness. In effect, he argues, we are living through profound changes within the nature of Western capitalism which, since the industrial revolution, has become the predominant culture of the entire globe. These dynamic financial and commercial processes drive the cultural shifts through which we are living and also lead to the increasingly severe environmental problems still untackled and becoming ever more menacing. Furthermore, in spite of the triumphant success of the capitalist mode of production, the fundamental contradictions inherent within it as first analysed by Karl Marx are still untamed and exert profoundly destructive effects on many aspects of human life[4].Whether contemporary capitalism also has a latent potential for overcoming the very problems it creates is the greatest issue of our time.
The inherent contradictions arise from an interaction between three prime characteristics of capitalism: (see Fig 1)

1. Growth orientation

The accumulation of capital upon which investment in new products is based depends upon profit. Capitalist production requires growth to function. The monetary value of the labour cost must therefore be less than the sale value of the product. Upon this differential depends the provision of dividend by the firm concerned and hence the continuing support for investment upon which further growth oriented production depends. Furthermore, since welfare provision by modern states is based in the taxation of profit, the very existence of social services of all kinds appears rooted in the success of the capitalist endeavour.

2. Labour exploitation

The need for growth if the system is to be self sustaining necessitates the difference between wages and the value creation of the process. Since the spin-off from profit goes to the ownership of companies a class differential between labour and ownership is inevitable. There will always be a struggle between the maximisation of wages by labour and the company seeking to maximise dividends for its shareholders through the control of labour.

3. Competition

Companies compete in commodity markets. Any company that can produce a cheaper commodity of comparable utility than others will achieve higher turnover upon which profit depends. Technological advances and organisational changes in production aim not only at more effective products but also cheaper prices, a process necessarily focussing on the reduction of labour costs. Labour, led by union activity, seeks to maintain its standard of living often by resisting technological innovation and organisational changes which may lower income and reduce the size of a work force and hence union strength. Yet firms which fail to pay high dividends to their shareholders become open to takeover bids from more successful companies. Firms therefore experience serious problems in attempting to finance research and development of new products while at the same time satisfying their shareholders. These problems are met by varying forms of financing in differing capitalist systems.

The interaction of these three factors tends to produce an alternation between periods of successful capital accumulation of products with labour control and periods of over-accumulation of products when both capital and labour lie idle and unemployment reigns. As commodity costs rise and production exceeds demand, sales fall, production drops, labour is laid off and companies move to introduce further technological and organisational fixes. When over-accumulation is excessive a major recession or depression develops as happened around 1930 on a more or less world wide scale.

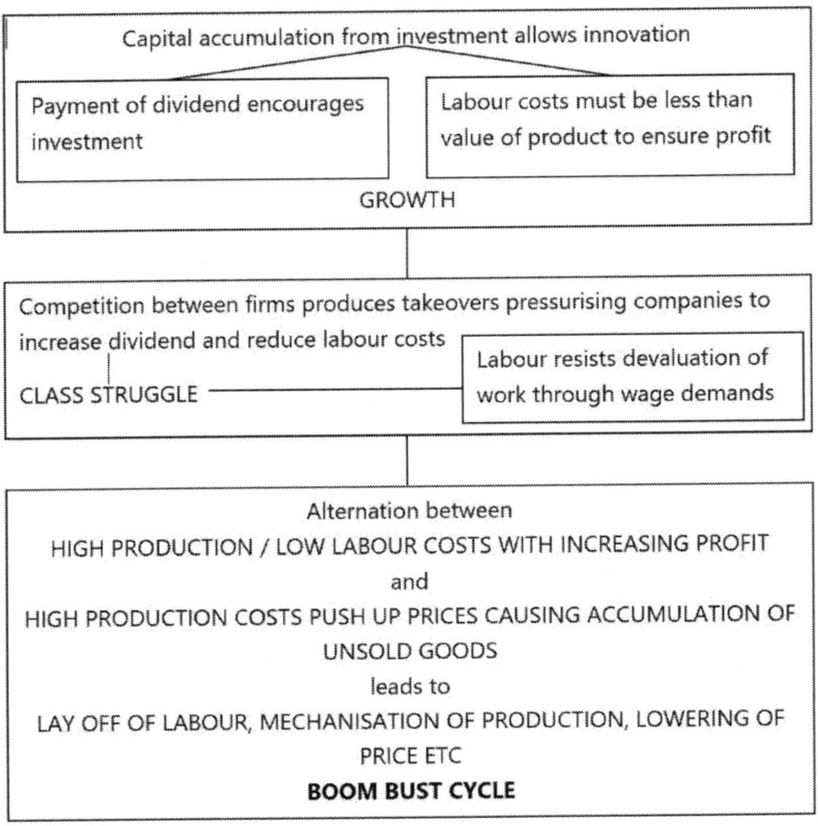

FIGURE 1 THE MAIN FACTORS IN THE BOOM-BUST CYCLES OF CAPITALISM

The boom and bust business cycles develop out of the contradictions inherent in the capitalist system.

People invest in a firm that yields a good dividend but which can only do so by maintaining a differential between the value of its product and the cost of labour. Labour by contrast seeks to Maintain or increase wages.

Competing firms survive by increasing dividends so that an inherent class struggle is built into the system. Public projects are financed by taxes that are imposed on company profits. Increases in taxation and labour push up prices until demand drops and products accumulate. There is then a stalemate until accumulated capital can be utilised by starting up a new cycle. Under a Keynesian system the harshness of the cycle is ameliorated by government use of public money sustaining personal incomes and thus profitability of private enterprise. Without government planning of this type the wealthy hold their own while poverty increases the size of the underclass.

In spite of periodic setbacks, the capitalist system up until the 1970s was generally expansive and recessions controlled by careful state organised balancing of capital accumulation and labour needs based on the ideas of John Maynard Keynes. For most of this period vast potential markets existed within expanding economies at home and abroad and the low cost of raw materials under global colonialism greatly assisted the industrial powers. The economic system spawned a culture based on class divisions quite unknown before the industrial revolution. New ways of life and social consciousness emerged based upon new class relations. The production system known as Fordism, after Ford's giant motor car works at Detroit, yielded a "modern" culture characterised by an interrelating set of features. A marked simplification of architectural style to suit the functionalism of the system produced huge factories ; vast assembly lines with individuals performing robotic tasks ; magisterial bank and office buildings; skyscrapers ; high rise blocks and formal estates; in general a gigantism in scale. The country side, regimented by railway lines, motorways and system agriculture became increasingly a dormitory land for the cities. An underlying ethic of 'progress' stemmed from an optimistic science delighting in nuclear power, chemical fertilisers and fixes of all kinds. The rationalist values of the humanist "enlightenment" generally held an optimistic sway with hopes for a changed world, removal of old poverty, new styles of "modern" living generating a rationality that cleaned up the untidiness of old regional practices under a rigidifying codification deriving from capital necessity. Inevitably a reaction set in with resistance to the machine like mould into which culture was falling, identical airports worldwide, city centres increasingly interchangeable and the globalised class problems.

Triggered by periodic financial crises, the early reaction was essentially romantic whether fascist or communist. Fascism emphasised the place, the 'volk', the locality, and negated the universalism of the enlightenment thrust. Communism, emphasising the class struggle, the inherent exploitation of labour and the critique of monopolism failed, as did fascism, to create a democratic system of government and, lacking a popular legitimacy, degenerated into proletarian dictatorship which meant, Stalin, Mao and others even worse. Gigantism paralleled that of the capitalist world but lacked a dynamism to sustain it. Yet, in spite of the immensity of the struggle between market capitalism and these alternatives, the conflict may in retrospect be seen to have been a sideshow in comparison to the playing out within capitalism of its own contradictions between competitive growth and over-accumulation.

Ways out of recession have been traditionally associated with devaluation, debt rescheduling, retooling of the production mechanisms and the placing of excess capital in other parts of the world where new foci of capitalist expansion could be kick started and pump primed from outside, the hoped-for benefits pushed into the future.

As new crises loomed in the 1970's the Fordist and Keynesian solutions no longer seemed to work as before. Harvey attempts to trace the exceedingly complicated interfaceting of conditions which brought about changes at this time and which are as yet still improperly understood. The triggering circumstances included the exhausting expenditure of the USA in the demoralising and unsuccessful Vietnam conflict; the renaissance of European and Japanese capitalisms kick started by vast American assistance after World war II; the consequent dollar devaluation and the OPEC inspired rise in the price of oil; but a major underlying factor must have been the very success of capitalism in becoming totally global with the consequence that spatial expansion as a solution to over-accumulation ceased to be an effective response to crisis. Instead the response took the form of what Harvey terms "flexible accumulation" in many shapes and guises. These changes are linked to the cultural shifts known as "postmodernity"[5].

Flexible accumulation is a change within the system whereby the gigantism and mechanistic structuring of old capitalism gives way to smaller scale networking in production, sub-contracting, diversification of products and processes, multiple company goals rather than single ones and looser more democratic even idiosyncratic organisational control with more participative and less authoritarian leadership. Labour becomes more associated with profit-taking through new forms of company ownership and management and a more flexible and enforceable relation with unions. Economics wider in scope than in scale become the norm, standardisation gives place to smaller batch production which is demand rather than resource driven. Labour focusses on multiple task learning, less robotic work tasking and wage payment is made more personal and less anchored in fixed rates for invariant jobs. On-the-job learning becomes typical as industries adapt more easily to new demands and situations.

The cultural spin off parallels these flexibilities, argues Harvey, and as the economic scene becomes more diverse and complex so does culture[6]. Old rigidities of class, ethnicity and gender open up as diversification proceeds and as teenagers and women are increasingly part of the network of commerce especially in the media, entertainment and service industries. Art picks up on the breakdown of rigidities and reflects it in a chaos of varying styles. All ideological assumptions become questioned and ephemeral personal values adopted through identification with short lived fads and fantasies. A myriad of life styles and gender variants emerge as "permissive" culture becomes increasingly on line with the new economics.

Philosophy itself deconstructs so that no certainties other than textual criticism remain. When the only resources for thought are found to be the fallible texts of outdated certainties the consequence is a rampant relativism wherein any belief, religion, ideology or idea is as good as any other. No basis for value remains and all values have the same value - doing one's own thing. Science, in spite of remaining the mainstay of the entire structure, gets a bad name since its values remain largely those of an outdated modernism. Vaguely defined "new paradigms" are in, their exponents usually ignorant of their origins in quite orthodox laboratories, cybernetics, holism and participative enquiry. In the superficial religiosity of our time New Age spirituality spawns old superstitions in new guises.

All this ferment anchored in changing economic practices has led to a great increase in personal liberty and expression, yet such freedom is also associated with profound uncertainties. Old role models and institutions, church, school, royalty, seem increasingly irrelevant to a churning world of high personal mobility, reduced communal values, image making, the attempt to fix oneself somewhere if only for a moment. Heavy investments in the image industries, advertisement, news selection, soap opera creation and media promotion has led to a distortion of culture through an increasing monetisation. Mini-cultures spawn around the elaborated intellectualisms of clique members talking to one another and selling their chat. Culture becomes something to buy and no longer something created by the cultured. The gutter press undermines values and taste by catering to the literally vulgar tastes of a semi-literate majority making the sophisticated appear fools or fuddy-duddy. Young fogies are in and false consciousness of all sorts appears together with imitation antiquity; every local bar becoming an Elizabethan inn with plastic oak beams and inglenooks filled with gas fired logs. Virtual reality blossoming on new televisual technology begins to provide a dreamtime in which image identifying persons float in a maze of projections ultimately controlled by commercial monitors.

And in the background, with looming menace, are the results of continued planetary denudation through unrestricted exploitation of non-renewable resources. Coupled with the ecological crisis is permanent, politically tolerated, unemployment. The technological complexity of electronic commerce has meant the employed earn excellent wages and acquire something approaching a yuppie lifestyle while the trend to complex skill has meant that the unskilled become the unwanted. The result is the rapid emergence of an underclass, the poverty-blighted street-sleeping cardboard box-housed population of disaffected individuals who, failing to make it in the system, have nowhere to go, nothing to identify with and no money for comfort. Furthermore, while many of the unemployed are actually highly educated, often with fine degrees from universities that remain excellent if underfunded, many belong to ethnic communities resulting from misguided immigration in earlier times of economic prosperity. For those without employment it seems there may be only a way of stasis if not of further fall. (see Fig 2)

The global spread of current over-accumulation means that kick starting enterprises elsewhere is much less of an option and interregional competition steadily increases. Even increased flexibility may not be enough in the future. As national income falls so does the tax to the state so that welfare provision for those most in need, elderly, sick and unemployed or unemployable unskilled is increasingly cut back or privatised. Imposing private insurance for the unemployed is a sick joke around the corner.

On our cinema screens appear nightmare cities of a not distant future where vast buildings of international corporations paying fat salaries to jet setting computer skilled executives overlook bludgeoning street scenes where small scale entrepreneurs come and go. Back of the streets drift the unemployed, the criminal, the addicts in an ever increasing resentful mass bursting out in joy riding and police bashing expeditions. It's us or it's them and one day may be them if only they could find out how.

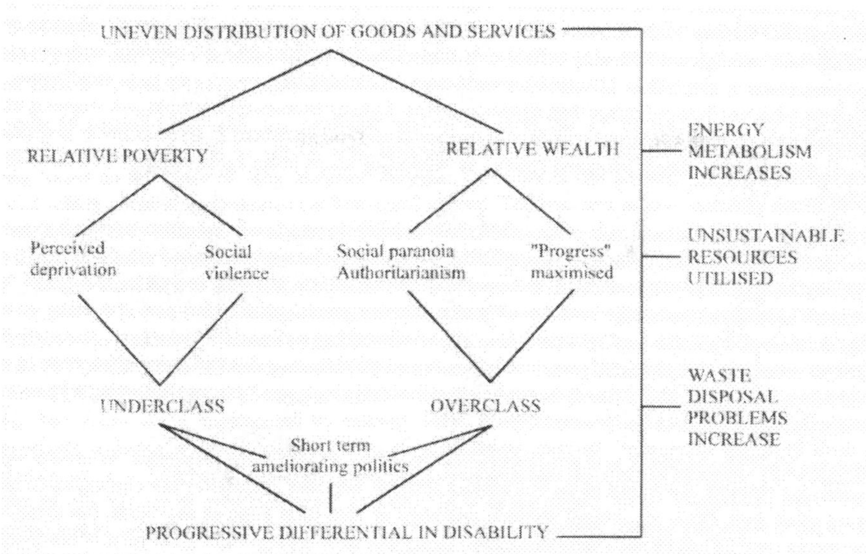

FIGURE 2

A Question of Values

All these trends have produced a depressive gloom, the "feel bad factor", permeating European and American society and a sense that the accumulating problems are possibly insoluble; that we shall leave to unborn generations a severely depleted planet[7] in which the electronic virtual realities of a teenage dream world may be the only compensation for the loss of quality in living[8]. We must ask what underlies this negativity, for in spite of wars and periodic setbacks, the trends of Western culture has been unremittingly positive for some three centuries.

The issues are compounded by the changing power structure of the world. The emergence of vibrant economies in SE Asia; the retreat of an economically unbalanced United States exhausted by military competition with the USSR and overspent in the Vietnam War; the slow and problematic re-awakening of Europe beset by renewed ethnic problems; chaos in the ex Soviet empire; the continuing socio-economic plight of Africa; the threat of international terrorism from Islam and the widening gap in both wealth and health between rich and poor in the Anglo Saxon world following the rash experimentation of Reagan and Thatcher; all reveal that the Western World has lost its hegemony of influence even if it retains a very expensive military strength, a strength which however cannot always be deployed with effect as Vietnam, Afghanistan, Bosnia and Somalia reveal. Local problems are subtle and do not respond to Western pressure as they tended to do in the days of the Cold War. Yet, at the heart of the matter is the suspicion that Western ways are in some sense wicked. What could be more wicked than the destruction of the precious rain forests, the ozone layer, the dumping of vicious pollutants in the third world, and the existence of vast food reserves only a few hours flying time from desperate starvation? The failure to meet these challenges suggests a profound lack of appropriate values the awareness of which creates deep unease.

In his recent study of ethical crises in civilisations Leslie Lipson[9] asks whether there is evidence for ethical evolution. He finds that ethical advances come in fits and starts and the conditions for improvement are not easily understood. He argues that there have been two great revolutionary periods in the cultural history of humanity, "axial ages" during which the root values of the contemporary world were established.

In the first we find great figures living widely apart within the same few centuries, Zoroaster, Confucius, Lao Tze, Gautama Buddha, Mahavira, Hebrew Prophets and Greek philosophers whose influence has set the tone of the ethical evaluation of conduct ever since. In spite of significant differences, the basic commandments for living which they recommend have a core in common to do with tolerance rather than killing and warfare, honesty rather than deceit, respect for property, care in sexual relations and for family integrity and generosity rather than meanness toward others. It is easy to see how such values became important as tribal structures became complex, populations increased and urbanisation with commerce began; any trend in an opposed direction always led to social and economic chaos or tyranny with misery.

The second axial age, argues Lipson, occurred in Europe after the Renaissance when the soporific power of the Church was at last broken within a rapidly developing Western Europe and inventive genius flowered with the expanding commerce of the middle classes. There was in fact a return to many of the humanist values of the classical Greco-Roman world with a key emphasis on the value and importance of the individual standing for himself before God and the world, the rights of all human beings for respect to their persons and for minimum standards of health, accommodation, opportunities and freedom from exploitation. These humanistic values rapidly began replacing the other-worldly focus of the Church with its intolerance of change, moralistic prescriptions on sex and marriage, and refusal to explore the nature of the world through science.

This movement, known as the European "Enlightenment", has been at the root of "progress" ever since; progress in understanding nature and utilising the resources of the planet, in health care, in removing gross exploitation of other races, children and women in slavery and work and above all, following the French and American revolutions, in promoting the rights of human beings everywhere. Changes in ideas clearly lead to changes in action.

It seems that for such great advances to occur several factors are needed, the first is a situation of economic and technological change which poses severe problems for an existing social order, the second is a cultural structure sufficiently flexible to accommodate social change and the third is the presence of outstandingly creative individuals who perceive a way forward to a breakthrough. Indeed a breakthrough often follows a breakdown but history is far from unanimous in this regard.

The current Western dilemma, argues Lipson, stems from the deeply schizoid nature of Western culture in which the humanistic tradition of the Enlightenment rests upon a largely rejected yet powerful otherworldly tradition seeking the transcendental solutions offered by the Churches. Somehow the rejection of transcendentalism is associated with guilty doubt and the absence of a settlement with God remains supremely unsettling.

The paradox is that the altruistic values of Christianity remain rooted in an other-worldly religion while the forward march of humanism has come to lack values of any strength other than individual freedom. Thus the capitalist thrust resulting from the handing over of nature to human exploitation[10] allows rampant self-promotion in business while the altruistic requirement to care for others as for oneself remains associated with an outdated religion. Indeed, in Britain, we have seen how the harsh effects of Thatcherite economics, allowing the rich to get richer while the poorer pay, have been resisted by the devines of a Church with its own values and finances in deep disarray.

None the less, even in Victorian times, the values of the "enlightenment" found expression in government initiated reforms alleviating the miseries of working people with the consequence that an opposition between liberal and hard faced capitalism became entrenched. Keegan[11]compares the social economics of Roosevelt which brought the USA out of recession in the 1930s with the crude market economics adopted in the 1980s. In the former scenario governments adopted the viewpoint of J. M. Keynes advocating considerable state intervention creating wealth through government led initiatives. The recovery of Europe after World War II was similarly inspired through the Marshall Plan. Such policy insured a reasonably effective balance between the need for economic growth and the need for employment. The particular problems of the l970's crises suggested that the Keynesian solution no longer worked and, although this remained unproven, radical right wing purists called for the withdrawal of government initiatives in favour of a market led economy which, it was believed, would right itself and generate profit for the successful which would "trickle down" to the rest. A lowering of taxes should therefore, it was naively expected, raise the government income from taxes - needless to say an outcome that failed to happen. The result was riches for the already rich, cutbacks in welfare and a return to Victorian style poverty for the poor.

Keegan points out, moreover, that rampant "Reaganomics" were adopted neither by Germany nor Japan where far more sensitive government involvement in the economy produced a wealth generating response without severe social aggravation. Yet the lesson has not been learnt; the dubious Anglo-Saxon approach is being foisted upon shattered east European and Russian economies regardless of the social strain approaching breaking point and which once again encourages romantically misconceived fascist solutions. Such a view of economics is so blatant a contradiction of the values of the European enlightenment that its continuing existence in the bland politics of the British Conservative Party is becoming profoundly disturbing to many people's sense of justice.

Will Hutton's impassioned and tightly argued analysis[12] of the profound inadequacies of British capitalism when compared with those of Germany, Japan and America puts the case for fundamental reform of the financial structure of Britain. Lacking a constitution, the majority party in the House of Commons can behave in a hegemonic manner with the potential for causing national disaster. The British financial system originated from a dominance of "gentlemanly" financiers who substituted shareholding for land holding and, while developing brilliance in share trading, failed to see the national importance of investment in industry. The demand for high dividends in a climate where banks and financiers are reluctant to invest adequately in industry has led to the steady run down in our industrial economy and the brain drain in talent to America. The British are failing in competition with far more effective German and Japanese economies where more Keynesian principles are actively used. The British have had to endure a far worse recent recession than elsewhere in Europe due directly to the monetarist policies of the Conservative government and its ideological rigidity. The extension of the market principle deep into society has produced massive differences between rich and poor and between regions with dire effects on health, life expectancy, social alienation, crime, family disunity and the despair of the long term unemployed." Altruism and the civilising values of an inclusive society have been sacrificed on the altar of self interest, of choice, of opting out and of individualism." (p15)

Lipson argues that the solution to contemporary problems requires a new axial age for which the conditions would appear to be right but for which the pressure from individuals has not yet developed to a take off point. It seems unlikely that the creativity for such a change in global morality can arise within a deeply authoritarian Chinese Confucian nor from the present resentful and unreformed Islamic stand point. Hinduism remains peculiarly Indian, Christian theology unrelated to science and the appeal of Western liberalism limited by its association with the very problems the exploitation of scientific discoveries has allowed. Clearly, however, the search is on. Many are in quest of an ethic for a better world, exploring, for examples, the relevance of ideas found in North American Indian religion, ancient Astrology, Celtic mysteries, Arthurian legend, the fragile guruism of New Age spirituality and the more orthodox traditions of mystical Christianity, Sufism and Buddhism.

At root, values are about our use of time space and people. How are we to find worthwhileness in an active life? How should we spend our time? What should we do about our environment? How should we relate to others? How should we maintain a "welfare state"? Is there meaning in the cosmos or do we have to create it? Are we victims of forces beyond our control or are we responsible for our fate and that of generations to come? How should answers to such questions be taught in schools? To a consideration of our awareness of time, space and relationship we must therefore turn.

Time, space and psychology

So fast have been the socio-cultural shifts in recent history that feelings of personal irrelevance and an unrooted anxiety at the very source of personal being have become endemic, especially in urban life. This is the "future shock" of Toffler[13], an aspect of what Harvey terms “space time compression” or the "annihilation of space by time".

We live within our personal 'ecologies of meaning'[14]construing our relations with the "outer" world on the dimensions of space and time. Yet, in everyday experiencing, place and time often seem separate modes of being rather than inseparably related . Standing in front of a fine landscape painting we experience a timeless space. The landscape is static, frozen in time, it is all space. Contrariwise, when we gaze from a window witnessing the movement of the traffic in a London street everything is change and change is time. Yet reflection tells us there is just one continuing "arrow of time" pushing us relentlessly to our personal deaths and, in whatever way we experience space, time never ceases. Yet, in slowing down time, we experience space while being pushed by time increases our awareness of mortality.

Even in medieval Europe time involved money. The cost of transporting raw materials, goods or products increased with time spent in travel. Likewise time spent in office tasks of administration and management, time consuming indeed with quill and parchment, cost merchants large sums it was desirable to reduce. Time measurement, the urban ubiquity of clocks, expresses the non -agricultural concern with hours and minutes on the job rather than the opportunities of changing seasons.

A prime mode of increasing turnover and hence profit lies in the reduction of transportation time and a speeding up of administration. As new technologies, canals, railways and so on came on stream so the significance of space and distance in the economies of scale became reduced. So too with the typewriter, telephone, radio, television, word-processing and faxing the speed of task completion and associated reduction in employment of lower skilled operatives have both been maximised. Work can often now be done from the home using word processors, fax and cash cards so that the old divisions between work and home life, town and country become abolished. Dormitory villages are more continuously occupied but the disappearance of the older agricultural communities continues apace. Seasonality loses significance, coffee breaks, tele programmes, and baby sittings rule the timing of the ex-commuters lives.

Space time compression has reached the point where satellite images from anywhere in the world can appear on personal screens all within a few moments news bulletin. Time zone differentials are overcome leading to a 24 hours market in shares. Only hours separate the openings of financial markets in New York, Tokyo, Frankfurt or London. The global uniformity of high speed transactional processing annuls constraints rooted in the old spatial dimension. Dishes from every corner of the globe lie side by side in supermarkets. Art forms, dance, expressions of lifeways and religions formally cultures apart flash on and off our screens becoming mixed in an extraordinary barely digestible collage. An averaging out of values occurs, for nothing from anywhere is more valuable than anything else. Everything is merely relative while the hunger of uncertainty is never appeased.

This is a world of stimulation, of sensation not of reflection, for there is no time to reflect. It is as if the qualities of becoming have become paramount while those of being are neglected. Being requires the opposite of space time compression. To be implies a dominance of space over time, a relative cessation of psychological movement within which to savour the relative constancy of a period.

A concern with place does in fact give this need some expression. Within a place locational constancy reduces the anxiety of change. The relief that this brings becomes itself a commodity. Great cities with monumental buildings and a relaxed atmosphere from past culture have an air of permanence and value is added to doing business there. Tourism focusses on the uniqueness of place. Places themselves may be falsified or even manufactured to stop time by the creation of the imitation old. Belonging to some illusory but seemingly underlying continuity becomes a marketable commodity, a resting place between birth and death where the flight of the arrow of time seems for a moment to have paused in some reflective space.

Sadly the actual churches of traditional Western religion seem often as much concerned with the rush of becoming as our culture in general. Indeed it is precisely in this general context that many have turned to the East in sad ignorance that a deeper Christian tradition remains extant in tucked away monasteries where the practices established by the ancient desert Fathers still provide a meditativety that may yet say much to our time.

Rather than space-time compression we now need periods for space-time expansion and it is precisely in this area that the age old message of the Fathers has something to say. Yet the same or very similar message is conveyed in Buddhism with a philosophical power uncluttered by the confusions of Christian theology and with a methodology of meditation honed by yoga to answer the problem of psychological suffering itself.

Identity and the responsibility of commerce

In the postmodern world with its extraordinary diversity of modes of life, overlapping ethnicities, uncertain class boundaries, travel channelled for comfort in tourist managed lands, televisual experience, we are faced with virtual realities of many kinds. An inconsistent schooling, focussed more on training for modern jobs than on enriching personal life, leads to the development of a fractured personal identity. We have one face for the work place, another for the home, we are pressured by the common values of the media into the specious conformities of a fashionable individualism. Unconsciously subscribing to a collectivity of isolated selves we hoodwink ourselves into the belief we are becoming "somebody".

The development of a personal self image needs the provision of role models that can give stability. The breakdown of marriage and the family home means that figures on the television screen, mere shadows, often become the only exemplars for the young, parents no longer having qualities that command respect. The quality of the images purveyed by the media is determined by the popular demand for reality-forgetting sensation, soap operatic cardboard persons living life styles unobtainable for the majority produce for many a 'dreamtime' unrelated to socio-political realities. Single parent families without fathers can rarely provide boys with masculine models worthy of respect, itinerant males being hardly likely to provide the relationship a boy seeking a positive identity needs. Worse still, socially deprived individuals may act out the horrors of video nasties as the murders of little James Bulger by young teen age boys and 16 year old Suzanne Capper by two disturbed women and their collaborators strongly suggest.

There is an evident need to inject into this social confusion some set of ethically related ideas that link the traditions of liberal humanism to those of a spiritual quest that is not a mere nonsense in the withering gaze of the scientifically educated.

A founding consideration here may be that not all forms of capitalism lack the inhumanity of Thatcherism. In continental Europe there is a much greater respect for society. In Germany the relations between labour and business have been carefully nurtured to yield policies of socially related public financing which have had great economic success. Only the problems of German reunification have delayed the recognition of the importance of the Neo-Keynesian stance exemplified here. William Keegan and Will Hutton point out that capitalism is an evolved relationship between commerce and the wider society that is not necessarily evil. It is quite possible to create a social capitalism based neither in discredited socialist ideology nor in a socially destructive Thatcherism but in a renewal of strategic planning that can manage the world's ills. Such a renewal can be expected to have strong effects both on culture and community.

Those who have now become the technological elite of postmodern capitalism, especially perhaps those working in transnational institutions, have not only great opportunities but also major responsibilities. Far less duped than most by the cults of our time, they are already seeing beyond the limited materialism of market economics. The age of complete relativism in which all creeds and customs had the same value, simply doing one's thing, is passing into a search, not this time for some overarching ideology, but for a flexible way within which, none the less, universal values are expressed. After deconstruction perhaps we are at last turning to reconstruction. Does Buddhism have a role to play here?

PART II. BUDDHISM NOW

The contemporary role of Buddhism in the West

What is Buddhism doing here? Given the circumstances we have outlined in Part I, let us begin by examining what it has to offer. I want to make six points of fundamental importance.

First, Buddhism is rooted in a "motion "theory, but one which is fundamentally different from the characteristic style of thought in the West for it is concerned with the subject rather than with the objects of knowledge. It is 'subjective empiricism'[15]. This empirical basis relates very well to the objective empiricism of science. Indeed, they are two sides of the same coin. Buddhism thus compliments and completes scientific investigation in a way no other religion can.

Second, Buddhism presents itself in a set of relatively simple formulae most of which have a self evident correctness. The intellectual elaboration of these principles is essentially a philosophical sport.

Third, the increasingly clear parallels between Buddhist and Western Psychology suggest that the Buddhist models of mind are good working descriptions of a universal human condition.

Fourth, a clear and plausibly correct view of the universals of human experience implies that the soteriology with which the working models of Buddhism are associated may have an answer to at least some of the fundamental problems of our time, in particular those centred on the nature of personal and institutional identity.

Fifth, Buddhism provides a yogic methodology for the psychological suspension of time providing respite from the shock of over-immanent futures and which examines critically the nature of the self responsible for human actions from the personal to the political domain.

Six, the practice of these yogas requires an altruistic ethic in which the maximisation of fame and gain shifts to an attitude focussing on the optimisation of welfare for all people through an educative process requiring a revolution in the conception of self.

Let us look briefly at each of these points.

Buddhist motion theory

Buddhism examines human experience in terms of the action of interdependent processes rather than in terms of persons as such. The no-self doctrine (anatta) and the principle of interdependent origination (pratityasamutpada) are among the earliest propositions of the Buddha. They are clearly accounts of the personal in terms of process, not in terms of named entities. All apparent entities are considered to be cognitive attributions arising from the interplay of mental factors (skandha). Such thinking is closely akin to the motion theory approaches we have discussed above. There are however two main points of difference between the historical materialism from which we have gained our perspective on our time and Buddhist motion theory.

Buddhism presents a subjective approach rather than an objective one. Mind and not matter has priority in the explanatory system because the world we comprehend is necessarily constructed by the mind. Buddhist theory is anchored in accounts of experience and not in mere psychologising; in an existential perspective therefore and not in academic abstractions.

In the West, a phenomenological philosophy similar in some respects to the Buddhist approach was developed by such thinkers as Brentano and Husserl and became the existentialism of Heidegger and Sartre[16]. In spite of Husserl's subjective enquiries, the line taken has remained abstract, intellectualised and distanced from mainstream science-oriented philosophy, thus appearing to be quite incompatible with an experimental deductive approach to knowledge. The anchorage of Buddhism in a thoroughgoing subjective empiricism thus offers a perspective with a basis that contrasts markedly with Western thought as a whole and in this may lie its key contribution to our time.

Basic formulae

The Buddha expounded his viewpoint very much as a doctor prescribing a cure for the unhappiness in the world. We do not therefore start with a cosmology nor with mega-philosophical metaphysics comprising a self consistent system but rather with simple statements of verifiable facts. The Four Noble Truths comprise the basic formulae[17]. Life entails inevitable suffering. This is due to craving, wanting what we have not and not wanting what we have. Suffering stops when this craving ceases. There is a way, the eightfold path, whereby this may be achieved. The path itself involves morality in intention, speech, action, and livelihood expressed with vigour and in mindful understanding of the nature of body and mind.

The mind is the expression of the interacting processes of sensation, perception, cognition, preconceptions built up from experience and consciousness. These processes result in the attributing of an "I" to the experience of self. This "I" is therefore no more than a useful cognitive imputation which however, through ignorance can be felt as a entity that needs enhancement, aggrandisement and protection. Since all things are impermanent such a quest is ultimately useless yet we spend our time concerned with it. Nirvana is the release from suffering that comes from the dropping of such ego related concern, the ego being seen then as merely functional in the everyday world of relations. In later Buddhism, reflection on the condition of humanity led to practices of compassion to save others from suffering even before one's own release.

Buddhism and Western Psychology

Contemporary Western psychology of identity and self concerns itself very much with the investigation of the very "I" that is the focus of Buddhist concern. Since the work of G. H. Mead our understanding of identity has moved ever closer to a formulation that parallels that of the Buddha surprisingly closely[18]. Although many cognitive psychologists and philosophers such as Daniel Dennet[19] would be slow to admit it, their work in many respects rediscovers the findings of the Buddha. The difference is that Western cognitive psychology stems from objective analysis and is little concerned with the subjective soteriological enquiry that was the basis of the Buddha's own understanding and that of Buddhists in general. The work of Margaret Donaldson[20], however, based in both a developmental and an historical perspective, reveals how the four modes of minding she describes have close resemblances with the five main categorisations of the ancient Buddhist model of mind. Likewise, in her philosophical study of morality, Iris Murdoch gives a sympathetic account of the Buddhist view[21]. Such comparisons suggest very fruitful lines of further investigation in which Buddhist thought can receive an appropriately respected place in discussion.

Human universals

The parallels between Western and Buddhist analysis of mind suggest that we have here a basic and plausibly correct understanding of the functions of human experience[22]. Since Buddhist "cures" are posited on the basis of a mental model, these parallels suggest the cures too may be based on a firm empirical foundation. Certainly they are there for the testing and cannot be rejected by mere intellectual bias or academic ignorance. Buddhism is thus hardly classifiable as a "religion" in the sense of a dogmatic belief in a metaphysical interpretation of the world. Like Stoicism in the Classical world it is more a way of life based on a quasi-scientific model of human existence which can be tested out in actual scientific enquiry at a personal level. Naturally this now involves a contemporary research sophistication well beyond that of the original propositions.

Buddhist yoga

The subjective empiricism of Buddhism is anchored in the practice of mental yoga. The Buddha himself argued that every proposition in his teachings should be tested against experience, and he meant not only everyday experience but also that gained through intensive meditation.

The yogic methods of Buddhism derive from those of pre-Buddhist Indian culture but these underwent a marked change in emphasis as a result of the Buddha's personal creativity. Instead of seeking a transworldly trance, the Buddha, in close self observation, noticed that no mental state was permanent, rather there was continuous movement. The problem of human suffering lay, he argued, in our seeking for an impossible permanence within an inviolable ego, a fixed security as an insurance against life's inherent instability and change. The acceptance of impermanence as basic implies that the way beyond suffering lies through not becoming attached to any aspect of it but to abandon craving, desire and attachment altogether in a discovery of a flowing-in-time that constitutes release. This approach remains very much on offer to the confused and conflictful experience of people today[23].

Altruistic ethics

The realisation that self promotion produces a negative and entrapping entanglement with the world results in the practitioners attempt to go beyond the everyday assumption of self. The practice of meditation shows what can be experientially possible here and as the release from "samsara" deepens there dawns a deeper insight into the suffering of others. A lowered concern with ego allows the adoption of an active role in caring. Because the ways of the world are rooted in self cherishing, fame and gain the practitioner almost inevitably comes to a thoroughgoing critique, not only of individual behaviour and mores, but of society itself and the institutions which comprise it. In modern times this leads to new forms of action in the world. The age old Christian concern with poverty is becoming matched by the even more ancient Buddhist concern with misery.

I argue that these six propositions reveal Buddhism as a very powerful source for a renewed visioning of human action. The schizoid ethical dilemma in the West, to which Lipson draws attention, involves an opposition between the worldly and the unworldly, between selfish maximisation of capitalist gain and the altruistic ethics of a Christianity confused in a postmodern world. Already the personal quests of many look towards a healing of this split which however cannot come from adherence to either side nor from the many forms of regressive contemporary superstition. Buddhism occupies a middle ground, indeed it calls itself a middle way. Three things stand out. Firstly it provides a simple working model for the release of an individual from the many forms of ego-related stress so prevalent in our time, secondly this model is open to sophisticated scientific enquiry because it is in itself scientific in its propositions and, thirdly, it provides a value system from which to re-examine the basic fault in our contemporary mode of life - rampant capitalism itself.

The concern with misery

When I work with stress groups for executives employed by a major London Borough Council the problem of the nine-to-five existence appears in raw form. Many executives hardly ever stop worrying about their work. They begin when they leave home to travel to the office, their minds run ahead of the train, the traffic on the roads, the crowds at stations and are already in their offices ahead of them reworking in rehearsal yesterday's or tomorrow's problems. Going home at night they may carry their work with them so that they may end up being present neither within their travel time nor within their home time. And at the desk there are no gaps between the often stressful telephone calls, interviews or engagements with a frequently fractious and difficult public. Their day lacks gaps for refreshment when the mind can pause and reflect a moment. Our workshop together leads into recommendations as to how that may actually be achieved and subsequent course evaluations from participants reveal the value of such an approach. To stop and actually see the street in which you work may lead to an important realisation concerning the profound alienation from actual experience that a mind overstressed with thought comes eventually to know.

The Buddhist concern with misery is focussed upon attitudes. A man in hospital after breaking a leg suffers pain but it is his attitude to that pain that largely determines the degree of his suffering and the form of his recovery. Attitudes are framed by activities in place, time and culture. The space-time compression of contemporary culture tends to preclude those activities that allow a recalibration of attitudes simply because time to experience anything in depth is denied. The alleviation of psychic misery thus begins with a re-allocation of space and time.

Buddhist meditation is one profound way in which time expansion can be created, bringing the participant into a mind-space of being rather than becoming. Such practice anchors the "I" within an experienced space-time continuum quite different from that of the victim of office routines that the unreflective person experiences as an alienating imposition. It raises deep questions concerning the value of the contemporary Western way of life.

In Buddhism, adherence to precept has the intention of generating attitudes preventing both personal misery and that created by mistaken action in relation to others. These precepts have implications for our times that run profoundly counter to the prevailing materialism of self before others at any cost.

For example - Do not kill: _______ What about the policies that lead to the assaults on South American Indian peoples? What about policies that prevent the sharing of the food mountains with poorer lands where starvation is rampant? What about the health differential between the south and the north of England?

For example -Do not steal:_______ What about the vastly inflated salaries of high ranking corporate executives and directors? What about taxation policies which over some years consistently favour the already rich over the relatively poor?

For example -Do not lie: _______What about the extensive corruption in high places by highly paid executives, Maxwell for an example? What about the consistent misinformation based on faulty interpretations of government statistics? What about Watergate, Irangate, Arms for Iraq-gate and the other obvious lyings of governments and ideologically corrupt local administrations?

For example - Do not drink: _______ Well only a little. But what about the economics of drug abuse; the failure of policies of education in relation to drugs. Tobacco advertising?

For example - Do not commit sexual abuse: _______ What about the whole gender problem today; the frequencies of rape and family failure, sex and violence on video, pornography and sick parenting?

The precepts do not refer only to personal motivation but also to the condition of society and the political-economic system that is responsible for the state of society. Clearly Buddhist radicalism and a social critique is both timely and called for. Socialism and Marxism lacked a sound underpinning in psychology, not so a Buddhist social policy. There is need for thought and action which the Buddhist rejection of self and other victimisation may well promote[24].

Expressing the Dharma

The role of the Dharma is our time can be no other than its traditional role; offering a medicine for the ills of humanity. Only a fool ignores a prescription based on a careful diagnosis but, sadly, part of the malady is foolishness itself. The doctor cannot afford to give up since the social ills deeply affect him too, so he must use his skills of reason and persuasion in making his offer.

The medicine of the Dharma tackles an illness called attachment. Buddhism does not deny the necessity of meeting basic human needs nor the role of an active ego in securing them; and this includes the effective practice of honest business. The problem is the development by the ego of attachments to self inflation through fame and gain which ignores the welfare of others and, as a natural extension, the excessive accumulation of capital and influence by the institutional egos of competitive international corporations to the neglect of planetary good.

The rationality of applying the Dharma is based in the depth of its psychological roots, its model of mind which, as we see, is well supported by Western psychology. The difference between contemporary Buddhism and other religious and humanist ethics lies precisely in the application of empiricism, open minded observation and experiment, to the inner world in amplification of the sciences of the external world. It is precisely this that was lacking in all socialist solutions that based themselves solely on an academic rationalism lacking an inner dimension.

The difficulty for the Doctor lies in getting the patient to understand the benefits of lessening competitive self cherishing in favour of attitudes that influence the common good even to the extent of reducing his/her personal wealth. To balance the world's economy this will almost certainly be essential. Currently our Western capitalist education and individualism makes it difficult for people to think collectively rather than in terms of personal benefit. This is why in a democracy no political party can easily adopt policies that demand self constraint by an electorate. None the less, it can be done and there are good indications. In time of war self sacrifice becomes well developed. Today our "war" is against the ruin of our planet by ourselves. Recently, we have seen the beginnings of a new peacefulness through negotiation established in South Africa, the Middle East and in Northern Ireland. If movement can be seen in these intractable problems so it can be expected on a wider stage. It seems however that things have to get very bad indeed and the future threatening to both sides of a dispute before action through negotiation is possible. Sadly this may mean the world has to get into a truly dreadful mess before anything is done. Hopefully those in power may show the pro-action of which the populace at large may not be capable.

Buddhism is strong on deconstruction - not merely as in the popular modern forms of academic philosophy but in the practice of meditation. The deconstruction of the self allows reconstruction on a contrasting base. As we deconstruct old gestalts at the personal, societal and economic levels of our global culture so we have a chance of reconfiguring the world, revisioning the meaning of our existence here in terms of setting our house in order. Time is short and Buddhists should not remain silent.

Conclusion

The tone of this discussion reflects the atmosphere of our time. Perhaps only in the newly wealthy states of S.E. Asia exists a more generally up-beat mood. Is the 'feel bad factor' merely a consequence of our current financial recession? In 1994 new advances in communications technology are promised and for many these will usher in a new age of shopping without visiting a shop, purchasing a house by walking though it on screen in advance of going there and other marvels. Expansion in the private sector may well produce a new run away boom in space-time compression. There was a time when such "progress" might have elicited enthusiasm and hopes for a changing world. Not so much I think now.

The problem is that such technological advance, even when associated with a burst of world trade following the new arrangements under the GATT initiatives, do not address the underlying contradictions in world capitalism and its production of divergent worlds of rich and poor, advantaged and disadvantaged on a global scale. The old split between economic management and ethics remains, leaving an uneasy feeling of collective guilt.

Passing the beggars in our flourishing streets we may well wonder who cares for the poor, the distressed and the needy as we rush into a new age of electronic tinsel. Unlike the Victorian period when the working class was basic to the functioning economy, these people have little economic value, no bargaining power, for they are largely unemployable and can be simply by-passed. It seems clear that the only method of drawing attention to their plight will soon be international terrorism. It only needs some genius to appropriate the methods of Islamic fundamentalism, the IRA, Animal Rights and Pro-Life activists to set the thing going. Then there will be a Law and Order crisis in earnest and another round of suppression. The rights of the downtrodden are often the least observed.

We return finally then to the crisis in values that prevents action on these issues in a way that will command electoral respect and political action. The issue is unresolved and deserves focussed attention in places where action counts. Deconstructive and reconstructive at the same time, the Buddhist stance provides a rationale for new thinking that can play a role in the active revisioning of human meaning. It is not perhaps Buddhism itself and its institutions that will do this but the coming together of a like-mindedness in a Buddhistic approach associated closely with Christian and Humanist values. Buddhist thought can fill the gaps in these ways of thinking that renders them so powerless today.

References

1 Bailey, W. 1986. Consciousness and action/motion theories of communication. Western Journal of Speech Communication. 50.1. 74-86. See also: Burke, K. 1969 A Grammar of Motives. University California Press. Berkeley.

Also Matson, F. 1966. The Broken Image, Man, Science and Society. Doubleday. New York.

2 Hobsbawm, E., 1994. Age of Extremes: The Short Twentieth Century 1914-1991. Michael Joseph. London.

3 Harvey, D. 1990 The Condition of Postmodernity. Blackwell Oxford

4 The importance of Marx here lies not at all with the later emergence of communism as ideology but with the profundity of his insight into the capitalist process. This is a great contribution to contemporary thought that to ignore it amounts virtually to an option of ignorance.

5 There is an interesting parallel here with the social history of warlike East African tribes. Once expansion was not longer possible the social structure began to become far more complex and the internal checks and balances elaborated. See Bonte, P. 1982 Non-stratified social formations among pastoral nomads. In: Freidman J and Rowlands, M. J. The Evolution of Social Systems. Duckworth, London.

6 See further Hobsbawm, ref[2], Chapters 10 and 11.

7. Crook, J. H. 1995. Psychological processes in cultural and genetic co-evolution. In Jones, E. and Reynolds, V. Survival and Religion. Wiley. London

8 For further discussion see Boyden, S. 1987. Western Civilization in Biological Perspective. Oxford University Press. Oxford.

9 Lipson, L. 1993.The Ethical Crises of Civilization. Moral Meltdown or Advance. Sage. London

10 Tawney, R. H.1926 Religion and the Rise of Capitalism. Harcourt, Brace and Co. New York.

11 Keegan, W. 1993. The Spectre of Capitalism: The future of the world economy after the fall of communism. Vintage. London.

12 Hutton, W. 1995. The State we're In. Jonathan Cape. London.

13 Toffler, A.1970 Future shock. New York.

14 Crook, J. H. 1991. Consciousness and the ecology of meaning: new findings and old philosophies. In: Robinson, M.H and L. Tiger (eds) Man and Beast Revisited. Smithsonian Institution. Washington DC. pp 203-224.

15 Crook, J. H. 1980.The Evolution of Human Consciousness. Oxford University Press. Oxford. Chapters 11-13,

16 See Paranjpe A.C. and. Hanson, R.K. 1988 On dealing with the stream of consciousness: a comparison of Husserl and yoga. In Paranjpe, A.C et al (eds) Asian contributions to Psychology. Praeger. New York.

Also Batchelor, S. 1983 Alone with Others. An existential approach to Buddhism. Grove Press. New York.

17 Cheetham, E. 1986. Fundamentals of Mainstream Buddhism. Booklet 2. Buddhist Society. London.

18 Crook, J. H and D. Fontana 1990 Space in Mind. East-West Psychology and Contemporary Buddhism. Element. Shaftesbury.

Also Carrithers, M.1985 An alternative social history of the self. In: Carrithers, M. Collins, S. and Lukes, S. (eds) The Category of the Person. Cambridge.

19 Dennett, D.1991 Consciousness explained. Penguin. London

20 Donaldson, M. 1992 Human minds: an Exploration. Penguin. London

21 Murdoch, I. 1992. Metaphysics as a Guide to Morals. Penguin. London

22 Relevant discussions of biological and cultural contributions to the evolution of mind may be found in: Jaynes J. 1976 The origins of consciousness in the breakdown of the bicameral mind. Houghton Mifflin. New York. Crook, J. H. 1980 The Evolution of Human Consciousness. Oxford. Donald, M. 1991 Origins of the Modern Mind. Harvard. Dennett, D. see note[17] and, more controversially Barkow, J.H. Cosmides, L and Tooby, J. (eds.) The Adapted Mind. Evolutionary Psychology and the Generation of Culture. Oxford.

23 Crook J.H. and J. Low 1997. The Yogins of Ladakh. Motilal Banarsidaddas. Delhi.

24 Jones, K. 1989 The Social face of Buddhism: An approach to political and social activism. Wisdom. London. Also ibid.1993 Beyond Optimism, a Buddhist Political Ecology. Carpenter Oxford. Also Sivaraksa, S. (ed.)1990. Radical Conservatism: Buddhism in the Contemporary World. INEB. Bangkok. and Fu, C. W. and Wawrytko, S.A. (eds.) Buddhist Ethics and Modern Society: an International symposium. Greenwood. New York.

XII

A NEW CH'AN HALL: MASTER SHENG YEN AND THE RETREAT OF JUNE 1995

Shi-fu came to Britain again this June to lead his third retreat at the Maenllwyd. Ever since January three teams of builders had laboured in all weathers to complete the new Ch'an Hall in time. The main building was ready for use two days before the retreat. The old barn, reborn in its new guise, positively shone for the occasion, the pine trees on the hill peeping down through the end windows and the sun often beaming in through the open doors.

Shi-fu told us he may not be able to visit us again since he is very busy in Taiwan developing the new monastic university on Dharma Drum Mountain. He took care therefore to instruct us deeply. He taught at three levels. Firstly, he was concerned to show us both the correct way and the right attitude with which to practice Silent Illumination. Secondly, he spoke often of the way of conduct in the world: the practical ethics of the Dharma. Thirdly, he went deeply into the profound texts of Hung Chih Cheng Chueh (twelfth century), literally retranslating them together with Ming Yee, to reveal the great subtleties of insight which they contain. Perhaps not all participants could follow him here, but we all gained a glimpse of the depths of the Dharma in the mind of a great teacher.

Shi-fu left us with tangible marks of his visit also, a portrait by Ros Cuthbert perhaps destined for the interview room, some beautiful calligraphy of a verse by Hung Chih, and his own poem, read to us in Mandarin and then translated by Ming Yee - the inauguration verse for the Ch'an Hall.

Birds are chattering, sheep are baaing
Streams sparkle, mountains spirited,
Cool and refreshing, self at ease
Everyday is a good day!

Transmitting the light, spreading the Dharma
Vast ocean, vacant skies.
Mind illumined, self-nature realised,
Everyone is Buddha!

Even in this English version the delicate balance of these matching verses comes over. There is great depth here as well as the Dharma joy which so beautifully reflected the happy occasion and the clarity of mind that many participants experienced on this retreat. The verse will be an inspiration and I have already given a "teisho" on it to the Ch'an Group in Bristol. In many ways it conveys the silently illuminating vision of Hung Chih which inspired us all so much during this retreat. We thank Shi-fu, Guo Gu Sse and Ming Yee Wang for having come and very much trust they will be back again. In the meantime we have our own work to do.

In June the long Welsh evenings only slowly give way to night. As the Celtic twilight faded and the last 'Boards' of the day sounded in the yard we could all experience:

> Half moon rising and one lone star
> Evening fades in the green valley.
> Birds fall silent, sheep are settling down,
> One lamp shines in the Master's room.

A FELLOWSHIP OF WESTERN CH'AN PRACTITIONERS?

The time seems ripe to put a suggestion to the readers of New Ch'an Forum that has been germinating for some time. Practitioners have often remarked that they would like some form of community based on their experience of retreats at the Maenllwyd with which they could feel closer identification. There are indeed now many people who have come and continue to come to the Maenllwyd regularly for that mixture of insight, peace of mind and companionship that the practice of intensive retreat provides. Furthermore, on our mountain pilgrimages and on convivial occasions at Rickford there has been a real sense of a community of common purpose reflected in the retreat reports of a number of participants.

I therefore propose the formation of a charitable institution of simple form to be called something like "The Fellowship of Western Ch'an Practitioners". This would have the function of arranging and managing a pattern of retreats and sociable events designed to meet the needs I have just described. The advantage of such a procedure would also be the formalisation of the practice of retreat and a network of practitioners in close mutual contact able to meet conveniently at a number of centres where we already have small groups; Swindon, Manchester, Edinburgh, Cardiff and supportive of regular training at Maenllwyd. There are also financial and administrative conveniences (as well perhaps as some difficulties to be looked into) in having charitable status. Basically membership fees (small) and retreat bookings (standard) would be paid centrally and used to fund the hire of Maenllwyd and the services of the Teacher, Cook and sometimes a Guestmaster. We may also be in the position to support local groups and events of a different nature from those we run at present - solitary retreats, longer term communal events, mini-conferences, teaching, pilgrimages, support of parallel organisations in the Mahayana etc.

The "spiritual" direction would remain as it has been, focusing on the teaching approach of Master Sheng Yen and his lineage with additional supportive training in Tibetan Mahamudra and introductory Western Zen Retreats. This pattern could be developed in several ways. We would create an advisory body from our membership, perhaps with two or so external advisors, which would consider the views of trainees and their needs, possible developments and, in specified instances, challenge the mode of teaching should it be felt that any mistake was being made. Behind this creation is the question concerning the role of lay monastic practice in the modern world and our work on this should be thought of as an experiment. We have not only the Asian models to guide us but also the long tradition of Western spirituality and monasticism in relation to lay practice.

The core of Zen training is to be found in intensive retreat, a tradition from which major personal discoveries can be taken out into the world. This is a key position of the Maenllwyd perspective.

Here then is the outline of my proposal. It seems a natural way forward after the inauguration of the new Ch'an Hall at Maenllwyd and the establishment of an effective teaching pattern there. I want to make clear however that it is not my intention to create a vast organisation; merely to improve the efficacy and value to individuals of the system we have already created. Retreats will not change their form or atmosphere nor grow into meetings unwieldy because of numbers. In any case the severity of the training will see to that!

I would welcome responses from anyone who feels they would like to join in such an adventure. Please indicate whether you would like to commit yourself to membership should we decide to proceed. Please respond soon. I would welcome opinions and look forward to reporting back. Needless to say, if there is insufficient interest, things will continue as they already quite happily are.

DAD

1.

You carry me on your shoulders
through the dark
and explain to me
the stars.
The owl in the old oak
calls in the night.
You chuckle, joyful
in that mysterious bird.
One day you received a stuffed fox
and, to everyone's horror,
set it up in the hall.
You wanted to put tiny
light bulbs in its eyes and make it see.
Later the owl came
to sit above the grandfather clock
striking the hours
with its hoots.
When I was six
and staying at the big house,
the Blue Room I remember,
you came and slept in the great bed
next to mine.
Before dawn I lay awake
a little sick or something,
you took me into your sheets
and together we watched
the light come.
Dawn, never so mysterious,
never again so filled with rapture,
your explanations of the rising sun,

the globe that spun, the east-west
meaning, time and openings
of day and night revolvings.
When the sun came
striking the gauze curtains
and filtering into the room
I was one with the planet's turning
lying in your arms.

2.

Long after the uncertainties began
I still went to church with you.
It seemed there was nothing else to do
and anyway there was love.
Stumbling hesitatingly through the Creed
one day I heard you say
"- in so far as it can be believed"
and my heart leapt
letting go all fears of losing love,
thrilling me with the vast courage
of that great doubt.
I sang the hymns so high
into the rafters I think
the tiles moved.

25.12.93

NCF XIII

AN EDITORIAL FROM THE CH'AN HALL

The "Question of Lay Zen" which has been the concern of our recent issues is a burning one. The majority of Buddhists in this country are lay practitioners so that the means of training available to them and their affiliations to training institutions become of paramount importance in the transmission of Buddhism from the Orient to the West.

However there are many ways in which training institutions might mistakenly provide inauthentic Buddhism. Yet, within so rich a tradition as the Dharma, it is difficult to define what authenticity may be. The recent mistakes in transmissions of authority to teach to persons who subsequently became faulty exemplars makes this issue important. Within our tradition of Ch'an (Zen) one fundamental perspective must never be laid aside:

"Followers of the Way! There is talk of the Way to be practised and the Dharma to be realised....Young students, not understanding anything, put their faith in wild fox sprites and so become entangled in their random talk and fancies......You say that everywhere there is training and there is realisation. Do not be deceived. Though something can be attained by training it only creates the karma of birth and death....I am afraid those teachers are like newlywed brides, uneasy and worried about being chased out of their homes and starving to death....When the sword of wisdom flashes there is nothing at all. Even before the light shines darkness is already bright. Because of this an old master said "The ordinary heart is the way". (Lin Chi. 9th Century).[1]

Lin chi, like the Buddha before him, emphasised individual attainment, searching out one's salvation through diligence, depending neither on words alone nor on institutions, nor the personal guru. A true teacher is a facilitator of such individual understanding and not an authority purveying a dogma to be believed.

Some developments in British Buddhism are a cause for concern to those who see Lin Chi, that profound iconoclast and personal facilitator, as representing the Buddha's own perspective. The growth of cult-like mega institutions focused on deviant teachings of modern charismatics is highly suspect. There is more than a hint of fascistic self-promotion in these closed systems, which bodes ill for the future of open Buddhism. I have recently apprehended what Stephen Batchelor meant when, in conversation at Sharpham, he once suggested to me that "the Golden Age of Buddhism in the West may already be over!" For these reasons I am most grateful to Ken Jones for his precise delineation of the problem in this issue.

My own perspective is quite clear. I am a child of the Western Enlightenment, that rationality that since the 17th century has thrown out the superstitions of the churches and given rise to science, the rights of man, social democracy and all those ethical attitudes we may perhaps take too much for granted in our post-modern scepticism. Of course all this history, despite (or perhaps because of) its emphasis on individual freedoms, has also provoked the serious problems of our time. However a regression to an age of authoritarian superstition is no answer. I stand for the integration of the Buddha's Enlightenment with that of the modern Western Enlightenment perspective. Bringing these enlightenments together is the function of my exploratory role as teacher and will always be so. Only in this way do I believe that Buddhism can flourish in the West in a manner that can fulfil its soteriological[2] role in our time. The Buddha as the great doctor needs a hearing. Yet the one who is healed in the end does it from within.

What then is authenticity in training? This issue is devoted to this question. We hope it will stimulate debate and we welcome your comments and discussion of what we are presenting. Our views have no authority, we play here as fox sprites but in a world of hungry ghosts they too must have their say and work their passage to understanding. We can only do it together. Let us have your views. Do not sit around in a passive hobbyism. Please write.

1 Selected from Schloegl, I.1976 The Zen Teaching of Rinzai. Shambala. Berkeley.

2 Soteriological: Doctrine pertaining to salvation.

AUTHENTICITY AND THE PRACTICE OF ZEN

The need for an examination

The authority of experience depends upon authenticity. If we base our action or feeling inauthentic experience it can only lead to play acting or pretence with potentially catastrophic consequences. Sadly, many of our justifications for action rest on the outcomes of past personal, familial and social tensions that have remained unresolved and which distort our perception of ourselves and other people. They lead to a biased repression of emotion and a ritualisation of personal behaviour into rigid moulds that may later produce an inability to recover the repressed experiences in understanding. Such "stuckness" commonly leads to damaged lives inhabited by persons in permanent low level stress and whose behaviour is often socially damaging. Such a condition is widely prevalent, almost a norm in human society[1] and some have argued that it amounts to a disease.

Buddhist thought has accepted this position for some 2,500 years arguing that the human mind is normally in a state of delusion from which it is difficult to recover[2]. The Buddha has often been called the great doctor and the task of Buddhism as soteriology is to replace illusion by clarity and this process is what is meant by "enlightenment"[3]. Yet so normal is the state of illusion that Buddhist institutions and teachers are by no means immune from it and there are those who would argue for the necessity of a constant and watchful cultivation[4]. Such a viewpoint is often ignored especially in heady periods of Buddhist history when the Dharma is expanding rapidly into new cultural settings. Since Buddhism and especially Zen claims to restore authenticity to consciousness we need to ask how successful it is or whether the teachings and teaching personalities hold us in some illusory thrall.

Today there are strong reasons for pressing such an enquiry. The behaviour of teachers, both Oriental and Western, participating in the dramatic spread of Zen and Tibetan institutions in America has often fallen severely short of the ethical ideal. Stuart Lachs[5] has recently reviewed developments that reveal widespread lapses in conventional morality. The causes for this are not solely due to an irresponsibility attributable to teachers, their followers have also been severely at fault. The context of such problems lies in the almost desperate Western need for personal meaning in a world which lacks the old certainties of Christianity and Humanism. The post-modern context is ruled by a relativity of values at all levels. Out of the plethora of religious and ethical possibilities, Celtic traditions, the nostrums of Merlin, orthodox faiths, unorthodox creeds or North American native practices, which one gives a meaning to me?

In spite of the democratic tradition in the West a prime problem in the arrival of Buddhism in the USA has been that the authoritarian attitudes natural to traditional Eastern cultures have been passed from Eastern teachers to those they appointed as first generation Western "masters". Their conferred infallibility as an "enlightened" person was often uncritically accepted by naive westerners desperate to believe in a human representation of the sublime but who, in the course of time, only discovered the ridiculous. Some such teachers came to dominate the institutions they led establishing neither democratic means for self-criticism nor advisory boards to provide feedback. In many sad cases the result has been the sexual exploitation of naive young followers of both genders and severe financial irregularity. Furthermore, some Oriental teachers themselves, succumbing to the permissiveness of the West they failed to properly understand, also revealed comparable faults. Clearly when such behaviour is revealed not only is the validity of the transmission to teach called into question but the whole system and the texts that sustain it become suspect. Finally, not only have many men and women become disoriented and distressed by the deceits practised upon them but authentic teachers truly worthy of their titles are smeared by gossip, suspicion and doubts.

What is Authenticity?

"Authenticity" has a range of overlapping meanings. The Oxford English Dictionary gives:

-real, actual or genuine as opposed to pretended;
-original as opposed to copied;
-proceeding from its reputed source or author;
-of established credit and genuineness;
-in accordance with or as stating fact;
-having legal validity, authoritative.

There is also a usage in music meaning a sound or note belonging appropriately to a scale, mode or melody. This meaning may be extended to appropriateness of a verbal expression within a form of discourse. An authentic statement is one that comes from the "heart" expressing a genuinely held, unambivalent belief or undistorted feeling.

Experiences that lack such characteristics are questionable, one may doubt their validity and suspect that they stand in for something else, a hidden agenda, motivation or bias. Yet how can one be sure that an experience is genuine? Most experiences are representations of internal and external circumstances in complex relations that may easily be mistaken or incorrectly perceived. How can we know that we know? Furthermore, how can we know when others, especially teachers and guides of all kinds, are authentic in their accounts of their experiences and practices? In what can we trust? In attempting to define ways of life appropriate to the problems of these millennial years an understanding of what is and what is not authentic is critical.

In the practice of psychotherapy the importance of the "unconscious" and the power of repressed experience to modify thought, behaviour and action has been well attested since Freud's original work. Studies by Winnicot, Guntrip, Miller and many others of the "object relations" school[6] have shown how negative experiences in childhood create buried scenarios that fester in repression creating attitudes, failures in self-knowledge and behaviour severely debilitating to the practitioner and harmful to his or her relationships in adult life.

The humanistic orientation in psychology emphasises the existential realities of personal lives. In particular this view focuses on the need to develop awareness, expression of feeling, capacities for choice and relating all of which are seen as essential for effective self-development in the expression of human potential. "A person is authentic in that degree to which his being in the world is unqualifiedly in accord with the given-ness of his own nature and of the world. Authenticity is the primary good or value of the existential viewpoint."[7] This perspective argues that authenticity entails a way of being in the world in which the person is in harmony with himself, others and the world. Inauthenticity means conflict within self, with others and the world. Yet here the idealisation of the term in language may become a danger. Authenticity is no mere adaptation or some mystical transcendence. Rather, we are concerned with a direct facing of the immediate realities of life with a willed affirmation of difficulties, an acceptance of them and their past origins and a letting go into a pro-active acceptance of change. It is not inauthentic to be faced with problems of ambivalence and paradox, indeed these are the very food of life. Modern therapy is essentially any effective interpersonal process that aids this process of comprehension and personal change.

The living circumstances into which human beings are thrown have been described in terms of four main issues; finiteness, potential to act, capacity to choose, and the realisation of existential aloneness.[8] We only have finite, limited understanding of ourselves and the world and such understanding as we do have is contingent upon circumstance, the availability of others, health and wellbeing, none of which can be taken for granted and none of which are permanently available. We are subject to the "fate" into which we are born and realise ourselves only briefly before death. Yet we have a capacity for action and gradually realise our responsibility for action in the world. No action can be perfect so we are faced by the risk of condemnation and anxiety generated by guilt or shame. We can only act within that context. So we have to choose a path and in such choice we experience autonomy. Yet within that very autonomy we experience our finite limitations and may thus be faced by a sense of meaninglessness. Seeking a meaning beyond our finite worlds we may get lost and experience such emptiness as a great fear. Yet, even while we experience our loneliness we discover we are not alone. We are "alone with others", as Steven Batchelor puts it.[9] In this, however, there remains the threat of the disappearance of the other or withdrawal from us leaving us in total isolation. Such anxiety is terrifying and the terror genuine.

Inauthenticity, emotional dependency and the disintegrated self

The life task of every human individual is inevitably to confront these uncomfortable truths of existence and to find the way through the givens of personal limitation in a manner that evades pretence, avoidance of difficulty and uncomplimentary truth to create an authenticity of being and expression that is both accepting and open. Perhaps that is what creativity is. The same task faces all those would-be carers in the helping professions and to this we must pay particular attention.

Therapeutic models and processes have struggled to find ways to alleviate the difficulties individuals face in coming to terms with these irreducible facts of life. Many have become caught in behaviourist, cognitivist or other reductionist fallacies that fail to meet the existential realities of human being.[10] Some therapies of dubious or partial validity impose years of expensive time consuming work often with little deep consequence. The burgeoning market place of therapy has encouraged careerists who, in inventing new glosses on old Freudian insights, often benefit their pockets more than their clients. The creation of ever new therapeutic and counselling methods all in competition with one another has created a commercial world in which the selling of new dependencies flourishes.

In spite of the genuine concern, expertise and courageous dedication of many therapists there is also emerging a puzzling inauthenticity within the whole "business" that only occasionally receives a degree of exposure. A skilled therapist may have a good idea, start to promote it in a small way only to find that his/her clients begin to develop wants to become therapists themselves. In such contexts the cryptic power of the therapist's role and the issues of transference may not have been adequately addressed. There thus develops the temptation to start a school for therapists who may well have been the sponsors' own clients. Such developments cannot but be viewed with suspicion. What has been going on here?

There has been a search for more direct methods less dependent on long term therapist-client relationships and centred on self-help often in group contexts. In this area work on chemical dependency (alcohol and drug addiction) has begun to turn up valuable insights of wide social application.

In working with addicts and their families it became apparent that family members who look after, treat, placate or otherwise manage the addicted person commonly show psychological symptoms of excessive caring for others, reduced independence, fixated referencing to family issues, depression and cagey if not dishonest behaviour, lying about the family etc., which do not necessarily improve when the alcoholic improves. The syndrome has become known as co-dependence

- the individual being dependent on the addiction indirectly by way of a fixation on the addicted. There is often a mutual or co-dependence between them.

It is now suspected that such a syndrome occurs widely in society and not only in relation to chemical dependency. Anne Wilson Schaef[11] considers it to be an aspect of a hydra-headed personality disorder produced by addictive processes widespread in society. Co-dependents have been defined as all persons in close emotional relationships with alcoholics or who have alcoholic parents or grandparents or who grow up in emotionally repressive families.[12] Co-dependency has also been described as an emotional, psychological and behavioural condition developing from prolonged exposure to a set of oppressive rules determined by social situations or family members which prevent the expression of natural feelings as well as the discussion of personal family or group problems.[13] It arises, therefore, as a set of coping skills under an enforced restriction of emotional expression.

Others have argued that co-dependence operates not only in families but in communities, businesses and institutions. Alcoholism thus begins to look like a response to this condition, as an especially negative coping skill in relation to forbidden or unexpressed distress, rather than as an essential determinant of co-dependence. If co-dependence is prior and as widespread as Whitfield[14] and Schaef believe then I prefer to refer to it as emotional dependence, a personality disorder that produces distortions in social perception, behaviour and feeling in others as well as the prime sufferer. It is socially infectious and socially tolerated. Its presence in a group commonly remains unidentified. The problem begins to emerge as truly vast.

Such distortions preclude an open awareness of personal problems because these are filtered through a wide range of unconscious pretences developed to prevent pain and distress. The individual becomes addicted to these responses and the object relations within which they occur due to the temporary and illusory relief they provide. The repeated performance of these patterns provides an illusory security as when someone who has lived for years with an anxious mother comes to placate and attempt to relieve the tension of significant others in life. With the mother such behaviour may have been essential for the child to have survived at all but, in adult life, the addiction to such a habit of security creation becomes destructive of straightforward relationship.

Schaef's list of personal traits achieving such ends is formidable. Emotional dependants are so focused on the activities of others (which may include their health, their approval, their withdrawal of control or punishment etc.) that they feel their own being to have little or no meaning. The meaning of their lives comes from outside and their intentionality is entirely determined by this. Relationships tend to conform to a pattern in which the clinging cannot be free from the clung. Personal boundaries are then so weak that psychological invasion is inevitable, the emotionally dependent quickly taking on the moods and responses of others. To sustain their dependent relationships they are forever trying to manage the impressions they make on others and are excessively and cleverly sensitive to another's moods and adapt to meet them. The insecurity and low self-esteem associated with such responses leads to depression and the consequent induction of further dependence in others who respond as carers. Caring for others is in this context not a valuable and helpful trait, rather it is a protective obsession designed to control the very one cared for and on whom meaning has become dependent. Self-martyrdom and seeming indispensability are actively cultivated to obsessive and overworked degrees. To sustain this picture, dishonesty of self-expression including active lying may become habitual - it becoming quite impossible for such persons to say how it is for them. The actual state of their distressed feelings is no longer available for expression in any direct way and referencing all activities on others becomes a form of endless self-concern.

These symptoms may appear in mild to severe forms of neuroticism. In particular the widespread distribution of the milder versions suggests that most carers may be suspected of being to a degree emotionally dependent and caught in the very addictive process they attempt to cure in others. Therapists, counsellors, ministers, therapeutic colleagues may all be affected unknowingly thereby basing their views of themselves on entirely inauthentic grounds. Whitfield indeed argues that the "untreated professional" virtually characterises the staff of caring institutions and may be sustaining the malfunctioning of those they treat. Recent dramatic examples may include the problems of responsibility in some cases of False Memory Syndrome where the recall by adult children of sexual abuse by parents has sometimes been shown to be due to an induction of such belief by involvement with the therapist. Much further research on this topic is essential.

We have reached a point where we are suggesting a condition of society whereby individual and social malfunctioning is widespread. While emotional repression and the disguising of motivation may have had some functional value in the social environment of human origins[15] we must suspect that in the developed societies of modern civilisations it can constitute a maladaptation through informational distortion of a serious kind. We may therefore be facing a "design fault" in our mode of social being that has been present for millennia and to which we have yet to construct an adequate remedy.[16] Certainly this appears to have been the view of the Buddha 2500 years ago and to this we must now turn.

Authenticity and Buddhist discourse

The Buddha was a man with vast experience of the yogic psychologies and philosophies of his time which were both rich in content and in debate. His personal search culminated in experiences which, as in an experiment, confirmed the views he was developing. In his very first sermon he argued that life was characterised by suffering, that suffering was due to craving, wanting or, in other words, addiction, and that it was possible to go beyond addiction by following a careful path. This looks very relevant to our discussion above.

His model of mind was essentially dynamic in spite of the rather static way in which the abhidharma expresses it. Sensation, perception and cognition build up the roots of conscious experience and inference about the world. In addition however, and crucially important, ongoing experience produces attempted solutions to problems that become relatively fixed patterns of response. These samskara are thus both the root of personal idiosyncrasy and also the source of change. In that they are essentially volitional they are both the repository of past karma and again the process wherein karma projecting into the future can change.

We can see here a close similarity to the discussion of dependency above. Karma distorts the appreciation of the present through inducing habitual, biased prejudicial or destructive modes of being that may have been valuable once as a response to a situation but which, at a present moment, may be distorting, unrelated to what is and thus illusory. The task therefore is to establish the mind in the present actuality and penetrate the snares of karma so as to go beyond them.

The discourses of the Buddha and subsequent Mahayana literature and commentaries are all essentially discussions of this endeavour. Sometimes leading into abstract phenomenological and metaphysical philosophies the core remains a practice. Buddhist thought is soteriological, designed to save; the take-home message is to penetrate illusion wherever it arises for illusion is considered widespread.

The main task advocated by the Buddha was to live "rightly" according to the Eightfold Way and the means to doing this was through the cultivation of awareness. The Maha Satipatthana Sutta[17] gives very precise instructions which focus on meditative attentiveness to the body, to the environment and eventually to the way of life itself. It is clearly proposed that attentive awareness is a tool with which to penetrate illusion.[18] It is essential first to calm the mind and then to gain insight into its process so as to distinguish the prejudiced from the authentic. From Satipatthana to Mahamudra, to the Silent Illumination of Ch'an and the Koan practice of the Japanese the essential quest is the same.

In Ch'an it is pointed out that attachment to quiet sitting, however agreeable it may be, is a "cave of demons", an addiction to tranquillity that must be broken up. The essential task of awareness is not trance or samadhic states but the perception of actuality directly. This means that in meditation one faces in various ways the actuality of existence. Contemplating the koans is one way of doing this.

The koans are paradoxical questions which cannot be answered but which can be resolved. The most basic are the Who questions." Who am I?" Of course at one level one knows exactly who one is but, at another, one realises much is hidden from one. There are several contrasting ways of using Koans but the modern method developed by Charles Berner and known as the "communication exercise" is especially valuable for beginning Westerners and I use it as an introduction to Ch'an (Zen) in Western Zen Retreats at my centre in Wales.[19] It leads through a vigorous examination of personal illusions to an exhaustion of opinion and language in an immediate apprehension of "just being." Finding this essential base line of existence throws all other concerns into a realm of mere relativity and the grip they have on one's life relaxes. Recalibration of a practitioner's attitudes and action in life then becomes possible from a phenomenological base that lies outside opinion. Since it cannot come from another it is also a rediscovery of an essential self and the basis for renewed autonomy.

The communication exercise is done in groups that divide into couples, dyads, who sit together. Over a 30-40 minute period a bell is rung every five minutes. In each five minute period one of the partners asks the other his or her question which may be; " Tell me who you are?"; "Tell me what life is?"; "Tell me what love is?'";"Tell me what another is?; "Who is dragging this old corpse along?"; " What was your face like before your parents were born?"etc. Most beginners and many others use the "Who am I?" formulation. It is basic. The practitioner works with his or her question throughout the retreat unless a resolution appears. After each period the partners change over. The rules are that the one who is questioning never says anything other than the question, only asks it a few times and maintains an open, interested demeanour without expressions of encouragement or scepticism. The one who answers is encouraged to respond in whatever way most truly expresses his or her state of mind. This need not be by words alone. The answerer is however asked to sustain contact with the partner through frequent eye contact. The five minute alternation imposes emotional discipline as each partner occupies in turn the complimentary role to the other. The exercise is repeated over a period of at least three days which, in the case of the Western Zen Retreat (5 days) also includes exercise, meditative sitting (zazen), meals, walks and periods in which the group process is reviewed.

Individuals usually spend many hours describing their various roles in life and their experiences in these roles. They then begin to express their feelings under a range of remembered conditions until some feeling is actually engendered in the present moment. To express that feeling, sadness, tears, joy, anguish, self-doubt directly is to give one self unreservedly to the other in trust. This is especially difficult when feelings of guilt or shame are around and a practitioner may spend many hours fearfully and cunningly editing his responses to the question. Finally, unless the practitioner is severely blocked, he trusts enough to share. Such sharing rapidly becomes mutual and personal secrets of a lifetime's duration may be shared for the very first time with accompanying emotion.

It is a fact that the rehearsal of the past within the session does not have to be repeated once full expression has been given to it. It is as if the latent energy locked up in an issue has been released. The consequence is a sensation of increasing freedom and openness both of which probably relate to the rising levels of trust in the group. Often, however, the flow of expression finally dries up and there is a silence but no feeling of having resolved the question. This is called "crossing the desert". It requires sensitive reappraisal of all that has been said and maybe just silent musing and waiting. The role of the retreat director or "master" is to interview practitioners and to interact with them in such a way as to facilitate their process. Naturally this requires considerable skill and imagination. The role cannot be undertaken by an untrained or an inappropriately trained person.

When the practitioner is fortunate, has managed to focus the question well and penetrated blockages the result is a gradual or sudden awareness that he or she is everything that has been said and, since the negative energies associated with the themes of life have been ex-pressed, there is a glowing sense that what one is is indeed alright after all. There is a moment of relief and acceptance in which the question drops away. One "knows" who one is in the same way that one "knows" water only when she tastes it. Such a person may be very joyful and experience a number of states of consciousness that may be entirely new - a spacious clarity, bliss, love, emptiness; words which in truth have meaning only for those who have been to the same spaces.

Most of these experiences are moments of personal integration around a sense of total oneness with what one is. In Zen this is called the "one man."[20] Such work facilitates but cannot in itself produce the experience known as satori or kensho in which self-reference itself disappears so that, "empty headed", one simply regards the world as it is, unfiltered, all personal bias gone. Such an experience, usually felt to be of inestimable value, may be said to arise through "grace" since any egoistic quest for it is bound to fail.

The ego cannot lose itself, it sometimes just gets lost. The practitioner is overcome by emptiness in much the way one may suppose that a blackbird is overcome by its song. Such rare moments are known as "enlightenment experiences". Because the texts consider these events desirable, practitioners naturally but mistakenly make a great effort to attain them: with the result that many such claims may be invalid. Most such experiences are probably of the "one man" type.

I believe this is also true of the results of the other meditation methods in Zen. Master Sheng Yen doubts, for example, whether many of the so called satoris in Japanese Rinzai Zen retreats are really such. In discussing the effects of the "Enlightenment Intensive" of Charles Berner, which uses the Communication Exercise exclusively, Roshi Kennet felt that most of them would have been" satori orgasms" - that is to say emotionally induced experiences. In both cases it seems likely that most such outcomes are likely to be experiences of the "one man" type induced by the stresses of such retreats. Some masters may collude in passing responses to koans as successes.

In fact all notion of success or failure in relation to kensho is illusory. Such events may occur spontaneously as the natural mysticism described in the writings of Walt Whitman, Richard Jefferies and Krishnamurti attests. Indeed many people may have had such an experience without being able to perceive its nature or its value. This is perhaps likely to be particularly true of those whose work in the country involves manual labour of skills requiring high present attention - rustic sages as it were.[21] Training is thus significant after all and Master Sheng Yen argues that for an experience to merit the label "kensho" it needs to occur with reference to a Zen perspective, otherwise the conceptual frame of the event is insufficient.[22]

The process of Zen training appears to involve a number of steps:

1) Direct acknowledgement of how one is, however negative that maybe. One simply says "Yes" to the negativity and holds it in the frame of meditative focus.

2) When the matter is sufficiently explored, the negative emotional energies tend to resolve themselves and die down as the practitioner penetrates their meaning in an acceptance of personal inadequacy. This of course does not mean approval of oneself.

3) Once this acceptance is total then, in a natural humility, the practitioner simply knows who and what he is. In such acceptance, energy (chi or prana) flows free and a positive yet curiously apophatic[23] self-affirmation arises. In time one can then face another question, "How is life fulfilled?"

Needless to say the habits of a lifetime are unlikely to be totally removed in one go and repeated training and the development of day to day mindfulness are also required. Those who think an experience of the type described is sufficient to break their habitual illusions are deluding themselves. To realise that Zen means long term cultivation is for practitioners in a hurry an unwelcome surprise. Furthermore, the very texts and ritualistic imagery of traditional Buddhism may need challenging in the way the ancient masters have always told practitioners to do.

It looks nonetheless as if the practise of Buddhist meditation when skilfully taught and directed[24] may have a considerable effect in breaking up the social addictions that are the cause of so much misery. The stages of acknowledgement, acceptance, realisation in humility and self-affirmation have much in common with the Twelve Steps recommended as training in recovery from emotional dependency.[25] These include: admitting that life has become unmanageable; making a fearless inventory of oneself, acceptance of one's negativities and awareness of their powerfully addictive nature; continual cultivation of such awareness, direct attempts to make amends in life and the placing of the whole endeavour within a spiritual context believing in the possibility of higher power and its influence for good. Here the Christian would refer to God, the Buddhist to the Three Refuges. These parallels suggest an important convergence between contemporary psychotherapeutic insight into the social processes of our time and the ancient wisdom of Buddhism. On this basis much could be built.

Authenticity in Zen Practice

The pervasiveness of emotional dependency is no new thing. It invades the practice of spirituality at all levels. As Christians might say - the devil is cunning indeed. The sensationalism of the modern media and the gossipy desire for the exposure of fault at all levels in society - so characteristic of the mediocre attempting to justify themselves - lead to endless accounts of inauthenticity in church and state. A reading of Chaucer shows such faults to be no new thing but the modern addiction to journalistic social pornography has produced a debilitating and depressive process in which the potential for good in anything is undermined by its inevitable lack of perfection. Yet the press performs a valuable function. We cannot pretend to ourselves for long and the appearance of iniquities among Buddhist lamas and masters who should be the exemplars of their tradition has been a shock to many. We need to examine it critically.

The Master

In the Mahayana tradition the lama or master, the guru, was to be treated with total devotion as an infallible teacher. This was conceivable because such a one had attained enlightenment through his or her practice and received a transmission to teach from his own teacher, a person of the same quality. That which was to be transmitted was nothing less than the enlightenment of Buddha himself coming down through the ages. From this notion came the significance of lineage and the vital importance of ensuring the purity of transmission.

We have here at least the scriptural tradition. Individual teachers were often much more reticent, being aware of their faults and showing a genuine humility. Indeed it was this humility and personal discipline through loyalty to the terms of practice inherent in transmission that preserved the idea as valid in the training of others.

Clearly the validity of this viewpoint could only be maintained if the behaviour of lamas and masters was indeed inspiring and irreproachable. The Rimpoche, precious jewel, really had to be above the common herd if he was to function as the tradition demanded. Doubtless falls from grace were commonly observed but the institutional framework of peer supervision among monastics usually corrected or managed these faults and the regard with which common people treated their teachers suggests this was usually both successful and authentic.[26]

The arrival of such teachers in the West gave rise to problems. The fantasy world of the hippy generation, courageous and searching as it was, needed holy teachers to represent the sublime. There was a need for such a person to combat the horrors of our time and the post-modern shift in the Euro-American scene with its rampant scepticism and subscription to ethical relativity. There was need for spiritual dependency.

Tibetan and Japanese teachers came from a monastic world, highly disciplined, authoritarian, with supervision from peers and teachers alike and little opportunity to know the world outside the walls. The monasteries were supported by the local population and by land owners or nobility through social subscription, gifts of land, service to monks of many kinds and unquestioning faith.[27] In the West such teachers found a questioning faith, multiple ethical and religious positions, no authority apart from self yet great dependency need. They themselves were usually cut off from both their own teachers and from their peers and the walls were paper thin. Furthermore, the most usual centres in which they worked were not monasteries. For the most part they were centres offering meditation instruction to lay people of varying ability, understanding and degrees of social neuroticism sustained by fluctuating and uncertain sources of finance much subject to shifts in fashion.

James Low and I once interviewed Zhabdrung Rimpoche in his north Indian home. Unlike many of the traditional Tibetans with whom we had been working, this Bhutanese lama, the reincarnation of former religious rulers of Bhutan, had led a troubled life of political exile for many years under risk of assassination. He was fluent in English and knew the West well. He was extremely critical of his fellow lamas who taught in the West. He argued that the tendency to create large organisations with a high profile lama as guru was typically Western and detrimental to true understanding. Such lamas become figures of fame, spiritual celebrities who jet set around the world from one idolising centre to another, spending little time in each and knowing their many followers only in occasional brief encounters.

"The true guru-pupil relationship is between two people who get to know one another intimately. The disciple can then be of value to the guru through reflecting the latter's faults. It is important that the disciple should be free to be critical from his side within his devotion and to share his feelings with his teacher. In this way a teacher keeps in touch with his own defects. Where a teacher retains a footing in his tradition his fellow monks will keep him in order. Where teachers in the West have cut this connection and gone flying off on their own they can substitute fluency in Western culture for an in depth understanding of their own original practice. Although a lama may have received initiation for personal practices unless he maintains them he can lose contact with their meaning. Such a person's spiritual growth has become superficial and lacking in comprehension of some of the difficulties involved in transmission. Initiations he gives may then have little power and may open their recipient to delusion."[28]

Much the same can be said of Zen masters coming from Japan. It is significant that so far Western Theravada monks have been immune from these criticisms. This is because they have established genuine disciplined monasteries in the West with tough old abbots well able to keep order and respect so that a deviant simply opts to disrobe. From this comparison there is perhaps much to be learnt.

From 1975 a series of scandals has erupted in both Zen and Tibetan institutions in America and to a lesser extent (there are fewer of them) in this country (UK).The details of these are mostly well known now and need not be reviewed except in outline here. The Western teachers had all received transmission from Japanese or

Tibetan masters and therefore held the lineages they represented. Their followers, imbued with devotion, allowed these men to become authoritarian rulers, real bosses, of the institutions they ran. They received little feedback or criticism and were treated as beyond reproach. Soon covert sexual liaisons with students were revealed, relationships, literally cases of spiritual incest, commonly deeply disturbing and damaging to the young people involved. The extent of sexual predation by some of these teachers was extraordinary. Such activities became associated with lying and the misuse of funds. Once the scandal broke their institutions became divided by factionalism concerning the best course of action to take. Some individuals whose faith had been broken in this way became severely distressed not knowing where to turn. Sometimes elaborate cover ups were engaged upon, the teachers not being reprimanded or corrected by their own teachers or monastic order. Some Oriental teachers themselves also committed similar misdemeanours causing comparable anguish.[29]

A major puzzle revolves around the question how can it be that a person who has received from a master a recognition of his or her "enlightenment" and transmission to teach within a lineage behaves in this way? There seems to be no reason to doubt the original insight of such a person nor the fact that this was recognised by an Eastern teacher in eye to eye contact. The error lies in the supposition that past karma is wiped out by such an event. Zen scriptures are sometimes unclear on this issue but early Buddhism makes a clear distinction. Enlightenment is indeed a breakthrough beyond the self but afterwards the karmic traces reassert themselves and need constant attention. It is said that even the Buddha spent his life following enlightenment working through the traces of his former karma. A person who has had deep experience in Buddhism may remain problematic in his or her ethical dimension. Eastern masters have perhaps paid insufficient attention to the vital importance of precepts, personal values and vows in transmitting Zen in America. A brilliant insightful pupil may be ethically unsound in everyday life especially when subject to the stress of becoming a master without local supervision.

Master Sheng Yen distinguishes clearly between the recognition of kensho and the transmission to teach. The former confers no authority- it is simply a mutual understanding between master and disciple. The giving of transmission does not depend on this alone but also upon the moral character of the practitioner, his/her continued training, capacity to teach and opportunity to do so in terms of pupils being available and willing and the existence of material circumstances within which teaching may occur.[30]

The answer to these problems clearly lies in a radical overhaul of the structure of Western institutions led by teaching masters. Democratic criticism, the formation of advisory boards, open discussion of personal matters and careful auditing of finance are all obvious remedies. As important however, as Lachs has pointed out, is a critical appraisal of key themes in Mahayana Buddhism. What exactly does Master or Lama mean? What is a monk? Should the rules for monks and nuns be the same or different? What is transmission? What indeed is enlightenment?

Current Western scholarship, developing biblical criticism in the Buddhist context and in detailed study of history through ancient textual material, is revealing how the meaning of such terms has varied through the long Buddhist history thus raising questions as to the best way to interpret and use them today. Such scholarship is to be welcomed although the danger of developing an arid understanding without a life of devotion has to be avoided. Reducing bibles to "texts" can take the life out of them.

I cannot finish this section without an appreciation of those many outstanding teachers, Eastern and Western, men and women, who in their authenticity have brought and continue to bring the wisdom of Buddhism to our shores. This very critique of developments that many of them could not have suspected is a tribute to their success.

Renunciation and the monkhood

Although the Buddha left teachings for the laity he clearly focused primarily on the training of the Sangha, the body of monks or "left-home-ones." To become a monk one forsakes all the activities and relationships of lay life - celibacy, no companionship with the opposite sex, no drinks, perfumes, high beds, dancing etc. and etc. into a great list of restrictions. From a lay perspective the precepts of a monk appear to be highly onerous yet their intention is to give the practitioner an especial freedom - freedom from the addictions of lay life.

Yet joining the Sangha could never be the path for everyone because somebody had to provide support for it, this had to come from the donations of laity. Somebody had to procreate, have babies, run businesses, rule the country, provide food. None of this was the business of the Sangha. Yet the relationship was not intended to be one-sided. The Sangha in its turn benefited the laity through providing them with opportunities for earning merit through supplying monks and monasteries with the wherewithal of daily life, through giving sons to monasteries as novices, through financing long liturgies. Merit was a means whereby individuals could ensure a higher rebirth - and that usually meant birth into a higher caste. The old Indian system was still very much alive although the Buddha was clearly not one of its supporters and the Sangha was in principle at least open to all castes.

Was there a deeper meaning to "merit"? Did the selfless behaviour and psychological wisdom of the monks provide insight, peace of mind and education to the laity? Plausibly yes, although the scriptures do not emphasise this point. In traditional Ladakh monks often function as shaman in ceremonies to control weather, benefit crops, effect cures. The wisdom of Rimpoches is sought in the selection of lha-bas, the healer oracles who operate in trance, and many matters of local ethics and social valuation are settled in conference with monks. They are ethical arbiters within the society.

Yet, in contemporary Ladakhi villages monks are also judged for their goodness. False monks who sell monastery property, defraud their clients or behave excessively in any way are treated with scorn and disrespected. Maintenance of an authentic role is essential.

In Zen, monks work their own lands and do their own labour. It was this that allowed the Ch'an sects to survive various holocausts in China when other orders dependent on the receipt of gifts went under. Zen scriptures use labour as a motif in teaching. Dogen, who brought Soto Zen to Japan, learnt much from cooks whom he met in China. The way a monk worked illustrated his capacity for mindfulness.

Mindfulness is the means whereby monks sustain their discipline. As in the corrective training of the army "glasshouse" attention to detail is the focus of the disciplinary regime. Why should anyone find the monkish life attractive? It seems to be fact that many young monks coming from lowly families, as indeed did the Dalai Lama, suffer no harm from being reared after infancy by men alone. They often turn out to be remarkable meditators, scholars, teachers, friends with a surety of self-possession that most would admire. It is the motherliness of these mindful monks free from the daily anxieties of village mothers that perhaps plays a key role in achieving this.

The practice of meditative mindfulness within the freedom of sustained discipline takes a monk through the stages we have discussed above. He thus comes to know blissful states of conscious awareness that are rare among the laity. The disciplined freedom from social addiction allows a relative "enlightenment" that gives them an unique charisma and beneficial social influence in a strife torn world.

Modern Western Buddhists rarely contemplate becoming monks nor as yet are there many suitable institutions to receive them. Only the Theravada goes quite vigorously down this path. Western practitioners of Tibetan Buddhism and Zen are predominantly members of the laity.

What is Lay Zen?[31] A lay practitioner has not given up the pursuit of material delights and continues to "keep up with the Jones" in a social competitiveness that may creep into his Dharma expression. Yet he or she pretends to follow scriptures and practises clearly designed for "left- home-ones". It is little wonder that they may find the practices unrewarding or difficult when the rest of life is devoted to work, play, arguing with the wife or worrying about the children. Such practitioners may become "hobbyist" Buddhists[32] who may soon depart to investigate some more promising path enhancing in some subtle way their spiritual egoism.

The dependency of the Western laity on their teachers is understandable since they give themselves so little opportunity to actually experience Dharma practice. For a lay person the only way to approximate to monastic training and hence gain some of the insights available to monastics is through intensive retreat, not once but many times. They then find that change becomes apparent. Not only do they begin to " taste the chocolate", as Lama Thubten Yeshe used to say, that is benefit from conscious states of joy and peace, but they begin to recalibrate their lives quite naturally around actions beneficial to themselves and, crucially, also to others. Life gets happier whatever falling aside may also from time to time occur. The vows begin to take on meaning as progressive change becomes apparent. The illusion of chasing enlightenment experiences or expecting spiritual rewards and the favours of charismatic masters subsides in a realisation that the grind of cultivation is essential. In such authentic practice monk and layman become indistinguishable in the perspective of Zen.

Understanding Dharma

Many of those who attend meditation classes at Buddhist centres are coming to benefit themselves through improving their self-image. To assume an identity as a Buddhist makes one feel better as a member of a positive group in the swim of the current "turn on". Unaware of Buddhist teaching they do not see this as merely another form of the addiction to self-interest.

Others come for their health or to reduce mental stress. Certainly meditation is relaxing, may save one from a heart attack, and gives one a new perspective on life. And none of this lacks merit. These are sound things to do - but they are not Buddhism - and in particular they are not Zen.

Even those who practice intensively and come on difficult retreats requiring will power and disciplined determination may not yet have any insight into the teachings. It is thus vital that anyone training in Zen quickly attempts to gain some insight into the message of the Buddhas. Basic Buddhism is fortunately expressed in a number of relatively simple and memorable formulae- the Four Noble Truths, the Eightfold Way, the Four Vows, the Ten Precepts, the Principle of Interdependent Causation. These need digestion and contemplation. From here topics such as Impermanence, Emptiness, and the meaning of meditative practice may be entered from a firm base.

The Dharma never constitutes dogma in the way that the Bible or the Koran is often used. Buddhist teachings are suggestions, signposts for those who wish to test them out. The Buddha's last injunction was not to follow his teachings mindlessly but to "work out your own salvation with diligence". The practice gradually becomes more meaningful and one can test it out in day to day living. Although reading books and scholarship can be helpful, we are in the West today beyond the book addiction phase of development. Opportunities for real practice and receiving sound teaching are now available in most cities of the realm and there are a range of teachers to evaluate. Hobbyism does not express authentic interest for it is merely playing games with spiritual ambitions.

In personal practice

At a weekly meeting someone comes up to me and says something like-"I'm sorry John I have not been able to do my evening half hour all week!" Others may only attend retreats when a famous or charismatic Eastern master is running it. Needless to say such persons find retreat more difficult than they need. Someone else may object -" People have troublesome enough lives as it is – why make retreats so difficult for them. We could get up at 6 am rather than 4. You could attract more participants that way!"

All such attitudes miss the point of Zen. The ego craves self-esteem. We want to do things that make us feel well regarded. When one friend found that he was not going to become a Zen rabbi quickly on retreat he gave it all up. The toughness of Zen is deliberate for it provides in microcosm those confrontations to self that are always with us - but gives us them in a context where they demand recognition and reflective management through insight Little things like worrying about the place one will get at the meal table: Did I have enough to eat? Am I going to have time for a shower? Do I have time for a banana before Shi fu closes the meal? Can I have a pee within the next half hour? Can I stand this aching knee for another ten minutes? Oh Oh When will the bell go? Poor me, I am such a noble sitter. Such questions are not nonsensical but the way they invade the mind shames one into a recognition of their addictive nature. The training is to "let through, let be, let go". Negativity arises, it is comprehended, it is released. Meditation continues. Not at all easy. The mill wheel of the addicted mind spins on taking its time to come to rest. One begins to learn patience- with oneself.

Such training in self-recognition not only reveals gradually the benefits of intensive practice but can also be transferred into everyday circumstances - shopping, washing up, going to work, whatever it may be. And it is for this reason that on retreat one is told to be "present" not only on one's cushion but when cutting carrots or filling oil lamps. I was once reminded that in washing up the enormous pots and pans in Throssel Hole Priory kitchen that I should do it as if I was arranging an altar. The mind should never be somewhere else. When no-one is cutting carrots yet carrot cutting is happening in clarity and with precision one is making progress. The rest is idle self- concerned chatter. If one does these things insights sometimes come quite suddenly, surprising one with joy.

In the result

Success is not success. Failure is not failure. Someone who has experiences on retreat that are deeply rewarding is often at great risk. Self-congratulation sets in, followed perhaps by comparison with those others struggling away not knowing who they are and then by a subtle pride that immediately denies itself. Master Sheng Yen says that pride and low self-esteem are the opposite ends of the same road - the road of ego involvement. To get off that road altogether is often difficult for the successful practitioner. Perhaps fortunately, good experiences are commonly followed by bad ones. A wonderful insight-yielding retreat may be followed by a gloomy depressive one. The practitioner simply has to learn, often painfully, that that's the way things are - not only in Buddhism but in everyday life. As is said Zen is no different from everyday life. It is the attitude that counts.

There was once an individual who had a profound experience which he decided was enlightenment. He therefore proclaimed himself a Zen master and began to run workshops. These were powerful events for he indeed had talents as a group facilitator. I was phoned by one of his adherents asking did I want to meet a real Zen Master. I found this man to have experienced no training under a qualified Zen master, to have never attended retreat, to have no respect for lineage or tradition and to be touchy when faced with searching questions. Such a person is like someone who awards himself a cap after playing a practice game.

Another individual who had trained well with the Tibetans and who had undoubted attainments both in meditative skill and teaching ability suddenly began to promote himself through various assumed titles right up to Rimpoche. Since he actually had some wisdom- why these games? Here an addiction to personal image would seem to be rampantly in play. The inauthenticity is damaging to the lineage in which he works.

A fine Tibetan teacher, trained in Lhasa, has reputedly taken to having himself described as a Buddha. Need I say more. When such affectations can overcome even the great and good it behoves us lesser mortals to take care. Self-deluding teachers, self-deluding helpers, self-deluding pupils are all caught up in a linked set of difficulties.

Authentic self-acceptance has nothing to do with either pride or self-reproach. It is the straightforward recognition of how things are. The practitioner simply moves along as best he or she can with whatever presents itself. Occupying the present with such presence is authentic being.

Honesty and "One great mistake after another"

Buddhist practice begins and ends with honesty, but this honesty is not easy to achieve. There is ordinary honesty and insightful honesty. The latter arises when through some form of training the illusions that bedevil one's life have at least to a degree been recognised and some progress in relieving them achieved. We have argued that much of human behaviour is inauthentic in the sense that insightful honesty is not available. In Buddhism this is the state of "not seeing" or ignorance. In both Buddhism and within the modern concern at the state of society, individuals are seen to be often addicted to patterns of thought, feeling and behaviour that have arisen in some familial or social circumstance in the past, patterns the Buddhists refer to as karma. The pain involved in coming to self-recognition often seems extraordinary and working with it may remain problematic.

The attempt to reach the "enlightenment" of a straightforward relationship with the world involves practice on a hard path full of illusory successes and failures. Sometimes whatever a practitioner does it seems to fail or to have no effect. Sometimes success leads to another experience of failure. The mind is extremely tricky - a maddened monkey as some have said. Whether one is attempting to work with oneself or with others it is never possible to be sure that the path taken is the right one. One time, walking in those wonderful hills above Green Gulch Farm north of San Francisco, I was discussing how to teach Zen with the Abbot of the monastery there, Reb Anderson. He remarked that he had found that if you say one thing it is bound to be wrong and if you say its opposite you will find that is wrong too. Whatever you say is likely to be wrong. To be silent may be no help either. One simply goes ahead in trust as best one may. Here is the fundamental honesty of the Zen position. You try it and see - in a trust that knows you may be wrong. Only the authentic self can do that in the faith that has lasted two thousand five hundred years. As some master said in defining Zen-"One great mistake after another."

References

1 Scheaf, A.W. 1985. Co-dependence: -Misunderstood -Mistreated. Understanding and healing the addictive process. Harper. San Francisco.

2 See Low J, 1990. Buddhist developmental psychology. In: Crook, J. H. and D. Fontana (eds) Space in Mind: East-West psychology and Contemporary Buddhism. Element Books. Warminster. (Distributed by Penguin. London)

3 See discussions in Crook, J.H. and J, Low. 1996 in press. The Yogins of Ladakh. Motilal Banarsidass. Delhi.

4 See discussion in Buswell, R. E.1983. The Korean Approach to Zen: The collected works of Chinul. University of Hawaii Press. Honolulu.

5 Lachs, S. 1994. A slice of Zen in America. New Ch'an Forum Issue 10. 1994.

6 Winnicot, D. W. 1988. Human Nature. Free Association Books. London
Winnicot. D. W. 1990.The Maturational Processes and the Facilitating Environment. Karnac books. London.
Guntrip, H. 1983. Schizoid phenomena, object relations and the self. Hogarth Press. London.
Miller, Alice. 1990. The Untouched key. Tracing childhood trauma in creativity and destructiveness. Virago. London.
For a wider ranging anthropologically oriented discussion on the nature of the self see Carrithers, M. Collins, S and S. Lukes. The Category of the Person. Cambridge U.P. Cambridge.

7 Bugenthal, J. F. T. 1965. The search for Authenticity: An existential-analytic approach to Psychotherapy. Holt, Rinehart and Winston. New York. p32.

8 Bugenthal, see note 7 above.

9 Batchelor, S. 1983. Alone with Others: An existential approach to Buddhism. Grove. New York.

10 Harré, R and G. Gillett. 1994. The Discursive Mind. Sage. London

11 Schaef. A. W. loc cit.

12 Wegscheider Cruse, S. 1984. Co-dependency-the therapeutic void. In: Co-dependency - an emerging issue. Health Communications. Pompano Beach. Florida.

13 See discussions by R. Subby and others in Co-dependency - an emerging issue. Health Communications. Pompano Beach. Florida.

14 Whitfield, C.1984. Co-dependency -an emerging issue among professionals. In: Co-dependency- an emerging issue. Health Communications. Pompano beach. Florida.

15 See for discussion: Trivers, R 1971. The Evolution of Reciprocal Altruism. Q. Rev. Biol. 46.35-57.
Trivers, R.1985.Social evolution. Benjamin/Cummings. Menlo Park Ca.
Byrne, R.W and A. Whiten. 1988. Machiavellian Intelligence. Social expertise and the evolution of intellect in Monkeys, Apes and Humans. Clarendon. Oxford.

16 Crook, J. H. 1995. Psychological Processes in Cultural and Genetic Coevolution. In: Jones, E and V. Reynolds. (Eds) Survival and Religion: Biological Evolution and Cultural Change. Wiley. London. For a wide ranging discussion see Berman, M. 1989 Coming to our senses; body and spirit in the hidden history of the West. Unwin. London.

17 See Ling, T.1981.The Buddha's Philosophy of Man Early Indian Buddhist Dialogues. Dent. London pp71-85 (translation)

18 For a contemporary exploration of this viewpoint see Blackmore, S. 1995. Paying attention. New Ch'an Forum. Issue 12.

19 Berner created this approach through comparing the practice of zen interview with a master with co-counselling. He invented a group workshop called the "Enlightenment Intensive" which uses this method exclusively. I was taught this method and to run intensives by Jeff Love in the 1970s. Berner has made some revisions to it since and such events are still offered from time to time. Berner has provided a manual for those directing such events.

20 The "True man of the Way." See Schloegl I. 1975. The Zen Teaching of Rinzai. Shambala. Berkeley.

21 Crowden, J. 1996. Mind in Agriculture. New Ch'an Forum. Issue 12. The term 'rustic sages' I owe to John Clark's 1983 A Map of Mental States. Routledge and Kegan Paul.

22 Master Sheng Yen is the director of the Institute of Chung Hwa Buddhist Culture in New York and Taipei. He leads retreats in New York and has done so three times at my centre in Wales. I have participated in ten of his training retreats and continue to work with him. He has published many books on Ch'an.

23 Apophatic: Stating things negatively as in "no-mind" or "emptiness."

24 This caveat requires close examination as the next section of this article will make clear.

25 Schaef, A. W. loc cit p 30

26 Shengpen Hookham writes to me (in litt) that any qualified lama (guru), whether a recognised incarnate "tulku" or not, can use the title "rimpoche" but, although there are no hard and fast rules, this usage is normally bestowed only on a high ranking teacher. Peer pressure means that teachers would not normally adopt such a title unless they felt their peers would support it. Peer pressure is probably mostly indirect. Lamas do tend to behave in more culturally subscribed ways in the company of other Tibetans. There is much more direct supervision among Tibetan yogins. "Yogis seem to recognise each other on a deeply intuitive level and advise each other from that standpoint." Yogis of high reputation are known and sought out for instruction. Among yogis the title "rimpoche" is rarely used and "tulkus" as such are of little interest to them because the latter have not often received yogic training.

27 For examples and review see the chapters on monastic life in Crook, J. H. and H. Osmaston (Eds). 1994. Himalayan Buddhist Villages. Bristol University and Motilal Banarsidass. Delhi.

28 Crook, J.H. and J. Low.1996. In press. The Yogins of Ladakh. Motilal Banarsidass. Delhi. p 248.

29 See Lachs, S. 1994. loc cit.

30 See Sheng Yen, Master.1994. Transmitting the Lamp. New Ch'an Forum. Issue 9.

31 Over the last year the Bristol Ch'an Group has been asking this question and members are attempting tentative answers. Some American masters and their followers have also addressed this issue. See New Ch'an Forum, Issues 10, 11,12. Also: Abe, M. 1985. Zen and Western thought. MacMillian. London Kraft, K.1988. Zen: tradition and transition - an overview of Zen in the modern world. Rider London. Tworkov, H. 1989. Zen in America; profiles of five teachers. North Point Press. San Francisco.

32 A term used by Simon Child in his article above. New Ch'an Forum Issue 13.

Acknowledgements

I am grateful to all those who have helped me realise the extent of my own emotional dependencies and led me to sustain continuing work on such vexation. Carol Evans introduced me to the current literature on co- dependence and additionally Ken Jones, Peter Reason, S. K. Hookham and John Pickering have commented helpfully on the text. My understanding of Zen, such as it is, owes much to Master Sheng Yen whose exemplary personal stance and masterly teachings are an inspiration in these troubled times. An especial debt is owed to all those hard working practitioners who attend the demanding retreats at the

Maenllwyd and whose resilience and authenticity command my respect and appreciation. To work with you all is an inspiration in an often difficult task.

WELSH WINTER: MAENLLWYD

Grey stone mountain
rain
and the gathering fogs
Drip drip the gutters
and the gurgling stream.
Two ravens out of the mirk
strut about warily
not seeing the face behind the window,
deftly grabbing a wad of rice
fly off into cloud.
Dark light at noon
no sign of sun,
full moon falteringly filtering
through the dismal night.
Warm and muggy
Welsh winter
washing itself away.

Not very good weather we're having!

No o.

Better 'an snow tho.

Not so sure
Cold's a better time
ice and hoar frost
bright days.

S'long as you're not driving isn't it?

Aai.

Can't expect much else, mind you
the time of the year.
I always say!

Sheep OK?

Damp's no good for the feet like
but woolly coats does 'em fine.
Look cheerful enough don't ey?
Up on your tod then - nobody with you?
Meditation is it?
Ah - wri-ting too then. Well
quiet enough up here
for sure.
Time to get on with it-
up the hill for a look round.
Missus'l be waiting for her tea.
Til next time then - is it.

Grey day
day barely day
cold wind slicing the grasses
puddles iced, walking with caution
ears and fingers freeze.
I puff on my hands.
Cold mist
clings to the hill side trees,
no sky at all, dull light

draining colour from the land.
Deep in their roots
sycamores sleep
bare twigs clutching at the wind.

Hull down in hollows
sheep are motionless,
backs to breeze
shrammed heifers stand like statues,
where no sun rises
hoar frost lies on the land.

Down a hedgerow
evening Blackbird squawks
despondency,
Crows pass lolling on the wind
watchful, waiting.

A time for ghosts
howling down the whitened hills
maddened in the grey freeze.
Deep in my hearth now
frosty fire tongues leap
at the coming night.

John Crook 1993-1996

NCF XIV

EDITORIAL FROM THE CH'AN HALL

The articles in this issue circle around a number of concerns that are occupying those of us attempting to see more clearly how Ch'an can be taught and practised in Britain. A number of us recently met at Maenllwyd and decided to create an institutional structure to help with these matters. It is to be called The Western Ch'an Fellowship and a report of our first deliberation forms part of this issue. The New Ch'an Forum itself is to become the journal of our new body. In February 1997 we met again to establish an executive committee prior to seeking charitable status. We intend to devote a large portion of the following issue to the new fellowship and many of the matters arising from our deliberations.

The creation of our fellowship raises issues concerning the points in Buddhadharma and in practice which we wish to emphasise. Basing our approach in the teachings of Master Sheng Yen gives us authentic roots which we need to water regularly. But, as Shi Fu has already impressed on me, we in Britain, with our distinctive culture, have to find out own way to be creative in our expression of the Dharma - just as the Chinese did when Indian Buddhism first began to spread in China.

It is with joy therefore, that I welcome Stephen Batchelor's article in this issue. We need to experience for ourselves the extraordinary discovery that "everything is as it is"; that the Buddha never said anything religious; that he realised for us that religious belief can be highly illusory predicating properties on the mind and the universe which cannot actually be found there. The mind in its ignorant search for identity, security and perseverance imputes properties to itself and the objects and persons that come within its ken. These are actually no more than the predications of the mind itself and the realisation of this is both alarming and freeing. Indeed the opening to such "emptiness" in full force is, as Stephen says, truly shocking. Enlightenment is just such a shock. To realise that "not knowing" is the root of being and creativity is an extraordinary liberation yet one difficult to come by because of our "need to know". As Krishnamurti so often says, freedom lies in going beyond the "known" for the known is a trap that ensnares us all in hope, fear and, ultimately, in a consolation in pretence. Institutions that foster such illusory certainty are ultimately devisive.

Stephen's use of "agnosticism" as a theme is thus of the greatest interest and Shi Fu, in his talk after my first retreat in New York in 1986, is saying very much the same thing. Not knowing, freedom in the suchness of things and creativity, seem pivotal points in the dharma to be worked upon in our new fellowship.

The New Ch'an Forum has not been tardy in attempting to clarify some of the concerns of Buddhists around the scandals that have affected us all in recent years. Reform depends on social critique and in our last issue Ken Jones extended this to some British Buddhist institutions (although without imputing scandal to them). Not surprisingly, we have had a vigorous response from one of them. We welcome this sharing of views but do not want it to descend into acrimony or personal comment. The texts on this subject are the last for a while - it will be interesting to see if our social criticism leads to any positive effect.

A happy 1997 to everyone.

OBITUARIES

In the last few months old hands at the Maenllwyd have lost two much loved retreat companions. Don Ball and Jane Turner had been coming to the Maenllwyd ever since we started retreats there. They both knew the days when accommodation consisted of a barn with a much holed roof through which snow might drift or an owl come in to share the shelter. They both knew the crowded retreats we used to have in the Buddha Room and the early morning runs in rain up the hill. Both worked hard at their life koans and loved to return again and again to Western Zen Retreats. Don indeed never tried anything else at Maenllwyd but Jane "graduated" to Ch'an Retreats and Shi Fu from whom she learnt much.

I was very fond of Jane, we shared bird watching interests and the love of countryside. Although often troubled by tensions and anxieties her inner life gradually became more peaceful so that during her last years she discovered a truly spiritual stance in life which brought her much joy and peace. I was very happy for her and our last interviews were as much an inspiration for me as they were helpful to her. Jane, I shall miss you and feel your spirit still with us in the quiet moments of retreat. Her daughter Sue has written the article that follows.

Don too was a tireless explorer. He loved the koans of Western Zen Retreats and stuck doggedly to them, often finding a resolution some days after ending a retreat and writing to me about it. As the years passed he emerged from struggle into light and was often an inspiration to his many friends. Again some of the interviews I had with him in his last years were as insightful to me as to him - maybe more so.

Once he was working on "Who is God?" Near the end of the retreat we sat together in interview and I asked him his question. "I am your friend!" said Don.

His exemplary death, described in the obituary to follow, showed how his training had moved him to a point where he could accept the last journey with an equanimity that has moved all who knew him. I am grateful to his son, Veda Ball, for the details of his early life. Don's spirit too floats in the zendo as we sit together. "There is no time. What is memory?" Don would have given a sprightly answer to that.

Don and Jane continued coming to retreats into great age. Neither was ever troubled by the tough rules and hours yet both suffered as much as anyone on the first days. They knew their value. Youngsters who want an easy time take note!

ENJOYING DYING: DON BALL 1914-1995

Don Ball, a great supporter of the Maenllwyd and a personal friend for many years died, peacefully on December 14th 1995 in a way that fulfilled with a quiet heroism his many years of spiritual quest. His was an unorthodox Zen training that went all the way to the end.

Don was born on March 25th 1914 in Hampstead, London, the oldest child of four, a brother Keith, who was later my team doctor on a research expedition to Ladakh, and sisters Jeanette and Heather. His parents were Leonard and Eileen who followed the Baptist Christian faith.

Don and Keith both trained as doctors at the Middlesex Hospital in London. Called up in World War II, Don sailed in a convoy for Burma but his ship was diverted to Bombay when Burma fell to the Japanese. He spent the war in India and loved it, later bequeathing that love to his whole family. He worked as a medical officer rising to the rank of major in the RAMC. He saw service at the key military bases in Poona, Deolali, Madras and North India. Don married Margaret Reid on July 29th 1941 in England. Margaret stayed behind in the UK for the duration of the war and the eldest boy, Luke, did not meet his Dad till he was four. When the war ended Don, joined now by his wife, stayed on for three years teaching medicine at Vellore Christian Medical College where his second son, Veda, was born in 1948. Later there was a daughter, Neera. At this time Don's spiritual interests were quite orthodox middle class Christian.

After 1950 Don returned to England by ship and remained one year before taking up an appointment at Makerere College, the University of Uganda, where he taught medicine and wrote a thesis on chest disease which was to become his speciality. On his return to the UK in 1955 he took a consultancy at the Miner's Chest Diseases Treatment Centre in Cardiff and established a beautiful home in Dinas Powys.

Luke also trained as a doctor and while at medical school met the woman he was to marry. As so often happens, when the original family begins to expand to include newcomers a difficult period of transition occurs. During this time Don and Margaret went through several years of reassessment of their lives and values. This was to become the first step on a path of personal growth that continued ever since.

Don's interest in Quakerism led to an involvement in "T" Groups which he came to know through the Anglican Franciscans of the Community of the Resurrection in Mirfield. T groups gave him access to the whole range of the Humanistic Psychology movement then burgeoning in Britain. In a deep and what was to become a prolonged search for spiritual values Don became interested in the ideas concerning human potential coming from Esalen, California and especially in the many forms of encounter group available at the training centre in London, Quaesitor. He experimented with LSD therapy, worked with Frank Lake and also took part in the People not Psychiatry movement led by Michael Barnett and experimented with communal living. Margaret also participated in these explorations with an approach more private and with a more cautious understanding than Don's adventurousness was to allow. These contrasts were to lead to their eventual separation. Their children, growing up in the hippy atmosphere of the time joined in these activities becoming ardent also in their quest.

When the encounter movement started taking an interest in Indian and eastern spirituality, Don's experiences in India stood him in good stead. He heard of Bhagvan Shri Rajneesh in 1971, well before this teacher was known by this title and attended his camps in India before the founding of the institution in Poona. For a time, indeed, he functioned as Bhagvan's personal physician. His children were to follow him to Poona but Don did not at first take the sanyas (vows) that Bhagvan gave his followers. That came later, but Don was perhaps never totally submerged in the Rajneesh movement although he contributed much to it both personally and financially. He visited Rajneeshpuram in Oregon before the troubles started there and was impressed by the enormous dedication of the whole movement before wealth, corruption and Bhagvan's failure either to control developments or perhaps to understand America led to the ultimate catastrophe. Don was saddened but not distraught. By that time he had deepened his understanding to the degree that he was able to use the positive side of his Rajneesh experiences and let go the rest. He began coming regularly to the Maenllwyd and, elsewhere, led some group experiences himself.

I had first met Don when I was training in Encounter, Gestalt therapy and Sensitivity Group methods at Quaesitor. We kept bumping into one another at groups and especially on the Enlightenment Intensives created by Charles Berner and brought to Britain by Jeff Love. In the heady atmosphere of the time these intensives were magical experiences. There was little doubt or pessimism in the air, anything seemed possible and on those retreats it seemed to happen. Perhaps it did.

When the charismatic founder of Quaesitor, Paul Lowe, and Michael Barnett both went off to India to become two of Bhagvan's most influential early followers, Don moved his focus there too. I also was attracted by the Rajneesh movement and later visited Poona where I was amazed and delighted by the extraordinary energy of the place, for it seemed as if human potentials were at last being fully expressed and explored. Yet I also noted that no one seemed to have a mind of his or her own. Every conversation began with "Bhagvan says..." The hypnotic influence of that man seemed total. I was too bloody-minded a loner and wary of psychological invasion to be convinced.

Having attended groups in California and at Quaesitor I had founded the Bristol Encounter Centre together with Ken Waldie and Hazel Russell. In the early 70's we offered a wide range of groups and intensives to become briefly the third largest such organisation in the country. Jeff Love taught me how to run Enlightenment Intensives and approved my plan to draw these nearer to their origin by creating the Western Zen Retreat which places Berner's communication exercises within the framework of an explicitly Zen retreat.

Work with the communication exercise focuses on the question "Who am I?" and related themes. It can lead to an experience of authentic being in which the games of life are set aside giving rise to a renewed confidence and sense of self-worth with accompanying openness to others. People work through and beyond words to a direct experience of self perhaps, in a few cases, identical to that known as Kensho or Satori in Japanese Zen. Don's work with these questions was characteristic. He remorselessly ploughed through the story of his life, complete with long anecdotal digressions, journeys down cul de sacs and vague intellectuality commonly without focus. I often despaired of him as he seemed lost in the complexities of his own mind. But his process often worked its way through to a conclusion that brought him much peace and happiness. He had the knack of allowing his thinking to become increasingly lateral so that he surprised himself with new insights again and again. I believe it was this capacity for inventive insight that allowed him so much success with his admittedly rather heady approach.

Once Don came on retreat following a severe heart attack and a period in hospital. He arrived wan, tired and worryingly unfit for the intense work entailed on the retreat. He told me, "I shall work on the question "What is death?"

And he set to work, exhausting himself until I became concerned for him. Then quite suddenly he broke through. The way he expressed it was to say, "Death is Now". The question fell away from him and with a profound sense of the interdependence of all things and times, he drove off rosy and full of renewed health.

In his last years Don suffered from Parkinson's disease, the shaking sickness, which must have troubled him greatly. But he did not allow it to get to him: practicing his Zen attitude with characteristic fortitude he set up a joyous eightieth birthday celebration just over a year ago. A short time before Christmas 1995 I was rung by friends to tell me Don was terminally ill. So I went to visit him.

Don's condition had reached a point where he could no longer swallow. He had the choice either of being put on a drip as his life slowly and speechlessly failed him over a number of weeks or months, or simply ceasing to take nourishment and pass into a final coma of his own volition. He chose the latter course saying that it was better to go that way with all senses alert than by the alternative. He decided to let his own life come to its natural conclusion.

When I reached his room the frail old man was in a chair attended by his son Veda and Veda's wife who had come over from Boulder, Colorado, where Veda is a therapist. They showed me a paper to which Don had given his signature to his decision. Don could hardly speak but through Veda, who could read his lips and sounds, conversation was possible and I soon learnt to understand him.

I asked Don if he remembered the retreat on which he had worked on "What is death?"

Don's eyes took on more life. Yes, he did.

"Do you remember the answer?" I asked him.

Don said, "On what one cannot speak on that one should remain silent"

Bowled over by this quotation, the last lines of Wittgenstein's Tractatus, I remarked, quite unnecessarily, that the German verb for "remain silent" (schweigen) could have the very strong sense of "Shut up!"

Dons eyes sparkled "Why don't you shut up then?" he smiled. We held hands together allowing the stillness of the room to grow upon us.

"Don," I asked, inquisitive as usual, "Do you remember the words you used at that retreat when you dropped that question?"

"Yes," said Don, "Now!"

Later that afternoon, Don's last, he remarked to Veda,

"You know I am enjoying dying!"

"I will tell your friends that."

"They will never believe you!"

"Coming from you - they might."

Don had achieved dominion over his own death and went out fully aware and joyous in his self-determination. Such deaths are rare. We read of them here and there in the lives of lamas and masters. Most of us lack such a focused understanding of the appropriate and the timely. Many of us do not have the good fortune to be able to make the choice. When it is possible and comes about where then has death a victory?

SOCIAL CRITIQUE AND BRITISH BUDDHISM

We are grateful to Vishvapani for his response to Ken Jones' critique of "movements" (FWBO, Soka Gakkai and NKT) in British Buddhism (NCF 13) and my own editorial comments.

I am sure most Buddhists would agree that Western Buddhism is going through a phase of re-assessment after scandals concerning both Zen and Tibetan teachers of both western and eastern origin. Social critique is an essential part of reform and in the New Ch'an Forum we have several times addressed this issue. In my view it is just as important to pursue a critique of contemporary institutions as it is to focus on individual failings. The purpose of such critique is to ask questions, to speak out firmly but in such a way as to encourage debate rather than acrimony.

Vishvapani argues that it was absurd for Ken to "tarnish three movements with the same brush". There are however similarities as well as contrasts between these institutions and, although we both recognised that there are indeed contrasts between the three, the point was to focus on wider generalities. Furthermore, there are indeed many positive aspects of the FWBO which we readily celebrate. In particular, the Karuna project assisting new Buddhists in India, is especially praiseworthy. Our point was to bring into sharper light some current objections which are by no means only our own but generally discussed by "open" Buddhists.

Who are "open" Buddhists? I refer here to those whose orientation and affiliation is to a main stream tradition of practice, whether it be Ch'an, Zen, Tibetan or Theravadin, but without the formulation of tight rules of membership, obligations to particular charismatic leaders and an obvious competitive sectarianism such as does indeed characterise the institutions we discussed. We are perhaps especially aware of these points as we ourselves are attempting to create a democratic fellowship of Ch'an practitioners.

Open Buddhists view the trends shown by these movements with some suspicion and may indeed suggest that some of them, such as those shown by NKT over the Shugden dispute, cannot be conceived of as having been remotely favoured by the Tathagata. Such posturings are clearly harmful to Buddhism as a whole and it is shocking to see such matters pursued more by Western adherents than anyone else.

Rather than being over sensitive to our critique we would invite FWBO to consider our points more openly. There are widely voiced objections here which the organisation might well consider in its own time. Neither Ken nor I have any wish to "beat other Buddhists". This is an absurd suggestion that fails to see the spirit in which our critique was presented. Those interested in a full statement of the FWBO's position may care to read the 48 page document by Sangharakshita entitled "Extending the hand of Fellowship. The Relation of the Western Buddhist Order to the Rest of the Buddhist World", Windhorse Press. That so lengthy a justification was considered necessary is perhaps an indication of a felt need for a cautious reassessment of some features through which the FWBO presents itself to the world.

In a covering letter Vishvapani points out to me that many Buddhist organisations are faced with genuine problems of scale. How do we cope with success, he asks? The question is very much on the agenda of the FWBO and many of the ways in which the FWBO has evolved are attempts to deal with it. I respect this endeavour. Peace to all beings.

THE WESTERN CH'AN FELLOWSHIP: CONSTITUTIONAL DISCUSSION

(First meeting June 1996)

In June 1996 John Crook called an assembly of Ch'an practitioners to a meeting at the Maenllwyd to consider his proposal to respond to numerous requests for a development in the field of Ch'an practice in the UK by setting up a charitable institution to promote Ch'an in Great Britain. The following persons attended:

Tim Paine, Frank Tait, Caroline Paine, Simon Child, Sally Masheder, Alec Lawless, Mike Masheder, Iris Tute, Bruce McLaughlin, Ken Jones, Peter Bannerman, Eddy Street (first afternoon only), John Senior, Nick Salt

The following were invited but were unable to attend: Jake Lynes de Ver, John McGowan, Tim Blanc, Bruce Stevenson, David Brown, Guido Montgomery, Ros Cuthbert, Hilary Richards, Alison Jones, Charles Vincent, James Monks, Peter Howard. Some of these sent in written views for consideration at the meeting.

Considerations

The agenda focused on the proposal from John in the New Ch'an Forum 12 (Autumn 1995) to establish a charitable fellowship in response to requests for greater continuity, community and interaction between those who participate in the Maenllwyd retreats and who practice Ch'an (Zen) on an intermittent or daily basis.

The meeting began by asking the question: What is missing from the present arrangement of occasional retreats supported by small city groups around the country?

The responses to this question took the following form. People have valuable experiences in retreat at the Maenllwyd but many face the problem of establishing some continuity between retreat and daily life and from one retreat to another. There is a yo-yo effect whereby a good retreat experience may be followed by the attrition of daily life which negates the benefit until attempting another retreat, or in some cases giving up or looking elsewhere. The notion of "fellowship" was attractive in that it implied sharing experiences in a communality of commitment; travelling together on a common path; a sharing of problems along the way.

Intensive retreats offer opportunities for self-acceptance, forgiveness, contact in equality with others, experiences of what we may term 'grace' or 'realisation' to varying degrees of depth or clarity. Sharing in group silence was particularly stressed as a valued aspect of retreat. After retreats there is a felt need to share the difficulty of NOT sharing such things during one's everyday life.

A fellowship could allow opportunities through various means and media to: share experiences; share the difficulties of not-sharing in daily life; share "ordinary life Zen"; express personal difficulties in times of mutual trust, caring and hospitality. The assembly concurred in expressing a felt need to relate concerns regarding social responsibility and community to those of personal, maybe solitary, practice and depth experience on retreat.

Prime Task

The prime task was defined as the attempt to bring the themes of solitary endeavour and communal practice together. In that Zen has been primarily a monastic pursuit there is a need to adapt ancient monastic methods to what may be possible in a lay community integrating outer and inner paths in a laity based middle way. It was agreed to set up a fellowship to carry forward these hopes and endeavours. After some discussion the title "Western Ch'an Fellowship" was chosen as a name.

Institution

The required institution was seen as resembling a mandala with a central core and a number of peripheral activities all connected as a web. The activity in such a web would constitute a "net-working." At the centre of the mandala lies the silent retreat process at Maenllwyd with its opportunities for receiving practical teaching, interviews with teachers, self-confrontation and transcendence and in-depth realisation. Around the periphery were such systems and organisations as: the network of city groups; the New Ch'an Forum as both journal and newsletter (perhaps involving two publications); Dharma study groups and advice on reading; address lists and sources of contact, tapes and books including a supply of resources for regional groups.

It was argued that the Maenllwyd retreats lay at the core of the structure because here the focused silence provided opportunities to drop concern, allowing "things" to fall away without the need for any egoic reference or social framing. As concentrative ability develops in retreat (joriki) the practice focus of the regime makes it difficult to evade oneself in self confrontation. This facilitates a view of the path in direct experience, a taste of "the state", a touching of the "mysterious principle."

The city groups were seen as providing opportunities for isolated practitioners to get together in practice sessions with someone capable of teaching basic methods, posture and attitude together with the provision of appropriate reading and opportunities for conversational sharing. The executive would be required to supply suggestions for readings, tapes and taped dharma talks for use by the city groups and to offer training weekends for those leading them.

City Centres

These needed an enthusiastic initiator competent to present basic instructions in sitting, posture and attitude. The provision of a suitable location would be vital. The initiator would create a nucleus of practitioners which would rise in number to a critical mass at which time the formation of a city group under the umbrella of the WCF would be appropriate. Following training leaders may become qualified to offer local retreats.

Maenllwyd Activities

These would be centred upon the introductory Western Zen Retreats leading to Ch'an retreats and hence to focused retreats on such themes as Silent Illumination, Koans, Mahamudra or Tantra. The central practice would be Ch'an.

In addition the new facilities at the Maenllwyd could be available for Dharma Study Retreats, Discussion Retreats or Mini-conferences, Solitary Retreats or longer term low number (say 4 persons) communities in an extended monastic retreat. In addition a month long community in monastic form containing two weeks intensive practice and two weeks looser communality was proposed.

Functions of the Fellowship

The functions of the proposed fellowship were envisaged as follows:

Primary focus

1. To promote training and practice in Buddhism
2. To promote and support training specifically in the Lin Chi lineage of Ch'an under the Dharma leadership of Master Sheng yen
3. To provide opportunities for ancillary practices furthering the above aims

The means of accomplishing these main purposes would include;

- Employing a recognised master or teacher (at present John Crook);

- Renting buildings (i.e. Ch'an hall at Maenllwyd);

- Receiving and managing membership fees and fees for retreat attendance;

- Requesting an appropriate programme of "spiritual" instruction from the master/teacher and putting it into effect.

Further aims

- To sustain contact with the Chung Hwa Institute of Buddhist Culture through Master Sheng Yen.

- To be mindful at all times of the Four Vows.

- To publish a journal and solicit appropriate materials for same.

- To raise funds for use in realising these objectives, providing an educational and/or research programme, assisting local groups, supporting low waged and retired practitioners through bursaries, financing teachings abroad, hiring or purchasing property.

- To initiate pilgrimages to Buddhist lands to increase understanding of Buddhist culture, history and origins.

- To engage an advisory board to comment on the Fellowship's activities, such a board to include at least one "devil's advocate".

The Teacher

The task of the teacher will be to supply an appropriate programme of retreats and education meeting the general aims set out above. As a lineage holder he/she would anchor the approach within the Ch'an tradition of China descended in this century through Master Hsu Yun to Master Sheng Yen. The teacher may however also use other methods from Western and other Buddhist sources to attain this end.

The teacher will be responsible for providing opportunities for practitioners to take some (at least) of the Buddhist precepts, offering event specific liturgies, training city group leaders and initiating training for those interested in, qualified to and capable of running retreats.

The teacher holds authority regarding the spiritual orientation of the Fellowship under its constitution while being responsive to democratic feedback from members and the advisory group. In the event of severe and justified criticism the teacher will be expected to 'consider his/her position' and to withdraw from the organisation.

The institution however has no power to transmit the lineage of Lin Chi Ch'an to another teacher. This power rests solely with the teacher in communication with Master Sheng Yen. In the event of a need to appoint a successor it will be vital to appoint someone able to sustain the lineage within which the Fellowship works even if such a person is not a transmitted teacher. If the retiring teacher had not yet appointed such a person it would be highly desirable to find one. Under the constitution the WCF cannot change its lineage orientation as expressed above.

Membership

It is proposed that membership be open to practitioners who have attended at least two Maenllwyd retreats or their equivalents and who have taken some (at least) of the Buddhist precepts.

Organisation

The WCF will require the usual organisation of a charitable institution namely trustees, an advisory board and an executive committee consisting of at least a Chairperson, Secretary, Treasurer, Journal Editor, Retreat Co-ordinator and other persons appointed or co-opted for specific purposes. The executive committee, in the first instance appointed by the current teacher, will be subject to election at subsequent Annual General Meetings in the manner usual for such institutions with some members up for re-election every three years.

Present Plans

Following the assembly it was resolved to consider the WCF as established, circulate the present document for comment among members of the assembly, publish an appropriate statement in the New Ch'an Forum and to proceed to negotiate charitable status based on a constitution framed from the above considerations.

The second assembly took place on February the 21st to 23rd, 1997. An account of our deliberations will appear in the next issue of New Ch'an Forum.

NCF XV

COMET ABOVE THE YARD

Up at the Maenllwyd -
funny how the days roll by.
I don't seem to be doing anything,
cleaning and writing and cooking
and sitting and walking
sleeping and waking.

Where does it all go?

The time so clear
nobody here
hours - hours
or merely minutes?
Today it is warm;
yesterday cold;
the wind changes,
clouds keep going -
in different directions.

Tonight a comet hangs over the yard
tail streaming in far off sunshine.
Down here, the moon throws dark shadows
and the windless sycamore stands against the stars.
An owl calls.
What was on its mind?
Out of the woodwork, curiously,
comes love.

March 1997 Maenllwyd

EDITORIAL FROM THE CH'AN HALL

When Master Sheng-yen visited Maenllwyd for the third time in 1995 he told us he would provide us with further instruction on Silent Illumination methods of the Ts'ao-tung school of Chinese Ch'an. He had already given us an introduction to this approach during his second visit, but on this occasion he intended to take us further.

We now have available the freshly edited text of his talks and can at once perceive how outstandingly Shi-fu fulfilled his intention. We have here not only a quite remarkable interpretation of the fundamental insights of the great twelfth century master Hung-chih Cheng-chueh but, in addition, a subtle treatment of the way in which relatively naive meditators, such as ourselves, can begin this practice with benefit. Shi-fu provides us with a graded series of stages, principles for use and, most important, an account of the attitudes needed if we are to proceed well along this path.

Silent Illumination is the prime method of the Ts'ao-tung school. Because of this some might wonder how it relates to the Lin-chi lineage which Shi-fu has passed to us. In Japan Shikantaza, the Japanese method which developed from Silent Illumination and resembles it very closely, is the sole Soto (Jap. for Ts'ao-tung) method whereas the Rinzai school (Jap. for Lin-chi) specialises in Koans. Chinese history has been different, encouraging an eclectic approach rather than one of separations and specialisation. In the last century, after a period of Buddhist decay and persecution, many surviving methods were brought together in the revival of Ch'an in china under the influence of Master Hsu-yun. Thus Silent Illumination, koans, Hua-tou and even a Ch'an version of Pure Land practice can all be used within the lineage transmitted through Hsu-yun's reconstruction of Chinese Buddhism.

The Lin-chi lineage is intact and cannot be disputed while, due to accidents of history, the line connecting Ts'ao-tung masters is less secure. Pedantic academics might therefore criticise a transmission bearing the Ts'ao-tung label but cannot do so when the Lin-chi transmission is under consideration. Since Shi-fu inherited both the Lin-chi and Ts'ao-tung transmissions from his teachers we can reasonably consider that both have also been transmitted by him to us.

During his first visit to Wales, Shi-fu remarked that he did not often teach Silent Illumination because it was easy to lose focus and become either too silent, lapsing into blankness or mere somnolence or, on the other hand, to mistake active intellection and an excited mind for illumination. In his offering us this method we may therefore feel Shi-fu's approval of our motivation in practice which, hopefully, allows us to achieve the balance required in this approach.

The text now offered has yet to be fully examined by Shi-fu so some alterations may follow before full publication. A new version of Catching a Feather on a Fan (now out of print) is proposed which will include this text and commentary. Element Press has again expressed an interest in this project but this has yet to be confirmed[1]. I felt however that the Fellows of our new institution should receive these teachings and am delighted that we can get them to you in the pages of our journal.

1 Subsequently published as: Master Sheng Yen, 2002, Illuminating Silence: The Practice of Chinese Zen. Watkins Publishing, London

NCF XVI

CREATING A NEW ZEN INSTITUTION:

THE WESTERN CH'AN FELLOWSHIP

EDITORIAL FROM THE CH'AN HALL

The scholars Melvyn Goldstein and Paljor Tsarong have argued that Buddhism is one of history's most ambitious and radical social and psychological experiments because it attempts to create a society in which ideals of non attachment, non-desire, material renunciation and transcendental wisdom are institutionalised. It tries to socialise recruits into an alternative set of norms for understanding and creating a world in which attachments are considered sources of suffering. But then they ask, "Is this successful?"1

The idea certainly appeals to the West. The spread of Buddhist institutions of many kinds has in the last decade been phenomenal. The number of Zen and Tibetan institutions now numbers over a thousand2 and one may argue that, apart from the venerability of vast old monasteries, Buddhist activity in the West far exceeds that within China and India and, even though understanding may often be poor, has a more creative and exploratory style than in the lands of its tradition and origin. Yet all is not particularly well. In recent years an embarrassing number of cases of sexual and financial corruption, particularly in US centres, has tainted this renaissance and the nature of some new institutions given cause for critical reflection. These have been the focus of several articles and debate in this journal.3 As we ourselves attempt to take a step forward in the creation of a charitable association of fellow practitioners, the move needs to be made with mindful caution.

Study reveals that, taken together with the ethical inadequacies of certain teachers, the main problems in the USA arose from a certain naivet, in the followership of both Eastern and newly transmitted Western masters. I have argued that we need not doubt the significance of the original transmission to teach of these men4.The problem has been an exaggerated and uncritical acceptance by their followers that the implication of their "enlightenment" has been that Western teachers would behave in ways that would not merit reproach. Operating outside the traditional supervision and peer control of monastic organisations it seems that basking in the approbation of their followers simply went to these people's head. In the case of

Easterners, a failure to understand the contemporary post-modern world of ethical and behavioural relativity appears to have contributed to their seduction by the self-indulgent permissiveness of our time. Spiritual inflation is a parent to corruption.

The answer must clearly lie in creating an appropriately effective institutional organisation with in-built checks and balances which prevent this sort of stupidity from arising. This has been our endeavour in the two assemblies at the Maenllwyd and we have come up with the accompanying constitution for the Western Ch'an Fellowship.

Some may ask why I should have proposed such a move. After all, the retreats at Maenllwyd were running well and, by suggesting these changes, I was giving myself a lot of trouble. It would have been easier to continue in the freestyle manner we had adopted and this could have meant that I could opt out and retire to the mountains (or the beaches) at any time. Maybe time will show that such an arrangement would have been more effective. A Zen teacher operates in many ways: remoteness, hidden practice and difficulty of access could well produce a more effective teaching even if it were limited to the few who took the trouble of tracking him down.5 I must tell you I find this notion attractive and may yet go for it.

At some point, however, I was asked by Master Sheng Yen to lead orthodox Ch'an retreats in the UK. Subsequently, he passed the transmission of the Lin-chi lineage as descended through Master Hsu-yun to me as the second of his Dharma heirs.6 In accepting this truly great honour I was touched by Shi-fu's trust in me and resolved that I had to try and carry out his mandate, transmitting Ch'an down to the generations up coming in Britain. I am the same age as Shi-fu: both of us are in our mid sixties and there is no saying which of us will last the longer. The task is for now and cannot wait. When I asked Shih-fu how to do it, he merely remarked "Since this is your culture and you know it better than I, that is something you will have to find out for yourself!"

At our first assembly7 I suggested an organisation that might be able to balance two essential requirements; the caring preservation of the lineage and the prevention of inappropriate behaviour in any teacher or master appointed by the fellowship. Given that we are a group of lay practitioners and not monastics under strict vows, a form of limited democracy seemed to be the answer. On the one hand the teacher, by virtue of transmission, has something especial to say and holds the traditional authority for saying it and transmitting it. No unqualified person can question the teaching as such, only request its more effective presentation. Scholarship and experience form the style of the one chosen to be a teacher and these cannot be arbitrarily altered if a lineage is to be sustained. Yet a teacher is only a human being and may suffer from defects in character. In past history these would have been balanced against his attainments through teacher and peer supervision. In the modern world, an Executive Committee elected by a lay membership must have some of this function and operate in contact with an advisory body of highly qualified non-members. Both teacher and members then have a court of appeal in the event of criticism or disputation. With such a democratic structure, an organisation of fellow practitioners is protected from the risks of inadequacy in the teacher and from the foolishness of individual fellows. This then is the prime feature of the constitution we have devised and which we put forward in this issue for your comment and criticism.

The Fellowship is open to those who have some attainment in Dharma practice through attending retreats at the Maenllwyd. This ensures that, before joining, some realisation of the value of practice has developed, leading an individual to appreciate the importance of the Refuges, the Three Jewels and the Precepts. Knowing full well that lay persons do not have a taste for restrictions that appear to be imposed by doctrinal commandments, we debated whether these requirements were too strict. Yet to think so would be to misunderstand the nature of preceptual practice. The Precepts are guidelines to help one avoid karmic mistakes that will generate future retribution. They are not rules which it is sinful to break. The difference is psychologically significant and, once understood, the Precepts should not be seen as a barrier. Even so, we appreciate there will be some who, while favouring Buddhistic approaches to life, do not wish to commit themselves. At present we are not considering some category of associate membership. We wish to be a practice organisation. None the less "friends of the Maenllwyd", genuinely hesitant about calling themselves Buddhists, are of course welcome on the retreats we offer.

It is vital to stress that the Fellowship does not exist simply for the benefit of fellows. In no way is the Fellowship a preserve for the exclusive advantage of those who opt to join us. Indeed the function of fellows is to support a programme of Buddhist education open to all. Starting with the Western Zen Retreat, practitioners qualify for more demanding retreats which they might not be able to undertake as beginners. To make the more intensive sitting retreats valuable one has to get used to the sitting posture; to understand the significance of sitting; to have some grasp of the essentials of the View; to have begun examining one's place in the Cosmos. Training is thus necessarily progressive, a beginner cannot start at the end. Literally a charitable organisation, we exist to help suffering humanity. Indeed we might well consider calling ourselves the Western Ch'an Sangha.

One concern that has arisen is that the formation of an institution may be divisive. I cannot say but Krishnamurti's well known argument against institutionalisation is one I take seriously. He felt strongly that to create an institution was to produce an object of attachment about which, furthermore, people's opinions will vary thus creating pros and cons and hence social divisiveness. To Krishnamurti spiritual understanding undercut all that; no institutions; no favoured methods; no dogmas or doctrines to be believed; beware of the known and the conventionally believed, only insight counts. I consider Krishnamurti to have been the greatest Bodhisattva of our time and I am happy in my memories of having met him personally, yet I cannot help noticing that, without his presence, his teachings, stored in video, audio and the written page have lost their immediate urgency now that there is no vehicle to proclaim them.

In Ch'an, the lineage is the vehicle by which insight is passed down through time in the form of a living, vibrant person, full of failings maybe, but one who stands for the View and presents it afresh again and again. We need therefore to face up to the undeniable risk of divisiveness as soon as options are created by the pros ands cons of institutional policy. Can we do this? Do we have the skilful means?

Unfortunately, sectarianism and the formation of cult-like clubs around certain Buddhist charismatics already promote the kind of divisiveness between institutions that Krishnamurti saw so clearly. As Ken Jones has argued in our journal, there is no point in not arguing one's case.8 Buddhism is corruptible and in the post-modern environment of sloppy New-Ageism only too easily so. Everyone nowadays can invent or put together their own blooming religion and fail to notice the self-indulgence that entails. Yet, in such debate, compassion is absolutely essential. Even fools have merit.

Within a carefully crafted institution there remain risks. Yet I have confidence. After several of our retreats we have allowed a more communal and sociable atmosphere to arise- just being together on a walk or mountain pilgrimage for example. I have noted that the genuine tolerance and compassion, even love, that develops on silent retreats and during a WZR can still hold up, in spite of the re-emergence of individual idiosyncrasies, if supported by a programme that sustains a quality of space and silence allowing frequent private renewal. Assemblies geared to silence thus have a chance of developing a sociable mindfulness and community coherence that allows tolerance, understanding and friendship to be maintained and our actions to be guided by kindness and wisdom. The best of monastic models can inform us here. At least, this must be our endeavour.

In the coming months I shall, be considering very carefully the way in which teaching and practice within the fellowship may be presented. We will experiment with differing forms of retreat and meeting while always anchoring our practice on the orthodox Ch'an retreat and the WZR. I realise more and more that all the Mahayana meditation methods spring from a common root. We need to understand this clearly so that nobody supposes themselves to be practising with a superior or inferior method. Once the family relationships between them are understood the whole meditative process can be seen as one historical sequence. Similarly Indo-Tibetan and Sino-Japanese teachings all have their roots in the same Sutras and, in spite of some divergences, again take the form of fruit of the same tree. I will endeavour to teach from this perspective giving a broad understanding of the Mahayana and using a variety of methods to help individuals build their most personally effective way of being.

The history of Ch'an has been markedly eclectic. Syncretism has proven useful and the broad scope of the teachings especially helpful to those in the West who react against narrower sectarian approaches. Now that Ch'an has arrived in Britain we need not feel tightly restricted to particular forms so long as the essential core remains clear and vital. Such an approach will allow us not only to adapt to changing conditions without risk of fossilisation but also to renew again and again the source of inspiration itself. Forms are empty and from our insight into emptiness we create forms. So long as we are clear in our pivotal perspective our institution will thrive.

1 Goldstein,M.C. and P.Tsarong.1985.The Tibetan Journal 10.1.14-31.

2 Rommeleure,E. 1997.Guide du Zen.Les Guides Selene,Paris.See also the advertising columns in Tricycle and Shambala Sun among other publications.

3 New Ch'an Forum 13 and 14. 1996-7.

4 Crook, J.H. Authenticity and the practice of Zen. New Ch'an Forum 13. 1996

5 See the opinions of the yogin Geshe Ngawang Jugne in Crook, J.H. and J.Low.1997 The Yogins of Ladakh. Motilal Banarsidass. Delhi p138

6 New Ch'an Forum 9. 1994.

7 New Ch'an Forum.14. p26-29. 1997.

8 Jones,K.New Ch'an Forum 14.p24-25.1997

Bodhgaya

Marble floors surround the Bo tree,
birds' calls, deep shade and fluttering leaves.
Was I ever anywhere else?
Dusk falling buffaloes, wandered home,
feed from large bowls fronting the houses.
Old ashram doors open over a river of sand.
Smoke stacks hiding brickwork fires belch in the night,
old clay to new homes,
empty time moving.

Paradakshina
slowly pacing footfall on marble
soft swish of passing robes around the square
mandala of the lamp-lit temple grounds
one side, citywards, noisy, the other not.
Nirvana and samsara
come up and fade away
as round and round I go.
Deep in the ancient cell below massive stones
candles weave shadows where the still image glows
in the bright silence - no one moves.

Calcutta

Today
a thousand eyes met mine
sitting in my high bus chariot
viewing this mouldering city
of cheerful faces, Bengali smiles
monsoon washed with brown-eye brilliance
down by the river throwing images of Durga

into the rising tide.
The bats are out in the darkening sky
flamed rose and misted by greying dusts.
Sitting on the swept pavement for their evening meal
this small family feeds from brass bowls
gleaming, our morning's gift.
From our high balcony we saw them
mother washing kids in the light of dawn
folding the canvas awning of their shelter
preparing another street-wise day.
Seeing us far above them, Olympians,
the children waved.
No way could we not respond.
Mother smiled, her pride
a way of life Calcutta time.

PILGRIMAGE TO KAILAS: The Holy Mountain of Western Tibet.

If a mountain trek may be described as an "epic" this surely was it. Almost every anticipated hazard and difficulty was encountered together with several that were unexpected. The plan was to enter Tibet by way of Humla (N.W Nepal) during a window of opportunity between the ending of the monsoon and the onset of the Tibetan winter. In 1997 the winter came early and caught us nicely exposed on the plains around Kailas and Manasarovar. As a consequence of the severe weather with snow around the mountain the yak men declined to take our equipment over the Dolma la since snow on the rough descent on the far side might lead to the yaks breaking legs. This meant we were unable to fulfil our aim of circumambulating the mountain. We did however succeed in placing the ashes of Lord Ennals and the hat of Bryan Beresford at the Dolma rock on the top of the pass. This was a prime function of my personal expedition and of several of the clients.

A break in the weather had suggested a window of opportunity. Several of us walked up to the cairn at Drirapuk where the Sherpas did ser.kyem and others made offerings, mantras etc to the mountain, the remarkable north face of which appeared splendidly before us. This had been a long approach walk and I for one was very tired by the time I reached the cairn. I knew I would not have the strength to go on to the top of the pass that day. As the weather stayed improved I allowed Alec Lawless, our strongest walker who was keen to go, to make an attempt at reaching the Dolma rock on the top of the pass to leave Lord Ennals' ashes and the hat of Brian Beresford there. He set off after emotional hugs from the group. Sangye Sherpa, who had done the route before, accompanied him. I had a worrying four hours until Alec and Sangye arrived back in camp at dusk having completed their mission under very tough conditions, racing back to get in before daylight failed. I had felt like a Commanding Officer who had ordered men into action and didn't know whether they would succeed against the odds. Theirs was a fine effort allowing us to claim one success for the expedition.

On returning we had seen four men descending the track on the far side of the river carrying a kind of stretcher. It looked as if they were bringing a body down. And so it turned out. Two Germans, apparently without a guide, had succumbed to exposure on the Dolma la the night before. Police had visited our camp while we were away checking on us. I was relieved when all of us were in camp again.

The return trek into Nepal over the enormously intimidating Nara Lagna la proved hazardous with snow on the narrow track above steep precipitous slopes. I was extremely concerned lest a single slip or mis-step cause a damaging fall to an inexperienced trekker. I myself had the scariest few hours I can remember for many a year. Fortunately it was a bright day with sunshine. Had there been ice on the track I doubt whether we could have crossed the pass without accident. Even the sherpas remarked that it was dangerous for Western trekkers- especially rather elderly ones however fit.

In spite of being a very heterogeneous party, morale was sustained throughout although some four members were very disappointed at not completing the kora, - even though three of these were not fit enough to attempt it. Most members had read little before coming, had little interest in the cultural aspects of the tour and were somewhat taken aback by the ferocity of the Tibetan climate and the demands of the trek but most greatly enjoyed the walking and responded well to the risks inherent in the adventure.

The scenery was outstanding throughout and some of the walks the most wonderful I have personally experienced and well appreciated by the group. The temples at Tsaparang and Toling were formidably impressive. As trek leader I gave two lectures on history, Buddhist art and thought and a guided tour of the mural paintings at Tsaparang and Toling and could have said more but was somewhat disappointed by the apparent lack of interest in such matters within the party. Even so all members appreciated the magnificent scenery and weathered the alarming, anxiety provoking and sometimes downright scary times well. I was indeed quite impressed by the philosophical attitude to their adventure which became general in the group. This is not to say that there were not times when most of us would have preferred to have been back home in a warm bed!

This was not a demonstrative group of people. Private in their feelings and attitudes I none the less sensed that the experience of hardship on this adventure meant a lot to them and that they were encouraged by their own fortitude and resourcefulness.

On our return trek we stopped for lunch at Yangar Gompa and some of us with two sherpas visited the Rimpoche. He was very sympathetic regarding our trials in Tibet, saddened by the news of the Germans' deaths and impressed by our attempt at the kora and by the fact that we had left memorials on the top of the pass in spite of the conditions. He remarked that many great sages and spiritual persons had come to Kailas throughout history. When there is real spiritual intent there are always difficulties. The purpose of the kora is purification from the past so that one returns "reborn" in life. Often purification is difficult and this is expressed through encountering obstacles, sometimes inner, sometimes outer. What counts is then the way one struggles with obstacles.

The Rimpoche told us that the way we had striven on the mountain more than outweighed our failure in not completing the circuit. Often indeed this struggle completes the purification itself, he said. We should not feel that we had failed but rather nobly succeeded. He was amused at the idea that we had done half a Buddhist kora and half a Bonpo one - thus making a full circuit with two aspects. Even sages with great wisdom never had an easy time on Kailas, he said. Only through such experience did they reach ultimate wisdom. He wished us well.

As for me: I am deeply grateful for the experience of leading a group with whom I had rather little natural empathy but which I came to respect in their individuality and own right. I learnt that leaders cannot choose who they lead and must adapt to whoever they are placed among. My main resolve was to sustain a friendly distance and a tactful response to all and to sustain morale when difficulties appeared. Although often quite anxious about weather conditions and their implications, the vehicle problems and the Nara Lagna pass I kept this from the party and pretended a greater optimism than I sometimes felt. "You came for an adventure and now you have one!" was a useful refrain. This seems to have been effective and appreciated. Client briefings in some detail were held every morning after breakfast at the same time as a sweet distribution. Sometimes the Sirdar was also present. The actual trek in Humla was a demanding and a wonderful experience in country of exceptional grandeur. Tibet showed its fierceside which I knew about but had not experienced so directly. I thank Himalayan Kingdoms for offering me this opportunity. [Mount Kailas, photo by John Crook]

CH'AN REVIVAL IN MAINLAND CHINA

Ch'an Buddhism is undergoing a marked revival in mainland China. Monasteries are renewing their fabric and providing services to the public. Meditation is starting again for young monks in the Ch'an halls. In July 1997, with my old friend Yiu Yan-nang as interpreter, I visited two of the most famous monasteries in southern China and was surprised by what we found. When I entered China from Hong Kong the customs officer barely glanced at the visa in my passport. I had held my breath at the crossing point expecting all manner of difficulties to arise. I began to realise that the new China really is undergoing extraordinary transformations. Fearing police supervision at every stage, thought controls on all we spoke to, and a deep official suspicion of my Western face, I had been unconsciously awaiting the type of experience I had had in Moscow during the Brezhnev era. Instead, I found complete indifference to my presence. Gradually I realised I was free virtually to do whatever I wanted - except perhaps talk politics.

We had arrived at Shenzhen, a brand new electronic city where, less than twenty years ago, only farmhouses had stood. Emerging from the glossy station we overlooked a central square in the centre of which stood a vast television screen showing advertisements and propaganda and blaring forth the loudest of pop music. Hoardings proclaiming "Come to Marlboro county" and "Carlsberg" suggested the spirit now abroad. Around them cruised innumerable taxis implying a lack of public transport but ample funds for car hire. From the square, huge canyons of multi-storey buildings, punctuated by stylish skyscrapers, lined treeless avenues stretching as far as the eye could see. The shops were full to overflowing with every sort of merchandise and thronged by eager shoppers. The waiting room for our train into China was a huge space filled to the brim with seated travellers. No sign of poverty here, everyone wore well-made relaxing, even sportive, clothing with good shoes and carried ample baggage. Children looked fit and jolly. During the whole of our trip we only saw one, equally neatly dressed, beggar and even he was hardly pressing his trade. As the train drew out of the city we saw no slums:

endless suburbs of high rise buildings stretched to the horizon draped in a pall of polluted air.

We were travelling soft-seat first-class. The train was not overcrowded although all seats were taken, often by whole families travelling as a group. Comfortable reclining seats lulled us and attendants moved regularly up and down the corridors politely even charmingly offering sweets, drinks and other delights. Air conditioning protected us from the inebriating humid heat of mid-summer. Nobody took any particular notice of us although I was the only Westerner on the train, so far as I could see. I revelled in the absence of attention, the quiet acceptance of myself as just another traveller and the stress-free self-contained attitudes of my travelling companions. Everyone was "minding their own businesses" in a manner quite unexpected to one trained in the ordeals of travel in India. Even in the restaurant car, where my handling of fish-bones with chopsticks left something to be desired, nobody looked my way or made a comment. Yan-nang too enjoyed the train ride saying how much things had changed in Chinain a mere five years. Capitalist competition was promoting good manners from officials and attendants alike and he much appreciated the improvement.

As we crossed the Pearl River delta towards Guangzhou (Canton) we looked out on a strangely patterned landscape in which the suburbs of small towns mixed with paddy fields, lotus pools and duck farms in an almost continuous unstructured urbanisation. There were many factories and, along one stretch of the route, a sequence of huge cement works stretched for miles emitting copious quantities of fine white smoke. A thin smog generated a visible pollution greater than that I have experienced anywhere. Spreading out high over the landscape it combined with other sources of city and traffic emission to hide the blue sky of a naturally misty and humid air, The price of China's economic advance will be deeply costly to the quality of the environment and peoples' health within it. Throughout our trip birdlife was prominent by its almost total absence.

Now and again fast trains roared by smoothly. The train from Beijing drew in while we were at Guangzhou station. The first class sleepers looked very comfortable if not luxurious and all spaces seemed to be taken. Even hard seat accommodation looked bearable to this veteran of Asian travel. Twice an extraordinary express rushed past, a double decker serving the line between Shenzhen and Guangzhou. The service will soon be extended to Hong Kong.

Beyond Guangzhou our line followed the North River, one of three that disgorge to the ocean by way of the delta. Gradually the pollution lessened, the river ran more briskly and cleanly and tall monumental mountains like those on old Chinese scrolls emerged and gathered closely around the speeding train. Lulled by comfort and untroubled by my fellow passengers the trip was truly enjoyable.

After some hours, pollution reappeared as we approached the mining and steel smelting town of Shaokuan. The newly developing city was again spreading far and wide over the surrounding countryside. Vigorously active but charmless streets lined by new multi-storey buildings carried little traffic. The taxi driver was politely intent to secure our services in the following days. He told us competition was intense. We drove out of town into the countryside, paddy fields and traditional village buildings appeared and, after a short time, we suddenly found ourselves confronting an enormous monastic archway, an impressive gated entrance to a compound of ancient tree-shaded buildings. We had reach our goal, Nan Hua Si, the monastery where the famous Master Hui-neng (638-713 AD) had settled to teach.

Nan Hua monastery

The most surprising thing about this marvellous monastery is the fact of its survival. Although the monks suffered grievously and one revered master died, the property itself, although decayed, has remained basically unharmed. Chou-en lai, had ordered its protection from the Red Guards then seemingly intent on destroying the entire heritage of China's extraordinary history. We owe to Chou-en lai the preservation of several remarkable sites within Chinese territory, including indeed the Potala at Lhasa.

Beyond the entrance gate lies a beautiful courtyard surrounded by trees beyond which one can see the sprung roofs of ancient temples. A bridge leads over a pool to a large arch with halls on either side containing protective deities. The figure of Wei-tou stands in the centre of the arch and here devotees make their first offerings of joss sticks. The second court leads to a further archway pavilion. On either side the central entrance the deities of the four seasons, giant figures perhaps twenty feet high, glare down inspecting all those who enter. In the centre of the entrance passage sits the fat smiling Buddha so loved by the Chinese. Again offerings are made and one passes into the main courtyard of the monastery.

The array of antique buildings here is magnificent. Although many people may be passing through the court at any one time, the scene is one of tranquillity and peacefulness. Small trees, potted shrubs and other plants are placed thoughtfully around a bridged central pool in which large goldfish rise from time to time to jump or gulp in air. Among the flowers huge swallow-tailed butterflies of several kinds drift delicately, braving the dangers of webs slung between twigs by spiders quick to respond in the warm air of summer. On either side the court stand two large pavilion towers, the one to the right containing an ancient bell dating from 1167 CE and the one on the left a huge drum, both used to assemble the monks for ceremonies.

The facing temple is the main Buddha Hall of the monastery where major ceremonies take place. The impressive frontage raised along the back of the court extends for eight deep bays between tall columns. Great statues of the Buddha and two attendants, each some 25 feet high, reach to the ceiling behind an ornate altar and gaze down majestically on the officiants beneath. Around the walls, and, again reaching up to the ceiling, is an extraordinary mural decoration. A stucco cliff face filled with grottoes from which peer the figures of hundreds of Buddhist saints, masters and worthies, stands above a wave-rolling sea. The variety and ingenuity of the figures knows no bounds. The entire temple in the Qing dynasty style was reconstructed under the direction of Master Hsu-yun in 1936. The mural decoration enshrines the idea that from the bitter sea of life you can find a hand to help you ashore if only you repent.

Behind the Buddha Hall lies a further courtyard of two levels culminating in a library above a hall of remembrance. Behind that, in a further courtyard, stands a vast pagoda of great beauty dating from the eighth century. It dominates the whole complex providing a focus from whatever viewpoint. Behind this, in a further temple, one finds the embalmed statue of Master Hui-neng.1The whole complex rises from front to rear so that as one ascends there is a feeling of progression in depth. When we explored the woodland at the back of the whole complex we found a stream gushing from a spring and an unfinished temple dedicated to Master Hsu-yun to whom the preservation of the monastery is due.

Our taxi driver took us round the back of the buildings and stopped outside the door of the Guest master's office, a roomy building with statues, heavy Chinese furniture and small buros opening off it. A tiny monk received us. Although we found him off-hand at first, he soon warmed to us, showed us to a large air-conditioned bedroom, gave us various instructions for our stay and finally presented us with several books in Chinese and English all, interestingly, printed in Hong Kong. Later he showed us round the complex and told us much about it.

Although of great antiquity, the monastery has had a chequered history with periods of affluence alternating with times of stagnation and decay. The original foundation by the monk Zhi-yao San-zhang followed his discovery of this beautiful place below the spring of Cao-xi river in 502 CE. When Hui-neng began teaching here after his years in hiding following his secret transmission of the patriarchs robe and bowl, the monastery achieved fame and was reconstructed.2 Later however it again fell on hard times. In 1601 CE Master Han-shan arrived at Nan-hua and found that the nine-hundred year old monastery had been converted into a meat market. "Squealing animals were being slaughtered, dressed and butchered. Stinking piles of worm infected guts filled the stately courtyard"3 The few resident monks did nothing to stop the profanation so Han-shan approached the Viceroy of the province for aid. This was forthcoming and Han-shan went on to do major construction and repair work re-establishing the fame of the monastery. He himself was a remarkable patriarch and his revered statue stands together with others in the monastery. The present reconstruction and preservation of ancient relics is due to Master Hsu-yun who having collected funds repaired the ravages of decay in 1934.

Although it was the prestige of this Master that probably caused Chou-en lai to preserve the buildings, various outrages none the less occurred. In one chapel we found the white marble statue behind glass of the revered Master Wei-yin. A photo beside the statue reveals a face of profound compassion and sweetness. He was beaten to death during the Cultural Revolution. The present abbot, Master Fo-yuan, now in his late eighties, was also severely treated but survived. Hsu-yun himself was beaten and only a miracle seems to have kept him going at a very advanced age (112 years) - eventually dying at 120 years in 19594.

We were surprised by the excellence of our air-conditioned accommodation. A whole flanking wing of the complex comprises second floor dormitories opening off a gallery each containing four large hard beds, rush covered and equipped with soft duvets. We had one of these for our use. Along the gallery and outside the doors of several occupied rooms were stacks of paper money for offerings to Buddhas and local deities. The monastery was visited by many tourists and devotees who stayed overnight in accommodations of varying quality.

Many devotees came to make use of the ceremonial authority of the monks in offering prayers and other services for the dead. Veneration of ancestors remains deeply embedded in Chinese life and benefits for the dead may be secured by burning offerings of paper money and other paper objects ritually in the large incinerators placed around the monastery. We felt that ceremonies of this sort must yield a substantial income for the monastery. Here the great tradition of Buddhism meets the ancient folk religion, itself a mix of Taoist practices, old superstitions and ancestor worship. The offering of these services in the august atmosphere of the monastery was clearly a source of considerable spiritual nourishment for the common people. Who were these? Mostly ladies of a very well-off appearance, business women of undoubted skill, independent minded persons very much the equal of men. This freedom of women must be one of the positive results of the Communist years.

In the guests dining hall these ladies showed a great interest in us. They were extremely friendly, willing to help us in every way and to show us the inner workings of the monastery. They had considerable influence and through their kindness we met several leading monks and were twice driven in the monastery station wagon over to Yun men Si later in our stay. Each devotee has a "shi-fu" or master who is a spiritual advisor and to whom they give financial gifts. It seems these donations are quite unspecified, no fees are asked, rather one gives whatever one feels is appropriate. Judging by the willingness of the "shi-fus" to help the ladies we had little doubts that the formers' income could be quite substantial. There was no doubt about the genuine devotion of these lay believers to the Dharma, the Precepts, to their teachers and to the ceremonial rituals they enthusiastically supported. While we suspected one monk of avaricious motives, others seemed generous and open hearted in this curiously balanced relationship. We had a problem paying our accommodation bill because the same system operated. It was difficult to get an idea of how much we should pay. Nobody would tell us, saying it was up to us. Using several contrasting modes of assessment we hoped the sum we eventually handed over was appropriate. For groups of tourists there is however another system whereby fees and receipts are exchanged.

One of our charming acquaintances offered to introduce us to her "Shi-fu". One evening therefore we met a burly young monk in his room. As the conversation developed and became a little technical, the ladies excused themselves and left us to it. The Venerable Zhen-de Shi began cautiously but soon began to talk freely as he saw the depth of our interest. He felt that the spiritual condition of the monastery remained poor. It was difficult to get good teaching and although materially the monastery was well off he doubted the quality of life led by the monks. Before meditation could become an important part of monastic life again, proper attention had to be paid to the Precepts, to a compassionate and tolerant life style free from petty corruption.

Yes, the Ch'an Hall was used for meditation and there were serious winter retreats. However less than a quarter of the monks actually used the Ch'an Hall. Most were concerned with other tasks around the monastery and the offering of rituals to supporters. In terms of Ch'an these things could not alone promote much in the way of spiritual development.

This was a Dharma-ending age, Zhen-de told us, and the best one could do was to preserve and perhaps develop basic values. He described how a Korean Master had visited the monastery with a large group of disciples. They had met with the monks for retreat. The teacher had suggested they should all solve the koan "What is it?" and to demonstrate he had held up a cup and shouted "EEEK - This is it! What else?" Zhen-de said that everyone had been confused and that, as head monk at the time, he had had to challenge the Korean master. He argued that such teachings were all very well when many monks were close to enlightenment through intense practice and the influence of great teachers but in China today that was nowhere the case. They had to begin with the fundamental teachings on the spiritual life as enshrined in the Four Vows and the Precepts. Zhen-de had himself undertaken a three year solitary retreat and admitted that where a monk devoted himself to such a practice spiritual discoveries could be made which might provoke the appearance of new enlightened teachers. He added however that things were very "difficult" and we took him to mean that opportunities for serious practice and teaching might be restricted.

I was keen to explore his personal practice. He said he repeated the name of Buddha over and over; "Amitabha Amitabha Amitabha" continuously until a shift in awareness overcame him. I was interested to see this mantric Pure Land practice adopted as the activity in retreat of a Ch'an monk. I enquired whether he ever used the koan "Who is repeating Buddha's name?" He did not reply directly to this, remarking only that the sincere meditative repetition of the name did in itself induce clarity and purity. Master Hsu-yun had also considered such practice important. Zhen-de said it was an effective practice when carried out with devotion.

Some older monks however had koans or other methods which they had used earlier in their lives. Everyone could use their preferred method when sitting in the Ch'an Hall, Zhen-de affirmed. He also remarked that simplicity of mind was an asset and that northern and southern monks differed in this respect. Northerners, among whom he counted himself, come from the poverty stricken regions of China, are used to dogged survival, and make good use of simple practices which work. Southerners, in their agriculturally rich homeland, can be devious, looking for short cuts or using complex methods for which there are no teachers available. The result can be a mental muddle.

The Ch'an Hall at Nan-hua Si lies to one side of the main courtyards in a court of its own. The rooms of the monks are nearby. We sat twice in the cool dim atmosphere of this place. I was inspired to sit in so ancient a hall with five or so ancient monks. One old boy spent most of his time on his seat lolling over in slumber but he had been most annoyed, complaining bitterly, when the young disciplinarian had almost closed the door on him at the start of the hour long session.

The monastic day begins at around five with knocking on a wooden board. This develops gradually until after some forty minutes the great bell begins sounding followed by the drum. Bell and Drum tower thunder forth their messages with increasing sound and speed as the monks and lay practitioners assemble in the Buddha Hall and stand in their respective ranks. In front of the altar a space is left for the leader of the ceremony. On either side of this there are rows of wooden boxes with an inclined top well padded for kneeling. Each person stands behind one. The chanting starts with the monks facing each other across the space. At times they turn towards the altar and bow or kneel on their padded boxes. The monks stand nearest to the Buddhas beaming down mindfully from above: lay practitioners wearing robes are placed at the end of the last row of monks and I was ushered to join them: after that come the laity without robes.

The services early in the morning were deeply impressive. Some old monks had amazing faces like those on ancient Chinese scrolls. I was moved to think of the privations they must have faced during the years of oppression. Young monks behaved with lively discipline not without tricks and teasing as mistakes were made in the conduct of liturgy. On one morning an extraordinary offertory was in progress instead of the normal morning service. A temporary altar covered in gifts of fruit and flowers stood outside the door of the Buddha hall and all the monks and laity faced it. The chanting was rich and finely done, rhythmically accompanied by wooden fish and bells. The donors were led repeatedly around the grand exhibition of their donations. The offering was to the "Heaven of all the Buddhas". I reflected on how strange it was that after years of Communist indoctrination this magnificent ancient ceremony full of religious superstition, the "opium of the people", should be treasured so deeply and offered with such devotion and expense.

Yun-men Monastery

Due to the kindness of our ladies and the willingness of the Guest master to please them, we drove over to Yun-men Si in the new monastery Toyota Landcruiser and, finding the place delectable, decided to return for a stay of several days.

We drove over in the company of a senior Taiwanese monk very neatly dressed in elegant robes. He had a kindly professorial air well used to the deference of his juniors. He was visiting the area to see work being done on monastic buildings being partially financed from Taiwan.

Yun-men Si is laid out in a pattern of courtyards and temples similar to that of Nan-hua Si. As with Nan-hua Si the monastery had been restored from decay through the activity of Master Hsu-yun in the 1930s. He was evidently fond of the place and one of his poems, the characters of which were translated for me by Yan-nang, reads:

Yun-men monastery heaves into viewdeep Buddha's throne in a high mountain. Green fields spread widely, the pine forest glows dark green, deep copper-verdant bowl and red wooden fish are calling, the flying waterfall pushes upwaves singing.Lovely fairyland!Come here to attain the Ch'an mind.

The monastery was largely destroyed during the Cultural Revolution and we were amazed by the scale and the success of the recent reconstruction, a truly vast undertaking. The buildings, in modern materials, lacked the atmosphere of antiquity prevailing at Nan-hua Si but the welcome given us by the Guestmaster and the disciplined seriousness of the monks was very encouraging and we rapidly came to revere the place. We were given a small room with poorly functioning washing facilities. The hot humid air was cooled by a ferocious fan and we missed the quiet air-conditioning of Nan-hua Si. How quickly one becomes spoiled by such luxuries - none of which I had expected when we planned this trip.

The Guestmaster was a young man of charm and energy who, to my surprise, had also undergone training in Tibet for two years. We were able to exchange a few words in Tibetan but our pronunciation differed so greatly and my vocabulary was so small that in no way could be talk directly together. Yan-nang too found his dialect of Mandarin difficult and they took to writing down characters from time to time to make things clear. Ming Shu Shi was a source of joy for with him we were able to talk seriously about meditation training in contemporary China.

The Yun-men school of Ch'an has always been exceptionally disciplined and strict. Master Yun-men was one of the greats among Chinese masters and his inspired teaching, his rough edged methods of investigation and confrontational style still seem to keep the Yun-men monks on their toes. We found that not only was there a scholarly school of Dharma teaching in the monastery but that the Ch'an hall was the active centre for a group of young monks undergoing intensive retreats in winter and, at this season, carrying out regular daily sitting.

There were three sorts of monks at Yun-men Si, the Sutra students in the Dharma school focusing mainly on scholarship, the precept monks who were practitioners of a pure life and sustained the administration and the Ch'an practitioners, specialists in meditation in their search for enlightenment. About a quarter of the monks belonged to this last category but unlike Nan-hua Si they were mostly new recruits and as keen as mustard, well led by men only a few years older than themselves. There were also some remarkable older residents who had survived the cultural revolution. These grand old men often led the ceremonies and their faces, again like those of the ancients depicted on scrolls, carried signs of extreme psychological endurance, courage and a zany kind of wisdom. These elders seemed to do their own practice apart. I spotted one alone in the woods behind the monastery standing by a pool reading a scripture with rapt attention.

I arose early in the mornings and, wearing my robes, attended the morning liturgy. The chanting was more disciplined that at Nan-hua Si and the monks behaved with great decorum. With no comment I was simply placed appropriately in the ceremonial hall in accordance with the robes I wore. No discussion or especial notice was taken of me and again I found this to be a freedom from attention I greatly appreciated. There seemed to be a kind of unspoken respect for everyone's individuality that took the form of simply letting persons be.

Yan-nang and I attended the Ch'an hall regularly. We must admit that this was partly because, due to its air conditioning, the hall was the most pleasant place to be in the hot humid heat of the sticky summer season. As at Nan-hua Si the large hall was square. A long bench extended around its wall and here the monks took their places for meditation. Behind the bench on two sides of the room were raised sleeping platforms for use during intensive retreat. To the right of the entrance was the place for the disciplinarian with bells and clappers for signals set close by. In the centre of the room a statue of the Buddha sat in a glass case and to him one bowed on entry. Behind the Buddha, non-residents, both monks and laity, could find places to sit on either side of a sort of booth for the abbot should he wish to attend. Morning, afternoon and evening sits were being held. As the clappers sounded monks hurried to the hall for fast walking round and round the Buddha. After some twenty minutes, when all the monks were present, clappers sounded and we all halted, going directly to a chosen place. This sorted out who was going to sit where; for there was no other ordering of places. One simply picked a vacant one and collected blankets to act as a cushion and another to cover one's knees. After a pause, sitting in our places with our feet to the ground, there was another ten minutes of walking until the clappers cracked again. This time one carefully arranged ones shoes below the bench and sat facing towards the room with legs crossed in the correct style. Another signal started the session which was to last one hour. The door was shut and bolted with an intimidating crash.

During sitting, a disciplinarian slowly, silently and gracefully circled the room along a marked track about three feet in front of the sitters holding an "incense stick", that is the baton for striking shoulders, high in the air, one end pointing at his ear. Occasionally an individual was struck, seemingly on account of somnolence, but there was no requesting its use on a regular basis. One lad got a fit of giggling and, as he would not shut up, the disciplinarian approached his place, struck the stick on the floor before him three times and the lad had to descend and kneel before the Buddha for about twenty minutes before he was allowed to return thus chastened to his place.

The room, which had been cooled by four large air conditioners during the rapid walking, fell silent as they were turned off and the hall settled into a profound stillness in which an occasional movement or fidgeting could be clearly heard. The muffled sounds of the monastery came in as if from afar through the walls. I found these hours a wonderful experience. To be sitting with the monks under disciplined training in these traditional halls was inspiring. I sat within a deep inner repose and the still happiness of silent illumination grew within me. The hour passed by as if it were only a few minutes and my body never complained at all. Yan-nang was not so fortunate. Troubled by wandering thoughts he found it difficult but, by persistence, he held out without moving for at least half an hour in each sitting. He stretched his legs out for a few moments and then resumed meditation. The disciplinarian did not object and later Yan-nang said he had never sat better.

Yun-men Si is situated at the base of a tall forested mountain and a rushing torrent originating high in the rocky wilderness cascades down one side of the buildings and provides the water supply for the place. Girded by high cliffs and near vertical slopes covered in dense vegetation, the mountain is accessible only along a built path that, starting from an intimidating flight of steps, twists and curls steeply up to a place where a beautiful waterfall drops down a surface of bare cliff.

Yan-nang and I climbed the path:

Bamboo forest
voices sound
in silence.
Between trees
monastic eaves
ripple in green sunshine.
Looking up the steps of the path
disappear in the mountain.
Somewhere near the sky
a waterfall
begins falling from heaven
the torrent filling
a darkening pool
white water
black rock
polishing.
Clear laughter
people bathing naked
babies pee.

One afternoon we walked to the base of the steps with Ming Shu talking about meditation and the practice of the monks. Again he affirmed that the main method they used was repeating the Buddha's name. I queried whether it might not be better to ask who was doing this repetition and so gain an insight into one's own nature. Ming Shu said that some people might indeed use such a koan but, by using the method he had described, a diligent meditator would in any case eventually perceive the source of repetition in a great limitless space. In this way one discovers the origin, rigpa as the Tibetan say, he told us. But it needed great persistence and his own practice had not yet "shown him the nature." Ming Shu then said something that was to touch me deeply.

"When you practice you need to have great faith in Kuan-yin5. Kuan-yin is universal compassion. While she is simply a symbol, the meaning is profound. When you see her as the kindness of the Universe offering all life's experiences to you then you find gratitude. You cannot be proud at such a moment. This teaching is profound and needs to be the background against which meditation is practised. Otherwise the practice is in danger of becoming something quite mechanical.

"Our problem today is that we lack enlightened masters to guide us. We have to teach from books and from our reading. None the less we have found this allows some progress so we are persisting in our training. Who knows what may turn up?"

During our first exploratory visit Ming Shu had taken us to meet Master Fo-yuan, the aged Abbot of Nan-hua Si who had rooms at Yun-men Si where he often stayed. Ming led us into a large apartment near the buildings of the Dharma School. An old monk was pottering about tidying things. He looked so ordinary and accepted our arrival with so little ceremony that at first we could not suspect this was the great master and abbot himself. None the less he quickly invited us to drink tea while he plied us with questions. Who was our teacher? What was his lineage? How did we practice? How was the Dharma in foreign parts? His main interest was in Master Sheng-yen and he took care to trace out his precise lineage from Master Hsu-yun. Master Sheng-yen is a third generation descendent of Hsu-yun while, at his advanced age, the late eighties, Fo-yuan was a first generation descendant. We were in the presence of the most senior master of Ch'an still living.

Master Fo-yuan had a rather strange presence. At the same time interested and disinterested in us, he had a matter of fact manner, yet he was none the less pleased to hear of the Dharma going to the West. Lacking entirely social graces and mannerisms he spoke to us with great earnestness and directness. His eyes had an unusual brightness and a querying look that suggested a capacity for demanding presence.

Afterwards I thought much about the times he had come through. He had been selected as abbot by lot in 1952 after Master Hsu-yun, who was retiring, had written from Beijing ordering that each of the seventy or so monks be given a lot. The drawing of lots continued for two days with all the monks standing in the front porch of Nan-hua Si. On the third day one name came out three times in a row. It was Fo-yuan to whom Hsu-yun had transmitted the Dharma the year before and who was by far the ablest of the monks. Whether the falling of the lot three times had really been coincidental seems questionable but the choice was considered by all to have been a sound one - made by Wei-to, the monastic guardian, perhaps![6]

During the cultural revolution Fo-yuan, together with other senior monks, had experienced not only the desecration of his monastery and severe maltreatment but had also endured the tragic death of his fellow monk and friend Wei-yin (see above p. 35) at the hands of the Red Guards. Then, in recent years and at an advanced age, he had pushed through the most remarkable programme of restoration at both Nan-hua and Yun-men, and was doubtless responsible for the monastic organisation and especially the excellent training now available for the young monks at Yun-men. Yan-nang and I were fortunate to have met such a towering, almost legendary, figure in the renewal of Ch'an in China today.

Yan-nang translated one of Fo-yuan's short poems in praise of the Buddha in the pavilion of the guardians at Nan-hua: Smiling mouthalways openEveryone calls melaughing Buddha.

Sitting shirtless
fat belly on view
Every thing about me
wishes you an easy way.

We repeatedly came across short poems hanging in strings of characters down columns in the monastery and in the pavilions hidden in the bamboo forest behind it. In the Dharma Cloud Pavilion we found the following. On the right hand pillar -

The body is like a cloud
empty come and empty go.
Where then do you find attachment?

and on the left hand side facing it -

The mind is like flowing water
no front
no back
no stop.

Ming told us that the winter retreat was very demanding lasting for six weeks of intensive effort. It began at 4.45 in the morning and went on till 11 at night. He wrote down the daily schedule for us. It consists of meditation periods divided by periods for talks, short ceremonies, light meals or tea breaks. Meditation periods are preceded by quite long sessions of fast walking around the Buddha. Most sits last a hour but they become shorter in the evening.

I asked whether visitors could sit with the monks on intensive retreat and Ming told us that was possible. Visitors would not be expected to sustain the whole programme but to do as much as they could. Ming welcomed the idea that I should bring a small party of Western sitters to participate in one week of a winter sesshin. So far only a very occasional Westerner visited the monastery and it would be good to have friendly contact with other organisations that took intensive sitting seriously. Retreats are held in winter when the climate is cold, the temperature going down near freezing sometimes at night. Since the monastery is unheated, rooms are cold and the monks wear padded garments. We would have to be properly equipped.

Shyly, Ming mentioned one difficulty. Women were not allowed in the Ch'an hall. It would be possible, however, for them to sit in another room which would be arranged for them. I mentioned that this would not go down well with feminist Buddhists. Ming remarked that at present they felt the essential thing was to restore authentic celibate life as the core of Ch'an monasticism. Once a healthy practice had been revived questions of gender could be reconsidered. He knew of course that outside the monastery walls there was no discrimination between genders in the new China. There was a difficulty here that has been resolved by Master Sheng-yen in Taiwan where monks and nuns in his monastery live together under discipline and attend all functions equally. No doubt these developments will eventually occur in mainland China also but, for the moment, I respect their discretion.

There is certainly an odd paradox here because women are among the most staunch supporters of the monastery. Admittedly their spiritual practices were focused on devotion rather than on the self-confronting tasks of meditation yet devotion, bhakti as the Indians call it, is a very significant aspect of religious life. Each of the monasteries had a nunnery attached and the relations between monks and nuns would form an interesting study. Traditionally nuns focus on the practice of the vows and precepts and there is no Ch'an hall among the buildings used by them. Yan-nang and I visited the nunnery near Nan-hua Si. The modern buildings in traditional style had a gentle charm basking in the late afternoon sunshine. The nuns smiled at us and let us explore the neatly kept buildings. I had the impression that their peaceful spirituality, even without a Ch'an hall, might be on a level equal at least to that of the monks and keyed to a natural humility and simplicity some of the monks seemed to lack.

On our last day some of the Ch'an hall practitioners sought us out for conversations. They had noted that we sat well and this attracted them to us. One of them remarked on the shameful behaviour of the boy who had giggled in the Ch'an hall. I said that Master Sheng-yen taught that a teacher must be hard on a group but understanding of an individual. The monk contemplated this point but then affirmed that at Yun-men there could be no room for lax behaviour. It was a difficult task trying to re-establish the Dharma and the correct practice. Each and every monk had to be dedicated very seriously if the endeavour was to succeed in such changing times. Discipline should be kindly but firmly administered.

Another young monk had been a sailor and had learnt some English which he wanted to try out. He was keen to know how the Dharma was fairing in the West and held the view that a strong western Dharma would help in the restoration of the practice in China where so much had been lost. I was deeply struck by the realism and seriousness of these young men.

Ch'an in contemporary China

Our visits to these monasteries hardly allow an assessment of the re-emergence of Buddhism in China. Certain things are however becoming evident. In Taiwan, Buddhism has become a very strong ethical force and, in Hong Kong too, there is great support for Buddhism. Compared with the alternatives, Communism, Taoism Confucianism and Christianity, Buddhism is winning hands down. When Master Sheng-yen and other major Taiwanese masters give public talks their audiences may run into thousands. While one may query the quality of much of this Buddhism there is a serious core that cannot be denied.

It seems very likely that the effects of the failure of Communism in China have some resemblance to cultural themes arising from the partial demise of Christianity in Europe. In both cases a powerful view of life with strong ethical injunctions has failed to hold the attention of the people and a spiritual vacuum has been created which only materialism and the quest for wealth has filled. This materialism, focusing on fame and gain, is however the root of much social suffering and the divisions between new rich and new poor. It lacks an ethical and a human dimension and no touch of the spirit enlivens it. It is this that Buddhism can supply. The interest in Buddhism in Europe parallels its re-emergence in the countries of its traditional practice.

The ancient superstitious liturgies and ceremonies for the dead touch a deep root in Chinese nature where the importance of the family and respect for ancestors and ancestral tradition form the roots of an enduring Confucian ethic of mutual respect. The magic and mystery of cult Taoism touches simple minds that cannot easily distinguish mummery from spirituality. The mixing of these old rituals with Buddhism provides some with an inner security that the changing times still demand. Sheltering within these trends are the serious questioners who are looking once again at the fundamental roots of Ch'an where the best of Buddhism and Taoism combine. Because these trends enhance social security the government does well to tolerate religious freedom and the restoration of those towering ancient edifices where the roots of religion lie.

Yet the authorities remain ever watchful. The National Buddhist Association of China is formed from representatives from lay and monastic institutions but there is also a strong governmental presence. At the local level the regional government supervises the activities of monasteries and promotes national tourism generating a renewed pride in Chinese culture. Some of the entry fee goes to the local tourist office. The taking of precepts is recognised by the giving of a certificate by the National Buddhist Association but the number of people who may take precepts in a year has been limited.

At the level of our own visit to southern China we saw no evidence of external control on ordinary folk engaged in everyday affairs. People spoke their minds with us freely but did not discuss politics nor did we trouble them with political questions. The result seems a paradoxical co-existence of freedom within a determinedly one-party state. Probably only the ancient Confucian instincts of the Chinese keep this in place. What the role of Buddhism may be in the times to come remains an open question. For now we may rejoice at the new found voice of the Dharma in China.

Postscript in response to Hsu-yun

Dozing in the summer sun
butterflies sip the temple flowers.
Cloud water from the bamboo hills
ripples through courtyards
filling cool pools with limpid clarity.
Soft gong and sudden clapper
call us to the meditation hall.
In dim light stillness falls
distant cicadas humming in the pines.

December 9th 1997

1 I understand that the original embalmed body was badly damaged in the Cultural Revolution and that the present effigy contains the rescued skeleton.

2 See Wong Mou-lam 1953.The Sutra of Wei-lang (Hui-neng) The Buddhist Society..London.

3 Cheung, R and C.Y.Shakya1993. The Autobiography and Maxims of Master Han Shan. HK.Book Distributor

4 Luk, C.1988. Empty Cloud. The Autobiography of the Chinese Master Hsu-Yun. (see pxiv,138-139)

5 Kuan-yin is the Chinese female form of Avalokiteshvara, the Indian Bodhisattva of compassion.

6 See Holmes Welch 1967. The Practice of Chinese Buddhism 1900-1950. Harvard East Asian Studies 26. Harvard University Press.Cambridge, Mass. p 169-170

THE FENCELESS GATE

(for Hughie)

High in the hills of Wales
somewhere above Ceredigion
a fenceless gate swings in the wind.
Bold spirit are you?
A rugged glance, good boots or a 4 time 4
and you're away
among sheep and ravens
cloudwise among crags
bogs and sudden mist
a falling white-out
lost in the desert
chilly too

coming down a valley   no-one ever saw before
the dead still sing   in the Inn
finding a way home   not so easy then
they make you welcome - see   beer's good
hard to get away   and the company cheerful
nothing to worry about - see the view in the rear mirror
mark me   fading,
boyo -   just you take care in Wales.
fenceless gates   swinging
are saying more   in the wind
than you take them for.   Having another are you?

January 1998

NCF XVII

EDITORIAL FROM THE CH'AN HALL

Charity status for Western Ch'an Fellowship

Good news! The Western Ch'an Fellowship has been granted charity status by the Charity Commission. So we are fully in business and we invite all our readers to join us as Fellows. Naturally you have to be qualified[1] - so come along to our retreat programmes, establish an effective practice and we will soon be welcoming you.

The Western Ch'an Fellowship has developed from some twenty years of experience in offering retreats at the Maenllwyd. In that time things have changed. At the start the pioneers were tough and determined indeed; no heating; sleeping bags in the barely roofed barn with an owl for company; a lot of snoring; thunderbox toilets or worse; little space for sitting; wild Rajneesh action yogas; a lot of alternative therapy and the spirit of the sixties and seventies. Frankly, there has been nothing like it since. People took risks, were amazingly open, even to the extent of nudity in the 'kundalini' exercise - nobody minded. People were just 'doing their thing'. Indeed, there was very often a freedom, dedication and sheer joy in those retreats that is not so common today.

Nowadays, participants are less willing to confront their desires for comfort, for having an easy time. People often refer to their problems with early rising, the absence of mattresses, and are already accepting the presence of showers as some kind of right! All those early simplicities and the problems of adjusting to them were part of an essential self-confrontation; not giving in to the aching body, the sleepless night. Those retreats were inner expeditions. In Tibetan 'Chod' one gives one's body to the demons. Most people find difficulty nowadays in offering it to the Buddha. Why? - the reason is obvious. We are all now 'consumers' and expect value for money. So, in addition to a retreat practice guaranteed to yield 'enlightenment', we want our home comforts. Sorry folks - at the Maenllwyd you pay for dis-comfort. Are you becoming soft? Do not think it goes unnoticed by the ancestors of twenty years ago.

Even so, perhaps the new comforts at the Maenllwyd have a good side to them. Retreat will undoubtedly be easier for beginners. And for the older generation it is a blessing. Perhaps then we can spread the Dharma in a gentler style well fitted to our time. Self-confrontation is difficult enough in the practice of sitting on retreat and attempting koans. A little more physical kindness may be helpful. Yet we must be careful not to turn what were expeditions into mere tourism. To confront the bodily is perhaps the first move in self-confrontation. If you want to cross the inner mountains the going is necessarily rough; your legs ache and you have no suncream. If you go by helicopter have you really gone at all? You are just imagining the route. So take care.

The Ch'an retreat is more formal today. We are introducing appropriate ritual during the two daily ceremonies and learning better chanting. This is a sign of greater respect for the tradition in which we focus most of our practice. It does not imply a leaning to traditionalism. As Shi-fu told me - we have to find our own way in Britain. We British are a critical people with no great love for ceremony unless it is felt to be meaningful. This journal sustains a social critique of Buddhism itself and I believe this is fundamental at a time when two significant Buddhist organisations in Britain have proved unworthy in important respects.

A vital question concerns the training of future teachers. We have instituted training for meditation instructors and each local group leader will be expected to gain the certificate for this. Training for retreat leadership will be more demanding. Even for those with the requisite qualifications as counsellors or therapists, it needs hands-on training during the event. We will be asking some more experienced fellows to act as monitors on retreat and then as Guestmasters. In this way it will be possible to learn about the retreat process from the 'other side' as it were. Further thought will be put into this question.

Sue Blackmore's wonderful radio broadcast about Maenllwyd was extremely popular and we have had many enquiries. Many letters showed little awareness of what Zen was about. People loved the story line of the broadcast, remote cottage, log fires, meditation, peaceful tranquillity, chanting OM - very new agey. Some however had a more focused understanding and are likely to join us as the retreats roll by. We must come back to Sue whenever we want publicity!!

This issue contains an important article by Shi-fu on Sutra reading. I myself have become particularly attracted recently by the original Sutras. They reveal to us the sort of man the Buddha was and I recommend them to you. Recent translations available from Wisdom Press are outstanding. David Fontana reminisces about a journey he and I took together in Greece muttering our attempts at solving koans to one another. Eric Rommeluere, now a member of our Advisory Board, allowed me to translate and publish an insightful essay that delighted me when I read it on a visit to him in Paris. Carol Evans tells us about her childhood experience of her father. It is a moving account but some may ask where is the Zen in this? Zen lies at the heart of every strongly-felt relationship whether it is known or stated or not. If you haven't grasped that you need to start all over again. Ann Dickman raises some important issues about retreats. Then we welcome a helpful retreat report that bodes well for the kitchen and some poems.

Every good wish to you all.

1 For details, see page 35

VISITING MOTHER

Copper whispers blowing in the wind,
beech leaves chase the rough grasses down the field.
At ninety two, I ask myself,
will she see another spring?

She rests there, quiet, her busy conversation gone,
anxieties softened now in forgetfulness of age.
Beside her in the garden, dozing off,
I see her smiling in a ray of autumn sun.

She set my character in grooves
so like her own, wakeful mornings worrying;
skilled diplomacy; collusion
in the many faces of a smile; all silent now.
Will she see another spring?
Falling like leaves - the boxed up photographs, cracked vases and old time
letters carefully stored away
in chests of drawers, yellowing archives

only she remembers, rarely now recalls; ancient faces;
raucous tones; the quarrelling;
the tears behind the racks of bathroom towels;
not her mother, remembered gentle granny her support.
And will she see another spring?
Suddenly, imagining her presence gone,
the house falls empty, only paper memories remain.
She sits here smiling in the autumn sun
Oh dear - such sadness at your gratitude for my having come.

1997

NCF XVIII

WHAT A MESS!

EDITORIAL FROM THE CH'AN HALL

A casual observer surfing the Buddhist scene in the West might well come to the conclusion that the whole thing was a mess. Indeed, some of us who feel ourselves to be serious practitioners may be beginning to feel like retiring to the hills. Yet that was not the Buddha's way. He stood by principle and stayed in town.

Holding fast to the Dharma brings us up sharp against Samsara within the Buddhist world itself. Nothing could be more absurd than the current Shugden controversy about the value of a medieval ghost, nothing less edifying than the apparent state of the FWBO, little less informative than disputes over whether Roshi Kapleau completed more than 32 koans, and there is no enthusiasm to be found in the dereliction from duty of corruption-prone sectarian leaders. Those of us who are happy in our simple-minded attempts to follow the Way may well be distressed by these news items that read like soundbites in the gutter press. Perhaps it is as well to be brought to earth with a thud. There is nothing special in institutionalised Dharma: reeking of ignorance it evidently perpetuates the mental suffering of disputants ego-anchored in opinion and prejudice. Where, one may ask, are the effects of following the path of wisdom and compassion to be found if not in the lives of its prime exponents? Is this all mere hypocrisy?

We need a pause for reflection. Buddhism is a growing force in the West and as it grows it picks up the prevailing trends of our culture. This is no new thing. It has happened throughout history as Buddhism, or indeed any other code of behaviour and belief, enters a world in which it is a stranger. In the late twentieth century an Eastern Way relatively unchanged since medieval times is encountering the full tide of Western capitalism and consumerism running as a cross-current through all its ancient values.

Westerners are increasingly educated to cultivate the independent self as an agent in an uncertain world in which fierce and unremitting competition sieves the talented from the less able, in which life-long employment is unlikely, in which state provision for accident and ill health is increasingly a thing of an out-dated socialist path and in which the 'post-modern' relativity of values means that any system of belief or behaviour is seemingly as good and as relevant as any other. In such a world any system of belief soon constitutes a 'market' to which 'consumers' come in hopes of a good 'buy'. And the first thing a consumer wants is concordance with his or her pre-existing comforts, beliefs or prejudices. Someone coming to a Buddhist group wants to buy a sense of understanding, belonging and uplift related to the ideas they hold on entry. Where standards are so variable that no cultural anchorage is available, the lost will grab at a straw. Strong minded, assertive individuals who appear to 'know' are exceptionally attractive in such a situation. A self-promoting teacher with the gift of the gab easily acquires charisma and followers and can infect a developing organisation of the 'faithful' with his or her own viruses. In Western Buddhism a common institutional structure is one in which a charismatic leader has full control of a blossoming, wealth-creating organisation without any form of check or balance from an evaluative membership. No one else 'knows' and the tin pot gods and goddesses of cults are created. This has occurred again and again on both small and larger scales. The loss of deep-rooted cultural means and standards for the evaluation of spirituality lies at the core of the problem. In so far as all of us are embedded in this world, the problem infects us all.

I was reminded of this in conversation recently with a young Californian social anthropologist engaged in Himalayan research. Kimber Haddix (of University of California, Davis) was comparing West Coast Buddhist centres with the small, home-spun village parish where her father, a Christian, ran the church. She told me that in the old time East Coast parish there was a real sense of community, people popped into each others' houses and helped one another, telephone chats were common on a "How are you?" basis. Families cared for their neighbours and the priest was a central facilitator for his small community of parishioners. Yet in all of this there was little talk of 'spirituality' and certainly no debate about God or theology. By contrast, in the Buddhist institutions each individual was chasing his or her own version of 'enlightenment', the key emphasis being essentially doctrinal and practice-oriented and there was remarkably little community feeling as such - more like the crew of a ship with a voyage to make and skills respected.

Similarly our own 'Community Experiment' for this June had to be changed into a shorter Ch'an retreat because an insufficient number of participants were prepared to spend longer time on a less intensive, community-building programme. In fact the extra two days some four of us spent together showed exactly what could be achieved: greater personal tolerance, liking for idiosyncrasy, respect for difference and a willingness to adopt a degree of discipline (spaced periods of silence) to sustain these things. Most of us are still gunning for the quick therapy of an enlightenment process - although without any real understanding of what such a process requires.

There is a paradox here because one of the reasons for forming the Western Ch'an Fellowship was because many people were asking for a greater sense of community. I put it to you that the 'consumer' attitudes that swamp most of our better feelings act unconsciously to prevent community developing. The reason: plain old, unconscious ego-indulgence.

There is a real danger that many beginners in Buddhism are being sucked into organisations that skilfully provide for their wants without the kind of self-confrontation that the Dharma demands. Lots of verbal 'teachings', visualisation practices involving creative fantasy; assertive even domineering leaders with strong sectarian partialities tend to produce uncritical dependencies in which a false, unchallenged self can flourish. When such an institutionalised view is challenged the adherents may defend it to the hilt because an assumed identity is now under threat.

And so we find seemingly rational Westerners engaged in the defence of protective visualisations involving a medieval and revengeful ghost or tolerating practices in which homosexual relationship is confused with spirituality or the value of the feminine ridiculed. The Buddha might well have been exasperated with bhikkhus who got involved in such things. And indeed there is ample evidence for this.

If we look into the Sutras we come to realise that stupidities of this sort existed even in the Buddha's time. At first there were no rules, a group of friends constituted the early Sangha. As the teachings spread and numbers grew, so accurate understanding of the Buddha's message was less immediate and the Buddha was repeatedly confronted by silly things his followers did. The Vinaya as a code of conduct was essentially a developing case law emerging from events in which the Buddha made a behavioural ruling to safeguard the spiritual progress of the monks.

If, therefore, we are faced merely by a modern version of innate stupidity what can we do about it?

The first thing is to remind ourselves of compassion, of Avalokitesvara weeping over the innate stupidity of the world. Tara was born from his tears. True Bodhisattvas do not lose patience; knowing ignorance to be pervasive he and she take it lightly and engage only mindfully in debate. This mindfulness does not mean a lack of critical acuity. There is a real risk that as large hegemonic Buddhist institutions, possessors of sometimes dubiously acquired wealth, might seek to dominate the rendering of the Dharma in the state, (in education for example) so governmental acceptance could lead to the purveying of false or inadequate Dharma in schools and the undermining of the true Way. The critical Bodhisattva will have to stand up and oppose such developments with all the skills that persuasive argument can deploy. If this means unfavourable assessments of some Buddhist institutions so be it. The name 'Buddhist' does not imply anything sacrosanct, indeed sadly, at present, sometimes the reverse. At another level, close attention needs to be paid to developing a mutual accountability between teachers and taught. Our own constitution is an attempt along this path and we must watch carefully to see how it works out. Authority needs to be appropriately employed. Thus the interlinking of the authority of the teacher to provide Dharma and the authority of an Executive Committee and Advisory Board in examining the means need developing as twin poles of a safety-conscious structure. It is exactly in this constitutional area that so many Western Buddhist institutions are currently severely incompetent. An institutional Vinaya needs to be debated and put into practice (see discussions with the Dalai Lama, page 10 and the article on pages 31-41).

We cannot ignore the world. Samsara and Nirvana are twin perspectives on one whole. What goes on in the world requires confrontation - even as the Buddha, a skilled politician, had to confront it. Yet it needs a quality of ego-disengagement if one is not merely to contribute to destructive debate. And here practice becomes all-important. It is essential to examine one's own life in the light of the Eight-Fold Way with great care. In particular, to know that only through concentration and meditation is underlying falsity disclosed and the Way made plain. To construct institutions without a personal humility, to advocate practices that are nonsensical given the state of Western scientific and psychological knowledge, and to engage in vicious and aggressive defence of held-onto positions is to undermine the whole project. Ultimately, true teachers have an option to retire to the hills and await those who seek truth to come to them. In such an option may lie the salvation of the Way. We have not come to that yet. Watch out!!

LEADERSHIP TRAINING IN THE WESTERN CH'AN FELLOWSHIP

This article begins the process of establishing appropriate training for those wishing to teach meditation and run groups or retreats under the auspices of the Western Ch'an Fellowship. This text deals with preliminary orientations and the task of teaching meditation in local groups. Other articles will follow. We are publishing it here so that group participants and beginners know what is expected of their local teachers and the training they are required to undergo.

Part 1 The Meditation Group

Introduction

The Western Ch'an Fellowship provides training in the practice of Ch'an/Zen. What is Ch'an all about? Most of us live lives that are to varying degrees unsatisfactory. It may be that we suffer considerably from personal disabilities, problematic relationships, troublesome family or social situations or from anxieties that our own minds generate. It may be no more than a vague feeling of unsatisfactoriness; that there ought to be more to life than the humdrum mundane existence some of us feel we endure from day to day. Maybe we feel ourselves victims of our life circumstances and feel resentful. Maybe we have not been able to achieve what we expected, or done something we regret, and then experience guilt or shame because of that. All of this the Buddha termed suffering (dukkha). The purpose of training in Ch'an is to lift the burden of such suffering through the discovery of a fresh way of being.

The method is based on the original formulation of mindfulness by the Buddha. Mindfulness means being aware of what is going on inside one's mind and also the influences that impinge upon it. Mindfulness requires paying attention to what is actually happening, not only through intellectual examination but through direct experience. In Ch'an/Zen this approach is especially emphasised and the training is focussed initially in 'sitting' (zazen). The mind is calmed and then inspected as to its activity. There are a number of methods. These are, however, not ends but means to cultivating a dynamic attitude of attentive appraisal in all aspects of life. In the end the everyday life is Zen.

It must be understood that a brief experience of 'enlightenment' does not remove all traces of suffering from our lives. Various difficulties remain and need continuing attention. Yet the determined treading of the Buddha's way leads to new realisations about oneself and the Universe in which we dwell and to new experiments in being. It is not the case that we have to create an extraordinary mind; rather we have to drop illusions that maintain unrealisable desire and in that letting-go we find out what an everyday mind free from such illusion can become. There is a task of clarification here and, as we progress, we may find we wish to help others on their way. The essential feature of Ch'an/Zen is enquiry.

Local groups usually form around those enthusiastic enough to offer time and space to set up sitting sessions. Soon a leader will be asked to offer instruction in sitting meditation and perhaps some teaching on Buddhism. It is important that he/she should be able to respond with some authoritative teaching that will be helpful rather than inventing some plausible story out of their own limited experience. Within the Western Ch'an Fellowship a number of local groups are now developing centred on the longer retreats at the Maenllwyd. It is essential that these local groups cover the same or similar ground in providing practice and training.

Likewise, the offering of Western Zen Retreats (WZRs) and Ch'an Retreats requires facilitation by someone who knows what he/she is doing. In both these forms of practice participants may come across memories or states of mind that are vexatious or distressing. This is inevitable when a key motif in such retreats is a confrontational examination of self. Help may be needed and the facilitator who leads such groups needs experience to handle these occasions. At present only one qualified teacher leads such events within the WCF. To allow the fellowship to develop, training of new leaders in all these ways of exploration is becoming important. This article begins the examination of what is needed for the facilitation of local groups by Meditation Instructors acting as group leaders. Part 2 (not provided here) will discuss training for retreat facilitation .

Local groups

Someone offers time and place for others to gather together and 'sit'. Initially that may be all and a group of friends may be quite happy with their own practice. One day a newcomer arrives and says he or she wants to learn. The initiator now has the responsibility of explaining to the beginner how to start. The WCF needs to have a policy that ensures that the guidance offered in such circumstances is reliable, conforms to a lineage and is not merely idiosyncratic. We are suggesting, therefore, that local leaders should attend a number of events exploring this question, during which they will learn how to meet the demands that may be made upon them. In particular they will need to know how to present what they know effectively and how to resist speculating about aspects of the path they may not have experienced or only read about. When a leader has shown suitable understanding, he or she may receive authorisation to teach meditation within the WCF. The following paragraphs list issues that need to be addressed in any syllabus for such training.

1 Find out where the questioner is coming from

Let us suppose that Mary appears at a session for the first time. Why has she come? How has she heard about the group? What does she want? What does she know already about Zen? Has she attended such a group or a retreat before? All these questions need to be explored in an introductory 'interview' which is best conducted privately in an atmosphere of confidentiality. The very asking of such questions requires that the leader show him/herself to be an open, friendly person who is quite happy if Mary remains reticent and does not wish to be very forthcoming about herself. After all she may, quite reasonably, only wish to dip her toe into Zen at the moment. The merely curious should be encouraged to sit and find out through experience what the group is 'on about'. Those who have come out of some painful experience may need time to disclose their pain. Time must be allowed. People should never be pushed into disclosure nor should exaggerated enthusiasm for Zen allow a leader to suggest that phenomenal results may be obtained by sitting. That may by no means be so. Cautious and kindly sharing is the best way to allow Mary to disclose, in her own way, whatever it is she wishes to explore.

2 The enquiring mind

Mary may not know why she is there. Whether she does or not, the first step must be the cultivation of mindfulness. Mindfulness is simply knowing where you are, what you are on about, what you want, need or fear. Later on it concerns the states the mind may be experiencing and recognising what these may be. A practitioner, whether experienced or a beginner, needs to know what she is doing at the very moment of asking herself the question. Pretences, avoidances, self-delusions need to be recognised and, whether the experience is pleasant or unpleasant, it is essential to say "This is what is going on now: this is my experience now." Whatever that experience may be has to be accepted as what it is. If she rejects her experience then she must learn to say "Right now I am rejecting my experience, that is my experience now." From such a place one can begin.

Mary needs to understand this before she begins to sit. Sitting is above all a form of enquiry. It is never a descent into a sort of trance - if that is what is happening the practice is incorrect. From the first the beginner needs to understand this point and the leader must represent it to her.

3 Calming the mind

The essence of sitting is to begin at the right place. If the mind is agitated, preoccupied with an issue, or grinding an axe in some form of self promotion, then the first thing is to challenge that very preoccupation. This is done by calming the mind, for which the time-honoured methods of samatha are useful. For beginners, many sessions will be taken up in establishing a relatively calmed mind. In weekly groups most people will be coming in from busy days and cannot expect to do much more than that in two half-hour sessions. None the less this is valuable. This process needs to be presented with accuracy and care.

4 Investigation

The group leader will have some knowledge of tsan (investigation) from retreat experience. It arises when a calmed mind gazes directly into its own condition. Shi fu's discussion of this in connection with Silent Illumination is important here (NCF 15). Some beginners may be able to begin this inner research and the leader needs to know how to advise them and how to use a koan-like question to assist in understanding. The leader needs to know when it would be advisable for the sitter to attend a longer retreat with an accredited teacher.

5 The use of ritual

The leader should provide simple texts for use in a short ritual with the stated function of motivating the practice and inspiring the endeavour. Ritual helps to provide the sense of a sacred space and time in which a particular activity is being undertaken. Respect for the sacred space in which the sitting session is being carried out needs to be expressed in bowing or prostration as taught appropriately.

Although Ch'an practice itself is relatively culture-free and we are engaged in establishing it in contemporary Britain, the attitudes to be cultivated had their origin in Indo-Tibetan and Sino-Japanese environments and this should be acknowledged and understood. Ritual establishes some contact with the historical and cultural context of Ch'an /Zen. The leader needs to make clear, however, that such ritual is to facilitate the practice and to create the thought as to how it may be maintained in everyday life. Ritual is a means, not the expression of some end.

6 The leadership of local groups

The task of a local group leader is to:

- Provide a relaxed setting for learning and practising Ch'an meditation, ensuring that the facilities are appropriate. Avoid overcrowding and accept that a very small group of two or three people is quite acceptable.

- Welcome participants in a friendly, open manner and attend to their needs during the event. Remember that newcomers may be shy, unsure of themselves and probably full of misunderstandings.
- Indicate the appropriate attitude to adopt, namely a light but serious mindfulness, awareness of others and a silencing of the over-active chatty mind. There should be respect for the place, the occasion and the needs of others for inwardness. The atmosphere should be cheerfully contemplative.
- Provide instruction in sitting (zazen) for those who request it, while allowing those who already sit to 'do their own thing'. An enquiry as to the acceptability of an individual's practice within a Ch'an event is none-the-less important and everyone should disclose what they are doing on the cushion. For example, petitionary prayer is not a Ch'an activity.
- Always remember to offer the Dharma. Do not act as a salesman advocating Ch'an in a persuasive manner. The offering should be low key, allowing practitioners to come forward for instruction or discussion in their own time.
- Do not get disappointed if people come and go.
- Do not talk about aspects of the Dharma or meditative practice that you do not understand, nor discuss states of mind you have not realised or had confirmed.
- Do not encourage or allow gossip about spiritual matters, institutions or gurus. Insist that the evening is intended for practice with a short period of teaching, reading, or discussion.
- Always remember that you are representing the Western Ch'an Fellowship and the lineage of that fellowship. This means you should never mix your evening with other activities however competent you may be in them. Leaders may well be skilled in areas such as Counselling, Psychotherapy, Tai-chi or Yoga and these are fine things to do elsewhere. Do not mix these activities with Ch'an, in some way grinding your own axe and creating some bastard activity of your own invention. If you do this, your certificate as a WCF Meditation Instructor will be withdrawn.
- Keep in touch with the WCF teacher and ask for consultation whenever in doubt about your training, your presentation of Dharma or the problems of your group participants. Attend retreats offered by the WCF to sustain your own training

- Remember that, as a leader in a spiritual endeavour, you may attract some dependent characters who may wish to rely excessively upon you and who will attribute charisma to you until perhaps you need to confront them. Such a person can then turn quite nasty, falling back into their own paranoia. Be very careful not to allow dependencies to develop; while being empathetic and kind, hand back the problems of others for them to solve. Do not let other people's problems become yours.
- Avoid establishing a relationship, especially a sexual one, with a group member. This will compromise your role as a group leader.
- Be aware of counter-transference in situations where you may be consulted by a participant about emotional problems. You should know when these should be referred to an appropriately trained counsellor or therapist. Maintain an attitude of humility towards your own abilities.
- Unless you are yourself trained in dokusan (ie Zen interviews) as a counsellor or as a psychotherapist, do not provide individual interviews. Group discussion, allowing the group to frame its own interests and conclusions, is usually helpful and you should provide facilitation and guidance where Dharma understanding is weak. Avoid argumentative intellectual debates which create competitiveness within a group.

7 Teaching meditation

When you start a group make sure everyone is appropriately motivated, respectful of the occasion and of the 'sacred space' and knows how to 'sit'.Provide the texts for a simple liturgy and encourage others beside yourself to bring short readings to share and discuss. You must know how to provide instruction concerning : i) The posture and the permissable variants. ii) How to focus the attention and hold awareness steady. iii) The deviations from effective meditation through fatigue, drowsiness, sinking of energy and wandering thoughts. iv) Use of breathing and exercise to reduce sleepiness and sinking. v) Watching the breath, counting the breath etc as a means for reducing wandering thoughts. vi) Kinhin practice and exercises for use before or between sits. vii) Take care not to be drawn into intellectual discussions where your understanding may be defective or misleading. In discussion, keep the focus on practice, emphasising discovery through experience rather than through reading.viii) Emphasise the key point in Western Ch'an teaching - that it is the expression of Ch'an in everyday attitudes that is crucial and, in the end, more important than 'correct' sitting. When Ch'an is well-expressed off the cushion and without dependency on either group or individual retreats then a practitioner is certainly getting somewhere. Furthermore he/she will then be providing unspoken teaching for others.

8 The Event

You may construct your event according to your own genius and insight concerning your particular group. It is better to stay simple than to become too complex with respect to ritual, teaching or meditation instructions. The Bristol Ch'an Group evenings usually begin with a short ritual (copies available and based on Maenllwyd practice) partly in English but including some Chinese chanting. There are then two half-hour sits with kinhin between. After a short closing ritual the leader will present either a short talk (if qualified to do so) or give a reading from a well-known author or from the sutras or Ch'an scriptures. This may be followed by discussion, which the leader should guide without being dogmatically assertive. People have to find their own way to the central ideas of Buddhism and this usually only occurs effectively when based on a developing meditative experience. Variants on this theme can be constructed to provide a custom-built approach suited to the participants who join you. When your group is well-established, has accumulated some effective practice and has reached around a dozen members you may want to provide occasional weekend or residential retreats. Initially these can follow the pattern already established. Retreats will however make greater demands on your own understanding and the WCF will expect you to attend further training sessions in the setting up and running of retreats. Discussion documents on this will be prepared as Part 2 of this paper.

DANGERS IN DEVOTION: BUDDHIST CULTS AND THE TASKS OF A GURU[1]

Western Buddhism: problems and presentations

In recent years a number of cases of individual corruption in sexual and financial matters have been exposed in Buddhist organisations, usually the result of the behaviour or indiscretions of individuals in leadership roles[2]. Ken Jones' recent discussion[3] has raised further important issues concerning the development in Britain of large Buddhist organisations that appeared to him to resemble cults more than they did a traditional Buddhist Sangha.

Two substantial articles have appeared in the national press[4] suggesting that Ken had every reason to be alarmed. The articles present a view of institutional Buddhism in Britain (the New Kadhampa Trust and the Friends of the Western

Buddhist Order) from the critical, debunking perspective characteristic of contemporary journalism. We live in a post-modern world of ethical relativity in which any creed or custom is easily interpreted in terms of ego defensive and self-serving motivations. Cynicism abounds as the ethics of religious forms are called into question in numerous ways. While the press functions in justifying the scepticism of non-believers in the mediocrity of contemporary religion, it none the less also calls attention to the very real problems faced by those inspired by forms of spirituality that still seem relevant to our time. Then, early this summer, a large, carefully printed pamphlet, anonymously authored, hit my desk. The 'FWBO Files' is a point by point, blow by blow, examination of the problems the Friends of the Western Buddhist Order presents to its colleagues in Buddhism. If it is to be taken on trust, there is clearly a very great deal amiss and it is right that these matters should be widely examined. If misrepresentation of the Buddhist tradition is actually occurring it needs to be exposed.

The Files make five main charges alleging:

- that the FWBO founder, Sangharakshita, lacked adequate training in the Dharma in India where his sexual activities came close to causing scandal;
- that Sangharakshita put together an idiosyncratic version of Buddhism which has become the central doctrine of the FWBO;
- that sexual experimentation within the order led to abuse of power and personal distress of heterosexual young men persuaded into a homosexual life style;
- that a misogynist and anti-Christian viewpoint dominates the teachings;
- that financial irregularity contributed to the FWBO's success.

The FWBO Files and the FWBO Response[5]

Reading the 'FWBO Files' is as distressing an experience as is the reading of the 'Response' in its defence put together by leading FWBO members. The tone of the two documents is very different. The Files presents a case for the 'prosecution' in a forthright style lacking in compassion but impassioned by a desire to put the record straight. The persistent anonymity of its author weakens his/her case but also raises suspicions about the possible coercion he/she appears to fear. The Response is surprisingly reticent, concedes that all has not been well in the organisation but insists that at heart the FWBO remains a substantial contribution to the spreading of the Buddha Dharma in the West and that its various experiments in social living are justified. It does not seek to whitewash the behaviour of its charismatic leader Sangharakshita, but rather to contextualise it with understanding. Sangharakshita himself continues to say nothing nor has he given any opinion on a dispute that centres upon his personality.

The assertiveness that some see as characteristic of the FWBO comes over strongly in the Response. The compilers argue "... some readers may feel that the mere fact of controversy lends credence to the accusers: 'there's no smoke without fire!' We would ask readers to pause before making this essentially lazy assumption and carefully consider what issues of substance actually remain..." And in Appendix 3 it is argued that the FWBO is the victim of a smear campaign rather than an organisation which has plausibly brought its troubles on itself. Given the strength of the prosecutors' case (and independent evidence from other sources[6]) few will doubt that the smoke has a genuine origin in fire. Yet the significance of the conflagration does remain in question.

A careful reading of the two documents leads me to a surprising conclusion. It is not a question of one being true and the other false. Both statements actually support one another in a variety of ways and on a variety of matters. Of course they draw different conclusions from their contrasting presentations and the Response succeeds in showing through textual quotes that Sangharakshita has in places been misinterpreted. Even so the documents often point to a common issue. I am concerned here with the questions concerning the representation of the Dharma and the problem of personal ethics shown by teachers. On the other issues readers of these documents must make up their own minds.

The pivot on which both presentations revolve is the person of Sangharakshita himself. As a charismatic leader his influence is all-pervading and appears to determine the argument wherever one arises. Who Sangharakshita was and what he has become are thus critical matters, as is the issue of his position in the institution both in the past and at the present time.

It is clear that his behaviour in India was not that of a normal Theravadan monk. Seeking to find the common roots of the Buddhist tradition he explored Theravadan, Mahayanist and Vajrayana approaches and sought to discover the quintessence of Buddhism. His restless exploratory mind thus showed a marked individualism and a failure to adopt the social identity of a conforming and practising monk. He remained an individualistic robe-wearing Westerner sincerely on a personal quest. Inevitably, given the vast scope of the Dharma, the diversity of its range of philosophical insights and practices, he necessarily picked and chose until he was personally satisfied. It remains a matter of debate as to whether he found a core to the diverse forms of Buddhism and particularly one which could be the foundation for a new order or for a Western Buddhism as such.

In fairness to Sangharakshita it must be said that such a quest is quite usual among Westerners attracted by Buddhism, and Sangharakshita's writings certainly show an impressive depth of scholarship. After World War II Christmas Humphreys had travelled widely looking for points in common between various traditions. Stephen Batchelor has investigated parallels between existentialist Western philosophy and Buddhism[7] and many writers, including this one, have explored parallels between Buddhist practice, psychotherapy and Western psychology[8]. There is, however, a distinction to be made between these personal and intellectual explorations and an ideological closure around a viewpoint subsequently made basic to the doctrines of an institution claiming to offer Buddhism to the West[9].

Sangharakshita's moral behaviour during his time in India remains debatable but it seems unlikely that any conclusive evidence concerning his private affairs will emerge. It is clear, however, that from the time of his return to England he was a controversial figure generating both powerful support and opposition. These controversies did not only concern his views on the Dharma and the nature of Buddhism in the 'hippy period' but extended to his life style. It is acknowledged that he experimented with sexuality in ways unacceptable from a professed monk but characteristic of the 'permissiveness' of the time. What does remain strange is that he continued to wear robes, hold a title and appear frequently in the guise of a monk even though his behaviour was typical of a young Western lay person of the period.

Sangharakshita's powerful and persuasive character led him into the role of leadership and once he had become the guru of the FWBO his views and attitudes necessarily began to colour those of his followers. I accept the Response's defence that his homosexual orientation probably never had the deliberate and coercive motivation imputed in the Files but it would be natural that his inclinations would influence those near to him. If his intentions had been more self-reflective and critical it is doubtful whether his sexual affairs would have generated so much distress.

On this matter the Files uses a highly personal approach documenting individual experiences in close relationships with Sangharakshita. The Response tends to side-step such personal accounts but admits that "there have been instances in the FWBO when relationships of kalyana mitrata have included a sexual element ... these instances have involved homosexuality. Some people will consider there is no place for this, and may even regard it as inherently abusive." The discussion then becomes general, outlining the common experience of Westerners during this period remarking that "the best safeguard against people being hurt through their sexual activity is maturity, awareness and the cultivation of keen ethical sensitivity."

While this may well be what "the FWBO seeks to encourage," the Files suggest such qualities were singularly lacking in Sangharakshita himself.

The problem here is that it becomes impossible to separate the FWBO from the personality of Sangharakshita. Individualist, scholar, homosexual, idealist, charismatic leader, authoritarian, prickly and often strongly liked or disliked, Sangharakshita emerges as an important figure in Western Buddhism. Such an influential person placed in charge of an institution inevitably affects his followers, especially those close to him in temperament and viewpoint. The result is the gradual formation of an institutional climate expressing not necessarily merely the informed, indeed scholarly, views of the leader but, more diffusely, his personality. If lacking in a necessary humility, the shadow side of such a leader may become expressed institutionally with little awareness of the process among devoted followers. Every human being has a 'shadow' and we are usually unconscious of its underground activity. It requires exceptional awareness to gain understanding of the transference and counter-transference that soon comes into play among mutually dependent persons seeking to create an institutional perspective under the eye of a powerful leader. In this area the FWBO continues to show a blindness reflected in the way both the documents under consideration focus almost exclusively on the person of the leader rather than on the institution and its organisation. It is this that leads many of us to see the FWBO more as a cult than as a Buddhist institution or school in accordance with tradition.

Cultic Buddhism : a brief analysis

In his book 'Religion in the Modern world: from Cathedral to Cults' Steve Bruce[10] argues that contemporary religion has moved away from monasteries, churches, denominations, to a predominance of cults, usually of the type designated as 'New Age'. Bruce is concerned primarily with Christian history but his analysis is useful here. He argues that the fragmentation of modern societies and the relativity of all ethical systems since the post-modern turn makes the institution of a widely relevant and meaningful "church" untenable. Cult, according to Bruce, is a "small loosely-knit group organised around some common themes and interests but lacking a sharply defined and exclusive belief system. Each individual member is the final authority as to what constitutes the truth or the path to salvation." A cult "hardly has members, instead it has consumers who pick and choose those bits of the product that suits them." Most cults focus on some 'mystical' practice that seems to be the way to salvation. It is togetherness in a self-serving practice that forms the core. Bruce does not however discuss a further dimension of the 'cult' - that is, its leadership. When the 'mystical' activity is prescribed by an individual of persuasive mien he or she quickly becomes the exemplar to whom charisma is attributed by seekers who rapidly develop dependencies, since to loose the affiliation with the leader would be to abandon a project in which self-identity has become deeply involved. Cults with such leadership soon create formulae for attitudes, behaviours, rituals and relationships inevitably reflecting the character of the 'guru'. And as a number of examples have shown this can lead to extraordinary collective action including millennial group suicide. Buddhism in the West has gone through parallel phases. An intellectual interest in Buddhism among non-Christians seeking a spiritual Humanism led to loose groupings of independent individuals exploring Buddhist ideas. As Eastern teachers, particularly Zen masters and Tibetan lamas, appeared or were invited into this scene a gradual growth in the traditional 'Buddhist churches' took place and today every city has its Zen or Tibetan temple and small groups of practitioners. But not all such teachers remain true to the strict discipline of the Eastern institutions to which they belonged.

In Britain the Tibetan lama Geshe Keltsang Gyatso broke away from the tradition of the Gelugpa Order to found the New Kadampa Trust of which he is the presiding authority and teacher. The purpose was to find a digest of the Tibetan Dharma best suited to Western consumption. Like Sangharakshita, the Geshe is a fine scholar and his publications continue to pour forth from an enthusiastic editorial team. He is alleged to allow his followers to consider him to be a Buddha and has authorised active disputes with the Dalai Lama over the nature of a protective "deity", the ethics of which are questionable. The cult surrounding him has cut itself off from the parent tradition and has become a free-floating institution dominated by his personal influence.

The FWBO has, on a similar pretext, created an institution which was at first very attractive to free-floating quasi-Buddhists and which has proven to be creative in spawning businesses and charitable enterprises of several kinds, many of which are beneficial. Its increasing authoritarianism and social biases which eventually led to the problems detailed in the Files may be attributed to the dominance of one individual. It therefore also has the form of a 'cult' independent from other forms of traditional Buddhism.

These Buddhist cults resemble the guru-based institutions of Hinduism more than they do their Buddhist origins. In Hinduism, gifted and charismatic gurus become the focus of a personal cult of devotional practice and at any one time there are many of these for potential devotees to choose from. The loose framework of Hindu belief and practice allows a high level of personal choice in such matters but not all gurus are free from the many forms of ethical corruption. How do such 'cults' arise? The psychology of such processes has become clear in recent years. Individual identity requires the formation of key values for which social approval is given and without which an individual experiences painful alienation. Traditionally these were given by the society in which a person lived, and we had monolithic religions dominating large areas of the world.Since in contemporary society the philosophical basis for values has become culturally relative and science has for many removed the belief in supernatural forces, individuals are forced to choose between a range of equally valid interpretations of the cosmos and of the way to personal salvation. Once a 'way' is chosen it becomes an area of profound psychological investment so that anything that threatens it also threatens the self. On accepting an institutionalised value system personal identity is largely replaced by social identity - that is the individual identifies with the social norms of the group. Value systems are based in what Muscovici[11] has called social representations. These are ideas and attitudes that are seen to represent the "real" and which are believed to be the truth. Social identity is rooted in the adoption of representations of "truth" and anything that threatens their credibility thus comes also to threaten the person. When the fount of wisdom is a particular individual, an unthinking devotion may develop which in worst-case scenarios leads to the establishment of an accepted tyranny. When an individual finally rumbles what is happening and attempts to break away into independence and an acceptance of his or her existential aloneness the reaction of other believers is apt to be intense. The question must therefore be asked whether cults of this kind and with this psychological causation are compatible with traditional Buddhist understanding in which freedom from suffering remains the goal. This question is vital not only in relation to the institutions which we have been discussing but for all attempts to form an organisation in which 'enlightenment ' is sought and within which teachers and their shadows operate.

Open Buddhism in the context of Practice

On his deathbed the Buddha told his followers to use the Dharma as a guide not the teacher. His profound advice throws the individual back into himself and his questioning appraisal of what Dharma can be. It does not lie in the views of a teacher, however helpful these can be and however fine an exemplar he or she is, but in the heart where the meaning of selfhood resides. The path to such understanding is essentially a lone quest, just as it was for the Buddha. Guidance lies in the teachings not in a teacher. Essentially the Four Noble Truths, the principles of impermanence, emptiness and the law of interdependent causation lie at the heart of the matter and require experiential realisation not mere intellectual assent. While vehicles for the transmission of the Dharma are essential, realisation is essentially an individual matter in which clinging to identity and all forms of representation is abandoned.

What then is the role of the teacher? The vehicles (Theravada, Mahayana, Zen etc.) are perspectives on the Dharma with the power to induce realisation. The teacher is a facilitator of this individual process. Any attempt to be an authority on the scriptures, a paragon of virtue, or a defender of a faith misses the point. A great lama or a solitary yogin consulted in some remote cave only have Buddhist validity if they facilitate the insight of others. There are many skilful means, as the Lotus Sutra makes clear. There is no absolute truth which has to be believed. All views disappear in absurdity. Attachment to any representation is thus an error. Krishnamurti was right in arguing that any institutionalisation of religion becomes divisive and yet a vehicle for the Dharma needs a structure.

All schools of Buddhism hinge upon and return to the understanding of emptiness. This insight is conveyed in a variety of ways and nothing can be picked or chosen as more relevant than anything else. That which is relevant is that which works. As Wittgenstein advised - look for the use and not the meaning. If a device or an idea works that is enough, for there is no ultimately discoverable meaning. This means that when a great Zen master and a fine lama meet there are no barriers between them. Although one may be riding a horse and the other a camel they both survey the same view. If this is not the case, understanding of the Dharma has at some point been lost.

The implication of this is that the Buddha Dharma must be 'open'. Even though individuals may subscribe to contrasting traditions of practice and viewpoint if there is openness to the underlying empty vision then understanding can arise. We need therefore to cultivate a tradition of 'open Buddhism' and only if we manage to do so will the Buddha Dharma find a place in the West free from cultic factionalism and argument.

It follows that all would-be teachers must understand what being a facilitator rather than an authority means. Essentially a Buddhist teacher is what in Christian terms is called a "spiritual director". It may therefore be valuable to consider the 'Code of Ethics for Spiritual Directors' compiled by the staff of the Center for Sacred Psychology in California[12]. They are concerned about what code of practise should determine the qualification for a person with this title. Although Christian in focus this document can help us formulate a Buddhist perspective on the same problem. This is not a matter of dictating how teachers should be but rather of defining their commitment to society in a way that people can understand and respect without fear of abuse. The following paragraphs are thus tentative suggestions concerning the attitude to be adopted by anyone attempting to be a Buddhist teacher in the West.

i) The essential relationship is a unique one-to-one, face-to-face confrontation or meeting between two people. One is acting as a facilitator while the other is seeking spiritual insight based in his or her own resources. This definition covers Zen interviews and consultations between lamas or monks and those seeking their guidance. A teacher may also provide instruction on meditation techniques and Buddhist philosophical psychology to groups but his or her essential function remains in a personal ministry in the context of the selfhood of another. The activities of meditation instruction and Dharma teaching are distinct from those of spiritual ministry but it is in the latter that the critical function of the teacher resides.ii) A Buddhist teacher has felt a 'call' to such activity through personal experience in the Dharma. The call needs to be authenticated through experiencing transmission from a 'master' or 'lama' in which the latter affirms the experience and understanding of the teacher and expresses faith in his/her ability to facilitate others.iii) Teachers need at all times to examine their own lives and personal relationships. Everyone has a shadow side and experiences psychological difficulties arising from their karma. These need to be seen, understood and accepted to whatever degree is possible. Help in this task from a practitioner of a Western psychotherapeutic process or counselling is a normal requirement for a teacher and should be entered into willingly. Western insights into the self process are now profound and Eastern practices do not replace this. Of course interaction with a traditional Buddhist teacher (as ii) is likewise essential. iv) In an interview the teacher is first and foremost a skilled listener who can experience others as themselves and not through his/her own interpretation due to theoretical or personal bias. It is the other engaged in his/her own exploration that is the focus. The teacher may be able to draw on his/her own experiences in discussion but must be aware of allowing these to intrude on the otherness of the other. v) Essentially the interviewee discovers his/her own solution in solitude and walks his own path. The teacher can, however, draw attention to the pitfalls, ego indulgence, failures to confront the self etc. that will be inherent in the interviewee's presentation. This requires skilful means in relation to the other's receptivity The relationship involves an implicit power imbalance in which one is a teacher or facilitator and the other to some extent a recipient. This imbalance creates numerous interpersonal consequences concerning which the teacher should be watchful and aware.vi) Even an experienced teacher should seek occasional supervision in which problems in his/her work can be discussed with an advisor. vii) Confidentiality in the relationship is essential and must be preserved. Furthermore the teacher should be aware of the phenomena of transference and counter-transference which inevitably occur in this work. In particular no sexual interaction should take place and if such seems to be consensually appropriate the relationship of teacher/ taught should be abandoned and the implicit power imbalance removed. viii) Teachers should be aware of other techniques useful in this art but take care not to turn the session into psychotherapy. The latter is essentially a means for adjusting the self to existing conditions of life and to better functioning in the social world. Buddhist spiritual counselling challenges the very nature of the self process as illusion and seeks to go beyond self concerns. It is transcendental work.ix) Teachers need to know when an interviewee requires help from other services and to feel free to recommend such help.x) Teachers and recipients should evaluate their relationship periodically, change it or terminate it as seems appropriate. Choice of a guru is mutual. The teacher has the option of accepting or rejecting those who wish to receive interview. Likewise the recipient needs to feel free in evaluating the teacher and in expressing his thoughts and feelings in this area. These ten points have much in common with codes of conduct used by therapists. This is appropriate since, although the goals differ, the therapist and the spiritual counsellor are both facilitators and facilitation of another's process in each perspective has many features in common.

Democracy in Buddhist institutions

There remains one final point. The problems of many Buddhist organisations have rested on the unlimited authority of the guru. This has often extended to matters of belief, practice, financial control and property. It is hardly surprising that mistakes have been made which have usually been as much a result of devotees' lack of responsibility as it is due to the leader's failure in self control and insight.

Cults can be profitably undone by democracy. All that is needed is proper attention to the creation of an institutional structure in which the power relations between guru and followers is balanced, in which problems and disputes can be raised and discussed and in which the formation of appropriate committees allows decision making processes reflecting the wishes of the membership. Many Buddhist institutions lack proper constitutional organisation and a prime recommendation may be that this issue be immediately addressed.

This task is not simple. The teacher is often the bearer of a lineage of teaching going back many centuries, maybe even to the Buddha himself. The teacher has received some form of transmission from his own guru to pass the way on to others. Those who have not received such transmission are hardly in a position to criticise the essential message. Too much democracy could mean that anybody's version of what the Buddha may or may not have said could gain equal credence with an inevitable regression to an ill-prepared salad[13]. It is rather the manner in which teachers present themselves, their attitude to others, their ethical stance and correctness in relationship and in financial concerns that become the legitimate focus of committees set up to monitor an institution's well-being. It is to this concern that an institutional constitution should be directed[14].

Given the nature of the psychological process active in cults such a change may not be easy. It will often require grassroots action within the institution. Indeed, if these institutions are to survive, this will become essential. Further publication of destructive arguments such as those we have discussed here will be to the detriment of all Buddhist institutions in the West. It is time to set our houses in order.

This paper has been much exercised with the internal affairs of the FWBO. My intention has not been to denigrate this organisation but to explore two of the wider issues to which the disputes within and about the FWBO draw attention. The FWBO has been and remains an important contributor to Buddhism on the world stage. Its social and sexual experiments have proven valuable to many[15]. There will be many Friends who are puzzled by the current uproar, many teachers entirely innocent of the errors that have been described. The position of their leader at the present time remains unclear. The whole matter is to be much regretted, yet the Files have drawn attention to abuses of power and to the serious problems facing any major 'spiritual' organisation today. It is to be hoped that the grassroots membership of all such organisations will from now on insist that social accountability be made a prime focus of attention. We can all then focus without dissension on the central task - the practice of Dharma itself.

Summary

This paper discusses recent controversies concerning the activities and orientation of the Friends of the Western Buddhist Order in the context of the character of institutionalisation in Western Buddhism. The two sides in the controversy show considerable convergence focusing on the role of the teacher and the authority of the teacher.

The nature of cult-like institutions in Buddhism is discussed and the role of teacher examined. It is suggested that teachers should function as spiritual facilitators and not as institutionalised authorities and that an 'open Buddhism' is required if Western Buddhism is to be true to its roots and thrive without bitter controversy. Democratisation of many current Buddhist organisations is seen as an essential prerequisite to change needed at a structural level, yet this is a task that will require careful understanding of the social and personal forces at work before it can be successful.

References

1. Paper presented at the conference ' The Psychology of Awakening II' at Dartington Hall, October 1998.
2. Lachs, S.' A Slice of Zen in America'. New Ch'an Forum 10, Autumn 1994.
3. Jones, K. 'Movements in British Buddhism'. New Ch'an Forum 13, 1996. Also: 'Response to Vishvapani'. New Ch'an Forum 14, 24-25 (1997).
4. The Guardian 6th July 1996 and 27th October 1997. See also a reply by Vishvapani, 8th November 1997.
5. Anonymous. The FWBO Files. Distributed by post. Available on the internet. The FWBO Files: a Response. FWBO Communications Office, 1998.
6. Personal statements made privately in interview by former members of the FWBO on retreat and in unsolicited email correspondence with two Americans detailing their reasons for leaving the Order.
7. Batchelor, S. Alone with Others: an Existential Approach to Buddhism. Grove Press Inc, New York, 1983. and Buddhism without Beliefs: a Contemporary Guide to Awakening. Bloomsbury Press, London, 1997.
8. Crook, J.H. and Fontana, D. Space in Mind: East-West Psychology and Contemporary Buddhism. Element, Warminster, 1990.
9. This is not the place for an extended analysis of Sangharakshita's views. A taste of his approach can be seen in a 48-page justification entitled Extending the Hand of Fellowship: The relationship of the Western Buddhist Order to the rest of the Buddhist world (Windhorse Press), which makes his claims clear.
10. Bruce, S. Religion in the Modern World: from Cathedrals to Cults. Oxford, 1996.
11. Muscovici, S. 'The phenomenon of social representations'. In Farr, R.M. and Muscovici, S. (eds) Social Representations, Cambridge, 1984.
12. Hedberg, T.M. and Caprio, B. A Code of Ethics for Spiritual Directors. Dove Publications, Pecos, New Mexico, (undated). Available from The Center for Sacred Psychology, Box 643, Gateway Station, Culver City, CA 90232, USA.
13. Indeed, this may well prove to be the defect of attempts at "mainstreaming" the Dharma through teaching meditation practices without acknowledgement of their roots in specific Dharma.

14 The Western Ch'an Fellowship has been much concerned with this issue. The constitution on which its charitable status is based is available in New Ch'an Forum 16:11.

15 See for example: 'Dhammadinna. Sexual Evolution'. Dharma Life, Summer 1998. Also published in the FWBO Response as Appendix 1.

Acknowledgements

The preparation of this article has been a painful and self-searching process. I am grateful to those who have aided me with their opinions and reflections. In particular I have benefited from correspondence with Ken Jones, Stephen Batchelor and James Low. Iris Tute introduced me to The Code For Spiritual Directors; and Fellows of the WCF, Simon Child, Ken Robinson and Tim Paine, have responded generously with their perspectives which have not necessarily always been in agreement with mine. Needless to say, I remain wholly responsible for what has been written here.

NCF XIX

MAKING STATUES...

Editorial from the Ch'an Hall

There appear to be two main ways of making statues. The first is to construct a supporting framework and then gradually to apply dollops of clay to its surface, carefully moulding them into the representation of a Bodhisattva or whoever. The flexibility of the approach allows very idealised forms to be presented in great beauty. The problem is that the finished product is fragile, easily cracks and is hollow inside. The second way is to take a log of wood or a block of stone and gently carve away the surface bringing to light a figure expressed from within. The sculptor's skill consists in negotiating with the underlying substance of the material so that the final representation is only in part the work of the artist and largely determined by the subtleties, distortions and inherent patterning within the material itself. What emerges is a disclosure of hidden potential.

There is a parallel here with spiritual training. Some people idealise a theme for its beauty or integrity and build up a frame of rules, prohibitions, injunctions and ritual practices upon which they shape a perfect image. The image may be beautiful and sustained for as long as the structure holds together but a sudden shock or blow may crack the perfect face or disclose an emptiness within. Followers of external rules who have not investigated their true nature for themselves are copyists, fundamentally followers of outer paths even if Buddhist ones. There is a shallowness of Dharma understanding here that can lead to upset and the appearance of the very opposite of an ideal image.

Others learn the hard way and realise that the image they seek is hidden within their own nature. No amount of application of external rules will bring this forth without a carving away of the surface of self. In reaching deeply within the hua t'ou, the Who? question, the true understanding of suffering gradually takes shape. Yet this shape retains the underlying patterns of karma, for these in truth are the very veins and sinews of the material to be worked. The result is thus inevitably idiosyncratic, not a perfect idealised figure but an often rough-hewn realisation from within, the forms of which retain beautiful distortions. The work has included a deep understanding, recognition and shaping. Knowing the shortcomings of his or her own material such a person is well equipped to help others on their own paths. Here there is no inner emptiness but a rock-like root.

When Jeff Love was teaching me how to lead groups using koans in the Communication Exercise, he once remarked to me that the most difficult participants were people claiming to be Buddhists! I wondered why this might be so. "Well," said Jeff, "their problem is that they think they know who they are... as a result of reading what the Sutras say or what some Dharma teacher has taught. They have never even begun to investigate themselves!"

Over the years I have appreciated increasingly Jeff's remark. Those who come on retreat from a confrontation with their own suffering or alienation investigate "Who am I?" with a searching honesty that is moving to encounter. Those who have adopted some Dharma ideology have terrible problems. One-time monks, for example, have been told what they ought to find but the external teachings always lead them astray. Having never recognised a Master, they have immense difficulty in examining their shortcomings and talk only of idealised experiences. At the Maenllwyd, officiously thinking they must know the answers - even though long disrobed, such a person may fail to look within. The question is either avoided or there are never-ending confusions. Nowadays, when I hear someone has been a monk, I feel pretty sure there will be problems. Sometimes such a person comes to reject the question and its relevance altogether and to resent my having faced them with it.

A true monk, long dedicated to exploring the path, has the advantage of being able to use both methods. The long-term training in rule-bound ritual eventually scrapes the surface clean and the true self begins to emerge. Monks and lay persons face the same task, only the context differs. Monks should not think they have any special knowledge but neither should lay people pity the monks' enclosed state. Each person's koan reflects their own karma. There is nothing to be proud about and nothing special to regret. There is the work to be done.

FLICKERING LAMP HOTEL

(To Carol)

Drifting clouds and in the purple light
white sheep stand emboldened 'gainst the green;
a flock of birds falls from the sky
hitting a tree in a murmuration,
the starlings are here again
alltogether fizzing and whizzing on the field;
ravens nonchalantly glide past
casting an eye on the farm;
a magpie lands on the back of a sheep.
Up there wet buzzards wheel
and somewhere in the ivy clad oak
last night's owl slumbers.

Beyond the high moors and the pine plantations
up a long gorge beside a lengthening lake
forgotten in the hills
the Flickering Lamp Hotel hides in the woods,
ivy clad oaks and dripping birches,
moss covered boulders, rushing streams, hart's tongued ferns.
The building, ordinary, nothing special,
front door ajar where the undimmed lamp
shows the way in
from the sound of water over the high dam
the silence of the unmoving lake
and the far off hawk's cries.

Power places in Wales are mostly small
hidden in woods, secret valleys, up rocky paths,
through bogs and streams, not easily found in the mountains.
Cwm-y-saeson, heather drenched in blood

Old Meg's grave high on Plynlimon's side
Taliesen's rock overlooking the ocean,
Ffynon garreg and Llangasty lake.
Find them
if you can !
Far from the weekending Brummy voices and damp
chapels of a sunny afternoon
holy wells in hiding from the world

drip yet with passion, blood, the veiled
bright-eyed cunning of the Welsh
and the roaring music stronger than the wind.

WELSH MANDALA

Akshobya

Dark light before dawn
no wind and in the silence
a fox barking on the hill;
suddenly in the candle lit room
the cold landscape unfurls
invisible rocks, burrows of badgers
trolling the turf for bulbs and insects
the starlit dome, dusk before dawn
Blue immensity.

Ratnasambhava

Sunrise, far to the SSE
almost at the point of turning
a midwinter sky lined by the tracery of trees,
northern thrushes search the drab field
four, five steps in a run, stop,
look-about and on again
occasionally the unwary worm
sun blinking sky bell chanting
in the cold season.

Old lady in the village shop
hairstyle not seen in a hundred years
dropping in for her 'weekly'
emerges from the hills, her man
the shepherd, dour, grey as the rocks,
immovable, sunray hidden in his heart
drove the landrover, mud covered,
sheep shit and collie in the back.
"G'morning" I say
"G'morning to you"- they turn smiling
extraordinary innocence
in their eyes.

Amitabha

Cars, lorries, sheep liners moving up and down the road
stopping at pubs for a cheery one
where the coals glow, damp logs fizz
mid-daying the sun laced light
on the grey-grass hills
dark firs sentinel beside the farms
cheerful sheep eyeing the black foraging birds
red god firing a thousand hearths.

Today, Mrs Sims, the Post Office lady
bustles around in the rain to open the door. "Horrible weather!" she says,
"Starting a cold too -"
Two letters for Poland - I tell her
"Poland is it then?" she eyes them doubtfully
"Where's that then? Europe is it?"
"Not quite - a bit beyond - but will be someday!"
"Ah - yes!" she finds it in the book,
triumphantly "43 pee then it is twice over."

Amoghasiddhi

Already in the early afternoon
light fades grizzling the land no shadows now,
A giant owl perches on a fencepost - no
just a fencepost really,
presences swarm in the groves
the crannies of the hills,
the old Welsh spooks,
the powers reaching the not-quite fearful heart
greening in the dark light
fading, yellow flames
in the village houses far below.

December 1998

BOOK REVIEW: LANGUAGE AND FREEDOM: MEANING IN ZEN

Dale S. Wright, Philosophical Meditations on Zen Buddhism. Cambridge Studies in Religious Traditions 13. Cambridge University Press (1998), 227 pages.

What is the place of Zen in contemporary thought, the relation of Buddhist metaphysics to philosophy and the value of ancient texts to thinking people today? These and related questions form the subject matter of this intelligent, subtle and provoking book. Dale S. Wright, Professor of Religious Studies, Occidental College, Los Angeles, provides a thought provoking read especially for those of us concerned with problems of representing Buddhism, and Zen in particular, within Western culture today.

Modern and post-modern perspectives

The starting point of Wright's argument asserts that there is a profound difference between the worlds of post-modern and modern thought. This requires texts written by Western interpreters of Buddhism prior to the 'post-modern turn' to be themselves re-interpreted in the light of current thinking. Without such a process the meaning of Buddhism in the contemporary context remains unclear and inclined to irrelevance. Wright chooses the work of John Blofield, in particular his translation of the Transmission of Mind by the great ninth century Chinese Master Huang-po (Huang-po Ch'uan Hsin Fa Yao), as exemplary within modern scholarship and provides a contemporary reinterpretation not only of Blofield but also of Huang-po himself.

John Blofield was a bold, spiritual adventurer who, after leaving Cambridge, went out to China in the 1930s and immersed himself in Ch'an culture and practice. Although deep insight appears to have eluded him, he became richly familiar with the Ch'an outlook and its textual documentation. Later in life he studied Tibetan Buddhism and lived in Bangkok. His translations from the Chinese are outstanding and popular while his autobiography makes fascinating reading. Blofield, Wright tells us, was a romantic very much in the style of the thirties. His approach to Zen was undoubtedly influenced by its earlier representation in the West by D. T. Suzuki whose 'spin' on the subject fitted the inclinations of the time. This viewpoint implied that 'oriental' perspectives, the mysterious East, could offer immediate access to a spiritual understanding that underlay all religions. This universal basis of spirituality was seen as culture-free and fundamental, a 'perennial philosophy' as Aldous Huxley was to call it. With its emphasis on direct experience beyond words and scriptures, Zen was interpreted as a major route to this experiencing of the real, the various terms for which usually began with a capital letter. Literature of this sort soon became challenged by 'scientific' historical analyses of texts in their socio-historical contexts which, as with Biblical criticism, adopted a sceptical, rationalist tone by- passing much of the inherent psychological insight of these writings. Such opposition still continues today when rational scholarship confronts the now often severely 'dumbed down' idealisms of New Age romantics.

Contemporary thought reveals that this romantic-scientific opposition was itself an expression of 'modernity', a schizoid world-view, which can now itself be examined in the context of the culture giving rise to it. This fresh, 'post-modern' perspective emphasises the contextuality of all philosophy. Whereas the "romantic quest" was to "behold spirit directly without mediation" through culture, so too did the scientific endeavour attempt to find an interpretation of history independent of context. The realisation that both perspectives share a common root in an avoidance of contextuality, turns the focus on how that root actually shaped the ideas of the time. Wright argues that any reading of a text cannot be free of its contextualisation within an inevitably culture bound, world-view of the reader. This insight leads us to question the very acts of reading, understanding and meaning-making. Blofield's interpretative bias itself needs deconstruction before we can again have a go at Huang-po himself. We then approach Huang-po in the knowledge that we too are doing this within the context of our own time, through our own coloured spectacles.

Wright shows convincingly that such an approach fulfils the requirement of Buddhism's own commitment to an understanding of the inter-relatedness, the co-dependence or interdependence of all things and processes. The co-dependence of text, a reader's understanding and culture are all matters that reveal the prescience of this fundamental viewpoint. To start with, the text Blofield translated so well hardly consists of Huang-po's own certificated words. The text has gone through innumerable re- workings right from the start and each one of these reflects the perspectives and prejudices of the time. To get back to Huang-po himself, as Blofield thought he was doing, is a very uncertain process which, however, does not mean that fundamental perspectives in Buddhism's history are not present in the work attributed to him and highly relevant to us now

How do we read Zen?

A major paradox in reading Zen is the constant admonition against reading itself, rough treatment of valued texts, even of the Sutras, and the suggestion that were one to meet the Buddha on the road the right thing to do would be to kill him. Yet these viewpoints are themselves presented in texts, in language, in often authoritative argument. We understand these remarks as criticism of a scholarly, book-worming, dry and lifeless, academic Buddhism that failed to read out of the books the spirit of life itself. The Master 'reads' his pupils, not merely the texts, he 'reads' the circumstances of the times. "When reading becomes a metaphor in this sense, it is synonymous with 'interpretation' and beyond that, with 'understanding' itself" (p40). What then is an understanding of Zen?

When the rich, textual products of one culture infiltrate another it is inevitable that their 'understanding' is influenced by whatever comprehension of its subject matter is already prevalent. On arriving in China, Buddhism was largely interpreted through the prior understandings of Taoism. The same process is operating in the arrival of Buddhism in the West today. When we read Zen stories in which, in answer to a perfectly reasonable question such as "What is the meaning of Zen?" the master tweaks a nose or beats the unfortunate questioner with his staff, we tend to be bewildered or to imply some hidden sagacity to the master. We may then apply to the story an explanation in conventional terms with which we feel at ease. The fact is we simply lack the understanding of context, the behavioural code, which underlay such an interaction. Only through familiarity and reflection can we begin to perceive the verbal and non-verbal communication that is happening here.

Following Austin and Derrida, Wright remarks that, "utterances can only be understood within actual speech situations where shared assumptions enable interlocutors to make sense of each other" (p48). And the same is true of situations, for these are always expressions of on-going culture. Interpretation is always based on pre-understanding and on the working out or floating with the various possibilities that this implies for interpretation. The implication here then is that any word, concept or story is 'empty' of any precise, culture-free meaning and is always relative to context. Once again the Buddhist emphasis on the implications of interdependence emerges clearly.

The absence of 'original meanings' or 'objectivity' in these texts becomes clearer when we examine their frequent use of allegory. When Huang-po is asked a complex question relating to some folk story about previous lives he replies by interpreting the story as representing the mind and its intentions or quest. In these texts we may see that the self who is interpreting or understanding them is "not just the subject of the activity but also the object as well" (p61). The 'Great Matter' of these texts is the self, the self who is doing the reading. When in reading Huang-po we eventually confront ourselves and our pre- understanding we sense "our immersion in the open space" of language (p62).

While Blofield often adds footnotes, today these only clarify Blofield's own interpretative stance based in his own cultural preconceptions. Today we may be more aware of the simple relativity of our interpretations and such a view must then itself be subject to reflection. Essentially this is what Wright means by the 'philosophical meditations' of his title. It is indeed a self-confrontation to realise there is no end to this!

The language of Zen

Our discussion leads of course immediately to the question of Zen language. The importance of language in Zen is often ridiculed in the texts, yet again this is a device pointing to the limitations of conventional uses of the formal or academic language of Buddhist description. There is a theme to be discovered here which is open to discourse in surprising ways because it has no solidified meaning - the relativity and flux of life itself is being pointed to and it is usually the tool of language that is used in such pointing.

Yet Zen rhetoric takes many forms. The language of Zen in Huang-po's time made use of ordinary speech intensified to a special purpose. The coded usage here had to be learned through the experience of being in a monastery, in having contact with the users among whom the masters were pre-eminent. "Words give rise to the experience and then issue from it immediately and spontaneously. 'Awakening' has not occurred in the absence of language, but fully in its presence" (p84).

The moment of awakening is a rhetorical occasion when the words of one speaker elicit a response in another. Wright classifies the varying forms of this rhetoric: the use of strange and puzzling expressions; direct pointing in which gesture rather than words is the means of transmission; the use of silence where words might have been expected; the employment of sudden disruptive even seemingly aggressive behaviour. All of these means are part of a 'language' with a clear intentionality - to effect transmission. For practitioners, language is therefore both the trap of samsara and the mechanism of release. Practitioners "sought a transformed rhetoric of 'live words' and 'turning words' through which awakening might be evoked." Some great masters, Huang-po and Lin-chi, were so powerful in the use of these methods that almost all 'faltered' before them. The master cut through convention so drastically that interlocutors were often unable to find any response - and yet through being thrown out of conventional language they might suddenly perceive its emptiness.

Wright remarks, "The Zen master is one who no longer seeks solid ground, who realises that all things and situations are supported, not by firm ground and solid self-nature, but rather by shifting and contingent relations... he no longer needs to hold his ground in dialogue, and therefore does not falter when all grounds give way... His role in dialogue is to reflect in a selfless way whatever is manifest or can become manifest in the moment" (p101).

Commonly the spoken words merely reflect the actuality of the moment, words and actions are contingent on occasion, they fit or reflect the interconnections in play and neither attempt to impose upon it nor to explain nor describe it. They co-emerge with it.

An important feature of a Zen story or koan is thus the 'turning word' upon which the point of the event 'turns'. There are no fixed words of this kind. They arise in the moment and one of the tasks of a master is to realise and release them. These 'live words' act as direct pointers but to what? They cause the interlocutor or the practitioner to focus so unnaturally on a phrase, a word or a story that it opens out of the conventional, common-sense relations of the actual linguistic usage, thus breaking the hold that ordinary language has upon the mind. When this operates on self-understanding, the positioning of self-concern within its habitual understanding is broken and, falling both into and out of relativity, its own emptiness is seen in a radical reframing.

Views of history in Zen study and Zen texts

John Blofield assumed that Huang-po spoke from a direct perception of truth that was pre-linguistic or extra-linguistic and that he would therefore not have an interest in history. In fact Chinese Zen, and indeed Huang-po himself, was always deeply concerned with matters of lineage and the accuracy with which transmission occurred. There is a vast literature that concerns itself with the historicity of transmission, much of which is myth or legend but which has an important function in legitimating practice.

These lineage records are essentially family genealogies of transmission complete with anecdotes, exemplary stories, methods of practice and rituals. Contrasting lineages are like branches of a tree which draw their strength from presence of the root. The ahistorical nature of experiential presence in Zen practice is thus always embedded in the narratives of the lineage. Enlightened identity is expressed in lineage identity and may include the occasional denial of the latter's importance for the sake of further transmission.

Contemporary historical study searches for the actual course of events and for documentation that may reveal the actual, 'true' history of Zen in China and Japan. From this perspective, lineage histories are simply bad history full of irrelevance, faulty timings, endless revisionism. The problem these lineages present for the practitioner in the present time are of a different nature. By idealising a certain approach, by a fixation of method and ritual, by an attempt at enlightenment as a resurrection of a particular moment in time, by a desire for unity and a specific identity in Zen, the capacity for a flexible relationship with the contingency of the moment - this moment - can be denied or made very difficult.

Yet, as Wright observes, a converse application of the Zen viewpoint to modern historical practices reveals the latter's stance as supposedly tradition-free and representing simple facticity yet lacking philosophical perspective and social responsibility. Such Western historians often fail in awareness of the extent to which historical study is reflexive to our time. This often comes about through a misuse of the natural science model in attempting to account for the origin and drift of human values.

"...both the Zen Buddhist and the modern, Western historical tradition deny implicitly some dimension of the impermanence of history, the radical mutability of temporal movement" (p117).

The encounter between traditional Zen historiography and Western methodology is already happening and as each begins to inform the other, particular traditions of historical reflection with contrasting purposes "may become... richer, more comprehensive and... applicable to cultural ends which are themselves open to similar transformation" (p118).

Exploring freedom and constraint

The Western idea of freedom dating back to the European 'Enlightenment' is closely tied to the significance of individualism in Western culture. There is always a dualism here, the individual is marked by his or her differentiation from others in society through the development of a unique identity relatively free from social coercion through self-possessed power and maturity. Liberation is conceived as the attainment of such distinction. This individualism plays a role in Western culture at a social psychological level to an extreme that differs markedly from Asian values with their greater concern with mutuality and social conformity.[1] In the West we have a dualism in our understanding of freedom that parallels the notion of a spiritual dimension independent from cultural constraint and definition. It was therefore easy for Westerners to interpret Zen enlightenment in terms of a liberation from social constraint into a transcendent spiritual dimension providing a sort of ego-free power. And indeed Zen texts are full of statements that may be read in this manner. With a naive but conscious guile or perhaps unconsciously, D. T. Suzuki promoted such a Euro-friendly vision and thereby laid an acceptable groundwork for the Western fascination with Zen in its romantic form. Like other Japanese teachers, his views expressed within Japanese culture were far more traditional and authoritarian.[2] Beat Zen, Jack Kerouac, and many Western Zen romantics continued this illusory preoccupation which has, even so, undoubtedly eased Zen Buddhism into Western culture in much the same way that Taoistic interpretation assisted the entry of Indian Buddhism into China.

A more considered examination of Huang-po and other Ch'an writers of the classical period reveals however a much more carefully nuanced idea of freedom. Statements that appear to promote individualism are carefully hedged about with requirements to obey the monastic rules, to conform to monastic ways of life, to imitate time-honoured practices, to obey the master and never to query the inheritance of the lineage as represented by him. The implication is that the practitioner submit himself to a powerful authority. And yet it is within this very submission that freedom may be found and the rules discounted. Freedom here is certainly not autonomy, nor is it the throwing off of constraint. Nor does this come to an end with the acknowledgement of enlightenment. When the enlightened master Huang-po is asked why he still bows before the Buddha although he has reached non-attachment, Huang-po simply remarks that this is his custom. Lin chi having slapped his teacher, Huang-po, in the moment of realisation, then settles down to study under the master for many years.

Wright emphasises the point that freedom is always relative to some form of constraint. In the Zen texts, terms such as cutting off, severing, exhausting, breaking through, are related to obstructions, screening, holding, fixtures, limitations, fixed perspectives, enclosure or bondage. Yet the result is not an independence from the monastery or a separation of individual from custom. Rather freedom is found within constraint. There is a triangulation in play here, independence and dependence are transcended in a third stance involving an emancipation from both through forms of inner renunciation. This comes about through an acceptance of limitation on individual will "in order to make possible forms of freedom beyond those surrendered" (p123). And yet within this very emancipation the monk continues in his personal dependence and independence.

Dependence on the master may be seen as a form of imitation through which a process with effects visible in the teacher emerges also in the practitioner. Imitation here is not copying, which is roundly condemned in Ch'an writings, but rather a following of a path revealed by another in order to make one's own discovery in the course of time. Again, the abandonment of the Sutras is not a rejection of them but rather a digestion of their meaning to an extent that they need no longer be consulted. It is the realisation of the essential 'emptiness' of phenomena that allows the 'burning' of the Sutras or the destruction of images and pagodas. The realisation that "form is emptiness and emptiness is precisely form", leads to the insight that monastic life and practice are empty of any objective value, are not anything of fixed merit and that, in the recognition of emptiness, there is no constraint in such a life either. Yet there is a path that has led to this insight, a path that seems at first sight the very antithesis of freedom. In the abandonment of self as independent, the interdependence of self with all things becomes clear. Within the insight of this renunciation any mode of being then becomes equal to any other.

Furthermore, the mode of realisation will not be of a fixed nature. Individuals will make their own discovery out of the uniqueness of their own experience, practice and karmic constraint. As time goes along and society itself changes so the mode of realisation shifts. In Ch'an texts we find old modes of enlightenment being updated so that ancient ancestors may be described as having realisations in the mode of the then present. Here again the Zen historian has often tried to fix too clearly the mode of transmission, ignoring Buddhism's own insistence on relativity.

Enlightenment today will come about in its own way and the psychology of renunciation is likely to take many forms. Mere imitators of the texts beware!

In realisation, the pupil 'goes beyond' the master. Here we can see that, although the traditional path remains vital, without a new creativity embodying the specificity of the moment the tradition will itself die through non-renewal. The storyline of Zen thus never reaches a final statement, has no fixity, remains in the perennial space of an openness always partaking of and never independent from the now. Wright asks: how does the call to 'go beyond' also apply to us in the context of our reading Zen?

The Great Matter

The pivot of Huang-po's thought and indeed that of the whole Zen project is the understanding of Mind, yet it is at once clear that this word does not denote the simple mind that all of us have - the restless thinking consciousness. Mind, and here perhaps we might consider a capital 'M', is treated variously in Huang-po's writings as something that cannot be fixed either subjectively or objectively; as encompassing all things yet itself remaining unfindable; as like space or as a source; as a ground of phenomena. Mind is neither identical with the forms of knowing nor separable from them, yet: "In correspondence to conditions mind becomes things" (p158). The repeated use of 'as' shows the importance of effective metaphor here: metaphor pointing to a target that cannot be clearly seen as an object. Being the all and the everything in both the inner and the outer of experience it is necessarily also nothing in particular. The 'One-Mind' is at the same time 'No-Mind'.

Wright barely discusses the sources of such ideas. They derive from origins in the Tathagatagarbha tradition of the Indian Yogacara view almost immediately, however, undermined by the application of the Prajnaparamita and Mahayamaka perspectives. Since, in the latter view, the six senses, their objects and the relations between them, all lack any inherent selfhood and have no controlling agency they are all 'empty'. In the Zen texts there is thus an inevitable tension between expressions locating presence and absence in the appearances of Mind. The insight into what the nature of this all-encompassing but unlocatable mind may be is both the focus of practice and the subject of much intellectual activity.

Wright explores the manner in which Huang-po's text and Blofield handle this issue. Wright's philosophical struggle engages the texts in a very Zen style, refusing to allow any definition to harden into an idea which would exclude its inevitable contrary or which would bring about a premature closure in thought excluding further mobility. In accord with his post-modern dialectic he repeatedly demonstrates that no term can be taken as standing on its own outside of language or culture and again, through this persistence, he cuts down the tendency to do exactly this. Similar tactics are inherent both in some ancient interpretations and in some parts of Blofield's own account.

For example, while "everyday mind is the Way", too much of an indulgence in everyday behaviour would lead to a passivity very far from the quest described elsewhere in the texts. Again, the attractive notion that Mind means the experience of the pure 'presence' of the here and the now can imply something outside the usual experience of time and space in an eternity set up as against temporality. While the experience of the present moment lies at the heart of Zen, this cannot mean that everything else has somehow disappeared; other aspects of experience such as the temporal nature of things have simply been set in the background for a time. Similarly, a focus on certain terms and their experiential concomitants does not mean that other modes of experiencing are negated - they are simply not then in focus.

The whole tendency to represent the Mind as any sort of id-entity is replaced in Huang-po by expressions implicating some sort of id-unity: a unity of diversity such that nothing is experienced in its separateness but rather in a merging in which everything is present as nothing in particular. Wright again and again emphasises that words and experiences are co-present in understanding. Such understanding is largely 'pre-conscious', shaped by and contained in old memories, stories and past behaviour of oneself and others. There is a 'storehouse'[3] of such resources that gives meaning to any event and which can take linguistic expression. Conversely, the recall of words can reset an experience in modes that are as much non-verbal as verbal. This 'pre-theoretical and pre-discursive' experiencing, while drawing on understanding, also re-forms it beyond the merely intellectual. Such action facilitates living within time rather than an endeavour to escape it (p174).

Indeed, if this relation between language, temporality and experience did not exist, it would be impossible for Huang-po to write of either experience or its presence now as an outcome of an event in the past - under the Bo tree perhaps. Paradoxically, his very words that point to 'direct awareness' are also understood by him as a doctrinal obstruction should the listener fixate upon them. And yet without them no transmission would be possible.

Wright says: "A dialectical relationship between the practice of thought and Zen experience is essential to the tradition. Thought pushes experience further, opens up new dimensions for it, and refines what comes to experience. Experience pushes thought further, opens up new dimensions for thinking, and sets limits to its excursions. The brilliance of Zen thinking is its tentative and provisional character, the 'non-abiding', 'non-grasping' mind. Knowing through thought that all thought is empty, Zen masters have explored worlds of reflection unavailable to other traditions - playfully 'thinking' what lies beneath commonsense" (p.179).

Whereas Blofield felt the 'Mind' to infer some 'absolute' hidden beyond the veils of ignorance, Huang-po and other authors in his tradition continued to insist on its immediate presence only distanced from us due to a tendency to adopt some idealising 'theory' closing ourselves off from the open freedom of staying with the flow of life. Yet to stay in such a space is scary, for the finitude of the self in its awareness of mortality then needs moment to moment acceptance. Traditional training in such awareness has required practices which are the outcome of exceptional life choices: to leave home; to live together with others in the acceptance of monastic rule, in the awareness of lineage and time, in discovering the co-arising of monastic and ordinary life and a sense of empathic compassion for all beings, and hence the insight that life is itself the ground of being.

"The ground is encountered, not as a separate relation, but in the midst of all other relations... practice is to cultivate the understanding and awareness that every relation to things in the world is simultaneously a relation to the ground of all things which has no 'existence' independent of the 'worldly things' through which it is manifest" (p189)... As the mind shifts in succession from one situation and object of awareness to another, the enlightened mind stays attuned to the 'one-mind' at the root of all things"(p 190).

Sudden and gradual

Wright argues that to be enlightened is to be responsive to life situations in an "open reciprocity" with them brought about by "certain dimensions of self-negation". In the history of Zen in China there were many disagreements concerning whether this understanding could be achieved by sudden or by gradual methods. Underlying these arguments were disputes between contrasting lineages basically political in nature. Careful reflection on the wording of the texts shows that sudden and gradual actually coexist in training. While a monk's everyday self-understanding is gradually called into question through hearing the teachings and living in a monastery in the proximity of a master, it was often by a sharp re-orientation of the manner whereby the individual conceived of himself against the background of his life that he came to an insight recognised by the master. Such momentary insight needed then to be related to an ongoing way of life and manner of experience before it could be said to be mature. Hence after 'seeing the nature' many monks remained in training often for years. Such a release into insight has the character of a 'letting go' which may only come about after much resistance: to let fall a secure conception of one's own identity is fearful and requires a trust that can only develop within time.

Wright once again emphasises the co-action within this process of meditative practices that are non- discursive with those that involve critical and creative reflection in thought. Practice is seen as not different from ordinary life, indeed the latter is to be experienced within the life of practice. To stress one or the other would be once again to fossilise an attitude in a closed perspective, the need for a 'going beyond' is again vital.

"Emptied of previous selves, monks were initiated into processes of constructing identities by... reshaping the variety of patterns bequeathed to them through the tradition. Established convention and distinctive identity were not held to be in opposition since the established models were distinct identities, and since one's own act of self-construction would inevitably push in some new direction" (p214). Indeed, the very creativity of the master would inspire a bright monk to innovation arising spontaneously within the life of practice.

The tension between the poles of tradition and innovation through 'going beyond' has sustained Zen through numerous historical crises and must be a key source for reflection at the present time. Yet a 'turning' moment remains essential for any individual on the path. The quest is necessarily always reflexive. Who is it that practices? Ever since the ministry of the great master Ma-tsu this has always been the critical question and the response to it constitutes the turning moment. As Wright says, the contemporary versions of this questioning remain at the heart of the Great Matter.

Conclusion: Zen cartography

If we have understood Wright's philosophical reflections accurately we will be sensitive to the realisation that the end of this present reading is no end to understanding. Wright's text is itself relative to the deconstructive trend in post-modern thought for which the many parallels in Zen have become more obvious than could be the case for Blofield's generation. Are there, however, contemporary limitations to Wright's viewpoint? Apart from continuing the debate it is hard to answer this question.

Wright's text is clearly a product of a post-modern, philosophical mind, albeit one almost certainly having a background familiar with practice. Zen is like a landscape and Wright has provided a philosophical map in terms expressing a contemporary philosophy highly influenced by Wittgenstein, Austin and Derrida. The same landscape can however also be drawn by different cartographers. In particular, while Wright does discuss mind and experience eloquently, this is not through the eyes of a skilled psychologist.

In the Lankavatara Sutra we find a psychological model basic to Zen practice and experience. Extrapolating from this model and relating it to modern psychology provides another equally fascinating map in which cross-references to Mead, Winnicot and the object relations school of psychotherapy would be in the foreground.[4] Again a more phenomenologically based stance would take us onto maps scored with place names derived from Husserl or Heideger and placed in close relationship with ideas expressed by the great Japanese Soto master Dogen.[5] Furthermore the experimental psychology of meditation has much to inform us about the underlying mechanisms of attitude change and alterations in consciousness.[6] A contemporary scepticism may also lead us to examine Zen through Thomas Huxley's advocacy of agnosticism.[7]

In collecting these maps together those practitioners of Zen who are not themselves cartographers may get confused. Where are the mountains on a map of county boundaries? What is the density of sparrows in a map of the vegetation of Wales? Maps do not answer all questions. They give us literally and deliberately a partial perspective. In the end, perhaps, we need to return to philosophising to gain an overview.

Wright teaches us not to allow closure on any perspective of Zen. There are always others in attendance. Zen in our time is Zen in our time - only just emerging from an Asian into a Western and increasingly global history. In China Buddhism went into a long eclipse under a neo-Confucianism that focused more on issues of social management and the economics of justice than it did on the dynamics of personal suffering. Indeed the economics of the monasteries were often hardly of value to the man in the paddy field.[8] Perhaps as these vital themes also emerge as paramount in the West the relation between Buddhism and our unhappy concern with a degrading environment should loom large lest what some may see as excessive introspection or self-indulgence leads to a lessening of current interest in the Buddhist view. Then again, when the vast majority of Western practitioners are lay people and never likely to become monks, close attention to a creative manifestation of Lay Zen is vital. This is likely to require a considerable questioning of ancient monastic practices in order to bring the essential clearly to the fore.

Staying in the open ground is in fact almost a necessity in the post-modern world of relativity where one can pick a religion off a shelf in the local church, mosque or temple; where one can choose from any number of systems of closure in a misguided and inevitably prejudiced search for escape into unworldly perfection. Zen tells us to fly by the seat of our pants in the world as it comes to us, staying open to its beauty, perversity and continuous flux, and finding that moment of global empathy in the loss of self- concern that yields compassion. If we are both personally and collectively to 'go beyond' the inherent suffering of human ignorance it will be essential to remember that while "setting the mind alive we do not put it anywhere."[9]

1 See further: Neisser, U. and Jopling, D.A. (eds). The Conceptual Self in Context. Cambridge University Press (1997).

2 Victoria, Brian A. Zen at War. Weatherhill, New York and Tokyo (1997).

3 The alayavijnana of the Vijnanavada perspective of the Yogacara element in Ch'an.

4 See: Crook J.H. The Evolution of Human Consciousness. Clarendon. Oxford (1980). Skinner, M. 'Spontaneity and Self Control', in Crook J.H. and Fontana D. Space in Mind: East-West Psychology and Contemporary Buddhism. Element (1990).

5 Peranjpe. A.C. and Hanson R.K. 'On Dealing with the Stream of Consciousness: a comparison of Husserl and Yoga', in Peranjpe, A.C., Yo, D.Y.F. and Rieber, R.W. Asian Contributions to Psychology. Praeger (1985). Heine, S. Existential and Ontological Dimensions of Time in Heidegger and Dogen. SUNY Press (1988).

6 Blackmore, S. 1990 'Mental models and mystical experience'. In Crook and Fontana loc cit.

7 Batchelor, S. Buddhism without Beliefs (1998).

8 See: Gernet, J. Buddhism in Chinese Society: an economic history from the 5th -10th centuries. Columbia University Press (1995)

9 Ref: The turning line from the Diamond Sutra that led to Master Huineng's enlightenment.

NCF XX

EDITORIAL FROM THE CH'AN HALL: This Suffering World

There was a time not long ago when politicians talked about a new world order of peace and prosperity worldwide. It was the end of the Cold War and all seemed set fair.

We were soon to discover our illusion - the Cold War had frozen not only our good but also many of our bad instincts. Almost at once the new freedoms released the bullies, the torturers, the capitalist egoists, the environmental destroyers from all constraint. Once more we were forced to look into the dark mirror of human history and see that evil had never been far away.

In this issue we follow the Buddha's advice and confront suffering and the way beyond suffering in an unflinching manner. Human life may be a dream chamber but the plumbing needs attention. On a global scale, the names of places tell their stories - Vietnam, the killing fields of Cambodia, East Timor, Tibet, the Gulag, Northern Ireland, Algeria, Iraq, central Africa, the Caucasian states, Bosnia, Kosovo... the same story; national pride, racial and tribal intolerance leading to abuse, murder, genocide and the long trail of desperate refugees. Yet so often these endless tragedies hardly disturb us as, comfortably, we look at the horrors sliding across our television screens like shining poisonous snakes. Only when we are moved personally, with a shock touching the skirts of human misery, can we start to empathise and in the heart begin to understand.

Suffering may be great or small - yet it has the same quality however intense. In this issue, articles and personal stories reveal both the shadows of our time and the hope that training can hold out for us. Perhaps we have to suffer before we can begin the 'salvaging of the sacred' as Marian Partington suggests. Yet empathy for the great pains can arise from the experience of the small. The Buddha had little interest in the mystery of the universe knowing that discussion leads only to endless debate. His great wisdom took on the ills of humanity. Today his message is perhaps more important than ever before. Modern technology means the stakes are higher and the speediness with which we live our lives constitutes a great danger. The heart needs time to understand. Give it time. Please.

WORKING WITH A MASTER

What is it like for a lay practitioner to work with a master over a period of time? A single retreat provides an introductory experience but what if one persists through a series of such events? This would indeed be a requirement if the aim was to train in Ch'an. Training takes time but does it take one anywhere?

To assist those for whom this question may be relevant, I attempt to answer it through presenting a series of excerpts from my retreat reports over several years training with Shi- fu[1]. Shi-fu is keen that participants should write a brief report on their retreat experiences. I have certainly found this to be a useful exercise. What changes may I have noticed over the years?

Naturally, everyone's experience on retreat differs and the training with different masters doubtless also varies. However, I believe the pattern of Zen retreats has much in common wherever they may be and whoever directs them: one person's description can therefore give a rough guide, although not an exact one, to what you may yourself experience should you set out upon this path.

I first attended a Ch'an retreat in New York in 1986 but I had previous retreat experience from working in meditation privately several times at Samye Ling Tibetan Centre in Scotland and from several retreats in Soto Zen at Throssel Hole Priory in Northumberland, one of which had been directed by Roshi Jiyu Kennett. Furthermore, I had spent time in the Himalayas with Tibetan yogins. My original encounter with Ch'an had been while serving as a national service officer in the army in Hong Kong 1953-54 when I had been introduced to a noted lay disciple of Master Hsu-yun and taken some teaching[2]. I was not therefore exactly a beginner, but I knew that work with Shi-fu could well provoke a Dharma struggle through self-confrontation of an order I had not encountered before. I was not disappointed.

Of course this article does not show how far I have come, but rather how far I have yet to go.

Conductor with a motionless baton. New York, May 1986

I knew that the Ch'an meditation centre in downtown Queens in New York was in an urban area yet, as a country-living person from Somerset, I was not well prepared to find myself in a converted shop with a factory on one side and the cacophonous main street of a commercial area on the other. Furthermore, a major street junction with traffic lights was just down the road and a fire station up the way. Every hour or so a fire engine would come roaring through the traffic, klaxon sounding, come to a reluctant halt at the lights and blare away at them in fury. "Of course Zen is everywhere!" I reassured myself as I sat through my first vibrating hours of passing trucks, car horns, full volume radios and the chatter in at least five languages of exceedingly lively passers-by. As my back began to ache and my legs to hurt I made a vow that I would at least survive this thing and that that alone would count as a sort of success. The first two days demanded naked will as sweat from the local heat wave ran down my face and I sat damp from perspiration in my minimal clothing.

I struggled to apply the method I had learned at Throssel Hole - shikantaza - the just-sitting wall-gazing approach of Soto Zen. I was searching to understand what the great Japanese master Dogen meant by "without thinking". My head was full of scattered bits of television serials; painful memories; bits of old dreams; an endless random collection of pictorial sequences without focus and seemingly without meaning. The scattered mind merged with the traffic noise into a hellish bedlam punctuated by growing physical pain.

Shi-fu's talks were always helpful, starting me off again with a touch of hope. He suggested allowing thought to subside on an out-breath and leaving it alone on the in-breath to create a silent space. I found this practice beginning to produce gaps in my scattered mind which slowly increased in length, deepening into moments of profound silence. After some hours I felt a swirling energy rising from my belly which changed into a glow of gratitude and release.

The following morning I awoke refreshed and, in the silence of the dawn, the simple song of the American Robin in the little garden sounded in a deep and sustained stillness. In a now rare dream sequence, I found myself seated beside a dark tranquil pool in a deep cavern in the earth. There was a full orchestra seated on chairs there ready to play. I was the conductor with baton raised - but motionless! No sound.

Shi-fu gave a talk about mu-shin, no-mind. My head started up again in a chatter of argument. This was no picture show but a vigorous debate. Did I know what mu-shin was? Certainly some past mystical experiences suggested so. But were these no-mind or merely some form of illusion? I puzzled on about this, working myself up into fuss and worry about how far along the Zen path I might be.

Some hours went by locked in this foolishness but, suddenly, I realised that what I was into was a quest for credentials and approval. As an academic I have a list of alphabetical combinations after my name signifying my attainments. I wanted to add mu-shin to the end of the list! The absurdity of this destructive endeavour got to me and, as I began smiling to myself and accepting that part of me that wanted to strut about exhibiting attainments, a new release arrived. I had an interview with Shi-fu and shared all this nonsense with him. Clearly, I could not tell whether past experiences were mu-shin or not, nor indeed could Shi-fu. He was not me and anyway it was all in the past. Nor, of course, could Shi-fu tell me whether I would experience mu-shin in the future. I could however be grateful for those past moments and press on anew with my method. The whole experience had been a barrier constructed out of my own karma. As it collapsed, I noted the deep truth of Dogen's phrase, "Whenever the opposites arise, the Buddha mind is lost".

Yet my body was now troubling me sorely. Backache, due to a small knotted muscle close to the spine below the shoulders, was generating a widening area of pain. I had travelled uncomfortably in the ill-designed seat of the aircraft flying me across the Atlantic. Sitting was soon so awful that I had to exercise sheer will to get through each half hour expecting it to end in an ignominious collapse. Periodic yoga exercises, rolling on my back in the breaks, back walking from a fellow participant and applications of one-handed massage became a desperate work programme to keep me going. The difficulty was not however overcome in this way.

At some point during the penultimate day, during a period of slow walking (kinhin), it suddenly struck me that my discomfort with the heat, my suppressed annoyance at the street noise and my anger at my back pain were all one thing - a burning rejection of being there at all combined with irritation at not "doing better". I saw myself as simply grumbling as if in some way it would get me out of the hole I was in. Yet grumbling at a self-imposed task was such a ridiculous activity that once again I was amused by this paradoxical and uncomfortable state of mind. I accepted as a blunt and obvious fact that I was just a fool seeing things the wrong way.

After all were any of these conditions bad? Neither the heat nor the sound of traffic were actually doing me any harm. Indeed, I was already aware that, in spite of them, an increasing clarity of mind was emerging. As I began to think in this way, a sudden turn-about in my feelings occurred. Everything that had been horrible a moment before not only became tolerable but acceptable - even inspiring.

As I sat down to face the wall after a break I found my world transformed. With my mind in stillness, I experienced the spaciousness of the room and the presence of others in it reflected there as if in a mirror. For a while there was the exhilaration of sheer joy. With some further hints from Shi-fu about body relaxation, I found it possible at last to let go of all these accumulated concerns as if they were all one thing - 'me' in fact. In the letting go of 'me', the world simply appeared as it was - all of the 'same taste', nothing special to praise or to blame. The experience seemed to reach from horizon to horizon without boundaries so that all the sounds and happenings were simply going on within it like the continuous flow of water in a river. The water was gently wearing away the stone and there was no need for hurry.

After the retreat was over, I spent a final hour meditating near the window of an upstairs room. It was open - and by now a road digger was excavating a ditch in the pavement immediately below. All the sounds were at full volume yet not for one moment was the inner stillness disturbed - in transparency the interdependence of everything flowed along. The hour seemed like a mere few minutes.

That evening I flew to Amsterdam. In the early morning I sat with my son and daughter eating pancakes for breakfast beside a canal. As we walked around, I found my breathing quietly centred in my belly and the stillness ever present in my mind. After every burst of conversation, it simply returned of its own accord. When at last I went to bed, I found I had been alert and active for twenty-seven hours, had crossed the Atlantic without jet lag and was continuing to feel a clarity of unusual perception. Only three days after my re-entry to my normal work schedule did recurrent worries begin to dim this way of seeing. I had truly learnt that "to know all the Buddhas of the past, present and future, only perceive that Dharmadhatu nature is all created by the mind".

Dogen offering to Dogen. New York, May 1987

I had come to the retreat bringing many tensions of my world with me; mental distress from a difficult domestic situation; remorse and shame at a seeming inability to solve such problems; a slightly frozen shoulder producing referred pain oddly in my upper left arm. Perhaps the physical pain was merely an emblem of pain in the mind?

As session succeeded session an increasing fatigue enveloped me, a deadly drowsiness with aches, pains and fidgety movement. My method of shikantaza was difficult to focus and punctuated by wandering thought, intense feelings of loss, grief and family distress. Whenever this faded away there were haphazard bursts of hypnagogic imagery in fragmentary visual 'clips' without apparent meaning. Even so each session was different and gradually some moments of calm emerged.

I began repeating the name of Amitabha, now and again stopping the repetition to gaze into the silence so created. This practice resembled the breathing technique

I had used previously but the results were very erratic. Again I found myself pondering Dogen's insistence that meditation is neither thought nor no-thought but a state of being without thought.

In one of my more silent periods the words of the hua t'ou "What is Wu"[3] arose spontaneously and it occurred to me that whenever 'without thinking' became established Wu was present. Just before Shi-fu called me to my first interview, the phrase "Dogen is offering to Dogen" arose, apparently meaning that out of Dogen's method a question had been given.

I told Shi-fu of this and he remarked that a hua t'ou or a koan could indeed arise spontaneously while practising shikantaza. He seemed to like the phrase about Dogen for his eyes shone. It had come from my sub-conscious, he said. As to my practice - "No problem!"

I returned to my cushion; the work was gruelling; sometimes I felt bored stiff and wondered why on earth I was doing all this. Could there be any benefit in so masochistic an exercise? I remembered a statement made to me by a yogin in Ladakh, "You must sit still within the boredom itself and wait for an energy to arise." I sat.

Silent patches continued to emerge and I felt grateful for them. Sometimes a hint of bliss appeared. "Ah", I said to myself "I am making progress!" and I considered asking Shi-fu for another interview. Yet, realising I had a strong wish to please Shi-fu like a schoolboy facing a powerful schoolmaster and wishing to impress, I desisted, waiting for this feeling, which felt rather silly, to subside.

Shi-fu's evening talk was based on the Song of Mind, just two lines of it: "Do not seek an experience of emptiness. Full comprehension emerges naturally."

This made striking sense and, in response to the charm and open friendliness of his presentation, smiling, playful even, so much the opposite of his stern, inquisitorial face in interview, I let go of my oedipal reaction and felt released from error.

On the third evening Shi-fu commented mockingly on the faint heartedness he had encountered in interviews with participants. Mockingly, he imitated the manners of the young Chinese women present who, like the rest of us, were complaining of leg ache, backache, headache, everything ache. "What is this?" he demanded. "It's not a retreat at all - more like a Day Care centre!"

I was stung by his remark. Whatever others might be doing I was determined that for me the retreat was a serious matter. However much it differed from the old monastic retreats, the horrors of which Shi-fu had alarmingly described, none the less I would do something. An angry determination arose as I contemplated my incompetence and faint heartedness. So, immediately after the talk, as I sat on my cushion once again, I punched my right fist into my left palm making a loud crack and, powered by anger, plunged into meditation.

The first target was my fidgety body. I stared again and again into the various aches and pains, fully allowing myself to experience them and then commanding their departure. To my surprise, one by one they cooled down, giving way to a quiet sensation that was not uncomfortable. I went to bed feeling that mastery of the body was not impossible and that aches and pains were largely the product of an uneasy mind.

I also became focused on two further lines of the Song of the Mind:

"When birth and death are cut off the principle is seen"

Shi-fu told us that this meant the cutting off of the moment to moment arousal and decay of thought. I could see deep sense in this.

I had a dream in which I had to cross a green landscape, wild open land, in which savage dogs roamed in packs and singletons. I had been given a sharp sword with which to cut them down so I set off with confidence. The dogs came close but none approached to molest me. In the early morning session I felt that this dream referred to my wandering thoughts and that the sword was Shi-fu's teaching. I sat with confidence.

It was a holiday morning; traffic was absent; the American Robin sang its evocative early morning song; to my surprise the pain in my body failed to appear and my body itself seemed to disappear. I was aware of its presence merely as a bag of guts plopped like a cushion upon the floor supporting a meditating mind. A strange image arose within me. It seemed as if a great grey mass like a tumour was filling out my stomach and gradually protruding from my body, almost as if I were a dividing cell. The experience was quite physical and alarming, a gross wrenching apart of something horrible in me that needed exorcism. As it separated from me, as a big round ball about a yard in diameter, it seemed to be made of grey paper. It was a wasps nest. I poked it with a stick and thousands of wasps poured forth and disappeared in distant air. A feeling of great relief filled me and my mind became tranquil like a mirror, simply reflecting all phenomena. I sat through two complete sessions without a movement.

After breakfast the same feeling continued but now the mirror felt rather tightly bound by its frame. Quite suddenly the frame dissolved and, with a vivid sensation of opening out, a loosening of constraint, a wide spaciousness appeared. The silent mirror now had no limit, there was no movement within it, no thought, no movement of mind at all, a sheer vastness which had not come in from outside but which had arisen with the disappearance of the mirror's frame. Words fail here for what words can stand for the wordless? I felt open to the entire Universe and, although the sights and sounds around me were all quite as usual, in the world where I had been I was not. There was no-one there. No wanting, nothing holding me for I was not there to be held. Happiness without attachment, for nothing arose to which attachment could exist. Gratitude, a continuing state.

I remembered Shi-fu's instruction to "Let the Universe do the work- not you!" and I felt at once that, where I had once been, there was now just this universal energy flowing of itself without constriction, time moving. I was time not in time. Wu was both the void of experience and the continuum of a flowing stream, both empty, both wide open.

At interview the experience was still with me for I was second in line and the experience had begun only fifteen minutes before. I described it to Shi-fu and added "Wu is universal energy endlessly flowing - it is also love." Shi-fu said "Good. Very good. Now you can start practising." I returned to my seat and almost at once the doubting, self-accusatory mind attacked me with every manner of demonic self persecuting thought and, for several sittings, I quite lost a hold on Wu.

I took up the phrase about birth and death again and could perceive how Wu was obscured not only by thoughts but also by their barely conscious bases that were generating diverse intentionalities and preoccupations not clear enough to take the form of thought.

In the afternoon, after a long series of prostrations, Wu returned. There was complete stillness and openness within a silent, sack-like corpse in and out of whose mouth flies flew as it breathed. I was this fresh corpse and a fear of such deathly emptiness arose together with so grim an image, a terror of losing all I held dear in the world, my pride, my intellect. Somehow, the image of the little blue iris growing in the garden came to mind and, "They toil not neither do they spin but who among you is arrayed like one of these?" I felt better, in touch with life once more.

Gradually, as session followed session I became able to track these movements of minding. The openness became lost not so much when thought arose but rather when attachments, old emotional needs, wants or fears were present. The presence of need, want or fear unrepresented by thought was especially subtle and signalled by bodily tensions, finger scratching, nail biting, fidgeting, the mind speaking as it were non-verbally. At these times there was a sensation of mental closure, as if being surrounded, hedged in. Yet, by allowing this state to develop fully, it began to lose strength, dissolving in the same way as bodily pain had done.

It was never possible to force an opening to occur, for this in itself represented an ego state. Yet, from time to time, a sort of letting go occurred, a putting down not only of ego states but of the entire self as felt in attachments. The putting away felt like something falling away - like sticking plaster being pulled from the skin but with no puller doing the pulling. With that the openness emerged again bringing a powerful sense of relief, "Ah - here it is again - how fortunate!"

This is a condition of total not-wanting. Death would be OK, entirely so, being neither good nor bad in itself. Only when this not-wanting has arisen does this openness flow. To say then "I don't know. I don't need to explain. I have nothing to discover, nothing to resolve and nothing to do, nowhere else to go absolutely at all." was somehow totally complete.

"Whatever arises in the mind gives rise to its own sphere."

Liberation lasts only so long as one is absent, saying of oneself "Who is here? Not me."

"Sometimes we raise the eyebrows of old Shakyamuni - sometimes we do not" (Dogen)

Oh - look at that! Maenllwyd, April 1989

This was a busy retreat for me. I was guest master and responsible for the welfare not only of the participants but also of Shi-fu and the 'team' from New York on their first visit to Wales, Ming Yee and Gou Yuan Se. I was of course concerned that all would be well.

In many ways my experiences of sitting resembled those of previous retreats. At first I was delighted to sit and blissful moments appeared but then fatigue and scattered thoughts arose and the usual struggle was on. I wrestled with my karmic problems, my unsatisfactory relationships, domestic disturbances and my neurotic desire to please everyone, yet the calming effect of meditation soon released me and at such times, while fully aware of the actual realities of my surroundings, I also felt myself as if floating on a platform above the valley; that the wall before me was insubstantial and that my awareness was reaching out over the rolling spaces of the hills and valleys into some limitless beyond.

At my first interview, I told Shi-fu how my mind was forever seeking explanations, especially since, as a scientist, to seek so had been the chief education of my mind. Shi-fu remarked that for me the most useful path would be silence, especially since my practice of shikantaza had given me some grip on the stillnesses that can arise in the mind. He felt that learning Silent Illumination would deepen this practice further. I returned to my cushion fortified with this thought which gradually yielded a feeling of stability and stillness only occasionally broken by mind wandering and dreamlike images. With a quietened mind I felt free to review my life in the Dharma and I resolved to tell Shi-fu of those rare experiences which had appeared as if by grace several times in my life since boyhood and which I have always been reluctant to share with anyone because of their incomprehensible nature.

I gave him a straightforward account of one event that had followed a retreat at the Maenllwyd. I had been down the lane on the point of departure and had returned from the car on foot to a gate which I had forgotten to close behind me. As I swung the gate, I saw two Red Kites wheeling overhead in the frost-clear air of the sunny, winter day. Red Kites I had never seen near the Maenllwyd before so I exclaimed to myself with joy "Oh look at that!" As I gazed at the circling birds my mind suddenly fell empty, I was no longer present within 'my' experiencing. There was only the landscape and the circling birds, a sense of wonder and amazement. I stood gazing for about twenty minutes as the birds gradually withdrew and felt the experience slowly fading as thought reappeared and 'I returned to myself.' This was a re-awakening, a joy to have found 'it' again, for such an experience has only rarely appeared, often with years between.

I also told Shi-fu of another occasion when I was visiting Naropa's cave at Dzongkhul. We had spent three days in July 1977 crossing the immense icefields of the Umasi-la pass through the Himalayas into the Zanskar valley of Ladakh. As we were being given tea in the upper hall of the little monastery I had glanced out of the window. The mountainside opposite was falling away as icy water rushed down in a massive waterfall from the glacier above. Again emptiness of self came over me and the great space of the mountains seemed to fill me with itself. I wandered alone for half an hour up and down the flat monastery roof until I felt myself again gradually returning as thought once more created self concern[4].

I asked Shi-fu what, from the point of view of Ch'an, was the meaning of these experiences. Without hesitation he told me that this was "seeing the nature" (kensho). I was overjoyed to receive his confirmation of what I had suspected but never been able to test in a direct meeting with a Zen master. Shi-fu also said that, from what he knew of me, he had already understood that I had had such experiences. He then said "Congratulations" and told me to make three prostrations before him, which I did with profound feelings of awe, joy and liberation. He also said that from now on he wanted me to run Ch'an retreats with his blessing and, as it were, as his representative.

While I experienced a great freedom, I also perceived immediately the responsibilities that this recognition implied for me. I also felt bewildered for what did congratulations have to do with simply experiencing the most basic nature of myself? I felt an odd shyness too for, while I was happy at Shi-fu's recognition, I did not want anyone else to know. In sharing with others minefields of potential miscommunication loomed before me.

After this interview the sitting sessions ran smoothly and clearly with a stillness of a mirror- like quality. One afternoon we did prostrations, carefully explained by Shi-fu. I experienced profound repentance, not only for immediate things but for the long perspective of inadequacies in my life. As the tears poured down my face, it seemed as if repentance must be endless. Oceans of karma from past generations seemed to sweep through me. It was as if this repentance was a beginning of atonement for previous lifetimes as well as for this one. The depth of feeling gradually changed to relief and gratitude towards the Dharma.

The naturalness of how things are. New York, November 1989

On the first day I was happy, rediscovering old friends. The atmosphere of the premises in the new centre, a few houses down the road from the old one, reminded me of the good things of past retreats. There was a large and attractive image on the altar so I went up to pay my respects and to look at the Buddha - and the Buddha looked at me! As I gazed into that peaceful, if curiously distant, face it was if a blissful harmony was transferred to me, a sweet peacefulness that seemed to permeate the room.

On this retreat I wanted to gain a deeper understanding of the Chinese word tsan - meaning investigate, enter or go into. How was one to do this in meditation?

Soon the usual troubles began, past and present vexations, dissatisfaction and despair emerged one after another like a host of waiting demons. My body stiffened and my back ached. There were subtle motifs working their way below the surface subverting whole hours of sitting. Two devils in particular were distressing me. The first was telling me that my endless tendency to try to placate significant others could not be satisfied here. It seemed then to me that without feeling that I was pleasing somebody else, I could not feel happy about my own being. Here of course there were no others to please - unless it were Shi-fu and to try and placate Shi-fu was so obviously absurd that I could not even begin. Sitting before the wall there was only myself, and I had to learn to value my own way of being. The second devil was a saboteur. In the middle of a peaceful kinhin a voice suddenly said "You don't believe any of this!" I was shocked by so traitorous a thought. My discomfort was taking its revenge on the ego's fortitude in enduring the process by denying the very belief that led me to value the work.

Furthermore, Shi-fu was presenting me with a very distanced appearance, checking my work in cleaning the bathroom on a work period and ticking me off for crossing my legs in relaxation during an interview. Afterwards he remarked that he understood that different cultures had different ways of sitting. It was just that in China to sit in that way seemed somewhat disrespectful. I was mortified by all this for it contrasted so strongly with his attitude towards my work on the previous retreat in Wales. I began to suspect that this was all a training procedure to test my resolution. Perhaps he would ask me to do some impossible task, just as Marpa trained Milarepa and Shi-fu's own teacher had likewise drilled him into self recognition!

I resolved that whatever he did or said would make no difference to my training. I would carry on regardless. With this I felt easier - even amused to try and spot what device he might throw at me next!

Shi-fu's talks on Master Hsu-yun's instructions on Ch'an meditation helped me greatly with my main quest. I had previously discovered that it was sometimes possible to detach from a painful thought and allow my awareness to expand to embrace the experiential moment, the nowness of the room, sounds and atmosphere, without the interpolation of thought. I began to practice bringing myself into the immediate presence of the place. As I did this, it seemed that the monstrous pervasiveness of ego concern began withdrawing into its lair, leaving the stage clear and unobstructed. It was strange how quickly this shift could occur. One moment my head would be in a fog of self concern, the next there I was in the room, clean, clear and present.

It seemed as if I was in a cage inhabited by troublesome monkeys. If I asked myself the question "What is troubling me now?" I could do one of two things. I could either perceive and name a basic problem, one of the monkeys, and worry about that, or I could look at it from the standpoint of the cage itself. This moves the locus of attention from the agitating monkey to the environment that surrounds it. The cage is not the monkey, it is uninvolved. However noisy the monkey may be, the cage is unaffected. Repeating this shift of attention many times led to an expanding and relatively enduring stillness. When I glanced at the Buddha now there was just a reflex of silence.

One morning the chanting of the ritual moved me to tears. All the tragedy and sorrow of the world seemed matched against the beauty of the passing scenes of life. Soon this sorrow changed into a growing feeling of bliss, deep, inward and physical in manifestation. At interview I asked Shi-fu the meaning of blissful experiences within the Ch'an perspective. Shi- fu said that such a feeling arises out of gratitude when there has been an insight into emptiness. Emptiness, gratitude and bliss are related, tending to arise one after the other in unpredictable sequences and with varying durations and intensities so long as the mind is one-pointed. Here was the invisible door out of the cage.

On the last night I sat till midnight. In the stillness of the meditation hall questions from Shi- fu's talks slowly circled. What was my original face before I was born? Before time what was I? If there was no time before time began, then there could only be space. But no - without time, no space. Simply the naturalness of the way things are. Wu is the inconceivable. Nothing to be said or done about it. Just the great NO of Joshu which seemed to be turning into my great YES. Did I say my yes?

Creating a fuss: seeing the stupidity. New York, November 1990

I arrived from England bringing a relatively calm mind, gentler of late due to some lessening of vexations and months of improving practice. This was to be Shi-fu's fiftieth retreat in the USA and, on the Tuesday, I was to celebrate my sixtieth birthday. It bode well to be an auspicious time.

Yet I had also brought with me something else of which I was not at first aware. I had spent much of the year away from home with visits to Taiwan and Hong Kong and in two long expeditions to high altitude in the Himalayas, one of them in the deep cold of the winter months. I really did not want to go abroad again: rather I wanted to consolidate at home and write. Yet I had a programme of retreats to lead in Britain in the coming year and I knew I needed further training with Shi-fu, both for myself and for others.

Although the first day was peaceful, I had a growing sense of unease. I was unexpectedly bothered by the rules, by the changed diet, by the feeling that I might make some mistake. I reacted negatively to the powerful authority of Shi-fu himself and became puzzled because, since I had attended retreats before, I had not expected to feel so resistant. Finally I recognised that I did not actually want to be in New York at all - at least not just then. I felt a certain resentment, a feeling of duress, that I had had to come at that time when I did not feel ready.

The realisation helped. Since I was undoubtedly on the Western side of the 'pond', the only thing to do was to work hard and enter the retreat as fully as possible. Yet, even if my head was telling me this, my heart refused to obey. It began creating a dreadful fuss. My discomfort grew and grew and, rationalise with myself as I might, it went on and on.

I was horrified to find myself repeatedly judging my companions even though I knew nothing about them and I was trying to follow the isolation rule, deliberately treating the retreat as if I was the only one on it. I soon recognised that these judgements were actually attempts to bolster my superiority because I feared exactly the opposite. To myself I was exhibiting privately a crude arrogance based in my own insecurity, exactly as Shi-fu, to my added shame, was to discuss in one of his highly pertinent talks. At times I felt as if I was the only victim of the strict rules. I did not want to be bound by all these strictures and I felt as if I was being subjected to the imposition of unnecessary authority. Yet, after all, I reasoned, I had deliberately come on the retreat of my own free will knowing full well what retreats were like. I realised that my feelings were nothing other than a paranoid reaction.

I began to develop an acute sensitivity to Shi-fu's presence. It was as if I were constantly worrying about what he thought of me. I went through seemingly endless and ridiculous mental posturings designed to seek his approval, hoping, for example, that he would notice how well I was sitting and relaxing as soon as he left the room! Of course I knew all the time how totally absurd this was. I knew that Shi-fu's relation to me was entirely straightforward yet I kept reading into his facial expressions the implication that he disapproved of me. It took me rather longer to realise that this was because I disapproved of myself!

Of course I knew all about such oedipal feelings, not only from my own experience of them with previous father figures, but also because, as a research supervisor for university doctoral degrees, I had considerable experience of receiving and managing such feelings in young men working under my guidance. None of this knowledge helped in the least nor did the fact that being sixty to the day put me in the same generation as Shi-fu himself!

I had a disturbed and self-conscious feeling that I was not doing the retreat well, that I was a most inferior participant. The silence and isolation meant that I had no means of checking this out and no means of playing my usual games whereby I get others to like me by subtly pleasing them, a game at which I recognise my unfortunate skill. I became increasingly anxious about everything, the possibility of being late perhaps at meals or wondering when I should go to the toilet.

Then there was the fatigue. The relentless effort to sit facing a wall with all this in my head exhausted me. The best things were the breaks in the programme for exercises and meals and of course the relaxing Dharma talks in the evenings. Yet I did have one great cause for rejoicing. I had very little discomfort from sitting itself. This was so wonderful a change from previous retreats that I reflected upon the possibility that it was the absence of physical pain that had set all this mental strife going. From time to time all these anxieties peaked in something close to a panic attack. I'm losing control, I thought, feeling desperate and seeking every inner means of steadying myself.

It was then that I remembered my mantra. Years ago I had received a mantra as the sound of my protective yidam in Tibetan Tantra. It had helped me cross passes in the Himalayas and to get me along precipitous tracks where I would have otherwise suffered from vertigo. Abandoning all methods, I plunged into reciting it. Wonder upon wonders, my mind, in the space of one sitting session, began to quieten and experience some peace. Something like the bliss of gratitude arose.

Shi-fu's talks were tracking my inner process with wonderful accuracy. He spoke of the lack of Dharma confidence, of the inner insecurity that gave rise either to fearful anxiety on the one hand or aggressive arrogance on the other. I followed his advice, classifying each bout of discomfort under a heading. I soon saw that all these headings stemmed from one single source. The common root was indeed an insecurity, a shaky self-confidence, that stemmed from childhood. Everything I had been experiencing came from this one source, me. I had brought it all through the door on arrival. If I was to know the Buddhas of the past, present and future I certainly had to perceive that all worlds of experience were created by the mind.

After each meal, I prostrated repeatedly before the statue of Kuan Yin in an upstairs room. I did these prostrations slowly, staying on the floor for minutes at a time. I understood clearly that what I had been experiencing was nothing other than a process of self-cherishing expressed in several ways. My ignorance of this was shameful, arrogant even, painful and depressing. What hypocrisy to think I could ever help others in the Dharma. I wept. I remembered those I had hurt, ancient sadnesses, failed relationships, the lack of love that feeds on fear. How could Shi-fu have authorised me to lead retreats in Britain when all this constituted so overwhelming a vexation?

But was it? I had an interview with Shi-fu. We talked of method. As to vexations, "Just tell yourself how stupid they are and put them down", he said. Stick to your method. Simple. Brief. No analysis.

During a period of group prostrations I relaxed into a minute attentiveness to every movement of the body. Hearing others weeping brought my own tears of sadness, regret and repentance to my eyes. Relief came. In silence there was only the movement of hands, knees and forehead. Gradually the rest of the body faded away. Hands flowed, knees bent, forehead touched the floor. It was like swimming, bodilessly, in cool water. Afterwards I sat on my cushion. There was nothing on my cushion. My body had quite disappeared. Above the cushion there was only an awareness in space; the thoughts that watchfully observed had no location; they were neither here nor there but hovering somewhere unlocatable. The thoughts were saying "So, here you are. All of this is me. This is where you start from - right now." In the now there was nothing but a vivid presence in which was peace.

If this was Wu, what was Wu? I knew how to tsan[5] a koan so I launched into it, gazing and gazing into that bright presence. What is it? What is it? Where is it? On and on to a central point locked-on to an absent target. Sound in the room. What is the Wu of that? Music from a ghetto-blaster going down the street. Where the Wu in that? Stillness now in the early morning. Where the Wu in that?

It was the sixth day. The mind settled and hour after hour sped by. I did exercises to ease the tired body but I did not strictly need to do so. I sat on and on in focused peace. Sometimes chi rose in the head so high that I refocused the questioning in the navel. It steadied there. On the last day there were hours of silence often suffused by blissful joy. The dreadful traffic noise registered hardly at all and, when it did, it entertained.

I understood Dharma joy. It had returned with a new confidence. I became aware of my companions in a new way, feeling love and respect for the great efforts that were being made all around me, for the heroism, if I may call it that, of these determined people. I saw Shi-fu once more clearly as the great teacher that he is. In interview I told him of my calmed mind. "That's good!" he said. "Continue." And indeed I guess that's it. Continue. Learn again and again to accept but not before there has been re-cognition.

I start from here. Always from here. At such a moment, looking in, there is the world beckoning.

Lilacs in the cruellest month. Maenllwyd, April 1992

"April is the cruellest month breeding lilacs out of a dead land." Elliot's words were with me as Shi-fu arrived the day before the retreat began. The weather was cold and light snow showers were dusting the hills, drifting past on the north easterly wind. Yet daffodils were out and, down in the valleys, the lilacs were indeed coming into bloom. Once again I was the guest master for Shi-fu's second retreat in Wales.

Everyone was helpful, some sleeping in tents or in the big barn where the cold wind blew through the holes in the roof. My normal room was allotted to Shi-fu as the

Master and, on the first morning, I awoke to frozen snow on the roof of my tent. People got colds yet the retreat began to unfold like a musical performance or the setting sail of a ship.

Shi-fu began talking of Silent Illumination illustrating his theme from Hung Chih Cheng Chueh's poem. The opening words always inspire me, startling the mind into a kind of expectancy, reawakening memories of 'it'.

> Silently and serenely one forgets all words
>
> Clearly and vividly it appears before you
>
> When one realises it time has no limits
>
> When experienced your surroundings come to light.

As I practised, the sense of the poem became clearer and more present. "Full of wonder is the pure illumination, like the dreaming of a crane flying in empty space, the still waters of an autumn pool. The feel of the valley beyond the walls of the Ch'an Hall came into the room. The room was wall-less.

Where does the wonder exist? The words woke me up, the question becoming a hua t'ou. Was the wonder inside my mind? Not exactly. Was it outside my mind? Not exactly. Between the two? Instead of a bounded experience, there again appeared that boundless space in which the observer has no specific location. Sounds came and went merging in a present continuum outside any measurement of time. Only a not-ness was apparent that no words could fit; a not-ness of the usual; no habitual mental movement; Wu in fact? A wonder was simply here, now and wordless, a suspended note of music or a beam of sunlight falling through a window.

In interview I told Shi-fu of this but an interval of time had come between my vivid experience and my meeting with him. Something had happened for I was suddenly overcome by sadness at the passing of time, impermanence and the frailty of things. Nostalgia has been with me throughout my life. Shi-fu remarked that, while my first experience was clear and correct, my mind had "gone down" after it. Sadness is a product of attachment. There is nothing wrong with such a feeling but it is not wisdom. The task is to see wisdom again and again and to understand the nature of emotion.

During the Menshang liturgy Shi-fu would go to the door of the Ch'an Hall and scatter the offering outside. I felt as if time stopped, centuries disappeared and ancient China was with us. My respect for the Dharma deepened and my gratitude to Shi-fu sometimes welled up in tears. Watching participants returning to their cushions I felt deep compassion for each and every one and a profound respect for the confrontation with self that each was making. In the Dharma love blooms like lilacs in the cruellest month.

A Game of Chess with 'me' at stake. New York, November 1994

Retreats are like games of chess that one plays against oneself. There is the beginning game, the middle game and the end game. In the first one settles in, endeavours to overcome the trepidation at facing another period of quite severe physical and mental hardship and to set aside both positive and negative expectations. In the second phase the struggle with self emerges, karmic predispositions appear in florid form, the body aches, there may be drowsiness and depression, all of which must be gone through as gates that are gateless. Finally, in the end game, if one is fortunate and has worked well, you come home.

Soon I was caught by the memory of a hua t'ou "There is no time. What is memory?" which I had first encountered years before in Hong Kong[6]. My mind became engaged in an intense investigation trying to penetrate the logic of this question. This was thought alright but not wandering thought, it was a racing mind intellectually engaged.

If there was no time, then all that has happened is literally no more. The past is dead; yet so often it seems that history determines the present moment as if all those dead persons were still with us determining our fate. False: the past is totally gone and since the future is not yet here there can only be this existing moment. All the shaping and conditioning of this moment springs from the recreation of the past. But if memory is only thought, what happens if thought, that colourful cognitive representation, that neurotic working out of unfinished business, is dropped? There is just the silent moment of existence, life but no-mind. What is that?

At that moment, I thought, there is only the unfolding of the Universe which, like a bubbling spring of ever fresh water, never stops arising and changing at the very moment of its appearance. Time becomes momentariness when we freeze it into solid memories. I am no more than a fragment of this vast unfolding which keeps reinventing itself in the virtual reality of memory. When I stop there is just the flowing. I bowed to the Buddha. "No path!" I said and the Buddha seemed to wink.

In my racing mind there was a focused excitement of exploration. Chi was running high and as each inference fell into place there was a real shift in experience, a thrill of discovery and an opening to whatever might come next. Finally, with nowhere else to go, the wholeness, the gestalt, of reaching an end gave a sense of realisation and joy. Yet, I suspected, all this was no more than "namtok" as the Tibetans call it, illusory intellection in which the 'I' was preening its golden feathers.

In interview I tried to speak of this with Shi-fu. He was not impressed. Metaphysical speculation, however exciting and revealing, was not enlightenment. Was I experiencing doubts about my method? I returned somewhat deflated to my cushion. I was clearly not using my hua t'ou properly. I shifted to "What is NOW?" using the directions helpfully given by Shi-fu.

On the last afternoon Shi-fu told us the story of the monk who, lest he be beheaded, had to carry a bowl of oil over a set distance without spilling a drop even though startled by various threats and surprises. Shi-fu bade us do likewise with our meditation so I focused my hua t'ou and worked hard. Silence descended in a profound samadhi within which thought sometimes moved softly. Holding my hua t'ou, I seemed to be a helmsman of a small ship bidden to steer towards the peak of a distant mountain. Waves and wind constantly moved the bowsprit off the marker and, as I adjusted the wheel, the bows swung past the marker in the other direction. Steering is a constant flow of minor adjustment to the lively movement of ship and sea. I had a vision that the ship was my body, steering was my mind and that the two were linked in a flowing process in which the 'I' need not be present at all. There was simply the flowing expression of cause and effect in the endless selfless flow of a sea-borne dance.

As I emerged from this samadhi I felt the room around me, the cars roaring and honking in the streets outside, the voices in many languages of the passers-by. All this was the sea on which I steer the ship under the guidance of the hua t'ou. But no one was steering the ship, no one was sitting on the cushion, there was just a cushion-sitting under an open sky. Instead of being locked in meditation everything opened out in joyous freedom as I sat there, beyond meditation, marvelling at the view. As the last moments of the retreat passed it was as if the ship came home to an island harbour. Unobserved, I bowed quietly to the Buddha, to Shi-fu and the assembly.

Nothing matters and everything must go, yet love is having the heart touched in the valleys of suffering.[7]

****

Final reflections

Personal critique

What lessons can I learn from these reports that may be useful for a beginning practitioner?

Firstly, on retreat one will indeed discover that one is not in control of one's own mind. Gradually, under the caring eye of the Master, you learn to practise with a method that calms the mind and establishes an awareness that includes refreshing and novel states of consciousness. Liturgical chant and prostration provide opportunities for deep feeling which is likely to include repentance and a renewal of forgiveness and hope. The whole process provides an often startling insight into the operations of one's mind.

It is also clear, moreover, that this process is not accomplished without a struggle with your own concerns; about who you may be; how you are regarded; what is comfortable or comforting to you and what stress may be supportable by you. Indeed, you may soon realise that the retreat is set up deliberately to challenge the self-referring mind by providing circumstances that challenge all its wants and desires for stability, security and sense of permanence. The challenges are tough and increase or lessen at the apparent caprice of the Master. You submit to his authority willingly, yet at the same time inevitably resist his power and influence. Who is he to order me about?

The participant is being challenged to recognise the validity of the Four Noble Truths. Life is suffering because desire is endless. Only when addictive desire is challenged at its source is there a hope of going beyond desire and finding freedom from habitual attachments. On retreat, desire is subtle: we are not speaking of major lusts after sex or chocolate but discrete underground movements; hurrying to a preferred place at table; wondering whether one needs another cup of tea and whether it should be Earl Grey, English Breakfast or Camomile; preoccupations with whether the Master approves of you; how near you might be to an experience of enlightenment; all this against a background of physical discomfort which you would dearly like to avoid. All these take over the mind and become barriers to insight. This is no easy ride, it is rather a Dharma struggle, trying to see the truth of the Dharma in its experiential reality rather than reviewed perhaps sleepily in a late evening armchair. Only when the difficulties, errors, stupidities and need to repent have been passed through in acceptance can they be laid aside. Indeed the putting aside begins to occur quite naturally as the acknowledgement of one's foolish egoistic self becomes unavoidable and accepted. That is when meditation starts.

These retreat reports also show that similar patterns crop up repeatedly in successive retreats. There is no question of a sudden immediate enlightenment just because you have elected to sit facing a wall for a few hours. This is long term work requiring dedication over a period of years, even a lifetime. Yet there is a kind of spiralling progression. As one spirals onwards, there is a change in each returning spin. The anguished dreams and pointless madness of the mind's career begin to centre clearly in the problems that are the result of a personal past, a personal karma, the very nucleus from which self-concern springs. Again and again, one brings this karmic complex through the door of the Ch'an Hall. Again and again, it goes through its destructive paces but gradually a clearer insight into its nature emerges. The sense of self-importance and protection diminishes. What does it matter where I sit, which tea I drink or whether Shi-fu is watching me? The body too gets trained, so that sitting is no longer a trouble, aches and pains become rare events. When you see yourself clearly, maybe you begin to find that rueful grin that is the start of acceptance. Yes, I am a joke, sometimes pathetic, almost always foolish, but, hey, this is where I start from.

Wilful dedication is needed on retreat and, with persistence, the mind indeed calms down. The way the mind works and leads you astray becomes clearer, depression gives way to confidence. Yes, after all I'm alright. A thrilling sense of freedom emerges. One returns to everyday life open and joyous. Working through karma to acceptance allows an integration of the fragmented and often rejected parts of one's mentality, recreating a unified sense of being in the world. Yet this is not completion.

One of the problems that began to manifest clearly as I progressed through several retreats was that my mind easily began to race under the influence of high chi. These were exciting times when the enthusiastic mind spun webs of intellectual insight, created poetry and imagery and became quite delighted in its manifestations. Shi-fu had indeed warned us that when there is too much "illumination", silence gets drowned out and the meditation becomes unbalanced. After such times I reflected: fun it certainly had been but none the less I seemed to be losing my way. Freedom did not lie in this direction: the dangers of an increasing self-satisfaction and an addiction to high intellectual energy were becoming clear. Furthermore, I had the impression that, as retreats became easier for me through familiarity, this difficulty was increasingly present. All that stuff about the ship coming into harbour with no one at the tiller. Highly suspicious!

I began to do some short solitary retreats in the hills to watch my mind-games more closely. I began to be able to relax without excited elaborations in the silence of the Total Body Awareness and the spaciousness that followed its emergence. In those silences there was little thought, perhaps a movement or two on the back burner but nothing up and running. In that space lay a new sort of freedom; nothing special; just an open presence; just "being time" as Dogen might say; a freedom from the need to do anything; abiding in not knowing; a bare awareness that simply let the world go on turning, a sense of vivid enquiry. Perhaps in that lay the secret of the Buddha's smile.

At least I feel now that this is the clear path. With practice such freedom begins to arise at any time; thoughts just drop out and there it is; nothing in particular; nothing to talk about; a private intimacy that feels complete.

Enlightenment? What's that?

One is told again and again that for an enlightenment experience to occur the self has to be forgotten. How can you do this when it is clear that, when you want such an experience, the ego is unavoidably present? Enlightenment cannot be a product of thought and intention. It arises out of its own nature when it wills: it comes over one in its own time often in a moment of amazement. Unplanned, unexpected, nothing to do with 'me'.

What then is enlightenment? There is so much confusion around this term in the literature and also, it often seems, in the teachings, that careful contemplation is needed and the facts of the mind's journey on and off retreat need to be well understood. Enlightenment refers to two separable processes, firstly to the gradual emergence of a self-understanding that leads to openness and caring for others. Secondly, it refers to periods, often quite short, when all egoistic reference falls away, the mind and environment merge in a mirroring wisdom felt at once to be an ultimate realisation, "seeing the nature". In any generation there may be a few individuals for whom this state is stable and long enduring but for most, who are so blessed as to realise such vision at all, it is of short duration, even momentary and comes only infrequently and capriciously in a lifetime. The records of the masters indeed show that for many of them such an event was infrequent, yet it formed the root inspiration for their stance in life.

A simple conclusion follows from this. As Roshi Reb Andersen once put it "You can't do it!" If you, that is your ego, is present, kensho cannot happen. If you want it even a teeny bit, its possibility is entirely precluded. Training can achieve a one-pointed mind and that which follows from that but does not necessarily predict a self-transcending insight. One may indeed return to the market place from one's mountain cottage as an unfragmented person well capable of practising the Bodhisattva's way and helping others but without having had an enlightenment experience. 'Seeing the nature' cannot be won, you can only be open to a possibility. Maybe you become enlightenment prone, maybe not.

It is for this reason that the wisest of Ch'an masters have always insisted that training should continue after realisation. Indeed, after a brief experience of kensho, training is even more important lest illusions of grandeur and a return of self importance corrupt the path. As Shi-fu so wisely says "Continue, continue!"

After one retreat I discussed with him the fact that experiences of self-transcendence occur not only in all religions but also among nature mystics and poets. It seems a universal property of the human mind however rarely seen. What then was special about the Zen enlightenment experience? What is the especial insight of Ch'an that gives Ch'an its peculiar claim to truth. Indeed, what is truth apart from opinion?

I had asked Shi-fu whether it could be said that kensho resulted from training. If you say 'yes' then it is possible to say that kensho is a goal of training but, if you say no, then training cannot produce it. In response Shi-fu remarked that, rather than as the result of some technique, it was training broadly in the Dharma as a whole way of being that facilitated the emergence of kensho. A transcendent experience within the Dharma is rooted in an understanding of impermanence and it is this that constitutes the especial claim to truth of Ch'an. Other similar religious experiences may be attributed to God or some outside agent and are therefore aspects of an 'outer path' with a dependency projected beyond human life. In Buddhism, Ch'an, life, the universe are all experienced as one pervasively interpenetrating, always moving, whole. There is no other. In kensho this is nature seen, yet what it is that is seen remains beyond any certainty of description, of any closure. There is only amazement within enquiry.

A dead mind?

On another occasion, Shi-fu had remarked that one of the reasons why the koan system had been created was that monks in monasteries had become no longer able to "maintain the dead mind" and hence masters had had to invent new ways of focusing. I said to Shi-fu that the thought that Ch'an requires the development of an extraordinary mind is a problem many people have. It appears that there is an everyday mind and an enlightened mind with training purporting to create one from the other. Yet, in his talks, Shi-fu had been insisting that there was only one mind, the ordinary mind of awareness. What then was this "dead mind"?

Shi-fu said that the dead mind was one that had become dead to attachments or, better put, a mind in which attachments had died. One should not differentiate this mind from ordinary mind for it is simply free from the dependencies that bind it to wants based in ignorance. Once freed, the mind becomes an awareness of clarity with unobscured insight into its own nature.

"Did this mean it had no thoughts?" I asked. "No", said Shi-fu, thought remains. Indeed there is always thought however quiet it may have become. The difference lies in what thought concerns. Attached thoughts express themselves in wanting or not wanting and they move about quickly. There is division and divisiveness. In a calmed mind thought remains but there is less conflict and it moves slowly. It may even become so slow as to be undetectable, but it is there none the less, latent. Even under the Bo tree thought was present. The Sutras show clearly that the Buddha was aware of his experiences in a way that could be expressed in thought. The essence of the contrast does not lie in the presence or absence of thought but in something else.

I said, "What happens then in the moment of 'seeing the nature'? Something has gone absent at this time. If it is not thought, what is it?"

Shi-fu replied that it was the self, or rather the sense of self, that had gone absent. There is then no self to which experience can be referred nor any self as a subject of experience. There is no self-concern whatsoever. Absolutely no wanting therefore. There is a pristine clarity of an awareness without any sort of desire for there is no cognisable basis for one who could want.

Shi- fu went on, "The 'me' is a sort of symbol, a script the thinking state invents to account for itself. It is just one, although a very major one, among many such scripts that appear to perception and thus to consciousness. When the mind puts it down, experience changes its quality, not so much its nature. It sees its own nature directly without a secondary activity of imputation and explanation."

I remarked that when self-reference is present that mind appears in split form, self as subject, self as object. Understanding can then only be a form of explanation. Direct seeing means the end of dualism.

"The 'dead mind'," Shi-fu continued, "is a mind without attachment and, in seeing its own nature, it has no self. The enlightened mind is never the less the ordinary mind of awareness: thought, perception and all other attributes remain in place. The beginner's mind can be an enlightened mind as soon as attachments drop away. The presence of a self-cherishing mind is the hallmark of Samsara while its absence is Nirvana."

I said, "This then has nothing to do with samadhi or trance states of any kind. Dogen was right to insist on no fundamental difference between sitting and enlightenment."

Shi-fu said "Only when a self-cherishing mentality dissolves of its own accord naturally and without willed effort can the insight occur. In a sense nothing special has happened - and that is why it is special. All one can do is the practice. Let the rest alone."

I said, "Shi-fu, you make it all so easy!" One of the monks present remarked "That is the sign of a true master." Shi-fu just smiled, remarking that in our conversation he had had the strange experience of understanding what I was saying even though he did not really know the English words. There was, he said, direct communication.

1 Some of these reports have been already been published anonymously in the Ch'an Magazine of the Chung Hwa Institute of Buddhist Culture, New York.

2 See Crook, J. H. 1997. Hilltops of the Hong Kong Moon. Minerva. London. Chapter 14.

3 Wu is the Chinese for the better known Japanese word Mu.

4 For a fuller description see Crook, J. H. and J. Low. 1997 The Yogins of Ladakh. Motilal Banarsidas. Delhi p37-40.

5 Chinese: Interrogate, examine, look into.

6 See Crook, J. H. 1997. Hilltops of the Hong Kong Moon. Minerva. London. p139.

7 Author's verse from the liturgy of the Western Zen Retreat, Western Ch'an Fellowship.

8 It must not be thought that "seeing the nature" arises as a direct product of training. Often such an experience arises outside a retreat and only obscurely linked to the training undergone. At other times it occurs spontaneously outside any training but usually in some life circumstance that has something of the quality of self-confrontation about it. When it does arise in relation to training it comes in different ways depending on that training. The intense methods of koan exploration in the Rinzai sect of Japan tend to produce the classic, dramatic and sometimes questionable breakthrough described, perhaps misleadingly, in popular literature. In the quieter, less driven, system of Soto it arises gently, almost surreptitiously so that the distinctions between a very complete personal integration in a deeply silenced mind and enlightenment are difficult to determine. Teachers are correspondingly careful about acknowledging experiences. In Tibetan Mahamudra again the

realisation comes gradually as a result of concentration on emptiness (see Note 3 above). In all cases however the subject will know the difference from the ordinary mind however steeped it may be in samadhi states. Even in absorption in emptiness, when no clear feel of self is present, a sense of intentionality may be there. In realisation, it is not.

NCF XXI

EDITORIAL FROM THE CH'AN HALL

Millennial Zen

So the millennium came upon us. I cannot say I felt any excitement or anticipation. I was in fact distinctly underwhelmed. All Christmas some hundred people sat miserably bound and gagged in a shit-stinking aeroplane slowly freezing on an Afghani airfield, innocent Indians caught in the continuing inability of India and Pakistan to sort out their confusions over Kashmir. The Russian army, true to a reputation for brutality, destroys Grozny with excessive bombardment forgetting that even the heaviest bombing hardly ever produces the results expected. Against these tidings the glitz of fireworks on the Thames and the splendour of The Dome and the Eye seemed merely the trivia of capitalism's controversial successes. Probably only a few revellers consider what this 2000 years represents.

Two thousand years ago Jesus the Christ was born. We Westerners dispute his historicity, we treat God as dead, we are left with the ruminations of the Don Cupitts of this world doing their best with this century's loss of conventional Christian meanings. Underlying this is severe disorientation. With no external source of meaning, self-identity loses value. We are prone to subtle depressions from which we run as if from hell - into sexual hedonism, a crudity of humour that even lovers of ancient bawdy must disdain, the administration of 400 brands of psychotherapy and the nonsense of uprooted religious ethics carelessly grafted on unsuitable roots. Even so the cheerful energy of London swinging into the new millennium yet beguiles. There is a careless joy here, like a sort of fiddling while the stock exchange keeps rising.

The excitement of the crowd on the Embankment as Big Ben toiled towards midnight was a thrill. The immense crush of good-natured, friendly, Christmas-spirited people showed what human good will could comprehend. Around us were smiling faces of many nations, many cultures reminding us of the amazing mix that is now contemporary Britain. How to use this good will, this creativity for the good of us all? Here lies the deepest question.

The Millennium is like a baby. Babies are born in many circumstances but whether these are of comfort or dislocation the baby always needs first attention. Whatever our view of our time the Baby needs help, needs love, needs our care. As time runs forward, babies are born every minute. What is our responsibility to them? Perhaps one responsibility is to look again at what Christ said. There are deep parallels with Buddha's way, his existentialism; and the Dalai Lama himself has been looking over the similarities of these two great religions of compassion. The secret must lie in a re-evaluation of which the churches themselves seem incapable. We should do it. Who else?

Our extraordinary century, now ended, leaves us in a state never before experienced. A global integration of economics and information means that the whole planet is now networked into a mix of complex opportunities and risk that is totally new. On the one hand, the steady spread of democracy makes the possibility of world war increasingly remote, yet the likelihood of internal strife in unstable states more probable. The danger of some confrontation between the West and an authoritarian China that fails to moderate its flouting of human rights in Tibet and other minority regions increases rather than decreases with time. Yet, we have to remember that, in spite of their discrete racial arrogance, the Chinese are not a people prone to war. The dangers of ever fewer transnational companies of immense ecopolitical power imposing their commercial wills upon the planet without thought for the benefit of the human race and indeed life on the planet as a whole, remain great but is at last being confronted- as the Monsanto affair and the events at Seattle have shown.

I have faith in the voice of people-power. Unfortunately the character of people power depends on people education. In many parts of the world it is an education in the meaning of global affairs that is lacking - witness Iran, witness Burundi, witness Afghanistan and what of Russia? - a country that needs to resolve an understandable and dangerous paranoia.

Zen means mindfulness of the everyday. The issues of our time concern us all - especially as lay practitioners who avoid the relatively unconcerned luxury of monasticism. We need to know clearly what we stand for - we need to have our definition of humanity and human needs always before us and informing our practices. While Buddhism is a 'refuge', it is also the basis for movement outwards into the world, the source of 'right livelihood'. We are not Prime Ministers or Presidents. We are ordinary members of the body politic and we need to get our values straight. For this reason buddhistic social criticism is an important aspect of our 'witness'.

Buddhism is not merely a source of togetherness in an alienating world, nor a source of comfort in a world lacking external meaning, it is a challenge to enquiry based on ancient insights and values that are demonstrably workable in our time.

The koan of our time is to live from generated meanings that come from empirically verifiable experience in life. In a world of ethical confusion dominated by markets rather than persons this project becomes the enlightenment project of our time.

Ch'uan-Teng Chien-Ti

January 2000

ONE THOUGHT FOR A THOUSAND YEARS

A Ch'an Hall meditation

Out of the corner of my eye I catch a glimpse of Bodhisattva Ksitigarbharaja seated upon the offering table in the Ch'an hall. As usual his serene countenance glows quietly there. I take a closer look. His expression of peace and tranquillity begins to enter and then to flood my mind. Time becomes motionless yet the soft wind gently moves the branches beyond the window, the distant rustle of the stream goes on. I am once again amazed at the power of this little statue to induce so profound a shift in attention, in awareness.

Whoever carved this little figure seems to have been able to place his own inner equanimity in the carving of this face. The inner peace emerges again and again from this iconic expression and becomes transmissible to those sensitive enough to receive it. The Bodhisattva enters the problematique of our minds and shifts something there. Time falls still, it seems.

The statue may be seventeenth or eighteenth century or possibly not so old, the iconography is not unusual and there are many such carvings on the offering tables of Buddhists in China. I have seen many of them but in most of them the face, even if well carved, does not radiate anything special. The genius of this carver was to create an expression that penetrates. How? I do not know. Perhaps it is not true for everyone. I am eternally thankful that this little statue came my way and now adorns our Ch'an Hall.

But what is it telling me? Whenever I carry through this communion I have an opening to stillness, a falling out of time. My thoughts of past and future fade away and there I am on my cushion hearing the breeze, seeing sunshine or rain and aware of the tranquillity emanating from the figure before me. And a thought comes to my mind, a single line quotation from the Hsin Hsin Ming - "one thought for a thousand years"!

A thousand years ago, maybe someone had that thought. What was it? No-thought in fact. Simply the dropping into the present moment, the moment that being timeless has no past or future in it. It seems not to move. One seems to have entered the eternity of the present continuum. Outside time indeed lies eternity. But the Bodhisattva here is not outside of time, rather he is within the timeless moment as it moves, the continuity of the timeless moment as it flows like a leaf borne on the current of a river. The leaf is still, in itself it has no time, yet it flows on the current of time. It rides the wave of time like a motionless fly on the inside of a train window doing a hundred miles an hour. Surfing the wave of time the figure on the board is motionless, it is the wave that moves. The wave and the surfer are one and in unity they flow towards the shore.

The continuity of the present moment arises experientially only when one flows with time in time. This is what Dogen meant by "Being Time" in his wondrous fascicle 'Uji'. This is not the timeless outside time, the eternity in which time happens, a void that has no continuity. Rather this is the flow of the universe itself. To enter that timeless moment of flow, this continuous present, is the same whenever one may do it. Within a thousand years one may enter the same 'thought' again and again. There is only one moment flowing in the timeless present, a movement synonymous with the expanding edge of the universe itself. Only as the mind drops into past or contemplates the future is one outside this moment. Yet for us samsaric beings that is for most of our existence. We categorise time to make it so.

This moment is the only moment one ever has. It is the only real. To be outside the present is to have the mind engaged with the past that is dead or the future that has yet to come. Such a mind is not alive to the living present where it actually resides. As soon as the rider dismounts the moment is lost, the surfer is stranded on the bank of time, the continuity of the present flows on without him. He has lost nirvana and is back in samsara's threefold time.

Finding this moment is when Ch'an begins. All the rest is preparatory, stage setting for the moment, seeking a way to it. The preliminaries of Ch'an fill most of our life on or off the cushion. Only the one who surfs the wave of the timeless present knows the continuity of time, being time.

Our practice is rarely thus. The World Honoured One climbs the seat. He appears about to speak. Manjusri strikes the gavel and the World Honoured One descends from his seat. Nothing can be said in the timeless moment flowing with the river. One word and one falls back into the three times, their divisiveness, their apparent movement from birth to death. All of that indeed is death. Only on the ridge of the wave is life. And to say a word is to dismount.

We train in Ch'an to be able to enter this moment. There is no other. Ksitigarbharaja enters our world of the three times to bring us out as surfers. Only then does meditation begin. Only in that one thought for a thousand years does meditation deepen. The rest is preliminary. In entering that thought, that moment, one enters the same moment the carver knew as he carved this icon. No past, no future, simply the present continuity of the wave's crest moving always onwards as the universe itself evolves.

This is what Ch'an as a way, as a practice, is all about. This is why Bodhidharma said, "Direct seeing, no scriptures, no words". And why Hui-neng knew there was neither mirror bright nor stand and nowhere for the dust to alight.

Do not be mistaken about Ch'an. Most of what we do is merely preliminary, a clearing of undergrowth on the way to the beach to find a wave. Riding the steed of time, surfing the wave, flying in a thermal like an eagle: these metaphors point the way. Our koan is to turn such reflection into the continuity of the living moment, old yet ever young.

APRIL SHOWERS

Everybody's back
everyone is singing
willow warbler, chiff chaff
flycatchers, redstart
and even the cuckoo too.
Hares are running in the April showers
the brook churns rounded stones
downhill, shafts of sunlight
crafting the green-grass view
late daffodils bent by an Easter snow.
Deep clouds obscure the moon,
it's chilly yet in the old hills
and hearth light glows warmly in the coals,
lamplight falling in yellow pools
the open book mirrors words in silence.

A BUDDHIST READING LIST

This reading list is for the guidance of those wishing to acquire a relatively comprehensive understanding of Buddhism, its past and its future in a global world. Naturally any choices from the vast literature available merely reflect a given individual's preferences. These are books that I have personally found useful. If you begin with these then you will soon go on to make your own reading personally creative.

The introductory list is intended for those attending retreats for the first time. The other lists are for those who want to study an issue in greater depth. All works are readably accessible for anyone with a O/A level education although naturally some texts are more demanding than others. A few of the more demanding, academic items are bulleted but many of these are important if you wish to gain a deeper perspective and some are difficult only in part.

The majority of these books are or will be available for consultation in the Maenllwyd Library. Arrangements for a study or reading retreat for fellows may be possible on request. Books may however NOT be borrowed nor taken from the library under any circumstances. A number of the titles listed have been contributed to the library only through kind donations from fellows. Most of the works stem from my own collection.

Books from more obscure publishers in print are often available from Wisdom Books. Some titles have been republished by other publishers. Amazon Books UK on e-mail is often an easy source of many titles

Introductory reading for Beginners in Ch'an/Zen

Batchelor, M. 1998. Principles of Zen. Thorsons. London.

Beck, C. J., 1989. Everyday Zen. Harper. San Francisco.

Cleary, T. Instant Zen. North Atlantic Books. Berkeley.

Crook, J.H. (ed) 1991. Catching a Feather on a Fan. Element. Shaftesbury.

Humphreys, C. 1949. Zen Buddhism. Heinemann. London.

Kabat-Zinn, J. 1994. Wherever You Go There You Are. Hyperion. New York.

Kapleau, P. 1965. The Three Pillars of Zen. Beacon Press. Boston.

Kennet, Roshi J. 1972. Selling Water by the River. Random House. London (reissued as Zen is Eternal Life)

Kukushi, M. 1996. Dream Conversations on Buddhism and Zen. Shambhala. Boston/London.

Lu Kuan Yu 1960 et seq. Ch'an and Zen Teachings. Three Series.

Sheng-Yen, Master. 1982. Getting the Buddha Mind. Dharma Drum. New York.

Stevens, J. 1993. Three Zen Masters. Kodansha International. Tokyo/London.

Suzuki, S. 1970. Zen Mind, Beginners Mind. Weatherhill. New York/Tokyo.

Thich Nhat Hanh. 1974. Zen Keys. Anchor. New York.

Uchiyama, Roshi K. 1973. Approach to Zen. Japan Publications Inc. Tokyo.

Watts, A. 1957. The Way of Zen. Thames and Hudson. London.

Study texts in Indian Buddhism and Theravada

Bunnag, J. 1973. Buddhist Monk, Buddhist Layman: A study of urban monastic organisation in Central Thailand. Cambridge University Press.

Carrithers, M. 1983 The Buddha. Oxford Paperbacks.

Dutt, S. 1962, 1988. Buddhist Monks and Monasteries of India. Motilal Banarsidass. Delhi.

Gombrich, R. 1988. Theravada Buddhism: A Social History from Ancient Banaras to Modern Colombo. RKP. London.

Humphreys, C. Buddhism. Penguin. London.

Ling, T. 1976. The Buddha. Pelican. Penguin Books. London.

Ling, T. 1981. The Buddha's Philosophy of Man. Early Indian Buddhist Dialogues. Everyman. London.

Nyanaponika, Thera and Hecker, H. 1997. Great Disciples of the Buddha. Wisdom Books. Boston/London.

Ch'an and Zen - Further studies and more advanced reading

Blofield, J. 1958. The Zen Teaching of Huang Po. Buddhist Society, London.

Blofield, J.1962. The Zen Teaching of Instantaneous Awakening (Hui Hai). Buddhist Publishing Group. Leicester.

Braverman, A. 1989. Mud and Water. A collection of talks by the Zen Master Bassui. North Point. San Francisco.

Buswell, R. E. 1983. The Korean Approach to Zen: The collected works of Chinul. University of Hawaii Press. Honolulu.

Buswell, R.E.1992. The Zen Monastic Experience. U.P. Princeton.

Ch'ang, G.C.C. 1972. The Buddhist Teaching of Totality: the Philosophy of Hwa Yen Buddhism. Allen and Unwin. London.

Cleary, T. 1997. The Five Houses of Zen. Shambhala. Boston/London.

Leighten,T.D. and Yi Wu. 1991. Cultivating the Empty Field. The Silent Illumination of ZenMaster Hongzhi. North Point. San Francisco.

Dumoulin, H. 1979. Zen Enlightenment, Origins and Meaning. Weatherhill. New York/Tokyo.

Holmes Welch, 1967. The Practice of Chinese Buddhism 1900-1950. Harvard U.P. Cambridge, Mass.

Kasulis, T.P. 1981. Zen Action-Zen Person. University of Hawaii Press. Honolulu.

Kraft, K. (ed) 1988. Zen Tradition and Transition. Rider. London.

Leggett, T. 1978. Zen and the Ways. Routledge and Kegan Paul. London.

Loorie, J.D. 1999. Teachings of the Insentient. Dharma Communications. Mt Tremper, NY.

Lu Kuan Yu. 1964. The Secrets of Chinese Meditation. Rider. London.

Nishiyama, K. and J. Stevens. Dogen Zenji: Shobogenzo. The Eye and Treasury of the True Law. 4 vols. Nakayama Shobo. Tokyo.

Sheng-Yen, Master. 1987. Faith in Mind: a Guide to Ch'an Practice. Dharma Drum. New York.

Sheng-Yen, Master. 1997 Complete Enlightenment. Dharma Drum. New York.

Schloegl, I. 1975. The Wisdom of the Zen Masters. Sheldon. London.

Schloegl, I. 1976. The Zen Teaching of Rinzai. Shambhala. Berkeley.

Sekida, K. 1975. Zen Training: Methods and Philosophy. Weatherhill. New York /Tokyo.

Suzuki, D.T. 1949-53. Essays in Zen Buddhism. Three Series. Rider. London. Victoria, B. 1997. Zen at War. Weatherhill. New York/Tokyo.

Waddell, N. 1996. Zen Words for the Heart: Hakuin's commentary on the Heart Sutra.Shambhala. Boston/London.

Koan manuals etc.

Sheng-Yen, Master. 1987. The Poetry of Enlightenment. Dharma Drum. New York.

Cleary, T. 1990. The Book of Serenity: One hundred Zen Dialogues. Lindisfarne. New York.

Shaw, R.D.M. 1961 The Blue Cliff Records. The Hekigan Roku. Michael Joseph. London.

Tibetan Buddhism

Ch'ang, G.C.C. 1970. The Hundred Thousand Songs of Milarepa. Harper Colophon. New York/London.

Ch'ang, G.C.C. 1963. Six Yogas of Naropa and Teachings on Mahamudra. Snow Lion. New York.

Cozort. D. 1986. Highest Yoga Tantra: An Introduction to the Esoteric Buddhism of Tibet. Snow Lion, New York.

Crook, J and Low, J. 1997. The Yogins of Ladakh. Motilal Banarsidas. Delhi.

David-Neel, A. 1967. Magic and Mystery in Tibet. Souvenir Press. London.

Gyatso, P. 1997. Fire Under the Snow. Testimony of a Tibetan Prisoner Harvil. London.

Harrer, H. 1953. Seven Years in Tibet. Hart Davis. London.

Lama Anagarika Govinda. 1959. Foundations of Tibetan Mysticism. Rider. London.
Lama Anagarika Govinda. 1966. The Way of the White Clouds. Hutchinson. London.

Lama Anagarika Govinda. 1977 Creative Meditation and Multi-dimensional Consciousness. Allen and Unwin. London.

Low, J. 1994. Simply Being. Durtro. London. (Also republished elsewhere now)
Mackenzie, V. 1998. Cave in the Snow: A Western Woman's quest for Enlightenment. Bloomsbury. London.

Rangdrol, T.N. 1989. Lamp of Mahamudra. Shambhala. Boston/Shaftesbury.

Samuel, G. 1993. Civilised Shamans: Buddhism in Tibetan Societies. Smithsonian. Washington.

Snellgrove, D. 1987. Indo-Tibetan Buddhism. Serindia. London.

Snelling, J. 1990. The Sacred Mountain: The Complete Guide to Tibet's Mount Kailas. East-West Publications. London/La Hague

Sogyal Rimpoche. 1992. The Tibetan Book of Living and Dying. Harper. San Francisco.

Wallace, B.A. 1980. The Life and Teaching of Geshe Rabten: A Tibetan Lama's Search for Truth. Allen and Unwin. London.

Buddhist History and Contemporary Culture

Batchelor, S. 1994. The Awakening of the West. The Encounter of Buddhism and Western Culture.

Parallax Press. Berkeley.

Bishop, P. 1989. The Myth of Shangri la. Athlone. London.

Ch'en, K. 1964. Buddhism in China: A historical Survey. Princeton.

Crook, J.H. and Osmaston, H. (eds). 1994. Himalayan Buddhist Villages. Motilal Banarsidass for Bristol University.

Fields, R. 1986. How the Swans Came to the Lake: a narrative history of Buddhism in America. Shambhala. Boston.

Friedman, L. 1987. Meetings with Remarkable Women: Buddhist Teachers in America. Shambhala. Boston/London.

Gernet, J. 1995. Buddhism in Chinese Society, an economic history from the fifth-tenth centuries. Columbia U.P. New York.

Goldstein, M.C. and Kapstein, M.T(eds). 1998. Buddhism in Contemporary Tibet. University of California Press. London.

Goyal, S.R. 1987. A History of Indian Buddhism. Kasumanjali Prakashan. Meerut.
Kitagawa, J.M. and Cummings, M. (eds). 1987. Buddhism and Asian History. Macmillan.

Lopez, D.S. 1999. Prisoners of Shangri la: Tibetan Buddhism and the West. University of Chicago Press.

Shakya, T. 1999. The Dragon in the Land of Snows. Pimlico. London.

Snelgrove, D. and Richardson, H. 1968. A Cultural History of Tibet. Prajna. Boulder, Colorado. Suzuki, D.T. 1938. Zen Buddhism and its influence on Japanese Culture. Eastern Buddhist Society. Kyoto.

Tworkov, H. 1989. Zen in America: profiles of five teachers. North Point. San Francisco.

Warder, A.K. 1980. Indian Buddhism. Motilal Banarsidass. Delhi.

Williams, P. 1989. Mahayana Buddhism. Routledge. London.

Philosophy, Psychology and Modern Issues

Abe, M. 1985. Zen and Western Thought. Macmillan. London.

Batchelor, S. 1983. Alone with Others: an existential approach to Buddhism. Grove Press. New York.

Batchelor. S. 1990. The Faith to Doubt: glimpses of Buddhist uncertainty. Parallax Press. Berkeley.

Batchelor, S. 1997. Buddhism Without Beliefs: a contemporary guide. Bloomsbury. London.

Collins, S. 1982. Selfless Persons: imagery and thought in Theravada Buddhism. Cambridge.

Crook, J.H. and Fontana, D. (eds). 1990. Space in Mind: East-West psychology and contemporary Buddhism. Element. Shaftesbury.

Eppsteiner, F. (ed). 1988. The Path of Compassion: writings on socially engaged Buddhism. Parallax Press. Berkeley.

Epstein, M. 1996. Thoughts Without a Thinker. Duckworth. London.

Faure, B. 1993. Ch'an Insights and Oversights. Princeton. NJ.

Faure, B. 1991. The Rhetoric of Immediacy. Princeton. NJ. Jones, K. 1989. The Social Face of Buddhism. Wisdom. London.

Faure, B. 1993. Beyond optimism: a Buddhist political ecology. Jon Carpenter. Oxford.

Murti, T.R.V. 1955. The Central Philosophy of Buddhism. Allen and Unwin.

Naranjo, C. and Ornstein, R.E. 1971. On the Psychology of Meditation. Esalen Book. Viking. NY.

Peranjpe, A.C., D.Y.F. Ho and Rieber, R.W. (eds). 1988. Asian Contributions to Psychology.

Praeger. New York/London.

Revel, J-F. and Ricard, M. 1998. The Monk and the Philosopher. Thorsons. London. Watts, A. 1961. Psychotherapy East and West. Ballantine. New York.

Wright, D.S. 1998. Philosophical Meditations on Zen Buddhism. Cambridge.

Some Sutras and Classics in English

Bhikkhu Nanamoli.1972/92. The Life of the Buddha according to the Pali Canon. Buddhist Publication Society. Kandy.

Bhikkhus Nanamoli and Bodhi. 1995. The Middle Length Discourses of the Buddha. Wisdom. London.

Cheng Chien, Bhikshu. 1993. Manifestation of the Tathagata. Buddhahood according to the Avatamsaka Sutra. Wisdom. London.

Cleary, T. 1993. The Flower Ornament Scripture (Avatamsaka Sutra) Shambala. Boston. Price, A.F. and Wong, Mou-lam (trans) 1969. The Diamond Sutra and the Sutra of Hui-neng. Shambhala, Boulder.

Suzuki D.T1932. The Lankavatara Sutra. Routledge and Kegan Paul. London.

Walshe, M. 1995. The Long Discourses of the Buddha. Wisdom. Boston/London.

Introductory Books for Children

Hope, J and van Loon, B 1996 Buddha for Beginners, Writers/Readers Publishing Inc Republished as 1999 Introducing Buddha, Icon Books

Blackstone, J and Josipovic, Z. 1986. Zen for Beginners. Writers/Readers Publishing Inc.

NCF XXII

EDITORIAL FROM THE CH'AN HALL

A number of important things have been happening in the Fellowship and all of them can be warmly welcomed. Shih-fu's retreat at Gaia House was successful and we are grateful to the management there for their assistance in running this important event. Shih-fu also enjoyed a mutually beneficial visit to Throssel Hole Abbey. We all appreciated the warm hospitality we received from the whole community.

Last year, for the first time ever, I was unable to run the January retreat due to a very severe and unpleasant attack of 'flu. I made it to the Maenllwyd and carried through a number of interviews but I was grateful to Hilary and Ken for running the event in my stead. Retreat reports show they did well and this has increased my confidence in gradually introducing new leaders to our programmes. I was especially grateful to Hilary for her TLC when I was feeling exceptionally low. "Patience!" she said. Under my circumstances of almost total, cough racked, immobility this was a wise reminder.

After this retreat Will Turner donated a Millennium Tree which we planted ceremoniously. Unfortunately it is not doing well and we may have to replace it.

Simon has led two short retreats solo this year thus embarking on a new Dharma career. Working respectively with Hilary and Sophie as Guestmasters, the two events were warmly received and reports indicate that a positive atmosphere was created by their work. Simon has trained with me as retreat leader for several years and is now fully qualified to help us all at such events.

As if on cue but quite independently, Shih-fu also informed me while in New York that Simon was among three Westerners he was going to allow to lead Ch'an retreats. The others are Gilbert Gutierrez in California and Max Kalin in Switzerland. While Shih-fu has yet to give "Dharma transmissions", he may be considering doing so when the three have had some experience 'under fire' as it were.

In Britain we are thus especially privileged in having two retreat leaders recognised by Shih-fu. Since Simon has had his experience in Ch'an recognised by Shih-fu as having "seen the nature", fellows and other retreatants can feel unusually secure in receiving Simon's help and guidance. Simon's first Dharma talk is given in this issue of our journal. I warmly welcome Simon as my colleague on the Dharma path.

Things move along. This year there will be a full programme of retreats in the UK and I will be visiting Warsaw, Zagreb and Berlin to support the Ch'an Sanghas there. It has also seemed to me that time was ripe to float a further suggestion (see below). Maybe this will prove to be a bridge too far - but let us see.

Ch'uan-teng Chien-ti

A NEW PROPOSAL: A LAY ZEN 'MONASTIC CENTRE'

It is several years now since I proposed that the casual retreat arrangements at the Maenllwyd might be of greater value to people if we created a charitable institution. Soon the WCF was in being and is now safely established and supported by small affiliated groups in a number of British cities. We have important European contacts and, thanks to Simon Child, a site on the web appreciated by many world-wide. We conduct retreats that almost always run. May be it is time to consider a further development.

I am making a proposal here for discussion among Fellows and all readers of this journal. What exactly do I mean by a "lay monastic centre" or lay monastery? First of all, it is clear that for the foreseeable future most Ch'an practitioners in the West will be lay people. We do have some models of actual monasteries - for example Throssel Hole Abbey, Tassajara and Green Gulch Farm etc, but even these places are sustained primarily by laity. From such lay practitioners I have received requests or questions about some kind of residential arrangement that would be rather more permanent and enduring than our current system of retreats allows and which would focus on longer term, personal retreats within a community practising silence and mindfulness but without the restrictions of a permanent commitment to training for a religious profession.

Perhaps here we may take Gaia House or the Sharpham Trust experiments as examples of the type of community that may be initial models for consideration. Gaia House runs many short term retreats but also sustains a system allowing long term private practice within a loose set of communal rules. Sharpham House has experimented with a community, a residential college and now a looser educational system with short-term residence.

I envisage a property with at least five or six rooms for personal occupancy, a meditation hall, a library-cum-office, accommodation for a Director, a sizeable garden or land and set in a suitable environment. Residency would not be permanent. Individuals would contract to stay for perhaps a two to three month minimal residential period open to renewal. The community would thus refresh itself regularly and be less likely to suffer from internal social problems than institutions of more fixed residency. Practitioners would all be lay persons of considerable retreat experience and personal dedication, supported by letters of recommendation and subject to interview. The centre would not be a place for teaching but for practice. Residents should therefore be capable of individual practice. The Director, especially if the first one was myself, would not be permanently in residence. Supervision through dokusan interview would however be more or less regularly provided. Each member would have a personal, agreed upon, practice and daily schedule set within a communal structure involving meals in common, a liturgy, two to three group meditation practices, group discussion and two hours work in the property. Individuals would take turns in certain essential roles such as cooking, obtaining supplies, office work, housework and gardening etc. One member would be a manager for whom some financial benefit may accrue.

Individuals might also be encouraged to do some creative work on their own during residency. This could be study, research or thesis writing, preparing a book or articles, a programme of reading, local field work or service or the continuation of a career through computer or other practicable means such as e-mail. Possibly some relationship with local Buddhists of a mutually beneficial nature may be established in time. While the main orientation would be Ch'an Buddhism as viewed by the WCF, persons of other Buddhist persuasions may, after appropriate discussion, also make use of such facilities.

The key question is who would be interested in such a project? Clearly a sustained occupancy would be essential for financial reasons. Who would like to come? People who have contacted me so far are mostly individuals who wish to deepen their spiritual lives but who do not envisage monkhood as a professional undertaking. They have had some deep experiences on retreat or otherwise in their lives and seek to explore the Buddhist way of being. Other individuals may have just emerged from some trauma in marriage, illness, through accidents or bereavements or war, terrorism etc and seek a period of sustained quiet under some supervision. Others may be approaching retirement and wish to reconsider how their lives may best be fulfilled. The intention to reside permanently at the institution would not be appropriate, although return visits may be encouraged at least in some cases.

The "Director" would be responsible for the Ch'an Buddhist orientation of the view and practice sustained in the "Monastic Centre" and act as spiritual guide to the community. The prime orientation would be that of the WCF as constitutionally established. Master Sheng-yen in conversation has approved the project. The manager would literally 'manage' the day to day arrangements. Various committees, advisory board etc would be established and the exact relationship with the WCF clarified.

Where could this be? Of course, were it possible to secure land and funding it would be good to develop Maenllwyd along these lines. Alternatively other properties might be considered. I may be able to supply some initial finance but any development would be dependent upon considerable fund raising. A major effort to raise sufficient funds would be required and this involves financial management at many levels.

In the short term, a property owned by my sister and I may be a suitable site for an initial one-year experiment. We own a beautiful house set in a large wooded garden in central Southampton. Although obviously urban, the property is secluded, surprisingly peaceful and has a happy atmosphere conducive to reflection and meditation. It is fully equipped and certified by the city council for multiple occupancy and is currently leased to students. While a considerable loss of rental might be sustained by such an experiment, should sufficient enthusiasm be shown this is a matter we are very willing to consider seriously. The advantage of this property is that no additional fund raising is required to set the project going.

The house currently comprises six bed-sitting rooms equipped as student studies, enough to accommodate one director and five "yogins", one large room suitable as a meditation hall, another as a social room or lounge for meetings, a library-cum-office, a kitchen dining room and a large entrance hall way. There are two bathrooms and three toilets. In the approximately one and a half acre wooded garden full of bluebells in spring is a hut which, after renovation, could be used as additional summer accommodation. The driveway could accommodate three to four cars. Southampton is a pleasant city, currently booming, with easy access to the sea, the Isle of Wight and the New Forest.

Preliminary study of the economics suggest that a number of scenarios for residency are possible. A calculated price for residency of say £15 per head per day (i.e. £450 per month), exclusive of catering but inclusive of council tax and insurance as well as basic house maintenance, is only slightly above current student rates and below most holiday rentals. (Prices might be lowered with a full house sustained as such over a period.) This would allow either:

3-5 people in residence each for single months throughout the year thus allowing thirty-six "yogins" to experience retreats.

or 3-5 people in residence for three months each thus allowing twelve different people to experience longer retreats.

or various combinations of such periods or longer.

The exact relation between this project and the WCF would need careful consideration due to the nature of the financing. It may initially have to be a separate project running in close relationship to the Fellowship.

Turnover times would be on an individual basis so that the community would have a fluctuating membership and hence a number of people would participate in management roles to provide a varying meditative environment. On the whole I believe retreats of this kind would be best when of at least three months duration.

This experiment could be set up quite soon depending upon the interest and enthusiasm shown. Obviously such a project is a dead duck without a committed and positive input from participants. Vague, half-hearted interest would not be sufficient.

So there it is -- I look forward to hearing from Fellows and readers of this journal in order to assess the nature of interest that the proposal arouses -- questions, alternative ideas, offers of financial help, or direct expressions of interest that might lead to an application to participate will all be welcome. Do contact me as soon as possible. None of us is getting any younger and the time is now.

THE PLACE OF CH'AN IN POST-MODERN EUROPE

Shih-fu has encouraged me to assist Ch'an Sanghas in Europe as well as in Britain. Naturally this has caused me to look more closely at continental Buddhism than I might otherwise have done. Some of the results have surprised me. A review of this kind is essential to formulating a Western Ch'an suited to Europeans and this is one of the tasks Shih-fu has asked of us all.

Introduction

When Master Sheng-yen got a shoe full of muddy water on alighting from his car in a remote farmyard in Wales in 1989 it was a but a damp prelude to the first presentation of Chinese Zen on intensive retreat in Britain. His subsequent visits have provided us with a fresh and profound discourse on the Chinese view of Zen hitherto dominated by Japanese versions. Few of us at the time also understood that these visits were perhaps unconsciously also a contribution to a considerable reinterpretation of the meaning of Zen for the West, or at least Europe.

When I was first asked to contribute to this volume I was rash enough to consider writing about the face of Zen in the mirror of contemporary "post-modern" Western thought. Reflection quickly revealed the arrogance of this idea. Yet the relation between the ideas about Zen current in the 1950s when I was first interested in the subject (Crook 1998) and the perspectives with which it is regarded today is an important field of enquiry for me personally. In 1994 Master Sheng-yen passed on to me transmission in the Lin-chi lineage of Ch'an to run intensive retreats and teach Dharma not only in Britain but where possible also in Europe (see NCF 9: 2-5). How to do this? I asked him. He replied by remarking that since I was British and he was Chinese it would be my task to find out! This article expresses some aspects of my attempts in this direction.

Since we are all lay practitioners the question of the nature of a lay Zen has much preoccupied us. For me, particularly, there has been the question of what emphasis to stress in the teaching of Dharma. The exciting opportunity apparent in the transmission of the Ch'an Dharma to Europe must necessarily engage the rapid changes in European culture and thought characteristic of our time. This change from a "modern" to a "post-modern" culture calls into question some of the interpretations of Zen and Buddhism that were accepted doctrine in the fifties. Without an examination of this critique there is a risk of failing to connect the profundity of the Dharma to our prevailing ways of life and thought. The skilful means are undoubtedly there but still to be fully uncovered.

Suzuki Zen and the Post-Modern Turn

The shift to so called "post-modernity" arose fundamentally from the enormous changes resulting from a growing globalisation as reflected in the growth of transnational corporations and the world wide success of market capitalism. One aspect has been the availability at all times and seasons of food products from anywhere in the globe in the supermarkets of the developed world. In parallel, each and every religious belief and practice is nowadays represented on all our book stalls. One can sign up for virtually anything. The manner in which business, political and cultural transactions have developed has transformed our world to set up a complex, computer led, global interdependence of economic and political activities so that nation states are becoming largely irrelevant and small minded local fascisms gradually a thing of the past. Philosophically these changes have led to a focus on the interdependence of culture and thought and hence to an emphasis on the contextuality of ideas, of historical interpretation, of taste, and of self-expression.

All Buddhists owe a tremendous debt to Daisetz Suzuki who, almost single handed, brought Japanese Zen to the West making a major impact on major contributors to the intellectual scene and thereby bringing a new found faith to many otherwise alienated from religious experience and thought. Among those touched by Suzuki were Thomas Merton, whose respect for the Japanese savant aided the emergence of a so-called Christian Zen, Christmas Humphreys, the London judge who was later to teach Zen himself, Carl. Gustav Jung (in spite of some resistance), Erich Fromm and Aldous Huxley. Arthur Koestler devoted a somewhat intemperate book to a trenchant criticism of Suzuki's approach and, in the post war years of "beat" Zen in California, Kerouac, Ginsberg and Watts based their inspirations upon his writings. Arnold Toynbee is said to have remarked that Suzuki's introduction of Zen to the West would later be compared to the discovery of nuclear energy! The philosopher Heidegger, caught reading one of Suzuki's books is said to have remarked, "If I have understood this man correctly, this is what I have been trying to say in all my writings." (Barrett, 1956). Be that as it may, Suzuki's influence and parallelism with some contemporary trends in Western thought can certainly be said to have been profound. Yet, upon mature reflection resulting largely from a better acquaintance with forms of Zen other than those espoused by Suzuki together with the advent of scholarly, historical study and textual criticism, it emerges that it was his undoubted charisma, open hearted friendship and lovability, as much as his views, that accounted for Suzuki's fame.

Daisetz Suzuki was a great scholar capable of original research in Sanskrit, Chinese and Japanese ancient literature and a subtle commentator on such works. His width of knowledge was great but his appreciation of Zen and Buddhism shifted during his long career from a profound antinomianism to a greater appreciation of the range of Zen experience and its historical transmission. It was however his early presentation that made such a great impact in the West. His later reservations have left little mark.

Suzuki's early view of Zen was lop-sided, favouring a presentation of Japanese Rinzai emphasising spontaneity of responses and the sudden and direct apprehension of reality (subitism). As Faure's detailed critique demonstrates (1993: 52-88), Suzuki interpreted Zen experience as the timeless, ahistorical, context free, basis of mystical experience and hence the very root of religion, of which Zen was thus the purest form (Suzuki 1949-53, 1: 73, 265, 270-272, 2: 304). The experience of enlightenment (kensho) was interpreted as a supreme individual achievement attained through heroic efforts but open to all irrespective of race, nationality or creed. "Because Zen is supposedly free from all ties with any specific religious or philosophical tradition, Suzuki argues it can be practised by Christians and Buddhist alike. -- Suzuki's view of Zen's "oceanic nature" reveals the extent of the exorbitant privilege that he confers on his own interpretation." (Faure 1993: 62).

Reading between the lines, his critics see in Suzuki's work a skilled apologia relating an increasingly triumphalist Japan of the post Meiji era to the Western world. In spite of living in the United States and marrying an American, Suzuki, in the end, is considered by some to have been a Japanese chauvinist who tolerated the militarism of his country leading to the Pacific war in WW2, did not condemn the use of Zen in military training and argued that the war itself was a consequence of Western intellectualism and lack of respect for nature (Faure 1993; 70. Victoria 1997; 22-25 etc). His work has been described as "militant comparativism"; comparative study in order to press home one's own case. And yet it is necessary to place the wartime Suzuki in context. To a degree the Japanese police were suspicious of him due to his prolonged visits to the West and his marriage to an American. He lived in seclusion in his home in Kamakura and recognised that Japan could not possibly win a war against the USA. While his post-war writings accepted a link between Zen and the state, after the war, although he wrote several times on the war responsibility of Japan and accepted that Zen practitioners had been at fault, he mainly blamed Shinto for the disaster (Victoria 1997 147 et seq). As an adopted Westerner, were he alive today, Suzuki would doubtless be greatly surprised by being read in this negative way as indeed are some of his ardent followers.

Suzuki understood very well the spiritual vacuum in the West of the first half of this century, the aridity of scientific materialism and the alienation arising from the general collapse of Christian beliefs before the impact of scientific knowledge. In seeking to go beyond the mere rationalism of the Western 'enlightenment', not only was science itself then an expression of Western romanticism, a seeking for ultimate knowledge outside social and historical experience, but the extreme individualism of Western culture meant that personal cultivation leading to so high a credential as Zen "Enlightenment" based in a heroic, inner adventure was alluringly attractive (Wright 1998).

In reading Suzuki it is not always easy to distinguish between the early antinomian radical and the later more cautious and more orthodox Buddhist writer. Suzuki's tendency is to emphasise the spontaneity and radical nature of Zen. Thus after providing an entirely orthodox account of Zen Buddhist origins in Japan he goes on "Zen undertakes to awaken Prajna found generally slumbering in us under the thick clouds of ignorance and karma. Ignorance and karma come from our unconditioned surrender to the intellect; Zen revolts against this state of affairs..... Zen disdains logic and remains speechless when it is asked to express itself. The worth of the intellect is only appreciated after the essence of things is grasped. This means that Zen wants to reverse the ordinary course of knowledge and resort to its own specific methods of training our minds in the awakening of transcendental wisdom." (Suzuki. 1938. p5).

But what is this 'Zen' to which his use of the word applies - a person, a system, a belief, a form of yoga? Later, in referring to the way in which a master answer questions, he says: "--- the answering mind does not stop anywhere but responds straightaway without giving any thought to the felicity of the answer. This "non-stopping" mind remains immovable as it is never carried away by the things of relativity. It is the substance of things, it is God --- the ultimate secret -". (p80). In these moods Suzuki appears to forget pratitya samutpada, the interconnectedness of things and the identity of opposites completely. While the intimations that arise in meditative practice may be psychologically transcendent, the world within which they happen is far from so - the everyday grind of monastic living. Can one distance 'Zen' from this supporting context? Doing so has become the root of many confusions.

Yet Suzuki did not go unchallenged. In 1953 Dr Hu-shih, a one-time President of the National Peking University, tackled him on his views concerning the non-historicity of Zen and its being beyond intellectual understanding. He gives a detailed account of the history of Ch'an and proposed historical reasons for the development of the idiosyncrasies apparent in Zen transmission which in his eyes had a rational, social if obscure basis. Suzuki's rebuttal is trenchant. "Hu-shih does not seem to understand the real significance of the 'sudden awakening or enlightenment' in its historical setting..... All the schools of Buddhism... owe their origin to the Buddha's enlightenment experience... no other than a 'sudden enlightenment'." He goes on to argue that this Zen "way of looking at life may be judged to be a kind of naturalism, even an animalistic libertinism." Quoting Spinoza, he argues "this kind of intuition is absolutely certain and infallible and, in contrast to ratio, produces the highest peace and virtue of mind." .... "History deals with time and so does Zen, but with this difference: While history knows nothing of timelessness, perhaps disposing of it as a 'fabrication', Zen takes time along with timelessness - that is to say, time in timelessness and timelessness in time." Zen is thus seen by Suzuki to be apart from its historical setting.

Yet Hu-shih and Suzuki seem to be at cross-purposes. Suzuki is speaking of experience, Hu-shih of context. They do not seem to be able to fit these together. Suzuki always felt that his version of Rinzai Zen provided an ultimate vision beyond history. His indeterminate status between monk and layman, between scholar and popularist, between practitioner and missionary, between Japan and America, led to a view in which all things remotely resembling Zen could be assimilated into one vision; and everything else rejected. The Kyoto School of Philosophy created by Suzuki's friend Nishida has largely followed this line. The result has been a kind of Suzuki monism closed to the usual forms of academic criticism through a direct appeal to an absolutism of the non-historical.

From the same basis Suzuki argued strongly against 'gradualism' which he saw as inherent in the Soto tradition (Tsao-tung) of 'just sitting' or 'Silent Illumination'. He backs Ta-hui in his ancient confrontation with Hung-chih (1091-1157) on this issue and emerges therefore as strongly partisan in his interpretation of practice and its meaning in Ch'an. Leighton and Yi Wu (1991) have however shown that these two great contemporaries were actually friends who co-operated as teaching colleagues sending students to one another. Ta-hui's criticisms were not at Hung-chih personally but at those who used the "just sitting" methods without appropriate mindfulness. He himself also "sat" and was aware that koans too have defects, leading in some cases to intellectually obsessive worrying over old stories. Suzuki also ignores Dogen who warmly approved of both these old antagonists while favouring Hung-chih as the founder of his own practice. Not surprisingly Suzuki's lop sided Zen has produced strange effects creating a certain bias in the transmission of Zen to European shores.

The key European philosophers of post-modernism, Wittgenstein, Austin, Derrida and others have all emphasised the importance of the role of language and culture in interpreting the significance of history in the understanding of metaphysical views. Analysis of texts and their historicity shows that all propositions are context dependent in often very complex ways; not only on the economic structures underlying culture but also on the interpretations of religion and self within those cultures. There is always a marked interdependence between philosophical statement whether popular or sophisticated, and its cultural frame. Even science is not free from this perspective as Thomas Kuhn (1962) in his analysis of scientific paradigms has shown.

Western romanticism, closely linked to colonialism and the heroic exploration of cultures in far off lands, Jerusalem, Timbuktu or Lhasa, was having its last throw in the fifties when John Blofield translated Huang-po and interpreted him through the 'romantic' vision of the time. We need to assess Ch'an and Zen and what previous Western writers have said of them, anew if we are to discover its relevance to our Western selves in our contemporary scene (Wright 1998). Zen, far from being independent from history, has, in its rich diversity, always been dependent upon it-- as indeed the Buddha, in pronouncing his principle of co-dependent arising, would have suspected and as Suzuki in his later writing also began to understand.

Zen in Europe

Much as we Westerners owe an initial understanding of Zen to the work of Daisetz Suzuki, we are also indebted to him for considerable confusion. It has not been easy to relate his monolithic vision to the contrasting expression of other Zen/Ch'an schools. Only in recent years, with the advent of outstanding, mostly American, scholarship, are we beginning to see our way through the haze.

One of the prime sources of confusion has been the absence of adequate Dharma teaching in the popular literature. Suzuki's emphasis and that of recent Rinzai tradition on the ahistorical nature of Zen has led to a situation in Europe where contemporary Zen is sometimes taught as if Zen as Buddhadharma was an irrelevance. Zen is seen as something basic to all religions, or at least both Buddhism and Christianity. This has meant that the historical tradition and philosophical underpinning of Sino-Japanese Zen is given little attention, the focus being upon various sorts of practice. Process and meaning have thus become divorced. One Christian Zen teacher even seems to pride herself on a lack of understanding of both Buddhist philosophy and Christian theology (MacInnes, 1996: 95).

This absence of a conceptual basis leads to an unanchored anxiety only too apparent in 'Towards a European Zen?', a report based on a conference in Sweden in 1993 (Karlsson 1994). With the exception of Ton Lathouwers interesting examination of Zen parallels in Russian literature, most of the other articles are worried examinations of the problems of adapting Japanese Zen ritual, koans and the authority of a Roshi into a Euro frame. These worries combine with considerable criticism of the social scene in Japanese Zen and doubts about the authenticity of Japanese practice. This anxiety could be greatly relieved by serious Dharma study and by a concerted examination of the deep contrasts between Christianity and Buddhism, in particular problems around the conception of God. None of this is being attempted; serious academic work on Buddhist history and culture being left to the Americans.

In fact several of the Zen schools in Europe are currently in deep trouble. Both the school established by Philip Kapleau and the widely influential Association Zen International (AZI) of Taisen Deshimaru are agitated by issues concerning method and teaching and whether the original transmissions to their founders were reliable. In the case of the Kapleau lineage one key teacher has been dismissed for unethical behaviour. The meditation offered by the AZI has been described by one critic as "loaded with and embedded into a complex ideological and authoritarian system of belief which is insidiously implanted into participants while being labelled as "true Dharma" (r.halfmann@nikocity.de 1999). Only Thich Nhat Han's centre in Plum Village (France) where Vietnamese Zen is taught, remains immune from such problems. Communication between Eastern teachers unfamiliar with the West and Westerners illiterate in Eastern languages and thought is another common problem. In Britain the Zen situation is more secure; both the Rinzai tradition led by the Austrian nun Myokyo-ni (Irmgard Schloegl) and the Soto based tradition of Roshi Jiyu Kennett at Throssel Hole Abbey, being well founded both in practice and teaching, while other new fangled British Buddhisms (The Friends of the Western Buddhist Order and the New Kadampa Tradition) have been subjected to severe criticism in the press in spite of their considerable wealth and popular following.

Nevertheless there are interesting explorations in some of the new Zen paths. The FAS society founded some fifty five years ago in Kyoto by Shin'ichi Hisamatsu is based on the Formless (i.e. the True or Formless self), All humanity, and Supra-history, meaning the creation of new history free from the ignorance of the past. Hisamatsu wanted to get away from Japanese formalism by an emphasis on all humanity and work in the world. In FAS there is no Master or any ultimate authority. Instead of the dokusan interview there is "mutual enquiry". Jeff Shore (1993) says "One can encounter a number of outstanding people and continually test and be tested--right now- not just at a special time or place, or with a special person" Instead of traditional koans, FAS uses one fundamental koan: "Right now whatever I do will not do; what do I do?"

The use of this koan is intended to foster a "genuine awakening, rather than the mere insight-experiences which often occur through improper use of the koan." While the koan certainly expresses the ultimate plight of the self and challenges it to solve the inherent paradox in the very wording, it may also be valuable at the level of everyday puzzlement, in relationships of emotional dependency for example (Crook, 1999). Yet, since there is no acknowledged person available to evaluate responses it is difficult to see how such a formless method can be reliable. Mistaken acceptance of koan answers are plausibly a commonplace even in the traditional system where a highly reputed teacher is present, how much more so must this be true in this admirably democratic but basically individualistic system. There is a confusion here between authoritarian rank and rank based on perceived attainment. When nobody is acknowledged as masterly who can be a judge of insight let alone awakening?

The Sanbo Kyodan school originated from the great Harada Roshi and his disciple Yasutani Roshi who created a practice integrating the methods of Soto and Rinzai. Yasutani has been especially influential in bringing Japanese Zen to the West, in particular as the teacher of Philip Kapleau. Unfortunately for their reputations in the contemporary West, it has been established that both ardently supported Zen training as an aspect of Japanese militarism, a position seemingly incompatible with the teachings of Buddha. Although the Sanbo Kyodan is an orthodox tradition it subscribes to the Suzuki fallacy of treating Zen as the ahistorical root of all religion and therefore offering a methodology applicable within basically any belief system. In Japan this had the consequence that the selfless application of the sword in the decapitation of prisoners could be seen as a Zen attainment. That such a situation could have arisen certainly merits careful historical and cultural analysis such as Brian Victoria has set in motion (1997).

The Sanbo Kyodan also appears to be the prime vehicle through which Christian practitioners have been taught Zen meditation and granted transmission. The resulting work of the Benedictine monk Jager Willigis, the Jesuit William Johnston and Fr Enomiya-Lassalle is admirable and has introduced many people, Christian and otherwise, to Zen practice but it raises many questions. Although the mystical experience common to all religions and probably basic to the shamanic origin of all of them, almost certainly has a psychological root which may be considered a fundamental human condition, this does not mean that the Zen cultural tradition and the practice of meditation can be meaningfully split in twain, adopting the latter while ignoring the former. To simply graft a Zen method of contemplation onto a Christian theological stance looks like thievery.

It is strange that Westerners respond more openly to the Asian model than to the profound practices of the desert fathers in the Neo-Dionysian tradition of apophatic theology. It is stranger still that apologists of Christianity should ignore their own profound methodology to ride the stream of fashion for Oriental mysticism. Undermined by the rationalism of the European "Enlightenment" and the emergence of scientific humanism it seems Christians need to look outside their own culture for spiritual inspiration. This has been a success perhaps only because of Suzuki's insistence on a Zen mysticism independent of history and culture. We do not deny the transmissions of these fathers in Zen nor their understanding of practice but we do need to understand that their realisation is that of a psychological or attitudinal state and not that of an insight into Buddhadharma. Needless to say this can cause profound disquiet in those of their disciples with minds alert to meaning as well as process.

It is likewise strange that basing their approach in the assumed a historical, culture free, character of Zen these teachers should still refer to it as a Christian Zen. If either Christian or Buddhist, Zen cannot be said logically to lack context. Only a completely independent Zen could be so. A similar criticism may perhaps be directed at an attempt to describe Zen in terms of agnosticism (Batchelor 1998).

In fact these Christian teachers have no intention of developing a Buddhist Zen understanding. As Batchelor (1994, p 213-220) points out, in spite of a greater tolerance of pluralism in religious belief, inclusivist Zen enthusiasts of the Roman faith are clearly placing sitting meditation in the service of a mission minded Christianity as basically as intolerant of difference as ever it has been. The superiority of Christianity is assumed on the grounds that it consists in 'revealed truth' rather than in 'natural' truth which is as far as Zen is said to go. For men like Father Lassalle and William Johnston, Christian contemplation remains the focus to which they are drawn - a focus paradoxically insistent on the importance of a remarkable if implausible "fact" as having happened in history. If there be any "revealed" truth, might it not be in the teachings of the Buddha and his great interpreters, Nagarjuna, Chandrakurti, Tsong.kha.pa or even Krishnamurti or the Dalai Lama? It seems a comparative analysis of the basis of so called "revelation" is surely needed.

It follows that a major source of confusion in European Zen centres on a question concerning whether Zen is to be considered Buddhist or not. One result has been an institutional eclecticism exemplified by the De Tiltenberg centre in Holland. De Tiltenberg in 1973 was a centre of the International Grail Movement, a Catholic movement for women. Christian Zen was initiated there in retreats offered by William Johnston and Fr Ednomiya-Lassalle. Subsequently retreats were led by Japanese Roshis, a Japanese Carmelite, and Toni Packer a former associate of Philip Kapleau who split away to form her own school. In addition conferences have been attended by major Zen scholars such as Professor Dumoulin and Professor Masao Abe of the Kyoto School of Philosophy. At De Tiltenberg one can sample a cross section of contemporary Zen teachings whether Christian in orientation or Buddhist. While this certainly offers a major educational opportunity, the question as to whether Zen itself is transmitted there remains an open and a confused one.

The debate begun at the Swedish conference continues and the questions it posed not yet answered.

Language, Culture and Interpretation

Suzuki's claims are rooted in a Zen discourse in which reading the Sutras is rejected, the teachings treated as irrelevant and even if one were to meet a Buddha on the way it would be advisable to kill him because any interaction would merely throw one off the path. The basic stance is well stated in the ancient characterisation of Ch'an attributed to Bodhidharma, the Indian monk who brought it to China.

> A special transmission outside the scriptures
>
> No dependence upon words or letters
>
> Direct pointing to the human heart
>
> Seeing into one's own nature.

Furthermore there are numerous stories in which Zen masters illustrate this viewpoint. No gradual approach, even the traditional methods put forward by the Buddha himself, can in this view lead to enlightenment, only the sudden realisation on the solving of a koan can do it.

And yet it takes little reflection to perceive that these very assertions are themselves embodied in texts, writings as voluminous as those on any academic subject. Furthermore the emphases in these texts have a clear history, lines of doctrinal development and preferences for practice are easily located in the traditions of the contrasting Ch'an sects. Even if we were to posit a completely non-cultural component in enlightenment, such an experience is clearly deeply embedded in traditions. John Blofield in his study of Huang- po assumed that the great master would not be interested in history (1985, original 1947). Wright (1998), shows that not only Huang-po but all Ch'an masters up to the present day are much concerned about the purity of the lineage of transmission concerning which disputes may easily arise. Yet, in deference to Suzuki we do have to account for the paradox in the transmission of Ch'an; its obvious embeddedness in historical texts with its roots in transpersonal experience.

Wright points out that any attempt at objective history is itself bound to fail. History is a discourse profoundly determined by prevailing philosophical and political views; witness the rewriting of Indian history after the end of the British Raj. The attempt to create history from legends of transmission is subject to similar processes; as recent studies of the Platform Sutra show. There is a dialectic between past and present and history is simply a discourse interpreting the records and memories of a past time. The purpose of Zen practice is to reach an experiential understanding of the basis of self as the source of mental suffering. Personal experiences of self-transcendence, by their nature beyond the reach of language, are not recordable as normal memories may be. They transcend the person, go beyond the record and yet, being considered exemplary, are transmitted through records. The famous encounter stories of Zen are records of meetings in which the dialectics of transmitting the transcendent are recorded as teaching devices. While the moment of insight goes beyond language and history its expression as teaching is yet dependent upon them. Without a hearing of stories no one would ever know where the signpost was.

If this relation between language, temporality and experience did not exist it would be impossible for the Masters even to speak of enlightenment as the outcome of an event in the past - the time when the Buddha sat down beneath the Bo tree. Wright (1998) says: "A dialectical relationship between the practice of thought and Zen experience is essential to the tradition. Thought pushes experience further, opens up new dimensions for it, and refines what comes to experience. Experience pushes thought further, opens up new dimensions for thinking and sets limits to its excursions. The brilliance of Zen thinking is its tentative and provisional character, the 'non-abiding', 'non-grasping', mind. Knowing through thought that all thought is empty, Zen masters have explored worlds of reflection unavailable to other traditions - playfully 'thinking' what lies beneath common sense". Without such play "memes", as Susan Blackmore remarks, can become forms of oppression (1999).

The Zen objection to Sutra reading and study lies in the perception that idealising theories and models of mind create forms of mental closure as 'beliefs', thereby preventing the exploration of experience that is itself the essence of the quest; an exploration that goes beyond language to where pre-theoretical and pre-discursive understanding operate. Since the time of the Buddha the nature of the self has been the key problem. A profound psychological analysis in phenomenological form underlies the practice and is treated at length in the Lankavatara Sutra of which Suzuki himself provides the major translation and commentary. It is of course not essential for a practitioner to know this, he may simply practice, but the cultural roots exist for him within the meditation instructions he will be given or the koans he may be set. Yet to abandon understanding for rhetoric alone may quickly become a confusing practice.

Going beyond self-concern necessarily leads to states that cannot be described in language constructed around pronouns, verbs and nouns. In the end the rhetoric of Zen is metaphorical or poetic often making use of actions or signs we can no longer interpret since we are not party to a particular ancient culture. Thus the knock-abouts that masters seemed to so enjoy and the rough speech carry implicit meanings we can today often barely grasp. Yet the matter is not intrinsically mysterious, the psychology of self- transcendence, the abandonment of self-concern, underlies the path, the view and the result. In Buddhism all this has received detailed philosophical attention much of which has striking resemblance to Western theories of mind in psychotherapy (Crook 1980. Katz 1983. Crook and Fontana 1990).

Momentary insights need to be related to an ongoing manner of life before a practice can be said to be mature. After 'seeing the nature' many ancient masters remained in training often for years. In traditions less subitist than Suzuki's there is nothing strange about this. While insight is characteristically sudden the maturation and digestion of meaning may take a long time. The ignorance of self-concern is not resolved in a moment. It takes time, and time is discourse, time is history. There are many methods for the personal elucidation of Zen and one is not necessarily superior to another. Rather, these differences often relate to individual capacities. Roshi Kennett once remarked how in her Soto monastery in Japan a monk who was not doing well might be referred to a Rinzai master - and vice versa.

It is important always to remember the returning line in the Heart Sutra. "Form is emptiness. Emptiness is form." The early Suzuki and those who followed him tend to forget the second line. All forms and experiences are ultimately 'empty' but the expression of emptiness is through these very forms. The two are indivisible.

The Contribution of Ch'an

Master Sheng-yen teaches in the lineages of both the Lin-chi (Rinzai) and Tsao-tung (Soto) traditions. In particular he has inherited the eclectic approach of the great Master Hsu-yun who, at the turn of the century, revived Buddhism in China after a long period of neglect. As many schools and lineages had disappeared Hsu-yun made use of the surviving traditions of both Pure Land and Ch'an to produce a valuable synthesis that is both deeply rooted and flexible.

On retreat with Master Sheng-yen the practitioner may choose a method of meditation the use of which is negotiated in interview. Watching the breath, Koan and Silent Illumination are all taught. But Sheng-yen does not believe in meditation instruction without a thorough understanding of the concepts that lie behind it. He teaches his followers not only how to sit but why sitting is helpful to realising a Dharma understanding. His talks range widely from the sayings of the Buddha through the Sutras and Zen dialogues to koan texts and philosophical works. He argues that meditation without conceptual understanding is a very limited activity and that attainment of insight requires both. To Master Sheng-yen, Ch'an is a Buddhism of exceptional clarity that seeks to fulfil the Buddha's intentions in opting to teach his realisation to the world. Today most Chinese Buddhists frequently refer to their practice as Ch'an but few concentrate on insight so strongly as Master Sheng-yen. Other groups are more concerned with charitable works and chanting in the style of the Pure Land sect.

While Master Sheng-yen agrees that insightful experiences akin to the transcendence of self in Zen occur in many spiritual traditions, Christianity, Sufism etc, he states that the enlightenment of which the Buddha spoke depends on realisation within an understanding of the Zen view. In particular this means an experiential insight into the emptiness of all phenomena including both self and universe. His teaching is thus based in the Prajnaparamita and Madhyamaka insights of Buddhism and their development in Chinese thought emphasising the Tathagatagarbha as the root of mind. Although I have not discussed the point with him in depth, I doubt whether he would consider an insightful experience of no-self within Christian Zen as "seeing the nature" (kensho) unless the God of the practitioner was perceived as 'empty'. And this of course would be a tall order for most Christian believers although less problematic for those versed in apophatic theology and contemplation.

Master Sheng-yen completed his own training in Japan studying for a doctorate at Rissho University and sitting traditional retreats. On coming to America he brought with him both the Koan tradition and the methods of Silent Illumination. Whereas Suzuki rejected the latter as a useful path, Master Sheng-yen has in recent years taught this approach increasingly, beginning in Wales in 1989. He has presented Silent Illumination retreats in Poland, Russia, Croatia and Sweden and in 1999 in Berlin where his coverage of the subject was exceptionally complete. We may argue therefore that it is through his teaching of Silent Illumination that Master Sheng-yen is making a profound contribution to European Zen.

Keys to Illumination

Rather than a precipitate gallop up the slopes of some koan mountain Sheng-yen lists four modest aims for beginners on retreat. These are: to realise that one is not in control of one's own mind, to discover how to train in awareness, to calm the mind, to provide opportunities for repentance and hence to regain the freedom of immaculacy, and to practice with an individually suitable method that will yield insight (prajna) (Sheng-yen 1982, Crook 1991). A beginner will usually start with watching the breath. S/he soon discovers the truth of the first aim and seek to develop awareness encountering the barriers of wandering thought and fatigue in the process. In addition, prostration sessions focussing on repentance are a means of facilitating the fourth aim. Only when a mind has achieved at least a relative calm may the method shift through negotiation in interview to the use of either a Koan or to Silent Illumination.

Koan practice does not differ from that taught in Japanese or Chinese monasteries. There is the requirement to develop the "great doubt" from which after intensive effort a resolution may come. Often stress is placed on a life-koan to be realised over many years of focussed effort. In Master Sheng-yen's retreats the emphasis is on working without tension, correct but not strained sitting, relaxed mind and "letting the universe do it". Since different participants may be using contrasting methods, the collective even obsessive focus on koans of a traditional Rinzai retreat with its accumulating mental power is less in evident and koans are unlikely to be solved with the explosive force described in some accounts of these retreats. The realisation under Sheng-yen's guidance seems likely to be gentler.

In teaching Silent Illumination Master Sheng-yen lists several stages of practice (See New Ch'an Forum 15, Summer 1997, about to be republished). While these may result in a gradual evolution of insight the stages do not necessarily follow one another. Some practitioners may quickly develop an advanced stage omitting or running quickly through the early ones. Usually however the first practice is to develop 'Total Body Awareness' - unlike the Japanese focus on posture the attention here is directed to the awareness of presence within the sitting body. A successful awareness here depends on focussed attention on the sensation arising within the sitting. Success leads to a calmed mind in which the boundaries between interior and exterior gradually disappear and time before and time after merge into one flow - what Dogen may have called "without thinking. "As one practices at this stage various meditation experiences of an encouraging nature appear and a realisation of "one mind" may arise in which the practitioner feels himself in confluence with nature and the universal process. These stages may arise through focussed intentionality. "No-mind" as in the experience of "seeing the nature" (kensho) cannot however be the result of any deliberative practice. When intention is present so also will be desire. Where desire is present so must the self be there. The concern with achievement, with getting a result has to be entirely abandoned but the attempt to do this merely completes a circle, the self still being present in the attempt to go beyond itself. Here is the ultimate 'gateless gate' likewise come upon in the intense focus within the Great Doubt of koan work.

Kensho arises spontaneously when the trained mind simply lets go without any willed intention. It cannot therefore be the object of any desire or wanting. Only the faith in its possibility seems important. One may wait for years but waiting itself is a mistake betraying desire. Yet one cannot forget the possibility nor its significance. "Seeing the nature" means seeing the immediate universal process as right before one's eyes, a boiling egg, a bird flying bird, a dropped tea cup. There is no self present then - simply.......... Words are transcended but the experience is never forgotten being often the very pivot upon which a life turns. Here then is the reason for Suzuki's insistence on a context free Zen. Yet, shortly, the self returns and practice continues, practice within a lineage, under guidance, in humility, with deference to history. Even great masters probably have such an experience only occasionally in their lives. It is sufficient.

Silent Illumination and Koan work in Ch'an are thus parallel paths. They seem to suit different people and the practitioner through experiment and experience will come to develop an affinity to one or another of them.

Western Paths

Master Sheng-yen once told me that the main difference between his Chinese and his American practitioners lay in persistence. A Chinese, once told how to practice, just goes and does it without question. Since the Master said so - it will be right. In the end, and that may only be after a long time, a profound result may arise. A Westerner typically shows a very quick intellectual grasp of what is being demanded. Western education enables quite complex ideas to be handled with relative ease. But Western education also inculcates a perennially questioning mind and an individualism that seeks personal distinction. When results do not come quickly a Westerner rarely persist into the Great Doubt but rather worries within conventional doubts: self criticism, scepticism concerning the master and the method destroys the very focus of attention he or she may have to an extent established. This worrying, based in self concern, sustains an agitated mind which may then quite easily decide to try something else - supposedly quicker and less disturbing.

In response to American needs for speed Charles Berner in the fifties created an interesting form of retreat which he styled the "Enlightenment Intensive". Within this practice individuals sit together in couples. One asks the other a brief 'koan' or 'hua t'ou', typically "Tell me who you are?" The recipient puts this to him/herself as "Who am I?" and has five minutes to make some response that does not necessarily have to be verbal. The questioner remains silent or merely repeats the question. After five minutes a bell sounds and the roles are reversed. Each partner thus has a sequence of five minutes alternating with the other for some thirty to forty minutes. There is then a short break until the participants reassemble to work with another individual in the same manner and with the same question. This process runs throughout the day with only short breaks for food, maybe a walk or a brief sitting session.

Typically, individuals begin by describing aspects of their roles in life. This gradually changes to comments such as "When I hear the news I often want to cry." The responses refer increasingly to emotion until someone expresses that feeling directly by weeping, laughing, being sad or angry. Clearly this is a direct statement of being at that moment. Emotion may or may not be expressed but it is deeply felt and the sharing of life's problems engenders an increasing trust in the group. Sometimes things are shared that have never before seen the light of day. Eventually a silence falls as people run out of anything to add. Some may then realise that everything they have said is who they are. "I'm me" may be a response which, if fully realised, leads to a letting go into an experience of wholeness that may be an entirely fresh opening onto previously unsuspected freedoms. Such moments may amount to the discovery of the 'One mind' in an orthodox retreat. Berner styled such moments as "enlightenment experiences" and their significance for the practitioner is undoubted. Yet they may only rarely amount to "No mind" since the intentionality in this process is so strong.

In exploring ways to present Zen, I trained with Jeff Love in Berner's process and later developed it as the Western Zen Retreat in which the format of the event resembles a Buddhist retreat but the Communication Exercise, as it is called, becomes a prime method of practice. After giving such retreats over some twenty years I can say that on average about 25% of participants have some insight into "One mind", 70% find the experience of common humanity deeply revealing and may undertake profound changes in their life styles, a few find the practice disturbing but usually manage to complete it with a sense of an achievement and surprise in so doing.

The Western Zen Retreat is now used as an introductory retreat by the Western Ch'an Fellowship. It provides an intensive introduction to the self-confrontation that all Zen training demands and we like beginners to start by participating in this process. The secret of the method lies in the progressive emptying out through sharing of worries, thoughts, concerns until even self concern is confronted. Letting go happens automatically if the process is followed with openness but there are many culs de sac and emotional blockages on the way.

The process has clear links to psychotherapy which is not surprising as Berner based it in a joint consideration of the dokusan and the Western co-counselling method. I have seen intense personal blockage, shyness and neurotic preoccupations dramatically shifted in individuals who have attended several such events. It follows that the relation between the theory underpinning Zen retreat and psychotherapy is a matter of great interest in the post- Freudian West (Crook. 1990, 1997, 1999, Crook and Fontana 1989, Epstein 1996, Pickering1997) and may become of wider interest as the globalisation of Western values continues to spread.

Interdependence and the Ecological Crisis

In bringing Ch'an to Europe Master Sheng-yen offers an ancient, less contentious, thread soundly based in Dharma and meditative experience and with unimpeachable authority. The prime features of his presentation are: complete anchorage in Buddhism while accepting the natural influence of Chinese culture, especially Taoism, on the tradition; a balanced position with respect to the 'subitism' of Koan work and the 'gradualism' of Silent Illumination; a progressive set of meditation practices graded to suit practitioners of all degrees of experience; a strict retreat structure with formal interviews and traditional rituals but with an emphasis on relaxed effort, tolerance of diverse abilities and humour; and last but by no means least, instruction on meditative practice related to and informed by examination of the main themes in the Dharma, anatta, anicca, pratitya samutpada, the Heart Sutra, Madhyamaka, the psychological basis in Tathagatagarbha, the significance of Hui-neng's teaching, and the recorded sayings of great Ch'an masters including both Hung- chi and Ta-hui. His public analyses of texts are often particularly illuminating. In this Ch'an package many of the implicit problems in European Zen are very fully addressed.

Yet there is an important aspect of Ch'an which he has yet to share fully with us. Although he has lectured on this subject to small groups in New York and mentioned it briefly at Gaia House in July 2000, so far as I am aware he has yet to present it on a seven-day retreat. The Avatamsaka Sutra is a backbone to much of Ch'an thinking but few European practitioners are aware of its profound meaning nor of the Chinese philosophical system of Hua-yen that is derived from it. In the USA some academics, writers on engaged Buddhism, and one or two masters have begun to focus on this system and it potential impact on the relationship between Buddhist and Western thought.

Hua-yen is a way beyond the negativism or nihilism of which outsiders sometimes accuse Buddhism and also a way beyond the problems inherent in the concept of 'emptiness' which Ch'an practitioners inevitably encounter. Hua-yen does a marvellous job in providing a positive image of Buddhism to which the present generation may comfortably relate and does so without contradicting the emptiness perspective that lies at the root of the Buddhist vision. It relates well to many problematical issues concerning the environment and interconnected global problems and it could well become a philosophy underwriting the perspectives of those troubled by the need for an 'engaged Buddhism' (Jones 1989, 1993).

Many who read the Heart Sutra for the first time are puzzled by the key lines "Form is Emptiness. Emptiness is Form", and there has been a tendency to concentrate on the first of these two lines without returning along the second. Hua-yen provides that all-important returning perspective.

The Avatamsaka is a vast compendium of Buddhist teachings originating in India but achieving its main impact in China. Thomas Cleary has completed the mammoth task of translating it into English (1993). Hua-yen abstracts from this multilayered compendium philosophical principles that are the chief focus of my interest here (Chang 1972). We may introduce these briefly by considering a few basic propositions.

1. First we must recall what 'emptiness' is empty of - namely inherent existence. No apparent thing set before our senses has permanent being in the world for everything is transient, subject to impermanence. Attachment to any object must therefore necessarily lead to distress especially if that object is oneself or any attribute of oneself such as good fortune, health, youth, wealth, a Mercedes etc. Yet an absence of inherent existence does not imply a "void" or non-existence as such. All events are mutually co- determining in progressive cycles of complexification and degeneration. This is the principle of the co-dependent arising of phenomena. Emptiness (sunyata) is such (tathata). One could say that the universe is like a river rather than like a rock. It continually flows and one can never enter the same stream twice.

2. Objects appear to us as images. The mind may be likened to a gigantic mirror in which the properties of the universe are reflected. We only see events as in a mirror. These images are not the things in themselves but rather constitute a virtual reality. This is all we have. While we may impute form and structure, causality and relatedness to images we do actually contact them only as they appear to our senses.

3. Descriptive knowledge is thus necessarily indirect. There is a metaphorical account of this in a description of a monk teaching a pupil. The monk appears in the mirror of the pupil, the pupil appears in the mirror of the monk. The teaching

is likewise mirrored and so is the acknowledgement of any understanding. The nature of knowledge is 'such'.

4. Furthermore different properties may be assigned to apparent things by different minds, persons or teaching. For example water may be said to be a liquid, H_2O, melted ice, congealed vapour, molecules or quanta depending upon the perspective offered. Yet all of these perspectives exhibit simultaneous mutual arising- furthermore they are each participant in the other showing simultaneous mutual "entering", and again each contains all the others. When we are aware of these relationships we have a 'Totalistic' or 'round' picture of how a thing is. Although any thing is empty of inherent existence it never the less may appear under any one of these mutually penetrating guises. Thus "emptiness is precisely form". The wonderful metaphor of Indra's net captures this vision nicely. Above the palace of Indra hangs a great net from which are suspended millions of multifaceted crystals. Each reflects all the others in never ending mutuality.

5. The events that appear to us as things- such as a man falling off a horse or an aircraft crash, has two aspects; the described event itself (with all the mutual penetration of potential descriptions) and the underlying causality that may be invisible - the principles that govern the happening. In Hua-yen the first is called the realm (dharmadhatu) of Shi, the second the realm of Li. There is no obstruction of Shi by Li as they are mutually interpenetrable. This leads to a number of contemplations: the principle that Li embraces Shi, the principle that Shi embraces Li, the principles that production of Shi must depend on Li, that Shi illustrates Li, that Shi may be annulled by Li, that Shi may render Li invisible, that while Li is Shi and all things/events are Li yet Li is not itself Shi nor are Shi Li.

The practical application of this is clear. Consider the life of a wood, the insects depend on the foliage, the birds depend on the insects, falcons depend on the small birds, the trees depend on humus which comes from the remains of living creatures. There is here a complex system well-researched in ecology through the application of systems analysis and cybernetics to structures such as woods, organisms, digestive processes etc. Yet we may still affirm quite logically that all these events are "empty". Systems analysis was foreshadowed centuries ago in the thought of these Chinese sages.

Here then is a powerful vision as to how emptiness expresses itself in forms. In meditation one may take up many aspects of the same phenomenon and through seeing their interdependence and lack of inherent existence allow them to merge into one understanding or experience. When the self also participates totally in that experience that one thing becomes uncharacterisable. Experience thus becomes empty, yet as soon as thought reappears the categories re-establish themselves. The understanding of emptiness must therefore necessarily also invoke form. The two are co-dependent. Meditation implies action and vice versa.

Master Tung-shan in T'ang dynasty China formulated a similar teaching known as the Five Ranks that depict the integration of opposed dualities as may occur in the practice of meditation. The first rank places the relative within the universal; the second places the universal within the relative; the third is the principle of emerging from the universal (i.e. the appearance of the ten thousand things from a unified sense of emptiness); the fourth is an integration of the particulate and the universal in one vision in which however their separation is still apparent; the final rank is unity itself without divisions. Each rank is never the less present in all the others.

Europeans appear to have had little to do with such an inclusive picture of Dharma. Perhaps our civilisation is somewhat tired after all the strains of this century and inclined to opt for the better known or apparently safer routes. In the USA a more exploratory attitude predominates which, although it may sometimes seem a little naive to European eyes, is also often highly creative showing a way forward that is not in contradiction with a full understanding of tradition. John Daido Loori, Abbot of Zen Mountain Monastery in New York State has written a wonderful little book (1999) in which the above principles of 'holographic' interdependence are shown to be basic to an understanding of wilderness and hence to all environmental study. Quoting Thoreau and Snyder he reveals an American vision of the wild that echoes in striking ways the Avatamsaka inspired Mountains and Rivers Sutra of Dogen and Tung-shan's realisation on seeing his reflection in the water of a stream. "I am not it yet it is all of me." - a profound metaphor for the relations between sentience and the universal.

Loori emphasises that the key to this understanding is no mere philosophy but rather an intimacy with insentient things, a feeling of closeness between oneself and the flowering of daffodils in spring or the falling leaves of autumn, between oneself and the mountains that are always moving, rocks, stones and trees. To develop such intimacy requires stepping beyond our dualistic, romantic aspiration and its culture of individualism. A certain sort of empathic imagination is needed for such an act, an imagination stimulated by meditation on the diversity in unity that Ch'an Dharma can inspire. Here we have an outreach from Zen to the problems of the environment that face us all and which need urgent attention.

Ch'an and the Future of European Zen

Zen in Europe is currently a patchwork quilt of somewhat competitive perspectives with much invested in contrasting metaphysical positions and ancient loyalties to church or humanistic faiths. While good Zen practice is cultivated in many centres the Dharma upon which Ch'an relies and its Buddhist history is poorly understood and in some cases ignored largely as a consequence of accepting Daisetz Suzuki's pan-religious mysticism.

Ch'an as presented by Master Sheng-yen can provide an important corrective through an emphasis on the anchoring of Zen practice in Zen Dharma and the proper investigation through intellect and experience of what that actually may be.

It remains of course unclear how attractive such a position may become in Europe. Tolerance of diversity between contrasting perspectives as well as between Buddhist and Christian exponents must be nurtured and sustained. Yet there is a real danger that forms of "inclusivism" that align meditation practices with Christian or Humanist mainstreamings may vitiate the entire Enlightenment project as understood by the Masters. Helen Tworkov's (1994) warnings from the USA apply to Europe too. Yet, even if it is at first only a minority who pursue the Ch'an way with its inherent difficulties as well as depth, the distinctive value of Ch'an as an open, well argued, perspective on the place of sentience in the universe, may well begin to win debates to create a much more sure footed unity of understanding and practice than at present obtains.

1 This text is a re-edited version of an article of the same name published in a festchift volume celebrating Master Sheng-yen's 70th birthday. Chung-Hwa Buddhist Journal, (2000) 13. 2 549-584. Taipei

References

Barrett, W. 1956. Zen for the West. In: Zen Buddhism, selected writings of D. T Suzuki. Doubleday. New York. vii-xx.

Blackmore, S. 1999. Waking from the Meme Dream. In: Watson. G, Batchelor S. and Claxton G. (eds) The Psychology of Awakening. Buddhism, science and our day to day lives. Rider. London. 112-122

Batchelor, M 1998. Principles of Zen. Thorsons. London.

Batchelor, S. 1994. The Awakening of the West: the encounter between Buddhism and Western Culture. Parallax. Berkeley.

Batchelor, S. 1998. Buddhism without Beliefs. London

Blofield, J 1947. The Zen teaching of Huang-po on the transmission of Mind. Buddhist Society. London.

Chang, G. C. C 1972. The Buddhist teaching of totality: the philosophy of Hua yen Buddhism. Allen and Unwin. London.

Cleary, T 1990. Book of Serenity: one hundred Zen dialogues. Lindisfarne. New York.

Cleary, T. 1993. The Flower Ornament Scripture: Translation of the Avatamsaka Sutra. Shambhala. Boston and London.

Crook, J. H. 1980. The Evolution of Human Consciousness. Oxford.

Crook, J. H. 1990. Catching a feather on a fan. A Zen retreat with Master Sheng-yen. Element. Shaftesbury. Crook, J. H., 1997 Authenticity and the Practice of Zen. In: Pickering, J. (ed) The Authority of Experience.

Essays on Buddhism and Psychology. Curzon. Richmond.

Crook, J. H. 1998. Hilltops of the Hong Kong Moon. Minerva. London.

Crook, J. H. 1999. Zen: the challenge to dependency. In: Watson, G, Batchelor S. and Claxton G. (Eds) The Psychology of Awakening. Rider. London. 197-214.

Crook, J. H. and Fontana D. (eds) 1990. Space in Mind: East-West Psychology and contemporary Buddhism. Element. Shaftesbury.

Epstein, M. 1996. Thoughts without a Thinker. Duckworth. London.

Faure, B. 1993. Ch'an Insights and Oversights: an epistemological Critique of the Ch'an tradition. Princeton University Press. NJ.

Jones, K. The Social face of Buddhism: An approach to political and social activism. Wisdom. London. Jones, K 1993. Beyond optimism: a Buddhist political ecology. Carpenter. Oxford.

Karlsson. H (Ed) Towards a European Zen. Zenvagen. Stockholm.

Katz, N. (Ed) 1983. Buddhist and Western Psychology. Prajna Press. Boulder. Kuhn, T. 1962. The Structure of Scientific Revolutions. Chicago.

Leighton, T. D. and Yi Wu. 1991. Cultivating the Empty Field: the Silent Illumination of Zen Master Hong Zhi. North Point. San Francisco.

Loori, J. D. 1999. Teachings of the Insentient: Zen and the environment. Dharma Communications Press. Mt Tremper. NY.

MacInnes, E. 1996 Light sitting in Light: A Christian's experience with Zen. Harper Collins. London. Pickering, J. (Ed) 1997 The Authority of Experience: Essays on Buddhism and Psychology. Curzon. Richmond.

Sheng-yen. Master, 1982 Getting the Buddha Mind. Dharma Drum. New York

Sheng-yen. Master, 1987. Faith in Mind: a Guide to Ch'an practice. Dharma Drum. New York. Suzuki, D. T. 1938. Buddhism and its influence on Japanese culture.

Eastern Buddhist Society. Kyoto. Suzuki, D. T. 1949-1953 Essays on Zen Buddhism. (Three volumes) Rider. London.

Suzuki, D. T. 1955. Zen: a reply to Hu-shih. In: Suzuki, D. T. Studies in Zen. Rider. London. Tworkov, H. 1994. Zen in the balance: Can it survive America? Tricycle. Spring Issue. Victoria, B. 1997. Zen at War. Weatherhill. New York/Tokyo.

Wright, D. S. 1998. Philosophical meditations on Zen Buddhism. Cambridge University Press. Cambridge.

THE SILENCE

Silence in my head
sweet sunshine and the jackdaws calling,
dew on the autumnal grass
muddy puddles and fallen leaves
scarlet on the lawn.
Silence in my head
nothing doing there,
the morning hour, mists dissolve
in grey-green hills, the rocks
show through the soil.
Silence in my head
clock ticking somewhere
in this empty house,
solitary today the open view,
moving shadows beneath the trees.
In the silence of the world -
nothing ever moves
the wind-drift stillnesses
the circling birds.

JULY AT MAENLLWYD

Evening falls in the silent valley
shirtless in the Ch'an hall
doors open

Sunbeams flood the floor
buzzing flies
dirty the panes

Bamboo wind bells
talk in the sycamore tree
tak, tok, tik, a good kip

Woodpecker shouting
ginger cat
visiting again

No water in the brook
no sound
looking up-somebody coming?

Haymaking humming in the distant air
binoculars to distant fields -
Where?

Dawn breeze through the open door
sweet sheep shit
flavouring honeysuckle

Wales, the green aquarium.
Birds swim along
singing.

NCF XXIII

UNCOVERING THE ESSENCE OF MIND

The essence of mind is tranquil, spacious, illumined by joy, unattached to thoughts or the thoughtless.

When it appears you may fill with a gratitude that slowly turns to bliss. If a thought of others emerges there may be love.

Love is embracing all and being embraced by all.

Love passes: tranquillity resumes: the spaciousness sustains itself.

The thought of 'me' is absent. Self-concern is no longer there.

'I' is and is not.

Desireless, one rests in that which is wherever it is.

Everything is as it is.

Time becomes continuous presence.

This may occur anywhere. There are no conditions.

It is not dependent on meditation.

It is not dependent on "kensho".

It arises in its own time.

All this is to be tested.

1/ A glimpse of the essence of mind is to know the mind uncovered by Buddha. It's clouding over is the return to Samsara. In spite of vexations, those who can 'turn it on' are baby Buddhas. Those who cannot have yet to start. Good intentions, casual practice and dharma gossip are not enough.

To find this innate basis of being it is necessary to uncover the essence of mind, the primordial root of experience. This is the "insight" or prajna that ships us to the other shore.

Mahaprajnaparamita.

This shore is the world of Samsara dominated by self-concern; the worries of self-concern; fame; gain; rank; credentials; pain; sickness; fear of ill health and death; the omnipresence of lack, suspecting this self is not what it seems and the dread that brings. Maybe I am not! When such thoughts and the emotions that sustain them are dropped or weaken then the essence of mind has a chance to reappear. At once we cross the river, we attain the other shore.

This that we call 'essence' has never gone away for it is the innate basis of experience. Yet most have never found it, never even suspected its existence. Others have stumbled across it, wondered at it, lost it. For them the sense of lacking something is more intense. They may make the error of developing spiritual desire and lose the path in projected wanderings among the fantasies of cultures as if there was something to be found outside themselves. So of course there is fear, sense of loss, spiritual wanderlust and futile practising.

Some people have even uncovered the essence of mind fully, "seen its nature" but, failing in subsequent comprehension, they may have made it into something to desire. They risk becoming despirited through effort after something elsewhere. They become like wandering ghosts having known but now not knowing. Pitiful.

The essence of mind underlies the mind of thinking and feeling, it is its basis. With the essence clearly bright everything comes and goes without attachment. It is likewise the womb of thoughts activated by memory, set going by fear. It is as it is. Like the sky sometimes clouded, sometimes clear.

Tathagatagarbha

The womb of that which comes and goes - Buddha.

Birth happens but the "unborn", the pre-born, is not lost. Retain the contact and the essence is seen.

But how?

Practice is the start. What to practise? Paying attention is the start.

2/ Paying attention means turning the gaze around to look within. Looking within is to see the mind's activity exactly as it is without judgement, saying "Yes" to everything that appears. Know that if judgement arises you will be lost in some cul-de-sac of your imagination. At first one sees thoughts, hears thoughts, thinks thoughts. Become aware of their nature, their focus moving and changing. Thoughts are like a screen hiding your innate basis of mind. Without engaging with them look through the screen, and penetrate to the realm where the emotions that generate the thoughts lie. Here again become aware of their nature, moving and changing. And these too are a screen. Look through this screen, penetrate to the realm below feeling where silence reigns.

All this is like diving into the sea. First there are the wave crests moving as thought, then there is the surge of the water below the waves, emotions. But deeper down the ocean is still. If you are watchful you will fine huge movements, a diapason, also surging here. There lies the true dragon, the root of life.

This practice is not easy. If successful you will begin to know who you are. You are these waves, these surging waters, but you also are an unfathomable depth, the silent deeps, the abyss. As you become familiar with the patterns so disclosed you get to know your complexes, neuroses, attachments, problems, samskaras, but you also will discover the deeps that lie beyond them. Do not get fixated by any pictures on the screen.

If you dive too fast you may have the joy of touching the tranquil essence but you will not fully comprehend it for you must needs return to the surface engaging the other layers. Yet such a dive gives us insight, courage. Here you may 'taste the chocolate'. Full comprehension develops later as the practice and the fruit become established and their meaning clearer.

Here are two ways to dive.

a/ Slow the breath and take a deep one. On slow exhalation follow the breath out and "watch" it disappear. 'Look' into the place where it has gone. Pause long enough to see clearly into that place where nothing moves. Then breathe again. Repeat. But do not set up a breathing exercise. Do this alternating with periods of normal breathing. With some practice the normal breathing also discloses silences. Later on the silence extends. It is there at the beginning as well as the end of a breath. It is around the breath. Soon you are breathing within the silence which now remains. You are in the doorway of the essence of mind.

b/ Contemplate the question "Who is repeating Buddha's name?" To find out start repeating Buddhas name. "Amitobha Amitobha Amitobha." Once you have established a rhythm, suddenly stop and 'look' into the place where the word would have arisen had you said it. There is 'nothing' there. This nothing needs to be entered. You will find the nothing expands until it too surrounds the repetition. When you stop the practice, the silence of that emptiness remains.

Later on you may develop the practice of holding other hua t'ou in this fashion, just as Master Hsu yun has taught.

3/ For many of us, attention never leaves the surging wave crests of our obsessive thoughts. It becomes impossible to penetrate deeper. It becomes essential to calm the waves. Once we know this to be true, we take up a practice of calming the mind - samatha. A sound method which we have developed at the Maenllwyd is the preliminary practice of 'The Circle of the Arms'.[1] This can be used to establish the Total Body Awareness that is stage one of Silent illumination.[2] It can also be a preliminary move in developing Mahamudra[3] or used simply as a calming practice in itself.

4/ Once a degree of tranquillity has been established we may enquire into the meaning of that tranquillity. This is a shift vital to the practice of both Silent Illumination and Mahamudra. Such enquiry is however not an intellectual matter. It is simply a close looking. It is as if a goldfish bowl containing two fishes were placed before you. You are asked "What is in the Goldfish bowl?" To find out you simply look. At first you will see only two fish. Later you will also be aware of the water. Seeing the "water" is a metaphor here for an intensification of silence. The tranquillity deepens and begins to 'shine', it stabilises. One feels as if "flying like an eagle" as the Tibetan lamas say. The essence of mind is appearing.

The onset of the uncovering may be known by a shift in conscious awareness. Sensory experience suddenly becomes more vivid, time appears to stop. One may find the eyes fixated on some object that 'glows' in a way not seen before. What is happening is that the evaluative mind that projects into the past and future and maintains thinking has withdrawn, has 'let go'. This withdrawal removes a filter from experience. Instead of everything being subject to an almost invisible but continuous evaluation fired by desire, filled by the needs of self, there is just an openness to that which lies before the senses. Objects thus appear clean-clear, precise, within a lucidity of awareness that does not judge. Intentionality, that is "going on about something", has ceased. One can say one's attention is completely given over to the awareness of what is - in all its singularity. If you feel the onset of such a condition, do nothing. Whatever arises needs to take its own course without "you" getting in the way. One move - and its gone.

5/ The main methods of Chan, hua t'ou, gong an (koans) and Silent Illumination all develop from this point and you should learn them from a teacher. You need to find out which practice is best suited to your karmic condition.

6/ All these methods are simply means to an end - the uncovering of the essence of mind, the basis of experiencing. Remember it is not found only at the end of a search for it has always been present beneath all your striving. The striving itself precludes its recognition. This is the paradox of Chan meditative practice. To know the paradox one has to recognise that the form of things, thoughts, feelings, neuroses are all empty and that the basic emptiness of the basis of mind takes up these forms as it adopts its functions. Form and emptiness are in a state of continual co- emergence.

At this point you can understand no further without practice. For most of us only through practice will the meaning, the reference, of these words, become clear.

This then is Dharma knowledge, a matter of heart much more than mind. And yet there are those for whom one word at the right moment, one bird call or a tile falling off the roof will do it. Suddenly you are there. This may perhaps take the form of what is called "kensho" 'seeing the nature'. Those with loose minds may find it surprisingly suddenly. Others, bearing heavy karma, complex emotional stress or fixated opinions will take a longer time, realising experiential truth more slowly. It is necessary to accept who one is in patience. To want to be someone else is mere foolishness.

The sceptic, the depressed or the disoriented may well say. Why bother? Are we not all going to die anyway? Perhaps these worries will never go away. What has the fate of the Universe got to do with us? Would we not be happier in the less sophisticated, non-yogic, belief system of some pre-modern Western religion?[4]

The answer to these questions lies within the experience only truly found by practice. In this Westernised 21st century world of spiritual alienation, distress, lack of identification with roots, cynicism and cultural relativity, no merely wordy answer can satisfy. Everyone has a clever argument. Most dharma talk is mere chatter because the speakers have no acquaintance with the essential. Yet one can perhaps respond as follows: in uncovering the essence of mind one discovers the root of personal being which in turn becomes the root of value, of a sense of worthwhileness. Why is this? Because in the laying aside of ego concerns one discovers that all things and all people are in a relationship that is at root the nature of the cosmos itself in universal interconnectivity. And such intuitive discovery parallels those of many scientific investigators today. (See David Brown's article below) Here then loneliness disappears, love arises, the dualism of self and other is transcended, the full potential of human being can be realised. This then is realisation. At its full extent we call it 'enlightenment'.

But these are all matters to be tested. Why not have a go?

Ch'uang-teng Chien-ti

Aug 13th 2000. Maenllwyd.

1 Details of this method may be given in a later presentation. The best way to know it is to come on retreat and practise.

2 See NCF 15: Illuminating Silence. Summer 1997.

3 See Crook J. H and J. Low 1997 The Yogins of Ladakh. Motilal Banarsidass. Delhi. Chapter 17.4

4 For example following Professor Paul Williams, intellectually expert in Madhyamaka, back into the easy simplicities of the Catholic faith. See The Tablet. Summer 2000

INTRODUCTION TO CHINESE MONASTERIES

These notes were given to participants on our recent tour of Chinese monasteries and may prove helpful as an introduction to the article that follows and be of interest to those wishing to know more about the institutions of Chan in China. They were abstracted from J Prip Moller: Chinese Buddhist Monasteries. Hong Kong University Press, a wonderful book now out of print and difficult to find.

The Monastery

The lay out and form of a Chinese Buddhist monastery derives from ancient models. The original Indian monastery consisted of a courtyard surrounded by monks' cells. In the middle was a teaching platform. Opposite the building stood a Buddha Hall for devotional ceremonial. The design is very clear at Nalanda in Bihar, India. The typical Chinese monastery consists of series of courtyards, often beautified into gardens, around which stand the ceremonial and accommodation /administrative buildings. The design reflects imperial patterns of residence and is modified to suit local conditions obeying the Taoist rules of feng shui.

On approaching the monastery one is commonly faced by a wall between you and the entrance gate. This wall prevents the entry of evil spirits and ghosts because these can only move in straight lines. Similar protective screens are found even in village houses. The main gate (T'ien wang tien) is often an impressive building of considerable size. Outside it or just inside it one finds the Door Gods, Ha and Heng, in the dress of ancient Chinese warrior generals. These are the protectors of the gate. Also, inside, one finds the "Heavenly Kings", four "gods" of the cardinal points of the compass, who are also protectors, and, placed centrally, usually a statue of Mi lo fo (Maitreya - the Buddha of the future) sometimes in the form of the Laughing Buddha. Behind Mi lo fo there is the figure of Wei to. He is the chief general of the many generals under the command of the Heavenly King of the south. Wei-to is in charge of monastery protection. He faces towards the central building where the Buddha is housed and hence stands back to back with Mi lo fo. These details vary in different monasteries and it is of interest to work out the variations.

Beyond the main gates one enters a spacious courtyard usually with beautiful gardens, often a lily pond and lots of butterflies etc. On each side stand buildings or towers. One houses a gigantic bell and the other a huge drum. These are played to wake the monastery in the early morning.

Passing beyond the main courtyard one finds oneself in a large courtyard facing an imposing building with large doors. This is the Ta Tien or main Buddha Hall. Here one finds rows of kneeling stools or cushions for the monks, the wooden fish and other musical instruments and the high altar with the image of Buddha. In some monasteries, as on Putuo Island, one finds Kuan Yin (Avalokiteshvara) in the place of the Buddha emphasising the spirit of compassion. Along the walls are often to be found the Lohans (Arhats) sometimes placed in elaborate stucco grottoes or other designs. The Buddha may be accompanied by other figures. It is interesting to work out who they all are. Often to his east side stands Yao shi fo the Medicine Buddha while to his west side stands O mi to fo (Amitobha) the Buddha of the Pure Land. Sometimes one may also find statues of O nan (Ananda) as a young man and Chia Yeh (Mahakasyapa) as an old one. Together with the Lohans one may also find numerous devas - local gods often numbering twenty four (Chu tien) etc. In this hall the main ceremonial events of the daily cycle are performed as well as other festivals.

Behind the Ta Tien one commonly finds the library where the Sutras and other works are kept. On the ground floor one finds the Hall of the Law or sometimes a Chan Hall, although this is more usually in a secluded courtyard away to one side.

Behind the Library, across another courtyard, is the Abbots Quarters or Fan Chang. Around the sides of the monastery are buildings for the residence of monks, their dining hall and kitchens. Also there will be a guesthouse usually with a separate kitchen and dining hall. There are also numerous administrative buildings. These complexes are constructed for many monks, running traditionally into hundreds.

The Chan Hall

The Chan Hall commonly has two parts. In one part are the Kang or sleeping platforms for the monks undergoing meditative training on retreat. The main part is a square hall with a central altar often set within large pillars holding up the roof. This increases the unobstructed floor space for fast circumambulatory walking (kin hin = Hsing hsiang). Around the walls are raised seats for meditators with a rack below for placing shoes.

A sitting session is commonly conducted in the following way although details probably vary between different institutions.

1/ The monks assemble and begin fast circumambulation. On hearing two strokes of the board and one ping of the bell they come to a halt (bell and Board = Chung Pan). A bamboo rod is struck on the floor by the officer holding it and everyone goes to his place, sits down and carefully arranges his shoes on the shelf with the feet not the hands. The Wei na (Head of Chan hall) then gives an instructive talk.

2/ When two Boards sound together with two knocks of the rod on floor outside the door the monks resume circumambulation. When one board strikes, everyone stops and the Wei na goes around the hall anticlockwise. The San Hsiang Shi (Rod bearer) goes outside the door as the Wei na returns to his place and hits the floor with his incense stick three times. Rod answers from outside. Monks may then go to toilets etc if they wish.

3/ On returning the Wei na goes around the courtyard followed by the Rod then returns inside. The monks sit and the Wei na walks around inspecting them (posture, shoes correctly placed etc) with the Rod bearer following. The Wei na gives some final instructions and the sitting session begins on the sounding of three boards plus one bell.

4/ A monk comes forward and makes three prostrations to the Buddha then resumes his seat.

5/ A disciplinarian (Hsun Hsiang Shi - a rotating appointment) circulates the room silently four times in the meditation hour carrying the Incense stick, alternating clockwise and anticlockwise directions. He may use the stick to wake sleepy fellows. The whole event is timed by watching the incense burning on the Wei na's table.

If the Abbot wishes to be present he uses a special seat provided for him.

Chan monasteries naturally have Chan Halls, but those of other sects and Nunneries do not have them. In some Chan monasteries monks are either working monks, students of the Sutras and Vinaya or Meditating monks. So there may be different professions for monks. Only some specialise in meditation.

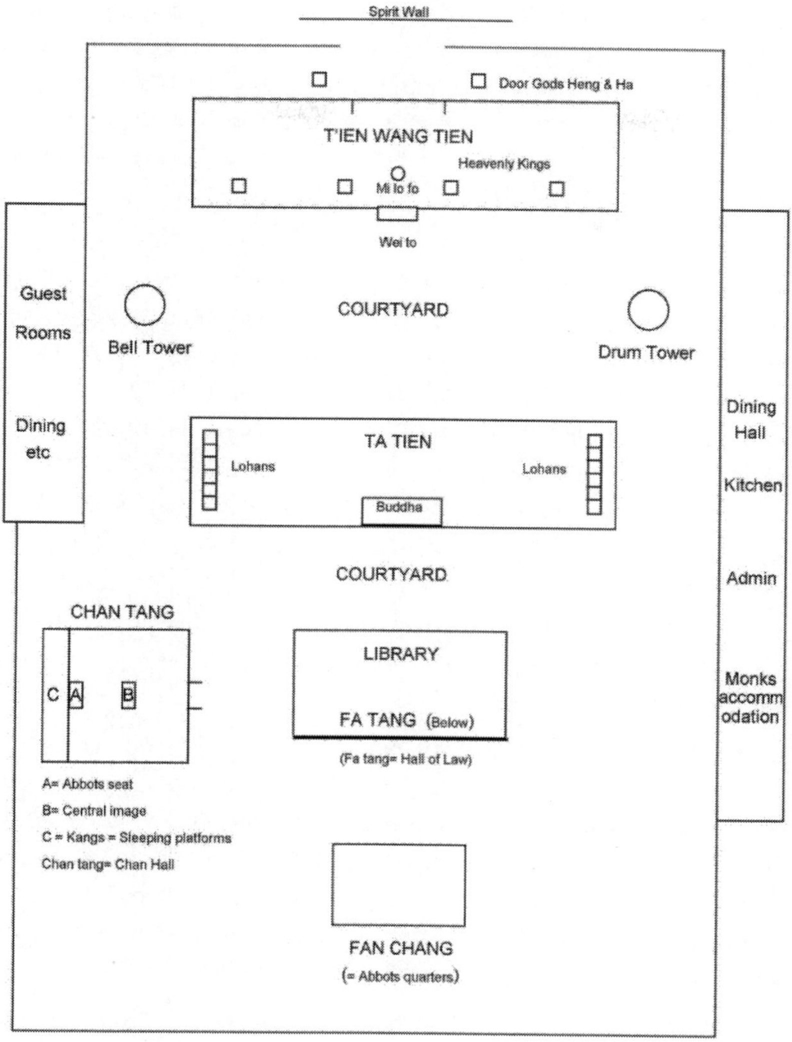

Monastic Daily Life and Offices

The daily life of Chinese monasteries varies in different sites and the account below is drawn from Moller's book. It resembles that which Yiu Yannang and I witnessed in Nan Hua Sse and Yun Men Sse in Kwantong province in 1997.

The daily round of a monastery begins at 2.30 am when the Watchman (Yeh hsun or Chao tou) rises and sounds his board three times going around the buildings. The Ta hou or fireman lights the fires under the boilers and ovens. The Chan hall Master (Wei na), the Guestmaster (Chih ko) and other main officers rise. At 2.45 am the Watchman sounds the board four times and the monastery as a whole wakes up. At 3 am the Watchman retires and the bell and board outside the Chan Hall is sounded. The monks assemble for washing and use of toilets while the great bell and drum in their respective towers begin loud sonorous booming. Everyone gradually assembles in the Buddha hall, the Ta tien, for the morning service followed by breakfast about 6 am.

After breakfast, most working monks go about their tasks while the meditators assemble at the Chan hall. The Chung pan is beaten and the meditation hour begins as described previously. The monks of the Chan hall ordinarily spend three hours there in the morning, one after lunch and two in the evening. The morning three hours is not all spent sitting however. The half-hour of exercises (Hsing Hsiang) is followed by the Tso Hsiang (Sitting) for an hour. Then there is a ten minute rest (Hsiu Hsi) followed by half an hour circumambulation, ten minutes sitting and an hour of rest. Not so exhausting after all!

Lunch is at noon. Evening worship in the Ta Tien is at about four or five followed by an hours rest period after which the monks return to the Chan hall for the evening sit at about six. At eight o'clock the bell and drum begin sounding in slow crescendo as the monastery prepares for bed. The signals given by the Watchman are in reverse of those of the morning.

The monks are of several categories The Ssu shou are the leaders comprising the officers of the monastery (Chih shih). The Ching chung are the ordinary monks while the Hang tang are the most menial doing such jobs as looking after rice supplies (the Fan tou), water for tea (Cha tou), bathrooms (Yu tou), toilets (Ching tou). The Hsiang teng shi are cleaners and the Hsu shan foresters. The Chu i are the kitchen staff. Generally monks are devided between those who work inside the bounds (Nei chih shih) or with an outside focus (Wai chih shih).

Among the more important officers, beside the Meditation Master (Wei na) and Guestmaster (Chi ko), there are the Tient tso shih or Chief cook, the Business manager (Ku tou) and the Chien Yuan or Treasurer of the Ku fang (Administration) who works closely with the Abbot. The Abbot usually has a young male assistant of considerable brilliance as a secretary known as the I po. The Liao yuan is in charge of the Monk's Guest hall and their registration while the Scribe (Shu chi) deals with letters and documents to do with commemoration of the dead, rituals and so on.

Today, after the ravages of the Cultural Revolution, monasteries are still being reconstructed and are mostly not as yet fully operational. It follows that the organisation is somewhat abbreviated from that of earlier years. However the pattern is still very clearly there and in process of renewal.

THE REVIVAL OF BUDDHISM IN CHINA

A WCF tour of some Chinese Monasteries in the year 2000

In the spring of the year 2000 a party of Western Chan Buddhists left the UK for China. Two Swiss, two Poles and one Maltese joined our group[1]. The purpose of our journey was to visit some famous Chinese Buddhist monasteries to see how Buddhism was re-emerging in China after the years of Communist totalitarianism. In particular we chose two of the sacred 'mountains' of China; Putuo Shan on a small island off the coast south of Shanghai and Jiuhua Shan high in the mountains of Anhui. We were especially delighted to visit Tiantong, the seat of famous Tsaotung masters and the site of Dogen's enlightenment. The findings were encouraging. Buddhism is showing a remarkable recovery and we had the good fortune to meet a number of outstanding monks. This article does not describe monasteries visited in Hong Kong as these have not been influenced by mainland politics in the same way, nor have we focussed on Chan alone. Many of the monks stressed the value of Pure Land Buddhism at the present time in China.[2]

Tiangtong Monastery

We flew into Ningbo in eastern China from Hong Kong not knowing how we would be received by the Chinese customs. I suspected some cold ghosts of the old Communist China might re- appear but there were no problems at all and soon we were in our bus bowling along a new, four lane motorway into the city of Ningbo.

At once we could see the effects of China's rapid development. In spite of the eulogies of our local guide, like all of our guides rather over-the-top with enthusiasm as if making up for some hidden lack, I could see nothing but the drab enormity of hastily constructed high-rise buildings and the pokiness of millions of little cubicles for the accommodation of China's millions. An endless suburbia spread an uninspired blanket in all directions punctuated by great factories, many of them spewing clouds of dusty murk into a sky already grey with pollution. Grey is the colour I remember whenever I think of Ningbo.

Mile on mile of intermittent factories, high rise buildings hit the sky, the smell of fresh concrete.

Our local guide had a surprise for us. The "Monastery of the Seven Pagodas" lay in the heart of the town. It was a dusty place, ancient, much of it being either renovated or removed, we could not tell which, and populated by people who eyed us with a barely hidden curiosity as if we were creatures from the moon. We realised Westerners were still a rarity here. People were offering incense and prostrating themselves before the Buddhas. The religiosity of the people was of the simplest kind - a request for better things through offerings. Yet I marvelled at the way in which temple worship such as I had seen previously in Taiwan was once more a commonplace in the new China. The years of Communist domination were so clearly a thing of the past and, while capitalist materialism now ruled and the pride in their rapidly burgeoning city was not entirely misplaced, the re-emergence of ancient, basically Taoist superstitions and their servicing by Buddhist priests seems yet a most remarkable thing. Old China resurrects within the foundations of the new.

After a comfortable night in a hotel overlooking the railway station, we drove out over a wide plain dominated at first by the widely dispersed patches of suburbia we had seen on our arrival.

Festooned with power lines,
the Ningbo plain.
No low flying eagles here.

Gradually the countryside opened up and small villages appeared set in a flat landscape of fields being readied for rice planting or covered by blooming crops of mustard shining a brilliant yellow even under the leaden sky. These big yellow fields remain my dominant memory of these plains in spring, as also do the spindly roadside trees, a kind of larch that was just beginning to sprout tufts of green. We drove on through a repetition of small villages (or suburban complexes in what had once been a village), long straight roads, scruffy trees and yellow fields stretching to the horizon. Hills appeared, deep woods and a lake and at last I could revel in true countryside free from the horrible, ubiquitous urban influence.

Mirroring the white sky
rice fields in spring,
soft spikes of green.

We topped a rise and sped down into a valley wooded by tall feathery bamboos and up a long approach to a great spirit wall, built to prevent the passage of ghosts, and on past tall gates beyond which which we could see an impressive array of buildings, Tiantong, the revered monastery of Hung chih Cheng chueh (1091-

1157),[3] the prime exponent of Silent Illumination (mo chao). To our great surprise the acting Abbot was on the steps to greet us, evidently responding dutifully to the China Travel Service phone call of the morning. He seemed unfazed by our arrival, non-committal as we were introduced, merely indicating that we should follow him in a tour of the monastery. Then he was off, walking at great speed, trotting up the flights of steps and along the corridors, through the palatial gate arches with their curved eaves, through the Buddha hall, up back alleys, through more temples, barely pausing for breath or any explanation. Eva tried to engage him with me as the group's leader. "Yes, yes", he said and hurried on, seemingly disinterested. But when I asked whether we could all have a talk with him, he at last smiled and said, "But of course, when we have finished." And off he sped again. Most of the tour participants failed to respond to the challenge and were soon left far behind and lost, gaping at the splendour of the great halls, the high ceilings and the benevolent Buddhas. Some five of us kept pace with the Abbot and at last he led us into a large room well furnished with wooden tables and chairs in a fine traditional style, elegant but formal. He seated us around the table, placed me to his right at the head of the table, began to smile at us and ordered tea. Some of our party never caught up with us, while others popped around the door at intervals as we talked.

I opened our discussion, as I was to do repeatedly in the monasteries we visited, with an expression of gratitude at our welcome. I said we had an especial interest in Tiantong because our main practice as taught us by Master Sheng yen was Silent Illumination (mo chao). Tiangtong had been the monastery of the great Hung Chih, the originator of Silent illumination and the author of wonderful essays about it. He had also collected many Gong ans (Koans) for "The Book of Serenity"[4] illustrating the fact that for him an important relation existed between the practice of Silent Illumination and the contemplation of Koans. Tiantong had also been the monastery of Master Ru ching, (T'ien t'ung Ju ching 1163-1228), one of the few in his time to maintain the Tsao-tung tradition of the practice of Silent illumination. When the great Japanese monk Dogen on pilgrimage in China, had heard of him he at once came to Tiantong where he attained enlightenment under Ru ching's guidance in the Meditation Hall. We had studied some writings of both Hung chi and Dogen and Master Sheng yen had taught us from the texts of the former. They were my favourite authors in Zen. I very much wanted to visit the Chan hall and requested that all of us could spend a little while there.

Vice Abbot Shu Shiang said he was deputising for the elderly abbot of the monastery who was away in Shanghai. It was the first time a party of European Buddhists had visited the monastery and he was delighted to receive us. It is not easy to practice Chan, he told us, and it must be even more difficult in a land without a tradition of practice or Buddhist culture. He told us that after the Cultural Revolution the first requirement was the restoration and renewal of damaged buildings. This had been a Herculean task and it was still far from completed. Now it was important to restore the Buddhist viewpoint among the people. Basically it had never disappeared. Communism was a mere blip on Chinese history. The Government now recognised that the roots of Chinese culture lay in Confucianism, Taoism and Buddhism and that all three were to a degree intertwined. In allowing the renewal of Chinese culture, communism was fading away and the old visions were being restored.

So far as Buddhism was concerned, Abbot Shu Shiang argued that the most reliable way to teach the masses who were coming back to the temples was through the Pure Land school. To the ordinary citizen the Pure Land is something to work for and the Buddha of the Western Paradise seems to be a source of strength and hope. Shu Shiang admitted this to be largely an "outer path". Only the more sophisticated could see that the Pure Land lay in the mind and that the method was in the end an inner practice. Chan was a technique that could be used within such a context. Many Chinese including monks would view Chan that way today. "In Chan we clear the mind to find the heart". Not all the monks sat in meditation but the Chan Hall was in use for practice. Silent Illumination was still an important practice at Tiangtong but many now would use a hua t'ou in the way Master Hsu Yun had suggested earlier in the twentieth century.

"And the contemplation of Koan remains valuable", Shu Shiang said, "Consider this story. As you know the paddy fields around here are crossed by very narrow paths. It is very difficult for people to pass each other unless one of them steps in the water. One day a monk and a girl were approaching one another along such a path. Neither of them would give way and eventually the girl fell into the paddy water, not only wet but very muddy. The monk said to himself ' Oh - I have a disadvantage.' When they came out of the paddy the girl came up and slapped the monk in the face. 'Ah,' he said to himself, 'Now I have an advantage'. What is the meaning of this story?"

I said, "I am wondering what is wrong with the paddy field?" Everyone laughed but the abbot did not take up such a line. This story is about people, he told us, consider when you have an advantage. Is it really an advantage? And when you are at a disadvantage are you really at a disadvantage? Was the monk right do you think? Did the girl end up thinking herself at a disadvantage. Perhaps not. So who is this story about? The monk or the girl? If we put ourself in the place of the monk perhaps we can get some insight. But then what of the girl? Now, come, I will show you the Chan Hall. You may meditate for a little while there. On this story perhaps?"

Lifting the heavy screen that separates the Chan Hall from the outside courtyard, the abbot led us into the dark interior of a very large room. Immediately we were enveloped in a heavy silence, a deep peace. He handed us over to a meditation instructor and left the room. The Chan Hall was of a type familiar to me from Nan hua Si and Yun Men Si[5]. It was a square hall in the centre of which stood a large glass case within which sat the figure of the Buddha. Around the walls were benches about a yard in depth, one of which, behind the Buddha, was walled off as a special seat for the abbot should he decide to join the meditation session. Most of the places were clearly used, cushions awaiting a sitter's return.

The meditation instructor motioned us to take places anywhere except along the front wall which is reserved for senior monks. He then delivered a short speech outlining the essence of Chan meditation. Precise and eloquent, he presented a clear viewpoint. He based his talk very much on Hsu Yun's writings. When we use the word "Amitobha" during a recitation of Buddha's name where precisely does that word come from? Can you trace it to its source? If you can do so you will find it simply appears before the mind. Do you know where it appears from? He told us it was not in the eye, ear or any other kind of consciousness. In meditation we abandon all kinds of discriminations and go beyond the mind of discrimination and all types consciousness that are involved in discrimination. If you practice with a good method you will find the heart. He then left us alone, so I gave a simple instruction to "Make the mind bright - thirty minutes!"[6] and, clapping my hands as a signal, we began our practice.

At first I was overwhelmed by the thought that I was sitting here in the very hall where the great Dogen had gained enlightenment. There was great presence in that hall, the accumulated silence of years of deep meditation, the 'one thought for a thousand years' hung in the very air. Gradually this deeply brooding atmosphere filled me with itself and for a while there was a profound sense of identity with the room, its message, its peace. I felt wonderfully grateful just to be there.

> Tiantong!
>
> Dogen once more
>
> speaks to Dogen.7

Suddenly the silence snapped. The blind covering the door lifted and a dozen or so young monks strode into the room. Purposefully and fast they circulated the Buddha swinging their arms with great vigour. Someone hit the floor with a rod and they halted. Removing their outer robes they swept towards their seats - and stopped! Many were already occupied by us. They hesitated. There was a word of command and, as swiftly as they had come, they swept out of the hall again. Silence fell. Shortly after it was time to go.

The abbot saw us off and we drove down the hill sadly: because too quickly leaving the handsome, reborn monastery with its great halls, its alley ways and shrines and, most remembered, the deep silence of the ancient Chan Hall. It was raining lightly as we drove through wooded slopes towards the coast.

> Hillsides glowing,
> peach blossom
> in soft rain.

Putuo Shan

I had been given the impression that Chinese restoration of old buildings had been shabbily undertaken, gross concrete with all the old arts dead. This was not our experience in Putuo shan nor at Tiantong. The artwork in the restored monasteries is of a first class nature; some of it brilliant, ingenious. The dedication and the financing is extraordinary. The total sum of material investment must be enormous. Some of the funding is from Taiwan and Hong Kong with millionaires gaining merit from their extensive donations. Much of it also comes from the donations of many pilgrims who come from large cities such as Shanghai and not only purchase great bundles of incense and burn paper goods for the benefit of the ancestors but also contribute directly to the coffers of the monasteries through donations given in the ubiquitous little red envelopes. There is also considerable government support for the material renaissance of these magnificent buildings and their palatial compounds. Much of this is doubtless to encourage tourism, mainly internal, but there is also an awareness, even shame perhaps, at the terrible waste and damage to China's heritage committed during the Cultural Revolution. The Government seems keen to reinstate traditional values so long as this does not lead to any suspicion of resistance to the government itself. There is in inevitable paradox here, given the appalling human rights record of this ruling clique.

In Putuo shan we have seen no sign of Western tourism. Not one Western face have we seen. The place is however full to overcrowding with Chinese, especially at weekends when they come from Shanghai by ship. There are numerous school holiday parties - young people brightly dressed in their uniforms traipsing around the monasteries in jolly little parties preceded usually by an attractive, young woman guide or student with a coloured flag held high to lead them. There are also large groups of sombre looking men dressed in regulation business suits of brown, black or grey cloth. They come in parties from their work place, business or whatever in groups exuding a strong feel of togetherness. The uniform tailoring of the suits seem to be the capitalist replacement of the blue Mao jackets in which Chinese used to attire themselves with unrelieved monotony. How different they appear from contemporary parties of adults in the West dressed with personal idiosyncrasy in sports clothes, suits, blazers, sweaters, T-shirts! The Chinese disguise their individuality in these monotonous displays of togetherness.

Up the old stone steps
stolid party gentlemen
in dark brown business suits.

These sights and sounds make us all wonder at the recovery of Buddhism in China. This is still nominally a Communist state and a highly totalitarian one in which individualism or even groupism is severely controlled - as in the case of the Falung Gong. Buddhism seems to be the state- tolerated aspect of a religiosity deeply engrained in the Chinese, who are among the most superstitious people on earth. Yet what we observed is not so much superstition as a deep devotion expressed naturally and without embarrassment in the kneeling, bowing and prostration before the Buddhas and lesser shrines and in the offering of great bundles of incense in the huge burners in the courtyards.

People buy the incense, light it and then move to the entrance to the great Buddha halls and bow reverently with the bundle held before them, three times quite quickly before returning to the burner and placing it therein. Scented smoke rises in all the major courtyards. A lot of money is being consigned to flame here. The devotee will then return inside the hall and bow or prostrate to the statues with great sincerity. This devotion expressed spontaneously and freely is not dissimilar to that shown by Tibetans at the Jokhang in Lhasa. On one steep incline we saw three women prostrating their way up and down the steep steps, going sideways on the steeper slopes.

Island groves, bird chatter.
Under the eaves of monastic halls
the dead are hovering near.

The island has a very strong atmosphere and I found it affecting me in unexpected ways. First of all there are the wonderful folk tales of the origin of the island sanctuaries. There was a monk who wanted to take a statue of Kuan Yin to Japan. The ship ran into a storm off the island of Putuo. After three attempts to get clear of the land he prayed to the statue saying, "If you do not want to go to Japan then please take us to the shore. I will build a wonderful temple for you there." The storm abated and the party came safely to shore. The monk created the monastery as he had promised. It is called the "Monastery of the Kuan Yin who did not want to leave".

Temple courtyard
soft chanting in distant halls.
Ancient heartache, yearning vision.

Large numbers of monasteries and hermitages came to be established on the island and many great masters came and stayed here including a great 19th century reformer who created the "Buddhism for all mankind" movement out of a syncretism of contemporary approaches. In Shi fu's book (in Chinese) about his visit here he describes the story of this monk's enlightenment on the island.

During the Cultural Revolution there was terrible destruction. The monks and nuns were defrocked and sent to labour on the mainland. It is almost as if the wonderful works of restoration now in progress are a compensation for those years. Yet Eva Song, our interpreter, argues that this can just as well be seen as an attempt to cover over the past, to make people forget and even deny the recent past in a celebration of the wonders of the economic revolution sweeping China today.

One morning Ken Jones and I went for a walk through the little island town and came across an old temple building not yet restored and still part of a heavily inhabited courtyard. Small shops bursting with all sorts of goods, crates and boxes of fish, dusty corners, upper stories with rustic furniture and washing hanging out, and animals wandering about amid early morning business did not distract us from the ancient roofing, pillars and carved cornices in the eaves that revealed what had originally been this place. It was interesting to witness what the whole island must have been like immediately after the revocation of the cultural revolution and all its malicious work.

The most important feature of Putuo Shan is the cult of Kuan Yin. As the holy mountain dedicated to her, there is an especial atmosphere emanating from the worship of this Bodhisattva, compassionate, feminine, gazing down on the world with her innumerable skills symbolised by her many arms revealed in some of her most dramatic and complex iconic representations and statues. Her arms of 'skilful means' are held to be so many that there is always one of them to respond to whatever sorrow or difficulty a human being may suffer. For this reason, to appeal to her for refuge is seen as virtually infallible. As the Kuan Yin Sutra says, all you have to do is to call upon her and, in whatever adverse circumstance you may find yourself, one of her skilful arms will save you.

This spirit of compassion is present all over the island: first of all in the tall statues standing in the main Buddha halls of the temples. A taped recording of her mantra sounds repetitively with a soft seduction which, strangely, does not grow wearisome. There is a gentle intensity about the chanting that speaks of the sorrows of the world and the possibility of redemption.

The tall Kuan Yin statues gaze down at one from a considerable height, the face revealing a gentle, half smile of compassionate caring. As I stood in those great halls and looked up into that face I often experienced a change in my heart. The gentle glance is calming and induced a gentleness softening my feelings about the sometimes noisy crowds around me and their seemingly banal religiosity. It was almost as if the spirit of Kuan Yin herself entered my awareness bringing a feeling of tolerance and understanding of the suffering needs of the world, reducing the egoism of self-importance and creating moments of a kindly humility. The face of Kuan Yin seems to become for that moment one's own face, one's own mind. The teaching of the statue is received through a direct apprehension of the expression on her face.

And this, after all, is no different from the response I feel when I see the same look in a human face. The vice-abbot at Tiantong had it and so did the tall elderly monk of eighty years we spoke to in the courtyard of Puji Si. In repose his face relaxed into a look very like that of Kuan yin showing that her icon is not a mere abstraction but a human glance, compassionate, strangely disinterested yet penetratingly aware. As time went on, this awareness of Kuan Yin's presence grew stronger almost as if I was in the compassionate embrace of the whole island, responding to everyone with empathy.

During my walk with Ken we had come down to the shore and heard from time to time a strange distant booming. Gradually we realised this was the sound of the sea rushing in and out of coves and funnels in the rocky cliffs. One such place, the "Cave of the Tidal Sound", has a small temple where people, thinking they saw Kuan Yin in the sunlit spray, used to leap into the abyss believing they would be received into her arms. This had become so great a problem that there is an ancient stone there with an inscription of the Emperor ordering people not to commit suicide in this way. While we stood listening, the dark shape of a submarine set sail from the nearby dockyard for patrol off Taiwan.

War drums sounding
sinister submarine

sets sail from Kuan Yin's naval base.

Near the temple at the "Cave of Tidal Sound" there is a round ornamental pool. As we approached people were gesturing and, looking into the pool, we saw reflected in it a perfect rainbow around the sun, a solar halo with the mists drifting through it. Looking up, there indeed it was, made even clearer by using dark glasses. I marvelled at this and at first saw it as the natural phenomenon it is- a rainbow created by the sunlight filtering through a light misty cloud. But then Eva came along very excited, this was an especial blessing to us given by Kuan Yin, she told us. Look how rare a chance it is - she said. At the very moment we arrived the halo around the sun appeared. It was a sign of her blessing. Eva very much wanted all of us to understand this and to experience the blessing. The solid English had barely noticed. They appreciated the phenomenon yes - but not really noticed. They were quickly off again poking about among the rocks and the little temple marvelling at the new carvings on its front wall telling the story of the first statue's arrival. Eva went off to commune with herself - but she left me thinking.

I said to myself - it is indeed a strange and mysterious event amazingly timed to coincide with our arrival, a synchronicity. My own meteorological vision was not the only way of understanding this. There were other glinting facets to Indra's net here. Already the cloud had thickened and the halo vanished. In opening itself to us at that very moment the universe had indeed let loose a blessing. Each witness had in their own way felt it. Suddenly I felt gratitude and a kind of wonder that merged with my experiencing of the presence of Kuan Yin. I went into the little temple and gazed at the Kuan Yin there. All these things came together and, indeed, I felt blessed.

What is it like to feel blessed? So difficult to find words. My mind fell still, quiet, peaceful, thankful, almost shy of my own experience which seemed to contrast markedly with my naturalistic explanation of a few minutes before. To feel blessed is to feel peace, to feel at one with the phenomenal, to be grateful for the beauty and uniqueness of the cosmos. These are mere words. The experience itself was almost empty - an emptiness coloured by the thoughts I have tried to express. At the time they were nowhere to be found; loose feelings floating through the equipoise of a moment.

Eva talked with me. This was our "Yuan Fen", she said. Causes and conditions had come together in a unique moment that blessed our pilgrimage. It was not chance but an expression of our own relationship with things. She had come on our pilgrimage as our interpreter on the spur of the moment knowing she needed a pilgrimage herself. Now she knew she had been right. The idea of "yuan fen" was to pursue us throughout our journey (see below).

We visited another little temple (Fanyin Dong) standing as a bridge across a gulch in the coast where waves roared past below us; another place where Kuan Yin appeared in the wave blown spume shot through by sunlight and where people had also thrown themselves into the merciless sea. We all felt the power of the place and fell into a silence filled only by our personal thoughts and the mellow fluted calls of the bulbuls in the bushes about us. Out to sea the distant islands of the archipelago rose against the horizon and the sharp-prowed fishing boats sailed past over the tawny waters of this riverine coast.

Estuarine mists
Yangtse brown
A good brew.

Wu Ming

In exploring the monasteries in the little town we had several time seen a mysterious, elderly lady dressed in a robe, with a tablet on her forehead and a remarkably self-confident yet reserved manner. We understood she was a Taoist and resolved to talk to her.

Eva got her into conversation and she agreed to talk with us. Her name was Wu ming which had a double meaning, either No name or No wisdom. Either would do she said. She had been married and had children but had suffered from many vexations. She had taken up the Taoist way in order to overcome them. She was, she said, an everyday Taoist not one of those who seclude themselves in the mountains.

Wu ming was short and round in stature but her figure was upright and blossoming with vigour. Her face was flat in the Manchurian manner, her eyes almost invisible between the lids, her voice authoritative, deep in tone and every word precisely spoken giving her discourse in Mandarin a commanding quality with all the tones richly emphasised.

She was still hanging around the temples, she told us, because it was her birthday and she would be off tomorrow. She came to the island because she revered Kuan yin and the atmosphere of the place. She told us that China had three great cultures which intermingled, Taoism, Buddhism and Confucianism. Taoism related us to the cosmos, the energy of the universe and its cultivation would lead to long life,

Buddhism emphasised kindness in human relations and the importance of transcending the ego while Confucianism gave us values for civic responsibilities.

Her main practice was to cultivate the life force, chi, and to live according to the vision of ancient Chinese culture. The main essence was to live in righteousness, honouring one's parents, obeying the laws and sustaining patriotism. Openness to everything without discriminations and with kindness to all sentient beings was the way of wisdom.

Wu ming said she meditated a lot but due to her short legs could not do this in the lotus posture. She meditated lying down in a 'sleeping posture'. "You prepare your mind through breathing practice and focus the chi in the tan tien two inches below the navel. This generates energy and provides the whole body with a strong life force through building up the power of the tan tien." Her main practice involved the regulation of "chi". Her flat shoes contacted the earth and held her head high towards heaven. Her forehead tablet was made of jade and protected her from previous psychic troubles. She said that much of what she did was to ensure her health and a long life so that she would die " crisply". She was very happy to be photographed and went off to change into a deep blue robe. She stood there smiling inscrutably making an emphatic assertion of herself before the cameras. I felt she was a lady of much integrity and no little wisdom.

Fayu Monastery

In the middle of the island, set back among deep woods, lies the monastery of Fayu Si, perhaps the most beautiful on the island. It is less crowded that many others and the spacious courtyards are adorned with great trees, spring leaves were coming forth and many flowering shrubs beautified the gardens. The architecture has been beautifully restored. We hardly had time to explore this place thoroughly when we met up with a striking monk in his early middle years, handsome and openly friendly. He was interested in what these rare Westerners were doing and invited us into the library cum book shop of which he was the keeper.

Nang chi Shi had a lively mind and his name means "Able wisdom". He and Eva got on tremendously. She, in her most charming style, thought she had known him before in a previous life. Perhaps they had been brother and sister. Nang Chi reciprocated these sentiments saying it was their "Yuan Fen" to meet at Fayu while Eva was on pilgrimage with us.

We talked about the devotion to Kuan yin shown by past generations in throwing themselves over the island precipices. Alan asked "How should one devote oneself to Buddha?" Nang Chi said that self-immolation was certainly not the way. The true

Buddhist path was a path of the heart. One had to develop a brave, determined, diligent and persevering heart. On the path one needs to use the body to take care of the heart, not to abuse it. To commit suicide is quite wrong. A belief that Kuan yin is out there in the mist waiting to save you is an "outer path" practice. That is not the meaning of Kuan yin. The universal compassion of Kuan yin includes care of ourselves in order to live better and to help others.

Nang chi told us a koan story. Once upon a time there was a poet whose great friend was a Chan master who lived on the far side of the river from his residence. One day he wrote the master a poem intending to reveal his Chan attainment.

> My head looks up.
>
> Heaven is the sky, a halo of light.
>
> I sit on a purple and gold lotus seat
>
> The eight winds could not dislodge me.

The poet sent a servant over the river with his poem. The master read it and appreciated the poet's skill. None the less, turning the paper over, he wrote one character on the back and sent it back. The character said "Fart!"

When the poet read this he was greatly shocked and rushed over the river to see the master. "Why did you write 'Fart' on the back of my poem?" he demanded.

"Well," responded the master, "Did you not say that no wind could blow you off your seat. See - one Fart could do it!"

It is interesting that these two stories told us in China both emphasise personal relations in which the problems of egoism were the key theme. Nang chi was very kind to us. It is valuable to ponder the meaning of such stories for yourselves, he told us. He emphasised that in Chan a disciplined equanimity was essential in order to reach the objective. He gave Eva a hand written book of his personal thoughts, goals and practices. Eva felt most touched by this kindness and teaching. Indeed it was a remarkable gesture of Dharma friendship.

In his notebook Nang chi reflects on why he had become a monk, perhaps to explain himself to others.

Why do I escape?

Maybe you think I am a coward who hides himself in an old monastery hidden deep in the mountains with the silent statues of Buddha, the light of candles and the sounds of the morning bell and evening drum; as if I am not doing anything all day long and find the sun setting when I wake up as each day goes by.

Maybe you think I intend to use this funny costume to build a wall separating myself from others, keeping a distance. You may feel we are different kinds of people living in two separate worlds. Actually I have not left the present world at all: I cannot. Enlightenment cannot be achieved other than by living in this present world. Such is the truth. One can only search for it through practice, from reality. To escape is not a wise choice. Only when reality is confronted, and problems resolved, can one achieve the best result.

To become aware is to know the heart. The heart is the source of everything; naturally it is also the core of worry and suffering. If the heart can be calmed, it will not be influenced by the outside world. Serenity will arise. Why bother to live in solitude, or sit quietly in the forest? I believe that if we contemplate mindfully even among the noisiest crowd, we can still discover splendour.

Why do I escape? I have merely chosen an unique lifestyle through living in this mundane world while maintaining a detached mind to pursue my own destiny. This is a frequently misunderstood and lonely path, hardly trodden, without flowers or applause. It is a choice I have made in full awareness, not an escape from frustration.

You may think that I intend to cover my face with a veil, with a touch of mystery, so that you cannot comprehend, cannot figure it out.

Amitabha!

Nang chi Shi. Lotus pond, Da Ming Monastery, Yang Zho, China. Spring 1990.[8]

Hangzhou

We drove to Hangzhou over the mustard-covered plains golden under the rainy sky. Gradually once more the same tedious suburbia appeared enlivened by traffic notices, here sometimes translated into English.

> Highway's end
>
> Hangzhou city appears
>
> "Urban area - NO Honking!"

Once within the city, its glorious past was gradually revealed. It is a place of elegance in spite of the tremendous surge of building in recent years. The West Lake, sombre under cloud, had a quiet beauty with pleasure boats slowly moving across its surface in the dusk. In the distance there were wooded hills and in the foreground great mansions in tree-filled gardens with flowering shrubs. Our hotel was most agreeable and our bathrooms contained the most advanced, electronically controlled bidets any of us had ever seen. Even the seats were warmed and little water jets so contrived as to clean out every possible human orifice.

Lingyin Si is the prime monastery of Hangzhou with an illustrious history. It was founded in 326 CE in the first year of the Eastern Tsin dynasty by an Indian monk known as Hui Li. Many times destroyed and renovated it has retained its original architectural style. It was largely preserved by the order of Zhou Enlai during the Cultural Revolution and active restoration was carried out from1975. Set in an ancient capital of China it is not surprising that Hangzhou's main temple has had a great influence on the history of Buddhism in China. In Shih fu's Chinese book about his short visit, he details the names of great monks of the past who trained and taught here. Perhaps the most famous in Chan history was Ta Hui (1089-1153) who received a purple gown from the Emperor. He was a great exponent of the use of Koans and took the contemporary Master Hung Chi of Tiangtong to task for teaching the Silent Illumination approach. But in spite of these polemics, when Hung Chi died he asked Ta Hui to become abbot of his monastery. These divergences do not seem to have influenced a real friendship and regard between these great representatives of the Lin Chi and Tsao Tung traditions.[9]

We were entertained by a deputy abbot, Jue Hang Shi, the actual abbot being away. We had tea with him in a magnificent room and talked. Although some monks at Lingyin Si practised Chan, the main emphasis was Pure Land. There was no Chan hall but there was a project to build or restore one.

I asked him, "Where is the Pure Land?"

"Lingyin Monastery!" he immediately replied. "Here we practice to create the Pure Land in the heart. Perhaps we can show the way so that others can follow."

"Would it not be better to ask who is repeating Buddha's name rather than just repeating it?" I enquired.

"To repeat Buddha's name in faith clears the heart of vexation." he replied. "The asking of questions is a Chan way. Indeed it may be helpful to those who are drawn to it. Some of us here practice that way. Yet in the end it is still the Pure Land that arises. You could say that practising Chan is a way to realising the Pure Land."

We enjoyed a vegetarian meal in the large restaurant and sauntered in the misty, rain washed courtyards of flowering shrubs where incense smoke rising from great burners and floating among the trees scented the air.

Today Lingyin Si is a cultural shrine visited by enormous numbers of pilgrims and tourists, ten thousand a day we were told. For the first time we encountered tour parties of Western and Japanese visitors, each tour being led around by young women carrying distinctive flags. At Lingyin there is an extraordinary, incompleted gallery of Lohans, gold leafed, life size figures in innumerable postures - a vast and continuing investment. The park around the monastery is extensive and includes a grotto with ancient carvings of Buddhas hidden among trees. I spotted a lantsa inscription from the early days when the Indian monks were here. There are said to be seventy two caves in the park, formerly used for reclusive meditation.

Huang Shan

The mustard-covered plains gradually gave way to low hills, woods, and bamboo groves. Wild magnolia, cherry and plum, azalea bushes and here and there carpets of flowers dotted the woods brightening them up ready for spring. Catkins hung from the hazels and other trees. Gradually fir woods appeared as we rose into the foothills of Huang Shan.

> Azalea red
> the wooded hillsides glow.
> No need for sunshine.

Driving through Anhui province away from the cities became a delight. The country became rolling, agricultural with neat tea terraces on the hillsides interrupted by groves of tall, feathery bamboo. Little rural villages appeared with neat black and white houses of a characteristic Anhui architecture with up ended ridges to their roofs called "horses necks" as a protection from fire.

We stayed at Cloud Valley Hotel (Yungu Hotel) arriving after dark in a deep mist that hung mysteriously around the fir trees. In the morning, still misty and rainy, we could appreciate the setting in deep woods in a steep verdant valley with rocky crags visible here and there. The forested mountains loomed above us.

> At three thousand feet, red coated hostesses
> decorate the hotel with formal informality,
> the occasional giggle.

We had learnt how to greet these serious, little gigglers. Ni Hau means Good day-so:

> "Knee High!" we all say
> greeting the red coated maidens
> in the dining room.

The local chair lift into the mountains was under repair so we drove around the foothills to another one. A splendid new structure designed by an Austrian-Swiss company lifted large cars holding a small crowd into the sky. The dense cloud hung its skirts entirely over the mountain. Up we went into the mist, nothing visible bar the passing vapour. Arriving on a stone platform, we set off on foot in dense fog along a narrow path between ghostly but beautiful conifers. The mist, hiding the abysses that we knew were somewhere near, gave a strange almost dangerous feel to the place. The fir forests were inhabited by wraiths of cloud, thickening and thinning as we went along, seeming to beckon and slide away. The hotel gave us a damp welcome but the rooms were good and the coffee excellent. We went for a walk in the fog.

On one of the legs of the track we came across a wash house with a WC. Needing a pee I popped up some steps to the toilet and on the way out found an attendant behind a counter. A price was written up and mistaking it for some kind of shop I waved my hand and started to pass by. Suddenly the attendant erupted in an elephantine roar and charged at me with what looked like an oncoming rugby tackle. I stopped, suddenly realising that I had to pay a charge for the use of the primitive facility. I gave him a small note and, getting matters straight, demanded the minute quantity of change. Grumbling with what sounded like a colourful swearword, he responded correctly and we parted. I was a little shocked realising that I had had a near shave. You do not disobey the rules in China. Don't test somebody's face in the wrong way!

Offended lavatory attendant nearly runs me down.
Humbly I pay one yuan for a pee
correctly demanding my 50 cent change.
In China - you take care of other people's face.

Back at the cloud-shrunken hotel we thought it would be good to do an hour's meditation together. So we requested the use of a small hall in which to do this. Alarm and problem! "That's a religious activity," they objected; not allowed in a public place. Well, we said, it would not be in a public place because we would be hiring the room in which to do it. Never the less we had to consult the local police. Aware of the fate of the Falun Gong, we carefully assured everyone we were proper Buddhists. Luckily the local constable was a friend of our regional guide. "All right," he said, "but keep the door shut!"

Police confirmation
meditation permit granted
but - keep the door closed!

After nightfall we found the stars were out in a bright sky and, walking to the cliff edge, we could see the remote shapes of craggy mountain tops all around us. Rising before dawn, several of us set off again for the cliffs already preceded by a host of energetic Japanese intent on viewing the world famous sunrise and on securing the best crags for photography. Sure enough the sky was clear, gradually lightening to reveal the pinnacles, crevices, gorges and fir clad peaks that surrounded us. The sun rose in gentle glory above the 'sea of clouds' that lay along the horizon and everyone cheered, clicking away in a million photographs.

Huang Shan is truly beautiful. It is no wonder many ancient poets and philosophers came here to write and think. In the old days the climb up the million steps must have been trying yet, I guessed, the rewards of the heights even more striking after so great an effort. Even today the modern hotels are supplied by coolies who trot up the steps with huge loads brought up from the valleys below. There is too much weight to be conveyed in the chair lifts so labour is used - much cheaper. Today it is difficult to distinguish coolies from tourists. Coolies, often trotting along without shoes, wear the same lightweight sports clothing, T-shirts and ragged jeans as do many of the younger visitors. For this hard labour they receive only the tiniest of wages and many pause as they pass the tourists and ask for money.

Once more we boarded our bus and crossed the yellow plains heading for Jiuhua Mountain. In the coach there was talk of Buddhism. Lively discussion raged between two of our older gentlemen who held decided and largely incorrect notions about the Dharma. How easily we become fixed upon our own mistaken notions!

> Two old tourist gentlemen
> discussing Dharma on the bus
> thinking to demonstrate the secrets of Zen.

Jiu Hua Shan

The mountain road twisted up between occasional small monasteries half hidden in bamboo. We reached an archway, the entrance to the holy mountain, where a large monastery, also a Buddhist Côllege, is situated. On again up the twisting road brought us to the Jiu hua village, handsomely proud with its large monastic buildings and stone paved squares, where we came to a halt before the doors of our hotel. Unlike Huang Shan, which is primarily a touristic mountain famous for its scenery, Jiuhua Shan is renowned as one of the great holy mountains of China, like Putou Shan dedicated to a Bodhisattva - in this case Detsang or Ksitigarbha[10]. The scenery is however scarcely less wonderful and in the hills we found the same craggy vistas, pinnacles, pine trees against the sky and cloud seas between peaks. The grandeur of the place rests however in its magnificent monasteries set in splendour on high platforms in the mountains and in deep groves of bamboo or pine.

The first monks came to these mountains in the fifth century, probably joining earlier Taoists as reclusive hermits seeking solitude. In the early eighth century a Korean aristocrat, Jin Qiaojue, related to the Korean royal family, settled in a cave on Dongya Peak. He practised devotion to Ksitigarbha, the Bodhisattva who descends to hell to relieve the suffering there. The monk's practice was so strict that the local people treated him as Ksitigarbha himself and built a temple for him. The local legend says he arrived with a white dog and a rich man, Ming Gung, said he would donate land. He was asked for merely enough for a small cave. A land area the size of a cape would do. But the cape was found to cover the entire mountain! After the Detsang monk died in a storm with bells mysteriously ringing and rocks falling, his body did not decay and it became the first of the "meat bodies", mummies, carefully preserved as cultural relics on the mountain. He is enshrined in the Roushen Palace near the original monastery of Huacheng Si The body is kept in a secret cave the door to which is opened only once in every sixty years. It is because of this monk's devotion to Detsang that the mountain became the holy site for this Bodhisattva - one of the five famous holy mountains of China.

The history of Buddhism on the mountain has had its ups and downs flourishing particularly in the Ming and Qing dynasties. Emperors granted money for the rebuilding of the main temple and two of them bestowed inscriptions there. At the end of the Qing dynasty it is said there were over 150 temples and three to four thousand monks and nuns on the mountain distributed in major monasteries and secluded hermitages. The Cultural Revolution caused immense destruction and the dispersal of monks and nuns mostly into manual labour. Since the fall of the Gang of Four, monks have returned, buildings been reconstructed or renovated, the Buddhist College re-established and facilities for religious tourism created. Today there are some 79 monasteries or retreat houses on the mountain. The affairs of whole mountain are regulated by the Mount Jiuhua Buddhist Society with its headquarters in Jiuhua village of which the Abbot is the Venerable Ren de Fa Shi, who is also Abbot of the Zhiyuan Si monastery. Many great poets, painters and calligraphers have worked on the mountain where to this day there are many important historical artefacts, stone tablets, calligraphy, religious objects and scriptures.

Master Moonshine and the Abbot of the Mountain

On our first evening we visited the Zhiyuan monastery and presented our letter of introduction from Shi fu. Almost at once we were received in his chambers by the Venerable Master Yuezau, a bubbly smiling monk probably in his forties, full of energy and delighted to receive us. We found that as well as being a Chan Master he was a writer, well known painter and calligrapher. He presented us with books and several magnificent calendars of his paintings which we later divided between us.

Master Yuezau's name means Shining Moon - or, if you prefer it, Master Moonshine! We talked about the Dharma and found him to be direct, earthy yet recondite. When we asked a question, he would pause and reflect before replying, evidently seeking to find the best way to express himself to these strange Westerners. When Alan asked him about how a lay person should behave sexually the Master answered very clearly and without embarrassment. Marriage was fine and totally acceptable but dalliance was out, he told us.

Yuezau had an infectious laugh - haw haw haw - which could be inflected in numerous ways. One of our wordy gentlemen asked a convoluted question based in some confused knowledge of Buddhist philosophy. It was one of those questions designed to elicit agreement and approval rather than a real enquiry. "Haw haw haw," went the Master, "and what kind of question is that?"

Trying to be helpful, I remarked that perhaps better teaching of the Heart and Diamond Sutras would be useful for those studying Dharma. "Too early!" said Yuezhau. "It is very difficult to study Chan in the West because you do not have a cultural foundation for it. All your expectations and your way of life face another way. In China, Chan grew from our traditional culture and expresses it with the especial insights from Buddhism. In China, when you get interested in Chan you are already half way there. It is much harder for you. Start at the beginning with the Pali Suttas. It is important to know what the Buddha actually said. Furthermore, in these early Suttas the message is very direct, humanist, less philosophical. The Dharma is more easily digested from the Suttas when you have no Buddhist cultural background. When you begin with the Buddha's own words as a basis the Dharma of later Sutras, the Mahayana, can grow naturally. Many people, Chinese included, want to hurry and start off on the difficult texts before they are ready for them. And then when they hear the teachings they misconstrue or misunderstand them, merely marrying them up with their already preconceived opinions. It is good that you are all such bold practitioners. Congratulations -- but do not try to run before you can walk. Take care!"

I could see that Master Yuezhau's heartfelt advice also applied to China where Chan is being slowly re-established in the renovated buildings. Doubtless his viewpoint would ensure that a firm foundation could quickly become once more established. Certainly it is typical of Westerners to try to run before we can walk and to meditate before we can even sit. Vanity is the main problem for those who natter about their Dharma knowledge.

We asked whether it would be possible for us to sit in the Chan Hall of the monastery during our stay. No problem, he assured us. We could come and visit him again at any time. Yet, when we arrived at the monastery next morning for a sit, we found that no one had heard of this promise and that the abbot knew nothing of it. We arranged to meet the Abbot - the Venerable Rin de, head of the entire mountain, aware that maybe we had been indiscreet in not seeing him first.

We were ushered into his office, a large room in which the phone kept ringing and cups of tea were brought. The Venerable Rin de, a tall, elderly man with a face that betrayed much past suffering and sadness, perhaps even a fatigue with the world and its onerous duties, began quite strictly, remarking that he had not heard of our request and that he could not allow anyone to use the Chan Hall without proper introductions. He was sorry but it was necessary to discuss our request first. Eva was interpreting with her usual tact and charm and I could see the old man was gradually melting. It was important to get things right. The sustaining of face in China means things have to be done in the proper order.

Abbot Rin de read Shi fu's letter without comment but when he heard about our practice, about Maenllwyd, and that each of us was a practitioner who knew how to sit, he began to relax and to welcome us saying we were the first party of Western Buddhists who had come to see him and certainly the first to ask to sit in the Chan Hall. He told us Westerners did indeed visit the mountain from time to time and come to see him but mostly they were students of Chinese language who were improving their skills and knowledge of cultural history, few were serious practitioners. He ended our discussion by allowing us to use the Chan Hall for two hours every morning between sits by the monks and inviting us all to lunch in his official residence the following day.

The Buddhist College

One of our first visits was to the Buddhist College situated in the Sweet Dew Monastery (Ganglu Si) hard by the big entrance gate to the mountain. We drove down and were met at the gate by a very serious, scholarly monk who took us around the courts and a classroom where dutiful monks were listening to a teacher.

Nobody allowed their concentration to be affected by our visit and this impressed us considerably. We even took photos without causing any disturbance. We were shown a fine Buddha hall used temporally also as Chan hall, which has yet to be fully renovated. The walls around the room were fitted with the usual benches so that the place could be not only used for ceremonies but also for sitting. At a higher level we were shown the future Chan hall, very spacious and currently serving as the dining hall filled with long tables. The kitchen lay off the one side and we could walk around the galleries surrounding these buildings admiring the view of mountains and forests.

The serious monk, Kuan rong Shi, was the Head Monk of the school and the temple. He led us to a hall where we were served tea and he happily responded to my many questions about the college. The acoustics of the room were bad and its shape difficult so that some us could not participate well in this discussion. Kuan rong knew Master Sheng yen and had shown him around the monastery when he had visited the temple receiving a very honorific welcome. He was happy to learn of our practice and our work in England. He told us that the college was not merely for academic studies but for the full training of up-coming generations of young monks. It was the school's intention to unify Dharma as practice and as teaching. The daily schedule followed a full monastic discipline with ritual, chanting, sitting, and strict discipline. There were forty-five young monks in residence. The course lasted two years but was to be expanded to three soon.

Young monks may apply from all over China but the selection procedure is very strict demanding a considerable intellectual background. Even so, a young man who showed great dedication to the Dharma would be accepted even if his academic attainment was not so high. After all, we were told, it was the heart that counted more than merely the mind. The college offered its students food and board plus some pocket money and the correct monks' robes. Medical care was included and when the young men returned home for their winter vacation there was a discount allowed on their fares.

The syllabus included the study of Chinese and Indian history as related to Buddhism. This also necessitated lessons in geography. At a more textual level, the monks studied Vinaya, the Pali Suttas, the stages of Buddhahood and the Platform, Heart and Diamond Sutras. Mahayana philosophy including the Cittamatra was taught and the comparison of the three main Chinese sects showed the students the range of Dharma within China. Since the mountain was dedicated to Ksitigarbha, his sutra was examined in detail and also the importance of Pure Land teachings emphasised. In addition the students received a detailed introduction to the classical Chinese language, philosophy and composition and might also study Pali. They were given meditation instruction in the Chan Hall and both chanting and calligraphy formed part of the syllabus.

After graduation the Jiuhua Buddhist Society sometimes found postings for them in other monasteries on the mountain for further training in work that was suited to their individual tastes and capacities. The Society awards diplomas and provides allowances so long as they are on the mountain. Skilled monks might be selected as teachers and there was a selection panel on the mountain to choose those for whom to provide further training. Some monks enrolled for further training in the college. Others might return to their home districts as monks in local monasteries or as teachers.

After our discussion we were invited to remain for lunch. We duly assembled and followed the young men into the dining hall for their ritual meal in silence. The food was excellent. We found the management of bowls and chopsticks tricky but most of us managed to get the placing of utensils and the manners required more or less right by carefully watching our young monk neighbours. It was a pleasing and interesting occasion and we were much impressed by the disciplined, dedicated way in which the young men conducted themselves. Eva suspected that, as was the custom, the food may have been improved or augmented for the occasion due to our presence as visitors, a contribution doubtless pleasing to the monks.

Meat Bodies

One morning we set off to visit the monastery of Baisui Gong, the "Hundred Year Palace" otherwise known as the Longevity Palace. It lies in the hills immediately above the village behind Zhiyuan Ssi. There is a short chair lift running up to it and, as we entered the car, we were joined by a monk who enquired where we were going. By good chance it turned out that he was the abbot on a flying visit from duties elsewhere. Here was another example of our good luck - or rather Yuan Fen. Abbot Hui Ching was happy to hear about us and personally showed us around the temples and, although on a busy mission, invited us to tea in the long meeting room with the usual austere furniture. He told us that the monastery was founded in the sixteenth century by a monk Wu Xia (1513-1623CE) who had built himself a hut on the site subsisting on wild fruits and become famous because of his practice. He spent twenty-eight years copying eighty one scrolls of the Avatamsaka Sutra with blood from his own tongue. The writings are still extant although we were not able to see them. He is said to have died at the age of 128 years and his body failed to decay. After three years the monks embalmed and covered his body with gold leaf and an emperor of the Ming dynasty proclaimed him to be an "Incarnation of Buddha". In a shrine room set aside for the purpose we were able to view his mummy set in a glass case in a striking posture with one arm extended. The gold covering is so thick it is difficult to make out the details of his anatomy but the meditative pose of the face is compelling and the whole cadaver presents a rather bizarre appearance of resolute sanctity.

These mummies, of which there are several on the mountain, are a sort of Jiuhua speciality, known as "meat bodies". Perhaps this rather unpleasant title would be better rendered as "Earth bodies". When a holy monk dies, it sometimes happens that his body does not decay. Naturalistically, this may be in part a result of the cold winters and moist summers but of course the phenomenon is attributed to holiness. When the body has endured some considerable time it is proclaimed to be a "meat body" and duly set up and embalmed with gold.

Elsewhere on the mountain we visited a small nunnery where a fresh meat body had recently arisen. A recently defunct, ancient and respected nun had requested that her body not be cremated on her death. As her end was approaching, she ceased eating so that her bowels were empty when she died. Her body failed to decay and she has been proclaimed as the latest of these miracles. It certainly seems as if, in this case, a deliberate attempt to create a meat body had been made. We were told her story by one of her likewise now ancient, nun disciples, a charming, serene old lady in her nineties, full of vigour and open friendliness.

The Cult of Ksitigarbha

Mount Jiuhua is the holy mountain of Ksitigarbha Bodhisattva and everywhere we found statues of him. The small monastery of Xiao Tiantai has an especial gallery devoted to his work. The story of Ksitigarbha tells us that that he made a vow that not until all denizens in hell have reached salvation will he rest from his work. He visits hell to relieve the sufferings of those incarcerated there. This story may be treated literally or metaphorically and it is far from clear in what way the multifarious pilgrims view him. That he is a source of relief from suffering is in no doubt and this is the focus of devotion to him.

Yet Ksitigarbha is in some senses a rather ambiguous figure. The gallery at Xiao Tiantai suggested a rather more nuanced view. Here we found him treated very much as the "King of Hell" overseeing a panel of judges who decided whether a person's misdeeds were sufficient to ensure descent into torture or not. In the gallery were depicted in enthusiastic detail the numerous tortures that awaited the condemned. These statues were grim indeed, bringing out the maso-sadistic frame of mind that infects the Chinese whenever there is a breakdown in society or they are placed in positions of unlimited power - as in their colonisation of neighbouring peoples disposed to resent it, the Tibetans, the Uighurs and the Mongolians. The Chinese seem very frank in their willingness to depict these cruelties but one must also recall similar, perhaps even more graphic pictures in the Gon.khang of Tibetan monasteries, flayed bodies with eyes dangling on their stalks and so on. In such pictures and statues we witness the dark side of the unconscious. Perhaps it is as well to reveal it with such frankness rather than hiding it away as Westerners are prone to do.

It may be that in the figure of Ksitigarbha two stories have become conflated; the stern judge and the compassionate Bodhisattva. Putting these images together poses problems. What to do about evil? Can it go unpunished? Although evil is "empty", it remains evil - the uncontrolled violence of a dehumanising ego - whether personal or collective. Something has to be done before recompense is possible. Karma is retributive and inescapable. Can it be borne? Perhaps this is where Ksitigarbha helps, easing the pain so that it can lead to restoration. Some of us with dark thoughts in mind found this presentation difficult. Ksitigarbha challenges us with the ethical problems in life, problems of guilt and recompense. We make our own hell and sometimes go so deep we could never come back unaided. For the Chinese, given their recent brutal history and their government's dismal record in human rights, these should be matters of deep reflection.

The High Peaks

To reach the ridge of the Jiuhua range there are many thousands of beautifully constructed flights of steps. Not all of our party being as young as they were, and most of us relatively lazy, we took the cable car which ran most of the way up. The rugged pinnacles, steep valleys, forests, dangling fir trees and bamboo groves created a splendid sight as we flew above them to arrive just below the Tiantai Zhending monastery dedicated to Ksitigarbha right on the ridge. Spectacular views, crowds of Japanese and Chinese sightseers and intense photographic activity were our reward for the ascent. There were enormous queues for the descending cable cars but fortunately we had, in any case, planned to walk down. Twisting flights of steps led steeply down the mountain. There was less crowding here but a busy passage of coolies taking supplies up to the monasteries and begging along the way.

The path twisted down between cliffs, around pinnacles and past a number of small nunneries where we saw real poverty for the first time. At the first little nunnery we found only monks, there being insufficient nuns to sustain it. They were Chan practitioners but the bare unkempt rooms told of severe deprivation. They told us that they practised as best they could but that the winters were hard indeed with frost and snow and no heating. Further down, we came across a strange building built as a bridge over a dry watercourse. When the gates to the building are shut there is no way up or down the mountain.

We came across a strange little nunnery with two very cheerful nuns inside. They asked us in, calling out "Amitofo, Amitofo!" in greeting and inviting us to eat from the rows of none-too- clean pots that stood to one side of the kitchen. The elder of the two was seated with her feet in a large tub, beaming away at us. She said it was a great chance, a wonderful Yuan Fen, that we had all met together at her monastery to chant to Kuan yin. And this we did - all joining in the chant. The old dear was radiant. The tub contained a small charcoal fire to keep her feet warm - and to dry the notes given her as offerings! Again she told us of the privations of winter. She was delighted when we handed her the little red envelope containing our own donations. Just beyond this place we came across a cave where another radiant old nun lived. It was only a few feet in depth but snug, probably warmer in winter than the rooms of the nunneries.

Lunch with the Abbot

We kept our lunch appointment with Master Ren de, Abbot of the Mountain. He was seated at table when we arrived together with a striking young businesswoman from Harbin who was one of his disciples. I joined him at table together with Eva and our two guides while the remainder of our party sat at a separate table.

It was a considerable honour to lunch with this monk. Although over seventy, he had shown great energy when we had met him in his office and his conversation was vivid. He was not only abbot of the mountain but also head of the Jiuhua Buddhist Society which was responsible for the affairs of the whole place. Jiuhua is also very significant in the Buddhism of China as a whole and Master Ren de holds influential positions in the consultative committees of the government institutions that regulate the practice of Buddhism. He was a member of the National Committee and Director of the National Buddhist Congress. He had also been in charge of the college for the last forty years. In view of the extent of his activities it was another example of our good Yuan Fen that we were able to meet him.

Our conversation turned to recent history. I said to him that many of the generation of youngsters who had been the destructive Red Guards must still be alive. I wondered how they felt in the new China Deng Shaopeng had brought into being.

Master Ren de thought a moment and then said "No remorse." In spite of the appalling destruction they had caused, the ruination of so many vital historical artefacts, the murder and the mayhem, few of them could later see in what way they had gone wrong and how Mao had mislead them. I asked if there were any practising Maoists around now. No, he said, most of them were dead. Everyone was a 'capitalist roadster' now. Communism was gone. Everyone was working on the economy.

"This human world is the 'can bear realm', he told us." In other realms the beings have no hope of enlightenment because they are either given up to the sufferings of hell, the ignorance of animals or the pride, pomposity and pleasure seeking of the asuras and gods. Only in the human realm where sentient beings "can bear" suffering is it possible to understand the causes of suffering and thus become enlightened." The job of the monks, especially those older ones who had survived the holocausts, was to restore Buddhism so that people could once again receive the teachings. He was personally dedicated to this cause.

Master Ren de told us about the problems that had faced him and his fellow monks when the Cultural Revolution swept over China. In his book in Chinese, later translated for us in part by Eva, he also details what happened on Jiuhua mountain at that time. At first the Red Guards just closed the temples destroying the statues, gates and confiscating the monastery estates. The monks were left with nothing to live on. One day a group of Red Guards drove all the monks out into the square of Jiuhua village. It was winter, bitterly cold and a freezing wind was blowing. The Red Guards surrounded the monks shouting in a frenzy, demanding confessions. The then Abbot of the Mountain was very old. Physically weak, he suffered severely sitting with his eyes closed amid the tumult. Ren de was quite a young monk then and a disciple of the old man. He did his best to shelter him from the wind. At first the monks were very frightened but Ren de noticed that, in spite of their passion, the young crowd was not behaving as if they believed they had really evil men before them. They were just letting off past resentments and following the fashion of the time. Ren de remembers that some monks had defected and joined the Red Guards in denouncing the old monks. Finally they ransacked the Buddhist Society building just off the square and left the monks alone in the cold. The monks returned to their unheated rooms with nothing.

That night Ren de sat in his room nearly in despair. There came a knock on his door and his old master, the Abbot of the Mountain, came in. Ren de said he should rest but the old man said, "I had to come to see whether you were 'holding up'." They talked and sat together affirming their faith and strengthening their minds. The old abbot then asked him to take on the task of the abbacy after he was gone - which would be very soon. Ren de was dismayed because his intention was to seek enlightenment through austere practice, maybe as a hermit hidden from the world. He did not want to live in the world in such horrible times. But the old master told him, "Remember the Buddha - Did he spend his life in seclusion or did he act to help others and improve life in his times?" Buddha work is not merely sitting in a cave meditating. Sometimes it is essential to engage the world. Ren de gave up on his ascetic intent and became the abbot. "Meditation is not the only way!" he told us.

At table Master Ren de told us of one experience he had had during those years. He and his fellow monks were set to manual labour. One day his closest monk-friend failed to turn up. Worried about him, Ren de went out at night, when he could not be observed, and climbed the mountain to this man's old hut, where he guessed he might be. He found him very sick indeed and incapable of movement. Resolving to help him, Ren de and some other monks made a stretcher and brought him down the mountain in search of a doctor. But all the doctors had been murdered or had died. Finally they found one but he said, "I cannot treat him without permission from the party. You must ask at the local party secretariat." So off they went again carrying the heavy stretcher with the seriously sick man lying on it. It was dark and late when they reached the place. The official merely shouted to them. "Go away. Why are you disturbing me? It is my time for sleep. Get away with you!" In spite of all appeals he took no notice and Ren de realised that in those times people were so calloused that one corpse was as good as another. No one could care anymore. Officials were simply saving their own skins. In the early morning his friend died.

Ren de then recalled another monk who had previously been a Muslim and had studied medicine. He found him and asked him to teach him medicine so that he could help people. This he did and he began to practice as best he could, helping those for whom there was no other help.

> Old abbots face - these sunken eyes.
>
> Then - temples burnt and statues broken –
>
> Today - the chanting monks once again
>
> perfume the flowering mountain.

The abbot asked me about how Putuo Shan compared to Jiuhua Shan. I said that there was a difference related to the character of the Bodhisattvas to whom they were dedicated. Putuo, the island of Kuan yin, had a softer character, very yin, the atmosphere was of great devotion. The place and the activities there had a very comforting feeling which was probably of great value to the confused and distressed. Here at Jiuhua, Ksitigarbha was a different sort of figure, rather more yang, with his great activity and dedication to the relief of suffering, particularly of those whose misdeeds had led them to hell. The atmosphere was different. The things we had thought about differed correspondingly. Ren de pressed further. "Was there any essential difference?" he asked. "No," I said, "So far as meditative equipoise is concerned they are the same." He seemed satisfied by this answer for he let the matter be.

The abbot's great dream and ultimate project is to build a huge standing statue of Ksitigarbha at a new site on the mountain. It seemed that to him this would be the final justification of his work: a statement that all those long years of suffering had at last been replaced by Buddha, Dharma and Sangha. I appreciated his endeavour but once more wondered at the Chinese tendency towards gigantism in their statue building. Is there a need to make objective the resurrection of

Buddhism in China through the creation of enormous statues? Maybe, and indeed there is a tradition of huge statues dating back to the earliest years in Central Asia, so perhaps this is the renewal of a tradition. I wonder at the vast expense and whether better use could not be made of such ample funding.

Ben (Miao Heng Shi)

One afternoon returning across the square to our hotel we were accosted by a young monk speaking fluent if strangely accented English. He worked in the Buddhist Society as the abbot's personal assistant. He amazed me when he told me he had learnt English almost entirely from books, tapes and listening to the radio. His vocabulary was extensive, his grammar mostly correct and his enthusiasm for the language quite touching. He badly wanted to talk with us. His name was "Ben".

Ben came with us on a walk and I was able to have an extensive conversation with him. It became clear from his comments that his insight into Chan was unusually perceptive - especially for so young a man. He had a lightness in his approach, a humour that recalled some of the old stories of the Patriarchs. Indeed these insights doubtless accounted in part for his significant appointment as the abbot's assistant. Yet when he turned to politics he spoke quite uncritically in the jargon of Government propaganda. For him Taiwan and the Dalai Lama were not negotiable. I said our politics differed and he agreed. "Not the best subject to talk about," he remarked, "especially when we can see eye to eye on essentials." Democracy has a long way to go in China. Maybe it has as yet hardly started. Only with freedom of information, toleration of difference and openness to political movement, all paradoxically essential to an open market economy, can real political change begin. Yet I felt that with men as intelligent and dedicated as Ben around, the growing freedom of religious expression provides a seed bed from which the ideas of the Buddha may percolate into society. And the Buddha was no autocrat.

Yuan Fen

Throughout our journey we had repeatedly encountered the use of this term. Chinese practitioners are especially fond of it. One evening Eva explained it to us and since then I have had letters from Eva and C. T. Song and from Yiu Yannang further explicating this quite complex notion. The term is invoked frequently whenever a beneficial circumstance arises; for examples, seeing the sun's halo on Putuo Shan, bumping into the abbot in the cable car on his way to the monastery, meeting helpful monks and nuns. Carl Jung would probably have called this 'synchronicity' and indeed the coming together of circumstances lies at the root of the idea. There is more to it however.

The idea is rooted in the Law of Interdependent Origination, or 'co-dependent arising' (pratitya samutpada), as described by the Buddha himself. This law states that the flux of the impermanent Universe is not random, rather everything is the result of co-determining mutual causation, the interaction of the basic event-atoms of existence, the dharmas. Yet, as Hua Yen philosophy emphasises, some causal events are primary and others contributory. The basic cause of an oak tree is an acorn but its growth, height, shape and productivity is shaped by circumstantial events that effect it through time. Causation and contextual influences are thus distinguished and as time runs along things get more and more complex as the universal process works its way through time.

Human beings are born with innate Buddha minds. Yet this is mere potential because adventitious events obscure our understanding of our self-nature by creating self-concern, egotism and all sorts of attachments. Even so, we also have a residual tendency to seek out the quietude, serenity and wisdom of our basic nature, the tathagatagarbha, for which we have intimations. As we progress through life, supporting conditions may arise to help us towards self-understanding. These are the joint result not only of our own search supported by past successes but also those of other sentient beings. We cannot tell what circumstances may assist us but potentially anything and anyone in the universe might do so.

As we go along in Dharma practice we move from simple faith to understanding to practice and eventually to the validation of practice in realisation. Causes and conditions (Yin Yuan[11]) are not under our control yet the tendency to look for insight and serenity enables us to respond to the circumstances that arise. "The world is the biggest offerer, soil, sun, sea air are all there for the seed to grow into fruit." (Eva Song)

The seed and the apple are of the same nature yet the seed of the apple is not the apple. The relationship arises due to the process of Yin Guo meaning cause and effect; every effect has its causes, every cause produces its effect. For a human being to become Buddha, the practices are vital and the karmic context is a key determining factor as to the manner of our growth. If our minds are clear, the supporting conditions will arise and we can then make use of them. According to common Buddhist belief, we have all been related together in innumerable ways throughout the incarnations we have suffered since beginningless time. Sometimes old companions from the distant past may turn up again to share with us our journey and maybe to help us or be helped by us. Hence the joy with which sudden friendships and meetings may be greeted by Chinese practitioners. Likewise, the feeling that one is blessed by some event arises from the sense that things come together to help us. Yet the personal intention must also be there.

Yiu Yannang remarks that in Chinese folk usage the terms Yuan and Yuan Fen are interchangeable. These common terms are used by all Chinese irrespective of educational background and interest in Dharma. The meaning is best illustrated by examples.

1/ John Crook and Yiu Yannang come from different sides of the world but have become firm friends for half a century. They have Yuan Fen.

2/ Two strangers meet, fall in love, become husband and wife and live together. They have Yuan Fen.

3/ Of two sisters, one is loved by the mother but the other is hated by her. The Chinese say the first daughter and mother have Yuan Fen but the second daughter and mother do not.

4/ A common Chinese saying: When there is Yuan two people can meet even though a thousand miles apart; but when there is no Yuan they will not meet even if they are together in the same room.

Little was said in our discussions about possible negative arisings and in Chinese lay usage the terms Yuan and Yuan Fen do have a positive connotation. In Buddhist thought, however, there is both good Yuan (San Yuan) and bad Yuan (Wu Yuan).

Logically one must suppose that if the will is evil or negligent so negative occurrences are likely to arise - retributive karma as it is called. Our lives, being mixtures of positive and negative, are subject to both processes and our need for skilful means underlies our training.

Shanghai

The train to Shanghai was a double decker, the first in which I had ever ridden. The first class was attractively decorated, comfortable with blue velvety seats. We were amply served by attendants and the train rode smoothly along. Cities came and went, Wuhu, Nangjin, and vast swathes of flat countryside. This was a land of little, man-made lakes, endless tracts of yellow mustard, a scattering of villages each with some ancient houses among drab, modern buildings.

> Brand new
>
> cities
>
> of the plains.

Peasants were tending their vegetable gardens, shepherding buffaloes feeding along the sides of ditches, preparing fields for rice. At railway crossings there were little crowds of bicyclists waiting to pass. In the distance the horizons were decorated with eruptions of cement factories, while in the foreground huge excavations for new road ways churned the soil and the tall, high- rise buildings intruded into the agricultural scene. Our great double decker rounded a bend and I caught a glimpse of its length and immense carrying capacity.

> Double decker, first class train to Shanghai.
>
> Fields of yellow mustard fly –
>
> cooking oil from the last thatched cottages,
>
> Communism - Goodbye.

Shanghai hums and bustles with energy like a newborn New York. A whole city, the Pudong area, replete with elegant skyscrapers has appeared on the far bank of the river in the last ten years. The Bund, the river frontage of the old British concession, sparkles with light, traffic roars, people stroll here in the evenings and in early morning ardent groups do Tai chi together in the open air or revolve in stately ballroom dancing. From high in the Peace Hotel with its art deco interior beautifully restored and its Old Jazz Bar open for Western dancers in the evenings, the breakfast room looks out over the river achurn with ships, barges, tugs and the incredible view of the skyscrapers of Pudong etched against the eastern sky, backlit by the sun.

We visited the famous Jade Buddha in its monastery, the Yufo Si. It is a fine Burmese statue of a seated Buddha made from a single piece of white jade. The temple was built as recently as 1882 to enshrine it and a similar standing statue. I wondered how on earth it had escaped the attentions of the Red Guards. The story is that the wily monks put a huge, enlarged photograph of Chairman Mao, the Great Helmsman, in front of it. The young guards were so awe struck that they never bothered to look behind it.

The Yufo Si, a huge establishment, is a training temple for monks which was only reopened as recently as 1980. There are about a hundred monks in residence and they train to work in temples all over China. Our guide did not know whether they had a Chan Hall but on enquiry we were taken to a side court and found a fine meditation hall in full working order. We sat there for some moments and then I was shown a hanging scroll of calligraphy that read "Who is reciting Buddha's name?" There was an elderly monk in the hall and I went up to him and asked "Who is reciting Buddha's name?" indicating the calligraphy.

At once, without batting an eyelid, "Me!" he replied, "The practice of Chan is to uncover the truth of the heart. " His prompt immediacy impressed me, so I told him a little about our practice in Europe. He took it in without comment and I asked. "Is it not difficult to practice Chan here in this busy city in the middle of China's great economic boom?" "Not at all," he replied. "We come here in the early morning. We close the door. It is silent and we practice. The city is no problem for us." And with that he walked away. I liked this man. It seemed that Chan is truly on its way back in China and that nothing is going to stop it.

Shut the door
the noise goes away.
The city itself is silence.

October 2000

1 The participants were: Simon Child, Roger and Ruth Green, Sophie Muir, Graham Morgan, George and Iris Tute, Hilary Richards, Linda Griffiths, Ken Jones, Elizabeth Crook, Beata and Maciejek Kazimierska, Hilde Thalmann, Rosemarie Auriau-Moser, Alan Quadling, Ralph Saliba and the author.

2 We were most fortunate in having Eva Song of Hong Kong for our interpreter. Eva is not only an ardent practitioner who soon became a pilgrim herself, but she has a good understanding of Chinese Dharma which proved invaluable in all our conversations with monks and abbots. In addition Jack Tang of the China Travel Service, Hong Kong, looked after all material aspects of our trip with exemplary enthusiasm. Yiu Yannang MBE, advised John on this tour and

provided inspiring help at all stages of planning and during our Hong Kong stay. We all remain most grateful to them for their unstinted assistance.

3 Otherwise spelt Hongzhi Zengjue whose life and teachings are admirably presented in Leighton T. D and W. Li (1991) Cultivating the Empty field North Point Press. San Francisco.

4 Cleary, T. 1990. Book of Serenity. One hundred zen dialogues. Lindisfarne. New York

5 I visited these monasteries in southern China with Yiu Yannang in 1997 and our account is published in NCF 16:32-45.

6 This is a translation of the command to start meditation given by the monk in charge at Bo lam monastery on Lantao Island, Hong Kong.

5 I visited these monasteries in southern China with Yiu Yannang in 1997 and our account is published in NCF 16:32-45.

6 This is a translation of the command to start meditation given by the monk in charge at Bo lam monastery on Lantao Island, Hong Kong.

7 This is a reference to an insight I had had on retreat with Master Sheng yen. See "Working with a Master" NCF 20:23.

8 Translated by Eva Song, slightly edited.

9 See Note 3.

10 Detsang is the Chinese name of Ksitigarbha (sanskrit).

11 In the Pali Canon these terms refer to hetu and paccaya. Yin meaning primary cause (hetu) and Yuan secondary cause or conditions. See Buddhist Dictionary by Nyantiloka Frewin. Colombo. 1972

WINTER POEMS

Red Berries

Treading the grey forest of my childhood's dreams where, melancholic under ghostly beech,
metallic hollies stand around
and frost crisped leaves rustle
to disclose wet humus unfrozen on the ground
the sudden discovery of a half iced pool
reawakens old moods under a carapace of time.

The dusk is burying the snowclad heath
and frozen air chills cheeks to flame the face before the waiting hearth
wind clapped branches suddenly feather snow in air
and puddles, wholly ice, lift like plates from moulds.
The wild beats of pony hooves ring like a bell the hardened land.

Here in December woods with the rare squirrel
and the straggling tit flock
hurrying to glean last morsels from the naked twigs
old perspectives emerge among cold sentinels
empty trees netting the tide turned sky.

Visiting the winter forest is like
rising at six of a Christmas morning
shivering down a cup of tea
walking the snow muffled streets to the cold church
for a piece of bread and a sip of wine

the fire below the altar suddenly
bringing blood red berries home.

1970

Christmas Cards - Around Again

You don't send Christmas cards to the dead
making up my list I remember them
wishing to see once more perhaps
their ancient faces telling me their news
or sharing mine, joys, sorrows, past times-

You don't send letters to the dead
though it might help not posting them-
after all you can say anything now
remembering that old companionship,
fire-light talk, long walks in mountains,
boggy moors in fading light
tea on a verandah in summer
the warm embrace in a cold bed.

Posting a letter in a crack in a tombstone
the lizards enjoy the feast
no gateway to the underworld there.
In far off caverns steaming
the voices of the dead ascend
as gull cries do over echoing cliffs
no way to climb there
where vapours turn to cloud.

Messages for the dead are not so easily delivered,
still-born they need a burial too,
aching memories in floating bottles
drift the inner oceans of the mind
fetching up on distant shores unannounced
disturbing the natives pontificating there.
Who is it strutting on the shore
in whom such ancient voices sound?

You don't lift the phone or send an e-mail
to those gone beyond redialling.
Where are they? We ask
concerned about our own destinations
the long walk to the station and the ever-waiting train.

December 1998

NCF XXIV

THE EXPERIENCE OF TIME

We live within our personal ecologies of meaning construing our relations with the "outer" world on the dimensions of space and time. Yet, in everyday experiencing, place and time often seem separate modes of being rather than inseparably related. Standing in front of a fine landscape painting we witness a timeless space. The landscape is static, frozen in time, it is all space. Contrariwise, if we gaze from a window witnessing the movement of the traffic in a. London street everything is change and change is time. Yet reflection tells us there is just one continuing "arrow of time" pushing us relentlessly to our personal deaths and, in whatever way we experience space, time never ceases.

There are many ways of classifying time and therefore experience. Some of them are as it were embedded within one another as in a Russian doll. The most basic time is the natural one of days and seasons, which depend on, and indeed measure, the rotation of the earth and its annual tilting set within the time of our solar system, our galaxy, and the universe.

Universal Time

Physicists tells us there is no sense in talking about whatever "existed" before the "Big Bang"; neither time or space existed then for matter had not yet begun. As if from a point the results of the explosion have flown outwards like the ever-expanding circumference of a sphere. Time is the changing, expanding surface of universal matter while space arises as the consequence of the movement of matter in time. And, apart from wobbles in the surface (which may have broken free as bubbles of space-time out of contact with the original universe and thereby creating other worlds, the number and existence of which we can only guess), that is all there is. Space is not only co-emergent with time but as time went on matter coalesced to form places.

Planet Earth was such a place, a globe that revolves and wobbles in regular rhythm in the light of the sun to generate days and seasons. As human life emerged people found themselves making their livelihood within this pattern of time and having their consciousness shaped by it. Master Sheng Yen speaks of such time as being of "the eternal"[1]. The agricultural round, emerging from a world of seasonal hunting, and becoming the prime mode of temporal existence for many millennia, still obtains in many parts of the earth and, in the alternation of green leaf and frost, underlies and shapes our consciousness and our imagination.

Economic Time

The emergence of exchange, the buying and selling of products surplus to subsistence, began the development of places where commerce could best occur and the establishment of geographical linkages for transportation of goods. Agricultural areas became focused on commercial loci where exchange occurred and the system of routes connecting them.

With the appearance of industrialisation the pace and nature of commerce changed radically. The relation between time and money became more critical and that between distance and time also. Within the "eternal" time of the seasons became superimposed the rigorous times of the work day, the hourly schedule, the annual holiday, time spent in getting to the office and back again for "time off", the precise regulation of meal times, pub times and sleep times and the leisure time of the rich with the emergence of leisure activity with its own separate timing, casual time.

The feel and atmosphere of place became dependent on human activity rather than on some natural quality of wind and water, rock and air. The relatively unchanging rhythm of time in a work place became experientially reified more or less as an entity, a period, an "event", more like a quality of space in fact than the movement of time.

Frozen Time

When we visit a place of character, a cathedral perhaps, or spend a holiday on an island or in an attractive city, the time we spent there appears to us afterwards as a singularity, an intact timeless memory, an apparent fixity, a constellation. Place may appear to stop time - even though of course we know it has done nothing of the sort. We remember a period of unitary character, being a student at Cambridge for an example, almost as a thing, we forget the impermanence of persons and events, the flux and the fragility of the moment.

Periods of still time and the places in which they occur can become very important for us because they suspend for a while the awareness of our mortality. Seasonal festivals, long holidays, certain experiences like an afternoon in an art gallery freeze the arrow of time and give us a fleeting sense of security, a momentary immortality. Because we can all share such times and places, a culture builds up around them so that they become embellished with the trappings of the sacred. In large measure they are what the sacred is. Memories are often like this.

Turbulent Time

The sacred place gives us the sense of something enduring. Identity itself comprises location and locality. Yet embedded in history are the processes of change. At certain times these come together to produce great shifts in our lives and in the form, appearance and importance of locations, places and institutions. Since we are identified with these forms such change, reminding us of impermanence, is threatening, frightening maybe and can generate stress, anxiety and depression. We may feel our world to be falling apart and us with it.

The same experience emerges during those periods of transition generated by our personal progress in life. The periods spent at school, in university, as a trainee, as a professional with his office or laboratory, all have their particular qualities and mode of being to which we become attached. During such periods our experiences become a constellation of patterns which in later retrospect appear as having one quality, the character of an "age" as it were. As we necessarily move from one life period to another the transitions generate uncertainty, again our illusion of fixed identity is challenged.

Such changes may be forced upon us by marriage, childbirth, divorce and separation, redundancy, bereavement, retirement, ageing, ill health. At such times the relative stability of a "time of life" is broken and our identification with that period has to be opened up to something new and other.

Catastrophic Time

Sometimes the turbulence takes the form of great economic and social crises, wars, famines and natural disasters. Time then freezes in a period of discomfort, deprivation, disaster or distress. There may be experiences of horror that shatter the personality so that the personal identifications of previous years are broken down. At such times only those who have inner resources upon which they can draw are likely to be able to survive psychologically in a positive manner. The victims of terrorism, of torture, of political imprisonment, have to face such issues and need the help and consideration of others - not their prejudice and racist concern.

Fantasy Time

In imagination and dream we create places and events that reflect and reconstruct our wishes and uncertainties often in highly symbolic form. The understanding of symbols is vital for the comprehension of our lives since our experience of the symbolic often conditions our responses to changes of a more immediate nature. The time we spend in fantasy has a particular significance for us.

Some sacred places become more real for us in imagination than as experiential realities. Places such as Jerusalem, Mecca or ancient Canterbury become places of pilgrimage where the timeless presence of the past can be evoked and the arrow of time seemingly annulled. Some places beyond our capacity for travel exist in this way almost solely in imagination, Timbuktu, Lhasa, imaginary spiritual abodes of the gods or the godly with whom a salvation from time can be imagined[2].

Symbols also express our values and these may be derived from collective ideologies of great persuasive power. A failure to receive loving care of an appropriate kind in childhood may cause an individual to seek out comfort not in physical and psychological intimacy with another but in some other safer "transitional object", a teddy bear or a pet for example, so called because in a beneficial sequence the transition leads back into adult intimacy. Where the personality is damaged the transitional object may take the form of a belief system which justifies the mode of restricted being which the person has adopted. Ideological symbols become "places" of refuge from the inner processes of the abused self. Such an individual spends great lengths of time in the service of such ideologies sometimes causing major cultural disaster and personal distress to others. Personal time has here been captured by the symbolic in an attempt to stabilise a distress that is repressed and not understood. Time becomes illusion.

Time spent in the symbolic may however also carry intimations that are not yet conscious. Archetypal symbols represent the root features of personal life acquired in childhood, experiences of parenting, personal heroes, strange old persons, the otherness of nature, sun time and rain time, dream time. The working through of such symbolic experiences can lead to a recovery of the repressed and the emergence of an adult mind ready to live a more open life in a space and time less characterised by fantasy.

Psychology and Time

The contrasting ways of experiencing time form a sort of evolutionary series. With the development of commerce there has been an increasing fragmentation of the 'eternal time' spent by agriculturists in relation to nature. We live in worlds of temporal dualities; work-play, travel-office. Such dualities together with others such as profit-loss, pleasure-pain, we-them are experienced in a characteristic frame of mind in which whatever happens is related to the individual's egoistic concerns.

Margaret Donaldson has classified the modes of human experiencing. In the first, the focus of experience is the ongoing present-continuum, attention to the moment is predominant. In the second, the focus is on relating the present to the immediate past or future while, in the third, the findings of the second are related to a context of structured memories that allows planned intention in relation to knowledge. In contemporary life most of us spend virtually all of our time preoccupied within the second and third modes of mental activity[3]. This is inevitably a highly evaluative process providing us with the basis for making choices between multiple alternatives most of which refer back immediately to self in relation to others.

Inevitably this process gives rise to considerations of approval or disapproval by others, of others by oneself and oneself by self and such thought entails a constant low-level stress punctuated by times of crisis or demand. Mihaly Csikszentmihalyi has shown experimentally how concern generated by the relationship between the difficulty of a task in relation to expectation of personal performance may give rise to a sense of alienation. Where a task is easy, boredom and mistakes may follow. When a task is too difficult, anxiety may arise in the expectation of failure. Where task difficulty is matched by confidence in an expectation of success, the experience of work tends to be one of optimum enjoyment or "flow" however difficult the actual task may be objectively[4]. Clearly such relationships depend greatly on the attitude brought to the life situation by the subject, especially when the tasks in question are essentially to do with social relations and with self. Modern life involves most individuals in a constant anxious and often largely unconscious enmeshment with self-concern.

Meditation can break this insistent self-concern by anchoring ourselves in the actuality of the present moment. In the simplicity of "being now" release can be obtained and here lie the seeds of "enlightenment". Few realise that such another mode of life exists in which recurrent contact with the ongoing present by an undivided mind can reveal an inner peace even in active living. Such a mode of being is not attained however without training.

Unfortunately today the conflict between a failing humanism and forms of superstitious spirituality increasingly divorced from either a scientific understanding of the Cosmos or meditational realisation creates a paralysis in creative thinking against which a few struggle often in vain. The task of Buddhism is to meet this challenge and open up the world to a recovery of the human heart.

1 Crook, J.H. 1991 Catching a Feather on a Fan. A Zen retreat with Master Sheng Yen. Element. Pp 60-61

2 Bishop, P 1989 The Myth of Shangri-La. Tibet, Travel Writing and the Western Creation of Şacred Landscape. Athlone. London.

3 Donaldson, M.1993.Human Minds: an Exploration. Penguin. London

4 Csikszentmihalyi, M.1975. Beyond Boredom and Anxiety. Jossey-Bass. San Francisco. Also Csikszentmihalyi, M and Csikszentmihalyi, I.S. (Eds) 1988. Optimal Experience: Psychological Studies of Flow in Consciousness. University press. Cambridge.

TRAINING TO LEARN, LEARNING TO TRAIN

EXPERIENCE IN CHAN TEACHING

John Crook

Most of us have read the story of how the great yogin Milarepa trained in Dharma practice in the household of his teacher Marpa. It is one of the classics of Tibetan religious literature and extremely important as a guide for those concerned with questions of how to advance on the Dharma path.

As a boy Milarepa had to endure extreme pain in family life as an uncle deprived his mother of welfare following the death of his father. In revenge Milarepa learnt black magic and achieved the downfall of his uncle's household. Ashamed of his behaviour he sought teachings from Marpa.

Marpa had gone to India, survived the diseases of the Plains and returned with the profound teachings given him by Naropa. These were to become the foundation of the Kargyudpa lineages in Tibet. When Milarepa arrived at his house Marpa greeting him mockingly, "Oh Great Magician, what do you expect to do here?" 'Great Magician' became the nickname with which he taunted Milarepa, while setting him impossible tasks to do, only to tell him to undo them or do something more useful. It seemed to Milarepa that it was impossible for him to please his teacher and he was on the point of leaving. Only the kindness and wisdom of Marpa's wife kept him back. Marpa was an irascible man, his methods were rough in the extreme but he had a clear purpose. He knew that unless Milarepa could overcome his personal pride and self-concern he could never inherit the Dharma and receive meaningful empowerments. Magic and pride go together, the Dharma requires absolute humility. In training a magician there could be no half-measures. In the end he succeeded and his pupil became one of the most renowned figures in the history of Tibetan Buddhism, the inspiration of generations down to today.

Shi fu's account of his training under Master Tung Chu (see above) reveals the same method only this time in the context of Chan. As we have just read, in spite of the severity of this training, Shi fu acknowledges it was critical to the acquisition of a selfless mind that is essential for advanced training. If fellows of our lineage in Europe wish to advance beyond a mere middle class "hobbyism" they too must understand the import of such training. This is especially vital when we are conditioned, almost unconsciously, to forms of self-indulgence that are inevitably concomitants of the consumer society and its world view and within which we aspire to practice.

Some Personal Stories

To my great good fortune I have experienced a number of encounters which impressed upon me the great need for self-confrontation in the manner so heroically endured by Milarepa and by Shi fu in his turn. I cannot claim to have made the best use of these teaching experiences but I believe that together with other forms of confrontational training at school and in the army something has rubbed off on me. I have come to consider it essential to hand on an understanding of these methods to those who train with me because not to have done so has led to a weak and relatively ineffective training in Dharma in the fellowship. Some recent pettily emotional events in the British Sangha and a tendency to argumentative disputing in the Polish Sangha have demonstrated this most clearly. We need to correct and understand this - at least those who are serious about training must do so.

One day I went to see the Austrian nun Myokyo-ni, formerly Irmgard Schloegl, who, at that time taught in the Buddhist Society in London. I knew she was of the Japanese Rinzai tradition and would give me outspoken comment. I told her about the Western Zen Retreats which I had then recently started to run in Wales. I waffled on at length, telling her about various aspects of these retreats and my role in them but she made no comment. She simply looked at me as I went on talking - perhaps with increasing anxiety. Finally, I stopped and asked her '"What is your response to what I have told you?" She said, "I have no response!" - and that was the end of our meeting. I was devastated, not by what she had said, but by the way in which, in one move, she had exposed to me my underlying need for her approval. She was warning me that I had to find my own approval for myself.

In another solicited interview I discussed my practice with her and my attempts at Zen teaching. She remarked, "You are like a person who sits at his desk writing innumerable articles and letters with great enthusiasm while ignoring the accumulating pile of unwashed underwear in the corner of his room." O dear, that hurt. I still recognise the truth of that remark today. Although I cannot say I loved Myokyo-ni for her comments, I remain immensely grateful to her for what she taught me about myself and about the training of others. I once had the opportunity to thank her and reminded her of these stories. "My goodness, did I really say that?" she had replied, smiling. A great teacher.

In training with Shi fu I have also had my petty ego pricked on several occasions and have had to learn how to handle such an event positively so as to learn from it. One day on retreat in New York my task was to clean the bathrooms. I had just finished polishing one bath and toilet when Shi fu looked in. He scowled and fiercely pronounced it "Filthy - do it again!" and marched off. I re-examined my work and could see no blemish in it. I felt angry and hurt and began swearing away in my mind, furious with my teacher who only half an hour before had been so kind and welcoming in interview. But then I remembered both Milarepa and Shi fu's own account of his training. I could not tell whether Shi fu was actually playing me a teacher's trick, was genuinely of the opinion that my work was defective or whether he was just in a bad mood. Whatever it was, I resolved to take no notice. Whatever he throws at me will not make the slightest difference to my practice - I decided.

There were to be several occasions when Shifu put this resolution to the test - sometimes by his deliberately grim failure to acknowledge my presence when I had just arrived for retreat, sometimes by his ticking me off in interview, and sometimes in fierce letters in response to some naive but innocent comment in one of mine to him. Always I returned to my resolve, realising these were ego confrontations which I simply had to set aside as of no importance, relying in humility on my own feel for what I was about - mistaken as it might possibly be - and upon my trust in Shi fu's underlying wisdom.

On one occasion I had felt it necessary to ask him in a letter whether he so disapproved of me that he did not want me to continue teaching Chan. In that case, I had added, I would continue on my own! Shi fu responded with a warm appreciation. Once I had incautiously mentioned the word "God" in a letter. I received a rollicking reply. I wrote back explaining that for me the word God was "empty". I got a reply warning me to make clear what I meant. Some months later, in my first interview on retreat after this correspondence, I was met by a smiling Shi fu, "Is it alright about God now?" he asked.

Training of this kind is training in the development of what I call the "Zen attitude". This starts with courage to be oneself and to submit to the ego testing of difficult experiences, of hardships on retreat, on pilgrimage and in relating without resentment, irritation or rejection to a demanding yet insightful master. It continues into learning to develop this containment of subtle egoism in everyday life. This is a very different set of demands from merely learning how to sit. It is deep training in reflexive mindfulness. Problem - how to teach it?

Problems in Teaching Westerners

Several Eastern teachers have remarked to me on the difference between teaching Asian people and Westerners. Shi fu has said that Western would-be practitioners, most of whom have had a good education, have little difficulty in grasping the intellectual ideas underlying Dharma practice. In addition, initial enthusiasm may lead them to quite quick realisations and to an apparent deepening of practice. Often however this is not maintained, practitioners failing to sustain practice through inevitable habituation and boredom. In worst cases, psychological insight is not matched by ethical advance. When such an individual becomes a teacher serious scandals have occurred. More usually, however, individuals begin prospecting elsewhere for spiritual experiences, whether within Buddhism or outside it - in Sufism for example, or various forms of "do-it-yourself" pseudo-Christian mysticism.

Such behaviour is natural in persons conditioned to the values of contemporary "consumer" society. There is a broad market place of "spiritual" ideas and practices ranging from the more religiously inclined psychotherapies through the emotional group experiences offered in many "new age" practices. Anyone acquainted with the spiritual shenanigans available in Glastonbury or Totnes will recognise the peculiar mix of wisdom and foolishness that is on offer. It follows that when one approach does not deliver the goods quickly there is another to try out round the corner on another shelf. This absence of consistency at the behest of self-indulgence is a deep enemy of serious practice.

Our Western society is also rooted in a marked "individualism" that characterises the Western, especially the Anglo-Saxon, self[1]. The strengths of individualism lie in the maintaining of independent judgement, in a self-confidence that allows effective personal action and in a social responsibility that underlies functional democracy. Sadly however such individualism may also lead to merely petty egoism and self-indulgence and a challenging of authority by mere amateurs with little understanding of a matter in hand. Every Joe Bloggs can have an opinion on the economy as if he were Chancellor of the Exchequer - a tendency encouraged by the gutter press. Opinionated persons with inflated egos fail to recognise their own mediocrity and can wreak havoc if they have any power, money or influence - which is often sadly the case.

These two aspects of contemporary culture mean that within Buddhist practice a Western individual may consistently overrate his/her insight and progress and reject or misunderstand a teacher as soon as they are corrected in any matter whether theoretical or practical. Unfortunately such an attitude towards teachers means that any challenge provided by a teacher is often unrecognised or perceived as some sort of an affront. And there is always another self-promoting teacher of poor quality waiting to attract cheap followers of this sort. Teachers are in the market place too, their overstretched smiles decorating the pages of their advertisements.

Challenging the Subtle Ego

In Tibetan Buddhism indulgence in such petty egoism is considered a major enemy, a thief of Dharma understanding. Anyone learning Dharma can soon recognise the effects of gross egoism, pompous self-importance or aggressive assertion demeaning others and will do their best to eliminate such behaviour. Subtle egoism is however commonly unconscious and only realised through mindful and reflexive self-examination. This is the egoism of small scale, self-concern, none the less insidious as an enemy to practice.

Examples include such things on retreat as worrying whether or not one has eaten enough porridge, rushing to get a preferred seat at table, arguing in favour of a late start, thinking about going walking rather than sitting, fussing about the sniffs of a neighbour with a cold, failing to cope with snoring companions in a dormitory or worrying pedantically about hygiene, warmth, or any aspect that disturbs one's sense of personal comfort. It is not that some such matters may not need attention, it is the obsessive concern that disturbs practice that becomes the enemy. The underlying attitude is that one should not be disturbed from perfect sitting through minor inconveniences - failing to see that coping with such matters is the essence of training.

The assumption of consumers is that everything should be directed towards their personal comfort, all inconveniences should be eliminated. The purchaser buys comforting experiences that shield him or her from the basic facts of life and death. In paying for defensive avoidance the consumer sustains a world of illusions. A teacher who confronts such an attitude is liable to be rejected, ignored or becomes a butt for argument and rationalised criticism.

Subtle egoism avoids the basic insights of Buddhism. A practitioner with subtle ego intact is merely comforting herself with nice experiences that give an illusion of spirituality. At most such a Chan practitioner may learn something about calming the mind but can never progress to insight whatever intellectual knowledge they may possess. The wayward heart remains unconfronted and devoid of clarity. These are mere "hobbyists" to use Simon Child's expressive term.

We see the world through our own psychological mechanisms, it is not the same world as that of frogs, cats or horses, they have their own worlds too. Depending on the focus of experience, this 'virtual' experience may be interpreted as an expression of agents (selves) in interaction or as motion within an interpenetratively active field of causes and effects interpretable at many levels. While Buddhism stresses the latter viewpoint it does not argue that one perspective is more true than another. Both are aspects of the experiences we draw from virtuality. The essence of insight lies in an understanding of the relation between varying modalities. We learn to handle different ways of seeing our modes of being, seeing things "in the round" as Huayen philosophers express it. Tibetan Buddhist practitioners of Mahamudra, for example, speak of the 'co-emergence' of particularity and emptiness as aspects of experience. That which is perceived depends on how one looks.

What then does it matter if one has had a sleepless night? What does it matter if one has ingested a few grams less of porridge than would be felt as optimal? If Shi fu is irritable - why let that disturb me? He is in his own space, I am in mine. Even if I disagree with a decision by a teacher do I need to pursue an argument, to ring up others for support, to set up a social disturbance which others may never have considered. Do I need to play the petty politics of Dharma gossip? Since my thoughts define my 'self' arbitrarily as a result of personal karma may I not reframe my own reflexive understanding in other ways? When the "view" is corrected one can perceive the relativity and inconsequence of so much that we do in defending our petty ego and its fears of affront, discomfort and the possibility of being wrong.

It follows that a Buddhist teacher must help his or her practitioners to confront the insidious undermining of insight through the operations of the subtle ego. The teacher needs to confront this negative process at every turn. That is what Milarepa had to face in accepting Marpa as his teacher. It is what Shi fu endured in the house of Master Tung chu. A Western teacher has a problem, however, for he or she belongs to the same consumer culture as his followers and can suffer from spiritual undermining in the same way. If he or she stands out against this and confronts practitioners in whatever manner, some of them will resist, basically on the grounds of their precious sense of what is comfortable. Such resistance can easily become destructive and personally insulting. There is the danger that such confrontation may be perceived not as it is but as an abuse of power.

The question arises as to what authority a Western teacher of Dharma may possess? Eastern teachers tend to be idealised as remote and mystical figures of perfection who know the answer to life and death. A mere Western teacher, whatever his transmission or empowerment, is viewed more sceptically - especially in Anglo-Saxon society. Unfortunately abuses of power by some Western teachers have created a not unreasonable basis for such scepticism. We have to distinguish the false from the true and this is part of the training a good teacher must provide.

The nature of a teacher's authority needs careful definition. It is not the authority of a boss. Our own constitution has carefully eliminated that possibility for the WCF teacher. Nor can a teacher tell a practitioner what he or she should or should not do. A Western teacher is primarily a facilitator. He/she facilitates that which the practitioner needs to develop. When the practitioner is clear as to what that may be, the relationship is not problematic, but, when a practitioner is confused, opinionated or resistant, the teacher has to proceed with great skill - often determining what may be a minimal move towards Dharma understanding. The role is not unlike that of a physician who seeks to facilitate the health of a patient but cannot dictate whether he takes the medicine. The Buddha was known as the "Great Doctor" with good reason.

Yet the teacher is authoritative in his or her understanding. He or she will have trained, sometimes for years and with great persistence against difficulties, with one or more Dharma masters in lineages of revered transmission. His or her experience will transcend that of beginners and of most old hands in practice to a very considerable extent - although this does not mean that a teacher's learning from practitioners is not also always present or that his judgement is perfect. It follows that when a teacher offers a challenge a practitioner needs to consider his or her position with mindfulness and not with some immediately prejudiced reaction. The authority of a teacher's experience demands respect.

Teachers of course come in various shapes and sizes. Some may be kindly and gentle by nature. Some may be quite aggressive and forthright. Some may be plain bad tempered like Marpa. Some may quite idiosyncratic in a variety of ways. The practitioner needs to seek the wisdom inherent in a teacher and not to be put off or concerned with their psychological traits as characters in the world. Of course if no one can see any wisdom in a teacher then it is time to look elsewhere!

There are two main ways in which a teacher confronts and challenges a practitioner. The first is through the programme of an orthodox retreat. Everyone knows that retreats are demanding and many people would like to see them made easier. This would however eliminate one of their main purposes - to challenge the attitude of the practitioner in a test of their zen pretensions. So we get up early, we spend many hours in practice, silence and retreat discipline are maintained. The subtle ego is confronted again and again and observed in interview. If you have not experienced this sufficiently at the Maenllwyd, go try Throssel Hole! This is not the only way of running retreats but certainly an important one that cannot be missed from any well-planned programme. Shi fu once told me, "In running a retreat be tough on the group but kind to individuals". I have experienced his own conduct in running retreats in this light many times.

One thing is essential in a teacher. He or she must be incorrigibly themselves. It is pleasant to fulfil others expectations, to please people so that they smile at you and love you. Yet this way dependency lies. Being oneself inevitably confronts others sooner or later. Shi fu's often dismissive stance towards practitioners when they are arriving on retreat is one example. Whether it is deliberate or not I have not determined but it is often quite a shock causing one to recollect one's attitude. Sometimes a teacher may have to make rapid decisions about whether to run a retreat or not, whether to accept an individual trainee or not, whether to offer criticism or not or utter a sharp correction or command. In this the teacher must act from his or her heart. The task of the practitioner in training is to respond mindfully and not to react from the dictates of subtle egoism. Many Westerners fail in this, start posturing in ways that reveal their inadequate training and shock the teacher into an awareness of the inadequacies of his methods. His skill in means is then tested to the full.

Of course a teacher is not always right. Marpa could have been kinder to poor Milarepa. He was a bad tempered man and chose to be true to his nature. Shi fu sometimes seems distant and uninvolved. I believe at such times he is simply being himself - perhaps needing some space in which to be. I like to please others but am learning to be blunter and more direct in my stance within teaching. I believe this is essential - if I may seem bad tempered or irritable, unusually sharp tongued maybe, it is because I am bad tempered and irritable - right there and then. Yet that is not all of what I am. Maybe it is worth your while to hang in there. Equally, maybe not. It's up to you.

In conversation with Roshi Reb Anderson, I once asked him about teaching. He said. "If you say one thing you can be sure it will be wrong. If you say the other, again you can be sure you are wrong. Whatever you say will probably be wrong. Why say anything? Well - you just do so in trust." And I was reminded of my favourite definition of zen -"One big mistake after another!"

Conclusion

The experience of being a transmitted teacher is not easy. Although there is often affection and friendship, being oneself incorrigibly, sticking to a 'zen attitude', challenging the stupidities and confusions of others, does not necessarily earn one praise, more usually blame or criticism. Yet the target is the subtle ego both in oneself and in practitioners. Without such confrontation there can be no true insight for that depends on the setting aside of self. I do not believe there is any essential gender difference in this matter. I am sure women's concerns cover a different range than do men's and that retreats for women and men separately are sometimes well worthwhile. In matters of fundamental egoism there is however little difference and women who attend our Chan retreats do quite as well as men. In whatever way it may be appropriate both genders have to confront their essential self-concern and to explore in what way that may be most clearly achieved. Gender relations in the Western world are often tortured and problematic and exploration of these issues within the Dharma is appropriate. Where selfishness is concerned we all have to come to terms with our innate intolerance of others. What else is the Dharma about?

Since I received transmission I have come increasingly to see where the difficulties in teaching really lie. They lie neither in showing people how to meditate, in giving Dharma talks, nor in arranging retreats or pilgrimages from which people gain a certain benefit. They lie much more deeply in the dynamics of self, my own and that of others. I have experienced all of the difficulties mentioned above and some others not treated here and I have done my best to understand them and to respond within the range of my own potential. I propose to continue in this way for only in confrontation is "ignorance" exposed. Whether this can become the heritage of the Western Chan Fellowship I cannot say - and no doubt there will be more to discuss anon.

May 10th 2001

1 See: Neisser, U and D.A.Jopling.1997. The Conceptual Self in Context. Cambridge University Press.

PASSING THE PESCADORES

A Voyage to Japan. MV Hermod. 1954

Uncoiling waves hover a moment caught between sunglance and foam.

Catch the incandescent moment in a loop of light and hold it to yourself alone,

Catch the spangled spray in the finger tips at the mind's end

And lie spread-eagled on a second's dome.

Passing the Pescadores a flying fish leapt and flew, a drifting tern tripped a wing on a wavelet

and turned again towards her barren home. The dreaming Pescadores!

Sunwink on spray and lighthouse blink,

a flying fish leapt and flew before the prow's dividing wave.

The first sea-mists of Japan, the smoke haze of our ship swirl together above the small light at the mast head. This much the ship has always known

but that far off coastal light and I on this damp deck

usually see the one without the other.

Between the word and the realisation there's a space where none may go. Even authors in their blind conceiving

know not the meaning of the seeds they sow.

Maybe the universal music master cannot understand the pain

that rings from his own bell's chime

and durst not seek an answer in a world he cannot know.

NCF XXV

REFLECTION IN THE CHAN HALL

Chuan-deng Jing-di

I have received several articles and poems about the current crisis and reams of world-improving e-mails. I wondered whether to publish some of these heart felt statements in this journal. Thank you all for them - but events have moved so fast. The writing is so quickly out of date, the feelings of today not clearly related to those of tomorrow; horror; fear; relief; hope; worry; succeed one another bulletin after bulletin. At this moment it seems that there is some hope for Afghanistan and its people after all and the possibility of retributive justice may indeed arise. Not that we will ever see the Buddhas of Bamyan again.

It seemed more important here to look at more restricted contexts wherein our reflections might make more direct a difference. Our issue this time takes up themes where our thought and our actions can have some effect - in "cultures of enquiry" (p13). The Dalai Lama's wish for us to practice, Shi fu's careful description of the Precepts and their meaning, a deeply felt encounter with Prison life, concerns about Schooling, some personal experiences and a book review revealing dangers in some western thought about the Dharma - all these take up themes that are the contexts of our lives. In considering these themes the Dharma becomes active and maybe we can see opportunities here for its actualisation.

The notion of context is important. The Buddha's Law of Dependent Co-Arising argues that causes lead to consequences under the influence of conditions - that is context. The understanding of context thus becomes very important for us. If we can adjust context the outcomes of past Karma may be very different. Context is always present but in our concern with events we sometimes fail to notice its importance.

At the level of mindfulness let us note that practice is the context for precept just as precept is the context for practice; that the sickness in society is the context of prison just as criminality is often a context of society; that schooling is the context of emotional growth just as emotional growth can effect schooling; that the Guestmaster conditions a retreat just as the rules of retreat are the context for him; that food is the context of meditation and meditation the context for cooking - which is why a Chan cook is so important; and, finally, that the adequacy of thought and philosophy determine Buddhist understanding just as insightful Buddhist practice conditions philosophy. So it goes. Practice at these levels has wide implications.

Please think about these.

1 December 2001

NCF XXVI

ASPIRATIONAL PRAYER FOR DAILY USE

Suggested use: on rising each morning of everyday life.

> May I awake to clarity and throughout this live-long day sustain mindful awareness.
>
> Let me observe my karmic reactivity so that I may insert reflection before I speak or act.
>
> May I restrain my natural pomposity, prejudice and pride so that I may return to openness, empathy and joy.
>
> May my words and actions reflect consideration and understanding for the stupidities and waywardness of others.
>
> Let all beings be as my mothers, fathers, brothers, sisters or children and let me so care for them.
>
> Let me perceive the Dharma in the life of my teacher setting aside his/her mundane characteristics.
>
> Let me pay attention to my teacher's words even if I disagree with them.
>
> May I train my thinking so that my thought corrects itself before any harm is done.
>
> Choosing one path with which I feel affinity let me pursue it with diligence without self-centred picking and choosing.
>
> Let me put all beings before me on the path to enlightenment.
>
> Setting aside my own ambition may I sincerely help others on the road.
>
> Leaving aside my wish for the future let me realise that life is only now.
>
> Homage to the Buddha, Dharma and Sangha
>
> Throughout my remaining life may I tread the Buddha's way.

THOUGHTS FROM THE CHAN HALL

Perspectives on the World Predicament April 2002

I have just returned from China where the Great Leap Forward is going on all the way from the coast to innermost western China. I had not heard the news for three weeks and felt relieved and benevolent as a result! So as I read what I had prepared for this issue (below) I felt out of touch with all the global anxieties I had raised. But then I realised nothing had changed, merely shifted from Israel to Pakistan and India – without of course any resolution to earlier issues. So I have kept the text as it is but intend to focus elsewhere in our next issue.

Western Buddhists may belong to a variety of political persuasions, for these differ not so much in good intentions as in policies to fulfil them. Even so, we all start from the Buddha's advice to cultivate compassion and insight, a position necessitating critical appraisal of the political initiatives currently being followed. These appear to arise from the best of intentions but so often lack wisdom of a reflective nature. Politicians, following the latest analysis of people's attitudes, tend to reflect an emotional reactivity that may earn them votes rather than a considered stance based in statesmanship. Is this a process of political deterioration in populist democracies lacking in courageous leadership?

The task of Buddhists in the present situation is to reflect and influence others through careful argument, clear positioning and tolerance. We must bear in mind that the Buddha himself did not eschew politics but often proffered opinions variously taken up by the rulers of his time, not always in a manner he perhaps intended.

I recently visited Robben Island off Cape Town and was shown around by an elderly African who had occupied a cell a few doors down the bleak corridor from Nelson Mandela. He emphasised " I am not a terrorist and was never a terrorist. I was and I remain a freedom fighter. " We need to consider this distinction wisely. Where the law is unjust, Robin Hood arises. Who becomes a hangman then? And who should be the hanged? When should laws be changed rather than upheld and who should change them and how?

Consider then the following issues upon which you may wish to consider your own Buddhistic perspective. You do not have to agree with them: you do need to think your own stance through.

* Violence, intolerant political activism and terrorism breed where the representation of the people's will is not expressed by a ruling government. Representation in a democratic style allows people to be heard and appropriate action considered in a participatory process which eliminates the need for extremism even if no one gets 100% of what they would like. Consider now the governments of the Middle East. There is no true democracy anywhere in the Islamic world, dictators, religious fanatics, royal aristocrats, dominant and unrepresentative politicians rule. Some Governments are more representative than others, as in Jordan and Egypt, but the repressive and heavy hand is never far away.

The need for a restructuring of politics is, as the European position argues, one of the most profound needs in this crisis. This can only come about through long term, democratic participatory negotiation. Few Arab leaders would welcome this and the means for representation has barely been considered.

* It is not anti-Islamic to point out that high-level terrorism will only produce counter terrorism backed by state power against which ultimately the cause will be lost, and the moral high ground vacated. It would be better for Islamic peoples to put their own house in order rather than replaying justified complaints about US dollar imperialism alone, serious as this charge may be.

* It is not anti-American to point out that the republican policies since George Bush's highly questionable election have put national selfishness far ahead of any sort of global responsibility. While everyone sympathises with a great nation humbled on Sept 11th and its angry response, the destruction caused and the innocent casualties suffered by a poverty stricken peasantry in Afghanistan now more than balances that offence. There is something morally repugnant about high flying, unassailable bombers flying in their arm-chairs, carpeting remote deserts with often unexploding bombs left for children to pick up. The failure to follow up such destruction with adequate nation-restoring policies other than money is losing the USA any moral high ground it originally held. And then there is Kyoto - and all that stands for

* It is not anti-Semitic to point out that by destroying the Palestine Authority's political structure the Israelis have denied Arafat the possibility of controlling terrorism and created a martyr's myth around him. The invasions of West Bank towns and the televised behaviour of Israeli soldiers bring to mind the Nazi occupation of the Warsaw ghetto. It is tragic that so historically abused a people should fall back on such suggestively similar methods when they become oppressors themselves. Participatory negotiation with the current Saudi plan in mind is the only course tolerable to world opinion. Although Israel, backed by US finance, is one of the last colonial states, in humility rather than arrogance it needs to negotiate its entirely justifiable continuation.

* It is not anti-British to point out that, whatever may be said in private telephone conversations, there is no need for a British Prime Minister to be so uncritical of American policies in public when the rest of Europe is clear cut in its opinion. The Special Relationship resembles a wobbly bridge ever increasingly, and the too easy use by the US of this country's kin-based fondness for America needs to be answered by more alertly critical replies to cross Atlantic opinion.

* It is not stupid to suggest that while uncontrolled proliferation of weapons of mass destruction by rogue nations must be stopped and an insistence on the implementation of United Nations demands upheld, the careless throwing about of military power "going it alone" may not be the best answer, especially when the outcome has neither been foreseen nor replacement regimes created. Forceful diplomacy should at least be properly developed and tried out before yet another war with unpredictable consequences is started. Iraq, Iran, North Korea are separate issues. There is no axis of evil.

Taking a broad, reflective position, Buddhists need to consider what justice, participation and democracy mean in this world and in what way a careful building of a new world political system based in representation and negotiation can undercut this trend to military industrial dominance within capitalism, cheap national interests, dictatorships of various kinds, ethnic and religious hatred, violence and death on an ever widening scale.

Meanwhile, the way the "world" will end is becoming apparent as every hectare of the Antarctic ice shelf falls gracelessly into the warming ocean unheeded by a seemingly obsessed humanity stupefied in its inherent ignorance.

What has happened to the "United Nations"?

Chuan-deng Jing-di

IN A DARK TIME

Making the mistake of continuing
we wander now in a meadow of thistles
yet even here we may listen to the songs of larks.

I am afraid of flooding the mind too suddenly with images
letting these black rooks
flap in their myriads, cawing

to some festival
claws clutching at midnight twigs half budded only, green tips coming slowly to the sun.

What have we done that suddenly
these figurines take life gyrate, kaleidoscope and waltz clashing their symbols, omens of bird flights
feathering under heaven.

Having strangled God he gets back at us with whips and great canes
beating slowly our twisting bodies on the bed

til we are crying
No No No
and enter this unending inner scream.

In my cupboard I keep it,
only under the pressure of someone's kindness do I let it out
cracking the glass in the windows.

My scream is as unending as a wheel spinning in a monastery.
I am as trapped as monks
in their wheels of prayer.

My scream makes no sound
I don't disturb anyone
it just goes on and on in silence.

I don't know what you will do when you hear it
Our hearts are so close it will kill you.

YES

I simply want to say "Yes!"
wordlessly tonguing the flute
where words could go on endlessly
into the deep woods.
Such warm silences of the heart this unison in joy
and the sea-bird's weeping.
Now this tangible absence –
looking for the caress
of lips with pain blossoming. Let be to let be

From an unpublished collection: Shamanic Verses - revised 2002

NCF XXVII

PASSING DOWN THE ROBE

Introduction

The Maenllwyd, our retreat farmstead in Wales, had been home to "Zen" retreats for some years prior to the arrival of Master Sheng Yen on that wet April day in 1989. I had been presenting Western Zen Retreats (WZR) based on Charles Berner's "Enlightenment Intensives"[1] at the Bristol Encounter Centre since the mid seventies and these had found a natural base in the Welsh hills. Newcomers were faced with lamps and candles, holes in the barn dormitory roof, haylofts for bedding, cold winters and sometimes a lot of snow. These "toughies", as we later called them, had a fierce Zen streak in their genes it seemed, for, in those immediately post-hippie days, such people would tackle anything for a glimpse of enlightenment. Yet these Zen events were hardly orthodox and legitimate questions could be asked as to whether they were Zen or Buddhist at all.

It was with this doubt in mind that I first attended Master Sheng Yen's Chan retreats in New York. Not only did I have a personal need to deepen my understanding and experience of Buddha Dharma but I felt that if I were to continue my retreat presentations at the Maenllwyd I needed to know how they stood in relation to orthodoxy. I believed that what I was doing was no mere idiosyncratic, self-indulgent, and possibly dangerous group process as adversaries were prone to suggest, but a very real contribution to the personal development of others. How to check this? In the event Master Sheng Yen was interested in my work and recognised the utility of the method but he agreed that the WZRs could not be considered to be Zen unless they included Buddhist vows and led on to the taking of Precepts.

After I had trained with him on several retreats and he had seen our work in Wales, he asked me to lead orthodox Chan retreats at the Maenllwyd in addition to WZRs. I was to be, as he put it, his "representative." And so our story began. The Bristol Chan Group was formed by a small group of enthusiasts[2] who asked me to be their teacher (NCF 1. 1990).

One of these was Jake Lyne who, in this issue, now presents us with a valuable and searching examination of our endeavour since those exciting first days and our subsequent creation of a national charity - the WCF. It is significant that we conduct such an examination now, not only because some of our senior members have come through a controversial period, but also because both Master Sheng Yen and I will be 72 this year and "time waits for no man". Furthermore I face personal questions as to how best to fulfil the trust placed in me by Master Sheng Yen consequent upon his transmission to me of the Chan Dharma (NCF 9. 1994 p 2 - 4) in the Dharma Drum lineage.

Among the questions Jake raises are matters concerning the relevance of our activities to our time, the effectiveness with which we attempt to fulfil our constitutional objects and the question of transmission to 'second generation teachers'. Implicit in considering these matters is also the need for a clear definition of the particular focus in Dharma teaching which the Teacher is endeavouring to convey.

Making the Dharma relevant to our time

We live in a peculiarly materialistic age dominated by scientific reductionism and an economic system rooted in the unsustainable maximisation of profit by competitive private companies. In such a world spiritual values of traditional religions have become largely ignored, sentimentalised or distorted into dogmatic belief systems of social intolerance.

Certainly under the impact of social changes led by these forces the cultural roots of Buddhism, and perhaps all major religions, are declining - as Jake has suggested.

Yet there is ample evidence of an increasingly vivid awareness of something lacking in our modern world. Not only are the times exceptionally violent with problems of control over weapons of mass destruction, but poverty is inexcusably widespread, politicians fail to deal with the major issues of environmental degradation world-wide, and the capitalist ethos of the modern world view offers no remedy leading towards long term solutions. The result is commonly a personal sense of alienation, confusion as to values, drug addiction, a macabre fascination with rape, murder and child abuse and, among thinking persons, existential anxiety and a sense of cultural failure. Peter Reason, in an article in the last issue of this journal, quotes a student essay which told him that "despite a whole array of 'graduate opportunities' there is a growing sense of claustrophobia and sense of powerlessness; for all the relative luxuries of the western world we are still unsatisfied: there is an unmistakable sense of longing, a deep craving for some kind of release or escape" (Sara Atkins). And Reason locates the source of that craving for escape in the "all encompassing frame of the modern world view - which stops us listening to the world" and which therefore requires us to confront the entire modern set-up. This widespread search includes a lively interest in Buddhism in all its forms.

So is Buddhism, and especially the Zen of this essay, relevant? Jake correctly points out that some traditional themes in Buddhist teaching do not sit well with a scientific understanding of the world nor with the modern needs of self enhancement in career, family, the gaining of credentials of all kinds. Classical ideas of reincarnation and the monastic emphasis on asceticism look strange to contemporary entrepreneurs, and career climbers, even when they themselves feel an alienation of mind from heart. These issues do need to be reframed and understood anew and a deep acquaintance with Buddhist philosophical psychology can certainly clear the way.

One of the useful ways of understanding "reincarnation" is to consider this theme as a metaphor for the descent of cultural traits and problems from one generation to another[3]. I once heard Shifu remark to a Chinese doubter that perhaps many of the traditional ideas concerning reincarnation need not be accepted as literally true, but he insisted that to be a Buddhist one needed some idea of "continuity". The kind of continuity I believe he meant was the way in which, for example, the character of a great grandmother can so warp that of her daughter that her children develop odd characteristics in adult life which are ultimately responsible for some of a descendants own oddities at the present time.

Awareness of such inter-generational descent can give a broad picture of the onward passage of "karma" (although this view differs in some important ways from traditional formulations). Likewise the descent of cultural themes can impel karmic roots from the past into the present; for example the way in which the British imperial period is significant to an understanding of multicultural modern Britain; and, correspondingly, the way in which the history of democracy and the labour movement in Britain influences the character of that multicultural scene. Interpreted in this way the notion of "karmic retribution" in the present for (mis)deeds in the past retains its meaning and its relevance. Who but the British can be held responsible for our own history and our current state? Only I can undo the karmic confusion engendered originally by the character of my grandmother. We cannot set aside these ancient themes without a deeper penetration into their meaning and their relevance today.

Furthermore, to avoid Buddhist ideas and to stress only those physical methods that relieve stress and reduce anxiety is equally a faulty path. Efforts at "mainstreaming" Buddhism through introducing mind calming meditational practices to prisons, hospitals etc without the teaching of the ideas of the Dharma can only cheapen Buddhism - much as yoga tends to become an activity of beauty parlours. This is not to say, of course, that any effective remedial treatment should not be used in helping distressed minds - but this is a presentation of psychophysical medicine, not of the Dharma path of the Buddha.

An interest in the asceticism of the monastic life is today actually quite lively. Athos is almost booming and Christian monasteries are receiving attentive interest if not necessarily ardent recruits. Asceticism is based upon a principle of restraint. Within the extraordinarily successful Indian order, the Brahma Kumaris, for example, there are many European adherents otherwise active in careers and family life who choose the path of celibacy in direct opposition to the near pornographic sexuality of so much of the social scene. Many others see in periodic withdrawal from the world, in nature, solitary cottages, retreats or monasteries, a means of facing the alienating pressures of city and corporate life. Monastic asceticism in itself seems unlikely to be a barrier to an interest in Buddhism. Furthermore, Tibetan Tantra emphasises a way of transformation through mindful participation in life rather than self denial, although a wise lama will tell you that this is barely possible without a mind also trained in restraint.

A romantic Western fascination with monastic practices, especially those of Japanese Zen monks on heroic retreat, has blinded many enthusiasts from the fact that no Sangha ever existed without a substantial lay following and support. The Buddha himself had much to say to his lay followers and, in both China and Tibet, enormous congregations would attend the reading or chanting of lengthy sutras or the giving of empowerments. Such events supported the 'everyday practice' of laypersons in their homes and work places. Buddhism has perhaps never focussed particularly on family problems, but it has never been unfriendly to family affairs.

The key practice for a layperson, whether at home or at work, is to maintain 'self at ease' at all times however difficult or fraught with tension. There are many ways to facilitate 'every day' Zen: daily sittings of short duration with family participating; the maintenance of a family shrine; etc but it is true that few contemporary western practitioners bother with such things, especially when the spouse/partner may not be a practitioner. Until they do so, they are dependent on bringing home with them the good practice uncovered on retreats. Our own intensive retreats certainly function to a degree in this way as retreat reports often testify. Shifu has remarked with humour on a westerner who, when asked why he came on retreat, replied, "Well, you see, Shifu, after a retreat there are a few days during which I do not quarrel with my wife!"

A deeper problem concerns the disproportion in the numbers of each gender that come on retreat. There is a paradox here in that women who do our retreats certainly get as much value from them as men do (see p 27 - 32 and p 36 - 41 in this issue): but the proportion of women attending retreats is low and seemingly falling. Yet women occupy a disproportionately large number of leadership roles in our Sangha: so that while we need more women members, we also need more suitable men to come forward as leaders.

The reasons for these anomalies may well lie in the reputation "Zen" has for being a particularly masculine type of activity - and it is true that, so far as monasticism is concerned, it has been a predominantly male one. There are therefore good reasons why women need to investigate what forms of practice are most suitable for them. If there are unconscious male biases at work then our women practitioners need to come forward with their own suggestions and preferences so that they can be carefully considered. There are reasons for thinking that women's groups function differently in self exploration than do predominantly male ones and we do need to investigate this in the context of our own fellowship. It is interesting that gender ratios are at parity for our Mahamudra retreats which involve basic Tantra. There are clues here which we need to examine.

Yet, when this is said and done, it may be that our Chan retreats are particularly well related to male problems in our current society wherein many young men seem disoriented and uncertain in ways that lead to an unpleasant "laddishness" that has now gone so far as to generate government concern.

Buddhism comes to the west in many forms, Chinese, Japanese, Indian etc and each arrives festooned with cultural concomitants, festivals, liturgies, meditation methods etc. Different individuals will find some such aesthetic accompaniments attractive and others not. The smorgasbord of Buddhism can accommodate many tastes and provisioning such preferences becomes the basis for a developing marketplace of superficial spirituality. In bookshops, magazines, films, we find innumerable means of providing for such a range of preferences - all the way from smiling lamas to new types of meditation cushion or a new "western" way of doing things and making them easy. The main Buddhist journal in America, Tricycle, is, for example, full of such adverts and presumably largely financed by them. The market soon catches up on Buddhist taste just as it did with the aesthetics of the sixties. It is not easy to escape what Trungpa Rimpoche styled "Spiritual materialism".

The question emerges as to what is meant by 'relevance'. It is certainly no part of traditional Buddhism to pander to the aesthetic tastes of a market in sentimentalities. Nor is Buddhism deeply concerned with the therapeutic adaptation of individuals to a more socially acceptable or acquiescent life. The Buddha proposed a remedy for suffering out of his own experience of suffering. Is that remedy relevant to the suffering of today?

We need always to return to the core teachings when considering this issue of relevance. Suffering remains with us in ever more complex forms. The Buddha said again and again that the only thing he knew was the relief of suffering - metaphysics, history, the origin of the Universe, were not his brief. So what is relevant today can only be the "great doctor's" prescription for the relief of suffering. We return then to the Law of Co-dependent Arising, the Four Noble Truths, the basic formulae and their emergence in the Prajnaparamita sutras and Madhyamaka philosophies of the Mahayana, for these provide a profound analysis of the human condition of suffering. Furthermore the Buddha stated no dogma, things that had to be believed to achieve salvation, rather he suggested a path and invited individuals to test it. His open ended offering of a spiritual empiricism remains basic to Buddhism today - although not all institutions fully understand it. Does the WCF teach this effectively? Are these themes being presented in the "direct, simple and relevant way" that Jake envisages?

Retreat and practice in the Western Chan Fellowship

The WCF is a young institution and we can be reasonably happy about our development so far. We have created a fine Chan hall for retreats at our meditational base in Wales, we hold many retreats, we have a number of small but active city groups in most regions of Britain, and we run an internationally recognised website and a challenging journal. We seek to open up questions concerning lay Buddhism in the West and have not failed to criticise what we consider to be corrupt, inadequate or failing practices. Although we have had one or two internal rows and individual defections, the warmth of our Sangha was well expressed at my birthday party in November 2000 for which I feel great gratitude. In addition I run retreats in a number of European cities and Simon Child and I are again to run a WZR in 2003 at Pine Bush - the heart of Chan in America. So far so good - but are our approaches and methods effectively representing the Dharma and conveying it to those who join us?

The main message practitioners need to receive remains the core insight of the Buddha as contained in the basic formulae. The source of suffering and our sense of alienation lie within the self and its habitual attachment to self-concern rooted in profound illusions about its nature. This is true whether one is speaking of personal self or institutional self. Impermanence implies that the self is empty of inherent existence as a discrete entity. Rather the mind and all things exist within a universal flow as described by the Law of Co-dependent Arising. Attachment to things as if they could be permanently acquired or safeguarded remains an illusion and this illusion is the prime cause of our sense of lack in a world focussed on acquisition. Such a world therefore needs challenging by an alternative image. This means that the self of which we are so fond needs to be confronted as the very first step in practice. And this is why newcomers at their first WZR immediately face the question "Who am I?" And we can say that twenty years of these retreats certainly shows that individuals can be greatly changed through this practice gaining new views on themselves and the world which may lead on to further Buddhist investigation.

Table 1 (below) depicts the range of training that the WCF provides for its practitioners. These retreats offer experiences of calming the mind and insight into its nature, which thereby facilitate self -confrontation through various well-tried routes. Retreats are supported by activities in local groups.

Unfortunately the deep import of such training quite often remains misunderstood. The prevailing culture biases people towards the satisfaction of needs and wants, often with little awareness of the difference. We hear that Zen can provide wonderful experiences, we want them; Zen seems to imply a hierarchy of ever deeper and wonderful realisations, we want them; we want relief from a troubled mind; we want to "get" an answer to our problems. Me, me, me. Sometimes on retreat we do indeed find some relief and for a while the self is satisfied. The dog has his bone. But to encounter the basic source of the confusion in one's own mind requires high levels of mindfulness not only in the retreat process but also in one's everyday life. The practice and the teaching has to inculcate a way of thinking and being in the world that makes a difference through satisfaction of a deep need; not merely a selfish want. This deep need is for a fresh comprehension of what being a self actually is and how it operates in illusion and in insight. No easy job.

Taking on the training

The difference between the life of a trainee monk and that of a western lay practitioner lies in continuity. The monk has the monastery always in his face. The casual retreatant may return to his office to begin advertising new brands of some commodity to feed new addictions without being fully aware of the discrepancy between his quest on retreat and the social negativity in his employment. There are countless variations on this theme. Yet, only in the intimacy of one's personal life can the world as self be confronted.

In monastic training the mind settles for long periods and a fresh understanding of increasing insight and clarity emerges. A truly new attitude may arise in which the diminished self allows an opening of the treasure house- as Dogen puts it. And out of gratitude for this peace of mind, clarity of awareness and freedom from bias, attention turns to others - and indeed the social system. To care about others and the world more than about one's self is the discovery of the truly "awakening mind" (bodhicitta) of the Bodhisattva. At this point one's stance in the world may indeed begin to make a difference.

How to facilitate this transition? It seems that the requirement for longer/deeper continuity of practice, which can facilitate the emergence of such an opening, implies something like a (necessarily limited) monastic endeavour. For this reason I am proposing the provision of solitary retreats within the WCF for those seeking this dimension of change (See p 25). In a supervised solitary retreat the gains from group retreats and daily training can deepen and become entrenched as wisdom begins to replace ego - exactly as Shifu describes it. And once established, this may last. In this practice the almost addictive desire for high religious states and insights falls into the background as an attitude of kindness and selfless compassion takes their place without thoughts of reward. One begins to experience 'self at ease' whether enlightened or not.

Of course it may be said that good-hearted souls can accomplish beneficial change without going on solitary retreats. True indeed. Yet intelligent personal and social engineering is not the same as a shift in the heart that eventually comes to influence others in a qualitatively quite different way. We can trace here a route back to an enchantment with the world through freedom from the obsessions of self. Life in relation to all things becomes a poem in which all participate. We are talking here of a spirituality in which a heart change creates another world - much as the appearance of HH the Dalai Lama, a man with so many responsibilities, can shift one's mind merely through the apprehension of his smile.

Transmission and passing down the robe

In Zen there has always been an emphasis on "mind to mind transmission" whereby a master acknowledges the Dharma insight of a follower thus empowering him or her to teach[4]. There are no written examinations in Chan Buddhism; any testing is of a quite different nature yet, in its own way, highly sophisticated. Even so, this transmission of authority has been considerably questioned in the West in recent years and not without good reason. There are numerous examples in which Western and sometimes Eastern individuals suborned by the permissiveness of our culture have shown themselves severely lacking in the personal constraint which their acquired charisma as teachers demands of them. Financial and sexual scandals, dis-robings and covers up have manifested not uncommonly. The result has been personal distress for many and serious doubts about the whole matter of transmission. And I believe it has to be said that the masters passing down such transmissions have done so mistakenly - mistaking experiences such as kensho or personal devotion for a maturity in which ethical behaviour and compassion would have naturally developed.

Such faults have emerged particularly but not solely among the "second generation teachers" of Jake Lyne's concern. Yet younger teachers of great competence, inventiveness and authority have also been arising whose integrity can be respected. Among these we may perhaps list Reb Anderson, Bernie Glassman and Daido Loori as well as Martine and Stephen Batchelor, among a number of others whose creative teaching and personal influence has done much to sustain the reputation of the Zen Dharma.

A key feature of Zen necessitates a heart to heart personal confirmation from Teacher to disciple. This is because the essence of Zen is conveyed and realised in direct experience not in any indirect description, writing, gifts in verbal presentation etc. which are the hallmark of a more typical educator. Zen seeks to educate the mind in the immediacy of apprehending the world and not into some system of ethics, behaviour or dogmatic belief or even the holding of opinions. To find out whether a trainee has the capacity to convey Zen insight in this manner requires face to face encounters in meetings of direct experiential sharing. It has to be 'now or never'. It is through such encounters and meetings that a master comes to trust the insights, and integrity of his or her follower and becomes willing to let them take on the job. "Passing down the robe" is not agreed upon in committee but through a master's discretion. Yet, as we have seen, and as some masters admit, mistakes can be made[5].

The issue turns on an integrity that needs to be based in the long-term training we have been discussing. A young man dressed in flashy robes, sporting a reputation for being "enlightened" and giving verbally brilliant discourses may not be a teacher to trust.

Someone of warmth, few words, and tolerant of stupidity may be far more reliable. A true teacher will know this and it will be apparent in whom he may choose as a dharma descendant: well aware of the disappointment he may give to secretly ambitious others.

It is therefore not so important that "second generation teachers" provide talks that find ways of speaking Zen in the fashion-conscious "speak" of the time or who as a result of their personal contacts with great teachers can present a bridge to the older cultures now fading, the aesthetics of which may have diminishing appeal. A "second generation teacher" needs only to be true to him(her)self in an honesty which includes a profound personal acquaintance with both the actuality of suffering and the response to it through Dharma understanding and practice.

The way to "present Chan Buddhism differently, in a way that will appeal to a new generation and that is not so much at odds with modern thinking" lies through a rigorous training based in the easily comprehensible truths of the basic formulations of the Buddha. Someone who does this can meet others face to face and declare the presence of the moment without fear or favour. Of course mistakes will be made, inadequacies surface, karmic retribution strike, but the integrity of the intention to be true to the essence of mind is what counts here. The ancient folk beliefs of Asian culture are, in this context, merely an aesthetic background. The matter in hand is culturally present, simply because the Buddha's own insight was so cogent and relevant to the human condition in any culture and in any time.

So does our approach work? Well, at the last WZR at Maenllwyd the majority of participants were newcomers between the ages of around twenty and thirty-five. This is the new generation and they went away showing changes in attitude and experience much as had the generation before them. If a teaching has the psychological truth of suffering by the tail, the response of one generation will differ little from another. How else could Buddha's teaching have survived 2500 years?

What changes in the world are contexts, fashions, opinions and modes of self-justification? Suffering has not changed, personal and social stress remain rooted in a psychology well described in the Buddha's basic formulae. It follows that adherence to the heart of the teaching and the practice is the way to ensure that Chan continues into a future generation. By all means change the decorations, wash the curtains but, above all, examine the foundations if you want to build a home.

The training of "second generation teachers"

A correct understanding of the relation between personal insights and a role in the institutional transmission of Chan is essential. A person who has experienced a deep 'kensho' may not necessarily be a person well equipped to teach Dharma. Dharma teaching skills rely on an ability to gain the trust of practitioners, a certain attributed charisma that can only be earned slowly, an ability to interpret and empathise with the suffering of others, a strictly ethical but flexible life style and a lack of egoistic ambition. We are describing here someone who is maturing in wisdom with "self at ease" rather than someone bent on winning the credentials of spectacular insights. It is the intention to live life as a Bodhisattva in the service of others that is crucial here. Hidden, or even partially unconscious, egoistic ambitions to earn a title or be seen as "enlightened" must be rooted out if a would-be teacher is not to be quickly set aside by a discerning master. No holds will be barred by a master in attempting to ensure that this is so. Why? Because if he appoints a teacher who fails, the entire reputation of the tradition is questioned - as indeed it has been.

If we believe in the deep value of the traditional teachings, the manner in which they are passed on becomes crucial. No amount of glitzy mainstreaming will help - only an essential authenticity.

Master Sheng Yen has made clear[6] what is needed for a teacher to be given a role in the transmission of the Chan lineage. Individuals with deep experience and Dharma understanding but without a 'kensho' experience may teach and lead limited retreats. They will perform a vital role since authenticated 'kensho' in a person also capable of teaching is rare. Only the latter however may be considered Dharma heirs within the lineage authorised to create future masters with the same or better qualifications than themselves. The reason for this is that the enlightenment experience of 'kensho' (however realised) can only be understood between two people who both know what is involved here. Yet this is not really a matter of ranking since kensho arises by "grace" and not by attainment. In this lies the shamanic mystery of transmission best left in many ways as mysterious - like the universe itself indeed.

Modern relativists are apt to negate the significance of lineage because of a belief in the value of individualistic effort. A number of westerners have styled themselves, or permitted their followers to style them, as Roshis or Rimpoches. While some such persons may have been splendid teachers they end by allowing the Dharma to evaporate into a form of self justification only too easily followed by practitioners not free from illusion. Adherence and understanding of lineage acts as a constraint on the ever-present tendency of the ego to inflate itself in endlessly subtle ways. Lineage is awesome when one considers the names on the chain. The attainments of great masters such as Huineng, Hanshan, Linchi, Tahui or Hung-chih are so far beyond most Dharma followers today as to inspire an essential humility. As Master Sheng Yen reminded me on my own transmission "Only in these difficult times could one with attainments as shallow as your own be considered even useful for the transmission of Chan. Yet in these times a person such as yourself can achieve something in a world so set in illusion" This applies to all of us who read this text.

Similarly, I was once discussing Western interests in the Dharma with a Ladakhi yogin at Lamayuru Gompa. He said "The difference between a western lay practitioner and a yogin is that the yogin is a consecrated person". Here we get a glimpse of the life-long commitment and total dedication of a true practitioner whether monk or lay. Consecration, furthermore, is a communal matter; one is recognised by one's fellow yogins and teachers because of a common attitude that has undoubtedly been hard won. In such company the careerist quickly exposes him or herself. And, although not necessarily immediately apparent, this difference becomes understood by others even if they cannot describe it exactly. This is something implicit rather than explicit.

Yet, we must not, through an excessive concern for authenticity, set the barriers too high for those genuinely touched by a wish to serve the Dharma. The root of the matter is a disposition to be kind to others and to be present for them in places of suffering as well as joy. What then should one with such aspiration do to fill the role of a budding Bodhisattva in the West of our time? The following matters need attention:

i. Motivation. How is it that such an interest has arisen? What exactly is the intention behind this interest? Has one faced up to the inherent egoism in all such endeavours?

ii. Training in retreat. Experiential training in a variety of retreat practices with qualified masters is essential and understanding must be confirmed in interviews.

iii. Personal daily life practice. What is it? How does it relate to the practices of others and one's daily life and career? Does it work?

iv. Dharma understanding. There is a need for thorough and ever deepening insight into the basic formulations of the Buddha and the Mahayana sutras. A good grasp of the meaning of the Heart Sutra and a number of fundamental koans is essential for any Dharma teacher who is more than a textbook repeater.

v. Global awareness. It is important to break out of the parochial concerns of one's class, country or profession. The whole world is culturally and economically interdependent these days. The bookshelves are loaded with knowledge and one needs to acquire a global perspective on the relevance of Buddhism in our time. This means study, reading and discussion.

vi. Pilgrimages. It is important to travel to India, Tibet, China, Thailand etc to appreciate the atmosphere of lands and societies where Buddhism has deep roots.

Naturally this takes time, dedication and funding but it is important if one is to gain a global insight into the Buddhism of our time. Without this there is a risk of underestimating the depth of Buddhist tradition through misunderstanding the role of myth and metaphor in older civilisations; and hence to trivialise Buddhism within the seductive world of post-modern capitalism wherein we are embedded.

vii. Never teach or even discuss that which one does not know. Dharma gossip is idle talk that aids no one. Back to the cushion of direct experience every time.

viii. Receive direct teaching from a master on how to present Dharma effectively, how to teach meditation and run retreats and how to listen to practitioners who may seek one's help.

ix. Recall the Aspirational Prayer given in NCF 26 and use it daily.

With these nine points in mind "second generation teachers" can feel they can acquire the basis for a compassionate practice in the interest of others which in the end is their only qualification. Furthermore, as such training deepens, they will acquire a fund of anecdotes about experiences, places, teachers, atmospheres etc which can form the roots of their own inspired and spontaneous talks leavening the core of dharma with life and wit.

Of course such a programme cannot be fulfilled all at once. This is a developmental process over time. Yet, as one goes along, these points of focus can act as a useful guide.

A Chan Community

The retreat leaders, guestmasters, local group leaders and meditation instructors are as important as the teacher in our Western Chan. Their efforts would have little effect without the practice and focussed understanding of practitioners all the way from beginners to "old hands." In the creativity of the Chan practitioner lies the future of the WCF. Already we have practitioners developing valuable means for helping others using their own initiatives based in their training. Most local groups arise in this way as an individual decides to offer a room where people can meet for meditation and feels able to help with instruction. This opening initiative is perhaps the first step on the Bodhisattva path, a sign of emerging bodhicitta[7].

In the Bristol Chan Group, for example, a number of individuals have used their own initiative to create very useful Dharma activities; social walks to get to know one another; a Buddhist art exhibition and poetry reading; a dharma study group which ran for a year or so; short retreats for children and teenagers all carefully thought out; and a recent initiative with Ken Jones of Aberystwyth proposing a short workshop on the experience of ageing. Our 'Mount Kailas in Wales' expedition and Ken's inventive use of landscape (p 27 this issue) as a source for retreat meditation in semi-solitary conditions in wilderness are perhaps especially noteworthy. All these initiatives reveal that anyone can use their talents towards the common good if they set their minds to it. This in fact is the root of community, a sharing of talents and skills towards a common object, the well being of one another. In the end the test for the WCF is whether practitioners feel able to contribute to the common good, both Buddhist and more generally, in ways that reinforce communal feeling as well as gaining a personal benefit. If this begins to happen more widely we will have created the basis for a culture in the West with roots that can continue to grow.

October 2002

1. I had trained in the leadership of these retreats with Jeff Love at Quaesitor and other centres of the period and Jeff had approved my idea of creating a Zen retreat based upon the Communication Exercise, the main method of Berner's process.

2. Paul Cohen, Hilary Richards, Jake Lyne, and Tim Paine. Of these two were medical practitioners, one a psychotherapist and one a psychologist.

3. For an extensive earlier discussion of this issue see:

   S-C Kolm 1979. La philosophie bouddhiste et les 'hommes economiques'. Social Science Information. 18. 4/5: 489-588.

   Blackmore, S. 1992. Beyond the Self: The Escape from Reincarnation in Buddhism and Psychology. In: E and J Berger (eds.). Reincarnation: Fact or Fable? Aquarian Press. Bexley.

4. Master Sheng Yen has provided a detailed examination of the details of Chan transmission in Chan comes West" (Rebecca Li: editor) Dharma Drum 2002.

5. Which is why I have insisted that in the constitution of the Western Chan Fellowship there are clauses that can ensure the removal of a seriously faulted teacher.

6. See discussions in Chan comes West.

7. Bodhicitta means the quest for enlightenment through assisting others to achieve it before oneself

FLOW CHART OF PERSONAL DEVELOPMENT IN WESTERN CHAN FELLOWSHIP

The WCF functions through Local Groups and through Retreats

Structure	Function	Responsibilities	Nature of learning	Instructors qualifications
BEGINNERS CLASSES	To welcome beginners and provide basic meditation instruction suited to their interests but oriented towards development within WCF	Group leaders and Meditation Instructors	Through Sitting to develop mindfulness and reflection on own needs and actions counteracting reactive habits and emotional dependencies	Meditation instructors certificate
WESTERN ZEN RETREATS	Introduces individuals to self confrontation as the basic method and requirement for personal change through Chan	Teacher with Guestmaster and monitors.	Through Communication Exercises to challenge habitual assumptions about self, to discover one is not exceptional. Development of self in the world, compassion and "one-mind". Wisdom of being	Certification for leadership of WZR or EI mastership + Chan training.
CHAN RETREATS	Based in meditation methods basic to Buddhism as taught in the Beginners Classes. Participants are introduced to Chinese Chan as in Dharma Drum Lineage viz: Silent illumination, use of koans and hua-tous	Teacher with Guestmaster and monitors	Through traditions of Chan to develop the wisdom of sunyata, insight into one-pointedness, higher effects of practice and understanding the wisdom of "Seeing the Nature" if not that experience itself. Introduction to *Bodhicitta* and bodhisattva vows	Chan transmission or Permit to run retreats by a Master or Dharma heir
MAHAMUDRA	Teaches basic Tantra and meditation methods of Mahamudra to deepen participants practice and personal integration.	Teacher, Guestmaster and monitors	Development of greater heart through tantric visualisation and physical methods. Wisdom of "Big Mind"	Higher practice. Empowerment from Tibetan lama or certification by an empowered Vajra heir.

Summary: There are several layers to training in the WCF and movement from one to the other is by practice and empowerment through personal recognition aided by interview. Permission to teach at any level is given by the elected Teacher of the WCF but open to comment in Committee as per the constitution. Current situation requires attention to be given to improving the classes for beginners through providing suitable materials. It is essential to be clear about the probable motivation of beginners: viz: sense of meaninglessness and quest, emotional distress or problems otherwise dealt with through counselling or romantic curiosity based in *folies de grandeur*. We live in a consumer age in which the predominant motivation is for self-satisfaction, indulgence or improvement rather than understanding through confrontation with illusions. Each of these has elements totally contrary to the thrust of Dharma. Unless a Dharma teacher is prepared to question and confront the very society in which we operate he/she is not worthy of that role. The skills required combine being a social radical with a compassionate understanding of illusion.

Chuan Deng Jing Di, October 2002

Fig 1 FLOW CHART OF PERSONAL DEVELOPMENT IN WESTERN CHAN FELLOWSHIP

SOLITARY OPTIONS: A SCHOOL FOR YOGINS?

John has recently become the sole owner of his property in the Mendip Hills of Somerset. The farm is well suited for development as a meditation training centre and in this article John offers suggestions as to how he may augment the Intensive Retreat programme of the WCF with a provision for personal training in supervised solitary retreats.

Winterhead Hill Farm lies on the western ridge of the Mendip Hills overlooking a gentle valley leading down to the Bristol Channel with distant views of the Welsh mountains. The location is surprisingly remote for this heavily populated area, tucked away together with two other properties at the end of a gated track and invisible from roads. The seclusion is perfect for a monastic setting. It is also quite beautiful with rolling pasture, bluebell woods and bare limestone hills providing excellent walking country. While the weather can be wet and stormy, there are many quiet, peaceful and sunny days too. It is within half an hour's drive from the cities of Bristol, Wells and Glastonbury and an hour from Bath. Access to M4 and M5 motorways is easy and Bristol Airport is twenty minutes away with access to the continent on KLM shuttle flights.

The farm has outbuildings sited around a courtyard and I sometimes dream about establishing nothing less than a small monastery here or at least a regional Chan Hall for the South West. Such a project would be quite possible but require considerable funding. Whether there is a demand for such a thing is however far from clear. The take up of the new facilities at the Maenllwyd for individual retreats has for example been minimal and a suggestion concerning a project in Southampton stimulated no interest.

My belief remains that a number of people would welcome intensive meditational training on a personal basis through solitary retreats under supervision in a small community of retreatants. Such a system does operate well for example at Gaia House for Vipassana, but is not particularly associated with Chan training.

I propose therefore to offer two new training opportunities for Buddhist practitioners familiar with the retreats of the WCF at the Maenllwyd and who wish to develop a deeper personal practice. My suggestion would be especially appropriate for any practitioner wishing to undertake solitary practice in a small communal setting under supervision, any Buddhist facing a life crisis for which a period of withdrawal from the world with intensive practice seems appropriate, and people simply wishing to take their insight into the experiential Dharma to deeper levels only achievable through longer term seclusion. Many practitioners gain considerable insight from weeklong intensive retreats but are unable to sustain this for long on returning to an abrasive daily life. The following suggestions would allow insights achieved on 7 day sesshins to be sustained and better understood through incorporation into a daily life practice.

Supervised Solitary Retreats. Accommodation will be provided for individuals interested in furthering his or her existing practice through solitary retreat. The retreat schedule would be agreed with the director (Retreat Master) who would be available periodically for consultation. Methods of practice could be Chan mindfulness, Silent illumination, Koan work or Mahamudra.

Yogin Training. The practitioner undertakes to deepen his/ her practice of Chan or Tibetan Buddhism through a course of training modelled on the training of Himalayan yogins. Practices would include basic preliminaries, tantric visualisation, breathing yoga, bare awareness and Mahamudra. The practitioner would undertake to learn, receive and practice teachings in Mahayana meditation under close supervision. The idea would be to develop a yogin's orientation to life as a basis for daily life practice and the teaching of Mahayana meditation.

Currently three rooms (bed sitters) will soon be available for individual occupancy. Durations of stay would range from one to eight weeks, the eight weeks comprising a term after which the Centre closes for a period. Preference would be given to those registering for the longest period of time.

Accommodation will be on a self-catering basis with self-provisioning. Apart from the individual "cell", there will be a Buddha Room, a meditation area, a communal lounge and a kitchen available for retreatants' use. The contract will include a two-hour work period on the property per day. Individuals may use the kitchen communally or on a rota as desired.

Current estimated cost: £10 per day for those staying for eight weeks. £15 per day for between four and eight weeks, £20 for two to four weeks and £25 for one to two weeks. These values are based on similar charges at Gaia House.

Schedule. A simple monastic regime will be followed with a morning and evening communal meditation, sometimes with liturgies. Apart from the daily Work period(s), the programmes will be individually constructed with the Retreat Master so as to suit the particular requirements and endeavour of the retreatant. Except for an occasional supply run to local stores, retreatants will be expected to remain on the property with walks in the vicinity being part of the programme. Visitors and pets will not be allowed. The house will be 'silent' except for agreed periods.

The Director will be in (private) residence most of the time but may be absent running retreats etc. for periods. If there is more than one retreatant in residence, one will be appointed as Guestmaster during the Director's absence.

Suggestions, enquiries, exploratory applications are all invited. Start date - 2003

John Crook
WCF Centre for Yogin Training
Winterhead Hill

LES ROCHES FLEURIES

After moonset stars shine more brightly in the still air,
Earth turns slowly rolling into day,
the great fly-wheel spins,
stars drift around the pole,
western mountains rise against my feet
and in the east the long horizon falls.
Onward she rolls, vast galleon
pivoted upon her pole,

time in empty space sits still
watching the moving dayline on the planet's rim.

Slowly, from the dark mass of brooding hills,
the vineyards and the running brooks appear,
dry, white rocks pierced by cypresses,
grey to old gold the distant hills,
sunlight greeting the trees yellowing the parched land.
Last owl poops its hidden cry,
with hesitation first cicadas trill,
breathless the air hangs waiting,
the landscape unfurls.

Heat collects, stirs in the rock strewn
valleys between pines, spills over,
pushing the air around.
Now under the baking sun
breezes fleck silver the olive trees
waves ripple over the lines of vines,
toss in sudden squalls domed planes.
Shuttered farms close inward
keeping cool their dark interiors,
the light hurts.

Crowning the hill top, Notre Dame de Graces
sits in her oak groves, shadowy pines,
short terraced gardens, crumbling walls
for lizards, nooks for images.
Resinous airs linger in the shade dark oaks incubate.
Wind in the tree tops heralds an afternoon's mistral.
Nobody about, empty the tables
set with chairs upon the terraces,
empty the gardens, pine shaded courts,

the only discord here must be my own.

Nothing moves in the stone mind
of the old centurion, guardian of the gates,
stone is still, inactive information.
A mason gave this rock a life that touches mine,
these questioning eyes, forbidding gaze,
"What are your credentials
that, passing me, you wish to tread
the steps to the sanctuary?
Many there are who pass within
making their noise
polluting the quietened atmosphere.
Go slowly now and make
these few steps sure a pilgrimage.
If rock has voice
consider well the silence in the stone."

Not any wood would do -not any hill.
Although I do not share the simple faith
of these crude images
I understand their transformations.
Cicadas purr in your stone head as well as mine.
Outside time you stand here guardian,
whoever comes may read your face,
your right to question, forbid frivolity.
I come neither on my knees
nor aesthetically sampling the handiworks of another age.
I sense the stillness of your stone time;
cicada cry among the oaks;
wind drift resin in the wine;
the hill top sacraments of fragile immortality
where form and substance interact in history

and shapes, frail in time's mistral, bloom.
I bow in gratitude before these crude configurations
constant recurrence, same place and time,
here, there, somewhere,
hands carving the connecting minute
one arrow hits another in the air
and all is gone.

Swallowtail curves a brief trajectory
above the jagged aloe spears.
Images flicker among breeze quickened leaves
"Defence d'allumer du feu!"
Why disturb a still pool?
Endlessly spreading from still centres of place and time
Cicadas call, circles radiate and disappear.

One man only
peasant with a fruit basket
has passed this gate
in an hour of musing.
A door slams along the hill;
a breeze shifts leaves yet nothing moves;
the air falls dreamlike into insect time.
Ants make pilgrimages,
flies from time to time
alight on table top.
The Virgin in the rocks
hasn't moved and no birds sing.
High above and passing
a raven calls.

Under a cone-covered fir where the path turns-
a wide-armed cross without inscription

backed by the heavy foliage of an oak,
bare wood, sun dried,
rock the soil in which it's driven.
The figure moves among the trees beckoning
no words - a total statement.
Death and time and history
deep rooted in a believing land,
the saviour's instrument.
Where the lines cross the trail begins.
Old lady coming from the house
does not look at me, composed
she passes by leaving the stranger quiet beneath the trees.

All but the desert plants wilt in the heat
roses struggle along dried up terraces.
Beyond the Cross the hillside drops away,
the great view looms.
Forests, rock cropped mountains,
far distances jagged and curved.
What is a World?
Down there the motorways exude
the roar of cars, polluted air,
the sea crazed industry generates its violent rhythms.
Airplane flies along the coast
dragnetting for customers
"Patron - et trois Duvals."
Crowding the beaches people are purchasing the sun.
At Notre Dame de Graces almost no one.
No price on this commodity -
silence tuned by insects and the warm wind.
A summer of opposites perhaps -
within such silence human insects cry
What is a World that contains all this?

Here in the wilting rose garden
the hardened plants need rain.

Wind falls with the fading light
gold to slow silver the rising nightline comes.
Day lingers greying the land, cicada silence,
hill crest firs collect the remaining breeze.
Down in the valley among the olive trees
shutters open from white walls
lights glimmer in dead houses
the troglodytes emerge.
Under deep well-heads dark water lies.

Cotignac
To HR
Revised 26.12.93, 11.6.1996, 6.8.02

IS ZEN FOR EVERYONE? Two book reviews

Saso, M. 2000 Zen is for Everyone. The Xiao Zhi Guan text by Zhi Yi. New Life Center, Carmel & Tendai Institute, Honolulu. ISBN 1-929431-02-3.

Haskel, P. 2001. Letting go. The story of Zen Master Tosui. University of Hawaii Press. Honolulu. ISBN 08248-2440-7.

The translation and interpretation of Zen texts from China, Korea and Japan continues apace demonstrating conclusively the wide range of views inherent in East Asian Buddhism. At first, when few works had been translated, interpreters tended, perhaps understandably, to produce simplistic understandings based on inadequate knowledge of the sources. Such mistakes are no longer so tolerable today.

In the first of the works reviewed here, Michael Saso provides a translation of a very early manual of meditation by the revered Tientai (j. Tendai) Master Chih I (j. Zhi Yi) who lived between 538 CE and 597. At this early date Chinese meditation was still strictly modelled on methods of Indian origin and lacked the later forms developed to suit Chinese culture. The Indian practices of Samatha (Calming the mind) and Vipasyana (Insight into the nature of mind) were known in China as the related activities of 'Stop and Look', terms summarising the nature of these twin approaches based in earlier Abhidharma literature. It was not until the Master Hung Chih Chen Chueh (1091-1157)1 combined these two approaches into a common system known as Silent Illumination (Mo chao) that the modern practice of Chan meditation developed, being taken later to Japan and reformulated as Shikantaza by Master Dogen.

Chih I's presentation of 'Stop and Look' is profound yet straight forward and certainly accessible to beginners, including lay practitioners. Indeed, using this text, it would be possible to start meditation without a teacher. He provides ten chapters detailing the manner by which a beginner can establish a good basis for meditation through purification of the senses and desires and harmonising body and mind through care in regulating eating, sleeping and breathing. He ends by relating meditational methods to teaching and by offering useful tips about meditation and health.

Essentially to 'Stop' means to examine closely a present situation without judgement and to come to rest in the present moment whether this be on the cushion or in everyday life. 'Look' means seeing experience in the light of the Buddha's teaching, especially the "Law of Co-dependent arising". This enables the practitioner to perceive in a heartfelt manner that all things are basically lacking in any inherent existence as entities but are rather all part of an ongoing process wherein cause leads to consequence under the influence of context. Such insight reduces the habitual tendency to attach to wanted things or people as if they were permanently available.

The text bases the practice firmly in the established thought of the Mahayana, particularly the Prajnaparamita and Madhyamaka literature. This creates a paradox when we find Michael Saso in his introduction arguing, as did Daisetz Suzuki early in the last century, that a Zen based in ineffable experience could be practised within any religion. Saso remarks, "Christians, both Protestant and Catholic alike, use and teach Zen methods in a purely Christian context. Zen is thus a contemplative method, not a belief system" (p xiii). It is this erroneous bias in Western understanding of Zen that has allowed so called Christian Zen to develop within a kind of philosophical vacuum- inadequate theology and non-existent philosophy adulating uninterpretable experience. To find Saso repeating this viewpoint is disturbing for, as post modern writers and contemporary Chan masters such as Master Sheng Yen, have pointed out, no practice can develop without a relationship to the ideas that sustain it.

Of course the mere process of Zen meditation, formal sitting and the regulation of mind, may be used by anyone of any religion and indeed has its parallels within most of the great world religions. And it is indeed beneficial. Yet the adoption of this method by Christians is a sign of a weakness that denies or overlooks their own meditative traditions. Chinese and Japanese meditation methods are rooted in the Dharma of the Buddha and cannot lead to an understanding of "enlightenment" outside that context. Whatever may be experienced by Christian meditators faithful to a deistic theology, however blissful or insightful, cannot be the same experience of liberation that comes through insight into sunyata (emptiness). It will be some other condition determined by the context of their faith. As Chih I himself says, the practice of meditation develops within reliance on the teachings of the masters.

Haskel's translation of the story of the Japanese Master Tosui introduces a parallel theme in which the question of the relationship between an institutional life of monastic formality and the nature of Zen insight comes into focus. In an extended and historically fascinating forward, he describes how Buddhism during the Tokagawa period fell under government control and became organised hierarchically as a highly formalised 'church' system. The free and open style of interaction between master and disciple had already become rigidified through the use of formalised expressions in the solving of koans and in the understanding of Dharma so that the spontaneity and naturalness of Chan was being replaced by a ritualistic and authoritarian form of transmission.

These social contexts of Japanese Buddhism seem to have been one main reason for the appearance of highly rebellious monks who deserted the formal institutions of their time to recapture a sort of crazy naturalness that accepted transience and mortality as the natural run of things. Their subsequent notoriety, fame and appreciation showed that these men were well and truly genuine practitioners of Zen. Tosui (d:1683) seems to have been the first and perhaps the most extreme of such masters, perhaps becoming an exemplar for later revolutionaries such as Ryokan (1758-1832) and Ikkyu whose lives were in many ways similar to his. After severe training Tosui had become the abbot of a monastery yet he decided to leave and live simply as a beggar or cheap artisan, homeless and unkempt, among the ordinary people, shunning all who tried to trace his whereabouts and learn from him. So successful was he that relatively little is known about him.

None the less his notoriety as a great and exceptional master did not escape those remaining in more orthodox surroundings. The celebrated scholar and Soto Zen master Menzan Zuiho laboriously put together all that could be found out about Tosui and eventually published his Tribute (Tosui osho densan) which is the text translated here.

Undoubtedly the social conditions of Buddhism in Japan were the seed bed for the activities of these sensational masters who took the daily life of the poor as their environment of practice far from the securities of monastic or 'church' establishments. The fact that they manifested profound practice under conditions of an often quite pathetic daily life is a lesson for contemporary practitioners. Perhaps they show a way out of the sentimental New Ageism and self-comforting idealisms of many contemporary Westerners and suggest a View and a Way whereby the Dharma may confront the destructive trivialities of consumerism. These lives should be read and carefully considered by all of us who live so comfortably attending our sitting groups once a week and believing we know something of Zen.

BUDDHIST JOURNEYS IN THE HIMALAYAS 2003

1) Ladakh: Mountains, Monasteries and Space

Dr John Crook, Vice President of the International Association of Ladakh Studies, will almost certainly be attending the biennial conference of this society in Leh, Ladakh between July 21st-27th, 2003. Following the conference he may be prepared to lead a small group on a tour of the remarkable monasteries, art treasures, landscapes and villages of this Buddhist land. Apart from the main Gompas, we will probably visit a remote monastery where yogins practice, some mountain-ringed lakes only recently open to tourism, and penetrate north into the little visited territory of Nubra where we may do a short trek.

The tour is open to fellows of the WCF and others interested in Himalayan culture. The logistics of the tour will be organised by our old friends Tanu and Zorab Rigdzin of Highland Adventures, Delhi.

Approx dates: July 30th - August 12th. Guesstimate price around £2000

2) Trek to Mustang

In a remote corner of northern Nepal a highland valley extends into Tibetan territory. Although politically part of Nepal, it remains largely under the jurisdiction of its own monarch of ancient lineage who lives in the little walled capital of Mustang known as Lo.

Unlike our tours to ancient cities in China, where most traces of anything older than thirty years is fast disappearing, Mustang remains totally medieval: no roads, no airport, no sewerage, no Western comforts -- starkly original and almost "untouched" by the crudity of the modern world. To go there is to go back many centuries into the cultural world of ancient Tibet.

The only access is by a long, quite strenuous five-day trek up the gorge of the Kali Gandaki river.

Although this is a demanding journey even at moderate altitudes by Himalayan standards (10-13,000 feet), it offers a quite unique experience which will probably not be possible within a few years as "development" moves ever onwards.

John and Elizabeth Crook plan to attempt this journey in the Autumn, approximate dates:

21 Sept - Oct 12th. London-London 22 days. Trekking 15 days. Strenuous. Max altitude about 13,000 feet. They will be using ponies for part of the trek.

The trek will be organised by Himalayan Kingdoms and led by a Sherpa team. If sufficient persons apply the tour will be restricted to our own members. The cost will depend on whether one is sharing tents or going as a singleton and on whether a pony is requested.

Minimum participation 4. maximum 12. Basic trek: approx £2850

Pony hire on trek: £20 per day. £300

Single room/tent supplements available. Approx £70.

Please note: if you wish to travel with John to these lands on which he is a cultural expert you should apply this year. 2003 may be the last year he will lead visits to these altitudes.

If seriously interested please put your name forward IMMEDIATELY so John can get an idea of numbers. Write to John at Winterhead Hill Farm, Shipham, Somerset, BS25 1RS.

SILENCE AND ILLUMINATION AN INTENSIVE TRAINING RETREAT IN CHINESE ZEN

Haus der Stille, Hamburg

July 4th-12th 2003

Led by John Crook with assistance from Simon Child and Max Kalin

Our retreat will endeavour to recapture the inspiration of two periods of traditional Chan training led in recent years by the Venerable Chan Master Sheng Yen in Berlin (1999) and in Gaia House, UK, (2000) and will be led by his senior Western disciples each of whom has received transmission from him to teach as Dharma heirs in the Linchi (Rinzai) and Caodong (Soto) lineages of China.

The retreat will take place in the beautiful retreat centre of the Haus der Stille in wooded country south of Hamburg. The setting and the accommodation are exceptionally attractive and comfortable. We hope for an international gathering of Shifu's Dharma followers yet all meditators are welcome.

Silent illumination is a key to understanding the deeper reaches of the self. In a gentle process of calming the mind and watching one's illusions at play the participant gradually enters a world of clarity and insight leading to the development of compassionate wisdom. Needless to say this is no easy matter. Practitioners need to be strongly motivated and willing to experience both physical and mental confrontation with their engrained self- concern. In our strife-torn world Silent illumination opens a way to personal peace that does not avoid the problems of modern life.

The retreat is silent but includes interviews with the teachers. The programme begins in the early morning and continues till ten p.m. The method of practice will be carefully presented for beginners and adepts alike and will be supported by physical exercise, work periods, ritual and chanting.

Each day will include a Dharma talk. Food is vegetarian. Languages: English and German

The retreat will be led by John Crook who is Master Sheng Yen's first European Dharma heir. He is the Teacher of the Western Chan Fellowship in the UK and leads Chan retreats regularly in the UK, in Warsaw, Berlin, Zagreb etc. He is the creator of Western Zen Retreats and Koan Retreats designed for Western practitioners. Together with Simon Child he recently led a Western Zen Retreat at Master Sheng Yen's centre in upstate New York.

Simon Child is secretary of the Western Chan Fellowship and co leads with John as well as presenting his own retreats.

Max Kalin is the teacher of the Chan Group in Zurich and edits the Chan Zeitung. He will be the main interpreter (English-German) on this retreat.

Interpretation into Polish may also be provided if required. Interviews can be in English, French or German.

NCF XXVIII

SELF AT EASE

Editorial from the Chan Hall.

What is this journal for? Why do some of us work so hard to keep on issuing these copies of New Chan Forum? What is the policy of this publication? First of all, it is not a house journal retailing our meetings, events and personal experiences as if in a chat room. Rather, it has a serious teaching intent augmenting our programme of retreats and the work of our regional groups. It attempts to develop clearly the means by which we fulfil our charitable constitution.

There may be some who would prefer 'lighter' material, others might seek philosophy. Our intent is essentially existential: to further the experience of Chan, to deepen our understanding through sharing and to show what we have felt and thought while doing this. So we include serious but not 'academic' texts, poems, accounts of retreat experiences, comments on the times and Buddhist iniquities as we see them, as well as hopes for the future, sermons, stories and laughs. Certainly we invite contributions in all these modes. Perhaps especially it would be good to have more accounts of the experience of trying to practice Dharma in everyday life: at the shop counter; in the bank; building a house or a car; negotiating business or counselling the bereaved. Whatever it is - how did your understanding of Dharma, such as whatever it may be, play a role in your work and thought?

At our recent AGM I tried to explain my understanding of what the WCF is endeavouring to teach through its retreats and other offerings. Based profoundly in the Dharma revelation of Master Sheng yen this is an attempt to make clear the Buddha's subtle message to our time within our own particular Sangha. It seems worthwhile providing some of what I said then, here, for a wider audience.

These are very difficult times in which the understanding of human spirituality is deeply confused, especially in the West, and in which the politics of contemporary consumerism create forms of self-concern which the Dharma confronts with perspectives that may seem counter cultural in spite of their psychological depth. These are times when presentation matters, because unless ideas are perceived as relevant they will not be heeded. Hence I am emphasising certain aspects of the Dharma more strongly than others (see NCF 27: Passing down the Robe) in order to clarify the purpose of the Dharma to contemporaries more clearly.

Chan is an enlightenment project and the requirements for a deep understanding of such an endeavour are essentially self-confrontational. The root project of the Buddha is the setting aside of the self which is both the root of illusory attachment and the source of ignorance. The process is necessarily one of self-understanding - which means you, which means me. Yet we live in a time when self-concerned individualism, encouraged by every commercial means possible, is the basis of our capitalistic, competitive striving. As David Loy has been pointing out in recent writings, our strong sense of 'lack' is rooted in the despair that the illusory attachment to self ultimately generates. Today it is not so much alternative outer-path religions that comprise a problem for Buddhism, but rather the unconscious cravings for wealth, status, self-esteem and aggressive acquisition necessary for capitalism to continue. And capitalism is a proven means of limiting the poverty for some while increasing it for others. How then can we confront the ego, not so much the rampant evil ego of a Saddam Hussein, which produces its own gross opposition, but the subtle ego of semi-conscious self-enhancement at the expense of others that manifests in everyday affairs and sustains our unease.

In modern Zen these issues are compounded by an almost competitive seeking for 'enlightenment' as a product of propaganda by some Zen institutions. An illusion about enlightenment is projected as the 'product' of training. Yet Chan/Zen teaching makes clear that an enlightenment experience, let alone a continuing enlightened state, cannot arise through any sort of self-based desire. Given the nature of our culture this is not only a difficult task to undertake but quite problematic for conventional understanding. Furthermore there may be a number of paths which individuals may take, paths that are relative to their karmic character.

To many westerners, Zen still seems to be solely about the attainment of a precise experience known from the Japanese as "kensho", by which is meant an event, commonly of very short duration, in which ego concern totally vanishes in the extraordinary clarity of an unfiltered perception revealing the universe just 'as it is'. This experience became emphasised for Westerners as the goal of zen in the influential writing of the great scholar Daisetz Suzuki whose personal training as a layman in Rinzai Zen followed that suitable for young monks who needed a quick qualification in order to inherit the temples of their fathers. High-pressure training induced experiences but many of them, according to Master Sheng yen, were probably shallow and arising while the young men were as yet hardly mature. Furthermore, Suzuki had failed to mention another focus of great importance in Japan, the Soto Zen approach brought there from China by the great monk Dogen. In this Cao-dong tradition all of us are considered basically enlightened from the start, it is only the complexity and depth of our 'vexations' that prevent us knowing this. In other words, enlightenment does not have to be sought for it is already there. We need to learn to 'lean back' into it - as Roshi Reb Anderson has expressed it, an outcome barely possible for those desperately searching for something that has never been lost; a search furthermore clearly driven by subtle egoism.

All this is not to suggest that a kensho experience is not extremely significant, merely that for some it becomes too exclusively the focus of Zen training as a desired outcome. The insight gained through such an experience is life changing in its realisation that the mind does not depend on the ego for its function and that the world just goes on in its impermanent flux anyway. It naturally leads to a falling away of suffering through an increasing concern with the needs of others. Yet, since it happens to one as it were 'from its own side' and in its own time when the mind is ready, its occurrence cannot be premeditated or grasped by any sort of wanting. Indeed to want it is to preclude it.

People vary in the likelihood of having such an experience. In both the Chan and the Tibetan traditions three grades of individual are described. There are those for whom the insight arises spontaneously, maybe outside the realm of teaching altogether, and it only needs the refinement of a teaching from a master to set the individual on the path of a Bodhisattva. Master Huineng is a good example. For others, intensive long-term training in meditation methods is required (for example Dogen) but, even then, such training cannot without fail yield such a paradoxical experience. There are also some whose karmic obscurations are so heavy that it is unlikely their egoistic referencing can ever be laid aside. Master Sheng yen says that it is within a life dedicated to Dharma that kensho arises, not through any specific method or meditational training. It is also vital to realise that the egoistic self returns so that continued work is needed. One experience does not mean you are enlightened person - you have had no more than a glimpse of what that may mean.

It follows that our WCF training, particularly for newcomers, should start with a method and a focus that grants some success without the immediate need for the radical undermining of self that is ultimately demanded but which may seem unreachable in everyday life. In our retreats over twenty years, the number of persons who have, or may have, experienced an enlightenment moment (kensho) is extremely small. Yet many have felt that extraordinary oneness and clarity that comes from an insight into the interdependence of self and universe - the 'one-mind experience'.

This valuable insight may arise through intensive training on retreat at a stage well before the letting go of self at a deeper level is likely. While teaching the dharma of enlightenment, it seems additionally important to encourage retreatants and Dharma practitioners in this less paradoxical direction. Such an insight I call 'self at ease'. There is a sense of oneness with all things, a profound experience of peace and a clarity of perception due to a marked reduction in the fog of ego concern, even though the practitioner may be quite self-congratulatory in the bliss of attainment. 'Self at ease' is attainable directly through adequately focussed attention once the confusion of thought has died down. As Dogen puts it "When you do these things for some time the treasure house opens naturally". Self at ease can then become a basis for further practice, 'not meditation' as the Tibetans put it, a bare awareness without purpose that eventually allows the realisation of higher states (jnanas), 'manifesting from their side', and which, with insight into emptiness, become the revelation of our basic unselfed condition (tathagata garbha).

These points suggest our training must focus first on calming the mind. This requires a precise attentiveness to the mind's process that arises in the practice of Silent Illumination or Mahamudra. No glitzy, worried mainstreaming to fit contemporary culture is required here. What is needed is the entirely conventional application of the Buddha's methods as revealed in the Sutras, developed in the Abhidharma and emphasised in the Mahayana sutras that lie at the basis of Chan/Zen. Since these methods can produce a 'taste of chocolate' as Lama Thubten Yeshe used to say, they can encourage practitioners into a deeper understanding of the Dharma eventually leading to a heartfelt letting go of attachments of all kinds - including 'me'. Gradual training and sudden insight are thereby related.

The application of insight requires an everyday process of mindfulness. Our training must therefore also encourage a daily practice that is not so much a time spent in 'sitting' as a moment to moment cultivation of self-awareness: a knowing why I do this, within a gentle critique that does not beat oneself over the head. Such mindfulness is actually the practice of the eightfold path. Any mechanical practice will not do the trick. Mindfulness is all in the everyday.

Finally a warning: if a practitioner settles down in 'self at ease ' he/ she will be like someone who, as Shifu has put it, finds a level place upon a mountain full of ferns, fresh water and sunshine and behaves as if it were the summit itself. Not so. 'Self at ease' must itself be let go, otherwise it too will grow stale in a false contentment. The path never ends. The mystery beyond the signless signpost pointing out over the ocean has not yet been understood.

In the end one suspects all this is forgotten. At home in the universe the bodhisattva is not concerned with him/herself nor with discovering anything. There is simply the task of working for all in the knowledge that everything is a sharing in all.

One may thus say - this is all words. Hughie told us recently of a story in which a Japanese teacher with little English was asked for his view of practice in the UK. He said:

> "Books, books, books,
>
> too much, too much, too much,
>
> dustbin, dustbin, dustbin!"

And, of course, this is spot on. If you find yourself at the top of a thousand foot pole all you have to do is to step off. One discovers:

> No top
>
> No bottom
>
> No gravity.
>
> Everything as usual....

But most of us have yet to reach the top of the thousand-foot pole - let alone attempt the stepping off it. Those who do need no words.

These remarks have been made to encourage those for whom the path may begin to seem too difficult or irrelevant to our times. The Dharma path is not only long and wide, it has many tracks. The root intention must be the development of bodhicitta - the spirit of the bodhisattva seeking enlightenment for all irrespective of him/herself. And, for this, those of humble attainment, as the world seems to know, may contribute much. Even those who seem to be in the third category, deeply troubled human beings such as the great monk Hakuin was for so long, may actually become greater practitioners than those with sharp Dharma intuition. Kindness, compassion and empathy are also the routes to great insights that may arise when time alone knows the moment. Let no one be proud.

Chuan-deng Jing-di

June 2003

THE CEASING OF NOTIONS[1]

This "teisho" has been given at Sharpham College and at the Maenllwyd in variant forms. Stuart McLeod has kindly transcribed the disks for us which John has edited for presentation here.

This little poem by the Chilean poet Pablo Neruda was shown me by a student on the Buddhism course at a Sharpham College. Introducing a weekend of Chan there I thought it showed me a way to begin. The poem is called "Keeping Quiet".

> "Now we will all count to twelve and we will all keep still.
>
> For once on the face of the earth let's not speak in any language. Let's stop for a second and not move our arms about so much.
>
> It would be an exotic moment without rush, without engines.
>
> We would all be together in a sudden strangeness. Fishermen in the cold sea would not harm whales
>
> and the man gathering salt would not look at his hurt hands.
>
> Those who prepare wars, wars with gas, wars with fire, victories with no survivors, would put on clean clothes
>
> and walk about with their brothers in the shade doing nothing.
>
> What I want should not be confused with inactivity.
>
> Life is what it's about. "

Neruda goes on to tell us that if we were not so single-minded about keeping our lives moving and for once could do nothing, perhaps a huge silence might interrupt this sadness of never understanding ourselves. He pondered whether perhaps then the earth could teach us that although everything seems dead in winter yet soon all is alive again.

"Now I'll count up to twelve and you keep quiet, I'll disappear."

A powerful poem. Yet in Chan and Zen there is something more than simply keeping silence. To investigate what that 'more' is we have to look deeply. Let's try and have a look at the Great Matter straight away. We'll probably not comprehend it at once but the endeavour is worth doing. After all how can one introduce Zen except by Zen. Zen often side-steps what one thinks is the 'point', yet any such "point" is just a thought.

Recall the story of Bodhidharma. Bodhidharma was the Indian monk who brought the Chan tradition from India to China. This is the legend that has come down through the ages. Legends are not necessarily history yet legends are part of history. Bodhidharma probably came by sea by way of Indonesia. There seems to be no record of him having travelled to China by the Silk Route as many other great teachers did. You may remember that when he arrived in China he had a rather uncomfortable meeting with the Emperor, who misunderstood what he had to say. It was a very frank meeting yet the Emperor could not understand Bodhidharma. Perhaps this travelling monk was too direct. One might criticise Bodhidharma and say that perhaps he lacked the skill to get his message across to so materialistic a mind as the emperor's. In any case, after this miscommunication, Bodhidharma went off into the mountains by himself and sit in a cave for the proverbial, famous nine years of gazing at a wall.

A somewhat distraught monk came to find him. This monk was eventually to become the second Patriarch in China, but at that time he was puzzled, disturbed as are so many of us. If you think of a time when you've felt ill at ease, disturbed, you know what this monk felt like. He came to Bodhidharma, and Bodhidharma took absolutely not the blindest bit of notice of him. He just continued looking at the wall. But the monk kept saying "Bodhidharma, great teacher, please." Nothing happened, silence, staring at the wall. So he got desperate and the story says he chopped off his arm and held it out to Bodhidharma. Bodhidharma said "Hah, Really! You must need something seriously to chop your arm off." Of course it might not have been his arm, it might have been his finger, it might have been anything. If you chop your arm off, doctors would tell you that you wouldn't be in a very good position to ask any questions!

Whatever he did was sufficient for Bodhidharma to turn away from the wall and say, "Well, what do you want then?" One gets the impression that Bodhidharma was certainly a bit of a grumpy old codger. "What do you want then?" So the monk said, "Please, my mind is so disturbed. Please calm my mind." Bodhidharma said, "Well, the first thing is, you have to show it to me. Find your mind and let me see it. " So the monk sat and looked for his mind - thought, thought, looked, thought, thought, looked, looked, thought, puzzled, paced up and down, maybe went away for a week, came back again and finally said, "I can't find my mind!" "Oh," said Bodhidharma, "Can't find it eh? Well therefore I have calmed it." And the monk realised something very important. He was suddenly in a state of not searching, he was somewhere else, and in that somewhere else was a great peace.

That story is picked up again in variant version in a Chinese text discovered in the last century in the Dung Huang caves of North China, a very interesting place where both ancient Tibetan and Chinese texts were discovered all mixed up. Some texts which scholars might have thought would be in Chinese have been found in

Tibetan and vice versa. This particular text has been recently translated and is called 'The Treatise on the Ceasing of Notions'[2] - the letting go of ideas. Let's just look at the first two pages. They clearly pick up on the story I've just told you.

It begins with a general statement.

The Great Way is without limit, fathomless, subtle, beyond comprehension, beyond words. Master Nuri and his disciple Emmon were discussing the truth. The master sat silent and was saying nothing. Emmon suddenly got up and said:

"What is it that we call the heart - mind? How is this heart - mind pacified?"

The master answered, "You should not assume the mind-heart, for then there's no need to pacify it. That is called pacifying the heart - mind."

Emmon said, "But if there is no heart-mind then how can we learn the Way?"

"The heart-mind cannot think of the Way, so why should the Way depend upon the heart-mind?"

Let's look at this. Here's Emmon, like our first monk, the man who was troubled and went to Bodhidharma. Emmon is not so anxious, not so disturbed but he is very concerned to understand what the mind, sometimes translated as heart, is. [3] "What is this thing?" he says, "what is this mind? The mind is so often disturbed you know, how can we pacify it?" The master says, "You shouldn't assume the mind." Interesting, fascinating statement, which requires a great deal of penetration. If you assume something to be present or something to be there you're making an assumption, it's a thought. I think I have a mind. So assuming the existence of something that we call the mind, prejudges the whole thing. And if we make a prejudgement that we have got a worrying mind then of course it goes on worrying. But if we don't assume it, we can question it. What is this thing that I'm calling a mind or a heart, which is this worrying entity? If I drop it or I stop assuming that it's there, is this pacifying the heart, pacifying the mind?

Let's see if we can enter into a discussion with Master Nuri. "Master Nuri that's all very well, but I mean I am worried, I am concerned, I have a mind don't I? I spend my whole time fussing." "Yes," says the teacher, "that's true, but look actually what you're doing. You're assuming there is a thing there called "you" - called your mind. You're making an assumption. Why don't you actually look at what experience is, the process of experience itself. What do you then find? Do you find a thing?"

Hmm okay, so let's sit and do that.

Now those of us who have sat and done a good deal of meditation will realise that you don't find a "thing". What you find is a kind of ongoing, flowing experience.

Yet, when we come out of that and start talking, we speak about the mind, the entity, myself, me, ego. And what we then do is grab hold of that thought as if it were a thing. We also give it a name - John. So by my own attributing of a name, an entity, to this flowing experience, I generate an object, a reification which I then grab hold of. "That's me!" And this me, called John, should be peaceful, must be enlightened, must be clever, must be handsome, must be perennially young. And if you're perhaps a lady, you must be forever beautiful, forever desirable, forever lovable. Me, this idea, must have those qualities, and if I don't have any of those things or if they are threatened or if I have a doubt about them, then this apparent thing called John gets depressed.

We can see there's an assumption here, the assumption of the importance of being John, or being Simon, or being Jane, or any one of us. The Jane-ity of our existence, the Simon-ness of my being, the John-ness of who one is, becomes terribly important as an object which has to be tinkered with, corrected, improved, made more beautiful. We spend our whole time fussing about it. It's called self-concern.

But supposing instead of indulging in self-concern, I actually look at experience.

The best way of doing that is in meditation, because in meditation we may manage to drop all the words. You will find 90 per cent of the words in your head are about 'muggins'- me. I challenge you to look at your thoughts to check this. Of course if you're studying for an examination or playing a piece of music, you may not then be thinking of yourself, but, okay, you stop playing the piece of music and you think, "Ah, I did that well!" or "Oh, what a mess I'm making of this essay," or "Oh dear, my meditation is so appalling," or "I'm so sorry, I've not done meditation for a whole week."

People sometimes come to me apologising as if they should be doing meditation the whole time, as if it concerned me! Self-concern. Check it out. I think you'll find maybe 85 per cent, but possibly even 95 per cent of the time that your mind is just spinning freely, it's about muggins. We all are making an assumption as to how important this heart-mind, this "muggins" is.

The beauty of meditation is that, after a while, (and those of you who've done a fair amount meditation will know this to be true) somehow that self-concern gets put on the back-burner or may even be dropped. And, although one is aware one is still Jane sitting on a cushion, one is not preoccupied with that, one is not assuming the importance of it any longer. And what do you then find? Well, you find experience of awareness just flowing. Instead of saying, "What is the mind?" we could say, "What is a river? What is its true nature?" You might reply, "A river is water." In the same way as one would ask, "What am I? What is my true nature?"

and you'd reply, "Well, I am a mind" Going further you might add, just as a river is water so a mind is experience.

Let's penetrate further. If I say to you, "Come, let's go down to the river today," It's not quite the same thing as saying, "Come, let's go to the water today," is it? The river is something bigger than just the water. The river is herons, otters, children splashing, willows, birds flying over, seagulls up from the estuary, fish, trout, salmon, and water. And the water that you looked at five minutes ago is not there. The water itself is not the water, it is water. It's a flowing ongoing movement.

If we take this metaphor for the river as being a metaphor for the mind, then we might ask, "Well what is this experience which sometimes churns up all these pains and agonies and worries?" I begin being concerned about this thing- this mind. Sometimes in Zen meditation I relax and go away from it, stop searching and it's peaceful, and I find something which could almost be called freedom. Freedom from being me, which is the most profound of all freedoms. And one knows that everything is part of the river. Maybe the freedom from being me is like seeing an otter. "Hey, there's an otter down there, beautiful, rare creature, an otter." Maybe it's like that.

So what is this awful noise that goes on all the time, this negative side of our preoccupation? In Buddhism it's called karma, the stream of karma. Karma is very similar to what in our Western vocabulary we would call neurosis. Neurosis itself would be particularly obsessive karma. Yet karma is not merely obsessive, it is anything that comes out of one's past and which is influencing one's present. In our psychotherapeutic mode, we talk about neurosis and conditioning and all the influence of the past which has come down to cause us distress. I dare say all of us here are neurotic in one way or another, well I'm quite certain we are, no doubt about it!

We know that when we're behaving neurotically, it is like an obsession. Something crops up and goes round and round. Yet karma is also the memories of joyous experiences which, when remembered, can become reborn in the present. Karma comprises the memories, complex, emotionally laden memories, which are constantly being reactivated by associations in the present time. They come up again and again and again, in various patterns. Karma, however, is also open to novelty arising in the now. It's quite wrong to think that one's present moment is totally determined by one's past.

Out of the past have come the moments which evoke distress in the present. One needs to allow that flow to occur. If one becomes fixated in certain attitudes towards that stream of the past which keeps cropping up in one's life, it's like "assuming the mind". One assumes that I'm a so and so, I'm a neurotic, I'm - whatever word it might be - I'm somebody who's been abused. I'm somebody who had a certain kind of mum, or a certain kind of dad. Karma is more than that. In karma, we also talk often about past life experiences. I'm not going to argue about what the nature of past life experiences might be, but certainly it is true that things that happened before our birth do affect us now. The karma of other people's lives comes down to us. For example, I know that that the life of my great grandmother affected my granny, which affected my mother, which affected me. Down through the generations comes the karma of the distant past, so far distant we can no longer trace it. It goes back through our culture. Most of us here are either English, or Welsh, or Chinese, we each have these cultural histories, sometimes of conflict, which goes down through the past, and crop up again in the present.

When we look at our experience in meditation, what we commonly see is the unrolling of some aspect of our karma. When we reach a point when we can drop that, no longer assuming the importance of the mind, we can see the mind's content is karma, all the unrolling karma is of the mind. This is what the mind is full of. When we identify with that content, making it "mine", we feel the distress and the worry. When we drop it, what do we find?

Well... we find something like silence, something like peace. We know of course that the content of the mind will come up again very quickly and very easily. A memory will trigger something that then emerges yet again. This silence provides a context for the content of the mind. If we put that content to one side, we then perceive the context within which that content operates. And the context is stillness, silence, motionless. As in this very room.... at this moment, the content of this room is the noise which my voice is making. Yet this voice, this noise that I'm making, appears in a certain context, this particular Chan Hall. And if I stop making that noise..... the hall is peaceful.

The Chan Hall furthermore also has a context. The context of this autumn day, the leaves falling off trees, the sun shining, and the brook running. The owl calling in the early morning before light. The experiential context of being in this room is never still. Like the universe itself, all is moving. If you want to grab hold of something and hold it still, permanently there, you're on the wrong track. That would also be making an assumption. You assume that you can get something. There is no "thing" standing in isolation by itself. The universe as a whole is continuously moving.

With training, we drop the content of our worries and discover the context within which those worries are occurring. Becoming context is freedom. The noise of the mind is its own prison. Put the prison aside and you find the space within which it existed. It's like visiting the river, and not being preoccupied with the nature of water.

Our two stories point to an essential, central pivot on which the whole practice of Chan balances, this curious relationship between thought and experience without thought. Dogen, the great Soto Zen master, points out that there is thought (shiriyo) and there is no thought (mu-shiryo) which is the suppression of thought. Yet the really important thing is to be without thought (hi-shiriyo), not to bother about thought or no thought, just be without it. Being "without thought" is when the mind begins to be open to the spacious context in which we live, and which is the current aspect of the universe itself. We exclude ourselves from the universe by identifying with the "little me" of vexation. When I let the "little me" go there is a sense of merging with these progressive layers of context - the room, the garden, the sky, the universe.

This capacity to free oneself from the worrisome content of self-concern, and to let oneself drift or fall into the spaciousness of experience itself, a spaciousness which is always available, is the essence of Zen. It is going to the place before one's mother or father existed.

It's a bit like those games we play as children, when you write a letter to Mummy, and it's addressed to the street, the town, the country, the continent, the planet Earth, the galaxy, the sky, the universe, and then you run out of words altogether. I dare say most of you have written such a letter and pushed it in the post box. God knows what the postman thought of it! Perhaps he got enlightened.

There are many ways in which such an opening comes about. Karma determines the way. There are those of us who have very obsessive minds, heavily preoccupied within the karmic stream. They have to work very hard to break out of their obsessions. There are others who by dint of great discipline on the cushion, can find peace and quiet. There are others who just spot it as an insight straight away, "Yes of course, it's obvious." Yet the first two types, the ones who are obsessively worried and the ones who sit in a silence of self- suppression, they also can have that insight at any moment. There's no way of predicting it.

What is the insight? Dropping the content and discovering the context. Context is the universe merging within us, and we will find as we go on talking, this word "merging" will come forward as a prime teaching. Merging with... what? Why can't we use a word for it? We have to go beyond words, because then we won't be caught up by them. Why review in words? Too long a journey. Don't assume the mind.

"Now I'll count up to twelve and you keep quiet, I'll disappear."

1 This talk was first given at Sharpham College in October 2002 and extended in teaching at the Maenllwyd. The taped version has been generously and skilfully transcribed by Stuart McLeod to whom I am most grateful. The transcription has been lightly edited to make it a readable text.

2 See: Myokyo-ni and M Bromley. 1988. A Treatise on The Ceasing of Notions. An early Zen text from Tun-huang with commentary by Soko Morinaga Roshi. Zen Centre. London.

3 In Chinese, the word which stands for mind is not very well translated by the English word mind. That's why sometimes it's called the heart, it's not just the intellectual capacity but the heartfelt mindfulness of being.

BOOK REVIEW: KEN JONES, ARROW OF STONES

British Haiku Society. 2002 (ISBN: 0-95223974-4)

Ken Jones has contributed much to engaged Buddhism in the UK through his noteworthy books and to the Western Chan Fellowship through his retreat and event offerings. Now he emerges as a prize-winning poet in a genre that is novel, difficult and highly imaginative. The haibun which Ken writes are a form of poetry that originated in Japan wherein short poems in the manner of haiku alternate with poetic prose poetry to create an image of unusual intensity and clarity. Such pieces are usually quite short, a page or two. The intensity of their impact could not be further sustained by a reader.

Haibun originated in the autobiographical account of his journey on foot to the north of Japan by the well-known seventeenth century Zen master Matsuo Basho but has fallen more or less out of literary usage in Japan in modern times. The emergence of haibun in English owes much to the Japanese originals although the poems do not of course follow the strict rules for the Japanese language. A number of collections have appeared in Britain and North America in the last five years. Some of these are relatively homely accounts of excursions or home life with no great literary merit, a form of diary writing one might say. Yet even these are adventures in creativity that are certainly to be encouraged. Ken Jones, in his introduction to this collection, is concerned with the more literary forms and he discusses the criteria by which they may be judged.

In his rugged style Ken's judgements are characteristically forthright. "A large proportion of Western haibun are bald narratives rendered in colourless and banal prose, with a bland earnestness devoid of feeling, irony or any subtlety." He ponders whether North American haiku sometimes show a "deficiency in ironic statement, black comedy and tongue in cheek ambiguity." Yet he concludes that the distinction between what is "natural haibun" as distinct from the literary form does not run across any clear cultural lines. The key question for Ken is whether a putative haibun has any literary form, any poetry about it. Does it enlarge our imaginative sensibility? Does it call on iconic imagery from the past to illustrate a felt situation in the present? Given the Zen origin of this form one may also ask whether there is sensitivity to transience, mindful awareness, perhaps compassion. Ken's introductory essay is invaluable for he sets out clear criteria by which such questions may be answered. The essay must be one of the most important contributions to the understanding of this field.

Ken's contributions in "Arrow of Stones" are an impressive achievement. Each one creates a specific "atmosphere" around an ordinary event, watching seals off Worms Head, receiving the results of a biopsy, coming across a ruined cottage in remote Wales, a one- night stand sharply remembered, sorting out old papers before moving house. Not surprisingly they all illustrate Ken's criteria for the literary form which he is strongly promoting here.

Underlying these poems one feels the Celtic imagination at work for Ken is very much a child of his native land. Indeed the Welsh background sometime resonates vividly:

"Close knit, we're always passing in this dead-end lane. Here comes Olwen and her cross- eyed dog. Been baking a cake for the Christmas party. 'Ah yes, Mr Jones, Arranging the almonds like little soldiers upon the icing.' 'Very nice.' I say .We both pause for thought. Then she goes on about Jesus".

Some passages are downright eerie. Ken settles into his high backed chair having thrown away old postcards and letters:

"The silence settles. The lawn is in twilight. And then I hear them.

Flying in low

over dusty fields

wild duck."

In such passages one can feel the rhythms of Welsh speech with its magical lilt and covert immediacy of expression. Indeed I feel these poems would translate very well into Welsh and I hope someone tries it for they are particularly a contribution to contemporary Welsh writing in English.

Yet - it is into Japanese they have gone. And the book amazingly includes the introduction and all the poems in full translation into Japanese by Sakaguchi Akiko and Professor Nobuyoki Yuasa, all printed in Japanese calligraphy. This is because an earlier book of which Ken was part author (together with Jim Norton and Sean O'Connor of Ireland), won the coveted Sasakawa Prize for "original contributions in the field of haiku" in 2001; the criteria being the presence of the spirit of haiku, the very nature of the writer shining through the life lived, a spiritual journey undertaken.

On the strength of this award Ken has recently visited Japan on a tour presenting Western haiku to Japanese audiences and naturally many of these were his own work. One cannot help wondering how the Japanese respond to the Celtic atmosphere of these poems and the translation from the colloquial must have posed severe problems.

> "From lamp to lamp
> a rakish fellow
> striding forward, falling back"

All lovers of poetry should have a copy of this remarkable work.

NCF XXIX

POLISH MEMORIES

Small town - Northern Poland

Almost forgotten,
moss covered mounds
in a forest
not so easily found,
no crosses here,
no stones of remembrance.

Cries of pain echo
the lamentations of tall trees
falling bodies leave
blood upon the leaves,
lorry departing
another load from the locked synagogue.

Revolver shot –
old man
unable to walk the path to the pit
one final solution.

Synagogue museum
respectful young Poles play
the wild music of lost
grey memories haunting the wintry woods.

Klamerz in Kazimierz

Kazimierz in Krakow
Another synagogue museum
Film clips from the thirties
Nazi documentaries 1943

Restaurants gleam with light
Goose necks washed down with kosher wine
Returned to the descendants of the Auschwitz dead
Property owners do well today

Rents are high
The district fashionable
One old lady from Schindler's list survives
Her memories of the film.

A photo on the museum wall
Close up - big head
His horsewhip under the chin - old woman
The guilt of not being there.

2003

THE UNIVERSITY OF BATH ACTION RESEARCH AND MINDFULNESS RETREAT

Closing words, Maenllwyd April 2003

This is our last morning together. So what abiding thought might one take away from visiting Maenllwyd? Perhaps it goes something like this. There is a strong tendency in modern philosophical thought to suppose that life is contained in texts, in language, and that all we need to do is to deconstruct and examine texts. This is completely an antithesis of Zen. Zen argues for a very intimate connection between language and silence. And unless there is silence, language can take off into what we have been calling "the secondary", so that one becomes progressively distanced from both the subject of mind and the object of mind, into a world that is somehow free-floating, nothing but cognition without contact, context without content.

The message of Zen, with its stress on clarity, silence, no words, no mind, is that all this effluvia of language is anchored in something which Buddhists call the essence of mind or the Buddha nature, which are simply words for silence. And this silence is simply the essence of suchness. One needs to be able to relax out of language into the silence of suchness, because this is where energy lies, life begins. So if you take away from Maenllwyd the awareness of the need for repetitive anchoring in silence, then the words can run, and there is no problem, because there is always the return to the safe anchorage. But if one forgets that, and takes off into increasingly abstract language, one ends up in the state which one started with, being an anxious academic. The anchorage lies in something quite non-academic, that is in simplicity, hearing, seeing, being in one's body, hearing the crows calling in the early morning, and the returning migrants tweeting in the trees. You know they come all the way from Africa, but you don't have to think about it.

So, before we have our tea, just take a walk around the yard. Be aware of the silence of the suchness of this dawn moment. The Tibetans have a lovely phrase. They say "when son and mother meet". What they mean is that the universe is always in the silence of suchness, that's the mother. And when the son, that is all of us, returns to the clear light of bliss, the clear light of silence, then the son and the mother meet.

NCF XXX

THIRTY YEARS OF MEDITATION IN WALES

It seems incredible that thirty years have passed since I began to offer meditation retreats at the Maenllwyd. We began with Enlightenment Intensives held in a ruin of a cottage remote from the world. One of them was led by Jeff Love who taught me how to master this process. This was all part of the programme of the Bristol Encounter Centre which I had created earlier with psychotherapeutic friends following my return from California. Gradually we moved to presenting Soto Zen meditation and eventually Shifu came over to support my endeavours and the Western Chan Fellowship was formed. So much history, so many feelings and states of mind embedded in those well juiced walls! It's odd to remember holding full retreats in the Buddha Room which seems so small today. Old hands have much to remember and be grateful. This issue is a celebration of these thirty years. It looks ahead with accounts of the training of Guestmasters, important book reviews concerning Buddhism and both therapy and social engagement, and a response to our recent articles on Buddhism and science. Shifu returns us to our roots with an account of the foundation teachings of the great Master Linji. Enjoy

GUESTMASTERS IN TRAINING

We now have in place a policy for the training of Guestmasters on our retreats. Here I outline the way whereby I am seeking to create retreat officers of distinction who will eventually continue the intensive work of the Fellowship well into future years. It feels appropriate to share these issues as part of our celebratory journal.

As most readers will know our Training Policy envisages inviting willing people to function first as Time Keepers or Workmasters in which roles they gain a thorough knowledge of how the retreat is presented, its schedule, timing and stages of development over the period of the retreat.

The role of Guestmaster is undertaken by invitation. It means working closely with the Retreat Master in the detailed organisation and monitoring of a retreat. There are two main aspects of this job. Firstly there is the care of the participants, ensuring they are comfortable in their lodgings and understand the rules, answering any questions, encouraging the faint hearted and levelling the pompous or misguided.

The second aspect is that of Disciplinarian who, gently at first, but with ultimate severity, corrects any failures in retreat procedure or rules on the part of a participant. A truly problematic participant will be interviewed by the Retreat Master and may be requested to leave.

Guestmasters develop their own style and usually welcome the greatly increased insight into the whole process that comes from caring for others. It can be a worrying job especially perhaps on the first days of a WZR when many newcomers to retreat may be present. The Guestmaster shares with the Retreat Master all aspects of the retreat as it unfolds and the two will often confer together, sharing their impressions.

After several retreats functioning in this way, a Guestmaster may be asked to participate in the interviews of participants, first as an observer and then in trying their own hand under supervision at interviewing participants and facilitating their process. This interviewing process lies at the heart of a successful retreat both in terms of a participant's new understanding and in terms of the communal experience of all. Training here must be highly critical and responsive. For example, psychotherapists may have problems in adjusting their skilled techniques to the demands of running a Zen interview. The purpose is not the same.

Ultimately a senior Guestmaster may be entrusted with Mastering a retreat under supervision and eventually alone relying on their own experience and training.

The principles are the same for all types of retreat. In the course of such training the trainee is faced by the powerful authority of the Retreat Master and this can easily give rise to fantasies and projection which sometimes take quite strong forms that the Guestmaster-trainee has to understand and control. All strong teachers are used to the mildly Oedipal reactions their best students commonly manifest and both Master and Guestmaster need to share these to undo any possible misunderstandings.

Guestmaster and Master form a strong team and the ultimate success of a retreat depends on their skills in managing the shifting moods and styles of experience revealed by participants. Although any one person's realisations are a result of their own willingness to work hard, there is no doubt that skilful interviewing and precise Guestmaster intervention can often bring a troubled practitioner through to realisations he or she might not otherwise have had.

In NCF 25 we presented a retreat report from Jake Lyne in such training, and in NCF 28 Nigel Jeffcoat presented his report on Guestmastering a Mahamudra retreat.

Here we present Fiona Nuttall's report of her first experience as a Guestmaster. Others no doubt will follow. Good fortune to them all!!

NCF XXXI

EDITORIAL LOOKING TO THE FUTURE

Chuan-deng Jing-di March 26, 2005

This text is based upon the Teachers Report to the AGM held at the Maenllwyd in February 2005.

Current successes

During the last year the Western Chan Fellowship has continued to function effectively according to its constitution and there have been a number of valued developments. The committee has also begun the task of considering the direction the Fellowship should follow in the long term. This discussion has arisen from articles in NCF by Jake Lyne and myself (NCF 27 Winter 2002) and from a request from Eddy Street following his election as Chair.

Most of our retreats at the Maenllwyd have been well filled or full and appear to have been successful in facilitating participants' understanding and practice of Buddha dharma. We continue to receive appreciative and often heart-warming reports of retreat experiences and learning. In addition, a number of retreats elsewhere in the country have been well supported and generated some enthusiasm leading to more people coming to the Maenllwyd. In particular, the Medway Towns group under the leadership of Stuart McLeod has held very valuable events at an excellently equipped location. Our association with Gaia House has continued. Bristol has continued to present excellent weekend events for retreatants mainly in the South West. Short retreats are being held in Manchester and York. Local groups have appeared in Totnes, Stroud and become well established in Cornwall and York but our London (Hampstead) group has folded after Will Turner decided to cease hosting them. London remains a blank on the map for us and we need to establish a good group there. We also have no group currently operating in Scotland and the Aberystwyth associated group is operating only uncertainly.

I have led retreats in Poland and Norway where the local Sanghas continue to flourish. In Norway the Hrydaya group, under the leadership of Thøger Nordbo, has now run two retreats led by myself, and Simon will be going there this year. Plans are afoot for a retreat in Lithuania based on the Oslo group. The Norwegian group is affiliated to us and Thøger and others are attending our retreats in the UK for leadership training. We are gradually establishing a firm working relationship with the small Norwegian Sangha, which we encourage to develop through wider recruitment.

Last Spring, Simon, Hilary and I led a Western Zen Retreat in Pine Bush near New York for the Dharma Drum Mountain of Master Sheng Yen. Retreat reports in the latest Chan magazine (Winter 2005) show considerable appreciation of this event although numbers were low probably because of poor advertisement. This year we will be returning again hoping for better support.

Simon and I attended a conference of European teachers of Buddhism near Munich in September and were able to witness the divergence of views and practices in European Buddhism as a whole. The atmosphere was warm, cordial and we all clearly shared a profound faith in the value of the Buddha Dharma which came to underpin our emerging relationships. Compared with this rooted faith, the divergences of view and practice appeared of little significance. Such meetings bode well for future collaboration between the differing schools of Buddhism in Europe. In the UK, Sally Masheder is doing major service in this same direction as the Secretary of the NBO.

Simon and I continue to train Guestmasters at several levels (see NCF 30 Summer 2004). In fact we would like to respond to one or two more individuals who wish to participate in such training. A problem here is that the number of retreats available for training purposes is limited and this is an issue we shall have to consider seriously in the immediate future.

Issues of Concern

All of this is generally to the good and we can be happy at the way the Fellowship is functioning so far as retreat presentation and the teaching of practice is concerned. In other respects however there are some sources for concern.

The number of people becoming Fellows remains very small and the total membership of the charity is little changed from the time of its inauguration. It looks as if people may be personally inspired on retreats but not in such a way that a commitment to an involvement with the charity emerges. This means the charity remains dependent on the leadership of its founders who are inevitably getting older.

The gender ratio among retreatants remains strongly male oriented. This is especially marked in the figures for our up-coming three-week retreat where nine males (to date) are attempting the whole period but no women are doing so. We need to keep encouraging women to attend retreats because those who do so benefit equally as much as men do. Our senior women fellows need to consider this issue further and make proposals.

The WCF has numerous facilities for the teaching and practice of Dharma that are barely supported, indeed neglected, by both Fellows and others who attend retreats. For example, there are now facilities for personal or solitary retreats available both at the Maenllwyd and at the newly established Winterhead Retreat House in Somerset. Occasional use of these facilities happens but they are basically ignored to a point of neglect. Personal retreats up to eight weeks long are possible at Winterhead and retreats of about two weeks duration are possible at the Maenllwyd - for two persons in residence in each place at a time. The beautiful new Hut at the Maenllwyd has come on stream during the year. Summer retreats in the hut would certainly be a delight for anyone undertaking to do one. Only about seven persons have used these facilities for never more than around seven days in the last twelve months. Such retreatants have valued their experiences but this has not led to a wider use.

There is a very good library available for consultation at the Maenllwyd. Individuals could therefore carry out reading and writing retreats using the library as a source for study. Books are also available in my own library at Winterhead. Two persons have used their retreat time for study at Winterhead but so far the extensive library at the Maenllwyd remains totally unused.

These considerations mean that Fellows and retreatants are not making use of the facilities available to them through the WCF. One conclusion would be that most people who attend retreats are beginners or people simply exploring occasionally the relevance of a Buddhist experience in their lives. However good a retreat experience may be, the demands of the Dharma may then subsequently be left aside as the claims of conventional life resume. Other, perhaps more regular participants, may be essentially Dharma "hobbyists" (to use Simon Child's phrase). That is to say, people who pop in and out of retreats much as one might pop in and out of a counselling room for occasional psychotherapy. This remedial use of retreat is of course entirely acceptable and helpful in these stressful times but hardly amounts to a commitment to practice or action in the true Buddhist sense. Those who use retreats as an adjunct to a seriously conceived and thought through daily commitment to the development of bodhicitta remain few. We are, none the less, fortunate that among those coming forward to train as Guestmasters are several insightful practitioners upon whom the future of the WCF will eventually rely.

Development Possibilities and Plausibilities

These reflections naturally bear on thoughts regarding possible developments of the WCF. It has become clear that major European Buddhist institutions are founded on two principles: firstly, a devoted group of loyalists who give up conventional life to live often communally as "home-leavers" in close affinity to a guru or lama, secondly, such institutions are housed in a communal dwelling similar to a monastic setting. Some such institutions have expanded by creating related institutions sometimes worldwide. They are major success stories with well developed "business plans" for their maintenance and profitable expansion.

In considering our future, one thought has been that we should to some degree follow this same line of development. There are plausible possibilities for property development at both the Maenllwyd and Winterhead but the detailed examination of such ideas reveal considerable complexity and solicitors advice would be needed. Alternatively the accumulation of funds for the purchase of a quite separate location could be envisaged. Either way a case is being made for the development of a considerable property fund to enable action to be taken in whatever way seems most appropriate. In principle I support this idea but there are problems.

Firstly our institution is not set up in this manner either in terms of a constitution nor in terms of the general motivation of Fellows or retreatants. Previously, plans for a local centre in Southampton along somewhat similar lines were completely disregarded by the membership. As we have seen, support for personal retreats is very limited. Certainly the idea of pushing towards something like a monastic–type solution is coming from the top. There is no evidence of any grass roots demand for it within the charity. Few show signs of leaving conventional life styles in some practice of "home leaving". Those about to retire might well consider such a course of action however and this could be successful. Yet we should not risk getting ourselves into the business of creating a retirement home! While the idea of creating a sort of monastery does attract me, there is no doubt any move in this direction must come from would-be monks. I don't see many of these around in our Sangha.

Secondly, although Fellows certainly express loyalty and a lot of kindness to me together with gratitude for the work I do, I see no evidence of a demand for me to function more in the role of a residential teacher. In any case, I am not at all sure whether I would like to undertake this - especially outside the context of the Maenllwyd or Winterhead.

One committee member has raised serious doubts about this whole line of thought. Perhaps it would be better to consider other lines of development, he suggests. It remains true that the WCF is a unique institution in the manner by which it brings the Dharma to many individuals. Perhaps we need to consider how this may be improved rather than changed to a different type of institution. The large scale financing required for property investment and utilisation would require a comprehensive and professional business plan managed responsibly by several competent persons. This would introduce a very different kind of government within the WCF and opportunities for personal rivalries around contrasting policies. Solving the koan Mu might move very much onto a back burner.

Models for Development

Even so there are several models of development that we should consider. For reasons already discussed, the creation of a residential monastery seems unlikely to be supported. In any case, Ken Jones has reminded me that such Buddhist houses as already exist are by no means always exemplary. Dependencies on teachers and institutions arise, community life generates its own in-group tensions and divisions over policy. Personal antagonisms or prejudices fester. Authority may be heavy-handed or not strong enough. The goal of residential life may become lost in communal discussion. Yet alternative institutional patterns are provided by Gaia House, the varying forms of Sharpham College, the Golden Buddha project and so on.

One form of institution that might work would be a natural extension of our existing practices. It could be that in a suitable establishment with facilities for retreat and adult education a small group of retired "elders" (say two persons) could provide a core for the quality management of a system involving various patterns of residence (one day events, short term group retreats, personal retreats, longer term staffing). They would commit themselves for a year or two and receive support from a further small contingent of existing fellows (say 2 people at most) committed to residence for say four months at a time on a rotating basis within the fellowship as a whole. The programme would be constructed by the committee, approved by the Teacher and supervised by our Dharma Heirs functioning in some form of abbacy for the whole. I can imagine such a social structure working quite well in a constructed centre on the ground available at Winterhead. I believe such an experiment could work but again the drive for it must come from the membership and not merely from within the committee. I place this idea in the open for discussion.

In the meantime the most important thing is to develop the relations between our various local groups through "networking". At the Leaders Retreat 2005 Ken Jones gave an eloquent presentation on what this would mean. In effect we have the roots of such a process well established. Some local groups already interact with one another, run retreats inviting outside speakers or facilitators and talk with one another. A more developed network of such interactions needs to be developed both formally and informally. Email linkages, visits between local leaders giving, in some cases, short talks or opening discussions and sharing common problems. The Dharma Heirs will endeavour to get around at least the larger groups hopefully to provide inspiration and Dharma instruction. We seek opinions on such developments and the committee empowered by the AGM will be making suggestions also.

Conclusion

I think we do need to establish a fund for eventualities that might include substantial property development or even purchase but a great deal more thought needs to be put into the whole matter and some demand for it stemming from the fellowship itself has yet to be demonstrated. Development may however take many forms and perhaps what we need at this time is a more mature policy to underpin with funding resources to be made available to support local events, joint ventures and networking projects in general. This discussion must continue for we cannot simply rest on our attainments so far.

BIRD DAWN IN MENDIP

At daybreak come the raucous crows
and jackdaws yacketing
down from the wooded cliffs
and tall, tossed branches
of their nightly stay
straight to our beech trees
and chimneys too.
In joyful disarray
they shout down rude comments
on a windy dawn
peer at curtained windows
telling us how to greet the day.

Only the ravens stay on high
solitary upon the escarpment's sweep.
Mates in tow they take the air
and play in updrafts off the crags
swoop and interweave
the patterns of their flight
until at last they perch upon a topmost bough
and stretch their necks
in honking chorus at the rising sun.

CAPEL HAGIA SOFIA

The Interfaith Chapel of Divine Wisdom

In early February, following the Silent Illumination retreat at the Maenllwyd, I spent a few days with Ken and Noragh Jones in their beautifully secluded home in the quiet valley of Cwmrheidol. Ken and I had decided to climb over the massive hump of Plynlimon to visit Ken's "cave" among the crags and his Kuanyin shrine in the valley nearby. But the morning dawned under dense cloud cover and we almost gave up. Knowing Ken was an old man of the mountain I none the less ventured up into the thick mists. Ken surprised himself by getting lost and we had left the compass behind, but by idling around a bit in the fog we finally located landmarks and came down the far shoulder into the one of the remotest, wildest, least visited cwms in Wales. We moved the small rock slabs from the entrances to the tiny, hidden shrines and conducted liturgies consisting of Buddhist devotions and some wild shamanic mantras in the style of Guru Rimpoche. For moments at a time the cloud lifted and the vast reaches of the mountain were adorned with mysterious light.

Next day we attended a remarkable little ceremony in the village of Pennal near Aberdovey famous during the brief rule of Glendower. Here Father Geraint ap Iorworth has established an interfaith chapel on the upper floor of his little house. It is dedicated to the wisdom common to all faiths as epitomised in Christianity by Saint Sofia. We assembled in church for an account of the reasons behind the event and then after a hearty meal of Cawl and rolls in the village hall we drifted along the main road to the little chapel bearing candles in the fading light.

I had been asked to bring my robes but in the absence of Hindus, Sikhs and orthodox Moslems I found that only Bishop Anthony of Bangor and I were dressed in style. "Showing the flag!" said Ken. Readings from Orthodox Christians, Quakers, Sufis and Buddhists in both English and Welsh followed the dedication ceremony led by Bishop Anthony. I read a lightly edited version of the Metta Sutta as prepared by Christopher Titmus. It seemed appropriate for such an occasion.

> May all beings be happy.
> May all be joyous and live in safety.
>
> Let no one deceive another,
> Nor despise another, weak as they may be. Let no one by anger or by hate
> Wish evil for another.
>
> As a mother, in peril of her own life, Watches and protects her only child, So with limitless spirit
> one cherishes all living beings.
>
> Love the world in its entirety Above, below and all around, Without limitation
> With an infinite goodness and benevolence.

Standing or walking, sitting or lying down

As long as one is awake

Let one cultivate loving kindness.

This is called the supreme way of living.

Such activities raise questions about interfaith work within Buddhism. It is not my intention to consider them in depth here for it is a multilayered question with experiential, ontological and philosophical components. There is however a text by Raimon Pannikkar, which everyone faced by an interfaith event should contemplate prior to participation. And this must apply to us as Chan practitioners. I offer it here, lightly edited, for your thoughtful perusal.

The Sermon on the Mount of Inter-religious Dialogue

When you enter into an inter-religious dialogue, do not think beforehand what you have to believe.

When you witness to your faith, do not defend yourself or your vested interests, sacred as they may appear to you. Behave like the birds in the skies: they sing and fly and defend neither their music nor their beauty.

When you dialogue with somebody, look upon your partner as a revelatory experience, as you would and should regard the lilies in the fields.

Try first to remove the beam in your own eye before the speck in the eye of your neighbour.

Blessed are you when you do not feel self-sufficient while being in dialogue. Blessed are you when you trust the other because you trust your faith.

Blessed are you when you face misunderstandings from your own community for the sake of your fidelity to truth.

Blessed are you when you do not give up your convictions and yet do not set them up as absolute norms.

Woe unto you theologians and academics when you dismiss what others say because you find it embarrassing or insufficiently learned.

Woe unto you, practitioners of religions, when you do not listen to the cries of the little ones.

Woe unto you, religious authorities, because you prevent change and connection.

Woe unto you, religious people, because you monopolise religion and stifle the spirit which blows where and how she wills.

SEPARATION

The silence that has fallen
here's forever:
carpetless your busy room,
embedded still the presences
of absent furniture,
empty bookshelves, departed garden tools,
flowering pots, patches of empty wall
where pictures hung -
so strange is time -
this ancient photograph lost behind a
list of phone numbers -
so long ago - the way you look at me
and I so vigorous - was that my prime?
The place is gently haunted now-
alone before the ten-o'clock news
memories of two cats gaze beyond the horizon
and distant donkeys bray.

I do believe it's much more difficult
staying behind -
the ghosts in your place
are unfamiliar
they will not trouble you.
Here they come through doors
unexpectedly
or creak along corridors
or run a bath.
The place vibrates in its past

immediate
the gaps in decoration
becoming doors
to sudden pictures
drown the heart.
The farm is restless now, reproachful,
distractedly a place in silence.

It's making cheerful phone calls
as if nothing in particular
has happened that does it --
At least you watched the ten o'clock
news with me where even timbers
now refuse to creak:
funny how these memories
are of happy things remorsefully recalled.
You will not be coming back.

It's final.

NCF XXXII

EDITORIAL: THE LONDON ATROCITIES

Within a few hours of the bombs in London, Simon and I received phone calls from Shifu's secretary asking after us and the welfare of Fellowship members especially in London. We are grateful that none of us have been killed or maimed in these events. Some of us, however, will be closer to the dead and to bereaved families than others. The fact that the bombers were British Muslims from Yorkshire has made us realise that the whole nation is involved in the process of neutralising such dangerous criminals and considering the reasons behind such an appalling event. It is of course a matter for national shame.

It will be a long time before the full story is told and the reasoning behind such an attack made clear. The confusion around these issues, politically, socially and ethically remains great. We cannot afford not to think about it. There are serious dangers of discord and even violence in areas where multiple faiths live together. It is not enough for religious leaders and politicians to make resounding statements. Everyone must be involved. In this matter there is no place either for thoughts of revenge or for denials concerning a certain degree of responsibility. We need a harsh realism if understanding is to emerge on so painful and so divisive an issue.

What seems evident is that a minority of extreme young Muslims, born and brought up here, educated here, lovers of cricket and sports, is so indoctrinated with mindless hate that they are willing to kill and maim large numbers of totally innocent fellow citizens – including fellow Muslims. How can this be?

It will do little good for Islamic leaders to proclaim that such activities are entirely outside Islam, that these people are not Muslims and that the Koran contains nothing that could be used as justification for such attacks. The perpetrators themselves proclaim an extremist version of Islam which, even if it is total anathema to the majority of Muslims and barely capable of any scholarly support, none the less has close links to movements within Islam in the Middle East. Such extreme activities have some historical basis in the strict sects of Arabia (Wahabism) and have found expression in the Taliban movement and in Al Quaeda. Today these ideas are widely disseminated on the Internet and have from time to time been preached in our mosques. What are the roots of such extremism leading ultimately to acts of such barbarity?

There is a deep sense of grievance in the Muslim world. It focuses on the failure of the West to enforce UN resolutions on Israel but has a wider significance in that a minority of extremists see the whole democratic world of the West as an hypocrisy and as an affront to the Islamic faith. In a very general sense of course Muslims are not entirely alone here – the entire anti-globalisation movement and the Western failure to meet the demands of climate change is also engaged, as is the debate over the legality of the Iraq war.

What gives this grievance an irrational and barbarous turn is the poverty, deprivation and lack of political representation for such issues in the dictatorial, authoritarian and often corrupt government of many Islamic nations. Where a significant number of people feel powerless to engage in adequate reform or heal the wounds of the Middle East a process is set in motion quite well understood by social psychologists such as the late Professor Henri Tajfel of Bristol University.

Where a minority is unable to achieve representation or influence within a majority there is a tendency to turn within, to reject the social norms of the majority, to seek revolution and to create a world view of revenge and destruction often with a 'spiritual' justification. These terrorists have principles and beliefs that their behaviour is not only ethical but blessed by God. A few verses in the Koran can evidently be distorted to give such extraordinary assurances.

To heal such world-wide, social sickness, the international community requires not only political action by the great powers but also an extension of the mere condemnation of atrocity to a proper examination of the moral, social and communal environments that allow these failures in political representation to take such drastic turns.

In particular, it is surely vital for the entire Islamic world to face up to its contextual role in such disorders and to engage in vigorous condemnation. Any preaching of an extremist nature in mosques needs to be actively rejected because disaffected youth is especially prone to respond with violence when it appears justified through only too effective propaganda. Within the British Muslim communities young people need to be included in dialogue so that the temptations of extremist views are exposed, openly discussed and the means to transcend them found. The challenge will doubtless be considerable, perhaps requiring something of a renaissance within some aspects of Islam itself. The whole relationship between Islam and the modern world of participatory democracy and its mechanisms evidently needs a renewed evaluation by the faithful.

Beyond the Islamic world itself, it will be essential for British citizens to resist the marginalisation of our Muslim communities. To this end Buddhists need to study and to express our appreciation of Islamic positivity in so many realms of thought and action. Islam is a religion of righteousness that merits an appropriate respect.

Britain can be proud of its multiracial achievements and the wonderful rainbow city that is modern London, so full of vigour, multicultural expression and the cohesion that engendered the Olympic bid's success. If this is not to be lost in divisiveness, strife and hate, of which Christians in our dubious history, we must recall, are equally capable, each one of us has to think deeply about our contribution to a better world.

Wednesday, July 13, 2005

THE TEN KOANS OF LAYMAN JOHN

In the course of his many years exploring the Dharma, John has had the good fortune to encounter many excellent teachers. At these meetings the conversations could be profound, deeply philosophical, include advice on meditation or simply a sharing in friendship. Now and again however John was thrown a ball he could not catch. These moments were deep occasions for thought and meditation. They remain for John the key turning points in his development of understanding. Since they all had the form of koans he has written them up here in case they may be of interest to others.

John's pilgrimages remind one of Sudhana the young pilgrim in the Avatamsaka Sutra who was sent from one teacher to another in search of wisdom. These teachers came from all walks of life, some reprehensible, some ordinary, some exalted. Every one of them had wisdom to provide, helping him on his journey. The lesson is that buddhas can be found waiting at bus stops, on trains, in the next seat of an aircraft. Sometimes they knock on one's door. Sometimes one glimpses them passing by. With so many buddhas in the world we all need to keep a look out for them and ask them for their help. Keep travelling. Keep asking! (Eds)

1/ Layman John went up to London to see the nun Myoko-ni. As they sat together he told her of his new retreat centre, the retreats he was running and his hopes for its development. He had come to ask for any advice she might have. As time went on Layman John found that Myoko-ni was saying very little. She made no comment nor did she give any advice. So he spoke some more – and then, somewhat hurriedly, again some more. Still no comment. So he stopped and said, "I am wondering what response you have to what I am telling you". Myoko-ni looked at Layman John and said, "I have no response." Layman John suddenly understood.

2/ Layman John was visiting Kyoto. His host, a professor from the biology conference he was attending, took him to meet an English-speaking master living in one of the compounds of Daitokoji temple. The weather was terrible, downpours of rain, lightning and thunder. They sat in a room where a skylight let in the rains that rustled away down some guttering. Layman John was introduced in a flamboyant manner as if he were a Western expert in Zen. He feared the worst. The master smiled in a polite greeting. Just then there was an enormous flash and a roar of thunder. The Master leant forward and said "Doctor John–Tell me - where does the thunder sound?" Layman John hesitated and then muttered something about it being both in the sky and in the head. "Very superficial, Doctor John, Very superficial." commented the Master.

Well then - where does the thunder sound?

3/ At Bo Lin monastery on Lantao Island intensive retreat was in process. Layman John sat entranced. It was his first "sit" in a genuine Chan hall. He was so happy to be there he barely noticed that the sitting lasted one and a half hours starting from four am. The monks were hidden behind the mosquito nets of their cubicles. Three cubicles away sat Master Hsing Yat, a wispy bearded ancient with long sleeves to his robes almost reaching the ground. His shape was dimly visible though the netting. After some time Layman John became aware of strange sound permeating the silence of the hall. "Gnrrrr Gnrrr, sklmp." Layman John wondered what this might be and gradually realised it came straight from the Master's cubicle. The master was richly and sonorously snoring. Layman John had rarely been so delighted. Behind his net he quietly bowed towards the master who suddenly awoke with a snort. Silence resumed in the hall. What about the Master's snoring?

4/ Layman John had been given a rare opportunity. Master Hsing Yat, believing that no mere Englishman could meditate, had none the less approved of John's sitting and permitted a very rare interview. All the monks were jealous.

What was Layman John to ask? He remembered his own teacher's emphasis on method so he asked "Can you tell me what your method is?"

"Method?" almost shouted the Master as if it were a dirty word. "That!" and he pointed to a Chinese scroll hanging on the wall. The characters read "Diamond Sutra."

"How?" responded Layman John

"Like so" responded Master Hsing Yat pointing to another scroll which read "What is it?" End of interview. Layman John bowed.

5/ Layman John was discussing the finer points of the Dharma with Geshe Damchos Yontan at his Lam Rim Centre in Wales. They were deeply into such things as prajnaparamita, madhyamaka and emptiness. They were both quite excited by their discussion. Suddenly Geshe-la stopped and looked at Layman John.

"John", he said. "When were you last kind?"

6/ Shifu and Layman John were walking in Westminster Square. A great swirl of traffic was passing around it, engines roaring, horns hooting. Suddenly in amongst the turning wheels John saw a pile of horse dung neatly stacked just as it had fallen and quite undisturbed by the traffic. It seemed incredible that a living horse should have passed that way in all that traffic and left so clear and neat a testimony to its presence. Layman John drew Shifu's attention to the unlikely pile saying, "Shifu, Look! Here's a pile of horse shit but where's the horse?" Shifu looked at it and said, "What need have we of the horse?"

7/ A small group had gathered at the house of Bodhisattva Krishnamurti to discuss the great matter. Layman John told the story of the Zen master who has ascended the rostrum to deliver his sermon to the monks when a bird had begun singing outside the open windows. He had stood with his flywhisk raised until the bird had finished. Then, lowering his flywhisk, he had said "Oh monks – that is all for today!" and retired to his room. Krishnamurti, that great speaker, said nothing.

8/ Layman John and his wife Eirene were visiting the shrines of Apollo at Delphi. They came to the tiered theatre and while John climbed up on the marble terraces Eirene declaimed the great speeches of the ancient playwrights from the circular stage below. At every point on the terraces the time-sharpened words rang out distinct and clear. John and Eirene were delighted. Ghosts of the ancient world swirled about them. But what about the breeze-filled silences of the pine-clad hills?

9/ The Stagna Rimpoche was in residence at Sani Gompa in Zangskar preparing the place for a visit to the old mountain kingdom by the Dalai Lama. He was busy sewing up brocade hangings on an old sewing machine when Layman John came to tea. Layman John asked the Rimpoche," Rimpoche-la, I have heard that Milarepa, the great yogin, once said that in the vast empty spaces of the high mountains there exists a strange market where one might exchange the vortex of worldly life for boundless bliss. Where might I find such a place?" Still whirring away on his machine, the Rimpoche said, "There are a great many books on such matters. It might be wise to begin there."

10/ Layman John and Yogin James were drinking chang with the yogins Nochung Tse and Gompo up at the little, tree shaded monastery of the Tigress on the Hill in

Zangskar. It was one of many convivial meetings. James said. "John and I have been talking about the mind and the yogins' path to understanding. We want to ask you what you understand by the mind." The two old yogin friends seemed to freeze in shock. Nochung Tse picked up his prayer wheel and begun intoning "On mani padme hum" in a loud voice without pausing. Gonpo looked most uncomfortable, rocking from side to side as if trying to make up his mind. Then he said, "Since the two of you have had the benefits of training in meditation, why don't you go and do it? Then you would have no need to ask such a stupid question!"

EXPLORING THE USE OF KOANS IN CHINESE ZEN

Talk given by John Crook during retreat in the Maenllwyd Chan Hall, 1997. Transcribed by Rob Alexander, edited, abbreviated and compiled by the author.

I'll talk this evening a little bit about the use of koans or questions in the context of Chan practice and I want to do that especially in the light of what we've been practising.

When one first explores the literature of Zen one gets the impression that the use of the Koan or questioning is completely the opposite approach of the type of meditation we've been mainly talking about and practicing here, namely Silent Illumination or, as the Japanese call it, Shikantaza. And there are some good reasons for that impression.

There were, in China, two different schools respectively emphasising a 'gradual' and a 'sudden' approach. In the sudden school the idea was that you could solve the problem with a question based on a koan story to yield an instantaneous discovery, whereas the other way was by study or by sitting on a cushion and slowly making your way to a solution through calming the mind in meditation.

Contemporary scholars have shown that nearly all the discussions that have split Chan into those two attitudes were actually mistaken; that there's much more in common between the two views than had formerly been thought, and furthermore a lot of the polemics was actually, you might say, Buddhist politics.

This distinction has none the less persisted, particularly because in Japan there is a very particular use of the Koan in the Rinzai school contrasted with the very particular use of Shikantaza in the Soto Zen school. Indeed, if you specialise, as it were, in one or the other approaches, they do become two contrasting even competitive methods.

I don't want to spend a lot of time talking about the history of these things. The point I'm coming to is that in Chan of this last century, Master Xu Yun brought many of the different approaches together in one practice that allowed different emphasises that could be chosen as practice depending upon the needs of the monk or meditator.

The reason for this was that the situation of Chan in China in the early part of this last century was chaotic. Even before communism there had been a great deal of destruction of monasteries. Master Xu Yun was instrumental in re-establishing many monasteries and many practices, but in order to do that he had to pick and choose from the surviving methods which were available. He focussed especially on the methods of contemplating the Koan and the methods of Silent Illumination. You could chose your focus and vary the relationship between them. So what we have in Chan today is a remarkably wide range of possible ways of practice.

So, how is the Koan used in present-day Chan derived from the 'reformation' of Master Xu Yun. How does Shifu Sheng yen present it?

If one reads the works of Shifu and Xu Yun together, you get a pretty good picture of how a Koan can be approached in Chan. The way I'd like to talk about it here is to develop the idea of enquiry. After all, questioning a koan is an enquiry. But enquiry also occurs in Silent Illumination. A very important aspect of Silent Illumination is the moment when one looks into the developing silence with the implicit question "What is it that is going on here?" The mind is alert with an enquiry, not a verbal question but an enquiry. It is this enquiry, this alert looking-into the silenced mind, or the silencing mind, that generates illumination. And this is very important for us to realise. It's no good sitting on one's cushion endlessly mulling over the same stuff, one has to really adapt a very questioning viewpoint; not a question as such but a kind of investigative look, what the Chinese called Tsan.

Sometimes you read in the stories of Chan that a master will suddenly shout "Tsan!" My original teacher in Hong Kong, Mr Shiliang Yen used to emphasise this point of "investigation". Investigation in Silent Illumination is an alert looking at what you're on about.

As I have said many times, investigation can be applied at whatever level you're at. In any retreat some people may be sitting there with their minds buzzing with thoughts, worries and troubles. Others may be in a pretty clear condition. There are always great contrasts between people on retreat. People have different karmas, different problems to work with. It would be most surprising if everybody was going at the same speed and doing the same thing. This issue of enquiry applies to whatever stage one is at.

Let's take somebody who is really very troubled by wandering thoughts and issues. As we've said before, what you do with that is ask yourself what on earth you're on about. "What's going on here?"

One doesn't just sit there and let the turmoil whiz round and round and up and down a cul-de-sac, a one-way street. One says to oneself, "Well there's no doubt I'm up a one-way street that's going nowhere, but what am I doing in it, how did I get here, how do I get out?" One takes a dynamic, investigative perspective. This requires a certain toughness, because there may be bits and pieces of that one-way street which you're particularly anxious to avoid, and you may not entirely know, until you actually bump into them, what it is you're avoiding. But that's still part of the investigative business. When the mind is in that state the investigative attitude is very important. Habits are very difficult to break.

Maybe there's another person sitting on the very next cushion who's had one or two blissful moments and is very peaceful, yet somehow it's a bit stale. A similar question applies there. Not so much "What am I going on about?" but "What is this that's happening, what's happening now?" Obviously it is a quieter and less confronting question, but it is appropriately investigative.

I sometimes tell the story of somebody who has goldfish bowl. A friend comes into the room and says, "Oooh, that's a nice goldfish bowl, what's in it?" You look at the goldfish bowl and you see two fishes swimming round, so you say "There are two fishes swimming in the goldfish bowl" and the person says "Anything else?" and you say "Hmmm.... not anything else, just two fishes". "Wrong!" he says, "There's something else in there as well". So you start looking.... you can't see anything but two fishes going round and round, chasing each other and making faces. So you spend a long time looking at this goldfish bowl and seeing two fishes go round in it.

Your friend, keeps saying "Look further, it's not enough, look further, there's something else in there as well!" So after a long time you think "Well, I've really got to look into this." So you sit quietly, collect yourself together, you sit back, and you look at the goldfish bowl, and you say "Well, what's *in* the goldfish bowl. Well first of all course there's the water..... ohhhhh. The WATER, of course, that's what's in there as well as the two fishes, the water, how obvious."

And it's like that. But it requires that investigative, peaceful, slightly withdrawn, let's have a real look at this, eyeing it from one side and then another, the kind of investigative attitude in order to spot what's absolutely obvious. But only obvious afterwards, as it were.

So, as we've been seeing all the time, this attitude of investigation is terribly important in the practice even of a so-called "gradual path"-- which is a dubious misnomer anyway because all realisations are actually sudden. Now what happens if, while you are sitting there, your investigation suddenly takes the form of an actual verbal question.

I once had a curious experience on retreat with Master Sheng yen. A phrase came up in my mind, "Dogen is offering to Dogen". It would not go away. It was going round and round in my head while I was trying to do Silent Illumination. So I went to Shifu and said,

"Look, this phrase 'Dogen is offering to Dogen' is going round and round. What shall I do?" Shifu smiled and said, "Well, you've got a question there, haven't you? What is it? What is it saying? There's a koan in this, you'd better look into it."

So, although I was practising Just Sitting, he had said "Take this up as an issue, as a question." Something had come to a focus in meditation and when something comes into focus like that it becomes a Koan. There's something to be gone into there. And that would apply to any such question which comes to a sharp focus.

Now, of course, that's a little bit different from having a question set to you by a teacher, or choosing one from a book or something. That's a bit different. But it's very typical of the Tsao Tung approach. Remember what Dogen said about this (of course it wasn't only Dogen, because it came from his own teacher in China) he said that "the Koan arises in everyday life". There are quite enough questions and problems welling up all the time without having to use a fabricated one from some ancient bit of history, stuck in some book by some collector of stories. You don't have to have such a Koan, the Koans are coming up anyway.

But the issue is that a Koan, to be really powerful, has to have, it has to point somewhere. It's no good taking up as a Koan, "Is today Tuesday?", because of course you can answer that question, you can look at a calendar and say "No it's not, it's Wednesday/Thursday/Friday/Saturday/Sunday/Monday", I mean you've only got seven options as to what it might be. And if you know what it was yesterday you can fairly well work out what it is today.

Of course, you might be totally lost on a desert island in which case it might be a real Koan. Because you have no calendar.... it begins to get interesting. "No calendar.... so what day is it today?" Now, that's a Koan. When there's no calendar, and you ask what day it is, there's a Koan.

Similarly, imagine you're flying in a rocket right out past the moon, somewhere in the direction of Mars, and you casually say, "What day is it?"

Well.... no light, no day. Just the rocket revolving; black/white/black/white/black/white as it flips round before the sun. That's hardly a day. So you have to think "What day is it on earth? There aren't any days up here. Indeed what is a day?" A day is the revolution of the planet, and the revolution of the planet is being shone upon by the sun so it is dark and light, dark and light, dark and light, every 24 hours. That's what a day is. But when you're out there.... the sun just shines, and it's black except where the sun hits the vessel. What's a day up there? It's become a Koan. Is it a meaningless question? Depends on what clock you're using. It turns into "What is time?" and there you have it.

Well, it's similar on a retreat; depends on what "clock" you're using. In other words, what is the context, where are you trying to get to, what are you using time for? So issues can arise in the sitting, or they can arise in everyday life. And if they point, as it were, beyond themselves, they're very probably Koans.

I've a picture of a Koan of this kind. It's a signpost, you know, just an ordinary road sign, except there's nothing written on it, and it's stuck on the top of a cliff, and it's pointing straight out over the Atlantic ocean. "Where would you go to?" that's the Koan, where would you go to with a signless signpost pointing straight out over the ocean. Which is actually the state of our lives, which is why it's a Koan. What is the purpose of this life? Is there any purpose in it at all? Is there any purpose in the cosmos? Well, one doesn't have to doubt the vastness of space, the immensity of the thing. What's it there for? Who made it? Why am I here? Have I any purpose? Or do I invent one? All of these are Koans. And of course they're terribly important, basic in our lives. It is the resolutions of those questions which bring meaning to us.

One of the tragedies of the present time is that the contemporary, materialistic kind of world in which we live has no ultimate meaning, apart from making money. So that we're faced, very often, with a meaningless existence. That is meaningless in the old sense, when meaning was given by the religion into which you were born. Nowadays one is not born into a religion, one is born into a chaos of ideas, people thinking one thing and then another. This particular age is in many ways as decadent as ancient Rome before it fell and there are some interesting historical parallels if you actually look into this.

The Koan is vividly before us the moment you open a newspaper or read the Economist or think about the state of the planet. And unless one has some kind of an approach to those questions, ultimately life gets meaningless, and depressive, and lonely, and unrelated, and one indulges in numerous compensations: drugs, confusing love affairs, co-dependencies, psychotherapy, all of which are palliatives for an absence of meaning.

But there's something also quite vibrant about this in a way. The very fact that there is no given meaning, means that one can face the Koans of existence without all that old superstitious nonsense of the past. Without all the stories of hells and heavens and angels and all that stuff. They were only prisons, after all, comfortable prisons of the mind. But we've thrown that stuff away, so we're left naked on the cliff top with the sign post, with nothing written on it, pointing straight out over the ocean. What do you do next?"

Well, someone has just sent me a cartoon showing two rather miserable looking monks sitting on their cushions. One is saying to the other- "Nothing happens next. This is it!" Go into that one. Sky gazing at the clouds passing the blue immensity of space might open it for you.

Books of Koans are nonetheless useful, if you want to use them, I don't want you to think that I'm in any way debunking the use of old Koans. I'm not, I'm merely saying that it's a relative approach and it's not necessary to use them. But they can be enormously valuable. Why? Because these old Koans are the puzzlements of past time, when two deeply reflective masters or monks had a conversation about one of these burning issues. And one of them came up with a question and the other answered it. They said "Ah, yes" and our question becomes "What the hell are they on about?" (laughs)

Sometimes I open a book of Koans, look at it, "Yeah, right, yeah", turn over the page, open another one "Cor blimey, don't get it, I just don't get it". It's like that with Koans.

One key Koan is the simple question "What is this?" A Chinese monk might have thought about this when he sat on his cushion and heard a bird singing outside the window. He may have thought, "Ah, what's this?" And that's a real question.

"So what is this?"

Now, the first thing to do when a question arises like that is to take a reflective, contemplative attitude. Forget meditation and all the techniques, just consider, "What's going on here? What is this? Well, there's a bird singing, but it sounds a bit different from usual. Is the difference out there, or is the difference in here? Mmmmm. Birds sing every day, every morning rather like that, but I haven't heard one so clear before. So the difference must be in here. Mmmmm. Wonder what that is? What is this? What is this? Well, it's nearly end of a seven day retreat, perhaps that's got something to do with it. Well, I have noticed some changes in the past few days.... "

So you mull it over, as it were, you actually think, surprise, surprise. You think "What is this? What's going on here, there's something puzzling, strange, my mind is so clear, clear as a bell, what is this, what is this clarity?" And, so, you kind of ponder it and explore it and ponder it and explore it. And this is valuable, but only the preliminary skirmish.

You sit there, and you're puzzling, "What is this? What is this?", and you've thought about it from every possible angle and nothing comes up. You've cleared the ground a bit, there's no more 'brush wood' around. The countryside is wide open, but the question is still vividly there.

Master Xu Yun suggests that what you do then is to let the question come up, but don't try to do anything with it at all, just let it come up, and kind of 'do its own thing'. You've tried everything else, you know, you've gone to the edge of your own thought, this way, this way, upwards and downwards. You've explored the ground but the question is still untouched.

As you let it crop up look at the instant before it arose, look just ahead of the thought. The question is really just a noise, almost a mantra, except that it's a very meaningful question for you because you've already explored it intellectually and thinking-wise, so it's a profoundly puzzling and meaningful question, there's a 'great doubt', around this question now, there's a great doubt inside you. "What is this? What is it?" You are profoundly puzzled.

So, Master Xu Yun says allow it to come up, but don't look at it any more, just let it come up. The place to look is just in front of where it is arising, that's where you should look, and that's the practice.

Now you can begin to see the close similarity between this use of a question and Silent Illumination. Here we have almost a Silent Illumination practice.

The beauty of the method is in the intensity of the question. The repetition of the Buddha's name for example is calming, quietening, almost silencing. Which is fine, it's intended to be so. But the intensity of the question and the doubt which is around it makes questioning a very pointed exercise, one-pointed. The mind is highly one-pointed, there's a different flavour about the work. That's why it may yield a 'sudden' response.

And indeed Master Xu Yun goes on to say that the response to such a question can be quite sharp, it can have the nature of a sudden breakthrough. Whereas Silent Illumination progress tends to be gradual, like a flower growing until suddenly it blooms: in the intensity of the Koan question, the whole thing can break quite suddenly.

In Xu Yun's own account he'd been puzzling over a Koan in this way, for many days, many retreats in fact. He was at a tea break. And, someone came to pour him out tea, but Xu Yun was clumsy, the teacup fell down and broke. His mind was so taut that it broke too. At that moment, he saw the solution to the Koan, an immediate experience of no-self.

I once asked Shifu, "What happens in these moments?". I was wondering whether it was the ending of thought so I said "Is it that thought ends?" He said, "No, it's not that thought ends. Thought is always sort of creeping about somewhere or other. It is not that thought disappears. It's that self disappears." At that moment in Xu Yun's account his sense of himself as a question vanished, and there was just the broken teacup.

These are matters about which we find a number of Chan masters have written and talked about. Somebody might have a wonderful flash of experience, but its impact may be short-lived and minor in the long run. Why? Because the other aspects of that person's training have not been developed. And this is almost certainly one of the reasons why, in our present time, a lamentably large number of western masters, for whom there is no reason to doubt their 'kensho' experience, have then failed miserably ethically and morally?

Why could that possibly be, one asks oneself. There's no reason to doubt the enlightenment experience. It's probably because in Zen training more than merely a focus on enlightening experiences is required.

I remember, once, I had some kind of an experience of that short, and went to speak about it with Roshi Kennett when she was over in Britain at Throssel Hole Priory. She said "Fine, but it's a bit like a kensho orgasm isn't it, really? The trouble with you is you're going 'one, eight, six, ten, two, five'. No no no, you mustn't go like that, you must go 'one, two, three, four, five, six'". Then I understood what she was saying.

It's no good having an experience which is maybe well advanced, well down the path, if you're neglecting the simple things like being kind, being thoughtful, struggling with one's difficulties, working with the everyday Koans: "What shall I do now that my child is in hospital with whooping cough?" or "What can I do about my lover, who doesn't seem to love me anymore?" or, the other way round, "What can I do about this relationship when I've started to love somebody else."

These are burning issues, and they're not at the end of the road, they're right down there at the beginning, raising questions of mindfulness, ethical behaviour, simply trying to be 'good'.

So Xu Yun would stress that there's no need to rush into using Koans. You can use the Silent Illumination approach, if that is appropriate for you. It may even be appropriate for you not to use that either; just watch the breath. Just calm the mind, forget about reading all about this Zen stuff; chuck it out. Just calm down man, okay?

There is a modern Japanese story of a man who kept coming to the master terribly confused. Whatever he did, nothing seemed to help him whatsoever. He had all sorts of high-flown ideas about being a monk, he was obviously the most unsuitable person to be a monk, but nonetheless he these ideas about being a monk, etcetera, etcetera, etcetera.

Finally, the master said, "You want my advice? You've been in this state, you've done twenty retreats, you're still the same, nothing's touched you. I suggest you do something very very simple". He said "What's that?" He said "Go and make prostrations to the statue of Kuan Yin, every morning, a hundred times, and just keep doing it." So the man who was at his wit's end, dropped all his arrogance, and said "Yeah, okay, I'll do that." He didn't come back to the monastery for six months. When he came back the master said to him "How are things?" He said "Fine, fine. I've begun to understand what illusion is." What had he done? Just done that which was appropriate to his nature. He needed to let go, and to ask "Please, help me." He didn't have to think "What is it that's helping me? Who is Kuan Yin? What is Kuan Yin? Kuan Yin is just a statue. What is the meaning of a statue?" None of that concerned him. He just found the statue, and did as the master had suggested. Fortunately, he had the sense to see the wisdom of the master. He let go of his self concerns and found a simple sanity.

A wonderful story, very important story, I think, for all of us. One of the beauties of Chan is having this wide range of possible activities, of possible ways of practising. One can choose a way which is suited to one. It's not like going to a rather more narrow approach which says "Do this, do that," and that's the right way to do it. But rather, it's more subtle. If you go with Shifu, have an interview with Shifu, you spend a lot of time kind of mulling over what would be a good approach.

This is why interviews in Chan are quite important. What both participants in interview struggle to do is to share an issue which the practitioner is bringing up, to find out what is the way through. Sometimes it really is very difficult. Who knows? Sometimes one just doesn't know. Neither the teacher, nor the practitioner.

No idea. What can one do then? Well, you can start bowing to Kuan Yin. Might do you a lot of good.

Koans are used in a very subtle way in Chan. They can be used in an entirely classical way. Master Sheng Yen trained in Japan in the Rinzai method. He's very well aware of the powerful value of the use of an orthodox Koan, and he'll sometimes recommend that. He'll talk at considerable length about the development of the great doubt, and how one can penetrate the Koan using a very orthodox Rinzai/Linji way of speaking.

Personally I have found Master Sheng Yen at his best in the more subtle negotiating of "Well, what is it we should do together, what is the question here?" That's where his mastery really shines forth, for me, to me. That's where I find him such a subtle teacher. And also of course, for me personally, his teaching in Silent Illumination is extremely profound.

So, this is evening I have been sharing with you a perspective on the use of Koans. Let's spell that out right now in practical terms for this retreat. Much of what we've been developing together is essentially the Silent Illumination approach. That's fine, there's no need to do anything extra; continue with it. But it might be the case that some of you find a puzzling Koan arising within that practice. If that happens, it might be a good idea to take up that Koan and focus on the issue which has come up.

I would suggest is that before you change your method, you come and speak about it with either Simon or I, and we will discuss whether that might be a good idea or not. It might not be a good idea; it might be better to stay calm, collected. It might even be better simply to watch the breath. Sometimes one has funny ideas about one's ability when a lovely question comes up, but actually you're not ready for it. One's Karmic state may be not such as to make it valuable to do that.

If you'd like to ask a question, feel free; if not we'll sit in a few minutes.

Questioner 1: What about when imagery comes up, not necessarily a thought, but are images similar to a thought?

John: Yes. Images can be treated in the same way as thought. I mean, they are thoughts, but they're pictorial, so there's no special recommendation here. Of course, images are quite interesting in a different way from thought in that of course they can lead on to dreams and fantasy. Perhaps the image is a more direct door to one's unconscious world. But apart from that it's just Makyo, as the Japanese would say, it's illusory, from the point of view of the task.

Q 1 again: Well you said to look in the gaps, but then this imagery, say of Amitabha comes up. No real thoughts, but imagery.

John: Ah, well look between the gaps between the images. If the image is continuous, you have to break the image somehow, which the Tibetans do very effectively by suddenly shouting "Phat!"

Breaks, breaks the image and throws you into a state of surprise. "Phat!" Breaks the image.

Q 1 again: Silently, we do that silently?

John: You can do it loud if you like. But you're only allowed one in every half hour!

Questioner 2: So you're saying that a Koan could be an image, because an image can be paradoxical can't it? One image can have two......

John: Strictly speaking, no, a Koan is not an image, strictly speaking a Koan is a question, which has a verbal form. But I think, if you mean you have an image that comes up which is deeply puzzling for you and which you wish to investigate and go into, you could use it in a similar style, yes.

The thing about images, they tend to change of their own accord, whereas questions say the same. Questions have a formal structure to them, a linguistic structure, so they stay constant. Whereas if you're trying to investigate an image in this way, the image is liable to shift and move, so it's more slippery.

Questioner 2 again: It might provide you with answer by shifting?

John: Well the answer actually doesn't lie in the image. Remember that what one's looking for is what lies between, behind, beyond, around, the image. And images are just pictures on pages. What is the paper?

Q 2 again: The space between the shifts?

John: Yes. You can try it, yes. If you have an image that you want to investigate, by all means do so.

Questioner 3: When you asked us to go outside this afternoon and sit down, a very strong question came up. I've been wondering about how to bring it into the practice. I mean, I recognise the question as one of the so-called "unanswerable questions" the Buddha did not discuss.

John: Well, a lot depends on what the question is and what its context is, where it comes from. A question can sometimes be a very personal one like "What shall I do about a certain situation?" That's not a Koan. It's a very important question but it's not a Koan. I don't know whether you want to talk about your question here or whether that's more suitable for an interview. Maybe we need to share what the question really was.

Q 3 again: I don't mind. The question has to do with the Mahayana idea that there's nothing that needs to be done, etcetera, etcetera, there is no path, and no suffering. And yet, the world that we live in is full of people suffering, it's full of people like us going to retreats, and going back, and coming back. That's a very personal issue for me.

John: Indeed that is a very genuine Koan. You need to sharpen it into a question that has only a few words in it, one which you can then use as a vehicle for the investigation. This is a deeply paradoxical and problematic issue which takes us into the whole issue of what is meant by emptiness. An ancient Buddha once said (Huang po)[1] "Do you not see that the fundamental teaching of the Dharma is that there are no entities having absolute existence. What are not entities from an absolute perspective are indeed entities in their relative aspect? One who understands this is a true monk and can practice rightly." If you can sharpen up your concern into a sharp-pointed, one-pointed question which feels right to you, than that would be a Koan to use.

Questioner 4: You have admonished us a number of times to make our minds bright. I take it from that that when I sit with my eyes open then that's brighter than sitting with my eyes closed, and when my eyes fall shut and imagery happens, that side of it is not very useful so I return and open my eyes. Is that the right approach?

John: Not quite, not quite right. 'Make your mind bright' really means 'investigate.' It means 'find out what you're on about, don't sit there doing nothing'. Investigate, make your minds 'bright!' That's what that means.

You refer to eyes open and eyes shut. It is true that the meditation is rather different if the eyes are open or shut. Basically, if the eyes are open then one can be more alert, and one is more easily able to feel the world around you, the room around you.

The value of the eyes shut is that sometimes one wants to go 'in'. One doesn't want the world, you want to go 'in'. Turning the gaze inward, into the darkness as it were, is also very valuable. By using both methods on a retreat, one can discover a broad view of one's own meditation practice. One can discover what it is like to go deeply inwards; one can also discover what it is like to come out again. There's an expression used in Mahamudra practice - 'co-emergence', it's all about relating the inner and the outer.

Q 4 again: When imagery happens for me, I'm not in enough control to investigate.

John: Oh. Well, one has to let it run, until a certain amount of calming-down occurs. It's true, at times, there's not much one can do, except just let it exhaust itself. Remember the image of the beer bottle. There's a lot of fizz in the beer bottle, you take the top off and the bubbles come up. If one sits patiently for long enough, the bubbles run out.

The thing you have to watch is that you don't keep regenerating them. The mind can have a way of 'regenerating' the bubbles, not letting go of the issue, but keeping on feeding the issue, milking the issue. Like 'poor me'. "Poor me, I never get anything right, my mummy did this and so I'm awful," or "My sister did this so I'm awful." You go round one loop and recognise what you are doing. Then you have a chance to say "Oh well, that's that, that's me doing my 'poor me' thing again." You have a chance to drop it and do something else.

But some people don't catch that moment, they go round again "Poor me, here I am in this awful Zen hall, with all these awful complicated talks and this dreadful Chinese chanting. Poor me." So you go round again! Now, the problem is, how do you break that. This is where interviews are very useful.

1 Chu Ch'an. 1947. The Huang po Doctrine of Universal Mind. Buddhist Society. London. p 51.

BOOK REVIEW

Originally published in TLS.

Hotz, Michael (ed) 2002. Holding the Lotus to the Rock: The Autobiography of Sokei-an, America's first Zen Master. Four Walls Eight Windows, New York.

It seems strange that so little has been published concerning the life and teachings of Sokei-an Sasaki who taught Zen energetically in New York from the 1930's till his death shortly following release from internment in 1945. He created the First Zen Institute in America and his influence remains strongly felt. As a native Japanese who adopted the USA as his home from 1906, Sokei-an can rightly be called the first American Zen master.

This valuable book will be of great interest not only to all contemporary students of Zen, for it contains much wisdom, but also to historians concerned with US-Japanese relations in the early 20th century and the mutual influence each country had on the other. It is also a very good read, full of incident, humour and subtlety in which a Japanese mind in a highly distinctive voice struggles to come to terms with the "noisy" West.

Our knowledge of this remarkable man comes from the records kept in New York and utilized by Mary Farkas for her articles in "Zen Notes", the journal of the First Zen Institute. Farkas, a student of the master, collected letters, photos and art and memories of anyone connected with Sokei-an and added them to another archive put together in the 1930s and 40s by another student Edna Kenton, a biographer and the Institute historian. Some of the teachings in this collection, particularly those concerning the Platform Sutra of Hui-neng, have been published in German under the title "Der 6. Patriarch kommt nach Manhattan" (Agatha Wydler, translator, Theseus Verlag. Kusnacht, 1988) but the present book appears to be the first work devoted to understanding his life, based likewise on this archive.

The book was not written as an integrated autobiography by the master himself. Michael Hotz, enamoured of his subject through repeated delvings into the archive, has put together the text from numerous fragments and the coherence of the work owes much to his editorial skill, diligence and, we can also say, love. It is the story of a lifetime's adventure.

Sokei-an was born in 1882 to a family of a Shinto scholar priest. Since the priest's wife was childless, his mother was imported. Two years after his birth, the husbands' wife returned and his biological mother left to become a successful singer and dancer. As with some other Zen masters, it was perhaps the unusual circumstances of his birth that gave rise to Sokei-an's restless character. His life history is replete with wanderings. He probably inherited his artistic side from his mother.

We find him as an adult in the army driving a dynamite wagon in Manchuria, but meeting Master Sokatsu, one of the early teachers of a reformed Rinzai Zen in the Meiji era, he became interested in Buddhism and proceeded to train. Eventually he travels to the USA together with Sokatsu to found a Zen farm which failed, and eventually a Zen community near San Francisco. In 1910 all of Sokatsu's group returned to Japan but Sokei-an remained in the States, wandering and crossing the continent doing casual work, living with his wife and child with Native Americans on an island off Seattle and endlessly woodcarving, a skill which often gave him useful employment. He wrote about America in Japanese, sending his writings back to Japan for publication. After his family returned to Japan, he lived in the bohemian Greenwich Village, New York, writing, reciting, translating in both English and Japanese and in many ways living the free-style life of a lay "dharma bum". From time to time Sokei-an returned to Japan for formal training and after some deep experiences Sokatsu conferred "inka" on him, confirming his Zen insight and enabling him to teach.

Back in New York, Sokei-an's new status was reflected in the profound seriousness with which he now undertook the difficult task of training American lay practitioners. It is clear that he had a considerable presence. Farkas refers to the Zen atmosphere near him "It was like standing next to a big gong and feeling its vibrations go right through you."

The autobiographical texts describe all these adventures in a very personal manner. Discussing teaching, he is very direct: "It is not so easy to find a Zen master. If a Zen master can teach by lectures, a boxer can teach boxing by correspondence. If you wish to study Zen, come to me and I will look in your eyes and find out whether you know Zen or not." Clearly strong stuff and Alan Watts only lasted three weeks of "sanzen" (koan training) with him. Others however passed many koans, a considerable achievement in the 1930's." To pass a koan given by a teacher is not so difficult, but to pass a koan given by actual life - that is wonderful.... Zen in the sanctuary of a Zen master is like learning to swim in a pool. But to swim in the ocean of life is the koan given by the tathagata (buddha). That is the koan we have to pass."

"Yes, there is a transcendental world. How can you get into it? If someone should ask me, "Have you entered it?" I would answer "Yes". If he should ask me, "Are you still in it?" I would say "Well - I haven't come out of it." Oh, Sokei-an, you are kidding. You are here speaking to me, with your eyeglasses, your nose, your voice. How can you be in the transcendental world? "I cannot explain.... I am here with you, I can see you, but you fail to see me, the man who is in the transcendental world."

This book is full of openings on the "transcendental." How can it be that it turns out to be so ordinary? To find out you must travel further with the Master!

NCF XXXIII

ZEN AT LAND'S END

The Story of Bill Picard - Master of Zen

Interviewed by John Crook.

Text transcribed from interview tapes by Eric Johns.

Edited by the interviewer.

I first heard of Bill Picard years ago while training at Throssel Hole Priory. One or two monks had left the Priory to join him in Zen practice in Cornwall. Later on, while visiting Bo Lam monastery in Hong Kong for meditation, I met Eric Johns (Hin Lek Si) who 'sat' with me in the Chan Hall and who told me much more about him. Eric had trained with Bill and learnt much from him (see NCF 18:21-22. 19:6-14). I was intrigued. Some time later I visited Cornwall and took the opportunity to meet Bill and his wife Biddy. At once I recognised a very serious teacher who was not well known in his own country. Hidden away at the far end of Cornwall he was not often to be met with elsewhere and he did not travel around teaching. Yet the group he founded, which continues to this day, was clearly of the highest significance. Together with one or two other teachers in the immediate post war years he helped spread and create the foundations for the Dharma, especially Zen, in the UK. He was thus a true pioneer. We do not know much about these teachers to whom we owe so much. Always independent, Bill's perspective remains valuable and I decided to interview him and ask him to tell us his story. It has taken a long time to get the tapes transcribed- a task nobly undertaken by Eric. Many thanks also to Bill himself for taking the time to carefully check this account. At last here it is — read, learn, mark and inwardly digest! JHC. Ed

The Interview

1. The War Years

John: Can you tell me how you first became interested in Buddhism?

Bill: In the early 30's I was an art student. I came across a very small yellow book by Christmas Humphries on Buddhism. It was, I think, the very first one he wrote for the Buddhist Society. Somebody told me about their centre in London and with one or two others we went along there. That was my first contact with Buddhism although my mother had talked about the Buddha as part of my early schooling at home.

I went to Spain in 1937 and was appalled at the political situation and the brutality of the Civil War. It made me ask a lot of questions and I came back and looked again at Buddhism. Then came 1939 and the war. I joined up and served in France then Africa then Burma. I was invalided out with malaria, beriberi, dysentery and a whole packet of jungly things and was sent to hospital down in Calcutta. I was transferred up to Darjeeling to a military hospital in the hills for convalescence. When I was starting to get my strength back, I became aware of notices saying that there were local British people who would like to take any casualty who would like to come and stay with them. I wrote to a Mr and Mrs Burk, retired tea planters who were offering hospitality to soldiers in hospital from the Burma campaign. This grey haired husband and wife arrived in their very dilapidated old car. We immediately liked one another and I got permission to stay with them.

I think I was able to stay nearly a fortnight with them. They had retired just outside Darjeeling in a typical bungalow found among the tea-planting people in the days of the Raj. Ghoom Monastery was just down the road. There was also an Indian officer, a very nice man, staying with them, which was slightly strange to me. Among the Brits with the colonial attitude, I hadn't seen Indians. I mean they would come and visit but not actually stay. I realised that the Burks were very positive about Indians and had Indian friends.

I was given the run of their library and I was told where all the thrillers, novels and magazines were. I went in there and I suddenly realised there were rows of books including some I had seen at the London Buddhist Society in Warwick Square. One of the books that had intrigued me when I had been at Warwick Square had been Evans- Wentz books on the Bardo Thodol. At that time, unless you were some well-known scholar, you could only read them in the centre. I had browsed through these and got very intrigued. What was my surprise when I saw these books on the shelves in Darjeeling?

My eyes nearly popped out of my head when I'd got this volume down. I was standing absolutely lost in it when suddenly a voice said over my shoulders, "Are you interested in Tibet?" There was my host. I was terribly embarrassed because he had not mentioned such books to me. He said there were one or two other books as well and we talked about Tibet. I had always had an interest in Tibet and years before I had obtained two ancient volumes on Tibet from about 1860, which I've still got. These were by somebody called Hack, a Frenchman I believe. I realised how inaccurate they were but it gave some account of Tibetan life long before we began to get it from more modern travellers such as Alexandra David Neil and all that lot. Anyway, my host told me I could help myself and read any of his books I wanted. This was marvellous and about two days later we were talking at table when the Indian Officer mentioned something about yoga and meditation.

Now I had heard about meditation, but there was very little done at the London Buddhist Society at that time. It was very much a place where you met other interested people, heard lectures and that sort of thing. My ideas were very vague about where actual practice came in. Mr Burk now said, "Would you like to meet a meditation guide? He is a Lama." Now, not long before I had read Lost Horizon, and I really thought Lamas might come floating in on magic carpets and things like that. I was full of a lot of very crazy and romantic ideas. I was told this guide was actually Chinese but he was none the less a qualified Tibetan Lama. He had also trained with the venerable old Zen Master Hsu-yun in China who was then 100 or so years old. I had heard this name mentioned but it didn't really mean a great deal to me.

Two or three days later I was taken to a small bungalow in the grounds and I realised that this Chinese Lama occupied it. He was actually in the Burks' garden. I found out that they had known this Lama for quite a while and that they both practised meditation with him. He was their teacher, their guru. They had an arrangement whereby they always kept this room available for him. He was sometimes at Ghoom Monastery and sometimes in Sikkim where I think he was meditation teacher to the Raja of Sikkim.

The British did not directly rule Sikkim at that time. It was one of the protected Himalayan states. You used to have great difficulty to get in. I joined a party of British soldiers who had got permission to go there and we backpacked up to the frontier with Tibet. Fortunately we had a District Commissioner with us so we were allowed to step over the frontier but not to go down into actual Tibet. It was a great event. It was my first time to actually step into Tibet. I've done it three times since but could never get to Lhasa. The last time my wife and I crossed the friendship bridge from Kathmandu with the Chinese watching us from the other side. We had taken a taxi from Kathmandu to go up there. I talked about the army with the Ghurkha guard on the frontier. He was terrified and made us leave our cameras behind and not have anything on us when we put our feet over the line!

2. Meeting Lama Rinchen

So I was taken to this room, went in and there was this figure sitting down at ground level. He had a flat table in front of him and some scrolls and things. He was obviously reading and studying but he looked up and beamed at me. I was very conscious of my army boots. I felt like a clodhopper coming in. Mr Burk just left me at the door, saying, and "This is the young man with whom you said you would have a talk," and vanished. I hadn't got the foggiest idea what to say but I was told to sit down. There was only a little old seat to sit on and I was trying to tuck my feet out of the way. His English wasn't all that good yet I think he understood a lot more than he actually said. He had a pupil who had been at the original Samye Ling in Tibet and who became the meditation teacher of Trungpa Rimpoche and Akong Rimpoche.

Lama Rinchen would not answer any of my questions but he started me off on meditation, breathing techniques using the hara and how to get to the point where you cease to have any mental activity. Although it was only a very short time that I was with him he told me enough and he was able to express enough and show me enough that it made a very big impression on me.

There is another side to this story that I really don't like to mention because it sounds a bit whimsical. Subsequently, I used to get a very strong feeling as though he was again present with me, so that questions that were in my mind suddenly got an answer. It was a very personal thing. I usually experienced it later on when practising my Zen meditation on the Cornish cliffs.

Eventually, I had to go back to the Army where, because of my language skills, I had a job in intelligence with the Kings African Rifles. Before I left I asked Lama Rinchen whether he would take me on as a chela (disciple) if I came back. The Lama laughed, patted my hand and said; "You'll find your East in the West!" I felt brushed off and at the time was quite hurt. I had felt worthy but I hadn't passed the test. He knew that my interest was wrapped up with a lot of juvenile romanticism and he probably thought that, if I persisted, I was going to find what I needed in the West. When I finally came back to Britain in 1946 I was demobbed but in the interim I got more and more restless internally as I was trying to find answers to all these things.

3. The Romanies

In 1933 I had got in with the Gypsies. I'd been near Dolgellau, cycling and climbing Snowdon and all the mountains, and I had had my bike stolen. While on the road I had seen a shiny bit of metal and out of curiosity I had picked it up. I had a vague idea that it might have come off an axle or something like that. For some unknown reason, instead of pitching it away, I slipped it into my pocket never thinking about it. About a mile or so further on, coming on a bend, I saw an old fashioned Gypsy caravan of the type that you saw a lot of on the road in the 30s. There was a little campfire and I could see this pregnant girl bending over and a young bloke doing something at the van. As I drew level, I realised he was struggling to push a piece of wood under it to lift one side of the van because it was on three wheels with the other wheel lying at the side. On the spur of the moment I walked across to him. I'd read quite a bit of George Burrows and I rather fancied myself as a bit of a linguist. If George Burrows could learn Romany so could I and I'd memorised a few words, which I probably mispronounced. I knew something of gypsies because the previous summer I'd gone hop picking with them down in Kent. I met a family of gypsies there, the Scamps, who were also doing the same thing. I mean I'd never looked like a gypsy. I had flaming red hair, but we had become fairly matey, and I'd learnt a bit about them so, airing my gypsy, I walked across and said, "Want a hand mush?" and the bloke looks up.

It was obvious what he wanted so I helped him. We pushed the piece of wood up, which lifted the van, and then he got the wheel up and slid it in. He said something to the girl who got up and went to the tool chest at the back of the van. I could hear her rummaging around and the only word I understood was "not here". The rest was a jargon I didn't understand. Looking at the situation, I suddenly thought I knew what was missing and I put my hand in my pocket and held out the object I had found on the road. "This is what you want mush" I said, and the bloke nearly fell over. The girl came up and just stared at me. 'Course he slid it in and it fitted the job perfectly. That was all right, so they both looked at each other, and he said "Would you like a cup of Chai?" And I said, "Yes I would". So I squatted down with them.

They were terribly diffident as if I was going to bite them, and I was desperately trying to think of some Romany phrases. I knew you never ask where a Romany is going, or where you are coming from. It was not etiquette or wise in those days on the road. If you volunteered information that was fine but you didn't otherwise so we just talked in general terms. Then I got up and I left them and a little while later they passed me and we waved.

I camped that night half way on the road up to Bala, and the following day, I was walking when suddenly there was a voice calling out from a gate I hadn't really noticed, down on one side. There were several male figures leaning on the draw-over and a voice called out. I looked round and there was the young man I had met and at his side a venerable figure with a white moustache and two younger men. I walked across and was introduced very formally to the elderly man who held a hand out. He gave a very funny limp handshake, and thanked me for helping his son. I said I was very pleased to have done it. I don't know what they thought.

Because I had been picking previously, I asked is there any work around here and the old man said you go up to the farm and say that Ithel says you are to join their working team. So that was fixed. I pitched my tent and kept away from them, as I didn't want to feel I was intruding. For several days we worked like that and then we moved on. Nothing was said but the young brother of the chap I'd helped, sort of got a bit matey. He was roughly my own age, 16 or 17. We got chatty and had gone out together once or twice in the evening putting snares out for the rabbits. He came across and said "Grandfather says to join them".

Now I used to do everything and cook my own food but we developed a sort of relationship. They would hop off and say they were going to be at such a place, and I would please myself if I did or didn't join them. We went through Llangollen and then down into England and in the end it finally came to the point when I was invited to come and eat with them - which was really a great thing.

I realised how strict they were. They had some lovely Worcester china and stuff in the van. I always remember the old man was squatting by the fire and he put his plate down. Just at that moment the dog came up and licked the plate. The old man just picked the plate up and smashed it like that. It must never be used again, he said because it had been polluted. I learnt a lot of things of that nature and we became quite close.

Well, one night we'd been sitting around the fire and talking about the day's events. Mainly the subject of conversation was to do with the clan or tribe, trade possibilities of business somewhere and that sort of talk, but they'd got on to talking about dukha as they call it. That's the fortune-telling for which they have two words. Dukha is really the more common form that the women do; it is based on sociological observation. For example, you walk up to a house, eye the clothesline and work out roughly the age groups of the occupants and things like that from the clothes you see. They polish up their information by talking to the owner and the next time they come round they visit the house. They know by now that the family has got a son in jail or a son that works or a son that is in the army. Their understanding surprises people. It's very clever how it's done but there is nothing more than at that level.

There are however some who really have second sight. The old Dai, that was Granny, Ithel's wife, was such a person. They were all a little afraid when she told the dukha but one night the younger women were goading her. They used to call me Billy you see. They said, "Tell the young Rai, tell Billy, the posh dukha." The "posh dukha" meant the real thing, and I didn't want it.

I felt uncomfortable and said, "I don't want to know, I don't want to know." The old woman was sitting across the fire and I was conscious of her very black eyes staring at me. I thought she would ask for my hand, which would have been palm reading, the normal thing. But she didn't. She just sat there. She was sort of rocking herself a little bit and began in quite a different way. She said "I see the boro pani, the great water, and it comes in." She was imitating the movement as of an incoming tide with her hands. "There are high hills, oh no they're not. There are high rocks and there is a head coming in through the water and a figure comes up out of the water and comes up the beach". She stops and she looks up at me with quite a different expression and said she wouldn't tell me any more. It left me feeling awful. One or two of the others said, "Well tell him a bit more, Dai, what happened?" She wouldn't say another word, and she never said another word. She left a very vivid picture in my mind though.

4. Cornwall

Now getting back to Cornwall. After I had been demobbed, I was finally able to hitch-hike away from London and arrived at Marazion. The day after, I spent quite a bit of time around Penzance harbour. I walked around Newlyn and on to Mousehole and up to the cliffs. It was getting to the end of the day by the time I got to Lamorna. There is a narrow cove there, and the rocks are up on one side. I went down into this little cove.

I was very intrigued as I had heard the name of this place, and I knew its association with artists and craft people because I'd read books by the different artists who'd worked there. It was part of my reading at art school for instance so I knew about the place and I'd seen a lot of paintings done by the Newlyn Art School.

I go down in to the cove and I'm standing there and at first there doesn't seem to be anybody there. There is a little stone quay on one side and, as I'm looking out to sea, I see what I think is the head of a seal in the water coming in. As soon as I saw it I got that deja-vu feeling. This had happened before - and then I remembered the incident with the gypsy. I remain riveted watching this thing. It seemed to be a complete resurrection of the image that I'd felt the gypsy woman had somehow implanted in my mind. It was just as Granny Lee had pictured it. The figure comes up out with the water dripping off, then onto the sand. I'd built up all sorts of things in my mind, for example that this would be the start of a great romance.

The figure came up onto the sand and I realised that below where I was standing there was a rug spread out and there was a little child on it. I realised then that this is not going to turn out like my dream, but I was very intrigued all the same, as you can imagine.

I carried on along the cliffs for a short way. It was near the rock of Carn Barges. I realised that it was getting quite late and I could hear somebody working in a field. They were what you call "tealing". You use a long handled shovel. A man was digging out potatoes, early potatoes because this would have been March. I asked him whether it was all right to camp and he pointed out a place among what we call quelets. These are little stone fields on a bend of a cliff and there was a nice little one about the size of this room with stone granite walls (quoits) that gave protection. I pitched my tent there and it was obviously perfectly all right. The man said leave it there, come up to the farmhouse if you want anything. He was a farmer, Bill Trevarroes who I got to know very well afterwards, and my tent was to remain there for two years!

So things seemed to fall into place, nothing more about the lady on the beach. Anyway I was full of ideas about being a monk, celibate and all that sort of thing. I was going to meditate like anything right there on the cliff top near the sea. I carried on walking the following day and did my journey to Land's End and around the coast. Then I came back to my tent and started this little meditation regime. I was being very dutiful about what I'd been taught, but of course I did a lot of odd things. I starved myself and various things like that and got into a depressed state, not a good one to be in alone on a cliff top. I could have done with a bit of advice and correction. Several months later I was going to take my life. At one time I swam out in the water of the bay, no light, no moon. Suddenly I desperately wanted to live and of course then I was trying to see where the shore was and I couldn't. Fortunately there was enough of a swell for a faint line of white to show on the coast so I swam back and dragged myself out.

A bit of a melodramatic thing to do wasn't it and quite honestly idiotic, but it shows what can happen. Often I used to go on to a particular rock to meditate. It is called Carn Barges and the local people always refer to it as the Druid's seat. It is a flat stone with a vertical back facing the sea; just like a huge chair, it was an ideal place for sitting. Yet I eventually decided not to go down there because there was a sheer drop over the edge. I felt that there was a part of me that had almost been taken over in a funny way that was dangerous. So I used to stay more in my tent.

Well - in the second year meditation had been getting better in the sense I was able to drop literally everything. As you probably know, you go through some very strange things, hallucinations, all kinds of things, but I kept going. I had been impressed by what the old lama had said about everything being a projection from my own mind. In other words it wasn't reality that was out there, I was projecting the reality. I had to calm this down and let it drop, and of course by that time I'd read Suzuki. I'm not sure about the reading. I feel that if you can get verbal teaching at the right moment from somebody that you trust in or whom you respect, that's better.

5 A Cliff-top Awakening

Out of all this came something I haven't talked about a great deal over the years. I suppose it was the most seminal experience for me.

Along the coast there was a garden that had been built by Colonel Painter, the old Squire of Boskenna. His was one of the old families that had been there since the year dot, and in the early part of the century, he and his wife had been to Japan. She fell in love with the idea of Japanese gardens and he'd bought a lot of stone things like lanterns and so on. He built her a Japanese garden there in the cliffs, completely surrounded by a wall, which could be locked. It was not attached to the estate gardens at all but rather a separate private garden. It had a little lake and a Japanese bridge over it and a Buddha Rupa (image) that he'd put in there.

Now some people, some woodmen, had been doing some chopping, removing some dangerous trees, and they had pulled down a bit of the Cornish stonewall so they could get a vehicle in to pull out wood. It was pure coincidence that an entrance was available there. I'd never been into this garden, but I'd heard about it so I knew that there was something like that there.

Well, there was this bright moonlit night. I think it was May or June. I'd been meditating and I felt quite a strong compulsion to go walking in the moonlight on the cliff along a path I knew very well. Instead of skirting the garden I crossed a field and found there was a gap in the stone wall. On the spur of the moment, I walked down to this and entered. At once of course my surroundings were transformed. I was in a Japanese garden and part of me wasn't quite sure whether it was a real garden or not. I had been meditating and been hyperventilating to a certain extent, hardly breathing, so I felt that I was floating, hardly conscious of feet on the ground at all. I went down there and there was this tinkling bell that I could hear, just a faint tinkle. I came around the edge and there was the bridge, and there was the Buddha Rupa. As I saw this, everything dissolved.................

John: You found the Buddha in the garden?

Bill: Yes, Yes I found the Buddha in the garden. That was just, in a sense, it.

John: How long did that state last?

Bill: Well I passed out. It seemed it was like a flash and then it was like being drawn into the brilliance. Then I'm not conscious of anything at all except that, this is it, and this is it, just it. Everything is just one, and I think that that was my main feeling. When I came to, I'm lying on the ground by the foot of this little bridge thing with the Buddha there. I was feeling very cold and I'm looking up. I realise that there is a golden light on the bamboo that was growing at the side. To my surprise of course it is dawn. So I must have been lying there for about three hours or so because it was the very first light of dawn shining on this golden figure. I had had a sort of amnesia. At first, I didn't know who I was or what I was or anything. Yet I was more conscious than I can remember - the feel - even now - of my fingers moving - and I put them on the rock with the Buddha Rupa above it. I could feel this sensation and then I got up feeling very stiff, and my idea was to get away somehow.

I knew that I had some way to go, so I slowly retraced my steps and gradually, of course I came to know I am me but with this great sense of lightness and weight and everything gone, no problems absolutely, all very vividly there. That was It. Everything was as though I was seeing it for the first time. I think that is the best I can say. There were absolutely no questions, no inner debate, and no doubt. I was empty so there was a sense of just lightly moving over the ground of this incredible creation as though it had just happened that instant.

Well - I knew enough to know the way out. I retraced my steps, got out of the garden, and, as the state faded, I had a sense that I am 'Me' now and I'll get back to my camp. That was fine and for the rest of the way, about 2 miles along the cliff, I thought I'd just enjoy this brilliant morning as though I'd never seen a morning like it before.

I got back to my camp. I didn't want to talk to anybody, I didn't want human contact but at the same time, if it happened it happened and that was it. Gradually I just got back to my self of who and what I was. I found that a lot of questions and problems suddenly seemed so obviously answered. Everything literally is one and there is no separation.

I think that subsequently I've looked at it as if from the point of view of physics. In an atomic sense, you know, we are all just whirling particles. That seems to be the answer. The thing that gives us all our troubles and problems is what our brain does. We split everything up and tie them into little packets. So meditation now became something that I did just any time. It was no longer the formal business of sitting as if to get somewhere. That was necessary at times because as the pressures increase, you know, one gets overwhelmed with things and you need the sitting meditation. But if you can carry that "state" knowingly within you then that is IT. What you have to do, and the problems that come up, you just deal with in the here and now.

The need to remain in segregation all alone on my little plot became less. I had already begun to do some work, I used to go up and teal potatoes and do things for the farmer every so often. In return I was not only allowed to keep my tent there but I could help myself to vegetables.

6. The Pottery at Mousehole and the Meditation Group

About the second year in Cornwall, my mother had moved down to Penzance with my widowed sister. They wanted help with the house they had bought. As a matter of fact I had bought the house. I put my gratuity into it to give them a base and also I could have the attic if I wanted it.

I had got to know Biddy, my future wife, and her first husband. I had already known the group of people with whom she worked. They were known as the 'Woodchoppers' and if you had ever read books by Ithel Colquhoun (Living Stones) or Denys Val Baker (Seas in the Kitchen) you may know their story.

'Woodcutters' or 'Woodchoppers' was the name given by locals to a group of young ex-pacifists who were sent to work on the land during the war. This was now a group of young, student-artist painters. Biddy was teaching painting at Badminton, long before there were hippies, and she'd met one of these woodchoppers there and came down to Cornwall to find him. She had been in Wales with another woodchopper friend and they hitched a lift on a Breton crabber from Haverford West round into Newlyn. For a long time the locals were convinced that she was a Breton. She landed here to contact this woodchopper, a big blond bloke with a long beard and all that sort of thing, so that's how that happened.

Actually I had known the Woodchoppers earlier. Up in Wales on one of my climbing trips after the war, I had a friend whose parents had a cottage on the Gower. I had stayed with him and we had gone climbing and I got to meet these woodchoppers then. I didn't know that in the interim they had all moved down to Cornwall and made their base at Lamorna.

I had cycled over to St Ives to see the famous potter Bernard Leach and we had hit it off. He became like a pater familias to me. We had a common interest in the east and Buddhism. He had started a pottery there in the twenties and was very influential in the pottery world. My mother got to know him also and I think she told him that he had better talk some sense into this son of hers living a sort of life that was not done in those days. You couldn't just opt out and live in a tent and just feed yourself, you know.

John: It must have been very cold on the cliffs in winter

Bill: Well - not as bad as subsequently. That first winter, the 1947 winter, was the first time that they had had any ice in Cornwall as long as they could remember. It had been a long spell of dry, good sort of weather and subsequently it began to get cold. But don't forget I'd been living in tents or living out in the open for nearly 10 years in the Army. I was in East Africa first and then, when we were in Burma, we were in monsoon rain all the time.

Weeks went by when our clothes used to rot on our webbing and get covered in mildew and you were never dry. Feet used to go white and pappy because they were always damp, wet soaked in mud, so in a way one was very tough. Even so at the same time I was getting periodical attacks of malarial relapsing fevers and I was still getting over dysentery and beriberi as well. I'd had to get medication. When I'd left the army I'd had a dossier thing that I'd take to the doctor and I'd have to have pills to cope with the malarial relapses.

Indeed, there was a lot of pressure on me not to be living that sort of life because I was supposed to be trying to get my health back and all that sort of thing. As it turned out it really was the best thing! When I got to know Bernard he had just started a pottery department in Penzance Art School the year before. He said, "Look you can apply, you've been in the army. They will help to fund you to come to the classes." Well I could do enough casual work to be able to attend 3 classes at the art school. I was rather a hit and miss sort of pupil. I used to come in some days and not others; they were very tolerant with me. But I enjoyed it. I liked the pottery and soon met the local artists and craft-workers.

I had trained originally to be a painter in London in the 30s but it was going to be years before I could make any money. I mean the first picture I ever sold was for £5. My son sold his first picture for something like £80! I would never have a sale for god knows how long and then I'd spend the £5 on treating my fellow students, my pals anyway, in some pub in the Kings Road! So it did not do me a great deal of any long term good! But it was perfectly true that with this background I could get a job with the potters. I refreshed my pottery with Bernard Leach and, when I'd finished the course, I got a job with what is known as the Lamorna pottery.

Chris Ludlow who had demobbed from the RAF a few years before had started it up. He is dead now. He'd manage to set himself up in pottery and employed local student artists. We weren't paid very much by modern standards, I think I got about £5 a week, but basically you could live on that.

My ambition was to get started up with a pottery as well but romance interfered with that. Biddy had split up. I had a number of lady friends at the time but the first time Bid and I met it was as though we had always known each other. We could talk. I mean she was still married to Ray then but whenever we met we could just talk quite naturally. It went on like that for a number of years. She had a marriage breakdown and another relationship with somebody and so on -- but eventually we came together and decided we'd set up a pottery down in Mousehole. You must know that it turned out that she was indeed the lady who had come up the beach at Lamorna! Strange!

She painted but also has a natural ability in pottery. These sculpts are hers, figures and things like that tree of life and all those sorts of things. So we set up the pottery down in Mousehole, in the fish cellar behind our cottage there. Hand to mouth it really was, hand to mouth. I mean if we could just scrape together roughly £150 at the end of the year, it could see us through to when next year's visitors were coming and we could start selling pots again

We had a number of friends who were in a similar position trying to sell stuff so we had a system of sale or return at our place. We also started off a number of young people who wanted to do work like this. One of them, Red Simpson, became quite a successful silversmith afterwards. He was a schoolteacher at the time and he played around with copper. He made some little copper dishes which we felt very sure we couldn't sell but he had a lot of cut off bits and Biddy suggested he made some earrings out of them. This he did, and they went like hot cakes. That started him off literally and he gave up teaching and moved on from copper into semi precious metal. He set himself up in St Ives and it became his life's work in the end. He became quite well known, and brought up his family on it.

We started up a shop as well as the pottery. This was down in Mousehole in the front of our house in our living room, which had stable doors. At the time, in those years after the war, everything was very drab. It was the same with our garb. We made sandals. We could buy leather so we made things like that. As soon as I'd left the army I'd started growing my hair long and if we could get a colourful shirt I'd wear a colourful shirt. Since everybody else was in suits with waistcoats and things like that, we looked quite esoteric long before it became fashionable.

I must tell you how the shop came about. We were sitting in our front room one day before we had started the shop and suddenly a gentleman walked in the door and passed us, peering about. We looked at each other: "D'ye know who this is?"

After looking around he said "Excuse me, have you seen my wife?" "No, no, what's your wife like?" And each of us thought that the other one knew it must be someone that they knew. Then he went out and we suddenly burst out laughing. He must have thought we were a shop. The place was so brightly painted and all that and we had pots and things in the window. And we suddenly said "Well that's it! Let's start selling ourselves." We built the shelves and I painted a sign that Biddy hated because it was very shi-shi. But that led to an interesting result. The sign was a pot with a mouse looking out of the top of it and we called it "The Mouse Hole" at first. Then somebody said, look you have got to call it the Mousehole Pottery. So Bid got her own way and my mouse and pot was thrown out.

The locals always made a distinction between them and us. I have a Cornish connection but they are very clannish like the Welsh. You either have to be one of them, or you're always going to be the foreigner. Now the artists were a sort of borderline case. I can remember one old Cornishman saying, "There is us-un, you bloody artists, and all the bloody foreigners up there". Now the foreigners were everybody that came in, whether English or not, but the bloody artists were part of the locals. We had not got much money so we lived much the same way as they did.

We often used women as models. Clothed models, mind, you did not get a naked model. This had happened for many years. All the well-known painters in the old school painted local people. When we used to hold exhibitions in the gallery in Penzance or Newlyn, a lot of locals came because they had relations that were models. They were delighted to bring them in and say "Oh, that is so and so!" Nowadays the 3rd & 4th generation still go there when they know one of the old pictures from about 1900 is there and they can see an ancestor. They take their friends. The local community always felt quite involved with the artists because of this.

Anything that people like us did was acceptable. Bid went into a shop one day and one of the ladies turned round and said, "Is it true me-dear that you live up in the trees?" And Bid said, "Oh yes of course". The rumour went around that when it was necessary we lived up in the trees. These legends remain.

7. The Teachers

John: How did the Zen business catch up with you?

Bill: Well, I just used to do my meditation. There were one or two people here that had been out East. Have you ever heard of Elephant Bill? Well he lived at Lamorna up the top there. When these people heard I was doing meditation, I was asked could they join? Would I tell them what I did? So that is really how it happened. They then decided they should have a society. The Tibet Society and the Buddhist Society in London knew some of us so we were often asked to host visiting Tibetan monks or Buddhists from India, Ceylon or Burma. Chogyam Trungpa as a young monk was one of them. The actual teaching grew from my personal practice. Over the years our numbers varied – from around ten to thirty. People came and went. In fifty years there were many changes.

We'd be a Buddhist society and we wrote to Toby Humphreys in London. He got quite interested because at that time I think there was only one society outside London, in Liverpool. Really people only wanted to come and discuss. It was a bit of a talking shop, and, quite honestly, I used to get a little bit bored. One or two of them used to air their bits of oriental language and one thing and another and I didn't feel I needed that sort of thing. I didn't feel I needed to go on with speculation any longer. I was quite content doing my thing, but there were odd ones in the group who felt they wanted to go further than talking. They felt there was something further to be explored, but for a long time I was very diffident about saying anything. I wouldn't talk about the garden business because I was afraid that I might be laughed at, or I would be told it was all a lot of hallucination or something like that. In my own way I was quite content with my "State".

As I have said, I had to get on with quite a number of things in order to make money so I used to work for potters. Then my mother wanted her house doing up so I went and worked on that but finally things began to coalesce. Obviously I wasn't going to be a monk and I had a number of girlfriends.

Eventually, as I have told you, Bid and I came closer in a funny sort of way. She had three children. It didn't make any difference. I'd seen them grow up. I was fond of them and they were fond of me. I've been very lucky; we've never had any clashes. Peter was working here and we're very fond of each other, and it's been a good father- son relationship. From that point of view I'm incredibly lucky.

Some years later a Japanese man came out of the blue; my mother-in-law was looking after the shop at the time. He was a lay monk attached to Shojiji Temple in Japan. Have you ever heard of Habbo Sensei? In Japan, he had had a recurring dream. It told him he had to go to the far west, "west" was the important thing about it. He had to take a copy of the Heart Sutra with him and he had to give it to somebody. After he had this dream several times he spoke to his Roshi. Anyway, he eventually got some business connection that financed the trip and he had come across to England by Trans Siberian Railway travelling westward. He'd gone to the Japanese Legation in London and they got a map and said, "You have got a choice, the most western point of England is Land's End." Now there was also a Spanish one or a French land's end also, but he said "I'll start with the nearest." Then they told him that near the English Land's End there was a place called Mousehole. He was convinced that this must be right for him because in his dream he had seen our sign. It was actually no longer our sign but it was the sign that we had had, the mouse that figured in the pot!

Sometimes it seems almost incredible how things tie in like this. Anyway, my mother- in-law couldn't make head or tail about what Mr Habbo was talking about. So she said "I think it's my son in law you want to talk to." I was told there was this Japanese gentleman who was going to come back later. When he did his drawing to show me his idea of the mouse and pot it was absolutely spot on. It was the old sign, which we no longer had because Biddy had thrown it out. I mean it was several years later you see. He had a phrase he kept saying "So happy! So happy!" and he kept putting his hands together and doing little bows to me. It meant a great deal to him.

Anyway we were obviously going to do a little ceremony and we sat on the floor and had tea. He bought out the scroll that he'd done and it was the Heart Sutra. Now he obviously felt I'd got to read this to him. He said do you speak Japanese? I remembered a few phrases from the war years, but I had quite a personal struggle with this. I'd got to hate the Japanese because in Burma we'd come across the most appalling things they'd done - like using the prisoners for bayonet practice and things like that. I just said Hrydrya Sutra and he looked at me and beamed. So I went and got the Edward Conze version so I could read the thing in English. He presented me with the scroll. I've still got it.

We started a correspondence; a very odd correspondence too. One day I got a letter in good English. It turned out to be from Jiyu Kennet. Apparently Habbo had told her how he'd been over here. She was sounding me out, to find out who I was, what was the set up here and was there a possibility of her being invited to come over and so on. This went on for several years, and at first I had thought it was an erudite Japanese writing to me. She asked questions; we talked about techniques and so on.

What I subsequently heard, although I didn't learn it from her, was that some Japanese were getting embarrassed with her and various young Americans who were upsetting traditional things and going there with their own ideas. They were not going to fit in and some of the Americans really behaved appallingly. I don't like saying this of Jiyu Kennet but she had a streak that she was going to be somebody of importance. This was what drove her in a way. I can't say it interfered with what she was teaching. That was good, but she very quickly broke off her links with anyone who was going to be an authority over her. She wasn't prepared to have a Dharma brother keep an eye on her at all. I got involved with groups raising money; we brought her over and we held the first retreat in Somerset in the 60s. I was always on the periphery of all this.

Another thing, a friend of mine who was stationed in Hong Kong in the army had met Lu Kuan Yu (Charles Luk) who wanted somebody to read some typescripts he had prepared. I think my friend gave him a wrong impression of my importance and so I got a letter from him. Would I contact a publisher? So I did what I could and gradually Charles Luk's books came out. That is really why he dedicated one of his books to me. All this revealed for me the Chinese aspect in contrast to Japanese Zen with its somewhat military approach. The Chinese go very much on the ceremonial side, the aspect that Eric Johns likes so much. Personally, while I think this is sometimes helpful, we always kept it to the simplest when I was involved in teaching Zazen, We always had a Rupa and lit incense to show when a meditation period had started and ended. We also had question and answers.

I was given permission to teach originally through Jiyu Kennet at Sojiji before they broke with her. They later renewed permission directly for me to teach independently and I kept up contact with them after that for a while. As time went on our group met regularly for meditation in a sail loft and in our houses. That was how the Mousehole meditation group was started. It began functioning around 1949. I think it was the London Buddhist Society that called us "The Mousehole Buddhist Group" and so it became known.

Most members lived at home as they came from Cornwall. Some still worked while others were retired. The older members made up the regular core of the group. Younger people only started joining in the 60's when Zen became popular and a few of these started living as monks or nuns. It was this that started us building our first Zendo - meditation hall.

Over the years our schedule of practice changed. Many original members died or gave up attending weekly meetings yet still attended our retreats. Once the Zendo was built there were weekly meetings. Over the years we used a range of texts, the writing of Daisetz Suzuki, Christmas Humphreys, and Charles Luk were the first. Luk's translations were most useful. Chogyam Trungpa was valuable in his first days in England. Over the years we invited various teachers. In meditation we used shikantaza and koans at different times depending on the teacher and who was present. Our methods were never hard but adapted to our ages.

The group has never closed down. Until I moved from Penaluna, I still sat with them but I am cut off now as my transport is by bus or by getting an old member to collect me. There are still weekly sittings but no one gives teachings any more. Indeed the present members who do sit can hardly represent the group as it originally was. Actually, I now know little of what they do as my age (92) prevents it. What started for me in 1948 has ended.

FALLING OUT OF YOURSELF

A talk given during retreat at the Maenllwyd. Oct 22nd - 26th 1998 transcribed from the original tape by Rob Alexander. Edited and abbreviated by the author.

It's probably true to say that the root of our troubles is the manner in which we think of ourselves.

After all, if it is true that we spend ninety percent of our thinking time wondering about ourselves, it's not really surprising we create a problem for ourselves. It follows that it's not at all surprising to find that the first major theme to which a Buddhist must address herself is the problem -Who am I? What am I? Where am I?

In the usual way of things we make an assumption. Because we have names Tom, Dick, and Harry, Betty, Esmeralda, Jane, we believe that a name refers to something, to a thing, an object; a self. We spend our time living as people who possess a self; who have a self. This is so very clear in ordinary language; I talk about "myself". I ask you "How do you feel", "Who do you think she is?" Or, even better, "Who does she think she is?" Possibly sometimes "Who do I think I am?"

There's a very good reason for this. It's what you might call 'common sense'. The only problem is that common sense is not always quite reliable. It is common sense to look around the room and see ourselves sitting here, Fiona, Simon, Hilary, Malcolm. We're all here are we not? Aren't we? But are we?

Well, of course, yes we are, yes. But what is it that is here?

I think I'm here, and I think you're here. At least, I hope you are, otherwise there wouldn't be much point in my talking to you, would there?

So, here we are. And yet, because we also know that we come into the world, and die, we only have a very short time, seventy years or so, to be here. Three score years and ten? Almost nothing on a cosmic or planetary scale. There was life on earth long before we ever came here. Think of the dinosaurs galumphing around, snorting and bellowing - but not doing much thinking, I suspect. Our extraordinary intelligence and language allows us to worry. "What are we here for?" "What ARE we here for?" "Did somebody put us here?"

Who was that?

These are not new questions. The Buddha addressed himself to them long ago, but they keep on turning up. There is something quite natural, indeed inevitable, about these questions. They have a long history. We cannot suppose a bit of study of Buddhist philosophy is going to solve these questions quickly.

It's natural to us to think that "John is here". How could I communicate with you if I didn't think I was here? There's a profound paradox in all this. Common-sensically, when John goes and buys an egg in the shop, it would be ridiculous if John didn't know he was John. Who would then be asking for the eggs?

So there's this common-sensical awareness of being John, Malcolm, Hugh. Such common-sensical awareness cannot be thrown away, clever-dick wise, by a bit of philosophy. We live inside this common sense most of the time. Yet, when we begin to look into this, and say "Well, it really troubles me: you know, seventy years isn't much, the quality of my life isn't all that good" we come up against the assumption we are making, - assuming a mind, assuming a self. Have I got it right? Is it as simple as it seems? Now - that's where the Buddha started from.

I want to remind you this morning that one of the very first ideas of the Buddha was the Anatta doctrine. Anatta is a Pali word meaning "no self", and the simple way of putting it is to argue "We got it wrong. We do not have selves".

Superficial understanding of anatta generates all sorts of mistakes, particularly amongst those who say "Ah, Buddhism is therefore Nihilism, it's all about nothing, there's nothing there, it's Nihilism." Actually although the Buddha said "No self", he didn't say there's nothing there. It becomes very interesting to investigate exactly what is there. What did the Buddha mean by "There is no self?" How did he discover it anyway, when it's common-sense to think that there is one? After all, -- here's John, -- there's Hilary.

We know rather well what the Buddha did. The Buddha was on a quest, like the rest of us. This young man had had a somewhat problematical childhood. His Mum died when he was very young. His Dad wanted him to become a king but he did not want to be a king. All very painful. Not very nice to be destined to be a king, which after all is rather a posh position, and actually not want to be one at all. Young Siddhartha became very concerned with suffering, his own and that of others. He fixed his mind on the question, Why suffering? He was completely focussed on finding out how to solve that problem.

As we know, he went off on a quest. He frequented all the teachers of his time, wandered about, teacher after teacher after teacher. And some of the main teachers of his time were the Brahmin forest wanderers who talked about Brahman.

What was Brahman? Brahman is similar to the idea of God. It is God and it's everywhere, the entire universe. Everything was Brahman; Brahman produced everything, everything returned to Brahman. So, they said, if you meditate well, if you do great Yoga, you'll find that your self, your 'Atman', this breathing being, will disappear into Brahman. And that is bliss.

Siddhartha said "Oh that's great, let's try it out". So he sat and he contemplated and he sat and he contemplated and he did his yoga and he was doubtless a very great Yogi indeed. We know he nearly killed himself doing his ascetic practices. Yet, after a while, he said to himself "Well, I seem to have done everything, but no Brahman, no bliss. Or rather, this doesn't seem to lead to anything transcendent or permanent. So maybe I'd better look more closely into what I'm doing with my mind. When I sit down in meditation, what is going on?"

So instead of going into a deep trance he began to sit easy and just watch what was going on in the mind. Every time he had gone into the deep trance states he had seen that "Pop!" he came out again. So where was Brahman, where was the permanent bliss? He watched what his mind was doing very, very closely, and he saw that one thing led to another. If you do a certain kind of yoga, it produces a feeling of blissful wellness. Then if you wait a bit, it fades, you're back to where you started from. If you do another kind of yoga, it produces silence. If you do another kind of activity, it produces joy. If you think too much about yourself, you get miserable. In this way he mapped his whole world of experiences.

"When I look at my mind," said the Buddha, "what I find is an endless pattern of change. Some of it is blissful, some of it is miserable. Continuous, changing patterns, flowing and flowing and flowing."

He also noted that nearly all of this flowing movement took the form of thought. Thought and feeling. The mind he was looking at was a thinking, feeling, concept-making, experiencing mind; the normal mind which we have, but now being closely examined within meditation.

He realised that instead of there being a something, a thing, a self, what was actually there was a stream of consciousness, a continuous flow. Furthermore, when he began to think about himself, it was as if that flowing stream in all its freedom suddenly congealed into a lump called Siddhartha. Identifying himself as a thing-like self he became a kind of lump on his cushion, he had lost the free movement. There he was, worrying about being Siddhartha.

This endless flow of experiencing began to intrigue him, and he made it the chief focus of his meditation. This was a new method of meditation, Vipassana. It is a method of inspecting the movement of the mind, so that you really recognise what's happening there. And when you do that you do not find a 'thing' called Tom, Dick, Harry, John, Malcolm, whoever, Theo, Jenny - you don't find it. All those words are just names.

What you actually find is this flowing continuity of experiencing which has many, many implications. It suggests that when you grab hold of experience and give it a name and make it solid, then all the problems begin to appear. Yet, when you get down to it in direct awareness this 'thing' dissolves into a continuous flow, just like a river. The name is just a concept, a mental construction, a sort of short hand way of speaking of a process of great depth and mystery. Thinking it to be a simple entity, me, is clearly a great mistake.

This principle is known in Sanskrit as the principle of interdependent origination or co–dependent arising, the process of continuous mental flux. These are big words, but the idea is quite simple. I first learnt about this experientially while walking in the mountains in India with a very fine thinker, Shri Tashi Rabgyas from Ladakh. As a boy, Tashi had walked from Ladakh to Lhasa to hear the teachings of the Dalai Lama. This would have been about 1950, and it took him three months to get there.

We talked a lot about Krishnamurti's idea of 'bare awareness'. Tashi said "You know this bare awareness, it's just the same as co–dependent arising". I said, "What, Tashi? What do you mean?" So he said, "Well, when you are just aware, bare aware, without bothering about your name or who you are or what you want, just being present, and allowing things to come through, that is observing the flowing presence of your existence."

And so we practiced this, just walking in the mountains. It was quite wonderful, to be walking in the hills without bothering about being me, just one foot after the other, one cloud after another, one stream after another, one camping place after another, flowing along.

When one thinks about life, that is actually how it is. One day follows another, an hour follows another, breakfast comes before lunch, dinner comes in the evening, we come on retreats, we leave retreats. It's a continuous flow of happenings and events. When you look more microscopically at what the mind is doing, it's similarly flowing from thought to thought and worry to worry; an endless, continuous flowing-ness.

What the Buddha had realised was that when you obstruct that flow by making yourself into a concrete thing, all suffering will appear. If, by contrast, you let go of yourself, if you let go of attachment to these thoughts and feelings, and just fall into the flow, then you find joy and peace. You have to fall out of yourself to find freedom from yourself.

Buddha said "Don't believe me, in fact you may disbelieve me, but I put it to you, this is what I've found. If you try and find it out for yourself, you can see whether I'm right or not."

The Buddha was not a dogmatist, he made suggestions based on his own experience.

When we think about ourselves, what do we think about? Well, it seems to me that there are two main things. First of all, we think about our bodies. We get terribly disturbed if we run a splinter into a finger. It's very painful, for one thing, maybe it's going to go septic and if it goes septic maybe I'm going to be ill and it's even possible I might die from it.

I'm reaching an age now when quite a lot of my friends now have gone and died, finished, caput. Once every few months, I read about some old friend who's dropped dead from cancer, or whatever it might be. "What about me, am I next?" Well, maybe I am next. But then I count up my ancient relatives, all of them were over eighty and some of them were over ninety by the time they died, "Oh, good, I've got a long time yet!" Forgetting, of course, the bus with my name on it, which is going to run me over tomorrow. Shaky business, life, very uncertain.

We, who live in peacetime, don't often have to think about immediate mortality. But I'm old enough to remember the war as a child. So I can remember things like the bombing and so on, but for a child that was a bit of fun.

A good friend of mine, Robert Hinde, the recent Master of St John's College, Cambridge, is a little older than me and served in the war. He navigated Sunderland flying boats flying out from Oban, in Scotland, looking for submarines. In those days, radio contact was extremely poor, no useful radar. They just took off and flew out a few hundred feet above the sea over the Atlantic. Coming home they had to stay below cloud cover otherwise they would have no idea where they were. Very dangerous. Of course there were many deaths.

These lumbering flying boats would come back after a six hundred mile tour out into the Atlantic trying to stop U-boats surrounding convoys. When the cloud was down you fly round and round, use up all your fuel, then you try to land. And commonly hit a mountain. That's the end. To such servicemen, mortality was an immediate possibility every time they went on a mission. They simply had to put that thought aside. We have it easy today - most of the time.

Yet mortality is right there in front of us all the time. The real worry arises from the attachment to being this person who wants to survive. The Buddha was interested in what happens if you drop that attachment.

The Buddha says, "Okay, see if you can drop the attachment to the body, the attachment to being a certain sort of person with particular kind of name and a reputation". What happens? Just try it. What happens if you drop it, just let it fall out of your mind? Where do you find yourself? That turns out to be the key question. If you do the experiment, and just let go of all that stuff, where are you?

This is something that can be found out only individually, personally. We can call it "the flow of experience", we can give it a big Sanskrit name; all right, that's fine, that's all literary stuff. But in actual experience, where do you find yourself, if you drop preoccupation with the things to do with the body and identity? Where are you then?

Look at it this way ......

What happens when the breathing goes out and you look into the space into which the breathing has gone? You find a sort of silence. It's not a big silence, it's just a sort of clarity with no concepts in it.

Hmmm.

You breathe in again... and maybe after a few minutes you start thinking again, -- because, as we said, thinking is natural. Even so you've learned something. Until that moment you never thought that such a thing as real silence existed

Just take a deep breath and then.... watching it go... what happens? It's like diving off a high board. Where's the water? If you have come to an end with the ending of breath where have you gone?

Look and see.

The great Master Xu Yun used to talk a lot about questions such as "Who Am I?" He would say, one way of working with this is to repeat the question; "Who am I? Who am I?"

'Who' is just a sound, if I look at it without identifying with it, the 'who' is just a sound coming up, but where has that 'who' come from? Well it must have come from me, where else? Okay, that's common sense. But look again, where, actually, in experience, does the 'who' come from? Try and see. You have to repeat the 'who' every little while, so "Who Am I?" "Who?" If the 'who' comes from 'me' what is that 'me'?

You know that in a couple of minutes you're going to say 'who' again. Where the hell does it come from? So - look into what's there just before it comes up. "Who am I?"

"Who". It's coming, it's not here yet, it's coming though, but where's it coming from? "Who". It came from somewhere, and where's it gone? Where is the mind when it's looking at the space out of which a word comes?

Before it comes, where is it coming from? And when it's gone, where has it gone to? "What is the experience before the 'who' arises?" If you can see it, note the implication.

If you can see the space out of which this simple word 'who' has come, you've also put your finger on the space that is always lying behind language. Here is that aspect of the self, the no-mind, out of which mind comes.

The Buddha recommends we find that space. It's not the whole story, but it is the beginning of the realization that mind is, as it were, floating in a silence. This silence is not the silence of the grave but the bare awareness of the continuous flowing of yourself and necessarily of the universe.

Is that Brahman? The Buddha would not assert such a thing because that would create an entity, an object of thought, a solidity and a source of attachment where there is no object of thought.

All he would say is "There is the unborn." Yes, indeed, there is the unborn. A beautiful word for that which is later born; the mind is born from the unborn. The unborn is the basis, and a familiarity with the unborn is a doorway to what's called enlightenment.

A WCF CENTRE FOR BUDDHIST EDUCATION

Proposal for Discussion:

On further reflection concerning the possible futures of the WCF (See NCF 31) I have recently come up with the following ideas.

1. The WCF does very well in promoting the Dharma through the medium of intensive retreats. Many retreatants come again and again to one or other of our events. This is all to the good. However many retreats simply serve a remedial function for those stressed by the contemporary conditions of life, personal problems, or a feeling that previous events have been beneficial. There is no harm in this; indeed it is good news that our work is of value to many. However relatively few retreatants have adequate knowledge of even the basic Buddha dharma and most are confused regarding the finer points of Buddhist thought or its potential contribution to modern times beyond that of a personally therapeutic role.

2. In the last two years I have been reading intensively for a book on "World Crisis and Buddhist Humanism" which may be published by Motilal Banarsidass on completion. I have realised that Buddhism, far from being a religion in anything like the usual sense, is in fact very close to Western Humanism but with a unique spiritual component.

I feel that the next WCF project needs to develop a distinctive educational focus developing such insights through the presentations of relevant teachers. The general direction of such teaching would be towards a Buddhist Humanism. In suggesting this term to some five potentially interested parties including Peter Reason, James Low and Jake Lynne, I found the idea appealed strongly to them.

3. In what would such a project comprise? Basically weekend workshops for about twelve persons focussed on the relationship between Buddhism and relevant modern ideas in philosophy, science and economics including the environment – that is to say the themes emerging in Western humanism from the 18th century European 'Enlightenment'. I would be happy to teach the line of thought presented in my forth coming book while teachers such as Peter Reason, James Low, Stephen Batchelor, Ken Jones and perhaps David Loy could be invited to supply comparable courses of whatever length. There is also the potential for a more careful consideration of our role in interfaith work – particularly Christianity, based on a more defined viewpoint.

The workshops would include meditation periods and socialisation. Longer courses could also be envisaged.

I would like to hear views on such a proposal, which may be formulated gradually as a WCF Teachers policy should there seem to be adequate support. John Crook.

Chuan-deng Jing-di. Teacher to WCF

NCF XXXIV

DEATH AND DYING

In the spring of 2006 the WCF fielded a conference in Bristol on the theme of Death and Dying presented and organised by the Bristol Chan Group. We had talks, workshops and much discussion. The closing dinner was a fine occasion for Sangha building and getting to know one another. Although the theme might seem gloomy, in fact everyone found the occasion to be of much personal value. Here we present John's opening talk and a discussion of "Euthanatos", the good death, contributed by Sister Ruth Furneaux. Eds.

The Conference on Death and Dying

Introduction

Let us begin with a quotation:

"One thing hastens into being; another hastens out of it. Even while a thing is in the act of coming into existence some part of it has already ceased to be. Flux and change are forever renewing the fabric of the Universe, just as the ceaseless sweep of time is forever renewing the face of eternity. All things fade into the storied past, and in a little while are shrouded in oblivion. Even to those whose lives were a blaze of glory this comes to pass; as for the rest, the breath is hardly out of their bodies before they are lost to sight and hearsay alike.

To what must we aspire? This and this alone; the just thought, the unselfish act, the tongue that utters no falsehood, the temper that greets each passing event as something pre-destined, expected- emanating from the one source and origin."

So wrote Marcus Aurelius in 161 AD, the Stoic philosopher and Roman emperor, campaigning against the barbarians on the eastern frontiers. The sentiments are ones of which the Buddha would approve. There is here a certain affinity between the Buddha's thought and that of one of the founders of Western humanism.

Meditations on death and passing form the fabric of many religions – indeed, they are perhaps at root primarily what they are on about. Yet many of them end by putting forward false hopes and illusions of which the Buddha would not approve. Three main preoccupations lie at the root of most religions:

- The fact of impermanence and lack of security

- How death may be met
- What happens after death?

It is probably the third that has the greatest influence on thought about the other two.

Let us be clear: Science, which is a description of nature, says nothing about what happens after death. Indeed how could it? Likewise, modern Humanism, which is sometimes critical of reductionistic science, remains none the less agnostic about what happens after death. Yet, outside the academies, we all continue to wonder. Christians still have their Miltonic Heaven and Hell. Islamic terrorists go to paradise with their houris.

Buddhism is not so clear. There are two traditions, which we may call Folk Buddhism or vernacular belief and in contrast the philosophical perspective.

In Folk Buddhism there is a strong emphasis on reincarnation stemming from traditions in the ancient world well established before Buddhism. Yet the idea here is not at all what many people actually suppose it to be: it is not the 'you' or 'me' in our complex selfhoods that are reborn in successive lives - far from it. What passes from one death into a new life is 'unfinished business' i.e. incompleted karmic retribution. Karma depends on intention, not at all on accident or unintentional acts. So, what passes on are the intentions of a previous time that have not yet reaped their reward or come-uppance.

The Tibetans express this is some detail. The embryo is formed from egg, sperm and social residues of your previous unfulfilled intentions that unite in fertilisation. It is therefore a threefold entity that emerges from the womb. This set of ideas can be translated quite readily into a modern understanding. When we are born, and indeed even prior to birth, we receive influences from the social conditioning of parents, and later on from teachers, that come down from previous generations. Indeed, a third – social – element quickly impacts on our biological lives coming from the psychological past, even a remotely distant past. A modern humanist is not however arguing that there is a direct link between what YOU did in a past life and the result in the present because the karma that influences the child has a collective origin.

In the philosophical tradition there is no self other than an imputation from the activities of the skandhas. The idea of 'me' is an inference or imputation arising from observing sensation, perception, cognition, and karmic origins in consciousness. Cognitive construction creates an 'I' much as electronic processes create an image on a television screen. The experience of 'me' is virtual. Yet we become attached to this image as all we have – we long to sustain it, fear its loss, dread its death. We invent endless scenarios whereby we can survive death to live again elsewhere and where we hope our enemies will suffer for their sins. We surround our lives with heavens and hells that become the objectivised prisons of our own making.

Yet, if we actually examine this precious self, this I or me, in yogic meditation as indeed the Buddha did, we discover that it consists entirely of memories, hopes, and complex projects to obtain our ends – all of which constitute a kind of narrative. We are one and all stories – hopefully believing we have existence. And of course indeed we have - but not in the form that we think conventionally. There is indeed EXISTENCE but only NOW – the past is dead, the future not yet arisen. Instead of flowing with this flux using skilful means to negotiate its rapids we resist it, invent fixities and defend them – sometimes to the death. Buddha said – let go of this illusory self – flow with the moment – right now even over the waterfall.

"What did the earwig say as he fell over the cliff – 'ere we go"[1]

Zen practices suggest we should take our vivid awareness of the present right into the moment of death. This is an idea of which Marcus Aurelius would have approved. If life becomes impossible, he said – let it go. Yet, in our present age with its emphasis on mundane individuality, it becomes difficult to think of self-dissolution without horror. So, we hide death away. Unlike Greek mountain villages where the elderly sit smiling on the doorsteps, we put our old people in badly smelling homes often far from being residences of kindness, indeed sometimes of loveless starvation. The fact is – culturally – we fear death even though death is as natural as birth. If you want life you get both. Yet, sometimes we do meet the challenge of death in such a way that its sting is surely removed and the fear conquered.

Don Ball was given the choice of living helplessly on a drip for six more months or quietly slipping away in a kindly coma. He signed his life away and waited. I was with him for a while on his last day. Some years before he had been on a WZR with me in Wales. He had chosen to work with the question 'What is Death?' His answer on the last day of the retreat was: "John- Death is Now!" As the day of his passing came, he was able to recall that profound experience and told me so. Just before he slipped away he told his son "You know I am enjoying dying – but I am afraid no one will believe it." His son told him "I think your friends will understand."

Another friend recently began to suffer from a severely debilitating form of lung cancer. He foresaw months of slow suffering not only for himself but also for his loved ones. He made up his mind to travel to Zurich to precipitate a legally assisted suicide. His wife, son and two others accompanied his wheel chair on the flight to Zurich. Afterwards they spoke with admiration of the kindness and compassion with which the whole matter was resolved. As the hour approached, he spoke individually with each of his loved ones and then they sat together with him as the glass of terminating drugs was brought. He sat up and lifted the cup. With a broad smile, "Cheers!" he said and departed.

But what to do where fear remains? The Buddhist seeks to apply both wisdom and compassion. Wisdom to face the koan 'what is Death?' and compassion to be with those who are nearing the end of their lives in kindly understanding. Mindfulness allows attention to the possibility that the sick and ill know more than you think. Recent research suggests that forms of consciousness persist often long beyond their apparent disappearance. Great care is needed. Care of the elderly should be in preparation for death and not in denial of death. Carers need to have come to terms with their own attitudes to their own death. They need training in the practice of empathy with failing minds and to support intelligence where it remains through discussion that is not condescending. There are deep problems in Western institutional care of both elderly and the dying to which Buddhist thinkers need to address themselves and make their voices heard.

I want to conclude with a further quotation, this time from the Mahãparinibbãna Sutta describing the response of monks to the death of the Buddha at Kusinara. After Ananda had discussed with the Buddha what to do with his remains after his death, the text reads as follows:

"And the Venerable Ananda went into his lodging and stood lamenting, leaning on the door post. Alas I am still a learner with much to do! And the teacher is passing away, who was so compassionate to me!" Then the Buddha enquired of the monks where Ananda was and they told him. So he said to a certain monk; "Go monk and say to Ananda from me: Good friend Ananda, the teacher summons you." "Very good Lord" said the monk and did so. "Very good, friend" Ananda replied to the monk and he went to the Lord, saluted him and sat down to one side. And the Lord said, "Enough Ananda, do not weep and wail! Have I not told you that all things that are pleasant and delightful are changeable, subject to separation and becoming other? So how could it be, Ananda - since whatever is born compounded is subject to decay - how could it be that it should not pass away?"

And he goes on to praise Ananda, encourage him and recommend him to the monks. Later on, after the Buddha's death, the Venerable Anuruddha uttered this verse:

"No breathing in and out – just and with steadfast heart the Sage who is free from desire has passed away to peace- with mind unshaken he endured all pains; by Nirvana the illumined mind is freed."

And the Venerable Ananda said, "Terrible was the quaking of the Earth. Men's hair stood on end when the all accomplished Buddha passed away. And those monks who had not yet overcome their passions wept and tore their hair, raising their arms, throwing themselves down and twisting and turning crying, "All too soon the Blessed One has passed away, all too soon the Well-farer, has passed away, the Eye of the World has disappeared. But those monks who were free from craving endured mindfully and clearly aware saying, "All compounded things are impermanent – what is the use of this?"

Then the Venerable Anuruddha and the Venerable Ananda spent the rest of the night in conversation on Dharma.[2]

Let us now proceed to hear what our speakers and workshop leaders have to show us.

1 A saying much loved by my father.

2 Walshe,M (translator) 1995. Mahãparinibbãna Sutta. In: The Long Discourses of the Buddha. A translation of the Digha Nikãya.Wisdom.Boston Mass. p 265f.

BOOK REVIEW - KIM GUTSHOW, 2004, BEING A BUDDHIST NUN. THE STRUGGLE FOR ENLIGHTENMENT IN THE HIMALAYAS

Harvard University Press.

"Being a Buddhist nun" is an extremely valuable account of the life of nuns in the Himalayan valley of Zangskar, a region of Ladakh in N.W India. The work is driven by a deep sense of injustice and a compelling focus on its nature and origin in a remote society still basically medieval in character. It is a highly gendered work in a necessarily gendered field of study. It is certainly true that the arrival of women scholars in such fields as primatology and social anthropology has opened up and corrected a perhaps largely unconscious neglect of the feminine by earlier male workers. Patriarchy is not something that ruled in the past, its presence may make itself felt even now in the liberal and democratic West. The gendering of a research topic is of course accompanied by a comparable gendering of review and assessment but fortunately reflexive self-understanding within post-modernity enables discussion to occur without the rancour of a previous generation. It is perhaps none the less unfortunate in this work that a major chapter on marriage, exchange, work patterns and responsibilities of the two sexes is entitled "The Buddhist Traffic in Women" and an illustration of nuns prostrating before a high lama is captioned "Bowing and scraping ". Such use of words reflects a western bias rather than indigenous perspective.

Kim Gutshow had the guts and the determination to endure some thirty nine months of research in one of the most demanding high-altitude environments of Asia, including three winters in the primitive accommodation of a cliff-top nunnery and making three trips down the notoriously dangerous Chador Gorge by way of the frozen river. Having studied Tibetan at Harvard she was able in time to develop fluency in the Zanskari dialect. This long term residence and linguistic ability has enabled her to present an unrivalled account of monastic economy and social anthropology in Ladakh. Her text is full of "thick" description, delightful anecdotes, biographies of courageous and not so courageous nuns and accounts of the personal joys and sufferings of individuals. Although she focuses on the often lamentable ways in which nuns suffer discrimination she is not unduly disrespectful of the monastic system to which they belong, rather she subjects it to a prolonged and penetrating examination and interpretation.

Gutshow focused primarily on the nuns of Karsha Nunnery but familiarised herself with other nunneries throughout Ladakh. She contextualises her prime focus with detailed accounts of the farming economics and social structure of Zangskar. Although the bulk of this material had been researched in detail earlier, work to which she makes rather scant reference, the specific details of life in Karsha add considerably to a comparative account. It is interesting to note, for an example, that the monks of the great Karsha Gompa use books in their accounting whereas in the previously studied Tongde Gompa across the valley the bulk of the accounting was simply done by memory.

Her prime thesis examines the causes of discrimination in Buddhist society which are often puzzling given the clear statement within Buddhism that men and women are equal and both capable of attaining enlightenment. There is also an equally puzzling contrast between the clear philosophical rejection of any objective reality to social categorisation and the 'emptiness' of co-dependent personal terms, and the rigid social enforcement of gender roles both within and without the monastic system. This puzzle is general to Buddhism and appears equally in China as well as in the Himalayas. Only perhaps in modern Taiwan are nuns now accorded a respect similar to that of monks. Folk belief differs greatly from the ethical philosophy of high lamas and it is folk belief that rules. There is a belief, for example, that women cannot attain enlightenment from their female bodies. For this they must be reborn as male. Many women despise their femininity and wish to be reborn as male.

Gutshow sees the prime problem as enshrined in the folk beliefs surrounding the idea of 'merit'. During a lifetime, merit needs to be accumulated so that future rebirths will be an improvement on the present. While this amounts to the clear expression of attachment to self and the operation of desire, both of which prevent any possibility of enlightenment, Buddhist ethics encourage the earning of merit through selfless behaviour. Generosity is therefore a pleasing aspect of Buddhist culture. However, merit can also be acquired through financing monastic ceremonies, teachings, and sponsoring numerous rituals many of which are only remotely Buddhist and hark back to earlier beliefs. Since monks are assumed to be pure, giving to monks acquires more merit than giving to others. Giving to nuns in their disadvantaged female bodies does not rank highly in a process of merit acquisition. There is thus an elaborately developed "economy of merit", which conflates with a differential distribution of gifted wealth to the disadvantage of nuns and the very great advantage of monks. Kim explores and elaborates this thesis in convincing depth. Much of the poverty of nuns and their poor ability to generate income or capital for their institutions arises from this non-doctrinal, folk basis of vernacular Buddhism.

The arrival of female anthropologists and accompanying do-gooders has promoted change in the traditional system so that financial aid is now given, often quite copiously, to nunneries in Ladakh. Gutshow herself has been able to help her nun friends considerably in this way. This has enabled nuns not only to improve their accommodation and buildings but also to spend more time in the study of scriptures and ritual. In general there is steady improvement in the life of Himalayan nuns and this is not only due to outside aid. Attitudes in Ladakh are changing, although the fundamental misconceptions of Buddhist thought seem to remain untouched. The whole doctrine of merit clearly needs re-examination and a new presentation. Kim is however by no means starry-eyed about the future. In her last chapter she points out that such changes in wealth and status have not occurred without resistance and resentment. The partial withdrawal of nuns from labour on their home farms contributes to economic difficulties for their families and a reduced support for monks. Outside influence is not always welcomed. As usual thoughtless or biased do-gooding can be counterproductive. In addition, wealth promotes greed and misuse of funds as well as occasioning theft and fraud. Even so there does seem to be a clear movement towards putting the Buddhist house in order with respect to women's rights. In this the Himalayan example is clearly well ahead of comparable movements elsewhere in Asia and the Middle East. As Kim concludes, outside support together with changing attitudes within the laity "will spell the difference between victory and defeat for Buddhist monasticism in the coming years."

Yet there is some evidence that Kim Gutshow's argument remains slightly parochial. During our recent visit to Tawang in Arunachal Pradesh we found large, comfortable well endowed nunneries near the town of Tawang with its famous Gelugpa monastery. At a major empowerment ceremony in the monastery nuns had been allocated some of the prime seating to hear the rimpoche's sermons. I had the impression that nuns in Tawang were well supported and respected in a way Kim did not find in the western Himalayas. These brief observations suggest that a further research enquiry into the differences in the ways nuns are supported between the two ends of the Himalayas would be well worth while.

NCF XXXV

ON MAKING A DIFFERENCE

Mindfulness and Meditation in the Practice of Lay Zen

This article takes a close look at the efficacy and function of key activities in Chan. It arises from reflections on discussions both within the Fellowship and with our consultants in New York last November. It was originally presented to the Leaders Retreat of the Western Chan Fellowship in February 2007 as a policy document for discussion and intended to be a guide for new activities in teaching by local Leaders. This final version is extended to include a broad survey of the relationship between retreat practice and everyday Zen in the understanding of Dharma.[1]

Problems in lay Practice

Some years ago a practitioner at the Maenllwyd on being asked why he was there, told me, "to make a difference". I have always recalled this reply and wondered how effective we may be in making any difference to the world or ourselves. At this time of reconsidering our orientation and commitment, it is appropriate to have a serious look at this question.

Do our retreats make a difference in the lives of participants? Do our participants use our retreats to make a difference? We know from our retreat report collection that our retreats are highly effective in opening retreatants to themselves, to fresh views of living and to the onset of some understanding of Buddha dharma. Yet the effect is normally short lived, people return to their karma-determined habitual ways and many soon feel the need for a return visit to this farmstead in Wales, which many come to call "home".

Many have remarked on the yo-yo effect of attending retreats; the up and down in mood, quality of being, depressive tendencies and personal relating that goes on between repeated visits to the Maenllwyd. Serious practice between retreats is quite rare. Many restrict themselves to half an hour of meditation in the mornings and perhaps also the evenings – the rest of the day being spent in the habitual rush of business or minding the baby. The brief appearance of calm is followed by the repetitive and ultimately exhausting daily routine. It is not as if routine life is commonly based in some values related to either retreats or daily mind calming, rather in this consumerist society all values pivot automatically upon self improvement; self satisfaction; concerns with comfort, beauty, status, health, competence and earning power, all subject to shaky self – confidence. It is a me-me-me society.

Yet it is also far from clear whether a more persistent Buddhist practice really makes a much greater difference. Geshe Damchos Yontan of the Lam Rim Centre once told me of a Geshe who, having a bad temper, took himself off onto a three-year solitary retreat. On his return everyone remarked on his calm, happy demeanour, yet, within a week, he fell out with someone and was back to his raging and backbiting. Shifu once asked a retreatant why he came regularly on retreats. "You see, Shifu," he replied "For some days after I get home I don't quarrel with my wife!" Certain young western Zen masters given both inka and transmission by their Japanese teachers have fallen by the wayside in spectacular fornication and money mis-use, leading to their being expelled and disrobed by their sanghas. Even a monk's training here made little difference to a basically immature person ultimately thinking of his own pleasures.

A number of critics have pointed out that the Zen training of laity as part-time monks in a monastic style in the West sometimes produces a split between a pseudo-spiritual life of meditation, liturgy and even significant Zen experiences approved by masters, and ordinary lay activity where irritation, karmic mistakes, hurtful relationships continue, even within the Centre itself. Such a practice commonly becomes abandoned after some years and the reputation of Zen necessarily questioned. Even sincere practitioners may continue to have such persistent difficulties in their life however honestly they may try to surmount them.

It seems therefore that a lay Zen practice following a monastic schedule whether on intensive retreats or over longer time spans makes only a limited difference. Lay practitioners of course have in no sense 'left home'. They are neither renouncers nor 'consecrated' to their practice as a monk may be. To a degree, a pattern of schizoid activity is almost inevitable. The question remains open as to how best a lay Zen practitioner can train in Buddha dharma. Yet, as Shifu has pointed out, monks too have their dilemmas and having left the house may not necessarily mean, "leaving home." Attachments may indeed persist. For monk and layman alike the issue concerns coming to terms with the karma of the self.

Vow Power, Mindfulness and the Clarity of Insight

It seems clear that meditational sitting upon a cushion may not by itself necessarily bring about a difference. Whether one does one's half hour a day or practices alone for three years there seems to be no guarantee that a deeply embedded change will necessarily arise. It looks as if the self-concerns based in karmic habits have not been sufficiently touched. What then is lacking?

The answer is self-confrontation. One may sit on one's backside for aeons, either in a state of hassling mind, a calm condition or even a thoughtless one but that does not mean that one's personal problems and prejudices are being addressed or habitual self reference being confronted. Indeed this was the root of Da Hui's objection to the quietism he believed to be present in Silent Illumination.[2] Meditation may suppress emotion and bring a degree of calm but it does not in itself address the fundamental origin of one's karmic reactivity in prejudice, anger or self-concerning love. Meditation in its basic breath-watching forms is the opening teaching in much Zen practice and may lead one into skilled awareness of silence or into states of trance without for a moment asking who or what the meditator is. Such self-confrontation is essential if any difference is to be made. So how to bring it about?

Our intensive retreats begin with the Western Zen Retreat[3] in which the key issue in the communication exercises is the question "Who am I?" "How is life fulfilled?" "What am I?" and related questions circling around conceptions of self. Statistically, some 25% participants discover forms of self-acceptance that contain the roots of great teachings and insight into Zen, others come to understand the human condition deeply and a few suffer much but find the struggle to have been beneficial.

Yet it has been argued from a Chinese perspective that the use of enquiry involving "Who?" questions slows down or may prevent a 'realisation' due to focussing on self concerns. It is certainly true that a question (hua-tou) such as "What is Wu?" being empty of any target for thought, may allow a retreatant to "drop the question" in a direct realisation of emptiness perhaps more easily. There is however a serious error in the view that working with "Who?" is mere psychotherapy or potentially a side-tracking of the mind into irrelevancy. The problem with immersing oneself too immediately in a dropping of all concern, as may occur with "Wu?" is that genuine personal karmic problems (samskaras) may remain far from resolved, being merely buried for the time being.

We have seen how inexperienced Zen masters who have undoubtedly experienced kensho have none the less subsequently committed serious immoral acts. Clearly, this is because kensho alone does not heal buried karma. The communication exercise in the WZR does allow buried karma to be processed by raising issues of personal distress through focussing on "Who am I?" Subsequently this then allows the mind to address "Wu?" from a condition no longer involving the repression of karma but from an inner freedom generated through self understanding. While this work can be described in Western psychotherapeutic terms, it can also be understood completely within the psychology of mindfulness utilised by the Buddha himself (see below). Moreover, a prime theoretical basis of the WZR retreat lies within the tradition of the Vijnanavada school of Mahayana Buddhism as found particularly in the model of mind presented in the Lankavatara Sutra.[4]

Yet, even these retreats do not necessarily prevent the yo-yo effect from developing and a practitioner may soon be back for more of an essentially therapeutic treatment. More is needed to extend the insights of the retreat into everyday practice.

There are two ways of embedding new understanding: Vow power – as Shifu calls the determination to fulfil precepts through vows, and Mindfulness. Vow power involves taking the precepts seriously and in depth every day. The Chan lay precepts are expressed conventionally in negative terms – no killing, lying, stealing, irresponsible sex or drunkenness. Each precept needs further interpretation as in no killing of a child's joy, no false advertisements, no stealing of other's beliefs etc. These are important no-nos but what we need in contemplating the precepts are positive and assertive injunctions. We need to express the precepts in positive terms: – give life; always speak truth; be generous, express love; be mindful. As part of an everyday practice one needs to recall these positive vows powerfully and be mindful of whether one fails in expressing them or not.

A serious practice of mindfulness requires a more or less continuous awareness of the quality of one's mind and behaviour. Normally when something happens or someone says something negative to one or about one, we immediately react with rejection, irritation, anger or, sometimes, even violence. These reactions come about instantly and recur unbidden in memory whenever the mind falls vacant to be immediately filled by wandering thoughts. A hurt person spends hours mulling over, nursing their pain and planning revengeful responses. A mindful person observes these states of mind, lowers their intensity, questions them, and alters the resultant behaviour. Instead of swearing or threatening, one may ask "Did I hear you correctly?" or "Lets have another look at this," - thereby opening the way to negotiation rather than dispute.

A longer pause allows one to note what aspect of one's self is responding so angrily. One can see that at the root of all such reactions lies fear. Fear is the father of all emotions: jealousy, anger, scorn are all fears for self. The reflex irritations arise without thought; they have become automatic through a deep repression of fears long ago experienced in childhood. These are the source of karma, the roots of personal 'samskaras'. When one reacts in this way, one is not aware of the deep origins of such responses. Long ago Freud pointed out that understanding the self involves the 'recovery of the repressed'. We need to know the origins of our fears and their attendant emotional derivatives. Once we do know them, it becomes possible to identify their re-expression as it arises and to create a tiny mental pause as if remarking to oneself –"Ah, here it comes again!" What I call the 'wry smile' may arise. Such an observation allows a modification of one's habitual reaction into something that with practice becomes a reflection rather than a reaction. To reflect on something allows a pause for consideration to arise. We need therefore to train ourselves to reflect rather than to react. The capacity to reflect in this way is the crucial aspect of mindfulness. It is far from easy.

A prime realisation that comes from such reflection is the shocked understanding of the omnipresence of a selfishness that persists even though a mind may have been skilfully calmed to yield a one-pointed focus on external or internal events as occurs in many practices of shamata or vipassana. Indeed such a sometimes blissfully relaxed focus can prevent one from seeing how even such a praiseworthy practice may be a self-serving activity. Furthermore, if the focus on "Who?" questions leads only into self-referential introspection without a break-through, the subtlety of the enquiry may be missed. It takes time, persistence and a willed focus to recognise the largely unconscious self-serving orientation of the mind even when the stated intention may be the induction of wisdom and compassion.

The specifically Dharmic intuition known as prajna is an insight that sees this obsession clearly and allows the mind to drop out of it into the more basic underlying no-self condition known as "No–mind", "Buddha mind", "Emptiness" or the "Unknown". This is a quite radical state of clarity in which the distinction between self-concern and its absence becomes observed in action. Although not a "kensho", i.e. the totally complete experience of self-absence that may last only a short time, this clarity becomes a form of knowledge of "the other shore" where compassion emerges simply as the natural form of the absence of self-reference. It may arise through intensive sitting practice or in any highly one-pointed reflection providing it does not get stuck in 'the cave of demons' of self-indulgent relaxation.

Once it becomes possible to rest in this clarity, the mind may expand further to a "one mind" state that embraces the whole of experience rather than the divided mind that is present in normal consciousness. When realised, the contrast between these states is at last understood or intuited and can then be sought for both within formal practice and outside it. It allows the practitioner to put the other fully before oneself since the relevance of one's self can be set aside. This is then the basis for an uncontrived, compassionate empathy that is the expression of a Bodhisattva's intentionality (bodhicitta).

The Buddha himself was a prime exponent of such mindfulness. Indeed, it formed the basis for his novel practice whereby he was able to observe the mind in all its expressions rather than bending it wilfully into trance – as was the prime activity of meditative yoga in his time. The essential ideas are expressed in the Satipatthana Sutta and Mahasatipatthana Sutta. The focus of mindfulness dwells on four foundations, mindfulness of body, the feelings, the mind and the objects in mind. These are observed precisely as they are without judgement. The attention is entirely focussed, for example on the body in breathing; "just as a wood turner concentrates on his blade as he makes a long or a short turn." The practice extends into mindfulness of the Four Noble Truths of Suffering, of the Cause of Suffering, the Elimination of Suffering and the path of practise. It is at this point that the omnipresence of self can be observed and the mind transformed. In a further sutta, the Mahadhammasamadana Sutta, the Buddha examines the ways by which activities may be undertaken through understanding what ways may be pleasant now but end in pain, unpleasant now and end in pleasure etc. the foundation of the ways lies in mindfulness. In these methods of close observation, the mind becomes practised in understanding its many ways of arising, their origin and their cessation. Such understanding brings about the power to alter behaviour through personal knowledge gained in practice. Clearly here is a way to make a difference.

Cultural Contrasts between China and the West

Our contemporary ways of life in the West are shaped by the extreme individualism of our times that have become pronounced in European and especially in American traditions since the European Enlightenment. There is thus an especial need for Westerners to understand how our egotism is cultivated in education and through consumerism. Yet, this is not to shift blame onto culture. We are the culture and just as we have created it so can we change it. In becoming mindful of the ways in which we respond and of their origins in our personal histories, both as individuals and as members of a culture, we can initiate change. In that such changes allow for understanding the responses of both self and other, real shifts in compassionate understanding become possible. In such a development, the task of training must inevitably emphasise the everyday practice as one not of lesser importance than training on retreats but rather as the foundation from which going on retreat is a further development. In the West, such work requires direct understanding of one's self and one's motivation.

When Shifu first asked me to lead Chan retreats in his stead, I asked him how I should do it. He said, "John, I am Chinese, you are British. You find out!" Although amazed by Shifu's level of trust in me, this is precisely what I have been endeavouring to do since that time. Perhaps, however, neither Shifu nor I perceived in what ways our differing cultures of origin might require contrasting approaches to the same Dharma. Extensive psychological research shows conclusively that East Asian peoples (Chinese, Korean and Japanese) educated within their traditional systems show very high levels of communal concern and a much less individualistic motivation than traditionally educated American or European citizens.[5] The aim is to merge with the positive aspects of the communities or groups to which an individual belongs, whether that is the family, the firm or a religious group. Identification with a collective psychology means that an individual is less concerned with standing out from a background and creating waves of his or her own. It follows that the question "Who am I?" has less significance for a traditionally educated Chinese than it does for a Westerner. Indeed, in interview with one Chinese gentleman he confessed that at depth he could not see a difference between himself and his engagement with his family. I suspect this East West contrast lies at the root of Shifu's playing down of the "Who?" question in favour of a direct approach to "Wu?"

There is also a difference between the requirements of monastic and lay practice. Monks, through extensive mind calming practice may have considerably reduced their karmic entanglements so that a focus on who is doing them would be less essential. Yet, perhaps one should not be too sanguine in considering monkish attainments.

Of course, neuroses occur just as frequently in the Far East as in America but their basis in ego- psychology is different and consequently the manner of working with personal identity needs also to differ. China, together with India, is in any case little influenced by post –Freudian developments in Western mental health psychology - so that models of mind well understood among the laity in the West have little impact in the Far East. What the appropriate question for a traditional Chinese in a WZR might be remains undetermined but plausibly "What am I like if completely alone?" or "Without a role, who am I?" might be startling.

Meditation

The practice of intensive Chan meditation is a yogic discipline for training the mind in one pointed observation through the cultivation of samadhi. In itself, it has no effect on the emotions, which are suspended or suppressed during practice. The yogic endeavour is to change the conditions of consciousness within which thought may occur so that for example, in a calmed mind objects normally giving rise to anger appear in a different light – just as they are. Repeated practice gives rise to an easier induction of calmed states as the condition for deeper realisation that, if one avoids the faults of falling into 'the cave of demons', may take one all the way to the cessation of ego reference in enlightenment. In returning to everyday life, these skills wane through lacking a basis in the meditative mind state. It is only with the addition of mindfulness that a persistence of a collected mind can be actively and successfully cultivated. As the Buddha remarked the four foundations of mindfulness, provide the direct path for the purification of beings.

For us practitioners in the contemporary world we can now see that an exclusive practice of meditation with neither self confrontation nor an everyday mindfulness under vows that can at least sometimes take one into clarity, is unlikely to make much of an impact on our lives. Yet a system of training in which everyday mindfulness, powered by determined resolution, is enhanced through the periodic cultivation of meditative mind states allowing a deep insight into mind in illuminated calm, may indeed place one firmly on the Buddha path. It is this approach therefore that the Western Chan Fellowship needs to promote if it is "to make a difference".

Supports for Practice

Many people have almost no insight into the causation of behaviour that often causes them deep distress. The practice of psychotherapy has become almost universal in the Western world and does indeed often assist people greatly. A key aspect of this is the recovery of repressed mentalities that, once understood and as it were 'digested', lose their power to cause anguish. Almost any method that effectively brings about such renewed understanding helps enormously; whether this is in individual counselling or in workshops designed expressly for the purpose. These can be given a Buddhist flavour providing a basis for putting feet on the Buddha path as, for example, participation in Ken Jones's skilled, Zen oriented workshops undoubtedly does. In Master Sheng-yen's eyes, however, unless vows are taken and precepts adopted such approaches do not amount to Chan itself.

The Tibetans too, understand very well that meditative practice needs support through other activities – the mind, speech and body supports – visualisation, mantric chanting and physical yoga. In this way, they cultivate a rounded path related to everyday life as well as the tantric endeavour.[6]

Among our retreats the WZR is, as we have mentioned, first and foremost an endeavour to understand the sources of one's karma. It is for this reason that I recommend it as the first or prime retreat on starting intensive practice. The WZR, through the "Who am I?" approach, establishes a basis for mindful self-awareness in subsequent everyday life. When this approach leads into or includes the taking of Vows, it becomes the first step in Chan study at both experiential and knowledge based levels. We need then to consider how, within the WCF, we can support the mindfulness practice that ensures the making of a difference. A new role for the leaders of local groups can be envisaged.

Leadership in the WCF

The local groups of the WCF are 'led' by kind people who often lend their homes or make other arrangement for the meetings of weekly or monthly groups. They may also provide elementary guidance in how to "sit", begin meditation, basic Dharma ideas such as the Four Noble Truths and offer helpful guidance. They are, however, neither allowed to teach Dharma as such nor to carry out intensive interviewing. This is because faulty teaching of Dharma subtlety can lead to quite major misunderstandings and because they are not trained to deal with possible personal distress.

We are however endeavouring to shift the major orientation of the fellowship away from a primary focus on intensive retreats onto the everyday practice of those who have or intend to take up intensive work on retreat. Indeed, there are also those who have no wish to attend an intensive retreat but who would benefit from basic teaching concerning everyday Zen. We are not of course reducing our concern with the vital functions of intensive retreat, but, rather, adding to it considerations that have so far been rather neglected.

It is here that the leaders of local groups can take up a further, highly responsible, activity. This concerns the promotion of Vow Power and Mindfulness in which they themselves may require further training. As we have seen, Vow power stems from the positive and active assertion of the Precepts in promoting life, truth, honesty, love and mindful awareness. Leaders need to understand these points in depth and consider the ways in which the precepts provide numerous metaphors for conduct in everyday life that can be monitored through personal mindfulness.

The practice of mindfulness requires skill in self-examination. This however should not be some sort of worried introspection asking whether one is good enough. Rather it should be a simple mental note taking as to mistakes, successes and misunderstanding in seeking to sustain ones positive vows. Mistakes, errors and inadequacies are inevitable. A careful watchfulness will however increase the beneficence with which one faces life and reduce the often distressing reactions with which one so commonly responds to other people. The mnemonic is the replacing of reaction by reflection. One's responses to others become increasingly considered and considerate rather than automatic and ego based.

During weekly meetings, means for the maintenance of vows and the practice of mindfulness can actively taught, considered and perhaps monitored. While confession can be an excellent practice not all may be inclined to go that far – even though it is a basis for monks' relations in Theravada monasteries. One suggestion is the use of the new Aspirational Prayer as a very practical approach to the Precepts. This is available in our Maenllwyd liturgy book. There is also the very helpful Tibetan practice of lojong mind training, with its use of memorised slogans as reminders of the work and the related tonglen practice of taking in and giving out – exchanging bad thoughts/feelings for compassionate ones.[7]

Of course, leaders have to be practised in these ways themselves. In particular, no self-righteousness should be allowed in relation to moral success! A kind of dispassionate and objective evaluation is what is needed. Above all the entire endeavour should be considered as a path of compassion, the practice of a Bodhisattva.

We have to discuss many aspects of this. What training do leaders need or want? Who is prepared to add these roles to their work as leaders? What difficulties can be foreseen? And so on.

I believe that a training in the vow based, mindful application of "Reflection not Reaction" to be provided by our leaders in their local groups can indeed begin "to make a difference"; to push forward Shifu's teachings among Westerners and to augment our practice of intensive retreat in beneficial ways.

Presented by the Teacher to the Leaders Retreat of the Western Chan Fellowship at the Maenllwyd Retreat Centre, Wales, in February 2007. Subsequently revised.

1 I have benefited greatly from extensive discussions on the theme of this paper with Simon Child, Rebecca Li, David Slaymaker and Jimmy Yu (Guo-gu) to each of whom I am very grateful. The more general discussions within the WCF provided the background for the initial enquiry, which had led to a consultation with Master Sheng yen, our Dharma patron, in November 2006 in Pinebush. NY. (see Teacher's Report to the WCF's AGM 2007.)

2 See: Cleary, C. 1977. Swampland Flowers. The Letters and Lectures of Zen Master Ta Hui. Grove Press. NY.

3 For a description see: Crook, J.H and D.Fontana (Eds).1990 Space in Mind. East-West Psychology and Contemporary Buddhism. Element Chapters 8 and 13

4 See Crook, J.H. 1990. Mind in Western Zen, In Space in Mind: East-West Psychology and Contemporary Buddhism. (Eds; J.Crook & D. Fontana). Element.

5 See: Neisser U and D.A. Jopling. (Eds) 1997. The Conceptual Self in Context. Culture, Experience, Self-Understanding. Cambridge University Press. Especially Chapter 2.

6 See: Crook.J.H and J, Low. 1997. The Yogins of Ladakh. Motilal Banarsidass. Delhi.

7 Chogyam Trungpa. 1993. Training the Mind and Cultivating Loving-Kindness. Shambala.

VISITING SHIFU AND ROSHI JOHN DAIDO LOORI

John Crook and Simon Child met Shifu in his personal residence at the Dharma Drum Retreat Centre at Pine Bush in upstate New York. The interview was interpreted by Rebecca Li and filmed and recorded by monks in attendance. The meeting began with formal prostrations: a warm welcome followed, during which tea and cake was provided. The meeting resulted from discussions about the future of WCF throughout the year and is presented in full in the teachers report to the AGM of the WCF 2007. (See website). John and Simon were also able to visit Roshi Loori at his monastery on Mount Tremper, NY and this article summarises their discussions also - and provides a concluding assessment of both consultations. Shifu's clarification of the meaning of transmission is especially significant in relation to lineage security.

Shifu's health is very poor. He remains resolute, strong in spirit and lucidly clear in his responses to our questions. We covered a lot of ground and here I can only summarise main themes. We showed him group photographs of recent retreats. He commented upon the relatively advanced ages of the participants – an issue he was to return to.

Although various interpreters have attempted to explain to Shifu the relation between therapy and Chan practice in the WZR, Shifu clearly considers the WZR to be a psychotherapeutic exercise. He emphasised the importance in all Chan retreats of 'Vow Power', that is the taking of vows and precepts as a basis for daily practice. To this end, he emphasised longer retreats using Silent Illumination or Hua-tou, encouraging larger attendance and teaching Dharma in them more profoundly. In response, John agreed that there is a strong psychotherapeutic component in the WZR: its great value to Westerners being increased clarity of mind and motivation using Western terminology prior to a clear entry to Chan practice. WZR retreats are especially useful for newcomers to Buddhism, and experienced practitioners also often find value in their fresh approach. He pointed out that our "flag-ship" retreat remains Silent Illumination.

The idea that the WZR is essentially psychotherapy has regrettably taken hold in some quarters of Dharma Drum Mountain in New York and may account for the rather poor attendance over two years. This is both unfortunate and erroneous and the precise function of therapeutic themes in this retreat is once again being emphasised both to Shifu and DDM with an insistence on the use of our own retreat description in advertisement of these events. (See further On making a difference: above)

Shifu took up the question of integrating Dharma and daily life. He stressed two main approaches. Firstly, to emphasise the use of both methods and concepts in daily life reminding oneself to 'pick up' the method as much as possible especially when facing problematic issues: secondly to create longer residential programmes. These may however have only limited benefit, he argued, unless the results extend beyond into subsequent every-day life. He suggested local groups should do much more to emphasise daily practice, even instituting early morning gatherings for those living close by. Group leaders should devise methods for re-enforcing individual participation in Dharma group activities through a variety of focussed events. Dharma gossip and mere socialising should be avoided through emphasis on the importance of the issues involved for each person and their relationships in life. Local leaders should help people develop a thirst for learning the Dharma and going deeper in both practice and concept. Again: develop Vow Power.

With regard to transmission in lay lineages, Shifu emphasised that transmission lasts longest when the recipients are young Dharma heirs with a long life ahead of them. Older recipients do not have much time left either to teach or to find their most effective replacements. Such young recipients should be encouraged to go to Universities etc. to understand the problems of the time. Failure of a lay lineage is by no means certain. Indeed properly established monastic lineages can and do also fail.

John discussed the problems in modern society of finding an appropriate Dharma heir. Most lay practitioners are primarily engaged full time in business or in family support. For most, a retreat is an occasional recuperative event however well the process is understood and applied. Shifu said that it is vital to locate enthusiastic supporters of Dharma who will put energy into continuation and future transmissions of Dharma. Some such persons may not have experienced enlightenment (kensho, i.e.: 'seeing the nature') but if they have enthusiasm, sufficient understanding of concept and method, and vows, then they can receive a form of transmission. Such serious students will do everything they can; they may teach, run events, do the accounts and support the Dharma programme in every practical way.

A student who has "seen the nature" has gone further and, having gone beyond residual doubt, Dharma becomes the focus of his or her life and career; profession and family are secondary to Dharma - Dharma indeed is then expressed through such activities. Such a person is a prime candidate for full transmission.

John asked, "Can those who have not 'seen the nature' themselves give transmissions?"

Shifu answered that such a teacher would not be able to lead a retreat at a deep level. They would not be able to recognise clearly when another has 'seen the nature' because they have not had that experience themselves. Such a teacher must know his or her limitations and be up-front about it with trainees. Such teachers are not qualified to transmit the 'Dharma of mind' – i.e. to give 'inka'. They can share the principles they know but cannot confirm another's experience. Only a sufficiently advanced and experienced practitioner can do that. Dharma heirs can be transmitted as teachers or administrators but may not necessarily be Dharma Masters – only those with kensho experience can be considered as the latter. This needs transparency and must be well understood lest errors occur. It is clear that lineage descends only through the transmissions of qualified Dharma Masters although others assist them greatly on the path. Even so, transmission does not depend on kensho alone. As previously stated by Shifu, a candidate needs to have a sound knowledge of Dharma, a well-established personal practice, be able to teach and attract a following and have a place in which to do it.

John suggested that maybe we need to emphasise Bodhicitta – the will to become a compassionate Bodhisattva - in contemporary Chan, rather than chasing after experiences. Shifu replied that it is easy to give rise to vows but hard to 'see the nature'. He recalled that we need both in the development of wisdom and compassion. John asked whether it was essential to go through a long ceremony and teachings before one can take the Bodhisattva vows in Chan. Shifu said John could make a proposal for a simple ceremony. The main elements are the three pure precepts, the ten virtues and so on. Guo Gu has translations into English. Shifu would then approve if suitable.

Concerning the differing points of focus of monastics and lay practitioners, Shifu remarked that there should be no difference in the depth of Dharma training. The difference lies in the styles of life. John remarked that lay persons with their families and businesses have to attempt non-attachment within attachments. Is not this a major koan about the nature of renunciation? Shifu replied that it was not the case that monastics did not have attachments! Lay people need to train in the context of their family lives. Since monastics have few possessions that is undoubtedly a help, - but they may still be very attached to self. So home leaving is in the heart – not physical – suggested John. Shifu agreed. Leaving the house does not always mean one has 'left home'.

John and Simon thanked Shifu for his inspired teaching over many years and told him they will continue to sustain the lay lineage he had created in Britain through their transmission.

Mount Tremper

Mount Tremper is about two hours drive from Pine Bush and set at a higher altitude among pine forests. The main building of the monastery is a massive, rather austere structure, originally an institution for correcting bad boys from New York. A number of other buildings are scattered among the trees. The forest is beautiful and the open-air shrine and cemetery above the main quarters is sublimely peaceful. In the winter, there is heavy snow.

Roshi John Daido Loori is a large, impressive man seemingly in late middle age. He greeted us warmly without the formalities we are used to in Chan. He responded at once to John's quote that he had argued that lay lineages only last three generations. Roshi said he had had much more experience of teaching both lay and monastic practitioners since he had written that. Never the less the monastics had a clear advantage in some respects. At Mount Tremper, they can pursue their studies without interruption from worldly affairs. During "Dharma combat" Roshi felt that monastics were usually clearer in their replies and understanding. None the less, lay practitioners do well. As many as fifty families had left their home locations and settled in nearby areas so that they could attend teachings. Many had gotten jobs or some form of employment in the vicinity. Schoolteachers spend their holidays at the monastery; those with their own businesses or the self-employed can find the time for practice and teachings.

Roshi spent most of our interview explaining the teaching model he had developed at Mount Tremper. Monks receive a $100 stipend per month but lay residents do not. Basically, monastics and laity follow the same teachings and practices. These are mainly Rinzai Zen, developed from Roshi's own teacher (Roshi Maezumi) and include progression through 750 koans, although this is too many for lay people.

The koans are tested through supplementary questions; there is the Rinzai rush for interviews that are usually brief. The process is supported by lectures, mondo, Dharma combat and a rising through a hierarchy of positions and roles within the institution. There are however those who prefer to practice in the Soto style using Shikantaza. Transmission in Rinzai may be to either monk or lay persons but on the Soto path transmission to non-monastics is not possible. The Shobogenzo of Dogen is a prime teaching text.

Roshi suggested that intellectuals like koans, those with faith in practice prefer shikantaza. Yet, he argued, the end result of either process is similar – the "capacity to enter samadhi".

He argued that a residential community guarantees a greater degree of continuity than any other institutional structure. It provides a disciplined community atmosphere in which it is possible to delve deeply into Dharma, experience self-confrontation within a community, and practice in the long term. Even if such an institution falls upon hard times or fails to produce good teachers, the existence of the physical presence of a place often carries the institution through till better times and better teachers emerge. This has often been the case in history, he argued – and indeed the survival of Chinese Zen through the intense communist period in China partly illustrates this. Most of the old monasteries, however badly destroyed have re-arisen in their own grounds.

The prime emphasis in this system is an educational one, intellectual, physical, artistic and spiritual. It is a gradual progression with tests, examinations and movements from one stage to another. The range of spin–off institutions is considerable and clearly a great many excellent people and teachers are involved.

Preliminary conclusions

There are few British institutions that can compare with western American Dharma centres or monasteries such as Mount Tremper, Green Gulch Farm or Tassajara in terms of Dharma training, monastic recruitment, lay support and financial security: nor are there many to compare with the Tibetan monasteries established in France. Our own institution is a small contribution compared with these but a significant one. There is no doubt the Fellowship is bringing intensive retreats with few attached strings to an increasing number of serious Dharma enquirers across Europe. There are doubts however about both the depth of our Dharma training and its viability into the future. Serious thought needs to be put into our approach, its institutionalisation and the responsibilities of leaders. The extensive membership, life commitment, organisation and financing of these other institutions provide models of modern practice to be seriously examined as we go forward.

Our discussions together and with Shifu and Roshi Daido Loori suggest a number of considerations to be developed as our policy for the future. As Teacher, I recommend the following:

i/ Transmission

Shifu's clarification of transmission within Chan Buddhism clears up several confusions. It is clear that, while transmission may be given to teach or administer within an institution, only transmission to someone having received inka confirming the experience of "kensho" amounts to the transmission of Dharma Mastership within the lineage. Only Dharma Masters may transmit such Mastership to others. Unfortunately, the term transmission still refers to both forms of "promotion' and relies on the honesty of teachers in making clear their status to disciples. If this is not present confusion can still be a result. It is to be hoped that a change in the Chinese terminology may clarify this matter still further.

ii/ Emphasise Local Groups.

Participation in Maenllwyd retreats has led individuals to offer their homes as meeting places for meditation and now local centres are active across the country. It is from these centres in turn that many individuals come for retreat at the Maenllwyd. The Maenllwyd lies at the hub of a large wheel that continues to acquire more spokes. This institutional structure has proved very successful in promoting important and deep Chan practice utilising retreat formats of four kinds - unique in Europe. The weaknesses we have been identifying stem perhaps from too intensive a focus on attending occasional retreats. We can conceive of a further wheel in which the personal life practice of individuals takes central place and retreats at Maenllwyd become one of the spokes - perhaps necessarily a rather distinctive one. These wheels are not alternatives but rather complimentary ways of envisaging and focussing our planning. One wheel on each side of our chariot - as it were. We should do two things: emphasise the importance of membership of local groups, and encourage their leaders to take on much more responsibility for the members' initial recruitment and training.

Membership of local groups should require active participation in Dharma events and participation in their planning and organisation. Members need to be pro-active in finding and recruiting young beginners interested in what Buddhism has to say in the modern world – especially in relation to the ongoing and increasing world crisis. The responsibility for this shift in orientation must lie with local leaders.

These need to undergo more training, study Dharma more deeply and play a very active role in the encouragement of local members. They need to provide the initial teachings, show the relevance of the Dharma to our time, demonstrate how Dharma can be practised in both family and business life and encourage participation in our central retreats. Attention may need to be given to providing leased or purchased premises for events of increasing size. This may entail considerations of local fund raising. Local leaders need therefore to upgrade their programmes with more Dharma social events, more frequent, even daily meditation meetings, giving talks and exchanging visits with other local group leaders and senior Fellows and retreat leaders, arranging meetings between neighbouring local groups etc. Local leaders may need to establish small local committees to help them. Each local group has unique characteristics so that each one can develop its own unique mode of participation in Dharma teaching. The focus should be on increasing the sense of community in a local group with a view to lessening the separation between Dharma and ordinary everyday life. Clearly this gets easier as a group enlarges to acquire aspects of a community; hence the need for recruitment.

iii/ Local Leaders' Responsibility

The responsibility of local Leaders thus emerges as a most important new emphasis in a developing Fellowship policy - and this will require improved ways of training local leaders. To this end we have discussed ways by which local leaders may consult with the Teacher or Dharma heirs when necessary, and sign up with a 'mentor' from among the senior Fellows with responsibility for Maenllwyd and local retreats. Mentoring can be a way to share and discuss difficulties, the advisability of suggested local programmes, how to deal with problematic members and improving Dharma teaching appropriate to the group. The Teacher will discuss these proposals further with an advisory sub group – probably the same as took part in the initial Teachers consultation. Conclusions will then go before the Committee.

iv/ Recruit Youth

It is especially important that young persons across all classes of society be encouraged to come along. There should be no unconscious class or community prejudice in our local endeavours. The more intellectual groups need to open themselves to practitioners that are more simple-minded. Those with only basic understandings need to obtain instruction in more difficult issues. Hopefully it will be among younger members that some future Dharma heirs may emerge. This is a point strongly emphasised by Shifu. He suggested recruitment should be focussed particularly on universities and colleges where Dharma involvement can become part of adult education. Group leaders active near such colleges should take this point seriously.

v/ Networking.

As discussed at a previous Leaders retreat, networking can be used to increase communication between groups and especially between local group leaders. Networking should be supported by visits from those designated as mentors who can evaluate the quality of the Dharma life of local groups and advise accordingly. Dharma heirs should also travel to local groups in the same way. While busy timetables has made this difficult John has visited Glastonbury this year, given three talks to the Bristol group and visited the Precious Wood of Eric's associated group in SW Wales. We hope to develop this further when not dashing across Europe to respond to yet another call for a retreat.

vi/ Month-long Dharma Retreats.

Shifu and other Masters recommend much longer retreats – rains retreats or 49 day retreats. The most we have managed is a three-weeker. Effective Dharma instruction needs embedment through living it and this is best acquired initially on long term retreat in which the intellectual and experiential understanding can develop together without dilution from worldly involvements. Such a strengthened practice can then be more easily assimilated to a daily life practice on completion of retreat.
To this end, I am considering offering longer retreats of three to four weeks focussed on Dharma teaching. These events would not however be intensive retreats such as the five or seven day events at the Maenllwyd; rather they would be more like monastic living in periods of non-intensive practice. We would have a loose programme centred on Dharma instruction backed by periods of zazen, work, administration, cooking and recreational walks etc. A test of such a retreat took place after the failure of the Skokholm adventure and will be tested again during the Chan Convivium of the present programme. Two advantages spring from this longer period of retreat. Firstly, there is time for experiential understanding to develop together with intellectual realisation of the meaning of Dharma concepts. Often academic instruction needs to be followed by experiential instruction of an entirely different order. One is form and the other is emptiness – it takes time to understand and also experience their relationship and meaning. Secondly, life in a small community necessitates the cultivation of tolerance for the individual idiosyncrasies of others. There is training implicit here in compassion and in mindfulness of others in a way not available in intensive, individually focussed,

short retreats. This aspect of monastic training undoubtedly contributes to the tolerant compassion often visible in older monks whether Buddhist or Christian.

vii/ Facilities

Such longer-term retreats need appropriate premises with reasonable mod-cons. The development of old buildings at Winterhead is a possibility that could meet this requirement. John is consulting with Nick Salt concerning such a project, which may or may not require some financial participation by the Fellowship.

It is far from clear however whether the present members of the Fellowship would wish to attend these rather differently oriented monastic type retreats and the offer may have to be made more widely. The signs are not especially promising as the absence of solitary retreatants etc. suggests. It would therefore be useful if readers of this report could state their potential interest in such a project.

viii/ Residential Community

There can be no doubt that Roshi Daido Loori is right when he argues that the establishment of a residential community is probably the best way to ensure the continuity of a lineage even through dark periods. This current suggestion for longer term, Dharma focussed, retreats may be a way towards establishing such an institution, which is clearly not possible for us at the moment.

These eight recommendations do not cover the entire range of issues discussed during the year but they emphasise the prime conclusions. In the coming year they will be considered further, discussed in committee and brought before the AGM. In this way, we are hoping both to improve our presentation of Dharma in the West and ensure its continuity into the future.

Final Remarks

I am well aware of an alternative perspective to the one I have outlined above. This would be based more on an appreciation of our success story so far and upon the hard work, indeed devotion that many have shown during its development. Indeed, maybe we do not need to do anything! Continuing as we are and allowing an organic growth of our current activities is certainly an attractive option. Could we rely on it? As one written contribution to the Teacher's Consultation put it: "A Zen attitude for me is an attention to my moment to moment reaction to the world around me in a precise and aware fashion that is appropriate, honest and authentic ... This is best expressed when self-concern drops out of the way. We learn about self-concern through the practice of Chan. We should be careful we don't develop a kind of organisational self concern that overwhelms our authenticity". These are wise words and they need attention. If only it were so easy!

What then drives the motivation apparent in the 'Preliminary conclusions' paragraph above. I have spent some four years writing a book entitled "World Crisis and Buddhist Humanism" which is at last in press and will be published in about a year's time. Investigating the current world crisis is indeed a sobering activity but it was encouraging to discover how closely Buddhism compares with the finest values of the European humanist 'enlightenment' in its empirical approach. There is hope here; although time for adequate correction is short. The overwhelming stupidity, ignorance and political inadequacy of our times, contrasting so pathetically with our scientific genius, is painfully apparent and the selfishness on which the institutionalised greed of our largely unconscious consumerism depends is clearly revealed.

We cannot perhaps rely solely on the authenticity of a well-meaning individualism however focussed on moment-to-moment involvement in living. In less stressful times, that may be adequate but such an approach may be too easily swamped today by the illusions and cults of the contemporary, self serving, global society. While it would be easy and doubtless gratifying to relax back into one's hermitage of authenticity, the cultivation of bodhicitta impels us to care for our world. This necessitates consideration of how we can best operate to make a difference. Here the role and function of our institution can play a part and we need therefore to examine it seriously. It is this that I encourage all fellows to do.

NCF XXXVI

THE BURMA SITUATION

Shifu's comment to the World Economic Forum (above) that "in order to save humanity from the danger of conflict and even annihilation, we must not only preserve the values of our own groups, but also respect the values of others..." establishes the importance of finding diplomatic means to bridge differences between faiths. It can also be applied to differences between political positions. The immediate situation in Burma is horrific and concerns us unusually directly in that Buddhist monks are being beaten, murdered and monasteries vandalised. World opinion is clear in its condemnation of a brutal and irrational regime but some states benefiting from access to Burmese commodities of economic importance are refraining from exercising a potentially powerful influence. A key case in point appears to be China. Is it possible to influence China towards a more active policy?

The answer is 'Yes' because China is very sensitive to any criticism that might damage its presentation of the Olympic Games in Beijing next year. If Buddhists worldwide were to encourage a boycott of the Beijing games unless China takes a more constructive role in Burma the effect could well be considerable. Of course, time will tell and by the time these words appear the situation may well have changed. The point to make is that the Chinese authorities are sensitive to world opinion regarding human rights and the Games are a rare opportunity to exercise leverage. Respect for the values of others certainly means values that sustain or restore the wellbeing of oppressed people whether Buddhist, monastic or of other faiths.

OLD MYOKYO-NI

Old Myokyo-ni
never came this way
the beds no doubt too damp the track too steep
and too much laughter. No doubt the kyosoku not long enough -
yet the gaunt pine stands sentinel. No nonsense cooking here
these hearts as empty bowls lined up for washing.

Doing their own practice in their own way -
mist laden groves,
cloud valley, village invisible. The bell rings a rainwet hand collecting sitters in still rows
tap -tap - precipitating silences.

Monks in mufti
adorn this quiet refectory
lifting spoons to silenced tongues dim light at noon requiring candles serving an extraordinary soup
bowl by bowl
the measured ladle.

In the library books
stand motionless in their places. Outside the Welsh monsoon greys the valley drab.
The sound of scribbling copies some ancient words.

Few farmers come up this hill
the sheep take care of themselves, scan the empty valley
hear the tumbling stream returning cloud waters seeking again a distant sea.

Too high for Kingfishers too wet for skylark flight
Wrens like mice run below the ferns mushrooms fairy circling scant grass thinking of soup.

Today silence hangs around these yards of meditation,
rain drops purl from the old roof. No wind - heavy leaves
breathe - sheep stand still
in their wet wool, water keeps the flies grounded.

OBITUARY - THE VENERABLE MYOKYO–NI

The above poem is not a criticism of the venerable Rinzai teacher, the nun Myokyo-ni – it is actually an endearment. Even so, it contains a friendly riposte to her long held scepticism concerning our efforts at The Maenllwyd.

Myokyo-ni came into the world in Leitersdorf, Austria, as Irmgard Schloegl. Highly educated, she took a PhD in physical sciences at Graz University and came to Britain in 1950 as a lecturer in mineralogy at Imperial College, London. Once here, she soon enrolled in Zen classes at the Buddhist Society led by the well-known judge, Christmas Humphreys QC, who had founded the Society in 1924. Christmas Humphreys taught discursively and enthusiastically but with little focus on actual meditation and with some intrusion of theosophical ideas. Even so, Irmgard became his strong supporter and soon assisted in teaching.

In 1960, Irmgard went to Japan to begin intensive training at the headquarters of the Rinzai sect at Daitokuji Temple in Kyoto. Together with Peggy Kennet she was thus one of the two outstanding women Zen teachers who went from Britain to Japan for training in those years. Their paths were very different however and I don't think they met. Peggy Kennet eventually became Roshi Jiyu Kennet in the Soto tradition founding Shasta Abbey in California and Throssel Hole Priory in Northumberland.

Irmgard spent twelve years training in an exceptionally demanding Japanese monastic Zen environment and always remained reticent about her experiences there. This may be in part because her life was eased by training with the American Buddhist, Ruth Sasaki, who led Zen study groups at the monastery. In 1966, Irmgard returned to the UK setting up full residence in London finally in 1972. She started a Zen group at the Buddhist Society focusing on serious meditational practice and lived with the Humphreys in St John's Wood where she also led classes. Her lay teaching became more structured in 1979 when she founded the Zen Centre to which institution Christmas Humphreys bequeathed his house when he died in 1983. This address subsequently became Shobo-an, Hermitage of the True Dharma, functioning as the centre's main administrative location and training temple. Irmgard also took control of all Zen activities at the London Buddhist Society and a group of her students assumed a dominant role in the society's affairs.

It was around this time that I met Irmgard, travelling up to town from Bristol several times for an interview at the Buddhist Society to discuss and seek guidance on my early work at The Maenllwyd, where I was setting up the first Western Zen Retreats based on Charles Berner's "Enlightenment Intensives". Irmgard was informative and helpful but would not commit herself on my activities. One of these interviews forms the basis for a training koan (See NCF 32).

"Layman John went up to London to see the nun Myokyo-ni. As they sat together, he told her of his new retreat centre, the retreats he was running and his hopes for its development. He had come to ask for any advice she might have. As time went on Layman John found that Myokyo-ni was saying very little. She made no comment nor did she give any advice. So he spoke some more – and then, somewhat hurriedly, again some more. Still no comment. So he stopped and said, "I am wondering what response you have to what I am telling you". Myokyo-ni looked at Layman John and said, "I have no response." Layman John suddenly understood.

What I understood was that in seeking her approval I revealed my own uncertainty and lack of trust in myself. Irmgard's response taught me an important lesson. Some years later, I met her at a gathering in London and told her this story. She beamed at me remarking, "Oh – did I really say that!"

As the Western Zen Retreat took shape and became functional, John Snelling, then editor of the Buddhist Society's journal 'The Middle Way', asked me to write a short article about it. I did so and John accepted it. Yet, when Irmgard heard of this she took forceful exception to it and forbad its publication. John apologised to me profusely but the dominating presence of Irmgard's Rinzai-coloured followers at the Society of that time prevailed.

I was, needless to say, irritated by this summary, literary castration but it had one highly beneficial effect. I decided to make sure of my own training in orthodox Zen and soon set off for my first retreat with Chan Master Sheng-yen in New York, thereby developing my acquaintance with Chan begun many years before. It seems Irmgard was never very tolerant of approaches to Zen that differed from her preferred school – Rinzai.

Irmgard's Zen teaching was as rigorous as her own training in the Rinzai approach must have been. There were those who found it too tough and several such deserters turned up at The Maenllwyd seeking shelter. They are still coming.

Morinaga Roshi had been Head Monk at Daitokuji when Irmgard trained there and in 1984, during a visit to London, he ordained Irmgard as the nun Myokyo-ni; Myokyo meaning "mirror of the subtle', a name he had given her previously, and ni meaning nun. She continued her teaching strictly, telling her students "The hardships are there to quell the fires within us." Many of her students became monks or nuns who admired her strength of character, which, although it could be overbearing, was also often fiercely insightful and deeply compassionate. She was said to embody an 'uncannily powerful presence during dokusan. One of her most influential students has been Professor James Austin whose exceptionally clear 'kensho' experience was the stimulus for his extensive work on the plausible neurology of Zen described in his book 'Zen and the Brain'. Irmgard had undergone a Jungian analysis before she went to Japan and would refer to Zen as a means of transformation of the psyche towards wholeness and compassion without neglecting the 'shadow'.

Myokyo-ni died aged 83 on March 27th 2007. British Buddhism has lost a formidable teacher and a powerful personality in the teaching of the Zen Dharma. Those of us in the Soto School and in Chan working to present a comprehensive Zen in the West may however perhaps now hope for greater communication with our Rinzai colleagues in the UK.

ST MOLAISE OF HOLY ISLAND

This spring many of us enjoyed a Chan Retreat at the newly re-constructed international centre on Holy Island, Scotland, now owned by the Samye-ling Tibetan Centre. The island gets its name from the residence in a cave there of the sixth century Irish, Celtic saint and missionary Molaise (died 639 CE).[1] His cave is a roomy shelter near the shore and we visited it several times. His saint's day arrived while we were there and, as no Christians came over from the mainland to celebrate it, we did so with chants of many sorts and origins, incense and music. The following poem celebrates the life of this ancient holy man.

A hard landing he had of it
Through the baying waves
Coracle smashed on grey boulders
The red cliffs rugged before.
Scratching a cross on a slab of rock
Thrice he prostrated his thanks to the wind.
Tell me what the Cross is...

West wind from Ireland brought him to this shore
Riding the high and rushing clouds

Cresting the black waves
Shearwater craft alone among wild waters
Arriving in the primrose time of catkins
Brown beech buds opening on fitful sun-showers
Tell me what the Cross is...

Between cliff and water
Boulders break the force of wind and rain
An empty shore roaring with an empty sea
Liturgical voices blowing through his head
And lone heart rejoicing in the fear of solitude
The bent and sombre musing trees.
Tell me what the Cross is...

Arrival without departure,
Bird boned coracle dead upon the strand
Rain washed rock already wet with waterfalls
Sunbreak at sunset, lowtide at dawn
Clawing sweet shellfish
From the fish-jawed stones.
Tell me what the Cross is...

Cliff climbing slowly
Gazing back at the sun-patched sea
Joy of journeying ripe in mind
Turning inland to the distant hills
The bee humming woods
Looking for people
Tell me where the Cross is...

April 1976.
Peppercombe, Devon.
Revised 2007 after Holy Island retreat. JHC

1 See: Mclaughlin, W. J. 1999. Molaise of Arran. A Saint of the Celtic Church. ISBN 0-9535437-1-4. Privately published.

NCF XXXVII

RETHINKING

The state of Britain certainly needs rethinking. The feral teenagers armed with guns and knives, some freely murdering those who object, the vulgarity of binge drinking, the vomit in our streets, the riotous prisons, the lack of respect for race, sex or age on trains and buses – these things are not common elsewhere – although other continental countries have their own problems. We need to rethink and force a rethink among the unthinking. But how? Depressive pontificating, moaning or gnashing of teeth gets us nowhere. It is sit down cogitation that is needed with both mind and heart. We can only begin in our known places. This edition of NCF includes some rethinks and some further thinks. As we continue to develop with an expanding network of small groups we will necessarily gain a larger footprint. We need to consider what print that is to be. In their own way each of our contributors has a message to offer whether as lecture, talk, pilgrimage, meditation, poetry or humour.

Chuan-Deng Jing-di

RETHINKING SELF

The Marianne Fry Lecture, 2007 [1]

This annual seminar of the Friends of the British Gestalt Journal commemorates the life of a well-loved psychotherapist. John was honoured to be invited to give this lecture before a national audience of around a hundred therapists in Bristol in the summer of 2007. The event took all day, included lunch and ended around tea time. The talk was followed by a long question and answer discussion session. John took the opportunity to review some of the main ideas in his forthcoming book, World crisis and Buddhist Humanism: End Games - Collapse or Renewal of Civilisation (New Age Books Delhi), which should appear in May this year. This article therefore allows our readers a preview of some of John's ideas and hopefully encourages a purchase of the book! Eds

The scene is set beside my father's deathbed. It was the time of the oil crisis in 1972. Dad was reading his newspaper; he'd had a serious heart attack and he was to die the following morning. That evening he was very lucid. He was reading about the world crisis of that time, and I was sitting with him. He put down his paper and he said to me, "John, you know, I always used to think I would like to come back in the future and see how everything is going on. But you know now I really don't think I want to come back; things look just too bleak." I was always sad about these last thoughts of my father, and I resisted them over many years. Yet, I have to confess that in the last three years I have come to have a lot of empathy with what he was saying. I am not at all sure I would want to come back in 20 or 30 years' time. And that's within the lifetime of my grandchildren. It's within the lifetime of the grandchildren of all of us.

The Problem of Decadence

It now seems certain that in the next 30 years or so the planetary world as we know it ecologically today will change dramatically. We can already see the changes happening. Furthermore, without being alarmist, we also have to say that scientists do not know what the thresholds involved in these changes are. There could be trigger points that may bring about far more rapid and catastrophic changes than we are thinking of at the moment. It is just very uncertain indeed. Let us hope things will proceed smoothly; let us hope that we manage to get on top of it, but there are no promises.

Why did my father feel that way? My Dad was an Edwardian who had come through the First and Second World Wars, who had seen the victory of democracy over Nazism and Fascism, who had also seen the fall of the Iron Curtain and the change in politics towards what appeared at first to be a much more optimistic scenario. This was a direction of change that would have fulfilled his humanist-Christian values. He had been an engineer and was proud of all the progressive advancements in the world. He'd seen all of those things but the changes that were then occurring were disappointing and seemed chaotic. I think he felt that the world had entered a period of marked decadence. Today I would agree. I put it to you that we are living in a decadent world. And I'm also going to suggest to you that the reason for that decadence is us, you and I in our time, I mean the current Western cultural attitude to this world of ours.

What is decadence? Well the Oxford English Reference Dictionary defines 'decadence' as "moral or cultural deterioration especially after a peak or culmination of achievement". The juxtaposition of these opposed ideas – moral or cultural deterioration after achievement – is a very sad one to reflect upon. We have to realise that, as Prime Minister Macmillan said long ago, we in the West have never had it so good. The scientific advances, the inventions, the extraordinary speed of communication, email and all that is really staggeringly significant and has brought about an ease and comfort in life that no previous generations ever had. Not only that, up until relatively recently the victories in the Second World War and the fall of the Iron Curtain did indeed suggest that we might be moving towards a more stable historical situation on the planet with a greater importance of the rule of law, the United Nations, a World Community, and the development of something approaching democracy over at least very large areas of the world. Yet, then what happened? Well I needn't rehearse for you the history of the last 15 years, but I do want to refer you to another definition – the definition of the adjective 'decadent'. The Oxford English Reference Dictionary refers to the adjective 'decadent' as "self-indulgent". Now, as we've seen, the title of this talk is 'Rethinking Self' and if our world is failing on account of a decadent self-indulgence, then it is attention to the 'self' itself that we will need to pay attention.

I don't want to spend too much time talking about the well-known problems of our time, the faulty politics, bad decisions, poor economics: Kosovo; Iraq; the state of the Middle East; Islamic religious fanaticism due largely to deprivation and poverty distorting Islam into the terrorism of resentment. This is matched by equally perverse and self-concerning policies of the Christian Right in the United States – the Neo-Cons. The collision of Islamic fanaticism and the Neo-Cons, if it continues, (and thank goodness it looks as though it isn't) could produce the ending of our cultural world, both in bangs and in whimpers. Fortunately, the victories of the democrats in the recent elections in the United States show the American people are at last waking up to the mistakes of their leadership: understandable mistakes because driven by the terrible disasters in New York of '9/11'.

Yet these dangerous political and terrorist issues are of relatively minor concern when compared with the problems of global warming and the concurrent political resistance to adequate action in changing our economic practices in relation to ecology. Again, sad to say, it has been in the United States that the major resistance has been seen – political resistance to doing anything about the planetary ecology. Furthermore, the lack of leadership by the United States is allowing or encouraging China to produce incredible amounts of pollution as it fills the US demand for cheap goods. This pollution does not stay in China but drifts around in the world's wind systems.

All this is the background to something else, which is perhaps the saddest point directly and immediately facing us in Britain. I refer here to the extraordinary social alienation of large sections of our young people – the lethal teenage gangs, the Ladism and the lunatic binge drinking. In Bristol, only a few weeks ago, I went to see a film and came out to the street at about 8 o'clock in the evening to find it full of drunk and half-clad young people. It was from any perspective socially disgusting. Then again, not much better was the behaviour of our football supporters in Barcelona a few months ago. The Spanish people were putting up politely with a good deal of shouting, violence and excessive bravado. Beyond these symptoms of decay, we have all the well-known effects of family breakdown. It seems that British teenagers of certain origins bearing knives and guns are becoming lethal, roaming dogs in the body politic.

I could go on like this but to do so would be merely depressing. We all know these things. So I want to make the one major point which makes our world decadent, truly decadent. We have been almost unthinkingly engaged in the spoliation and destruction of this planetary ecosystem upon which our civilisation depends. The way in which we are behaving economically and socially is bringing about climate changes that may be extraordinarily destructive over time. What is so extraordinary is that when we know we are faced with severe damage to our own planet, to our own cultures, to our own cities, we're doing so remarkably little about it. Two days ago we had headlines about the Queen getting cross during an interview. Such triviality is typical of the media. There is very little adequate focus on the truly serious situation that we are in.

We might ask - haven't things always been difficult? For my Dad things were pretty ominous in 1939. Yet, in 1939 it was not the state of the planet that was at stake. This is what makes the word 'decadence' truly potent in our time. It is unbelievably decadent, in my book, not to take this planetary issue enormously seriously as the most important issue of our current existence and one that will affect our grandchildren and our great-grandchildren enormously. Washington fiddles while Rome burns.

World-Views

These pressures, these gloomy pictures, do have personal effects on all of us. I myself find that listening to the 10 o'clock news bulletin is commonly a highly depressing experience; it's often grim. I want now to refer to the essay written by a young woman student in the University of Bath which Peter Reason, Professor of Management Studies in Bath, quoted in his inaugural lecture about two years ago. She had said: "As I approach the end of my studies I can't help feeling that freedom is a fallacy, and that somehow I've been walking a predetermined path to mortgage repayments and commuting nightmares. Further, I'm not alone. Despite a whole array of graduate opportunities, there is a growing mood of claustrophobia and a sense of powerlessness. For all the relative luxuries of the Western world we are still unsatisfied, there is an unmistakable sense of longing, a deep craving for some kind of release or escape." In quoting this essay and going on to discuss it, Peter Reason argued that what this young woman was trying to escape from was the Western world-view itself, that is the unthinking collusion in a certain image of our world that almost all of us entertain.

What is a world-view? We have to spend some time thinking about this. A world-view is that complex set of integrated social images and understandings that, as it were, passes as the norm of one's time. A world image of a period of time drives the history of that period. You could say that the world-view of the Victorian era had to do with imperialism, to do with white supremacy, to do with the cocky arrogance of the West, to do with Christian dominance. Yet, it is also to do with the rights of man, European enlightenment, free play, democracy, and the ending of the slave trade. Such a complex made up the prevailing world-view of the majority of educated people in the Victorian era.

What is the set of components that determines the world-view of most of us today? Well, I think very few of us ever actually sit down and ask what is my world view, or what is our world view, or what is the British world view, or what is the European world view, or what is the Western world view. Of course, there's a good reason for that – it's very complicated.

I want to list three features of our current world-view to put to you as being characteristic of our time and which are operating for the most part unconsciously in that we don't reflect upon them and are not educated to reflect upon them – Capitalism, Individualism and Dualism.

Capitalism

First of all, there is the overriding power of capitalism in its consumerist form. We have to realise that this economic system is amazingly dynamic based upon the system of business institutions that requires investment to yield products which in turn produce dividends for the investors. In order to make that cycle work, there has to be novelty, exploitation of ever more resources, and growth creating value addition beyond the cost of labour. The system naturally sustains the division between the relatively poor producers and the often tremendously rich investors. Needless to say, some of these industrial activities involve arms sales utilised in regional violence and the potential for atomic war. Nowadays so powerful is consumerist capitalism that many of the really big trans-national corporations are much bigger than national states.

If one asks who is responsible for the activity of a trans-national corporation it would be very difficult to put a finger on anyone because these are machines – machines driven by a very effective economic process. One could say that the people who are responsible are the investors, that is you and I. Yet we rarely know exactly where our funds are invested. They are invested by brokers. Only a few of us have actually conducted an ethical investigation as to what these investments are actually supporting. One of the effects of the system has been the enormous expansion in the search for raw materials into all parts of the globe involving the destabilisation of tribal peoples, the creation of enormous dams sometimes requiring the removal of whole populations, and the breakdown of the culture and language of many small peoples.[2]

This extraordinary system, we must realise, is historically completely new, a novelty. Before the industrial revolution the great empires of, say, the Sultans of Turkey, the Moguls of India or the Emperors of China, were all based on agricultural riches. Of course, there were trade routes, of course, there were banks, of course there was exchange – these systems were also dynamic. Yet, the limitations of agriculture and the seasonality of production meant that such empires could never gain more than a certain amount of power. Such economic systems couldn't become endlessly progressive in the manner of post-industrial economies. Britain with its dynamic world-view of industrialisation created something entirely new when compared with any of the agriculturally based empires. It is this very European novelty, adopted by all the powers of this world that is now destroying the natural systems that it exploits.[3]

Individualism

What is this consumerist capitalism riding upon? I put it to you it's driven largely by another feature of our Western world-view - our extreme sense of individualism. This is the second feature I wish to stress. We value our individuality enormously, perhaps excessively. One of the crudest indications of this is the way in which every time a British or an American soldier gets killed in either Afghanistan or Iraq, flags go up, ceremonies are performed, corpses are brought home covered in national flags, relatives are informed, great sadness is publicly expressed and, because of a few hundred American dead, new policies are presented in Congress. But what about the hundreds of Iraqi civilians run over by American convoys rushing at high speed to supply their fortresses and so terribly fearful of roadside bombs as to drive recklessly through crowds of civilians smashing any cars in their way? I was reading a whole set of such accounts in yesterday's Guardian, interviews with

American soldiers now back in the States currently recording the grotesque brutality in the way in which Iraqi civilians have been treated.

These are signs of our preoccupation with ourselves as individuals and our failure to generalise this preoccupation to others with whom we fail to identify. At a subtle level, there is an extraordinary self-confidence about the individual in the West. Our education encourages us to focus on becoming the brightest boy in the school or the most beautiful girl in the class. Some very interesting psychological testing has shown how this focus on the individual creates a very selfish attitude towards purchasing, buying, being – all focused on me, me, me. Furthermore, psychological enquiries reveal a very different situation in Japan or in China where research directly comparable to that done in America has been carried out. Briefly, the average Japanese or Chinese is not particularly concerned with 'me'. What they're concerned with is relating to the community within which they belong. First and foremost is the family – a strong communal sense of the family. And that extends outwards to the company within which individuals work. If individualism can be said to be the hallmark of part of our Western world-view, so communalism is actually the hallmark of much of Asian world-views.[4]

Of course, this means the Western media are very strongly focused on things that happen to individuals – the cult of celebrities, discussions about the differences between the last Prime Minister and the present one. The focus is far more on individuals than it is on policies and viewpoints. Our general assumption of the importance of the individual is one of the reasons for the success of Western capitalism. Individuals run it and earn cash fortunes never dreamt of before

Dualism

The third of the characteristics that seem to define our Western world-view at the present time is what I would call metaphysical dualism, and there are two forms of this. One is philosophical and one is religious. The philosophical form of metaphysical dualism comes from Descartes and the whole Cartesian way of viewing science. The object to be studied is completely distinct from the person or the process doing the studying. The two are kept apart. Mind and matter – the thinker and the studied – are kept rigorously separate in classical science. This, of course, promotes a kind of almost schizoid activity within science. What such a scientist actually does is not necessarily effected by what he or she values.

As you know, I'm a scientist and I have a great many scientific friends whom I respect enormously and who hold more or less this so-called reductionist attitude. But what are their values? Some people denigrate science as being somehow valueless and not contributing to our world. This is not true. The orthodox scientists of my acquaintance think very carefully about the world. But what do they feel about themselves in the world of their understanding? The scientific enquiry reveals a universe in which there is no ultimate 'point', just an extraordinary complicated mystery. There is no personal security offered in the investigations of science to bring comfort in the face of universal death. After all, however exciting and intriguing may be the wonders of the Big Bang or the recent discovery of some galaxy so far out it's light was created so many millions of years ago that one can't even imagine it – at least I can't – and which reveals something about what happened within the first few seconds of origin of our universe, what does that mean to an individual with a mere three score years and ten of transient existence?

Most of my scientific friends are, I would say, stoics. Really, they think very much in the way of a Roman Stoic. Many would say this is the way it is, this is the way the world is, we adjust our lives to fit it. We investigate what the truth is. The truth is something we have to live with and discover. Values and idealism here tend to become highly utilitarian, because the values that such people hold are about making utilitarian differences in the world, improving the water supply, flying better aircraft, speeding up communications. Scientists are dedicated to utilitarian results that make our lives more comfortable, more 'happy' in a material sense. The philosopher Charles Taylor argues that what we lack are 'hyper-goods'.[5] By hyper-goods he means values that have, as it were, a fundamental relevance in some sense, not merely things being done for some utilitarian effect but things being done because it is right and proper to do them, driven by some universal perspective. Such values are not so common among my scientific friends. A mere utilitarianism in values has percolated very widely throughout our culture. We can call this a philosophical dualism. Action for utility.

The religious dualism is more potentially dangerous. What is religious dualism? Well, it's the form of belief that has been traditional for many centuries in monotheistic cultures. The thinker reifies some abstract idea and promotes it into the key position in a discourse. For example, when we don't understand the universe, we may well say it must be due to 'God'. We reify the idea of a causal God and project him into the universe and go on to believe it. This is dualism in that the entity placed up in the heavens is a production, a projection of our reasoned inferences. It is not something up there to which we can be intimately related except in illusion. It is simply a metaphysical imputation. This mode of thinking is known to philosophers as logocentric discourse: a discourse which pivots around one key theme and everything else hangs on it.[6] So for example, in Christianity or Islam, everything hangs on the concept of God.

I must have been a really unpleasant student. When I was at university, I was troubled about this word 'God', so I used to go along to theological lectures. I used to sit deliberately in the front row and of course the speaker, being a theologian, would very soon use the word 'God'. I would put up my little 19-year-old hand and I would say "Excuse me, you have just used the word 'God', could you please give me a definition of God because without a definition I don't see how the lecture can proceed". Bastard! I never ever got an answer, which just goes to show that if you have a logocentric discourse you cannot query the logos in the middle of the discourse otherwise the entire thing falls apart.

The tragedy of these logocentric religious discourses, however, is that there is more than one of them. So we have Islam versus Christianity, where we have two versions of 'God' that share a lot of common history but whose rules and regulations have come down in a rather different way in the two cases. Then, because neither of them can be questioned within the belief, one side is always the infidel to the other – hence Crusades, hence Jihads.

Jihads and Crusades are fundamentally rooted in a particular kind of dualistic position and such attitudes in the modern world need to be very seriously interrogated. Yet, if you listen to the radio, if you listen to what's going on in the world, you will find a general assumption that this kind of dualistic religious thinking is fine, nothing wrong with it, perfectly OK. Yet, the troubles between them fester. We have to discover a philosophical position allowing tolerance between the two of them. It is very difficult to find tolerance between two ultimately absolutist dispositions. It requires a third perspective, a third philosophy that might compensate for and integrate the schism between the two. This will not be easily achieved and is not yet achieved.

I've chosen these three features – capitalism, individualism, and dualism – as three cardinal points within the Western world-view. Now we need to understand a little more clearly what world-views are and how they may have changed through time, because none of these world-views, none of these elements in our world-views which I've been talking about, are in any way sacrosanct throughout history.

The History of World-Views

There is a wonderful Russian philosopher called Mikhail Bakhtin who is not very well known in this country. He is mainly a writer on the structure of novels and the way in which the novel and similar literature is related to the world-views of the times in which they are written. As part of his project, he has considered the historical sequence of world-views. He argues for three main periods, chronotopes he calls them.[7] The first period is Shamanism – the ancient matrix as he says it. Shamanism is extraordinarily interesting. It's a pattern of varying beliefs in the cyclicity of nature. It creates relationships with 'gods', which are actually forces of nature – forces of nature which determine the annual cycle. Its practices bring about adjustment to forces of nature through visualisation and often the use of psychedelics to create a close association between the Shamanic yogin or 'priest', the natural powers and the manner in which village people relate to those natural powers. Some of the Shamanistic systems are extraordinarily well adapted to the ecologies in which they exist, as in the Amazonian forest or in the Siberian tundra – quite extraordinary examples of intuitively skilled metaphysical adaptation to ecology.

The shamanic phase in the history of world-views gave place to viewpoints that we can call progressive dualism. Once overproduction of some commodities was achieved through agriculture, markets were established through the flow of goods. You had banks, you had businesses. Life was less concerned with cyclicity of the seasons, but rather with the acquisition of money and power, hierarchy, of leadership or kingship. This was a linear vision instead of a cyclic one. You got a division between authority and those who were dominated. It was in this context that the logocentric discourses emerged. You also got the emergence of high priests, bishops, popes, authorities, dogmas, coercion within religion. Here emerged a kind of authoritarianism including such things as the assumption of infallibility and the inquisition, and so on; a system of power in which the state and the religion became highly intermingled.

In the third phase, Bakhtin argues very interestingly for a period characterised by reflection, a reflective world-view. In a reflective world-view the mind of the thinker becomes aware of the nature of what it has thought, the limitation of that thought. The thinker begins to accept responsibility for what he has thought. For example, a thinker might discuss God. God? God is in his heaven. Maybe yes, but that's just my idea. Actually - I don't know. Mmm. That's reflective thinking. It doesn't necessarily mean that the thought was wrong, it just means that it was a thought and no more than a thought, a concept reified into a truth, a 'reification'. It was the great philosopher, Kant, who really began to uncover this whole issue in Europe exploring how far we can ever understand ultimate reality when ultimate reality is always necessarily a production of our own minds. This viewpoint became a key element in so-called post-modern thinking, and therefore it's relatively common today. Yet, here's a surprise! As we shall soon see, it also appeared at least 2500 years ago, in the iron age of India, with the thought of the Buddha.[8] We shall investigate the implication of this shortly.

So, our current Western world-view is a strange one in which we have a conflict between religious dualism and the scientific understanding of the world creating for many a deeply schizoid tension between the values of scientific exploration, the utilitarianism of economy, and the quest for something spiritual in the absence of any 'hypergoods'. There's an enormously confused interest in the spiritual in 'New Age' movements of various kinds. Most of these are easily perceived to be projections of individual minds despairing of something more relevant to life and death within a world of utilitarian values.

West and East

This Western world-view is deeply divisive yet few realise that it's not the only one on offer. If you read learned texts about the history of world culture you quite often find they begin with Ancient Greece and proceed to the present time without a mention of the tremendous philosophical importance of India and China. Their cultures and philosophies are quite often bypassed and simply ignored. This is indeed amazing today when the literature of great Indian thinkers and great Chinese thinkers in translation is well available through superb scholarship, particularly in North America. No-one really has an excuse for assuming that world culture began with the Ancient Greeks. A lot of very important things did indeed begin with the Ancient Greeks but that's not the whole story.

The key thing about these Asian world-views is that they are not dualist. They are holistic. Let's take an example – Confucianism. Chinese Confucianism, which is touched also by Daoism, assumed an intimate relationship between the Emperor and the natural world. The Emperor held the 'mandate of heaven'. Heaven was the natural world. Heaven was the universe. When something went wrong in the rule of an Emperor it was said that he had 'lost the mandate of heaven'. This means that in Confucianism there was a connection between political power and the natural world. They are not separated by thinking that allows the natural world to be forgotten while the political world is retained. No, the political world and the natural world interact with one another. This is an important holism. And we find much of this also in philosophical Hinduism, in Daoism, and especially developed philosophically and experientially in Buddhism.

If we are looking for an alternative to our western perspectives or for a way to modifying them then I put to you that Buddhism is the most useful of these Asian visions because Buddhism is essentially a never-ending enquiry. As my friend, the philosopher Steven Bachelor, puts it, 'Zen is enquiry'. That's what it is – it is enquiry. We shall see in a moment it is a special sort of enquiry, but it is enquiry. It's not an answer: it's an enquiry.

The essential point to realise in approaching Buddhism is that it is not just a rationalised philosophy or belief system. It is based in a never-ending enquiry rooted in the methodological practice of mental yoga. It resembles science in being a subjective empiricism.[9] That is to say, an experimental investigation of the nature and practices of mind rather than an objective empiricism concerned with nature as perceived and measured by a mind. Unlike psychological science, however, its prime focus is not actually mind itself, but rather suffering. One could say, rather pompously, that Buddhism is a phenomenological soteriology. Sorry about that - but it's rather a good definition. What does it mean? What does it mean? Phenomenological means a psychologically based experiential investigation of suffering, and soteriology is the study of its function in producing 'salvation', a resolution of suffering.

So we have here a system of active enquiry, a philosophical inquisition which is aimed at understanding the suffering of the mind with the purpose of finding something which is termed 'enlightenment', the relief from that suffering. The most important thing is that it is rooted in mental yoga as a prime method. The yogic enquiry is the essence of Buddhism. What is the yogic enquiry? Well, to put it very simply, meditation is a yogic enquiry. Why? Because when you sit in meditation you are looking into the mind and you are saying what is this? What is this experience now? Where is it? What is it? How is it? It is endlessly going in to the nature of mind. That's what I call subjective empiricism. It's just as significant for us as the objective enquiry in psychology that is essentially the description of mind, and the analysis of people's behaviour. That's objective. It's fine. Nothing wrong with it but it is incomplete. The key point here is that the essence of Buddhism is subjective enquiry. Buddhism parallels Science in this very fact of enquiring. Of course, these two modes of enquiry are related and we must go on discuss their relationship.

The Perspectives of Buddhism in Relation to Science

One cannot simply assert that Buddhism is like science; one has to demonstrate it. The first thing to say is that there is no dogma in Buddhism. The Buddha himself said quite clearly that here's an argument, here's a viewpoint – if you like it, fine, come along and we'll participate in investigating it. If you don't like it, fine, find something else. This has remained true throughout the history of Buddhism; there is no coercion within Buddhism. This resembles Science in that the scientist can put forward a theory, an idea, and no-one has to believe it. It's put there to be evaluated. Of course, that releases enormous discussion between those in favour and those against but there is no coercion to believe and no personal problem if you don't follow it. In Buddhism there is no sin, but there is the making of mistakes. This shift in vocabulary marks a whole difference. No sin, but yes, one can make mistakes and one pays for them through karmic retribution.

What is the prime hypothesis of the Buddha? It's called the 'Law of Co-dependent Arising' or 'inter-dependent origination'.[10] This argues that the universe has no single origin; it has always been a flux of causes and effects. The cause A comes up, has an effect B. B has an effect C. C has an effect D. B and C may also affect something out to one side – a parallel discourse going along. So there is a network of causes and effects always going on and on and on. This is what is meant by 'inter-dependent origination' because A, B, C, and D are all inter-dependently related with one another. The process can also come back in a circle so that the original A is also caused by the sets of circumstances within which it arises. Buddhism is a philosophy of contingency. Causes arise and produce effects dependent upon conditions. This is an extremely simple statement, but it is enormously far-reaching. It means among other things that nothing can come out of nothing. There are always causes and effects and conditions. Equally well nothing can ever come solely out of itself for the same reason. And so on. There are therefore whole sets of logocentric, metaphysical theories which simply collapse in the face of the law of inter-dependent origination. Many of the great Buddhist philosophers spent a lot of time enjoying themselves destroying metaphysical theories through subjecting them to the arguments of inter-dependent origination.

This theory, this viewpoint, this 'law', is itself a hypothesis – it's a way of seeing. The fascinating thing about it is that it has some extraordinary parallels within Science. Now I'm not a physicist, so I'm on dangerous ground here, but there is support for this general view from quantum mechanics.

The Buddhist story itself underwent evolution. The simple law of the Buddha became very much enlarged in a wonderful philosophy developed in China called Hua-yen, which is based on the Indian Garland or Avatamsaka Sutra. It contains an extraordinary metaphor, a picture of the Law of Co-dependent Arising. Imagine a huge sky, hanging in it is a net known as the Net of Indra – Indra simply being the King of the Gods. This network consists of hundreds and hundreds and hundreds of diamonds, multifaceted diamonds all hanging in space. They are all mutually reflecting one another. Everything is reflected in everything else. The Empress Wu of China couldn't quite understand this metaphor and asked a leading teacher to demonstrate it for her. So he said - well it's like this. He fixed up a room with many mirrors – I think an octagon of mirrors. And in the middle, he put a lamp. Then he brought Her Majesty into the room and said, "This is the demonstration of the Net of Indra", because the lamp in the middle was now reflected millions of times in the octagon of the mirrors in the room.[11]

When these ideas first began to come to the West, people thought that's just amazing but how on earth does it relate to what we're talking about in Science? Yet then along came quantum mechanics, and the extraordinary thing about quantum mechanics is that the inter-relations between the quanta, the 'particles' or 'waves' of energy, which operate as the most fundamentally known constituents of matter, perform in a way that makes that metaphor very valid indeed. I'm not qualified to go into quantum physics but my reading of the matter and checking it out with physicist friends shows that the way in which quanta relate together is in a mutual interaction of great complexity that could very well be expressed through the ancient metaphor of Indra's net.

So, right at the foundation of Buddhist thinking we have an extraordinary parallel with some of the most advanced thinking in contemporary Science. Furthermore, if everything is dependent on everything else, one would expect that in evolution the emergence of novelty would have been dependent upon conditions. Indeed, the evolution of humanity has depended on certain conditions in the past out of which the causal processes of genetic selection produced our species.

A lot of evolutionary theory has been quite simplistic, that is up until about 10 years ago. The way in which evolutionary theorists – and I have been one of them – used to think about evolution was to think of the environment and the organism as a dualism. The organism adapts to the environment. It does this by producing broods of offspring in every generation of which the individuals vary. Some of them are more suited to the environment than others. The ones that are most suited reproduce and spread and the population becomes adapted to the environment. In this view, there is always a fixed environment and a dynamic process of reproduction which is endlessly adapting to the environment. Two things therefore – life and environment; a dualism.

Recent evolutionary theories have shown that this approach is far too simple. Why? There is a viewpoint being developed by a former colleague of mine, John Odling-Smee at Oxford, who talks in terms of 'Niche Construction'.[12] Niche is a term describing the way in which a species lives in its environment. For example, take the bird the Great Tit. It's quite a large Tit, a member of the Paridae family. It lives in trees but will also explore food on the ground, bird tables and so on. That's its 'niche'. The Coal Tit, a smaller darker coloured Tit prefers conifer woods. They are a prime feature of its niche. So the question is how do species evolve in their different niches?

John Odling-Smee has argued that species play major roles in creating their own niches. How does this argument work? Well, a very simple illustration of this comes from one of my own first PhD students – Steven Gartlan – who very sadly died recently. Steve was out in Africa studying a forest monkey and he noticed that along the forest fringe the monkeys used to bring their fruit out of the forest, go 100 yards or so outside and climb up on a termite mound and eat the fruit there. What happened? They dropped the seed. The seed germinated and the forest expanded. So the monkeys were actually producing the extension of the forest which was their own habitat. There's a feedback here. The monkeys were helping create the habitat within which they were eventually to live. It's not simply a dualism of habitat and selection, the monkeys were participating in creating their own habitat.

This idea goes further. If you introduced some burrowing animal into a small island, what would happen? Well, first of all you had a nice neat and tidy virginal island with sand dunes and hills and a few trees. You introduce these animals. What do they do? They start creating burrows. Before you know where you are, they've spread widely and the whole environment is full of burrows. Now the appearance of burrows in a habitat where there have been no burrows before will produce a lot of ecological changes. The humidity of the soil is altered. The topography of the soil changes. The presence of nesting sites changes. The whole habitat begins to change as a result of the activities of the animals. So that after 10 years or so, when you come back to see what has happened, you find an entirely different habitat on that island as generated by the behaviour of the animals. The animals in relating to their habitat as first encountered have created their own domain.[13] Those currently living had evolved not only in relation to the original matrix but to the changed environment created by their immediate ancestors. And the process goes on.

Now, in the case of humanity, we have extensively modified our environment to increase our use of it but increasingly we have failed to adapt to the constraints of our planetary system sustainably. Indeed, our behaviour has become adaptively dysfunctional to the extent that we are altering the climate of the planet in a manner that disturbs the entire ecosystem. By failing to curb our greedy aggrandisement, our limited capacity for reason appears to have turned into a malfunction so far as adaptive biology is concerned. We may be heading for the evolutionary denouement of extinction - a common fate for species that fail to support their sustainability in relation to resources.

Such a viewpoint is obviously a holistic position, not a dualist one.[14] What we evolutionists now have to consider is the way in which the activities of organisms themselves modify the habitat to create a changing world, the niche of the species. This example shows how something like the Law of Co-dependent Arising can be a relevant if simple expression describing a modern problem, the evolution of species in relation to their habitat.

The Buddha put forward a very simple yet elegant model of the mind. It is also based on the Law of Co-dependent Arising. He argued that there are five main features of the mind in constant interaction with one another. The first is sensation. If I pinch Malcolm, he'll feel a sensation. Secondly, there is perception. Perception is when Malcolm realises that it is John who has pinched him. Thirdly there is cognition. Malcolm is now calculating fast and comes to the conclusion that it's a joke and not an assault (hopefully he comes to that conclusion!). And fourthly there is the conditioned historical background to his cognition. If he was a particularly aggressive person, he might come to the opposite conclusion and bash me one. So you have sensation, perception, cognition, and what's known as Sanskara in Sanskrit, namely the pre-determining conditioning factors which affect cognition. Lastly there is consciousness. You have a whole system here in which these psychological aspects are interrelating, co-determining features of mind. Although this is a relatively simple model, it's not so different from those we use today.

But where is the self? No self appears in this system. Self, Buddha argued, is an imputation within cognition that arises from the activities of the five features. So I'm sorry, Buddha thinks you're just an imputation derived from your sensation, your cognition, your perception, and your predispositions and your consciousness – all that produces the impression that there's somebody sitting there. Sorry, says the Buddha, you're just not there in the way you think you are.

Now when a person holds onto this false impression that he or she exists as some sort of a 'thing', s/he will go on to examine what happened to him or her in the past and what might happen in the future and begins to create a narrative. This narrative emerges as the basis for the constitution of a self-image, an identity. Amazingly therefore in the Buddhism of 2500 years ago we find this very sophisticated idea of the self as narrative which, I think you will agree, is not far different from a lot of ideas which we hold today in modern psychotherapy and in modern psychology.

Indeed, after 2500 years, it seems we really haven't got very much further on. These parallels show that these fundamental ideas in Buddhism are compatible with scientific enquiry and parallel much modern phenomenological research. As we have already discussed, Buddhism is fundamentally concerned with subjective rather than objective enquiry. The Buddhist Law of Co-dependent Arising came from the Buddha's direct observation of his own mind. His Brahminical teachers had told him that if he looked deeply into his mind he would eventually discover Brahman and that would be the solution to everything. But the Buddha was a deeply sceptical thinker. When he did this meditation - and he was a superb meditator - he found that whatever was going on there was caused by something which had happened previously. There was always some kind of process or condition which shaped what the mind was doing, even to the extent that when the mind began to disappear, seemingly to become Brahman, that was simply because the removal of certain attributes of mind had left an empty space. This was not something absolute and final, rather it was part of the process of meditation. So the Law of Co-dependent Arising was born. Absolute Brahman was just another imputation.

I hope I've managed to persuade you that there is sufficient overlap between the empiricism of Buddhism and the empiricism of Science and, indeed, the empiricism that underlies the enquiry of psychotherapy, to justify an interest in the Buddhist viewpoint. What I want to do now is to suggest in a broad way that the manner in which our world-view needs to move is towards a holism that could repair the schizoid quality of our present split between economics and ecology, between self and other, between 'God' and person. What we need to do to replace that schizoid world-view is to regenerate some kind of a holism.[15]

Obviously, this cannot be the ancient Shamanism. Too much complex superstition is involved. Yet Buddhism, although ancient, is actually an exercise in the reflexivity of Bakhtin's third stage in world-view history, often supposed to be a modern development. Essentially the Universe is a mystery for us. We project images and ideas upon it, logocentric visions as powerful and often mutually rejecting alternatives. Yet in relation to mystery, there can only be rational inference and inquiry as a product of our own minds. Reflexive understanding knows this and does not promote either dogma or coercion.

There are real problems for education here. One can appreciate the danger of illusions that may be fostered by 'faith' schools for example. Yet, in school, inquisitive teenagers may be easily excited by the universal mysteries of world, mind and self. An educational approach presenting them as open inquiry permitting debate right from the beginning, would set the young thinking, wondering, get them going. Instead of having to believe this or that about Allah, God or whatever utilitarian project was to hand – however ethically sound such beliefs may be - the fundamental metaphysical assumptions of the dominant 'world' religions need to be exposed as out of date – actually by two thousand years! It may then be possible to create a world of values in a world that is honestly mysterious.[16, 17]

Postscript after the Event

What would be the result of uncontrolled decadence? We have the fall of the Roman Empire as an example. But this time, after the extinction of the Lion, Tiger, Elephant and Rabbit, the logging of almost all forests and the exhaustion of petroleum it may be the turn of Humanity itself. Destroying the means of interdependent life, exhaustion of energy supplies, loss of land to the sea and greenery to new deserts, the vast population disturbances will generate wars of survival and chaos. With no psychological discrimination left we will hardly be in a state to fly finally to another planet circling another star. We will die out here.

May be this is natural evolution. Life itself will not pass away. A new surge of evolution will follow just as it has after five previous global extinctions. Once more the planet will be beautiful, filled with myriad life forms of complexity, rarity and beauty- only we will not be here to see it. Gaia will have heaved a great sigh of relief. Humanity will be gone. But not the Buddha Mind, the spirit of life itself. Emptiness will find new forms facing new vicissitudes. In imagination, in visualisation, the heart of things is not lost. Yet, with wisdom, we do not have to tread this path. Will there be wisdom? Will there be compassion for remaining life? Who can say? Those of us who are sufficiently aware need to make our voices heard.

1 Presentation of this article here by agreement with Friends of British Gestalt Journal. Many thanks to Dr Malcolm Parlett who initiated this invitation.

2 Boyden, S. 1987. Western Civilization in Biological Perspective. Oxford.

3 Stiglitz, J. 2002. Globalization and its discontents. Penguin

4 See: Neisser U and D. A. Jopling. Eds. 1997. The Conceptual self in Context. Cambridge.

5 Taylor, C. 1991. The Ethics of Authenticity. Harvard.

6 See further: Belsey, C. 2002. Poststructuralism. A very short introduction. Oxford.

7 Bakhtin, M. 1981. The Dialogic Imagination. University of Texas. Austin

8 See discussion: Crook, J. H. 2007. Shamans, Yogins and Indigenous psychologies. In: Dunbar, R. I. M. & L. Barrett. (Eds) Oxford Handbook of Evolutionary Psychology. Oxford.

9 See: Crook, J. H. 1980. The Evolution of Human Consciousness. Oxford.

10 See: Loy, D. 1998. Nonduality; a study in comparative philosophy. Humanity Books. New York. Also: Macy, J. 1991. Mutual Causality in Buddhism and General Systems Theory. The Dharma of Natural systems. SUNY.

11 See: Chang, Garma C. 1972. The Buddhist Teaching of Totality. The Philosophy of Hwa yen Buddhism. George Allen and Unwin. London.

12 Odling-Smee, F. J; Laland, K. N. & Feldman, M. W. 2003. Niche construction: the neglected process in Evolution. Princeton.

13 For a psychological version of the above approach in application to humanity see: Crook, J. H. 1995. Psychological processes in cultural and genetic co-evolution. In: Jones, E and V. Reynolds. (Eds) Survival and Religion. Biological evolution and Cultural change. Wiley. New York.

14 A further notable and very important example of biological holism is the global perspective of James Lovelock. See Lovelock, J. 1989. The Ages of Gaia. A biography of our living earth. Oxford.

15 There have of course been Western holistic philosophies starting with Heraclitus. In recent centuries Jan Smuts and A. N Whitehead have put forward suggestions. A most recent advocate is Thomas Berry: see Berry, T. 2006. Evening thoughts: reflecting on Earth as Sacred Community. Sierra Club. San Francisco. They have contrasted markedly with the main stream Cartesian approach to Science.

16 My book in press, World Crisis and Buddhist Humanism (see introduction to this article), ends by focussing on the significance of buddhistic (not necessarily Buddhist) education as a global orientation.

17 For a contrasting approach to these issues, see: Hinde, R. A. 1999. Why Gods persist. A scientific approach to religion. Routledge. London and New York.

MAMETZ WOOD

In October 2007 my son and I took the Honda and drove to France staying in Arras in the valley of the Somme. We were looking for my Uncle Ernest's grave. He had been an artillery officer and died of wounds during the Ancre offensive near the end of the great battles on the Somme in 1917. I did not know any family member who had been there since the 20s. We found him, visiting him in his gentle resting place twice, and told him the news. The Somme on these bright October days was beautiful yet the memories in the cemeteries and monuments that scatter the war-riven landscape are both deeply troubling and strangely inspiring. One of the greatest fights had been in Mametz Wood where the disciplined Welch Regiment on its second attempt overcame ferocious resistance in a bramble filled wood with low visibility everywhere - a dreadful hand to hand business. Several notable accounts of this action have been written. In honour of these brave men and in memory of them I wrote the following.

Mametz Wood –
Human entrails hang in the branches-
Arms, legs and heads stuck in trees-
The dying lost among shell holes
Hidden by clutching brambles:
That dead German, still helmeted,
Green face streaked by black-blood snot
Propped against a trunk.
Odour of death everywhere.

Mametz Wood –
Peaceful now
Gentle below tall, same aged trees
Dark shadows here are now our own. Brambles still impede the path
Where maybe boar are hidden.
Shades of deer float through the trees
Platoons of ghosts in distant foliage.
They rear pheasants here today
For shooting.

Mametz Wood -
A flash of colour upon an oak tree's trunk
Welch flag painted there
Not long ago
Red Dragon high
Where shells once fell
And guns and blood stained bayonets
Did their work
To fill a hundred cemeteries.

This tranquil landscape of the Somme
Shines in the Indian summer sun
A mellow fruitfulness
Gentle cattle,
Ploughed fields,
Rolling down land and wooded rivers
Still green on this October morn.
The Sunday chasseurs stalk the ground
Their dogs at heel.
The memories do not fade
Tears still falling
Year on year

Monday, October 29, 2007

NCF XXXVIII

EDITORIAL - PATHS TO ENLIGHTENMENT?

Do our retreats make any difference? Do they lead to an insight into enlightenment? Or are they merely spiritual hobbies in an age lacking in true wisdom? Although the Western Chan Fellowship is increasing in size and we offer a uniquely wide range of retreats of several types led by accomplished teachers, do our practitioners and local leaders truly understand the implications of the paths we attempt to follow? In this edition of our journal we provide deeply reflective texts in order that we can refocus where necessary on the demands that Chan makes on us as individuals – whether in groups, on committees, on retreat, in solitary reflection, trekking in the mountains or in the hassle of everyday life. Whether an institution is large or small, in Chan it is only individual motivation and personally self-aware criticism that makes any real difference. Consider your personal case!

Chuan-Deng Jing-di

MEDITATION AND PERSONAL DISCLOSURE: THE WESTERN ZEN RETREAT

Supreme accomplishment is to realize immanence without hope. (Tilopa[1])

In the last couple of years several people have asked me to contribute something on the Western Zen Retreat to the NCF. This was indeed the founding retreat practised at the Maenllwyd before Shifu came there and the WCF was founded. We prefer all practitioners to begin by attending one of them before proceeding to other Chan retreats, Silent illumination and Koan etc. This is because in the WZR it is impossible to avoid an essential self-confrontation that can easily be avoided in a practice focussed solely on meditative sitting. A study of the manner in which Chan Masters have taught shows that self-confrontation is the way to opening a door to Dharma understanding based in a process that negates self-importance entirely. This is not a path that makes sense to many in our present individualistic age – yet it is the foundation of spiritual wisdom.

It is time therefore to take a further look at the WZR. I find the article I wrote for the book "Space in Mind" in 1990[2] still rings with an original freshness that does well as an introduction. I have simply updated it for our consideration today. Furthermore, it leads on effectively into Ron Henshall's scholarly critique of experiences in these and similar retreats. Hopefully, it will stimulate contemporary retreatants to reflect carefully on the nature of what they are attempting.

The Vietnamese Buddhist writer Thich Nhat Hanh (1974) has had this to say about Zen in the West:

Zen does not yet exist in the West as a living tradition. Many monks are teaching the practice of Zen there, but this practice remains oriental; foreign to western culture. The fact is that Zen has not yet been able to find roots in this soil. Cultural, economic and psychological conditions are different. One cannot become a practitioner of Zen by imitating the way of eating, sitting or dressing of the Chinese or Japanese practitioners. Zen is life; Zen does not imitate. If Zen one day becomes a reality in the West, it will acquire a Western form, considerably different from Oriental Zen.

The creation of a Western Zen also poses the problem of lay Zen because, although there are Zen monasteries in America and Europe following ancient traditions, the majority of those attempting to practise Zen (Chan) remain lay men and women. For these practitioners, instead of the protection given by the walls of the convent and the mutual endeavours of fellow trainees, there is the constant encounter with the many forms of egotistic energy with which most people relate to their everyday worlds. Tough as the monastic environment may also be, the often overwhelming effect of engagement in worldly relationships is commonly the one difficulty that can be reduced there. While strict training in the monastery can and perhaps should lead to a return to the market-place, those who try to train without the walls are often especially heroic in their endeavours. But many fall aside in confusion.

Several authors have already addressed this and related questions; some from an intellectual and academic viewpoint (Merrell Wolf, 1973; Humphries, 1949; Pirsig, 1974; Suzuki, 1953; Watts, 1957, Kasulis,1981 and the more recent scholarly works of Faure, 1996; Heine and Wright, 2000; McRae, 2003; and others), some with personal accounts of their own struggles (Kennett, 1977/78; van Wetering, 1972, 1984; Amphoux, 1986) and some with a close examination of Zen in the context of attempting to teach and practise it in the modern world (Brandon, 1976; Kapleau, 1965, 1980; Kennett, 1978, Sheng Yen with Stevenson 2001, Sheng yen 2006). In most cases, however, it is with the transmission of oriental modes of practice that these writings are concerned. Little attempt has been made to see what happens if the Western mind, using its own energies and contradictions, can realise Zen practically with minimum direction but accurate facilitation based on a clear comprehension of the goal of training. One particular effort in this direction has revealed startling insights and possibilities (Harding, 1974) and there have been important discussions in our journal, the New Chan Forum (NCF)[3].

For over thirty years now I have been running several specially constructed five-day Zen sesshins (retreats) yearly for lay people at a remote farmhouse in mid-Wales (The Maenllwyd). This article puts together some key ideas about the nature of the process of change I have observed in participants during the retreat, and which some participants have described to me in letters weeks, months or years after their participation in a sesshin.

The Participants

The retreat is designed for lay people who may or may not have prior experience of meditation or Buddhist teachings, or even consider themselves Buddhists. People come often because they hear of the retreat from friends who are former participants but nowadays increasingly from reading about our programme in the NCF. Although in the early days retreat numbers were sometimes as low as 6-8 persons, I cannot recall having had to cancel a retreat for lack of interest. We often accommodate around 17-18 people even under harsh winter conditions, and have occasionally had up to 25 people, some under canvas, in summer. Participants are usually `middle-class' but with an increasing variety of class origins and social affiliations, and a wide range of incomes. Originally many were university-educated and a considerable proportion were in the helping professions. The proportion of counsellors, doctors, psychotherapists and psychiatrists rose annually over several years - some individuals being prominent in their fields. Nowadays however due to the internet there is a very wide range of applicants some basically ignorant of Buddhism but intrigued by what they have read. The age-range is great, from about 19 to 80, and individuals may profess inclinations loosely discernible as atheist, agnostic, Humanist, Christian, Marxist or Buddhist. Many have received some training in the sciences, and originally professional scientists and university teachers are often in evidence - perhaps influenced by my own academic qualifications (which, however, have little to do with the process in hand!). There are usually rather more men than women and the reasons for this remain unclear. Possibly they may have something to do with the rather deliberately primitive physical conditions in near wilderness. Comfortably warm hotel rooms and bathrooms are not in evidence here.

People come primarily not because of an interest in Buddhism or Zen, but out of a feeling that the retreat may be helpful in relation to a personal problem. Basically participants are seeking to alleviate their suffering. Some participants have had strong counter-cultural or feminist orientations, or may have embarked on a vigorous search for new or different ways of living. In summary, participants are not:

1. necessarily committed to a particular path;
2. especially convinced that Zen (Chan) offers a solution to their problems;
3. experienced in religious retreats;
4. monks or nuns; or
5. practitioners of any sustained training schedule.

These facts are important in trying to understand the process. In particular the retreats can only be compared with caution to actual monastic Zen sesshins of the Chan, Soto or Rinzai traditions, conducted by monks either for other monks in training or for especially committed Asian Buddhists who may have been in training already for some years. It follows that descriptions of experiences by Western Zen Retreat participants cannot therefore automatically be equated with experiences reported by monks in the classical literature. I shall not therefore be assuming that reported experiences during retreat are necessarily kensho, satori or enlightenments. It can be said, however, that reports by WZR participants, and events occurring in interviews (dokusan) during the retreats, are sometimes very close in form and content to those described, for example, in Kapleau's 1965 transcripts of trainee interviews with a Japanese master and the retreat reports in Master Sheng-yen's book 'Getting the Buddha Mind' (1982). Furthermore, there have been one or two enlightenment experiences that have followed closely in time participation in a retreat. It thus follows that some of the underlying psychological processes may be the same. Furthermore, my personal experiences in a variety of forms of Buddhist training point to an underlying unity.

The Practice

The retreat is built out of a considered blending of three elements: zazen practice, the communication exercise (CE) invented by Charles Berner (see Love, 1976), and physical activity. These are combined into a daily schedule which changes slightly as the days progress. On the first day emphasis is on sustained zazen, on the second, third and fourth days on questioning in the communication exercise. On the last day zazen is emphasised once more. Interludes of physical exercise may include exercises or a run up the hill behind the house before dawn, manual work, and a one-hour hill-walk. Sessions of physical exercise are derived from Dharma

Drum exercise schedules, Hatha yoga, Tai chi or Mahamudra training, and often there is an evening session of one of the action yogas of Bhagwan Shree Rajneesh. These can be especially powerful in helping participants break through emotional blocks.

Zazen

The traditional sitting posture is adopted (see for example the Zazen Rules in Kennett, 1972) and a meditation method employed. There is a range of methods available: counting the breath; watching the breath; observing thoughts on an inhalation, letting them go on the exhalation and observing what is there when they have gone; repeating the Buddha's name; repeating a name of the Buddha, suddenly stopping it and looking into the gap so caused; searching the heart (see below); examining a hua-tou or mental device that evokes a witnessing of the mind before it is stirred by a thought (that is, an ante-thought - see Lu, 1964, p. 47); or seeking a response to a paradoxical question based upon a case history from old Zen records (koan).

In the WZR it is `Searching the heart' or shik-an-taza which is the main method employed in zazen. Here the practitioner endeavours to discover what 'just sitting' is; every thought that arises is allowed to do so until it is recognised as what it is (a worry over a child, a loss, a social blunder, a moment of sexual bliss, a theoretical inspiration) and then it is released, let go of entirely. The mind returns to the state before thought. The practice is summarised as `let through - let be - let go' - there is to be no encouragement of thoughts, but rather a repeated letting go of all states that arise. Searching the heart can be a long, exhausting process; with low energy states it is painful indeed, with high energy there is the occurrence of scattering. Eventually after many hours the mind seems to quieten down, the hassle reduces of its own accord. This is samatha, or stillness meditation. With persistence, the method leads towards deep inward trance. In zazen one is encouraged to look directly into this quietening mind to perceive its very nature. Penetrative insight can reveal a mind that is empty of thought and notional content - there is simply a reflecting process, like that of a mirror.

In the WZR, Zazen is used at first primarily to allow the participant to `arrive'; to let the diffuse energies which he has brought with him settle, and moments of tranquillity appear before the communication exercises begin.

The Communication Exercise

The onset of the communication exercise breaks up all this gentling, and sets the mind going again in vigorous pursuit of a question. But the initial practice of zazen has begun to clarify the enquiring mind so that penetration may now go deep. Zazen may also have loosened emotional feelings usually repressed or hidden behind layers of rationalisation or social pretence, and which are now clamouring for release. In Charles Berner's system, two participants sit opposite one another, each taking turns of five minutes to respond to a question from the partner who remains open and alert, receiving whatever comes with acceptance but absolutely no comment. This alternation continues for 30-40 minutes, after which there is a break before the process is resumed - each participant now, however, paired with a different member of the group but persisting with his/her original question. The questions are in fact root koans shorn of all traditional background. In the WZR the following questions are given and usually in the following order:

1. 'Who am I?' (= Tell me who you are);
2. 'What am I?' (= Tell me what you are);
3. 'What is life?' (= Tell me what life is) and
4. 'What is another?' (= Tell me what another is).

A useful question that is commonly used after `Who am I?' is `How is life fulfilled?', for which (3) may or may not be a helpful preliminary depending on the depth of the earlier answers. Other questions used in the WZR include `What is love?' From where does love (truth, life, it, etc.) come? 'What am I like if completely alone?' 'What is meaning?' 'What is Death?' or the more advanced. 'Tell me what the Cross is?' or 'What is working with karma?' These supplementary koans are given within contexts which arise in the interviews between practitioner and facilitator. The skill of the facilitator is needed to select a koan which has direct relevance at a heartful level for the practitioner - for example 'From where does love come?' given to someone recently deserted by a spouse or love or proposing to desert.

As Berner saw, the value of these misleadingly simple questions, lacking entirely the trappings and verbal paradoxes of traditional koans ('What is the sound of one-hand-clapping?'), lies in their direct pointing to the state of the practitioner here and now. 'Who am I?' or 'How is life fulfilled?' have no enticing frills - they point straight to the basic dilemma. Like the Kamakura warrior koans (Leggett, 1985), they can arise on the spot in the relationship between practitioner and facilitator, and their choice is a matter of 'skilful means'.

In traditional Rinzai Zen, the practitioner sits and meditates on his koan seeking to break through the barrier it represents. In the Enlightenment Intensive (as Berner called his system) and in the WZR the communication between two persons allows direct personal disclosure in which participants face the fear of risking to share their guilty, shameful or agonising thoughts and feelings with another. It may take several hours before a participant can trust partners sufficiently to disclose an emotional barrier which must be stated and released before further work on 'Who am I?' can continue. Such issues of disclosure, fear, risk and trust are present in traditional settings when the monk faces the master. In the WZR they are constantly present as the participants work with one another in the communication exercises.

The communication exercise arouses strong emotions. Once a participant has shared emotion it is rare for the partner not to be deeply affected. The sharing can move to a very profound level of mutual understanding and compassion. Very deep suffering, undisclosed for years, can be released in this way with powerful effects. Sometimes states of great intensity and confusion are aroused and the facilitator's experience of humanistic therapies such as neo-Reichian bioenergetics, gestalt or psychosynthesis is needed in the interview room where body-work as well as heart-to-heart confrontation may occasionally be used.

Action Yoga

The use of Bhagwan Shree Rajneesh's action yoga involves the whole group in vigorous exercises which help literally to shake out (the 'Kundalini' exercise) or blow out (the 'Dynamic') energies suppressed, cathected to unshareable ideas or simply too far below the surface to appear in verbal presentation. The permission to shout (wordlessly), rage, scream, dance, roll about and laugh is a shared act of trust with the facilitator, whose role as an authority-figure is thereby softened, allowing his care for the group to be more easily perceived. In addition, for some, it constitutes a previously inconceivable performance of fantasy themes involving experiences of regression to childhood. The personal meaning of these emotional events is subsequently explored when the communication exercises are resumed.

The Schedule

These main practices are combined in a timetable that begins at between 5 am and 6.30 am (depending on the season) and ends around 10.30 pm. The day opens with chanting, using orthodox texts from the various Buddhist traditions as well as hymns written specially for the purpose. The day divides into either Zazen sessions (2 x 30 minutes with a cycle of slow or fast walking between) or Communication Exercises (usually 2 x 30 - 50 minutes, with a five- minute break between) with walks, meals, work periods, and action yoga cropping up as appropriate.

Discipline and Leadership

The retreat is strictly disciplined in the manner of a traditional Zen sesshin. A set of vows - of silence, gratitude, compassion and diligent practice - is taken at the start of the retreat, and to break any of these persistently is taken to indicate an unwillingness to work and is followed by a request to leave (this has occurred only very few times). The prime rule is that of silence - which means a total absence of conversation rather than a prohibition of all remarks such as simple requests for information. Conviviality when it develops is not suppressed, but rather contained and reflected upon as a result of the silence rule and reminders to `Hold your Questions!'

Of necessity, the facilitator tends to have a high profile role, especially at the start of the retreat. This is in order to generate an outer discipline vital for the success of the inner work. Furthermore, an assertive expression of the role may be important in helping participants to feel secure. The facilitator must have confidence in the process, and complete openness towards anything a participant may produce. Once the pattern of the retreat is well established and the koans have taken hold, the facilitator can increasingly allow the group process to unfold naturally. He (or she) will be spending more time in giving interviews, and will ask assistants or senior participants to organise the time-keeping and other administrative tasks.

The two permanent figures around which the retreat unfolds are the facilitator (Retreat Master) and the cook. The role of maintaining discipline, and a willingness to exert authority in the interests of the group as a whole, may fall from time to time on either or both of them, and needs to melt naturally into a nurturing role as time goes along. Both facilitator and cook may in some ways be seen as occupying parental roles to the family of participants, and indeed oedipal expressions of feeling may sometimes make themselves felt. The facilitator needs to be able to use such responses creatively in the interests of the participant, and not to react with an authoritarian or overly 'parental' stance.

Anyone attempting to facilitate a process such as this will need to have completed periods of intensive Zen training including orthodox sesshins with a skilled master, training in counselling or therapeutic work with clients and some personal work on themselves in psychotherapy. Facilitators need also to be familiar with Berner's manual of leadership instructions available in the Maenllwyd library. He or she will also require a 'supervisor' with whom to share the events and experiences of running a retreat. Untrained individuals should not attempt work with the degree of interpersonal involvement that characterises the WZR.

Nowadays, most WZRs are facilitated by Dr Simon Child as 'Retreat Master' who trained at length with me in this process and who is a Dharma heir of Master Sheng-yen. We have worked together in training a further two facilitators who will soon be 'flying solo' under supervision. Training new facilitators revealed a number of unexpected difficulties. Leading a WZR differs considerably from leading a meditation retreat such as Silent Illumination wherein the change in participants' responses comes gradually and the teaching follows a consistent course. In the WZR the facilitator needs to be able to respond to surprising responses from participants right from the beginning. Furthermore, as the participants begin to work through their emotional origins at differing paces, the facilitator needs to keep pace with both the differing speed of shifts in individual reactions and the general movement within the group as a whole. This means that talks and teaching interventions cannot be fixed in advance but must move in accordance with the varying rates of changes that individuals and the whole group may show. This is no easy task and requires considerably more experience in training than either Simon or I had at first realised.

Another difficult task for the facilitator is to ensure that in interviews the participant is moved forwards in their personal enquiry. To return a person to the meditation hall without a renewed impetus from interview is a potentially serious mistake. If several people lose momentum they will inevitably share this with others during the CE and the risk of generating a 'group in flight' (i.e. losing trust in procedure and leader alike) increases. I am glad to say this has never happened yet but the potential danger is always present.

The Retreat Process

The evening on which people arrive is spent in organising bed spaces, getting to know the layout of the building and meeting fellow participants. Around 7.30 pm an assembly is held, and people asked why they have come and what their hopes and fears may be. This plenary sharing helps the facilitator to get a preliminary impression of individuals' attitudes - especially important where newcomers are concerned and to make sure that no one has come with severely aberrant or misinformed expectations. It also allows individuals to get to know one another a little socially before the discipline of the retreat is imposed, and to experience each other's seriousness in the endeavour. The sesshin begins with a short opening ceremony before lights out, after which silence begins.

On the first day Zazen is difficult, the mind chatters incessantly, the early start and a poor night's rest rapidly induce sleepiness and the struggle to resist leads to low energy states. During the day interviews to settle which koan people will wish to work with are given. This establishes contact between the facilitator and participant, helping to renew energy. Originally Communication Exercises began on the second day, but nowadays they commence on the first afternoon.

On Day 2 most participants experience an improvement in zazen, and some individuals may make rapid progress towards engagement with the koan. By the evening, however, the toughness of confronting the koan hour after hour, and the onset of difficult disclosure frequently bring about a return of low energy states. Again these may be alleviated by physical exercise and chant. People become deeply involved with their questions. Most answers to 'Who am I?' begin by references to roles and experiences, but gradually move to the sort of statement 'I am the kind of person who...' with verbal descriptions of feelings. Personal problems and situational dilemmas begin to be shared.

Day 3 calls for great personal application. Considerable emotional expression may occur, so that the sounds of weeping, rage, grief and distress often ring through the building. But these are helpful signs as individuals are freeing themselves to express their life dilemmas as they are actually felt in here/now experiencing. It is more difficult for those who cannot feel free to express emotion, cannot find emotions to express, or who feel imposed upon by the emotions of others. Rationalisers may get very angry, and this anger may be aimed directly or indirectly at the facilitator, who may sometimes feel he is riding a bucking horse. The expression of great emotion is, however, not always a necessary or even desirable activity. Those who have a clear perception of themselves, and those who get emotional blocks out of the way early, begin to look very directly at their moment-to-moment experience and try to see its form and source. Whether by reason of a highly focused intentionality or because of catharsis, some individuals may have breakthroughs into moments of serenity or joy - which, however, dissolve again into other hassling mental diversions as new thoughts come up for attention.

During Day 4 a subtle change comes over the group. Participants now tend to come forward for interviews (dokusan) either because of persistent perplexity, pain or distress or because insights seem to be arising. For those caught in circular or spiralling systems of thought, which like repeated traverses of a cul-de-sac seem to iterate endlessly without release, these interviews are often of great importance. The facilitator endeavours to mirror the individual process of the meditator, and by precise questions and other skilled responses, to bring the individual to insight into his own mental attachments and personal myths and the need for their acceptance.

Individuals now have the appearance of emptying themselves of self-expression. To an outsider they might appear drained or exhausted, but in fact they are entering a highly concentrated state with an increasing level of a type of energy that allows high attentiveness. Such a state may last for hours while the individual 'crosses the desert'. The level of focused energy in the room may seem almost palpable - the atmosphere is intense but no longer tense - highly creative and insightful communication exercises occur. It is now possible for some individuals in their quest for themselves in 'Who am I?' to go beyond words and experience the living moment non-discursively with a clarity of apprehensive immediacy in which the subject - object dichotomy may dissolve. Such experiences may be accompanied by moments of profound inner stillness, a rising sense of physical and mental bliss, and an awareness seemingly unlimited by previous imputations of self-regarding thought. This extraordinarily acute awareness may be associated with feelings of profound gratitude, openness to others and compassion. Only a few experience this state in depth, but many discover a radically quietened mind in which self-acceptance leads to a loss of personal anguish, together with the emergence of a new view of life in which openness and optimism are characteristic. There is in particular a remarkable feeling of having shed a burden, and a consequent feeling of freed energy.

Day 5 sees a reduction in questioning, with the koan now used more as a simple focusing device than as a question to be answered. Many have realised that in any case there is no answer - rather the paradox inherent in the koan may be resolved through a change in perception. This is like observing those illusory figures in psychology textbooks - seen from one mental stance an old woman stands upon the page - a second later there is a beautiful girl. The cognitive reorganisation now has an opportunity for stabilisation into a changed attitude, but whether this can be maintained following the retreat depends upon many factors in an individual's life. Usually the experience fades quite quickly and much now depends on how an individual's philosophy of life and attitude to living have been affected.

A koan is 'dropped' when an individual experiences a certainty that he or she is quite clear about 'Who I am' (say). This certainty may be associated with the experiences described above, and usually crystallises into a form of words given to the facilitator in a manner which indicates resolution. The participant is now energetic, clear in mind, peaceful, resolved, self- accepting and certain, and this shows in marked changes in posture, breathing, eye energy and facial expression; so that the form of words used is of relatively less importance. When a koan is 'dropped' in this way, the participant is usually asked to savour the result and to continue sharing it with others. This may go on until the end of the retreat, or occasionally a further koan may be given.

Generally, about a quarter of a group's membership has an experience approaching the above description, another half have reached a degree of self-acceptance that frees them deeply to face life's problems, while most of the remainder have experienced and learnt a great deal about themselves and the human condition. A limited number may be profoundly disappointed or leave as puzzled as they came - but even here very few of this number actually regret attempting the retreat. They rightly feel that to have come through it at all is something which, on a wider scale, is exceptional and which may have hidden benefits.

Are these results an opening to the experience of enlightenment known in Japanese zen as "kensho" (Chinese: kai wu)? Usually this is not so but the work of self-emptying on retreat may facilitate such an occurrence – sometimes soon after leaving the event or much later on. The prime initial feature of a successful retreat is simply self-acceptance: the retreatant has discovered that being alive as 'me' is not so dreadful after all, that there can be mysterious joy in forgetting oneself, letting go into simple bare awareness of the present - whatever it is. We call this 'self at ease' and it is an opening to 'clarity'. Deeper levels of this experience give rise to a sense of oneness with the world or cosmos in which the machinations of self are temporarily forgotten. An actual 'kensho' only rarely follows but may do so, sometimes taking the form of a sudden realisation after the retreat is over. In 'kensho' there is a personally surprising absence of all self-reference – an experience clearly distinguishable from the previous ones. (See further Crook (ed) Illuminating Silence p94-96 and Ron Henshall's following article). Such insights are again normally of brief duration.

What is the long-term effect of participating in Zen sesshins? This is a difficult question to answer since over a period of years individuals grow in many ways, simply as a result of further life-experience and of joining in social activities. In the late 1970s, I distributed over a hundred questionnaires to past participants from which the above assessment of the actual experience of a sesshin was drawn, but apart from a general authentication of the value of the retreat specific detail was difficult to obtain. Personal letters, sometimes of great length, have, however, indicated the considerable influence of these retreats on the life course of at least some individuals.

Very rarely an individual may be adversely affected by the retreat. There is a condition known to the Japanese as 'stinking of Zen'. After a WZR it is possible for the release of energy to produce excessive exhilaration, amounting to a manic euphoria which the subject projects in wildly ambitious expectations of others. Only two cases have occurred in thirty years, both young women, and a spell in hospital care was required before the condition subsided. It is likely that those subject to schizoid breaks are more at risk than others, but the rarity of these occurrences suggests that the proportion of people at risk at the WZR is no larger than that in the general population.

A Psychological View of Changes Experienced during a Retreat

The solving of a koan in a Western Zen Retreat has a strongly self-affirmative character, but one that appears in a curiously apophatic mode. Instead of assertions about identity and personal history, one finds a frequent use of process words - 'I am peace', 'Life is living',

'Another is an adventure', accompanied by a clarity of awareness which lacks easily attributed boundaries in either time or space. What is being affirmed is the quality of the living moment rather than the personhood of the experiencer - yet there is no self-doubt about who it is that manifests that quality. The conventional attributions of parts and processes to oneself as descriptive categorisations in social discourse are however replaced by expressions springing with direct immediacy from a realm of insight and feeling, which lacks the necessity of being named.

A way to explain this is by means of the concept of disidentification. The human individual is a self-conceiving mammal whose concepts of self function to maintain individual distinctiveness, both introspectively and socially, in a world of interpersonal relations. Infants come to impute to their body-mind experience the properties of agency in interaction with others - especially mother. The discovery of agency is followed by the imputation to the self so realised of properties or qualities which arise in social interaction (Lewis and Brooks, 1977; Horrocks and Jackson, 1972).

A powerful view of the way in which identification with such conceptual realisation occurs has developed in Western thought in the writings of G. H. Mead (1934), Homans (1961) and Tajfel (1978) and have been discussed in Crook (1980, 2009). Social acts are seen as events through which individuals learn the perspectives of others about themselves; and incorporate them into `identity constructs' which constitute their cognitive being. A person only becomes such through a progressively elaborated process of role-taking in relation to another. People not only conceive of themselves largely as others see them, but tend to act in accordance with the expectations that others may hold. More recent views, based both on observational evidence and sociobiological theory, affirm that, apart from needs for social approval, infants are from the beginning also strategists. They pursue nutritional, affectional and self- expressive goals that form the eventual basis for autonomous action in the world, the creation of economic well-being and the rearing of a family (Crook, 1980, Chapter 9).

Erikson (1950) and Sullivan (1955) show how the development of identity constructs is severely affected by the emotional content of the child-parent relationship. Whenever a child's need for support and explanation is met in an open, caring manner, its development can proceed in a constructive, positively self-evaluative way that leads to the learning of self- affirmative skills and expression, combined with tolerance for others. Where, however, the child is subject to loss (Bowlby, 1969, 1973), to repeated bad temper and punishment, to denigration or abuse, these threats to the emergence of a positive self-evaluation produce habitual anxiety which, when projected onto other figures, becomes the basis for the complex affect-laden habits in adulthood by which actual relations with others are distorted by fantasy. Furthermore, the contrasting, genetically based strategies of the male and female genders lead to contrasts in the fathering and mothering of children in a family. These are often sources of conflict and an important 'root origin' of suffering (Crook 2009, Chapter 19)

Masking operations, suppression, schizoid denial and excessive egotism are devices to protect the self from largely imagined threats derived from fears of the parent. Such devices become deeply ingrained in the character of the individual - basically as attempts to support a negatively valued but necessary sense of personal identity. Naturally, interactional styles based on such patterns in adult life tend to evoke similarly distorted patterns in others leading to the whole range of 'games people play' (Berne, 1966).

At the onset of a retreat, some participants are presenting themselves to one another through the screen of such self-protective social attitudes based on their guarded suspicions of others. Their shaky identity constructs, often based upon years of hurt, determine an often highly defensive or over-assertive stance. Other individuals may have varying degrees of self and other understanding based on life experiences or work in therapy or `growth' groups. In either case, to come to the Zen Retreat has required an act of trust or courage, because participants know that these restricting habits of personal closure are precisely those they will confront in the course of the retreat. In the communication exercise it is precisely these attitudes that are disclosed to another.

Jourard (1971) has described the therapeutic value of self-disclosure of this kind. As trust develops and deeper topics are broached, the individual experiences relief from the tightly bound defensive positions of self-constriction with which he or she tends to face the world. Self-disclosure is an important aspect of co-counselling, a system of mutual therapy which Charles Berner used as a model for the Enlightenment Intensive process, and which has a close resemblance to the communication exercise. As the disclosure moves from the merely conceptual to the direct expression of hurt through weeping, rage or distress, so the whole body-mind process is activated and the 'armour' (as Reich termed it) can literally relax - muscular, endocrinal, sympathetic nervous and mental tensions all move towards release or relaxation. Every authentic statement or presentation becomes literally a letting go of 'stuff', and a thorough release of a theme allows a dis-identification from it so that, for the time being at least, it does not recur. There is thus a progressive abandonment of restrictive identity constructs, together with the forms of their physical incarnation.

The motivation for self-disclosure seems to lie in an awareness of the need to share. This sharing can, however, only occur with another felt to be positively regarding; a person not necessarily warm but certainly capable of non-judgemental sympathetic listening. There may be also an element of confession present, as thoughts of shame and guilt are spoken often with profound expressions of remorse, longing for clarification or atonement. Participants have to learn that they can trust one another's common humanity.

Dis-identification leads to an abandonment of conceptual constrictions, and the mind is free to look into the emptiness so created - a consciousness increasingly freed from self-regard and even from the dichotomy between subject and object itself. It is the nature of this consciousness that is the focus of Buddhist self-examination and about which Western psychology still has had little to say beyond complex theoretical disputes (see discussion in Blackmore 2003)

Conclusions: Perplexity and Preceptual Truth

Whether one is an Eastern monk or a Western lay person, the root of the motivation for Zen training lies in perplexity. Perplexity arises within the unsatisfactory character of life itself with its inherent difficulties in self-evaluation, in personal goal-satisfaction and its termination in death. Buddhism itself seems to have arisen in response to an increasingly complex life resulting from the emergence of an urban, class-based hierarchical society in ancient India with its consequent problems of identity, self-esteem and meaning for individual lives (Ling, 1973). Contemporary Western life, with its rapidly changing social norms, breakdowns of social and familial structures and secular value system, raises similar issues in florid form.

The Buddhist response may seem a strange one to anyone who has not undertaken training - for the uncovering of a characterless 'unborn' mind 'empty' of itself seems an unlikely basis for life in a highly fragmented and competitive social world. To understand the purport here, it becomes necessary to penetrate to the depth of meaning attributable to such definitions of Zen as 'the self making the self into the self.' Fortunately, there is an ancient Japanese story which helpfully illustrates the meaning and value of Zen training.

Once upon a time there was a bed of squashes ripening in the corner of a field. One day they began quarrelling. The squashes split up into factions and made a lot of noise shouting at one another. The head priest of a nearby temple, hearing the sound, rushed out to see what was wrong. He scolded the wrangling squashes saying `Whatever are you doing. Fighting among yourselves is useless. Everyone do zazen!'

The priest taught them all how to sit properly in zazen and gradually their anger died away. Then the priest said, 'Put your hands on top of your heads.' The squashes did so and discovered a peculiar thing. Each one had a stem growing from its head which connected them all one to another and back to a common root. 'What a mistake we have made!' they said, `We are all joined to one another, based on the same root and living one life only. In spite of that we quarrel. How foolish our ignorance has been.' After that this reader hopes they all lived happily ever after. (Taken from Kosho Uchiyami Roshi, 1973)

The story illustrates the experiential fact that as a result of Zen training the habit of discrimination in producing dualistic distinctions between self and others diminishes, and may even disappear altogether for a time. In this freedom from self-concern there is a sense of participation not only in a social but also in a universal process. 'Emptiness' of self-nature means awareness of the interdependence of all the phenomena of experienced life. This is the stem of the vine. Unthreatened by the processes of others in a sense of community, compassion arises, anger dies down, love in its broadest sense appears.

A training such as this recalibrates the meaning attributable to a person's sense of reality. Dualistic functioning remains appropriate in contexts where action is needed and planning done, but action itself is now perceived within the wider context of a pervasive non-dual base. The Zen task is to develop the skilful means to apprehend this wider, psychologically validated, holistic view of reality and then to discover how to move creatively within it. This is the self making the self into the self.

Given the current norms of society - the practitioner of Zen will almost inevitably find himself to be the possessor of an outsider's vision. Faced continuously with the problem of value in contemporary society, life becomes a permanent koan - how to live according to preceptual truth within contemporary society. Since training leads to the Bodhisattva's concern for the welfare of others, it seems inevitable that a Zen trainee, whatever the details of his personal strategy, will adopt values of a generally altruistic nature - focused more on the common good than on personal advancement. Yet, as skilful means to this end, action in pursuit of an appropriate career, economic livelihood and family life are not to be seen as inappropriate. In holding the koan ever in mind the appropriate way becomes plain. In this there is no magic solution - the effects of karma, personal conditioning, are very strong and need endless review, witnessing the failures, the errors and the disappointments. Life is making life into life and there are no short-cuts - only the emergence of an understanding. As Philip Glass the composer has remarked, the meaning of a work of art is always completed by the hearer. In the view of Zen that too is true of the work of life.

Footnotes

1 Chang, G.C.C., Six Yogas of Naropa, New York, Snow Lion, 1963

2 Crook, J. H. and D. Fontana (Eds) 1990. Space in Mind: East-West Psychology & Contemporary Buddhism. Element. Shaftesbury. (Vega, 2002. Out of print).

3 Our journal New Chan Forum is a potent source of discussions of practice in Western Zen and Chan. For examples: John Crook, NCF 11,Supplement; NCF 13,15-30; NCF 22 ,14-31; NCF 27, 8-19 ; NCF 28, 20-25 ; NCF 30 ,p 10; NCF 35, 2-8, 12-18; David Loy; NCF 36, 6-34; Simon Child NCF 9, 16-20; NCF 13, 9-13; NCF 34, 4-7; Stephen Batchelor NCF 14.3-8; Stuart Lachs NCF 10.12-19; Susan Blackmore NCF 12, 9-15.

References

Amphoux, N. 1986. Diary of a Zen Nun. London: Rider.

Berne, E. 1966. The Games People Play: The Psychology of Human Relationships. New York: Deutsch.

Blackmore, S. 2003. Consciousness: An introduction. Hodder & Stoughton.

Bowlby, J. 1969/73. Attachment and Loss. Vols. 1.2. London: Hogarth.

Brandon, D. 1976. Zen in the Art of Helping. London: Routledge & Kegan Paul.

Crook, J. H. 1980. The Evolution of Human Consciousness. Oxford: Oxford University Press. Crook, J. H. 2009. World crisis and Buddhist Humanism. New Age Books. Delhi.

Erikson, E. 1950. Childhood and Society. London: Pelican.

Faure, B.1996. Vision of Power. Princeton – and related works.

Harding, D. E. 1974. The Science of the 1st Person. Ipswich: Sholland Publications. Homans, G. C. 1961. Social

Behaviour: its Elementary Form. New York: Harcourt, Brace.

Heine, S & D. S. Wright. 2000. The Koan. Oxford University Press.

Horrocks, J. E. and Jackson, D.W. 1972. Self and Role: A Theory of Self-Process and Role Behaviour. Houghton Mifflin: Boston.

Humphries, C. 1949. Zen Buddhism. London: Heineman.

Jourard, S. M. 1971. Self-Disclosure: An Experimental Analysis of the Transparent Self. New York: Wiley Interscience.

Kapleau, P. 1965. The Three Pillars of Zen. Boston: Beacon. Kapleau, P. 1980. Zen: Dawn in the West. London: Rider.

Kasulis, T. P. 1981 Zen Action Zen Person. University Press Hawaii

Kennett, J. 1972. Selling Water by the River: A Manual of Zen Training. New York: Vintage, Random House. Kennett, J. 1977/78. The Wild White Goose. Vols. 1 and 2. California: Shasta Abbey.

Kosho Uchiyama Roshi. 1973. Approach to Zen. Tokyo and San Francisco: Japan Publications.

Leggett, T. 1985. The Warrior Koans: Early Zen in Japan. London: Arkana. London.

Lewis, M. and Brooks, J. 1977. Self-Knowledge and Emotional Development. In M. Lewis and M. Rosenthal (eds.), The Development of Affect. New York: Plenum.

Ling, T. 1973. The Buddha. London: Penguin.

Love, J. 1976. The Quantum Gods. London: Compton Russell.

Lu K'uan. Yu. 1964. The Secrets of Chinese Meditation. London: Rider. McRae, J.R. 2003 Seeing through Zen. University of California Press.

Mead, G.H. 1934. Mind, Self and Society. Chicago: University of Chicago Press.

Merrell-Wolff, F. 1973. The Philosophy of Consciousness without an Object. New York: Julian Press. Pirsig, R. M. 1974. Zen in the Art of Motorcycle Maintenance. London: Bodley Head.

Sheng-Yen, Master. 1982. Getting the Buddha Mind. New York: Dharma Drum Publications (90-56 Corona Avenue, Elmhurst: New York.

Sheng yen, Master with D. Stevenson. 2001. Hoofprint of the Ox. Oxford University Press

Sheng yen, Master. 2006. Attaining the Way. Shambala.

Sullivan, H. S. 1955. The Interpersonal Theory of Psychiatry. London: Tavistock.
Suzuki, D. 1953. Essays in Zen Buddhism. London: Rider.

Tajfel, H. (ed.) 1978. Differentiation between Social Groups. European Monographs in Social Psychology, 14. Thich Nhat Hanh. 1974. Zen Keys. New York: Doubleday.

Watts, A. N. 1957. The Way of Zen. London: Thames & Hudson.

Wetering, J. van de 1972. The Empty Mirror. London: Routledge & Kegan Paul.

Wetering, J. van de 1974. A Glimpse of Nothingness. London: Routledge & Kegan Paul.

NCF XXXIX

Editorial - The Passing of Shifu and the China Journey

As we began to prepare this issue, the news came to us that our Shifu, the Venerable Chan Master Sheng Yen, had passed away. It is a sad time and we send our condolences to Dharma Drum practitioners, monastic and lay, wherever they may be. Such a time is nevertheless also one for renewed focus and resolve to activate the Master's Teachings in the world so that they may make a difference during these crisis years. We present various texts dealing with Shifu's Will, his obituary, memorial services and accounts of personal experiences of him as a memorial of a great teacher.

Last May and June several of our Leaders accompanied John Crook on a study tour of Chinese monasteries guided superbly by Rebecca Li, Shifu's key interpreter. Our journey ended in Taiwan at Dharma Drum Mountain thereby allowing us to meet Shifu, pay our respects to him and receive the blessing of his company. This was a journey during which we learnt much, received valuable teachings, met many fascinating people and began to truly appreciate the depth and presence of Chinese Buddhism in our time.

It is thus also appropriate that we share our discoveries with you at this time.

Chuan-deng Jing-di

Reply to the Venerable Abbot President

Chuan-deng Jing-di

Dear Venerable Abbot President and Friends in the Dharma,

It is with much distress that we hear of the death of our Teacher, Shifu and Patron of our Sangha. Although many of us were aware of his ill health, a death is always a shock. For me, Shifu was my spiritual father, my root teacher, and his departure brings feelings of loneliness and inadequacy as one generation passes to another. Yet also, there is immense gratitude. I have always been amazed that he passed the Dharma to me, a non-Chinese who cannot even read his language or speak it; yet, it is true, that sometimes when we met there was a direct participation with him in the Truth and this gives me courage to continue the work in the Great Matter. Shifu was to me an inspiration and a shrewd disciplinarian. He understood my wish to convey to our British Sangha the insights of Chan in ways that Westerners could best understand - and that has been my work now for years. Shifu always questioned me in depth and with challenging koan-like subtlety concerning my plans here. I am eternally grateful that my life coincided with his, we were the same age, and that I should have met him. I especially appreciated Shifu's essential simplicity. In spite of his attainments, his learning and his vast seniority there was always a flash of simple understanding between us.

It was an especial joy to introduce several local leaders of our British Sangha to him last June when we came to Dharma Drum, and to see him once more vividly himself and so present with us. My private moments with him then were an especial renewal of an understanding.

I have seriously considered coming to Taiwan for this ceremonial occasion but travelling with a very bad back and moving with a limp would cause more trouble than any help to you. I am to see a consultant next week and trust it will then be set right. Simon will be joining you. We are receiving much mail sending condolences.

I wish you, the Sangha and our friends at Dharma Drum all Dharma blessings at this time. We shall of course continue our deep relationship with you all.

The Venerable Chan Master Sheng-yen - A Brief Obituary

Chuan-deng Jing-di, John Hurrell Crook

On February 3rd 2009 at 4:00pm Taiwan time, the Venerable Chan Master Sheng-yen, passed away peacefully at Dharma Drum Mountain Founder's Quarters in Taiwan thus bringing to an end the life of perhaps the most influential Chan (Zen) master of our generation. At centres all over the world, communities are mourning the loss of their Teacher - 'Shifu'.

Shifu's health had been declining over the past three years. This rapid decline started from the time of the inauguration of the Dharma Drum Mountain World Centre for Buddhist Education, Taiwan, in late 2005, when Shifu received surgery to remove a non-functioning kidney, and the remaining kidney's ability to function became very poor. Since then, he had been going through weekly dialysis and various other treatments, making his body very weak. Over the following two years, his health condition has had ups and downs, and remarkably, in mid to late 2008, Shifu had been noticeably stronger and able to give many lectures and attend many public events. However, in late December, a routine check-up at the hospital revealed a problem. Yet, Shifu kept on with his agenda. Shortly after, he was hospitalized and his health deteriorated rapidly. His condition looked grave. After a few days it took a turn for the better, and there was a visible improvement. Afterwards, Shifu continued to attend meetings and receive guests and also took a leave of absence from the hospital to visit the local Taipei monasteries and centres. Yet, soon his condition again deteriorated, fluctuating between good and bad. He returned to his home in the monastery that he had founded and passed away.

In 2008, Shifu published his autobiography in English carefully prepared by his closest disciples[1]. Here we read of a man who, like His Holiness the Dalai Lama, always considered himself to be a simple monk but who has accomplished a remarkable renewal of Chinese Zen Buddhism in Chinese communities throughout the world and extended its teachings to the West. His many books have augmented and corrected the earlier Western Zen understanding based on the previous contribution of Daisetz Susuki. Together with other masters such as Thich Nhat Hahn, Shunryu Suzuki and Jiyu Kennett, Shifu has created a Zen renaissance worldwide thereby continuing the work of that great reformer Master Hsu-yun of the twentieth century in China itself.

Sheng-yen was born in 1930 near the estuary of the Yangtze River. Floods destroyed his father's lands and the family had to rely on a very small property and on fishing the river. This was a life of poverty soon to be made more difficult by the Japanese invasion of the area. As a boy, an old monk asked him whether he would like to be a monk. Although he had no idea what that meant, he grasped the opportunity and sometime later went to school even while battles flamed around. Eventually he became a monk at a well-endowed monastery, Wolf Mountain, near Shanghai. Here he became enamoured with the Dharma with some insight into its significance. Soon however came more trouble and the eventual arrival of the communists. The monks, forced into poverty, kept going by offering funeral services in Shanghai. They received no training. Finding the only way out, Sheng-yen eventually joined Chiang Kai Shek's nationalist army and was thus able to move to Taiwan.

In Taiwan after the usual military training, square bashing and so on, Sheng-yen became an officer in the Intelligence Corps. Although he had no understanding of the implications of the telegraphic material he was handling, the military would not let him resign his commission lest he betray national secrets. He began developing his practice in his spare time and visiting monasteries. Eventually he was able to go back to civilian life. On one occasion in desperation he sought the help of old Master Ling-yuan in whose helpful presence he relieved his mind and experienced 'seeing the nature' for the first time. Gradually he became known and through working on a Buddhist magazine eventually he joined a monastery mastered by the eminent monk Dong-chu who had previously been the Abbot of the famous Jian Shan monastery on a riverine island near Shanghai. Dong-chu taught him through vigorous confrontation, giving him pointless tasks to do testing his resolve and will. It was much like the ferocious way in which the Tibetan Marpa had taught Milarepa.

Shifu eventually undertook a six year solitary retreat in the mountains beginning with a long period of repentance leading into study, learning Japanese and developing a determination to study Buddhism at a university in Japan, there being no place of advanced Buddhist learning in Taiwan. He obtained his Doctorate at Rissho University but also undertook gruelling retreats in Japanese sesshins where his learning was ridiculed in true Zen style. He developed the wish to take Zen to the West but had his doubts because he knew no English. "Ha," said his Master, "Do you think Zen is taught by words?"

Shifu found a sponsor and began teaching in Toronto and New York. But his sponsor was disappointed. Shifu had less English than he expected and other disappointments between them flourished. Eventually a friend, C.T. Shen, arranged for him to live at the Temple of Great Enlightenment in the Bronx, New York. Although Sheng-yen had the qualities of a Master, the temple treated him as a mere novice monk giving him only basic cleaning work to do. Yet again, C.T. Shen stepped in and had him made Abbot. Gradually a few, then more Westerners began coming to the monastery. Although Sasaki Sokei-an had taught Zen, especially from the Platform Sutra, in New York in the 1930s, Shifu was the first Chan master to teach contemporary Chinese Chan to Westerners on the east coast of the US. The only other such teacher in the USA at that time was Master Hsuan Hua over in California.

Then he was called back to Taiwan. Master Dong-chu needed help in his monastery and it took time before the arrangement of alternating time in Taiwan with time in America became stabilised. When Shifu returned to the USA, he needed to live near the monastery and not with his sponsor much further away. He had then to finance his own life but having no money, he became a wanderer, sleeping on the streets, or 'nodding with the homeless through the night in coffee shops, foraging through dumpsters for fruit and vegetables.' For a man then in his fifties living this way in a New York winter was a hard life. Yet again, C.T. Shen assisted him finding places where Sheng-yen could teach and hold retreats. Shifu has always said that living in this way was a training invaluably testing his resolve, ingenuity and determination. In any case, as he pointed out, his life had always been like that and the self-discipline imposed by Dong-chu's fierce training came to his aid.

Gradually a Chinese community with some Westerners formed around him and in time they bought a small building on Corona Avenue in Elmhurst in Queens. Although the present Meditation Centre on Corona is not in the same building, his presence in that area was established for many years. A pattern developed. Through his writings in Chinese and in English translation, he became known and through his personal charisma, Shifu grew into an influential figure in both Taiwan and New York. In Taiwan, he headed the Institute of Chung-Hwa Buddhist Culture and also inherited Dong-chu's monastery outside the capital. Donations flowed in and, given the economic success of Taiwan, the sums contributed were large. Shifu was able to obtain a large mountainous estate on which, gradually, a magnificent monastery has been constructed. It is now an architectural showpiece and a functioning Chan Centre and monastery complete with a seminary developing full university status. In New York, he likewise obtained a large estate in the Catskill Hills thereby creating a beautiful meditation centre in the woods. It must be said, however, that Shifu's poor command of English and his long stays in Taiwan limited the success of his mission among Westerners in the USA.

It was during this period that I first went to New York to 'sit' in an intensive retreat with Shifu. He was very interested in my own work in Britain and in the little centre I had created in Wales. After I had attended several retreats, he came over to Wales in 1989 and led the first of four retreats in Britain. My work with him developed into a close understanding and Shifu made me the first of his Western Dharma heirs in 1993. I helped him lead retreats elsewhere, guestmastering for him in Berlin for example. But he was also developing retreats in Poland, Switzerland, Russia etc. This was a time therefore of increasing international involvement. As his name became known, he represented Chinese Buddhism at numerous conferences; in an important public dialogue with His Holiness the Dalai Lama, thereby healing a breach with Tibetan Buddhism that had lasted for centuries; and finally co-chaired conferences of world religious leaders under the auspices of the United Nations.

Chan Master Sheng-yen had become an international figure. In his addresses to conferences, his approach was always one of complete sanity, carefully attuned to the world situation and presenting the Dharma in ways his fellow religious leaders could understand and to a degree accept.

For me, writing this, what I recall are his more personal traits. On retreats, he could be a hard taskmaster but always understood the limits to which he could drive the participants. It became clear that this approach was deeply compassionate. As Master Dong-chu had taught him, confrontation with the ego is essential if wisdom is to sprout. In interview, Shifu could appear as a warm friend, as a critical schoolmaster, as a father, or present a remote even chilling distance after which one spent hours struggling to understand. Sometimes there was a depth present that left one groping to follow after him.

After his retreats in the UK, I was fortunate enough to be his guide for a few extra days. Once we drove through Wales to Hereford Cathedral, on through Oxford looking at the colleges and thence to London where we stayed in a 'pad' in Great Russell Street then occupied by my children in their late teens. Another time, I took him to see some of the amazing documents and paintings collected by Marc Aurel Stein in Dunhuang and Central Asia around 1900 and now kept in London. In Westminster Abbey, he bought the guidebook in Japanese. During these few days, Shifu was totally relaxed, a charming guest, a wonderfully insightful conversationalist and great fun to be with. At my children's pad, he noticed some unclean coffee cups hiding under a chair. He found this a great joke and humorously made good friends with my kids. In the museums, the bright ink of the ancient documents that often looked as if they had been written only yesterday delighted him. I was also able to drive him in terrible rainstorms up into the Pennine hills to visit Throssel Hole Abbey of the Order of Buddhist Contemplatives. He spoke warmly with the monks and was very impressed by the life of this British monastery.

Shifu's death creates a tragic loss for all those who had the great good fortune to be taught by him but it is also an inspiration. His wisdom lives on in books, tapes, and video and in institutions. It is now the task of his Dharma descendants to take up the roles he has left for us to occupy.

1 Footprints in the Snow; the Autobiography of a Chinese Buddhist Monk. Doubleday 2008

The Will of Chan Master Sheng-yen

1. I was born in 1930 in the Jiangsu Province of China, and my family's surname is Chang. After I pass away, do not issue the obituary notice, make meal offerings, build the grave, stupa, or monument, erect my statues, or collect my relics, if any. Please invite one to three eminent elder Dharma masters to respectively preside over the rituals of sealing the coffin, bidding farewell, cremation, ash burial, and so forth. All this must be carried out in a simple, frugal manner, and never in an extravagant and wasteful way. In the mourning hall, only hang an elegiac plaque with the words "Quiescent Cessation Is Blissful" written by a calligrapher as an encouragement. Request people not to present flowers or elegiac couplets, but just recite "Namo Amitabha Buddha" to form pure affinities for rebirth in the Western Pure Land.

2. If, after I pass away, there is any cash offered to me by Buddhist believers and any revenue from my copyright royalty, they should be donated to Dharma Drum Mountain Buddhist Foundation and Dharma Drum Mountain Cultural and Educational Foundation. I have no personal properties during my lifetime. All my belongings have been offered to me by the general public, so they should all go to the Dharma center of Dharma Drum Mountain (DDM), and be handled according to both the codes established by the Buddha and my will, which has been notarized by the court.

3. All the Dharma centers that I have founded and have been in charge of belong to the Dharma lineage of Dharma Drum Mountain. Except that they are financially independent in their operation, they should adopt a unified mechanism with respect to the sustaining of DDM's Dharma tradition, education of talents, mutual loving care, and personnel arrangement. However, the branch Dharma centers overseas should take as its principle to have a uniform style of Chan and make use of local manpower, so that the pure, authentic Chan teachings will not decline and Chan practice will take roots and spread in societies of different cultures.

4. Whether the post of the abbot president of DDM's headquarters is assumed by one who is elected internally or is an eminent bhikshu or bhikshuni invited from outside of DDM's system, he or she, while succeeding to the post, also succeeds to DDM's Dharma orthodoxy, and shall inherit and carry on DDM's Chan lineage, and shall not relinquish the vision and aims of Dharma Drum Mountain, which all shall abide by permanently. The Buddha said, "I don't lead the assembly; I am a member among the Sangha." The abbot president is the Sangha's spiritual nucleus, as well as supervising and advancing the monasteries' operation and Dharma affairs of the

Sangha, making sure that they are resolved and executed by monastic members in accordance with the Dharma, precepts, and regulations, and that all live in joyful harmony, diligence, and purity.

5. In order to avoid misuse and adulteration, any manuscripts of my writings which have not been reviewed by me personally shall not be compiled into books hereafter, except for those that have already been published and can be included in the complete collection of my works.

6. After I pass away, please request Professor Lin Qixian and his wife to complete the "Chronicle of Master Sheng Yen's Life" up to the time of my death, as historical materials for the reference of future generations. Therefore, please do not compile or print any commemorative collections and the like.

7. DDM's Sangha is entrusted to carry out the instructions in my will. Please perform the ceremony for my death not as a funeral, but as a solemn Buddhist ritual.

8. My monastic and lay disciples have nothing to dispute over regarding properties, funds, power, and positions. Rather they are expected to act in compassion, wisdom, harmony, and respect, and carry out the education based on the Four Kinds of Environmentalism. Virtuous followers, please cherish yourselves. We have the good karmic roots and blessed causes and conditions to walk the bodhisattva path together, and we have formed affinities while practicing under the guidance of innumerable Buddhas in our past lives. We will also be cultivating together the supreme enlightenment at the assemblies of innumerable Buddhas as fellow practitioners for one another in the right Dharma.

9. The wills that I made prior to this one can be used as a reference. However, this Will shall be the standard one.

As a conclusion, I compose the following verse:

> "Though nothing happens,
> we've grown old in our busy lives[1].
> We cry and laugh, all in emptiness. There is originally no self,
> So both life and death can be cast aside."

Bhikkhu Sheng Yen, Founder, Dharma Drum Mountain.

1 See alternative, improved translation by Jimmy Yu in Valedictory Address, below.

Valedictory Address, Master Sheng-yen

Feb 15th 2009, Bristol Chan Group Memorial Service

"Gaté gaté paragaté parsamgaté. Bodhi Svaha."

Here we have the great mantra of the Heart Sutra but today it is Shifu who is "gaté gaté - Gone Gone" and we meet together to mourn this great loss. He has been my personal guide and our patron for many years. Perhaps also he has been the greatest Zen master of our generation. Not only has he introduced Chinese Zen throughout the world, spoken diplomatically with the Dalai Lama thereby helping to integrate differing approaches to the Mahayana, attended conferences of World religious leaders at the United Nations but, most importantly, he has brought together the Chan teachings into a fresh unitary lineage at his monastery of Dharma Drum.

Yet the mantra ends with "Bodhi Svaha" – Wisdom arise! So at this time we must also bow in gratitude for the life of this man, a simple monk who has thought so deeply about the problems of humanity. Together we need to renew our focus on the great teachings he has left us and recall the long lineage that he has continued into our time.

Perhaps for us in a British Sangha, one of the most important aspects of his teaching has been the clarification of problematic issues arising from the history of Zen's arrival in Europe. Shifu was able to help here following his long solitary retreat and his subsequent period of research in Japan. The great Daisetz Suzuki, right until near the end of his life, only presented to the West the approach of the Linji school (Jap: Rinzai) of Japanese Zen in which koans and hua-tous are the prime methods used during meditation. When eventually the West discovered the Caodong (Soto) school, some arguments developed about what was proper Zen. This dispute had arisen in China in ancient times between monasteries competing for support and subsistence. The stories are well known. We find them in the Platform Sutra and again later, in the apparent disputes between Masters Hong-zhi and Ta-hui. We now understand that although there were political motives undoubtedly involved, the prime issue was merely a preference in meditation method – there was no fundamental dispute at the level of Dharma. Indeed, while disagreeing about method, it is clear that Ta-hui and Hong-zhi were friends. Never the less, these divisions in lesser minds promoted a dispute that has come down to our time. Shifu examined these issues carefully. Already in Japan, under the leadership of Master Harada, an approach integrating these schools was developing and Shifu had attended retreats with a successor of Harada, Master Bantetsugyu. He was therefore aware of the need for reconciliation.

When I received transmission in 1993 Shifu gave it to me in the Lineage of Linji, saying that that was the only lineage with an intact sequence of names. Further research, however, enabled him to correct our understanding of the Caodong lineage. Since Shifu himself was teaching and offering retreats using methods from both schools, Silent Illumination from Hongzhi and Hua-tou from Koans from Ta-hui, he then created an integral lineage including both approaches and updated my own transmission. This is the Dharma Drum Lineage, containing both Linji and Caodong, which we inherit from him today and within which both Simon and I are Dharma Heirs. (See further, Li, Rebecca (ed) 2002. Chan comes West. Dharma Drum Publications)

A further Dharma clarification has arisen from Shifu's meeting with His Holiness the Dalai Lama, going a long way to sort out a long stand-off between Tibetan and Chinese Buddhism and restoring Dharma good will between them. This is very helpful for those of us who have additional interests in the Tibetan approach.

I have been so fortunate in my life to have met such a teacher. Shifu was so alert, so focussed and at heart so deeply compassionate, yet often very strict and confronting in his personal teaching. When I first met him he introduced his retreat with such bleak authority that I wondered whether it had been wise for me to come. Yet, I soon realised this was a front to get participants truly focussed on the seriousness of their endeavour. Shifu could be quite a trickster. As he said when he first came to The Maenllwyd, that he had come not so much to give us enlightenment, that was ridiculous, but to show us how confused our minds were! He was very good at that.

On my first visit to New York I had told him about the Western Zen Retreat. This interested him and we had much discussion about it. After I had done several retreats with him, he agreed to come over to Wales to teach us. What a privilege! After that, the best we could do was to create the Bristol Chan Group to continue with what we had learnt. I have so many memories of Shifu: kindness itself; humour; profound thought and mutual delight in conversation; sudden rejection of my mistakes; sometimes quite fierce confrontation leaving me angry and disturbed until I suddenly saw his point and dropped my egoic reaction. What insights, what teaching! Sometimes he taught very indirectly leaving me to puzzle over what had happened between us. This was very insightful, causing me to reflect again and again until I got the point. I am still getting it today!

To illustrate Shifu's style, I will use a story I recently received concerning an encounter experienced by an early student, Merrick Lex, at the Queens' meditation centre in New York. Lex wrote:

"I continued to study with Shifu when he visited NYC. In either late '79 or early '80 the building for Dharma Drum Meditation Centre had been purchased, and we started to fix it up. One day, Shifu took me to the picture window downstairs and asked me to open up the old metal security grate that was spanning the window. I did that and we saw that the window was completely covered with grime and grease. It was a depressing sight. "I want you to clean that window up," Shifu said. He took a single edge razor blade out of his sleeve where he had been hiding it and gave it to me. I looked at the tiny blade and then at the huge window and must have looked pretty forlorn, but I set to cleaning it up. After many hours of scraping and wiping with rags, I finally had it cleaned up and spotless both inside and out. I was standing and admiring my work, when Shifu came in and asked me to get to work on the basement.

When I next came to the building about ten days later, somebody had painted the old metal grate with bright gold paint. Shifu asked me to take a look at it with him, then he asked me to open up the grate again. When I opened it, I discovered that the painter had not taken care to cover the glass window, which was now splattered with blobs of gold paint from top to bottom. My beautiful clean window! I turned around with a look of shock on my face. Shifu was only smiling at me for a moment, then, he slowly took the razor blade back out of his sleeve, handed it to me, and walked away in silence. I was filled with surprise, frustration, and finally humour and burst out laughing. Then I set to work to scrape the whole window again! And so it went with my greatest teacher!"

Shifu has followed a long tradition and left us his final verse at the close of his will. It reads:

> Busy with nothing, growing old
>
> Within emptiness, weeping and crying
>
> Intrinsically, there is no "I"
>
> Life and death, thus cast aside.

There is so much one could say about this verse. Some of us may 'get it' immediately. Others may not yet be ready for it. For me, it reveals both the clarity of his being and of his teaching. Rather than talking about its inherent philosophy, I would like to present a brief prose-poem written earlier that seems to sum up my feeling as I read what he has said. This poem symbolizes Shifu's gift of clarity that is always available for us. Let us open ourselves to his clarity and then sit for a little while with it – as it were under the light of the Moon.

"Knowing the full moon was shining and the hoar frost sharp, I went out in to the garden closing the door on the yellow light of the room behind me. Suddenly, a different world; silent, frozen literally into stillness, everything either dark or silvery bright where the moonlight landed, black shadows looming where it did not reach. Looking back at the house now massive in these contrasting shades, it seemed a presence as if unknown to me – as if I were some stranger in a realm often available but seldom visited. Surrounded by stars, some brilliant against deep black, some tiny almost blinded by the moon, Orion was hanging in its iconic place: a great spread of sky constrained by lines, shades, shaped shadows and the sheer bulk of the emptied house; the bird seed holder so far below, motionless, without a visitor; no one there, simply a witness to where the vast silence of outer space touched down upon the lawn."

The China Trip 2008

Some three years ago, I was in New York staying with Rebecca Li and David Slaymaker prior to running a retreat at the Dharma Drum Retreat Centre at Pine Bush. After the retreat, I suggested to Rebecca that, as she was Shifu's main interpreter, she would be the best person to act as interpreter to a party I hoped to arrange to travel to Chinese monasteries. We would pay her expenses. I was extremely happy when she accepted. Rebecca, David, Simon Child and I then began planning our itinerary. I wanted to visit the major Chan monasteries that had been important throughout the history of Buddhism in China. I had already led a previous party to two of the famous Dharma Mountains in China, Putuo Shan and Jiuhua Shan (NCF 23, Winter 2000) and together with my friend Yiu Yan-nang had spent time in both Nan Hua Si and Yun Men Si in the south of the country (NCF 16, Spring 1997) so I decided not to repeat those visits but to concentrate on the North, including the famous Dharma Mountain of Wu tai and the important monasteries west of Shanghai.

My aim this time was to take several of our group leaders of the Western Chan Fellowship to China to provide a living education in Chan today in its homeland, its current state, main monastic and archaeological sites, problems and revival. I believed this would also be an inspiration to them in their task of passing the Dharma on to the participants in their groups. I also realised that we could return via Hong Kong and cross over to Taiwan to visit Shifu at Dharma Drum Monastery near Taipei. This would be the final and most important port of call enabling us to pay our respects to our Teacher and Patron, The Venerable Master Sheng Yen.

The suggestion was warmly received and we soon had a party. It consisted of the following: Simon Child, Alec Lawless, George Marsh, Jake Lyne, David Brown, Pete Lowry, Hugh Carroll, Eric Johns, Stephen Ward, Sophie Temple-Muir and Sally Masheder together with Rebecca, David and I. Yiu Yan-nang and Eva Tang, who had been our interpreter on the previous visit, joined us for part of the journey and Jack Tang (no relative) was once more a splendid group guide and tour manager. Jannie Mead joined us in Taiwan.

Rebecca and I began an extensive e-mail correspondence about the preparations for this trip. We wanted to stay in at least some of the monasteries to witness their life and practice but this needed diplomatic correspondence in Chinese. None of these monasteries other than Dharma Drum were familiar with Western Buddhists, they might suspect our motives and the Chinese authorities might prove a problem to them. Rebecca did wonders and, although we did not actually sleep in more than two monasteries, we stayed close to all of them. We also decided to visit other cultural sites of touristic interest to boost our knowledge of Chinese history and culture and these included major locations in Beijing, the gardens of Suzhou and the city of Shanghai. Yiu Yan-nang once again offered valuable advice. Our eventual itinerary was as follows:

May 21 (Wed) Arrive Beijing

May 22 (Thu) Visit Forbidden City, Tiananmen Square and Lama Temple.

May 23 (Fri) Visit Fa Yuan Temple (the Buddhist Institute) and Hutong Tour by rickshaw in old city area including family visit, and drum tower.

May 24 (Sat) Visit Temple of Heaven. Train to Datong.

May 25 (Sun) Visit Yungang Grottoes, and, in Datong, the Upper and Lower Hua Yan Temple, Shan Hua Temple.

May 26 (Mon) Transfer from Datong to Mt. Wutai, visiting the Suspending Temple on Hengshan Mountains en route.

May 27 (Tue) Visit Xian Tong Temple, Ta Yuan Temple and Pusading.

May 28 (Wed) Transfer from Mt. Wutai to Taiyuan then flight to Nanjing.

May 29 (Thu) Visit Qixia Temple. (Overnight at Qixia Temple).

May 30 (Fri) Transfer to Yangzhou, visit Da Ming Temple and He Garden. In the afternoon visit Gao Min Temple. (Overnight at Gao Min Temple).

May 31 (Sat) Depart to Zhenjiang, visit Jiangshan Temple and Jinshan Temple.

Jun 1 (Sun) Transfer from Zhenjiang - Changzhou, visit Tianning Temple, transfer Changzhou – Suzhou

Jun 2 (Mon) Visit Humble Administrator's Garden, Garden of Master of Nets, Lingering Garden.

Jun 3 (Tue) Transfer from Suzhou-Wuzhen, visit Wuzhen, transfer to Shanghai

Jun 4 (Wed) Visit Jade Buddha Temple, Bund, and Long Hua Temple. In the evening, Huangpu Cruise trip.

Jun 5 (Thu) Transfer to Ningbo. Visit nearby Tian Tong Temple

Jun 6 (Fri) Fly to Hong Kong, followed by a visit to Dharma Drum Monastery in Taiwan.

Our journey was extremely successful, without negative incidents, and taught us much about China, its people at the present time and the marked revival of Buddhism. We found Chan to be thriving although its form tended to be the more simplistic Pure land type, without the depth of either Silent Illumination or strict Linji work with koans or hua-tou, but none the less very sincere. Even so, intensive practice was observed in several places notably Gao Min Si, Tian Tong Si, and on Mount Wu Tai, while in several conversations with us individuals expressed deep understanding. We also had the great good fortune of meeting two amazing ancient Masters who taught us with depth and great virtuosity. We visited two seminaries and, taken together with training witnessed at Jiuhua Shan previously, it is clear that scholastically inclined monks can receive a good education in the Dharma and that this must be gradually spreading again across the country. Furthermore, the big, enthusiastic crowds visiting monasteries during festivals together with extensive Chinese inland tourism revealed a widespread popular involvement with Buddhist faith-based practices of a folk nature. In Taiwan, it was a joy to renew my personal acquaintance with my Shifu once again and to introduce so many of our leaders to him.

I am extremely grateful to Rebecca for her great skill in interpreting this journey to us and to Jack Tang for his accomplished leadership of a complex cultural tour. Eva Tang helped us enormously by negotiating our interview with the ancient Master of Wu Tai mountain.

In the articles that follow, we draw on the reminiscences of several of our travellers to present an account of what we discovered and now wish to share.

There is also an online gallery displaying some of the photographs taken by the party – see www.westernchanfellowship.org/china2008

Ancient Teachers in Full Flow

On two occasions during our tour, we met extraordinary ninety-year-old masters who were clearly delighted to be talking with us. These two men were rarities indeed. Their monastic careers cover a vast length of time including the period of repression of Buddhism under the communists. In Yun Men Si some years ago, my friend Yiu Yan-nang and I had talked with the Guestmaster who had said that the lack of such masters meant that many monks in China nowadays could learn only from books. Here we had found two genuine, living roots of Chan enlightenment.

Master Meng Can

The first of these remarkable men lived in the nunnery of Pu-shou Si, well off bounds to tourists on Mount Wu Tai. Eva Tang, who had been our interpreter during a previous visit to China, knew of him and had kindly arranged for us to meet him. It may seem unusual for a monk to live in a nunnery but as a refuge for elderly monks and their attendants this seems to be not so uncommon. The nunnery itself was an exemplary institution. We attended the Evening Service and noted the almost military precision of the assembly, row by row neatly drawn up facing the Buddha and the delicacy, discipline and decorum with which the nuns behaved. The chanting was some of the best we encountered in China. As most of us were males, we were fortunate even to be admitted.

We were taken to a large upper room and made comfortable. When Master Meng Can (Dream Investigate) came in aided by an attendant we all prostrated and sat. As the leader of our party, I sat facing him below his raised rostrum directly under his gaze. That gaze alone was extraordinary for a ninety-year-old man. It was direct, demanding attention, vigorous and keenly involved in getting his message across to us. He seemed to enjoy the novelty of meeting a group of Western lay Buddhists. It was a gaze that could have been wilting had I not raised my game to hear him. My record of what he told us is shaky so I am relying on notes from Rebecca who interpreted. Here is a summary.

"You must know that the purpose of Chan practice is to illuminate and understand the mind and to see the true nature of experience. Indeed, for us, the meaning of the word "Buddha" is "Awaken and Understand". Naturally, this requires one to reflect upon one's past, including past lives, so that one can get a clear idea of one's personal karma. One should see this life as resembling a dream. It is illusory and when we wake up, as if from a dream, the illusion disappears. As the Heart Sutra says, Form is Emptiness and Emptiness is Form. They are two sides of the same coin. The experience of Form implies the experience of Space. To understand form one needs to understand space."

"The practice is one of letting go of body, family and career. These are all not 'I'. They don't belong to your essential nature yet they are your illusory 'me'. In my case, I just live in this monastery. It does not "belong" to me, not 'mine' in any way. I simply make use of its facilities and of my body for what they can be used for. This is letting go of self.

"Regardless of differing schools of thought, the essence of Buddhadharma is 'Nature empty - Conditioned co-arising". Nature is emptiness; the conditioned arising of our thinking experience appears as not-emptiness, a seeming solidity. This means that all forms of family and human relationships are the result of karmic connections. They have no other reality. Every person is equal in Buddhism. One has to pay back the karma one has collected in the past and this applies to the wealthy, the poor and to people of all nationalities."

"Before you practice, make sure it cannot cause anyone harm. Then, in each moment, let go of everything. When you do that, you are Buddha. When attachments return, that is Samsara. If one can let go of attachment moment to moment, one has accomplished one's cultivation."

"We are meeting today because of distant association in the past. This is good. I wish you well."

The vigour of the Master's mind was truly amazing for someone of more than ninety years of age.

Master De Lin

Gao Min Monastery in Yangzhou has the reputation of being the best in China for the propriety and discipline of its pure Chan regime and of its monks. This has been so, whatever the national situation, for well beyond a hundred years. It is one of the few with an active Chan hall recently re-constructed. The old master we met at Gao Min Monastery is Master De Lin (Virtue Forest). He is a Dharma heir of Master Lai Guo, one of the most important masters of the 20th century, an associate of the famous reformer Master Xu-yun. Again we were ushered into a comfortable room and treated with every respect. The ancient Master was led in by very attentive assistants and was seated comfortably. Again, the vigour of his gaze and the forcefulness of his presentation were remarkable. Master De Lin emphasized the importance of serious study of the Dharma (sutras and sastras) to build the foundation of one's practice and spoke clearly of Silent Illumination. What follows is an edited version of David Brown's recording of our interaction. I soon realized that his questioning was rhetorical – to enable him to provide the answer whatever I might say!

Master de Lin (MDL): "How is Sheng-yen instructing you?"

John Crook (JC): "He says the most important thing is to 'See the Nature' with a compassionate heart. Can you help us with how we should do this?"

MDL: "That is pretty good. It is better to practice Chan as a lay person because Chan is daily life. It is difficult to explain Chan. So first, I would like to understand your view of Chan. I understand there are a number of PhD's here so you should have grasped something! (NB several of the group had doctorates of one type or another, mostly medical or in psychological science).

JC: "Actually, none of us has a PhD in Buddhist studies."

MDL: "Is Buddhahood attained by practicing?"

JC: "Practice is preparation."

DL: "The word Practice in Chinese has two characters, meaning 'repair or rectify' and 'practice'. So to practice is to rectify our behaviour. Buddhist practice can be summarized in one sentence: 'Buddha - mind is pure whereas ordinary people have impure minds.' The mind of purity equals 'wisdom'; the impure mind equals 'vexation'. Where does vexation come from?"

Jake Lyne answered "From attachment", but MDL went on:

MDL: "Vexation comes from absence of wisdom, just as wisdom is the absence of vexation. The key to practice is to know that you have vexations and thus to find a way towards wisdom and be like Buddha. There are many paths and practices. You need to find one that suits you. You must engage in Chan practice outside retreat, in daily life. If you can do that then that shows progress. Even when one cannot go on retreat one can practice Chan in daily life."

With emphasis MDL went on "The most important thing is to maintain Unified Mind outside retreat not just during retreat days. It is very important to investigate what Chan is during our practice. For example: Is it the Buddha of your inner nature that you are investigating when reciting the Buddha's name or are you looking outside yourself for some Buddha in the Western Paradise? You have to think about the relationship of Chan and your heart. What is it you are doing?"

MDL then asked if we had learned any non-Chan methods. JC replied that some in the group had done Theravadin and Tibetan practice.

MDL responded: "Theravadin practice is different from Chan practice. What does 'Buddha' mean? The word Buddha literally means 'Awakened one'. Sentient beings are 'confused ones'. But what are we confused about? How do we practice to attain Buddhahood and lose our confusion? We must understand the direction of the path clearly. I want to share with you the many decades of my practice in one sentence – even though Buddhahood is only attained over many lifetimes. The one sentence is this: 'Do not engage in any unwholesome deeds whatsoever'. This applies not only to actions. I do not engage with any thought that arises in my mind whatsoever. Not engaging in unwholesome deeds means that you are not a bad person. But what do you do to become a good person? Engage in wholesome deeds! Do both to perfection as well as you can."

"There are several important principles to follow.

1. No unwholesome deeds whatsoever, using a very strict definition of unwholesome to include not giving rise to thoughts of attachment. Even a single thought of attachment means you cannot see your Buddha Nature. A single thought of attachment is like a small thin reed in front of your eyes that can hide a whole mountain from your sight. You must do repentance for any unwholesome deeds.

2. Engage in wholesome deeds. Use the 10 great vows of Samantabadhra as a guide to wholesome deeds. Do this to perfection for the benefit of oneself and others.

3. Purify one's mind. Because we haven't done this, we fail to see Buddha-mind. A pure mind is not a dull empty mind. Everything is there in a pure mind but it is not then illusory."

MDL then asked how we practice Silent Illumination as taught by Master Sheng Yen. Without waiting for an answer, he went on, "Use a method to gather and quieten the thoughts. There are many ways to do this. It is important to understand the difference between merely a quiet mind and a quiet but also illuminated mind that reflects everything. The path of practice involves adjusting our attitude and mindset. For ordinary sentient beings, the mind is 'out there' in the sensory world. But the mind of the Buddha is not anywhere, it is not abiding in any place or realm.'

MDL then mentioned the Diamond Sutra which says much the same, and the story of Hui Neng's enlightenment on hearing chanting of this sutra, and in particular the famous phrase 'Without abiding anywhere the mind arises'. He said: "This is very difficult to understand. You should read the sutras to get a sense of this.

Otherwise your practice will be more difficult. Silent Illumination means that 'in Silence there is always Illumination', and 'in Illumination there is always Silence'. And Silence and Illumination are Not Two, they are One. Consider the Heart Sutra that says that 'Form is Emptiness and Emptiness is Form'. You must have this understanding to practice Silent Illumination correctly".

MDL then went on to say that the last chapter of the Vimalakirti Sutra deals with non-duality. "If we have Silence without Illumination or vice versa we are in duality, not non -duality, not oneness. The path is to find a way to practice to attain silence and illumination together (non- dual). As Manjushri says in the scripture 'To my mind, all dharmas (the elementary, momentary events of existence) are without names, explanations, purposes, thought. They are outside all questions and answers.' This means that if you search you will not find. If you 'find' it is not correct Chan'. 'Chan is the present moment. You have to acquire a method to collect and silence your mind. Silence is an attitude, like 'agreeing silently' or 'accepting'.

Concerning effort in practise, MDL said that one's sharpness of roots makes a huge difference. He again used the example of Hui Neng who 'saw the nature' without practice because he had very, very sharp roots from practice in previous lives. "If you are unable to attain silence in Silent Illumination practice it is because you have a course mind. There are three layers of thoughts to be aware of. There are course thoughts, fine thoughts, and very subtle wandering thoughts. These must all be recognized in the practice. Wandering thoughts are habitual. Deal with the habit by developing another habit to replace the wandering thoughts, for example, by reciting Buddha's name. This leads to focusing of the scattered thoughts. It's simple if you understand it. Otherwise it is an impenetrable wall."

"Attachment to wandering thoughts is why we appear different to Buddha even though we have the same mind. All phenomena are the products of our mind. This is just as waves have the same nature as the ocean. When there are no waves (no disturbance in the mind) you can see to a depth of 10,000 feet."

Later several of us had a conversation with the monk who is head of the Chan Hall. Unlike Master De Lin who had such a clear understanding of Silent Illumination this monk was surprisingly sceptical. He suggested that Silent Illumination no longer existed anymore in the world. The belief in Linji lineage, he said, is that Silent Illumination method died out completely many centuries ago and that no one alive now truly knows how it was practiced by Hongzhi and other ancient masters of the method. Was this some sort of political statement? Was it the attitude of younger partisan monks in the monastery? We are not sure. MDL was perhaps especially interested in Master Sheng yens teachings on this topic and wished to pursue it with us. We are not too clear about what methods are used today in the Gao Min Si Chan hall – probably "Who is repeating Buddha's name "as elsewhere in China. Certainly, in speaking of Silent Illumination, MDL seemed to be concerned with the possibility of 'quietism' which is one of the traps in Silent illumination that the Chinese call 'The Cave of Demons'. Again, he clearly used Pure Land approaches as a Koan for inner development not for finding some refuge in a 'Pure Land' of imagination.

To meet such Masters was a privilege and a revelation. The idea that before the Communists came Chan was already dead in China, as some Japanese teachers used to argue, was clearly revealed as manifestly false. Again, today, in at least some of the most disciplined monasteries in China, a very clear Chan (Zen) from both a Rinzai and a Caodong approach is present in the hands of elderly Masters and differentiated from the more simplistic of Pure Land approaches. In some places at least the parallels with the teachings of Shifu at Dharma Drum are striking. We wished that more of the monasteries we visited in China had proper Chan Halls and the application of method we had seen only in these few. The significance of Dharma Drum in the revival of Chinese Zen was clearly apparent.

NCF XL

EDITORIAL - LIVING DHARMA

As those sad days of Venerable Chan Master Sheng-yen's funeral at Dharma Drum Mountain fade into the past we are all getting our practice and Dharma thoughts together again, remembering vividly his impact on our lives, his teachings and our debt to him as our Shifu. And we are not wasting time; whether it is in Taiwan, in Pine Bush or at the Maenllwyd, the orchestra resumes its play. In this issue, there are two things to note. Firstly, the range of activities and contrasting focus of our practice- investigations and, secondly, the fact that our journal has reached its fortieth issue – no mean feat of continuity and resourceful application. I want to thank everyone who has maintained our work through the years with contributions, thoughts, theories, poems and argument, editing and computing. Our journal is not here to praise our masters or our practice but rather to examine and criticise where necessary and to keep the investigative Dharma that is Chan alive. In this, we follow our Shifu whose originality and persistence in bringing Chinese Zen to the West has been so important both for us as practitioners and to Buddhism as it spreads its global wings.

Please continue supporting our endeavours and we await your thoughts and contributions.

To celebrate our 40th birthday we present a number of accounts of ongoing Dharma initiatives covering several contrasting issues that concern us. Read and Enjoy!

Chuan-deng Jing-di

COMING HOME

Mahamudra Retreat 2005 - Session One

When we were introducing ourselves last night, several of you remarked on how valuable you found it just coming to the Maenllwyd and how much you valued the place.

Let us begin then by asking why that might be so. I have a good story that helps us here. Some years ago there was a practitioner, Jane Turner, whom some of you might remember, who used to be a regular retreatant at the Maenllwyd, driving herself here from north of Glasgow. One year she got the dates wrong and arrived here after her long journey in the wrong week! She told me about it afterwards. In those days the track, was largely undriveable so she had walked up the track only to find the place deserted; there was nobody here! The Maenllwyd was completely silent; not a soul! Locked up! Yet she told me that she was so radiantly happy just being here that when she went back down the hill and got in her car and drove back to Glasgow, it was almost as good as if she had done a retreat!

Jane, perhaps, was a slightly extreme case, but a lot of people make remarks along such lines, I myself sometimes arrive here and discover myself smiling; and, as is my wont, I sometimes ask myself, "What on earth are you smiling about?" I have often gone into that because I have found that if I just sat and allowed the smile, as it were, to seep into my bones, then I began to experience a move beyond smiling, into something really very blissful. And of course on such occasions, it isn't necessary to know why; Something is happening, which is bringing about a feeling of bliss. And indeed that bliss ... that joy ... at thinking about Maenllwyd or being here is, in many ways, a very important component of Dharma. Many people experience bliss in the course of meditation, but in this case it simply arises out of the smile at being here, or maybe even just thinking about the place.

So what is going on here? Well, Shifu gave me a clue to this many years ago when I was talking with him about the fact that sometimes in meditation blissful feelings arise. I had been experiencing bliss on retreat in New York with Shifu; and I went to him and I said, "What is all this bliss about?" So he said, "Well, bliss arises out of gratitude". "How come?" I said. "Well, what it means is that, without really knowing it, in meditation there has been a moment of stillness ... silence. You've got yourself out of the way. And because you did that, you feel gratitude; and gratitude produces bliss."

I have contemplated those remarks of Shifu's ever since ... and tested them out. And I find it to be true. When one experiences those moments of bliss in meditation, it emerges from a process of which one is not fully aware. One has dropped the cares of everyday life for a little while, and the fact that they have gone gives one a freedom and a clarity. And spontaneously, out of that freedom and clarity comes a feeling of thankfulness, gratitude; and that expresses itself in bliss.

I think something like the same thing happens when some of us arrive at the Maenllwyd ... or perhaps when one even thinks about the Maenllwyd, or maybe one does a visualisation which might involve the place. And it is not, of course, only Maenllwyd. Those of us who travel around and visit various monasteries or power places for meditation sometimes find the same thing happening there too. In fact it has to do with the fact that what we have been doing here is creating a little monastery. Maybe not exactly a monastery as a place, but rather a monastery of the mind, in that when we come here we practice a certain "dropping of attributes"; we let go. Maybe we're not always sure about that, and maybe some of us find it very difficult, but essentially the key thing that happens here is the letting go of care. When you arrive here you let go of something; you let go of the troubles of life. And you find yourself arriving and you find yourself smiling, and you say things like "coming to the Maenllwyd is like coming home". Many people say that. Home, of course, is a place where there is no care because one is 'at home'.

This is a very interesting discovery to reflect upon, because we may ask what is going on when one "drops care"? What's happening? One could say "Well, it's just that I'm away from the kids for a bit", or "I've left the office and don't have to worry any more about the bloody finances", or "Thank God I'm away from him or her for the weekend" ... a bit of rest from the relationship. Any of these things might be, as it were, the stimulus, but that's a fairly shallow response. Because, of course, in problems of relationship, in problems of work, in problems of looking after the children, it is actually one's own performance that one is most worrying about and monitoring. "Am I a good enough Daddy?" "Am I a good enough friend?" "Oh, dear, I wasn't very nice on the phone last night." "Oh, I'm always stressed when I go to work; I'm no good at my job." Many of these things which we attribute to outside calamities, pressures, strains and stresses, are really actually internal strains and stresses. It is self-concern.

So I put it to you that one of the things that happens when we arrive here, when we find ourselves "coming home", is that we drop self-concern. And in dropping self-concern, what does one find? Well, if you drop your self, then you allow a great space to appear; a great space for just appreciating precisely what's in front of your nose, namely: the yard; the clouds glowing in dawn light; a kite flying over; the sound of chanting. All of those things can then make an immediate and direct impression because 'You' are not in the way. You're not worrying about, for an example, "Am I meditating well today?", because you've dropped self-concern. There is then no worry about whether you're meditating well or not! You're just sitting there. And if you're truly Just Sitting ... to use that Japanese expression ... if you are truly just sitting and not being there as a 'me', then everything is present to you, for you, of you ... in a kind of special freedom. It's what is called "emptiness" in the Buddhist jargon, the psychological experience that is thus named.

Unfortunately, 'emptiness' is also a technical term in the Buddhist philosophical vocabulary and this may be confusing. Whenever one wants to try to understand what emptiness is, one has to say "What am I or what is it 'empty' of? What is it that's 'gone empty'? And, if you've dropped self-concern, that's marvellous: you're empty of self-concern. And that's well on the way to enlightenment! We are smiling on arriving at the Maenllwyd because we have actually, unbeknown to ourselves, dropped care. And particularly, for a little while, dropped self-concern. So there's a very useful lesson in this; because, of course, dropping self-concern is precisely what the Buddha was talking about in his first two Noble Truths. That's really quite a discovery. If one has found, as it were, an indirect way into understanding the Noble Truths, that's really very useful indeed. So how come? Well, let's just remember the pattern of the Buddha's fundamental thought here. The Buddha, as you know, was concerned about suffering, and suffering, of course, is self-concern ... or in a very large measure, self-concern. So suffering and self-concern go together. So at the moment when self-concern is dropped there is no longer suffering ... or, at least, a big alleviation of suffering. And Buddha called that a dropping of "ignorance": we are ignorant of the fact of self-concern and the reasons for it. The Buddha worked out why. Self-concern is usually concerned with time. It is usually about something I did in the past, or the fear of something in the future. Self-concern is time bound. And time, of course, is the measure of impermanence.

The Buddha realized that absolutely the root for understanding suffering is to understand impermanence; because it is the fact that things are impermanent which causes us distress. Something beautiful happens, a lovely holiday on a Greek beach, and then it's gone and Winter comes. Spring comes, but then it goes again. The joyful love affair is over and one is left by one's self. One gets older and one realizes that, as somebody said last night, the idea that one is going to go on for ever (which one takes for granted when one is young) begins to fade, and one realizes that Time is shortening. It's all impermanence and, of course, what we do with impermanence, through our ignorance, is to grab onto things that we like and try to hold onto them and make them permanent, because then we can be "safe" and 'happy'. The reason why that is so ignorant is that we fail to face up to the fact of impermanence: things cannot be made permanent; nothing is permanent. The universe itself is not permanent; it's endlessly moving and God knows where it's going to ... and probably He doesn't either!

In our stupidity we try to make the things that we like permanent and to annihilate or get rid of the things that we don't like sometimes, even the people that we don't like. And this is ignorance, and the root of suffering. The Buddha called it anicca, But then the Buddha said, "Well, what is it that is so worried about impermanence?" Well, of course, it's Me. I'm worried about Me because I am impermanent; I am going to die one day. I'm going to get old; God knows what's going to happen. As somebody said yesterday, arriving on the retreat, "God knows what's going to happen here!" Quite Right! Goodness knows what's going to happen here!

It's scary, very scary; impermanence is scary ... if one is holding onto permanence. Of course, if one isn't holding onto permanence, it's not scary, obviously. The two go together. But time flies, troubles come, troubles go. Nothing to hold on to ... if one tries to hold on, it's like trying to grasp the wind. You can't do it. The Buddha's truth however, was to say "Well, who are you anyway? What are you? What is it you're holding on to?" Well, the Buddha realized that he was holding on to Siddhartha; I have to realize that I am holding on to John; you have to realize that you're holding on to Rebecca, or whoever it might be; Eddie. That's what we're holding on to. This thing which appears to be here; John, which appears to be here, is what I am holding on to because it is that which is changing, it is that which is fading, going away ... it won't be here much longer! So scary. But then, "What is this John?", asked the Buddha. This is where he made a very important discovery. Because when he examined himself through yogic meditation he was able to see very clearly that, actually, what was going on, what was called "John", was a process; not a thing, a process. And it could be divided up into five different aspects. Very simple; very simple psychology; but a very, very good model. It still works. It still works better than a good many modern models.

First of all, there is Sensation. Obviously, you feel something, a sensation; something happens. You sit on a drawing pin Ooooh!: a sensation.

But then there's Perception. Perception is "Oh, what's this? Have I sat on a scorpion? ... Oh, no. No, it's just a drawing pin; that's not so bad." That's perception. You perceive what the sensation is.

And then there's Cognition, which is working out why there happens to be a drawing pin on your chair: "Did someone put it there? Who could have done that? Somebody hates me, and put a drawing pin on my chair so I'd sit on it ... or is it just that I dropped one out of the box yesterday?" Or if it actually is a scorpion, "Oh, my God: scorpions! Better put down some DDT or something. Let's be nasty to scorpions for a change." That's cognition: working it out.

And then there are the so-called samscaras: we have to use the Pali word because it's rather difficult to find an English word for it. The samscaras are, as it were, the habit formations from all one's previous thinking, so you think now "What about scorpions? Yes, I remember about scorpions; well, they are supposed to occur in the South of France, so what is one of them doing here in England? It must have escaped from the zoo. But I haven't been near a zoo, so how can there be a scorpion here?" And so you start working out, by referring to the past, by referring to karma, why the present situation might be as it is. And of course it is these samscaras which become what you might call the "habit formations", because they determine what you worry about next. Thus karma is built up out of these samscaras, these past habits. So a mind, this John, is actually a complicated functioning of Sensation, Perception, Cognition, and habits of the past, which as it were make one decide what is good and what is bad. And all of it has a certain form: and that form ... bodily form ... bodily presence, that is what we call "John". But John is just a name; there is no John, there's just this process; the process of Sensation, Perception, Cognition and habits, going round and round and round. Quite temporary; moving through time, but no fixed entity, no John. John is just the name. So if John is just a name, where is John? Is John the perception? Well, no, that's not enough. Is it cognition alone? No, not enough. Is it the history? Is it the past? No, that's not John. So where is John? There is no John as a thing! It's just a name for the process. The Buddha called that anatta, No Self.

So. We have Impermanence; no self. Very radical; a very scary teaching. Because, of course, what we want is John, this thing, to be loved by everybody all the time (at least John likes that, to be loved by everybody all the time); John wants to be permanently young, permanently beautiful, permanently clever ... whereas, in fact, he is becoming increasingly idiotic, falling apart and getting dotty, and generally becoming absurd. That is the truth about John, it is the zen truth, total absurdity; one big dottiness after another! But that's not how we want things to be: that's because we get attached. So, ignorance is made up out of this attachment to something, which is a flowing, ever moving, process. There is no Thing to be attached to; there are just names. Language fools us: technically it is called "reification"; the making of things out of concepts. Just as another example, take the word Spring. We speak of Spring as a thing; but actually, of course, it is just a period in time, in which all sorts of other things are happening: we know there is Spring because the flowers flower. But we can't actually see Spring; Spring is just a word which refers to the period of time within which flowers flower. There is no Thing called Spring which you can grasp hold of. That's another example of reification. And me, John; you, Betty; whoever it might be, are just like that.

So, the Buddha's thought is very subtle here. But the problem is the illusion that there is a thing to which we can be attached, which we must be protective of. Now, in common sense terms, of course, conventionally, we do look after ourselves; that makes sense. But we don't have to be obsessively attached to the ego in the way in which we usually are; that's where self-concern comes in. Self-concern is actually illusory. Now this message of the Buddha is not so easily taken on board, because we are so easily convinced of the normality of John being John. This is why, in order to really understand the Buddha's message, we have to investigate the mind, to explore and find out whether these things are true or whether it is just the Buddha's fantasy. That's why we meditate. Meditation as it were is always the testing of a hypothesis. The hypothesis is "Where am I? I exist. Am I here?"

Am I here? Well, let's investigate it. And of course, what you find in meditation, as you calm the mind, as you practice, is that gradually the attachment to things begins to fade. You begin to find a kind of openness emerging. Something which is much more difficult to characterise; you can't find words for it. Language begins to fail because you're actually going beyond language. You're going into that which language tries to express but never entirely succeeds. Because it's just language; it's not the thing in itself. So we work at that and in our meditation we begin to test the Four Noble Truths for ourselves. In Buddhism, it is said you should never accept things on trust. There is faith in Buddhism, yes; but it's a faith in the method of exploration. It is not a faith in a thing; it is not an attachment. Faith is often an attachment to a concept. This is more like faith in an investigation, *an unending investigation, because there is no end to it. The universe goes on; we go on ... for as long as we're here. Then we disappear. But what an exciting adventure!

And the moment of smiling as you arrive at the Maenllwyd is a hint that there might be something in this. Because if it's true that you're smiling and enjoying being here because you've dropped your self, even for a moment, and just allowed the space of the place to impact upon you directly, you've actually tested the hypothesis. For when you drop attachment to self, the universe is there in all its wonderful turning, in all its manifestation as a place: Maenllwyd in December.

"Christmas is coming and the goose is getting fat" ... whether you're a vegetarian or not, the goose is still getting fat!

So we have then in this very simple beginning; this simple recognition of happiness at arriving home at a place we call Maenllwyd; the being open to the monastery and all that the monastery is for, we discover that we drop something. We can either investigate what it is that we have dropped or we can just enjoy the fact that we've dropped something, and let it take care of itself. That's fine also, although it may not allow one an understanding of what one is actually experiencing. So the letting go is an absolutely key thing in Buddhist practice. The Buddha himself discovered his insight through letting go, through the process of letting go. He didn't discover what eventually he knew by adding, as they say in zen, adding a head on a head, more ideas on top of more ideas, more philosophies on top of more philosophies. Intellectual construction isn't it at all. You drop the intellectual constructions and there It is the thing in itself; the Thing In Itself, which can never be quite caught by language, or fixed in philosophy. The experience of Being.

The experience of being is the experience of flowing. Being, in fact, is always becoming. It is never stationary; there is never a halt; there is never permanence. The challenge of Buddhism, the challenge of the words of the Buddha, is whether one can actually allow one's self to enter the flow of being, the flow of time, without trying to grab on to things which keep one safe. That's the challenge. And that's why an entry into Buddhism can be quite painful. * There are people who come in interviews and meditation and say, "A strange thing happened today: I seemed to be about to fall into nothing". So I say, "Yes?" And they say, "... very scary". So I say, "Why?" "Well, I might not exist". And I say, "Yes, you might not exist."

It requires a certain nerve to say, "Okay, I'll fall into that nothing". So that, in your meditation, you let go of your attachment to your little self, just let go of it, and then you find the extraordinary freedom of the flowing of time without attachment. But it is not easy to do. One has to have a certain nerve to jump off the high diving board; as I know, having jumped off the top of high diving boards. I've done it, but I must say it was quite difficult! And I'm not talking about diving; I'm talking about just jumping into the water: "Oooooh! All the way down there!" Big splash! Yes, big splash, but rather nice.

So maybe out of this comes a key message for this retreat; in fact, for all retreats. Jump!

HOPE FOR THE FUTURE

During my last visit to Dharma Drum Retreat Centre in Pine Bush, New York, I was introduced to Dena Miriam the head of the Global Peace Initiative of Women based in Manhattan. We discussed the world crisis and I promised her a copy of my new book, World Crisis and Buddhist Humanism, as soon as it appeared. In due course I sent a copy to her and received an invitation to attend the Conference of the GPIW in Copenhagen timed to coincide with the global Climate Change conference there in December and at which leaders of the world's religions were being asked to prepare an advisory document for presentation to the statesmen and politicians. Very sadly my back condition prevented me from taking up this invitation – a great disappointment, but I decided to send a brief statement of my views, which could be circulated among the representatives of religions gathered there. This is what I had to say.

Message to Honoured Venerable Teachers and Participants in the Global Peace Initiative of Women Conference in Copenhagen, December 2009

Thursday, October 22, 2009

It occurs to me that a brief statement of personal views concerning this meeting and the planetary condition may be helpful and be a small contribution to discussions. I send it therefore with good wishes to all fellow participants.

As the late Venerable Chan Master Sheng-yen's first Western Dharma heir, I have read through his various contributions as co-chairman of international meetings of religious leaders. He always sought to find an interfaith perspective that brought representatives of contrasting faiths together. I have oriented my thinking about this meeting from this viewpoint. I feel that if religious leaders are to influence the approach of political leaders to climate change and our global ecological dilemma, it will be essential to formulate a common viewpoint to which all at this meeting can agree. Any partiality towards one religion rather than another must inevitably contradict an essential interfaith perspective seeking to represent a global opinion.

It follows that world religious leaders need to adopt a somewhat contrite attitude of humility because it is strife between various religious fundamentalisms that underlies so much of today's warfare and regional killing that in turn prevent progress on global ecological problems. Generally, religions have done remarkably little to address this situation adequately. It is essential that comparisons between religious theologies and metaphysical interpretations of the origin and nature of the cosmos in which we dwell be set-aside in our discussions. Even the most advanced scientific comprehension of the universe can do no more than stress the mystery and wonder of it all. By contrast, however, the world religions have much in common when it comes to exploring the ethical basis of human life. Here we have the real possibility of outlining a global interfaith position that can provide politicians with guidance.

One of the tragedies of modern life is that the important perspectives arising from the European "enlightenment' of the nineteenth century have become distorted through the emergence of economic greed. The principles of democratic government, free elections, open debate in the media, the implementation of human rights, gender equality and the rights of women and the creation of international fora such as the United Nations are all basic to human happiness and political development. Unfortunately, economic theory, controls of finance and the political will sustaining such important principles have all failed. Instead, we have had economic collapse largely through corruption and greed, developed states becoming richer often at the expense of developing nations, the destruction of local industries and vernacular cultures and the over-exploitation of valuable landscapes essential to climatic stability. Indeed, the entire economic process seems little more than a "greed machine" favouring the wealthy – individually and collectively. Economic theories with known benefit to all nations have too often been ignored. Even developing nations, such as China and India, use the same defective financial tools. The ruination and pollution of rivers and natural environments in China and the great gap between rich and poor in India testify to this. The widespread denial of gender rights is chronic. All this can only be due to a failure to seek out policies that are good both for humanity and the planet and an absence of any adequate spiritual understanding of what the "good" may comprise.

Philosophically, one may argue that Cartesian theory in both science and in some Christian theology is responsible for much of this decay through creating dualisms between humanity and divinity, one religion and another, observer and observed, economics and ecology, right and wrong in contradiction to the currently emerging scientific focus on a holism revealing the complex interactions of all causes and conditions in world affairs that may only be understood through systemic analyses. Such dualisms have a very long history mainly in the West and in the Middle East.

The work of Lovelock and others in developing the Gaia hypothesis reveals the way in which our planet functions through the co-dependence of numerous systemic processes that include socio-cultural effects on climate. There is no doubt whatsoever that without strong political action our climate system is breaking down in a way that will bring chaos to our current world civilisation. This civilisation, brilliant though it is in scientific achievements, none the less lacks any socially adequate ethical structure to combat the corruption and decay now so evident. Traditionally it has been the responsibility of religions to provide the values and ethics that ensure well-being. For the world religions to overcome their differences and combine in bringing about an international and interfaith system of values is critical to our current situation. Are they up to it?

The world religions are each deeply concerned with the "Sacred" but espouse contrasting positions regarding its nature. From an interfaith perspective, the prime character of humanity's sense of the sacred must focus on the home that provides the basis for well-being. Such a home needs to be safe, protected from destructiveness, supportive of life, family and economic welfare, including insurance for the future but not essentially or specifically a place for wealth creation. The home may also include places of worship following whatever the local religion may be. The home necessarily depends on the local environment and eventually on the whole of the planetary system of which it is both part and contributor. It is this planetary system that is overwhelmingly threatened by the current "greed machine" and its supporting politics. The planet itself is the basis of the sacred but this is widely ignored through exploitation and greed. Without planetary care humanity's survival and certainly the integrity of current world civilisation is severely threatened. There is no current evidence that humanity could establish a home elsewhere. It is overwhelmingly the duty of the world religious leaders to insist on the protection of humanity's sacred home, its beauty through which our cultures are meaningful and to promote the selfless love that underlies both.

It is a remarkable fact that although theologies of various kinds are commonly in dispute, and defensive belief the basis for aggressive conflict, the world religions share preceptual systems of values, ethics and vows that show very close agreement. There is common emphasis on values that reject war, aggression and killing, espouse principles of financial honesty, truthfulness in debate and speech, compassion and assistance for the poor and the sick, gender equality and the rights of women, love in sexual relations rather than lust, and clarity of mind free from distortion by alcohol and other drugs. Christian compassion, Buddhist wisdom, Islamic care for those in poverty are all well known. The Taoist view that the 'mandate of heaven' will be withdrawn from an Emperor if his governance does not support the poor and unfortunate is especially instructive. We can see today how the 'mandate of heaven' is being withdrawn from world politicians because of their failure to control greed, pollution, ecological exploitation and strife. Given this common ethical inheritance, present day World leaders should be able to formulate a set of interfaith principles providing a preceptual philosophy that politicians may be persuaded to follow if they are to develop a worldview that moderates the rapidly approaching tragedy.

Perhaps we need to remind ourselves that rising sea levels can flood vast areas of low lying land (Bengal for example and many small islands) as well as some modern cities: that water shortage can bring starvation and deadly thirst to thousands; that intense heat can create deserts and uninhabitable waste lands and that all this is predictable by carèful research. The result would be overwhelmingly large migrations of people invading lands that are more fortunate, causing war and killing maybe on a vast scale. Social and political chaos would be inevitable and the probable appearance of tyranny led, as usual, by desperate if perhaps sometimes well-intentioned tyrants.

Specific recommendations are a matter for discussion but we can point to some essential needs.

1. The gross greed of bankers and vast transnational corporations needs an immediate legal curb. The short-termism and institutional selfishness needs to be firmly addressed. Perhaps 80% of all current executives' bonuses should be taxed and used to fund climate related projects.
2. Negotiation to yield global agreements concerning climate warming that are workable and a system of consistent monitoring for the next century or more.
3. Compensation from rich developed nations to developing nations called upon to slow or shift their emphasis on development in response to climate warming.
4. Political reform in the direction of democracies of truth rather than spin, together with balanced representation of gender in world affairs with especial attention to the welfare and contributions of women.
5. The development of UN supported treaties limiting land disputes through skilled negotiation and the adoption of reconciliation where huge crimes are in process.
6. Reform of economic theory to prevent the destruction of local cultures and agriculture brought about by market driven policies lacking any human concerns.

In conclusion, this meeting calls upon religious leaders to create a preceptual system aimed at restoring care for our sacred planet. The ethics for this can be based in the precepts of major religions restated to suit the contemporary world on a global scale. Within that context, special focus may be directed at the six prime targets suggested. The details of such a statement for onward transmission to world politicians will constitute the work of all assembled at this conference in Copenhagen. Compassion, tolerance and diligent persistence will be required.

IRIS TUTE – IN MEMORIAM

Sunday November 22, 2009

I heard of Iris's death today with great sadness. Even though I knew Iris had suffered long and with great courage, I feel her passing to be a very personal loss and know her many friends will be feeling the same way.

I deeply regret not being with you here today; especially because I know she would have liked me to be here. I send these words as a small contribution as we remember her life together.

Iris was a deep thinking human being of unusual spiritual attainment who, through her manner of life, her career and personal expression, has given much to those who knew her. Indeed, she continued to do so throughout her long and trying illness.

I knew Iris in a number of contrasting settings: on retreats at the Maenllwyd, during our Indian pilgrimages; with George and the rest of our group at Christmas dinner in a splendid Maharaja's palace not far from the inspiring caves at Ellora; at meetings of the Bristol Chan Group and in personal encounters both in Zen interviews and more casually in her beautiful house and garden.

I did not encounter Iris in the context of her work as a therapist but I know she was not only very competent but also inspiring, able, as she was, to draw on spiritual as well as on psychological knowledge of the weaknesses to which we are all heirs. She was not afraid to experiment – exploring for example the ways of introducing children to meditation in successful, pioneering short workshops.

Travelling with Iris in India could be both amusing and instructive. She was a stickler for cleanliness at all times, be it sheets on hotel beds or the washing arrangements – the state of most India toilets attracting her extreme ire. This, of course was rather like looking for a vegetarian restaurant in France. On arrival at many, often highly recommended, hotels, I would soon hear her calling the manager to her room and upbraiding him in no hesitant tones, while various lackeys ran around washing and flushing with brush and disinfectant with unwonted vigour. I always hoped that future guests would benefit from her heartfelt instructions. None the less, she loved India and the fresh insights it always afforded.

Iris was one of the early participants in our Chan retreats at the Maenllwyd. She soon revealed a deep understanding of what was happening there. I participated with her in communication exercises during which her insights were often profound. On one occasion, I noted a clear white aura around her head as she spoke. I make no interpretation of this, but I was aware of the connection between its appearance to me and what she was saying at the time. Iris understood Chan Buddhist meditation very well yet her insight was such that she was by no means constrained to one approach. As a practising Quaker, she showed me how the spiritual roots of the good life are not limited to particular viewpoints but can appear in many circumstances and through many disciplines. Several times, she brought small groups of Quakers to our Chan retreats during which our common understanding was clearly evident.

We have often had Quakers coming to experience the silence we cultivate in the hills of Wales. Iris's diligent practice soon led her to a very direct understanding of the Zen practice of Silent Illumination. Hers was not so much a matter of verbal or intellectual understanding as the finding of herself in a state of joy and bliss leading into that silent emptiness from which deep compassion springs. Although we rarely discussed such experiences analytically, it was clear that her vision often took her beyond the boundaries of her personal narrative and the discrimination of time into that elusive presence of the present moment that transcends the objectivity of suffering. She felt this not only as a Zen understanding but one that opened the secrets of Christian texts such as the 'Cloud of Unknowing' to her in a totally clear way. When she became ill and had to endure the painful consequences of medication, she did not lose this capacity for direct contact with what one may call the divine but rather her experiences became the root of patience and resolution. During our last meetings over this period, she was able to share her insights with me with such simplicity and humility that I feel humbled as I recall those occasions. I know that Iris inspired others similarly. Iris, I have no doubt, was a 'realised person' as we say in Zen. Many of us feel an appropriate humility, I believe, when we recall the depth of her spiritual being. I do not use such words lightly.

As we gather together here on this occasion, of course we feel deep grief, yet also we should also use our gathering as a celebration for a life well led and exemplary, one for which we should be thankful as we send her on her way.

Let us say to her, "Iris – thank you for being among us".

(Optional addition if someone is available to lead the chant and if it feels appropriate:

In remembrance for Iris, let us chant together the Mantra of Compassion of the Bodhisattva Tara – Om tare tutare ture soha – one hundred times).

NCF XLI

CONCLUDING APPRECIATION: THE SEARCH FOR NEW WORLD- VIEWS

I was exceedingly disappointed not to be able to attend this conference. As most of you know, I had been suffering from lumbar pain, bad balance and poor walking making movement etc. difficult. This has been exceptionally troublesome as I was additionally prevented from attending a brief meeting convened by Archbishop Rowan Williams at Lambeth Palace on the climate situation and the gathering of religious leaders by the Global Peace Initiative of Women in Copenhagen to consult on the climate conference there. I was hoping to discuss points from my recent book[1] with participants at all these events. For the same reasons, I was unable to complete a text for use at this conference, although I did send a brief audio disc with some suggestions.

In reading and editing these papers, I am struck by their detailed attention to serious matters with deep implications. Although perhaps not all the questions we hoped to be addressed by the conference were covered, these proceedings merit extensive reading and study by all. As we face the oncoming dilemmas of transition to some workable state of society that responds effectively to the Peak Oil and Climate crises, matters of psychology, work, education and the implementation of holistic philosophy will need more such detailed attention as the writers have given us here. We have made a good start.

I have recently been studying 'The Transition Handbook' by Rob Hopkins[2] in which he not only presents the truly alarming environmental crisis that we face with relentless clarity but also puts forward ways and means whereby local communities can make transitions creating functional adaptations to the inevitable effects already forecast. In particular, he faces the fact that many people are in denial of the seriousness of our dilemma. He puts forward ways by which workshops and individual initiatives can stimulate communal responses. He demonstrates his points by references to such activities in the Devon town of Totnes and other places. This is excellent stuff and everyone should consider how he/she might respond to his suggestions. What is lamentable, of course, is the way in which almost none of this appears in national politics as the recent, extremely limited, prime ministerial debates have shown.

Yet, there is a further difficulty. The current crisis has developed within the context of general dissatisfaction with the quality of life that consumer capitalism has entailed. There has been a general assumption that economic prosperity brings happiness. The evidence refutes this. Economic growth has in fact gone hand in hand with a rise in psychological distress, mental disorder, family breakdown, social exclusions of several types and falling levels of trust in government and politics generally. Strikingly, recent work in China shows that the lifting of millions out of poverty has been associated with decreases in life satisfaction at every level of income in both urban and rural areas. Comparable distress is only too clear in the UK; the nation has probably never before reached such a low state of social morale.

Professor Derek Bok makes a strong case[3] that it is time to rethink the function of politics to promote well-being rather than wealth. Research on happiness has shown that it has great social and environmental benefits and can contribute to prosperity, but most people have little idea as to what brings them lasting satisfaction .Bok's book parallels Hopkins's in its general stress on the need for a fresh world-view encompassing both environmental and socio-personal issues. Anyone familiar with the Buddhist Dharma knows that it is precisely in this direction that it points.

All of these suggestions tend to miss an important issue. It is not enough to consider only the local, the small and the personal. Everything 'small' arises within the 'big'. Co-dependency is not only local; it is planet-wide. What may suit Totnes may not suit London. Approaches at local levels will need to be related to overarching national and trans-national policies. This gap is still not bridged and there is little thought going on about it. As Niko Tinbergen has remarked, what is needed is 'a new type of citizen' and this, I argue, depends on changing our basic, global world-view.

A world-view summarises attitudes and practices of a community, a group or an individual and determines the overall effect of behaviours and policy. Our current world-view is based in consumer capitalism, which, beginning in the West, now determines virtually all economic and ecological policies. It is fundamentally based in the concept of endless wealth advancement through profit-based investment in non-sustainable energy exploitation and so structured that the unthinking greed of senior officials has lead to gross corruption and financial crises. What is wrong here is the absence of clear moral values based in an understanding of world-mind relations. The dualisms of the Western religions of Christianity, Islam and Judaism split thought between the worldly and the spiritual and cultivate mutually divisive metaphysical beliefs that have no scientific basis and which lead to conflicts distracting us from the truly serious problem we are considering. Much science too, based in Cartesian dualism fails to relate the mind with matter, society with the world. While the hypothetico-deductive methods of science are fine for the study of mechanism, they fail when faced with the problems of their place in a totally integrated cosmic or planetary system. Holistic scientific approaches are now developing again and they are essential.

As I argue in my book, the holism of Buddhist philosophy based on Gautama's original insights can provide an overarching understanding of world-mind relations based in the subjective empiricism of yogic investigation and clearly argued, reasoned understanding. Here is the basis for a holism that focuses on the total co-dependency of mind and matter on this planet and hence the co-dependency of thought, feeling and action, economics and ecology, wind and sun shine. Such co-dependency makes essential those ethical values that sustain qualities of homeostasis in the world. These too are provided by the precepts of the Dharma.

Of course, this does not mean that conversion to Buddhism is the necessary answer to all our problems. It does point however to the need for a holistic world-view that relates these Buddhist values and interpretations to other similar perspectives in some world philosophies and some existing world-views stemming from both the Asian and European 'enlightenments'. As we have heard, Lama Thubten Yeshe and Thomas Berry, coming from such different cultures, none the less focus their concerns within the field of the same holistic themes. In several ways our conference has emphasised this need for a profound holism as a world-view that can function at many levels, in education, in ethics, in participatory perception, in philosophical and personal understanding.

As Teacher of the Western Chan Fellowship, I would like therefore to recommend that the contrasting issues we have discussed here be increasingly inter-related within an overarching world-view that can be understood worldwide by all educated people. Science and economics in the service of capitalism have spread from the West to all cultures using the English language and provided a global overview. In spite of fears and denials, there is therefore a common, world-wide potential for reasoned communication on forming a global philosophy through using all the modern electronic devises now available. Furthermore, new universities world-wide, as far apart as Saudi Arabia, Singapore and China[4], are establishing intercultural relations that can foster such debate. Rather than current trash and clever hearsay, we need a serious debate among these educated and often deeply concerned people world-wide, understanding varying approaches to planetary holism and integrating them in an educative global path to eco-transition and global well-being. In this vital movement, Buddhists have the orientations and practices to play a major role. Let us all go to it, considering indeed our responsibility as lineage holders focussed on the universal good.

Notes

1. Crook, J.H. 2009. World Crisis and Buddhist Humanism. New Age Books, Delhi.
2. Hopkins, R. 2008. The Transition Handbook. Green Books.
3. Bok, D. 2010. The Politics of Happiness. What Government Can Learn From The New Research on Wellbeing. Princeton University Press. (Reviewed in Nature, April 29 2010).
4. Wildavsky, B. 2010 The Great Brain Race: How Global Universities Are Reshaping The World. Princeton University Press.

NCF XLII

MEANING, PURPOSE AND INSIGHT IN WESTERN CHAN: PRACTICE AFTER SHIFU

Annual Teacher's Address, Stroud 2010

Chuan-deng Jing-di, John Crook

The Annual General Meeting of the Western Chan Fellowship (2010) coincided with the anniversary of the death of the Venerable Chan Master Sheng yen, our Shifu, guide and Dharma advisor for many years. Shifu transmitted his first Western Dharma heir, John Crook, in 1993 and Simon Child in 2000. The WCF has thus had the unusual good fortune to receive instruction from two Dharma heirs of a great teacher. This annual Teacher's Address is thus in part an expression of our great gratitude to Shifu for his advice, retreat presence and Dharma instruction over the years and also an investigation of the way forward for Chan in the West now that the Master is no longer with us. This leads us into a timely examination of the ways in which expressions of traditional Chinese Chan may be presented to beginners in the West taking into account particular discussions and correspondence between Shifu and John over many years. We dedicate this lecture to the memory of our Shifu in profound gratitude and reverence. Editors.

Shifu and his Dharma Heirs: Relations between the Western Chan Fellowship & Dharma Drum Mountain

The death of the Venerable Chan Master Sheng yen (our Shifu) last year has been a traumatic event for all of us, especially those of us who had received personal teachings from him. A direct relationship with a great Master is rare and wonderful and the disciple comes to depend on feeling the Teacher will always be there 'on call' when problems arise. Needless to say, this illusion is inevitably trashed.

The departure of a great Master forces those Dharma Heirs he has left behind him to consider their own approach to teaching the Dharma. Throughout the history of Chan, as one generation passes to another, there have always been unavoidable shifts in emphasis dependent on the personal views, personalities and capacities of the inheritors. Indeed, it is remarkable how the fundamental teachings of the Buddha have survived given the powerful personalities of successive Zen masters. The reason for this lies in the fact that Zen does not depend on idiosyncratic teachings, personal approaches, or indeed any philosophical position subject to personal opinion but is rooted in a fundamental experiential understanding of life and world that is essentially universal throughout humanity (i.e. 'A special transmission outside the scriptures'). This spiritual basis can be found in all religions but the Zen perspective is particularly direct and free of over-interpreted fantasies. Insight into this universal experience has never ceased to be the key understanding and focus of great Zen masters.

The relation between Dharma Drum Mountain, Taiwan and New York, and the WCF is rooted in the involvement of Shifu in both of their creations. In the WCF, the question of how to integrate cultural contrasts between Chinese and European thought within Dharma teaching was present from the beginning. When Shifu affirmed my inka experiences, he asked me to lead retreats in Silent Illumination at the Maenllwyd as it were as his 'representative'. At that time, I asked him, "I am not Chinese. I am not a monastic. How can I best do this?" Shifu had replied, "I am Chinese. You are English. You find out". He was always willing for me to present the Chan Dharma in an authentic, personal way – not as a mere imitation of what he had done or said. We had much discussion along these lines throughout our relationship.

The first focus for discussion was the structure of the 'Western Zen Retreat' a basic retreat that I had compiled from Western sources before I began training with Shifu.[1] Shifu took a great interest in this from the very first time we had met. He believed it was a valuable Western approach, which only required the addition of Lay Precepts and an emphasis on the importance of compassion to make it 'truly' Zen. When Shifu eventually encouraged me to take this improved retreat form to Dharma Drum Retreat Centre, Pine Bush, New York, he showed his trust in what I was about. Subsequently, with rather greater interaction, he queried and finally supported the development of our new method of presenting Koans on retreat.

These discussions drew attention to certain contrasts between social aspects of the Western and Chinese minds that became clearer as we went along. It is on a basis of these contrasts that a certain shift in emphasis between the DDM approach and the WCF approach is inevitably developing. Even so, for reasons stated, our essential insight into the Dharma remains one. Only the methods are varying as we seek to convey the Dharma most appropriately to peoples of differing culture; our lineage loyalty is not affected.

My discussions with Shifu turned out to coincide with the development of a more broadly based academic interest in contrasts between Western and Chinese psychology and they had therefore the timeliness of a wider relevance we had not fully recognised. Recent research from the empirical literature shows that there are significant differences between Eastern and Western measures of several aspects of 'self'; self-esteem, self-efficacy and self–enhancement. Furthermore, research shows that these differences are less when measured between Chinese acculturated in the West and their hosts suggesting a social causation for the contrasts.[2] In addition, measures relating to concepts of 'happiness' differ between Western minds focussed on personal independence and the interdependent social focus of the Chinese.[3] Several psychological studies point to an historical shift towards Western mental structures among Chinese in recent years, reasonably attributable to the growth of consumer capitalism and Western business attitudes in China. The emergence of a complex personality type that is partially Western with respect to certain contexts such as business and Chinese with respect to general social life has been noted for example in Hong Kong. Conversely, we find the increasing importation of psychotherapeutic methods derived from Chinese Buddhism and Taoism in Western mental health care and an increasing focus in the West on the need for cultural change towards a more collective and less individualistic stance, such as that found in Chinese psychology, in political attitudes towards the developing Climate crisis.[4] There is thus currently a demonstrable tendency towards convergence between Chinese and Western approaches to psychological issues. The discussion on retreat practice that follows has a relevance to these concerns.

Self-Expression in China and the West

Chinese and Western people differ subtly in many sociological and psychological features underlying their attitudes to life.[5] The major one in question here concerns the understanding of the self. Research has shown comprehensively that, compared with Chinese, Korean and Japanese peoples, Westerners – that is Europeans and Americans, especially the latter – are quite remarkable in their often-excessive focus on self-importance. At almost every level and in almost every interaction the Western person is concerned consciously or unconsciously with how his or her self-image will be affected by any behaviour – either one's own action or how to respond to other's actions. This concern begins in the family, develops through education and is manifest in the highly dualist and competitive relations between fellow businessmen, academics, politicians or any professional person. By contrast, the Easterners show an equally clear yet contrasting focus based in a self-process that emphasises mutuality, sharing, and development of common aims, cooperative and team-based activities rather than ego competitiveness. This contrast has a wide range of consequences socially and politically.

Within Chan, it affects the attitude towards the purpose and function of group and individual activities. Young westerners often seem to be competing as to who will become enlightened first and develop quite fierce competitiveness as to whose is the best master or method. Commonly a Zen beginner arrives with an intense desire to 'achieve' enlightenment, which is perceived very much as a successful consequence of diligent training with undoubted benefits as a credential – at least in one's own mind. This attitude was greatly enhanced by the rather one-sided introduction of Zen to the West by the Rinzai focussed teacher, Daisetz Suzuki, with its emphasis on getting enlightened.

Shifu expressed this contrast to me once as follows. He said that when he suggested a method to a Chinese retreatant the person would say "Yes Shifu", go off, and do it uncomplainingly perhaps for years. A Westerner in the same situation was likely to ask "Why?" and privately consider whether Sufism might not suit him better.

The interdependent Eastern social relations rooted in generating mutuality have, none the less, a defect. Lacking in individualistic concerns the process can lead to groups of cohering persons worshipping over-authoritative teachers who are rarely subjected to criticism, and to sectarian stances that are not adequately debated, evaluated or criticised; for example the militarism of the Japan's Rinzai orders in the 1930's and 40's, yet its absence in the Soto sect.[6]

As I began teaching Zen, it became clear that one of the chief karmic blocks a Western beginner had to encounter in practice was his or her own ego-concern. This wells up in endless hassling thought circling around personal problems pivoting on fears from self-criticism in personal, usually relationship problems. By contrast, as we began working with Chinese people, it also became clear that many traditionally educated Chinese practitioners could not relate easily to the question 'Who am I?' For them, a really powerful question would concern relations within the family or the firm. For example 'What is freedom?' or similar. These contrasts suggested that for each culture slight differences in the presentation of Huatou and Koan retreats would be helpful. This is what lies at the root of many of our innovations.

Dharma Clarity in the West

Careful reading of English translations of Chinese instructions concerning method and focus in both individual meditation and on retreats suggests that the subtleties of Chinese language are often not being well conveyed to Western readers and that Western mental subtleties are rarely a focus of Chinese interest. For example the Chinese word Hsin has a variety of subtly related meanings. Some translators give the word 'mind' as its meaning, others 'heart', yet others try to present yet further subtleties. At root, Hsin refers to both of what we speak of in English as mind and also heart. To use one of these terms rather than the other shifts a Westerner into either thinking in terms of the intellect and hence philosophical explanations, or into emotional reference that ends up in some poetic or psychological view. The Chinese reader will be interpreting the word in a much more inclusive manner. Similarly, the word 'happiness' produces similar problems.[7]

This and related puzzles lead to particular problems when texts try to discuss experiences that are essentially beyond objective understanding, because they lie beyond access by discriminatory thought. (i.e. 'A special transmission outside the scriptures, no dependence on words or letters') Instead of gaining some psychological insight, a beginner may only find wordy obscurity. The problem here resembles a question such as 'What is the taste of water?' A reply might be 'No-taste', which is of little encouragement to some investigator of water.

Such problems become quite acute when experiences arising in meditation are in question. Since experiences of an ineffable kind lie at the root of Zen, the manner in which they are described, explained or discussed become crucial to teaching. Most such translation seems ineffective. Indeed many translations purporting to explain the significance of Buddhist wisdom use words such as 'awakening', 'enlightenment', 'emptiness', 'Buddha-nature' or other subtle metaphors, which do not allow a beginner a practical rather than a plausible intellectual insight on why he should follow training.

The Obscurity of Mu

A good example of a case where such difficulties arise for Westerners, especially beginners, is to be found in considering the koan 'Mu'. We will recall that when the Master Zhaozhou was asked "Does a dog have Buddha nature?" he replied "WU!" – a Chinese word simply meaning "NO!" (Japanese Mu). This is an odd response when Buddhists believe in the universal presence of Buddha nature. Yet, this is one of the most popular koans in China and Japan, stories given to monks in training to reveal the basis of enlightenment. What did Master Zhaozhou mean?

Some Chinese authorities argue that Mu is the best of all koans precisely because it is meaningless. Yet, then what is it that is NOT? If Mu implies an 'emptiness' that is NOT anything, what is the meaning of such 'emptiness'? The beginner is told that the solution is only to be found by breaking out of doubting enquiry in an enlightenment experience (Jap: kensho, Chin: kai wu). But if Mu is meaningless may that not mean kensho is also meaningless? Kensho is inexplicable in words – so what use is it? In what sense is the term 'meaning' being used here? What does MU actually refer to?

The ego-centred Western beginner always needs a 'use' or a function. He or she requires an understanding of what the usage of meditation is. Shifu's viewpoint is that the advantage of the meaningless Mu is that it prevents a practitioner wasting time with worrying about self. It gets straight to the point of forcing one to break out of reasoning discriminatively about an answer. The Western beginner may find this 'meaningless' response merely confusing and off-putting. Shifu's proposed list of alternatives would then be far more attractive.[8]

Western beginners commonly belong to a post-Freudian, post-Darwinian and post-Einsteinian intellectual culture that always rejects questions that are not meaningful in some practical sense. Many do indeed find Mu problematic, are not encouraged to proceed or get stuck in some fantasy about it which, without good teaching, may last for years. Given the self-focussed concern of the average Western mind, a meaningless question is given little patience. A koan that is so resolutely empty seems even to destroy its own paradox and it is an intriguing paradox that keeps the Western mind involved.

The traditional Chinese approach to Mu is based in the view that rather than wasting time with dogs and their attributes, the practitioner needs to experience that very real felt 'emptiness' that comes when thought and attachment are dropped. But a Westerner, even when falling into some such preliminary experience, may fail to appreciate it; rather asking what is the point of something so beyond any thoughtthrough 'usable', 'practical' or personal meaning. The Westerner, prior to undertaking any Buddhist yogic mind enquiry, usually needs to have a view as to why this understanding is actually of deep significance. This calls for a basic 'faith' in the method and needs some preliminary work. There is then a strong case for arguing that the Western mind needs to sort itself and its conundrums out to a considerable degree before it can generate the doubt appropriate to koan enquiry. The 'Who am I?' question is therefore a good one for a beginner in this culture.

New Retreats Using Koans

In traditional Chan, koans have been used in retreats in many different ways; as a series to be answered one by one, as a single paradox for long term study, as an expression of a life time's difficulty or as a basis for sermons. Recently koans in their full form, as opposed to the short excerpts (hua-tou) often used on retreats, had been somewhat neglected in Chan. I felt koans expressed wonderful paradoxes and that these puzzling stories often suggested guidelines both in resolving personal problems and in elucidating Dharma.

In our freshly designed Koan Retreat, I present retreatants with sets of koans that they examine on the first day. They are asked to choose one of them on which to work. This idea came from Shifu's discussion with me of the 'Life Koan' as the prime karmic confusion in a person's life. Every person, Shifu would argue, has a key set of issues that as a Life Koan creates problems for him/her throughout life. To me, it seemed that a practitioner's choice of a koan would therefore be based in a feeling for its personal relevance and that the choice could be none other than an indication of some connection with a Life Koan. It would not be essential for the person to have any understanding of this; a feeling of intrigue at the wording would be enough. The most intriguing koan should be therefore the one selected for investigation. Furthermore it seemed that for a Westerner to dive immediately into traditional koan observation might not be as helpful as a thorough, typically Western, initial search for some rational, ego based explanation. Given the nature of paradox no such 'answer' would be found and the practitioner would then resort to more meditative examination in the Eastern style.

The manner in which this approach has worked out on retreat 9 has provided good evidence for the accuracy of this viewpoint and has led to people making much progress in both self-understanding and in personal insight within the Dharma. The WZR, the Koan and Hua-tou retreats that we present have therefore come to focus on self-confrontation in ways that traditional Zen retreats consider much less clearly but of which Bodhidharma would probably have approved! (See below) These innovations have led us to further understandings in seeking to express the processes of change during retreat.

Clarity and Insight

Master Hsu yun has said that the practice of zazen, either as Silent illumination or in a koan or hua-tou investigation, is to illuminate the mind so that we can see our 'true nature'. This 'true nature' or 'Buddha nature' is Emptiness experienced – not a void without objects, nor lacking anything, but rather the basis of sentient being – 'emptied' of words. Experiencing and eventually understanding this and applying such understanding in life is the purpose of the Dharma.

In practising Silent illumination, Shifu always stressed the calming of the mind to reach a one-pointed awareness of the totality of a body's experiencing (Total Body Awareness). Once achieved, this awareness may be widened to admit sensory impressions. Once this is stabilised, changes in experience may appear spontaneously. These may include a loss of a sense of time, a widened awareness of space and later possibly bliss, gratitude, and a disinterested love of being itself. These shifts in feeling lead into a quiet tranquillity. The Japanese call these experiences makyo, illusions, since untrained persons may mistakenly think they are enlightened. I call this condition 'Self at Ease'. The feeling of being a normal self remains present during these shifts in awareness. It is clearly 'me' that is having them.

The hua-tou method may be either intense or relatively relaxed.[10] The concentration takes the form of an obsessive enquiry, known as the 'great doubt', into such brief paradoxes as "What is the sound of one hand clapping?" or 'What is next?' At some point, during either Silent Illumination or hua-tou work, some stimulus, usually quite small and either of an inner or outer nature, may trigger a sudden change. This change comes 'from its own side' without any self-involvement, wishing or desire and the continuing presence of 'me' is disrupted. It is as if at the centre of awareness there is a mirror where the 'I' had been and in which all impressions are reflected without any comment from the mirror itself. Shifu calls this experience 'self forgotten'. While the intensity of the experience may be suppressing the normal awareness of self, it remains possible that the egoic component of self changes in form to a bright witnessing with a mirror-like quality lacking self-reference. This experience of 'insight' (prajna) beyond ego is essentially ineffable – one can try to express it but it is essentially beyond the reach of language. Although this is an experience of 'emptiness' – an emptiness of access to word, thought, idea – yet the immediate environment is extra-vividly present in a unique way, extraordinarily brilliant, clear and vivid. One is uninterruptedly 'present in the presence of the present'.

What then has this 'insight' seen? It has seen the triviality of the wordy, discriminating mind of anxiety, its utter lack of solid basis and its impermanence and, by contrast, it has perceived a state that seems basic and fundamental, a mental truth. This is however not yet what is called kai-wu in Chinese or kensho in Japan, the 'enlightenment experience', although it is indeed the underlying essence of that experience. Although the egoic self has been 'forgotten' during the experience, self is still present as a witness and the experience is still reported as 'I felt'.

Although the translated words of these accounts appear clear enough within their theoretical presentation, there may remain uncertainty as to what 'doubt', 'illumination', 'true nature' and 'Buddha nature' actually mean in the personal life and practice of beginners. What should one do? While the Chinese terms may work well for them, we need to explore their meaning for us in the West. Let us investigate further.

Having a look at the way the Buddha and other thinkers of his time understood the structure of the mind assists us here. The mental attributes or skandhas provide us with a basic model of how the mind functions in everyday activity. The mental processes involved are sensation, perception (knowing what the sensation is), cognitions and will, (comprehension of the perceived experience in relation to one's lifenarrative and acting on it), and conscious awareness, which underlies the others. One's personal history is formed through the action of sensation, perception and cognition: they create the conditioned life story that we know and entitle through our names – John, Betty. When we think, we probe the storehouse of memories based in these three attributes and seek resolutions to problems. We construct ideas, viewpoints, illusions, intellectual insights and actions that lead either to anxiety or potentially to a homeostatic sense of ease. All of them are necessarily based in the presence of awareness.

The hassling mind of everyday is the continual judging or evaluation of these mental events as they go along moment to moment. The key result is the sense of being an anxious 'me'. 'I' am inferred to be an objective presence, a 'thing' with all these mental events as its attributes. Yet, as the Buddha told us, all of this is subjective and all impermanent. We cannot rely on any of it. We have developed attachments to what we like and aversion to what we don't like. The interplay of these in a world of impermanence constitutes human suffering. As far as we know, no other sentient beings, except possibly the Great Apes, even remotely suffer in the way our ego-hood forces upon us. To a huge extent, the ego is our problem.

The Buddha set out to solve it and the Dharma has been the result. In the texts of the ancient Abhidharma the fundamental analysis is expressed both philosophically and as a basis for practice. The central theme in Zen is the setting aside of ego-related suffering and acquiring the Mahayana practice of compassion that follows from that. The practice operates in two ways; stabilising, calming and letting go of anxiety, and, secondly, gaining insight into the fundamental nature of mind – its 'true-nature' (see Tables 1 and 2).

Most Buddhist meditation methods apply the two processes of calming the mind and gaining insight into its nature – although in slightly varying ways. Calming the mind is basic because the problems of karma need quietening. Once the mind is calmed, one may persist with silent investigation or jolt up that calmed mind with calculated questions – such as a koan or hua-tous. The process is gradual until suddenly insight occurs and the problem is resolved, as Hsu yun explained above. The sudden resolution comes from the entry of the second method acting from its own side, experientially.

Some individuals, whose karma is less obstructive than others, may experience that insight quite quickly, moving from Self-at-Ease to Clarity or suddenly falling into Clarity from a one-pointed mind. Fundamentally, this prajna insight is the personal realisation that all thought, feelings, ideas, are merely mental processes empty of any objective being or significance except on their own dreamlike level. This 'realisation' is presumably the completion of what Shifu called 'contemplating emptiness', which involves cognitive experiencing beyond merely intellectual insight.[11] The personal realisation is experienced as a sudden plunge into an emptying of all ideas – and ultimately even the idea of self, entirely. Only that which is seen in the remaining bare awareness remains shining in an undistorted clarity. What has happened is that all the operations of mind cease – except for the maintenance of a mirroring awareness present as an extraordinary and unique clarity free of ego orientation. This 'self-forgetting' is distinct from a yet further experience of realisation where self is 'absent' entirely and only recognised as it begins to reappear – this is then 'seeing the nature', an 'enlightenment experience'. In all this 'no-self' awareness there is a strong sense of 'freedom'. Returning to daily life, such a mind knows it is free to 'dream' anew. The prison gates are open. The meditation process can be described in these practical terms and the valued result emerges through the bliss of the final perception and its consequences in life.

Developing Western Chan

Most practices of Zen meditation in the West begin with Calming the Mind (samatha). Indeed given the complex, agitated sense of self among Westerners and their basic insecurity, it would be hardly possible for those who are beginning training to attempt any direct insight into such a troubled mentality until agitation has subsided. Yet, perhaps to our surprise, the founder of Chan in China, Bodhidharma, in one of the earliest descriptions of practice, did not suggest beginning in this way.

Bodhidharma said there were two aspects to Zen, the Principle and the Practice.[12] The Principle is the enlightenment experience itself, and he probably implied also the preliminary experience of clarity in a timeless present. However, he argued that only people of sharp intelligence could achieve this insight without prior training in practice. Actually, I think that there is a translation problem here. I suspect Bodhidharma was not talking about the intelligence of the clever mind but rather the fact that most people suffer from ignorance arising from problematic karma and that it is the karmic bias of the self that prevents insight. Certainly, those with severe karmic problems would need an initial practice. So what does he mean by practice?

It is not samatha. Rather, it is the use of self-criticism and self-knowledge in the context of examining karmic reactions. In the first of Bodhidharma's methods, the practitioner is asked to respond to the aggression of another through considering his/her own involvement in causing the other to be aggressive. In other words, he wants the investigative practitioner to respond to the antagonism of another with reflection on his/her own role in it. This is, of course, a form of self-confrontation. In effect, it is a 'Who am I?' question contextualised in a specific personal situation.

His second practice broadens the approach by requiring meditation on one's personal role in the everyday causes and effects of daily life – that is within context of the Law of Co-dependent Origination. This requires practitioners to investigate their karmic past and immediate relations with others. The third practice is to allow life to function within the Law without manifesting attraction or aversion to whatever happens. The fourth is the practice of a life in the Dharma through following the Bodhisattva path. Each practice requires self-examination and confrontation with karma in a series of widening levels.

This is a fascinating finding because it implies that self-confrontation is the basic practice recommended in the earliest Chan. This is exactly what we are emphasising in our forms of retreat so why has samatha become emphasised so strongly? The answer is that samatha is one of the key Theravada techniques rooted in the ancient Abhidharma – entirely traditional and valid therefore but not what our founder in China chose to emphasise, a fact that many Western teachers seem largely to have ignored. This difference is perhaps a sign of the pragmatic rather than mystical inclinations of the Chinese when compared to India. As a sole practice, samatha leads to varying depths of inner silence and ultimately the sensation-less trance basic to much Indian mental yoga. The Chan practitioner is asked not to go this far because beyond a certain point 'insight' is not possible.

This does not mean that samatha is not of great value to Chan practitioners. Indeed, to quieten the mind is extremely important for Westerners and is commonly the first technique to use in attempting Silent Illumination. Never the less, in entering Chan a more self-confrontational approach is clearly to be recommended as soon as possible. Presenting the WZR and our koan retreats in this way has therefore traditional support.

Whether the practitioner calms and simplifies his mental activity through samatha or by examining closely what his motivations may be, the outcome is an experience of increasing equanimity, peace and tranquillity. As we have seen (above), at a certain stage, the mind state begins to change. There is a timeless quality as, for example, when a thirty-minute sit seems to have lasted only two minutes. There may be a feeling of spaciousness as when one appears to have an awareness extending beyond the room, walls and building to the farthest horizon. Sometimes feelings of bliss may be physically experienced as if rising up the back or spine. Sometimes a total blankness appears, a deep dark stillness with no sensation at all. These experiences arise due to the dropping away of mental measurement in space and time thus giving rise to a timeless and spatially unlimited feeling coinciding with a letting go of depressive ideas limiting bliss.

The above process is termed 'gradual" since it develops progressively and takes both time and focus. Prajna, 'insight', by contrast always arises suddenly, it is subitive, 'sudden'. While there is commonly some trigger, a word, a thought, a falling tile, a passing aircraft, the change of state is immediate shifting the mind into a completely different mode. This mode is beyond exact description because the thinking mind of thought and language does not operate here. No thought, therefore no measurement, therefore no time. Although the mind state provides an immutable background condition in the manner of a mirror mirroring, the movement of the trees in the wind continues therein as a continuing present moment. There is thus a sort of complete stillness and peace and total relief from all time-based worrying.

Many such occurrences of this 'Clarity' are exceedingly brief, seconds or minutes. In reporting them in interview, practitioners will characteristically say, 'I felt'. The self is still there although it has been temporally set aside, forgotten or changed into mere witnessing. I call these experiences 'Clarity' because they are clear of karmic responding and totally anchored in the mirrored present moment. Mental time stops as awareness simply flows along in the impermanence of the world with no thought of past or future. Worldly time goes on. The ego is not active but the self is present as an observer.

A more sustained period of Clarity is called the One Mind Experience (Shifu).[13] The mind is still, peaceful, quietly blissful, the environment appears pure and at peace. It is as if one is looking at an alternative reality.

While these experiences are of great value and encouraging, they are not 'Enlightenment Experiences' ('No-mind' – Shifu) deserving the Chinese name kai-wu or the Japanese names kensho or satori. Kensho is present when the same clarity erupts without any sense of the self-function being present at all. The egoless state is experienced as a startling and mysterious absence. As this fades, usually quite quickly, self-reference softly emerges again and the blissful innocence is lost in evaluations.

Experiences of 'enlightenment' (kai-wu, kensho) are rare although their asserted frequency seems to depend on a Teacher's understanding of what comprises such an experience. Shifu always stressed to me the need for caution since to claim 'enlightenment' of an insufficient experience may harm a practitioner through subsequent faulty self-assessment. In discussing several possible cases, which we had both considered following the relevant interviews, he usually let any doubt lead him to confirm an experience as no more than 'clarity' or 'one-mind'. The deep experience of self-absence rather than a mere self-forgetting is the key distinction here, and often difficult to determine. Furthermore, kensho experiences themselves vary in depth and may sometimes lead to direct experiences of the universe as 'Buddha mind' rather than merely 'seeing the nature' in 'no-mind'. Such an experience is likely to appear following deep reflection on co-dependence in a 'contemplation of emptiness' (p 8) and several brief experiences of 'no-mind' enlightenments. This indeed seems to be the meaning of the Japanese term satori.

In assessing the nature of any such an experience, the Reverend Master Daishin Morgan of Throssel Hole Abbey once told me that he was less interested in his monks' descriptions of experiences than in their consequences shown in changes in character. He felt sure an experience was a genuine kensho only when character changes appeared. If none appeared he let it go. Western teachers have to be aware that Western practitioners have developed an excessive concern with having these experiences as a result of the Rinzai teachings of Daisetz Suzuki early in the last century. Mistaken assumptions about personal 'enlightenments' can be a major cause of Zen mistakes.

Professor James Austin, the author of Zen and the Brain has attempted to construct a neurophysiological explanation of such Zen experiences based on an experience he had himself had on a London station on the way to a retreat with the Venerable nun Myokoni (Irmgard Schloegel). He writes:

"The new scene is fixed gently, not fixed on hold. The purely optical aspects of the scene are in no way different from the way they were a split second before...They are being viewed directly with all the cold, clinical detachment of a mirror as it witnesses a landscape bathed in moonlight… but there is no viewer. The scene is utterly empty, stripped of every last extension of an I-me-mine. Vanished in one second is the familiar sense that this person is viewing an ordinary city scene…not pausing to register the further paradox that no human subject is doing it…a vision of profound, implicit, perfect reality"[14]

It appears to have lasted in a clear intensity for less than a minute and led Austin to further insights entirely traditional in form – indeed resembling the exclamations of Master Huineng on attaining enlightenment during an interview with his teacher focussed on the Diamond Sutra. On hearing the quotation "Let the mind arise without attachment to anything!", he exclaimed:

"Who would have thought that the essence of mind is intrinsically pure? Who would have thought that the essence of mind is intrinsically free from becoming or annihilation? Who would have thought that the essence of mind is intrinsically sufficient on its own and free from change? Who would have thought that all things are the manifestation of the essence of mind?" He concluded, "For someone who does not know the essence of mind there is no use in studying Buddhism. But knowing the essence of mind, he is Buddha – a teacher of Gods and men…"[15]

The Venerable Myokoni accepted Austin's account as kensho saying "I am very happy for you." Thus, the 'essence of mind' has been the same for at least a thousand years.

A Master once said that the visionary Clarity basic to all these experiences can take 'one all the way'. Indeed the basic feeling of sudden Clarity is also the fundamental quality of the kensho experience too. This means that an experience of Clarity is a kind of preliminary glimpse of enlightenment potential but not yet 'enlightenment' itself (kensho) for that depends on 'self-absence' not merely 'self-forgetting'. Shifu has also remarked to me that someone who has experienced kensho is likely to taste partial 'shadows' of it again in re-appearances of moments of simple clarity.

Table 1 Sequence of Transitions in Silent Illumination

A. Normal Egoic Consciousness (1–5)

1. Everyday mind, hassling mind, wandering mind etc.
2. Zazen sitting in posture. Mind calming. Body awareness.
3. Total Body Awareness.
4. Makyo experiences. Time and space changes silence, void, bliss, disinterested love.
5. Self at Ease. One-pointedness. Vast present awareness. 'Being present in the presence of the present'.

B. Diminished Ego Consciousness (6–7) Prajna – 'crossing to the other shore'

7. 6. Clarity. Mirror mind. Self-forgotten. One-mind state
8. 7. Kai-wu, Kensho. Clarity with ego-self absent. No-mind state.

Notes:

- Each meditation attempt may succeed for a while, then gets lost and return to wandering thoughts etc. It is then restarted. Progress is like a spiral. "Use the method, lose the method, retrieve the method" (Shifu). The makyo experiences may or may not occur in the sequence.
- Prajna can in principle 'strike' anywhere but usually follows a one pointed mind episode however caused. The transition to diminished ego consciousness is not therefore 'caused' by the sequence 1–6 but may be facilitated by it.
- Kai-wu by this route is sometimes difficult to distinguish from Clarity. It arises often from Clarity and may return to it. It is quieter than in Hua-tou investigation.

At root, Clarity is a sustained sense of the presence of the present moment. It is not simply a sharp awareness of immediate momentary sensations but, rather, a sustained state of bare awareness in which the present happening reflects. As we have seen, it has a mirroring quality. The practitioner enters a transformed state, an unmoving, un-reacting, mirror of a bare awareness in which the world moves. It is well termed the 'essence of mind'. This 'world' in the mirror has the simplicity of just being itself; one might say it is 'allowed' to be itself. No projection of personal bias, prejudice or theoretical understanding is imposed upon it. It has the simplicity of mere presence: bird song, rustling water, the wind in the trees, an owl call. In the complete clarity of kensho the additional absence of self is apparent as a strange feeling, no-one is there. Only the un-interpreted world remains. One may well say that after discovering one's 'true nature' one perceives the universal 'Buddha nature'.

Buddha nature then is the 'world' seen by the subject in one flowing relationship in the state called 'true-nature'. The sensory mind participates directly in the world process but without dualistic identification as something apart. Intellectually, one knows that vision is a perception of objects reflected in light from the sun the energy of which is focussed by the eye and interpreted by the retina and optic brain. One knows that the chemicals giving rise to smell touch the sensory nerves, which pass impulses to the brain for interpretation. The world that seems so glibly exterior and separate from 'me' in a dualistic relationship is actually deeply integrated with my being in a unitary pervasion. The experience of clarity and subsequently the 'enlightenment' of kensho is the experiential awareness of such oneness. What consciousness 'is' remains as mysterious as the cosmos itself.[16]

This then is the 'enlightenment' that provides the evidence for the monist perspective of Buddhist thought. Furthermore, one may argue that such a sensory world-awareness is potentially the same for all human beings once discriminatory thinking is set aside. And further, allowing for contrasts in brainpower, the seemingly always-bare awareness of higher animals may be similar. Looking at the sheep pondering one's presence in a field in Wales, one may be seeing a being in a similar state of clarity without an ego. This is one root for the Buddhist compassion of all sentient beings.

Westerners may like an evolutionary interpretation here. Clarity may well resemble the form of sentience experienced by big-brained animals such as birds and mammals; the ones that we intuitively identify with, or have as pets with 'whom' we talk. The uniquely human sense of an egoic self with its capacity to create a cognitively constructed and wordy reified identity (and thus karmic conditioning, attachments, liking, aversion, personal love and hate) plausibly developed out of such a more basic awareness of simple sentience and has varied in its social expression with contrasts and developments in culture.[17] [18]

Table 2 Sequence of Transitions in Hua-Tou Work

A. Normal Egoic Consciousness (1–5)

1. Hua-tou introspection. Ego based reflection
2. One pointed focussing.
3. Intensifying 'doubt'
4. One-pointed mind of Great Doubt.
5. Various relapses passing through tranquillity and one mind states

Or:

B. Diminished Egoic Consciousness. Prajna (6)

6. Clarity etc – or Kai-wu.

Notes:

• The Kai-wu by this route is commonly abrupt, emotionally dramatic and leads to deep stillness. The sequence commonly breaks into a relapse. Prajna again can arise at any stage and is facilitated rather than caused by the early ones.

Evolutionary psychologists[19] are arguing that this cleverness came about through social evolution. Many primates have evolved as group living populations in relation to patterns of distribution of resources in their habitats and as protection from predation. Within this context, competition between individuals is believed to have provoked the emergence of skills for deception, insight into deception by others, alliance formation and the brainy intelligence associated within being aware of one's personal self as an object in a social world. The individualistic, ultimately self-destructive, aggressive nature of human politics stems from this. Yet, in contrast, parental care, family and alliance formation drove the emergence of tendencies towards empathy and certain forms of altruism.[20] The conflict between these forms of social being produces the highly bipolar nature of human life. Generally, many world religions favour the mutualism of altruistic compassion yet become structured as highly self-oriented institutions often willing to murder those of other faiths.

In Koan 62 in the Book of Serenity[21] we have the story of a monk who asked a master "Do people these days need enlightenment?" The master replied, "Oh, it's not that there is no enlightenment but what can be done about falling into the secondary?" The story clearly recognises a primary holistic orientation of compassionate enlightenment contrasted to the secondary condition of a discriminatory, argumentative, hassling mind. In meditation therefore, we may be evoking something of enormous psychological antiquity, plausibly even a pre-human mode of knowing and being. The clarity of 'insight' (prajna) appears to pre-date the 'ignorance' (avidya) of discriminatory intelligence!

Extended Implications, The Bodhisattva Path

We have been using English terms that hopefully may clarify the nature and function of Chan meditation (bare awareness, clarity, present in the presence of the present, one-mind state), and tried to show how they can help translate Chinese discussions of meditative practice. Yet, we have to be careful. Like all words and ideas, their very use can be a barrier to insightful practice.

Essentially, the nature of Chan insight cannot be described. All one can do is to hint at it through various forms of metaphor. Any attachment to names or ideas sustains the discriminatory mind and this is just as true for the words we have been using as to older terminologies. The experiences arising through Buddhist meditation remain as mysterious as consciousness itself. Furthermore, practitioners may come across other experiences not discussed here that seem utterly inexplicable from a scientific or Western psychological perspective – for example during certain tantric practices or the unexpected appearances of moments of clarity seemingly evoked by place and circumstance, or the presence of certain charismatic teachers. It is necessary to acknowledge mystery and the strangeness of the human mind we share. To hold opinions generates ego-based dualism and prevents insight in practice – and this is always a difficult lesson for Westerners to learn. This choice of terms is intended to enhance precision in English expression. In practice, retreatants need to find those that help them most.

Insight (prajna) carries one across 'to the other shore' (secondary to primary) where sensory experience and the energies expressing the Universe appear clearly in union. There is no sense of separation or duality. One sees then how one's basic awareness is normally invaded or covered over by thoughts and feelings that express the personal concerns of practical life. The unified understanding of world-mind pervasion may be what is termed the 'ancient mirror' in Dogen's writing,[22] a term for 'Buddha nature' where 'Buddha' is a synonym for a cosmic awareness in humans. Dogen emphasises that to think of a practice that proceeds by stages to enlightenment is misleading. Such an idea arises from the way the mind shifts back and forth repeatedly from unitary to divided, multiple states. Enlightening insight is always potentially available; one is 'enlightened already'. All that is needed is a clear awakening to the way basic awareness becomes 'clouded' through invasion by mental discrimination.

Yet, that discriminatory awareness is not in itself 'ignorance'. It is the natural and evolved way by which the brainy physical body negotiates the competitive life of the 'world'. 'Ignorance' is the absence of perceiving that this negotiation is only a mode of experiencing within a much deeper original unity of mind and nature. The 'Bodhisattva Path' then becomes the practice through which insight is understood and selfhood steered away from harming others and indeed the planet through greed and aggression. This is then the profound path of enlightened compassion and wisdom. As Shifu would put it, here meaning and purpose unite in a life that is the ultimate practicality of Chan.

> Master! How can I understand enlightenment?
>
> Have you had your breakfast?
>
> Yes, Master.
>
> Then perhaps you had better wash your bowl.

Conclusions

In this talk, I have attempted to provide an account of Chan practice that may be helpful to Westerners puzzled by translations of Chinese Zen literature. It is important to close with certain comments. Firstly, we have been discussing methods of practice rather than the Dharma teachings of the Buddha and the Patriarchs. There is no alteration intended here to the basic line of Shifu's Dharma Drum lineage based in both the Linji and the Caodong schools. Secondly, we have been seeking to respond to a need for clarification especially for Western beginners, and thirdly we have noted that this is a quite natural process of re-expression present throughout the history of Chan and at the present time. Indeed, two of the main Chinese Dharma Heirs of Shifu in Taiwan are providing retreats that differ considerably from one another and from those taught in recent years by Shifu himself; one emphasising calming the mind as a prerequisite for Hua-tou exploration and the other the confrontational approaches initiated in antiquity by such great teachers as Linji in China or Hakuin in Japan.[23] Adding our innovations to the mix, we may suggest that Chan teaching is highly creative at the present time and that centres such as the Dharma Drum Retreat Centre in Pinebush, New York, benefit greatly from this diversity of presentations.

These changes of course will continue. What is essential is that they never fail to express the root teachings of the Buddha. The maintenance of traditional Dharma is vital lest deviations develop that could so easily import the greed and selfish arrogance of so much of the Western dominated consumer capitalism of our present era. Both Simon Child and I are highly sensitive to the dangers of incautious, popularistic modifications to traditional practice. We remain devoted to the teachings our Shifu gave us and will continue on this path.

Wednesday, January 20, 2010. Revised, Thursday, April 1, 2010

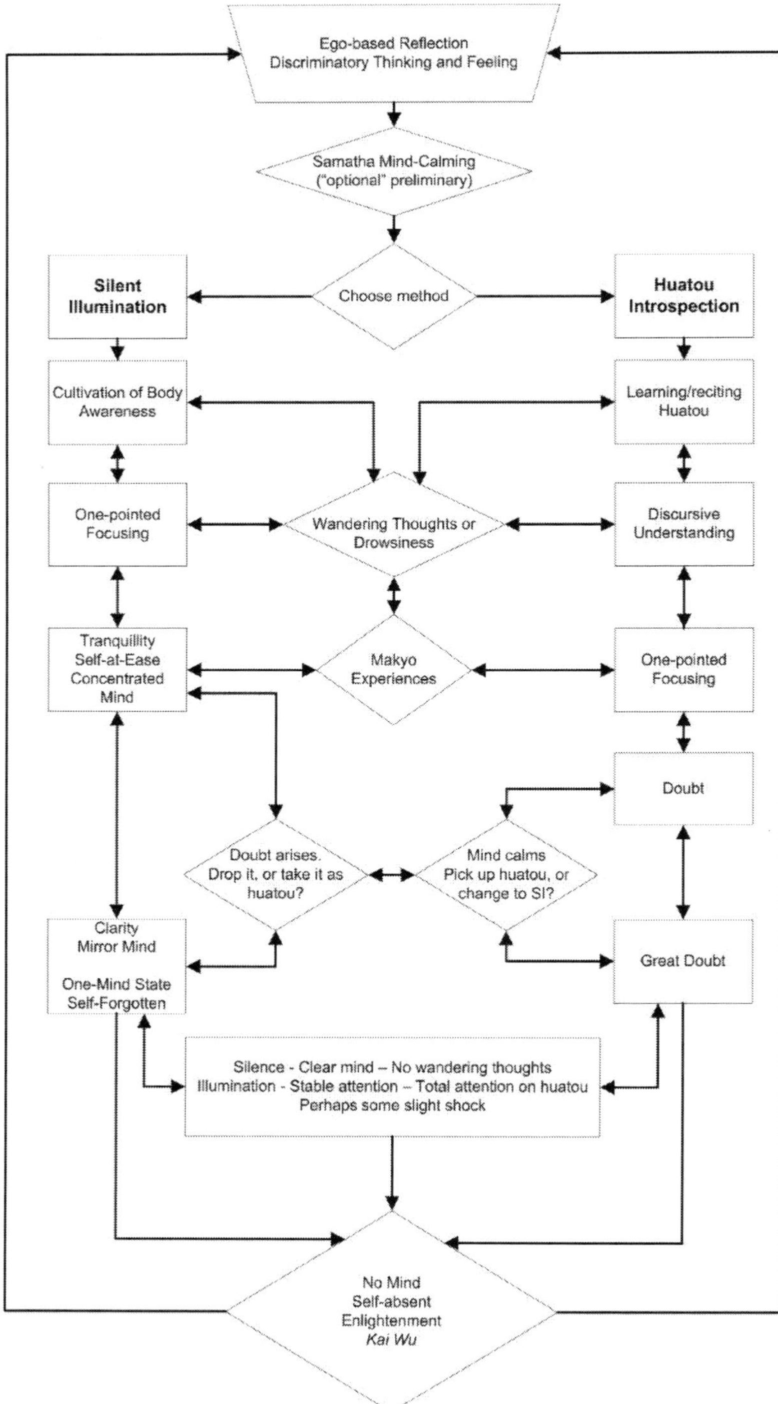
Ego-based Reflection
Discriminatory Thinking and Feeling
Samatha Mind-Calming
("optional" preliminary)
Choose method
Silent Illumination
Huatou Introspection
Cultivation of Body Awareness
Learning/reciting Huatou
One-pointed Focusing
Wandering Thoughts or Drowsiness
Discursive Understanding
Tranquillity
Self-at-Ease
Concentrated Mind
Makyo Experiences
One-pointed Focusing
Doubt
Doubt arises. Drop it, or take it as huatou?
Mind calms
Pick up huatou, or change to SI?
Clarity
Mirror Mind
One-Mind State
Self-Forgotten
Great Doubt
Silence - Clear mind – No wandering thoughts
Illumination - Stable attention – Total attention on huatou
Perhaps some slight shock
No Mind
Self-absent
Enlightenment
Kai Wu

This diagram summarises the sequences of likely transitions during retreats using Silent Illumination or Hua-tou methods. Note that both Clarity and Enlightenment experiences require the 'subitist' appearance of prajna insight. Moreover, this may arise at any time including non-retreat times and is usually preceded by one-pointed attention to the present moment and often some slight stimulus from the environment. The 'gradual approach' at the beginning of these practices thus requires non-intentional insight for their completion.

Acknowledgement: I am most grateful to Simon Child for his valued discussions with me concerning this talk in draft and for his great improvement to the diagram that summarises key themes in the text. Also to Jake Lyne for a helpful comment.

Notes

1. Crook J. H. and D. Fontana (Eds) 1990. Space in Mind: East-West Psychology and Contemporary Buddhism. Element books. Chapters 8 and 13. Also: New Chan Forum, 38.
2. Kwan, V. S. Y, Chin-Ming Hui and James A. McGee. 2010. What do we know about the Chinese self? Etc. Chapter 17 in Bond, M.H, (Ed) Oxford Handbook of Chinese Psychology. Oxford University Press
3. Luo Lu 2010 Chinese well-being. Chapter 20 in the Oxford Handbook of Chinese Psychology. loc cit above.
4. Crook, J. H. 2009. World Crisis and Buddhist Humanism. New Age Books. Delhi.
5. Neisser, U & D. A. Jopling. (eds) 1997. The Conceptual Self in Context. Cambridge U. P. See also The Oxford Handbook of Chinese Psychology. 2010. loc cit
6. Victoria, B. A. 1997. Zen at War. Weatherhill. New York. Tokyo.
7. Luo Lu 2010 Chinese Well-being. Chapter 20 in the Oxford Handbook of Chinese Psychology. loc cit above
8. Sheng yen 2009 Shattering the Great Doubt. Shambhala
9. See Retreat Reports. New Chan Forum 40.
10. Sheng yen. 2009 Shattering the Great Doubt. Shambhala
11. See: Sheng yen. In press. Things pertaining to Bodhi. Shambhala. p 23-24
12. See Sheng yen and D. Stevenson. 2001 Hoofprint of the Ox. Oxford. p 187.
13. Sheng Yen Chan Master. 2004. Song of Mind. Shambhala. See p 88
14. Austin, J. 1999. Zen and the Brain. MIT Press
15. Wong Mou-Lam 1953. The Sutra of Wei Lang. Luzac

16. In a curious way the wholeness of the mind-world relationship in Chan recalls the ancient, more dualistic Islamic interpretations of world-mind association in al-Faradi and Avicenna that came into European thought via Albert the Great and were lost in Aquinas. (See: Kenny, A. 2005. Medieval Philosophy. A new History of Western Philosophy. Vol 2. Oxford University Press).

17. Crook, J.H. 1980. The Evolution of Human Consciousness. Clarenden Press. Oxford.

18. Crook, J.H. 2007. Shamans, Yogins and Indigenous psychologies. Chapter 35 in Dunbar R.I.M and L. Barrett (eds) 2007. Oxford Handbook of Evolutionary Psychology. Oxford.

19. This newly named science has developed from merging studies of Animal Behaviour (Ethology) and Comparative Psychology with fresh orientations in Social Anthropology. See: Dunbar, R. I. M. & Louise Barrett. (Eds). 2007. Oxford Handbook of Evolutionary Psychology. Oxford.

20. Dunbar, R. I. M 1996. Grooming, Gossip and the Evolution of Language. Faber & Faber.

21. Cleary, T. 1990. Book of Serenity. One hundred Zen dialogues. Lindisfarne Press

22. Dogen Zenji. (Translations by Kosen Nishiyama) 1983. Kokyo. P 45-59. In Shobogenzo. Vol 3. Nakayama Shobo.

23. See Guo Ru Fa shi. 2010. Comparing the methods: Huatou and Silent Illumination. Chan Magazine.

Spring 2010

DAVID CLARK: IN MEMORIAM

When I was fourteen and safely at boarding school in Dorset, David was plummeting out of the sky on a parachute descending into a fierce and disastrous conflict in France. Several years older than I, this difference underlined the contrast in our lives. His wartime experiences were heroic in the ways of war but David wrote with humility about them all. His wartime autobiography[1] tells us so much about his character. His parents always wanted him to be intelligent, scientific and brave and he was to be all those things. Few of us have had the experience of visiting a camp of Hitler Youths in the 30s and gone on to help win the war against them! Doctor, socialist, humanist adventurer, psychiatrist not without a warm self-doubt, David was a striking personality.

I first met this large, friendly almost boisterous man at a conference in Dartington where we began to share our spiritual interests. David was a sceptical humanist but also a Quaker with a characteristically wide vision of spirituality. He had come out of a personal crisis partly though some experiences of bliss and insight that he recognised as characteristically 'Zen'. This was to bring him into 'sitting' with us on our Chinese Zen retreats at the Maenllwyd in Wales.

I have many happy memories of David. His warm, honest character and his deep concern with spirituality of an essentially practical kind made him a great companion in talking about such things. He wrote an account of his experiences for our journal[2] and joined us on a retreat in the lighthouse on Lundy Island where I recall the immense fun of cooking with him in the tiny kitchen there. He loved the island and always wanted us to go there again.

At the Maenllwyd, our local farmer with a lamb that had broken a leg tendon once challenged his surgical skill. Together with another doctor, he sowed it up and soon had it walking about again. David dug drains with enthusiasm and brought a lightness to what we were doing that many appreciated. He was one of the 'toughies' who appreciated the relatively primitive condition of the old farmhouse of those early days.

I have been sad not to see David more in recent years but we corresponded from time to time and I know his involvement in Zen meant a lot to him. Many of us fellow practitioners remember him with happiness and miss him and his presence amongst us with sadness.

Notes

1. Clark. David H. 1995. Descent into Conflict. A Doctors' War. The Book Guild. Lewes.

2. Clark. David H. 1992. Transcendence in my life. New Chan Forum 4. Spring issue. www.westernchanfellowship.org

WE REMEMBER SALLY MASHEDER

When Sally told me about her medical diagnosis we were together at the International Mindfulness Meeting in Bristol. I was shocked but also struck by the extraordinarily calm way in which Sally was responding to this dreadful news. Strangely, we had just listened to Jean-Marc Mantel's talk about moment-to-moment awareness and, in her own way, this was to be Sally's profound response to her illness. I have been deeply moved and touched by her manner of dying, deeply marked by Chan understanding all the way to the end.

Sally gave much of herself to helping Buddhist practitioners on their way, not only by becoming a valued group leader in Bristol but perhaps most importantly through her work in stabilising the NBO and bringing it through to an effectively organised and functional institution. All British Buddhist practitioners are deeply in debt to her for her wise, diplomatic and thoughtful management. Sally was professionally a well-loved doctor in a difficult area of Bristol. Her broad-based medical practice included much attention to the social and personal problems of her patients and included special thought concerning the more unfortunate people of that tough district, including the often-abused street women of the city.

Yet, it was her more personal understanding of Chan that became so notable in her last months. Sally was always a generous, thoughtful person, devoted to her work and willing to give advice and help and she had found herself suddenly confronted with a dire illness. From the beginning, she clearly realised the pain that her possible death would cause others and used her understanding of Chan to empower great courage in facing it. She was able to use her faith in the Dharma to support her own spirit of calm endurance and at the same time respond to the needs of others grieving around her.

For example, on one occasion, she was talking with Hughie who came to visit her. As she told him about her illness, Hughie felt overwhelmed by the sadness of so early a death. As he was about to weep, Sally leaned forward and said "But Hughie – you must know that life is perfect".

Such a remark in such a circumstance is only possible from a spontaneous practitioner for whom immediate sensitive compassion is as important as wisdom. One cannot help but be reminded of the Buddha's own compassionate understanding as Ananda grieved his potential going; "Ananda, have you not learned that all compounded things must pass away?"

Sally maintained her inner peace in spite of the difficulties of her treatment and finally decided to go her way rather than endure further chemotherapy. She took this decision with calm understanding and was quite annoyed at the slowness of her gradual passing that followed. She was anxious to get "on the train" and be on her way. Somehow, this was a response quite typical of her resolute and practical personality.

The manner of her passing is inspirational for us, for we all have to face our own departure one day. On this occasion, therefore I want to say how grateful I am to Sally for all she has given us – and especially for the wisdom and compassion of her last days. A profound practitioner has gone on her journey. We can all be happy and grateful for the example she has given us.

NCF XLIII

THE SUTRA OF COMPLETE ENLIGHTENMENT

An Introduction

The WCF receives the Dharma through the teachings and lineage transmissions of Chan Master Sheng-yen, our Shifu. We should all be familiar with his major works that help us practice and understand the Dharma. Leaders in particular should all study his books on Silent Illumination and Koan study.[1] His account of Chan history and philosophy with Dan Stevenson[2] provides a broad overview and some of us may wish to go on to his quite advanced presentation of the Sutra of Complete Enlightenment[3]. This is not an easy book so I attempt to provide a summary of it here that can help those who may wish to investigate this important work. This text is an edited transcription of an evening talk at our retreat on Holy Island in 2007.

How do we train to be Bodhisattvas, or at least baby Bodhisattvas? A look at the major book by Shifu called Complete Enlightenment helps clarify what is involved in answering this question. Firstly, I don't think the book has a very good title in English. It sounds a bit inflated. The book is more like 'A complete course in approaching Enlightenment', and that it certainly is.

The story tells us that a group of Bodhisattvas are puzzled by the new Mahayana teachings of the Buddha so they ask him to meet them all in a conference together. So here they are assembling together to ask questions of the Buddha. These are questions we might be asking him ourselves since all of us are potential Bodhisattvas.

We will find they are indeed puzzling questions. The Buddha's replies are by no means completely clear, they need interpretation. This 'sutra' was a major work translated into Chinese from India in 647CE, a very old text. That first translation didn't catch on, and the better known text, which is the translation here, is by an Indian named Buddhapratha in 693CE. The reason it became famous is that it subsequently received a major commentary by the great master Tsung Mi (824 CE) who was one of the leading proponents of the Hua-Yen school of Chinese Buddhism, very close to Zen.

Shifu tells us there has been some doubt as to whether this ever was an Indian sutra at all. Three or four of the major sutras used in Chinese Buddhism are thought to be précis of Indian sutras, recompiled especially for the use of the Chinese. So far as we are concerned that doesn't matter, because the subject matter is absolutely to the point, very direct and on the ball in a rather Chinese fashion. A lot of the mystification that you find in Sanskrit literature has been removed.

There are all sorts of fascinating Bodhisattvas gathered for the meeting. There are the great ones of course, Manjushri, Samanthabadhra, Maitreya and others more 'junior' but with wonderful names such as Bodhisattva-at-Ease-With-Himself and other titles like that. They all have a question to ask. Manjushri is the Bodhisattva of Wisdom, so we might well expect him to set the ball going and indeed, he asks the first question.

There's a lot of etiquette at the meeting. The Buddha is on his throne. Manjushri arises and makes prostrations, then circumambulates the Buddha all the way round three times, makes another bow then asks his question. All of this sounds a bit formal but Shifu points out in his commentary that such a polite approach was Indian manners in those ancient times. Great honour and respect was paid to a teacher. So, from tomorrow I'll expect all of you to question me in this way!

The ritual palaver over, Manjushri asks: "O Honoured One, please explain the Tathagata's practice of the original arising purity of the causal ground."

What a question! So we have to struggle with what his question means before we even contemplate an answer. Actually, it's not so difficult.

'Causal ground'? We must remember that the Buddha's first insight was the Law of Co-dependent Arising. He saw the world, not as a collection of objects, but as a unified process of intimately linked causes and effects. So the 'causal ground' is the totality of what's going on in the universe. And the 'original rising purity' of it means that the causal ground – the universe – is entirely without fault.

How do we relate to this as a practice? Look at it this way. Some of us were out on the island beach just now, looking at the sea, the birds, and the sunset. When one looks at that scene from the point of view of the Law of Co-dependent Arising, what one sees is a world in which everything is interconnected. The setting sun throws beams of light through the Aran mountains that strike the sea and set the waves sparkling. The birds are beginning to move towards their roosts. Nature is settling down for the night. The tide is beginning to rise again, pulled by the moon. And the alternating days and nights are themselves expressing the rotation of our planet. The whole thing is in motion. The whole thing is interdependent, co-dependently arising.

When we hear that rather heavy expression, 'the Law of Co-dependent Arising', what we need to recognize is the way in which we commonly fail to see sea, island, sun as it were all of a piece but rather as unrelated, separate bits. Oh yes, the sun setting, there's the sea doing this and the birds are doing that – they're all kind of distinct entities in our minds. But if you look at the scene from the point of view of the Law of Co-dependent Arising, the whole thing is working together. And the beauty of it is that it is totally pure. Indeed how could it be faulty? But what is purity doing here?

If you think about it, how could the universe not be 'pure'? Words like purity, innocence, clarity – these are words which we apply to human conduct. Nature, the universe, just is. It keeps on going. It has no side. It is 'causal ground'. It is the basis. It is the turning, mysterious, co-dependently linked universe without intention – quite pure in fact. In poetic language, it's quite simply a singleton. We can see the poetry of the unified 'things'. As Roshi Shunryu Suzuki has put it, "Things is!"

It is all one process. So, the question is asking: "Please explain the Tathagata's (Buddha) Dharma practice in relation to the arising purity of the causal ground – the original rising purity." It is always 'arising'.

The dawn comes, the night comes, the birds go to roost, the birds make their nests, the predators take the eggs – all are involved in the arising purity, the continual process.

As human beings, we might not like it when a Great Black-backed Gull goes and steals the eggs of a Curlew, but that's just our prejudice. For the Great Black-backed Gull, it's business as usual! It's the misfortune of the Curlew that it didn't hide its eggs better.

The universe is not sentimental. Human beings are sentimental. Nature is red in tooth and claw, but it is also gentle and kind. Tiger mothers are among the kindest of mothers to their cubs. Things relate together in ways that belong to nature. We do something un-natural in imposing judgements. And therein lies the problem.

So what does the Buddha reply? The Buddha says, "Well, we establish the great Dharani of complete enlightenment."

Dharani is an interesting word. It means something like a mantra, but it's much more than that. It means a whole process of learning, training, a moving along, a 'course' of enlightenment allowing us to relate to the suchness of the universe with wisdom and with release – the Nirvana that drops all. Such freedom is 'from' something – but what? That's the question.

The Buddha continues, "There is a problem. Human beings from beginningless time have suffered from Ignorance, delusion that prevents us seeing clearly."

The tricky bit here is to understand actually what this Ignorance is and why it is such a barrier to relating to the arising purity of the causal ground.

Surprisingly Ignorance arises from one of our greatest benefits, language. When you think about the Great Black-backed Gull or the Crows or the Oyster-catchers along the shoreline here, we can see they relate to the environment directly, immediately. I was watching an Oyster-catcher trying to open a mussel-shell this afternoon. They're very clever birds but they're not thinking about it, they're just doing it: no discussion.

When cats, dogs, goats or sheep do whatever they do, they just do it. They don't think about it, at least not thought in the sense of verbal thought, thought using language. There is a kind of innocent immediacy about the behaviour of animals, in that they are directly there en face de nature, the world around them. By contrast, when we think about doing something it is through a secondary medium. The language of words is really no more than a description of the world around us. We are from the very beginning separated from the natural world by the fact that we don't relate to it directly, we relate to it through a medium: the medium of words, of language. And that distances us from immediate contact with what we're calling the causal ground, this extraordinary causal process we are talking about.

Language is very paradoxical. It enables us to do an enormous number of things – to calculate, for example, using the language of mathematics. We can go to the moon, we can understand the most extraordinary things. We can build up these whole worlds of understanding, which do indeed make contact with that world out there, but it's through a kind of devious mesh of calculation. And it can be mistaken. As we know, no scientific theory is ever 100% proven. Always there are more ideas, more thought, more development: Newton, followed by Einstein, followed by quanta, string theory etc. Our analytical world is continuously moving and will continue to do so. Language is enormously creative. But it can also make enormous mistakes. When linked to desire it can lead us off into fantasies that may cease to relate to the world it purports to describe.

Even when we are describing things in a simple way, we colour them from inside with our preconceptions. Language is not merely a description of something outside; it is a description that is always coloured by something that is arising from within.

For example, think of the words Holy Island. Take away Holy for a start, just consider the word Island. We British people, living on an island, have a strong feeling for words like 'island'. The Hebrides have a great appeal to many people largely because they're islands. Places like the Scilly Islands are a delight, rather more than mainland Cornwall – why? Because they're islands. There's something special for us around the idea of islands, their separateness, their secretiveness, their privacy – all of those things give them a certain attraction. Now, when you add the word 'Holy' to it - wow, then you really start things moving! Holy – what is 'Holy'? You find yourself back with that dear old Celtic saint, who came here all those centuries ago. St Molaise, a tough old Irishman, came over here and sorted Christian things out somewhat, got fed up with it, and went to live in a cave – and here it is just along the shore there.

All of those ideas come up when we hear the word 'island' and even more so when we hear the word 'holy' and each one of us – because we're all separate poets – would actually have a different image, depending on what we may have read about islands and holiness. We each of us have a different poetry about islands.

So, when we say 'I'm going to Holy Island' or 'I'm going to an island' everybody has to negotiate exactly what this means. They may actually have quite different ideas in their heads about islands. Likewise, a description of the world is hardly ever objective. It's always got a subjective component plugged into it and we usually don't notice that. We make assumptions that what I mean when I say an island is what you mean when you say an island. Actually it's usually not so.

Ignorance then is the failure to understand how language works, and how tricky language can be. For example, the first thing to know about words is that words are only labels. Even if you take something as simple as a cup: a cup is a very simple object but the word 'cup' is just a label for it. There is an object and different variously shaped objects might be considered to be cups, or might be considered to be glasses, or even bowls. One person might call a cup a bowl and somebody else might call a bowl a cup, depending on how they approach the object.

These labels are pure conventions, indicating from one person to another what something is to be called. Even monkeys have a primitive possibility of doing that. There are some monkeys in Africa that have a different squawk depending on whether a leopard, an eagle or a lion is approaching. They have an alarm cry specific to particular predators. These are almost, therefore, like words.

When we use words, we impute a 'thingness' to things. For example trees are not 'things' at all but complicated processes. In ordinary conversation a word is a thing. A sounding bowl is a bowl. A wooden fish is a wooden fish. There's no discussion about whether the important part of the bowl is the metal or the space within it. We use these words as if they were things with 'inherent' nature – that is things that are potentially permanent or unchanging.

Now we've just talked about a tree: clearly it hasn't got inherent thingness, rather it is a complex living process photosynthesizing the air. It's endlessly changing, just like the landscape. The tree is growing or dying. The tree is suffering from storms or not. The tree is having a good summer if it's drawing a lot of liquid up etc. The tree is always changing and moving. It hasn't got inherent fixed quality at all. But we commonly use words as if they are things of that kind, as if they refer to some sort of a fixed essence.

Furthermore, we either develop liking or disliking of them. Someone who lives in a desert might think trees are horrible. Somebody who lives in a forest might find a desert horrible. Actually a desert is just a desert and a forest is just a forest; in themselves, completely neutral. And out of our approvals and disapprovals come, of course, attachments and rejections.

If we're talking about people, it begins to get complicated. If I approve of somebody and you don't, it's rather difficult for us to converse about that person. And so, we get into disputes. And from that comes Samsara.

Nothing is stable in language, yet we have these strong tendencies towards like or dislike. One may have had a particularly happy childhood or one may have had a very miserable childhood and that affects the bias, the twist, with which one develops one's attachments and rejections. And all of that is the world of Samsara.

In a sense, it's a dream world. It's a dream world because it's all in what the Buddhists sometimes call the 'secondary'; it's all in language, and language as we've seen is an untrustworthy medium. It's a medium of thought that you always have to question. The Buddhists say it's like flowers in the sky. Of course, there are no flowers in the sky but we invent our samsaric worlds in the way in which a madman might say there are flowers growing in the sky.

This is the meaning of Samsara and the meaning of Ignorance. So, Ignorance is not something simple like making mistakes or making a rude noise at supper. It's absolutely fundamental. It's rooted in language.

How to stop people getting tied up in language and creating their flowers in the sky? How can we stop that? If we can stop that, we wouldn't even need to discuss enlightenment. In fact enlightenment doesn't exist, again, it's just a label. Enlightenment is being natural. But we are divorced from nature by the fact of our falling into the secondary, falling into this world of Samsara, attachments, rejections, hatreds and even worse. Just look at the daily news to see what that's like.

Up stands Samanthabadhra, circulates the Buddha and says: "Hmm, having heard all this, how should we practice? If all experience is illusory, how can we use experience to remedy illusion? How can we do this?"

The Buddha says intriguingly, "You have to use illusion to dispel illusion."

Very interesting reply. You might think he might say something like "Well, you ought to forget everything about Samsara and go straight for Enlightenment." No, it's not as easy as that – because you cannot understand what words like 'enlightenment' mean simply from the side of words.

I bet everyone around this room has a completely different idea as to what the word 'enlightenment' actually means. I'm sure you all have your biases – some of you may even hate the word. Others of you may be so doting on it you're driving yourselves crazy. Who knows? But everyone's going to have a different view of what enlightenment might be.

So how are you going to get out of that entanglement? You can't just say 'Drop it and get enlightened'. You have to use words to help the disentanglement. And the words are precisely where the problem is. Hence, of course, koans using illusion to go beyond illusion.

As you know, koans are metaphorical expressions of insights; but metaphors are tricky. You can never be quite sure which metaphor it is. You have to use illusion to penetrate the illusion. And it leads us straight into the world of paradox, which of course is Zen's speciality.

Up gets the Bodhisattva-of-Universal-Vision. He stands up, approaches the Buddha, does his prostrations, circulates, another prostration, and then he says: "Honoured One, all this is very difficult to grasp at once. Please explain some gradual steps. What are the methods one could use? If one doesn't have an immediate understanding of how to contemplate, one could just get confused. Surely there must be some provisional steps?"

Very sensible question, don't you think?

The Buddha says, "Well, first of all, you have to realize that ignorance is pervasive. To penetrate ignorance, you have to use the illusory language but because so much of the trouble with ignorance and the trouble with Samsara is due to emotional entanglements, the first thing to do is to set up some precepts for yourself that will enable you to cool the mind down a bit."

So the first thing is to adopt some precepts that will stabilize one's world instead of hurtling from one entanglement to another like some addict on crack.

How to use ordinary talk to get out of that? Well, establish some precepts for oneself for a start. And then calm the mind. Samatha.

Bodhisattva Vajragharba gets up and asks another very interesting question. He says: "I hear it said that human beings are Buddhas already. After all, we are of the same nature as the ground of pure being.

We belong to the causal ground you've been talking about. Indeed, we are expressions of the causal ground. So since we are Buddhas already, how can this terrible ignorance arise?"

The Buddha says that Ignorance generates reason after reason until it becomes cyclic. He's talking about the cycle of life and death, whether you're thinking about reincarnation or simply the way in which our ideas keep regenerating themselves day after day. After a few minutes respite, all the nonsense starts going again. That's reincarnation for you. The nonsense is reincarnated every day!

The Buddha says the problem is that it's cyclic. And one has to be able to crack that cycle somewhere or other.

So then, not surprisingly, up gets the great Bodhisattva Maitreya, approaches the Buddha, does his prostrations, circles round makes another prostration and then says: "OK World Honoured One, how can we sever the roots of this karmic existence?"

The Buddha then begins to say some very interesting things. He says pure Bodhi – pure vision, pure mind – is without attachment left or right, up or down. It's neither that things are empty of what they appear to be nor that they are exactly what they appear to be.

To understand what Buddhists mean by emptiness we have to ask – what is something empty of? Well, it's usually empty of what it appears to be. That's the usual meaning. But when you see something and somebody comes along and says it's 'empty' beware the clever-dick Buddhist. A clever-dick Buddhist might come along and you say "I can't drink my coffee yet because it's a bit too hot". He might say "What a stupid fool you are, don't you know its empty!" Infuriating! Don't waste time with him.

Yes, well, it is only empty of what it appears to be – you don't have to call it 'hot' – 'hot' is relative to you. To somebody else it might not be hot. So it's 'empty of the appearance of how things are' yet, given mutual understanding, a word for that appearance works for you both. A label is never exactly what it appears to be and above all it's empty of inherent existence. It's always part of the causal nexus of movement, or conversation, it's never a still permanent object that you can rely upon – ever. Even a cup!

Buddha says don't lean too far forwards to emptiness and don't lean too far back from accepting appearances. Both, as it were, give you a vision of how things are. So what you have to understand is how things are – neither just as they appear nor actual empty 'reality' but rather co-dependent arisings – no less. You have to find your way through to a perception of how things are. Form is emptiness yet emptiness is form.

To do this requires standing back from attachments because, of course, if you're attached to something you always see things from the attachment perspective. One has to find a third place, in which it is neither good nor bad. When you can settle in the place where the problem neither is nor is not, then you find a certain kind of freedom. This is a tricky concept. The third way means 'to be without bias'.

If you take up the third position without bias then you have a chance of seeing the thing in itself, actually how it is, rather than influenced by any of these poetic prejudices, one way or the other.

The mind has to go through Samatha. When the mind has been calmed you can see the thing as it is. You don't have to think "Oh what a beautiful flower arrangement! Isn't it absolutely wonderful?" Somebody over there would say "I could do it a lot better than that." It's just a flower arrangement. It's lovely. Have no bias, just appreciate it – daffodils, willow, roses. Just be there with it.

When the mind is calm, you can just be there with things, or be there with people, or be there in certain circumstances. Some people, of course, are specially trained to practice that. Doctors, medical people, firemen have to practice just being without bias in a situation, no getting excited this way or that way – you need to try to understand the thing in itself, the situation in itself. Good training – also true of military combat.

It's the same for Buddhists in Dharma combat. If we can calm the mind, we can just be present in the situation without the heavy bias that we normally bring with us.

As I've said elsewhere, we replace reaction with reflection. And you cannot reflect if you're charging around with your mind full of tension, worry, anxiety, self-criticism, self-loathing, self-like, self-admiration – any of that going on and of course the mind is warped. You won't be able to see except through distortion. It's like wearing five or six different-coloured glasses one on top of the other, and hoping to see what you're looking at. You can take the lot off – of course, that may not help – you have to wear an appropriate pair of Dharma glasses! Then you might see something.

So don't react. Calm the mind into reflection and then it becomes possible to see a situation without all those biases. You're halfway there if you can do that.

The Bodhisattva At-Ease-In-Majestic-Virtue gets up and trundles round the Buddha respectfully and says,

'Please tell us, then, what is the range of expedient means?' And the Buddha says "Samatha, samapatthi and dhyana."

Samatha we've already discussed. Samapatthi means insight. It's similar to prajna. Or rather, prajna is the method used in samapatthi. Prajna is basically the careful insight into seeing things exactly as they are without bias. Samatha calms the mind, and then direct vision with the mind clear of all the fuss allows insight. Insight is not intellectual or wordy but rather an experience of clear knowing within which all these words at last make sense within their relativity. Silence and illumination emerge in understanding. No need to say anything. That's just it – neither good nor bad.

Mind you, moments of insight can happen out of the blue. But always because, for some reason or other, something has happened to knock the nonsense out of your head so that, for a moment, everything becomes clear. You can have a clear experience seemingly out of nowhere. You might have some good experiences here because on the beach at Holy Island you've managed to let go of all the nonsense. Letting go begins to become an important theme.

Dhyana is the combination of the two practices while remaining in understanding. It is being able to sustain a calm mind and being able to use insight into seeing things directly instead of through all these filters of attachments, likings and dislikings, bias and prejudice.

The Bodhisattva-of Sound-Discernment rises and says "How many approaches are there that we can use?" What is interesting about the Buddha's reply is his saying that there isn't just one way. You can combine them in different ways that suit you in relation to your karma. You might go slowly with one process and quick with another. You might be a sudden practitioner in one way and a slow practitioner with another. And another person may be the reverse.

One of the last questioners gets up, the Bodhisattva-Cleansed-of-All-Karmic-Obstructions circulates the Buddha, does his prostrations and asks the question "What is the main cause of the defilement of our minds, so that it becomes so difficult to work all this out?"

The Buddha replies that the problem is attachment to 'self '. The nub of the problem is that out of our limited understanding in Ignorance of the world we have inferred that this process of being me is a self. And we get attached to that, egotistically. Yet, here is no person called 'John'. There is just sensation, perception, cognition, consciousness and action, continuously going along in a pattern with a history.

That's what John is. There's no John other than that. 'John' is a name.

But I think I'm me! I'm John! I'm really important! This worries me. Am I nobody? So long as I'm attached to my view of John, my need for a safe identity, and don't start looking at it a little more deeply I'm liable to remain in Samsara.

This is quite a tricky matter to get one's mind around. The mind naturally reacts against it. The thought that I don't exist is a pretty horrible thought. The Buddha would say "Hey, no-one said there's nothing there. No-one said that at all. They said that the word 'John' is just a label – what is actually there is a process. Have a look at the process. If you can understand how that process works you'll understand why you have attachments, why you have reactions rather than reflections, why you're a bastard sometimes and an angel the next. If you understand those processes, you'll understand why."

If you want to label it all 'John', fine but it's just a label. It means that one can detach oneself from this obsession with one's individuality, which is a Western obsession. By thinking of one's process one can be more open to these other processes, which also have names. But what's there? It's not that there's nothing there, it's wrong to say naively that Betty is empty – Betty is very far from empty. Betty is there, but it's not 'Betty' that's there, it's a history, a narrative, a story, which is going along through time acquiring novelty, dropping ancient things, having children – that's what's there. It's just called 'Betty'. Useful if you want to ring her up.

The final Bodhisattva we'll mention is the Bodhisattva-of-Universal-Enlightenment, who asks a question that is perhaps very pertinent to us. "Since in the future the Dharma will be thoroughly dumbed-down, how can one be sure that sentient beings will still understand the Dharma?" The Buddha doesn't deny that. He says there will be great need, so seek out good teachers with correct views in which an understanding of the Dharma is free from contrivance and indifference. Basically, teaching should be honest and not cooked-up for self-fame purposes, or money or anything of the sort. Simplicity and love.

The questions that the Bodhisattvas ask are very profound questions and very searching. They are the roots of the Dharma. We in the WCF need to polish up on our Dharma, to understand much better and more clearly what the Buddha says in reply to these shrewd Bodhisattvas. We each have an issue here: how can we relate experience of life to what the Dharma is saying? And how can we actually have experiences described in the Dharma?

In the Dharma, many experiences are described. Many good resolutions to problems are described. They're not very difficult to understand on the page. But many of them are very difficult to grasp as experiences. A fundamental question for all of us as practitioners is how to relate what you might call the theory of the Dharma to actual genuine experiences of what's being written or spoken about. And how can we be sure that some of the experiences we have are actually the experiences described in the Dharma? These issues require a lot of patience. They require a lot of practice. And, to be blunt, a lot of thought.

Thought is something that Zen masters have often considered to be undesirable. Yet, there is a place for thinking and most Zen masters have clearly thought a lot. There is a place for thinking about how the theory of the Dharma and the experience of the Dharma relate. It has to be done both by 'no-thought' in the simplicity of experience, in the simplicity of watching the rising moon without comment, and in the course of a precise, subtle, largely introspective analysis of what the mind is doing. These things need to be brought together and anyone who wants to be a group leader or teach the Dharma has to take that difficult balance on board. It's not an easy balance. It's full of paradox. But it's also full of life, the kind of life that will give us some kind of self-at-ease in this decadent, contemporary world.

Friday, September 24, 2010

Notes

1. Master Sheng-yen, Illuminating Silence (London: Watkins, 2002).

    Master Sheng-yen, The Method of No Method (Boston & London: Shambhala, 2008).

    Master Sheng-yen, Shattering the Great Doubt (Boston & London: Shambhala, 2009).

2. Master Sheng-yen, Dan Stevenson. Hoofprint of the Ox (Oxford: Oxford University Press, 2001).

3. Master Sheng-yen, Complete Enlightenment (New York: Dharma Drum Publications, 1997).

SAYINGS OF JEAN-MARC MANTEL

John Crook & Carol Evans

Carol and I were attending the International Mindfulness Conference in Bristol. One of the speakers was Jean-Marc Mantel, a psychiatrist from the south of France. As soon as he began speaking I was impressed by something other than his mastery of English, he was speaking from somewhere different. I had only experienced this before when in the company of yogins in the Himalayas or with persons illumined by Zen: a child-like quality with extraordinary clarity; a speaking straight out of a direct awareness within the situation. This was no descriptive discussion of method or idea as if somewhere else, the method and idea shone right before us. Few seemed to recognise this and the questioning that followed was not related to it but rather had the usual dualistic, analytical tone of intellectual discussion. I felt that that was not what he was on about. So what was he saying?

Carol and I travelled to Vence near Nice to find out. We had a private meeting with Jean-Marc and he shared much of his view with us. He kindly invited us to join a Sunday meeting in a farmhouse high in the hills. Some thirty people, his 'sangha' one might say, were there. Their session was devoted to interaction and discussion, not meditation. Jean-Marc sought to bring people into direct contact with where they were with detailed, compassionate concern and attention. Some got his vision – most did not. Speaking both French and English we learnt a lot: the sun shone; the mountains breathed; rocks, wood, crags, trees, in a distant haze the far-off sea.

There are two ways of expressing knowledge – the usual one is analytical, splits up a situation into its parts and bits and explores their relationship. The other is holistic, seizing the whole pattern at once while examining the components of that picture. Some call this 'Goetheian science' after the holistic approach of Goethe. The first is interested in multiplicity within the one, the other in the oneness of the multiplicity – as one scholar has put it. In facing the issues of being, Jean-Marc begins with the wholeness of life and its basis in bare awareness. The resemblance to Zen and Dzogschen is unmistakable. Insight has a wider reach than specialists suppose.

At the Bristol meeting, Carol had noted down phrases from Jean-Marc's talk. I have edited these here to reveal the wholeness of the perception that shone throughout his presentation. Whether you will see this as you read depends on how your mind is dealing with knowledge. Let us see what you find out. What was Jean-Marc telling us? Do you get it?

The Sayings

Meditation is not an activity. You don't have to go there. You are already there. The silent background is always there. The witness is always there too - outside the meditation. Meditation is being one with what you are.

Being and your story are different. The silent background has no story. It doesn't move. You become silent awareness when you are present to the absence of thought.

Perceive that at the basis of being there is no thought. Silent awareness needs no such support. This silence does not impede sound. It is not imposed. It arises as happening.

Anxiety and depression are not real. They resemble a movie on the cinema screen. When something appears, do not believe it. It is necessary to welcome it whatever it is – yet while there is welcoming there must be no-one welcoming. Welcoming happens. Our reality is the permanence of mere presence in which the pure meaning of acceptance is oneness undivided.

Refusing something creates suffering. When there is no refusing, there is no suffering, no split. Stopping your refusing you do not find you are anything in particular - for it is a route to silent awareness. When you explore that which is not real, it brings you to reality. Peace, joy happiness all come from the silent background.

No need for beautiful experiences; just welcome the moment and be without a programme.

Your essence is not the thinking mind; you are not in its jail. As pure subject, you have no location. When you discover where happiness is not, you are happiness.

Tension in the body reflects tension in the mind – listen to it and it will dissolve. Stay with the tension. Do not seek to escape it – then it can leave you. You remain as simply being.

We are more like the projector in the cinema than the movie. The movie looks very real like the games- playing of a magician. Words and images are only pointers. The light from the projector does not need a movie. At essence, we are the light not the movie.

When you stop saying 'me', the ego is powerless and a response arises naturally from the silence. Such silence is love: being totally present to the present is love.

There arises a situation. An answer is needed but it is not a problem. No judgement is needed but a full awareness of the context of the situation. Full understanding without self-judgement yields release and action from silence.

Have a direct perception of the situation in its proper context. Forget the memories. The past is only an edited thought of the past. The emotion it produces is memories not the situation. Past is past. The picture on the wall is empty

Living moment to moment leaves no past. Stay with the present feeling of tension, contraction. Look into it directly. Narratives bring only temporary comfort. We are not our story. Acceptance is welcoming through being open to the now, not resignation. When sadness has gone there is no need to produce joy. It emerges when 'you' are not.

Suicide should be the ending of the 'I', not of the body – then there is peace.

A well-structured person is able to say 'Yes' completely, 'No' completely or 'I don't know!' completely. This is health. The root silence yields Joy, Compassion, Love. They are the silence.

Therapy is like learning to breathe when we have forgotten how. Expand into inhalation, exhale until there is nothing left – a space arises. Here we have the pattern of birth and death. The silence between the breaths is a gateway to the spaciousness and silence of the mind. Accept your non-acceptance for only then will it leave you.

NCF XLIV

EDITOR'S INTRODUCTION BY THE LATE JOHN CROOK: THE LONG WALK

The articles that fell together haphazardly here and came together in a natural composition seem to emphasise complexity; the irredeemable complexity of the human mind, the self, our world and the Universe. We struggle towards some kind of clarity through the dense fog of history, our contradictory ideas, our worried philosophising and our refusal to accept the simplicity of this moment. We like to achieve, to gain celebrity of any kind, to be clever and please ourselves by what we are doing. Our western minds seek explanation, certainty and respect through self-importances of which we are rarely aware. Reluctantly, we admit our blank stupidities, blaming others, the times, politicians, and our parents. Why are we too often such sad, conflicted, over-complicated persons?

These articles take us along many paths and struggle in various ways with these themes. Our two retreat reports reveal two very different situations. We can learn from both of them. It is so difficult for us not to be one-sided, stuck on one bank of a duality. Accepting the unacceptable often seems impossible yet that was the message of the Buddha and the Sutras. Yes – the world and we ourselves are complex yet, when we turn down our overactive left hemispherical concerns, we find a Universe immediately before us in the landscapes we see, the faces we know, the eggs boiling in the saucepan so brilliantly. Yet, thought returns to puzzle us and indeed is often necessary.

The place so difficult to reach is the third place – knowing that both sides, intellectual enquiry and spacious direct awareness, make up the whole, we need to pause there seeing both as one – not only the multiplicity in the simplicity but also the simplicity in the complex patterning of our lives: Just Now – no other time. The birds in the spring time trees sing at sunrise.

THOUGHTS ON JAPAN

The world was deeply shocked by the terrible catastrophe in Japan. We send our condolences to all who have lost loved ones and are still suffering there at this time. When I think of a 30 foot wave striking the Somerset coast, I see the land lost to the sea all the way from Weston super Mare to the Dorset hills, lapping up the valleys below Winterhead Hill and leaving Glastonbury Tor as a lonely island surrounded by total devastation. It is almost unimaginable but that is what the Japanese are facing. The nuclear disaster is a lesson for us all. The demonstration of human blindness in placing reactors in such dangerous places arises from the extraordinary carelessness with which humanity has approached nature for over a century. Let us learn from nature not ignore it. The planet has spoken in a decisive way that we ignore at our peril. We should all consider this and express our dismay at and resistance to our carelessness.

Om mane padme hum

DAVID FONTANA – A MEMOIR

I must have met David Fontana at a psychological conference where several of us decided to form a small discussion group to have a look at the then growing interest in Meditation and Zen. We worked closely together to set up an international conference on "Psychology: East and West" in Cardiff and David and I edited and contributed to the book that followed "Space in Mind" (Element Press, 1990). It was a joy to work with David and we had many attitudes and questions, if not answers that had much in common.

David always saw the best in people. Indeed, he was sometimes accused of being flattering but I don't think so. He always spoke from the heart and optimistically about others. Of course, this made him a joy to be with on a whole range of occasions.

We went together to two conferences on 'Consciousness' in Athens organised by the Brahmakumaris and both spoke there. Afterwards, we went on extended expeditions through fascinating regions of Greece. We flew in mid-winter, buffeted by alarming winds in a small aircraft, to the volcanic island of Santorini. There were no tourists and we had the wonderful island almost to ourselves. Another time, we drove a hired car around the Peloponnesus including a complete circulation of the extraordinary and remote Mani peninsular dining simply in remote tavernas closed for the winter but opened for us with that characteristic friendliness to foreigners that Greeks often show, especially perhaps because, having married a Greek with a mother from the Mani, my Greek was up to the job. This led us into the many fascinating encounters that can happen best outside the tourist season. We strolled around the old centre of Athens musing on ancient times and pretending to chat with Socrates.

During these journeys, David was working on the difficult Zen koan "Why did Bodhidharma come from the West?" He was having a hard time and evening after evening we returned to our puzzlement. In Delphi, appropriately, I tried to persuade him that he might do better if he answered, "Who am I?" first, but he persisted. He never found Zen easy being essentially a thinker and a writer – at which he excelled in his many well-prepared books.

We also enjoyed many further weekend meetings of our little discussion group at my retreat house in mid Wales talking and walking in the hills. At this time, David had much in common with the rest of our group – an enquiring mind open to all the strange phenomena and experiences that religious and non- religious spirituality can provide. Together we investigated several sources of healing experiences. As time went on, David moved more into a direct investigation of the occult, which intrigued him greatly. He found a factory in Cardiff where poltergeists threw things about and went there in the night to examine what had been reported to him. He told me of the experiences that persuaded him there was indeed something happening. Yet, David was wary of letting others in on this investigation. It was if he suspected a subjective component that the presence of others would subvert. He refused to allow Sue Blackmore, a well-known sceptical thinker but a good psychologist, to accompany him saying that if she were there nothing would happen. Although I expressed an interest, I never got the invitation!

This led on to further investigations of which I heard little until the publication of his valued book "Is there an Afterlife? A comprehensive overview of the evidence" (O Books. 2005). It is indeed probably the best review of this subject available. Here he explores the afterlife both through personal enquiry and through an extensive search through the literature. The accounts are fascinating and his own participation intriguing but he is honest in saying at the last that, although he was personally convinced, he realised that others may not be so persuaded. As usual in such an enquiry, the evidence does not quite make the grade, extraordinary though it is and brilliantly reported.

David turned to Christianity and died in the faith. He was cremated following a simple service in the Cardiff parish church that he attended regularly in the last years of his life. I mourn the loss of a dear friend on life's strange journey and a stimulating, deeply thoughtful companion.

NCF XLV

INSPIRING WORDS FROM THE TEACHER

No guru, no church, no dependency.
Beyond the farmyard the wind in the trees.
The fool by the signless signpost
Stands pointing out the way.

Here on the mountain where the path stops
You go on into the snow alone.
Hell's gate is open and Heaven shimmers in the mirage.
The Great Sky is totally devoid of cloud.

POEM

Only as nobody can I make the start
walking the street, merely the street's images

Only as nobody can I respond
to the face suddenly before me

Only as nobody am I free
from the chains that forge me

Only as nobody can I reach the bottom
of the sea without ropes

Only as nobody do I die happy.

Only as nobody can I truly live
with you – and you – and you.

POEM

The man in the park
stabbing bits of paper
with a pointed stick
on behalf of the UDC
has the freedom
to let
his mind
go.

Envying him
I would like to spend my day among waste papers.
Watching him
my own bilge
swirls away.
he doesn't know
somebody is grateful

TAPPING ON STONES ABOVE PYLLAU CLAIS

Tapping on a fence post with a hillside stone –
suddenly she came
invisible presence
sunbeam through cloud.

Look about you now
maybe you'll catch a glimpse
flitting behind grey rocks
or among the grouse chuckling in the heather.

Never far away about she roams.
Listen and she'll come to you

Turn suddenly
catch her silhouette upon the crest.

Sleeping in the heather
she caresses your cheek with flying mist.
The old Welsh certainly knew her name,
no one hereabouts can say it anymore.

Tap tap, stone on wood,
accidentally discovering the secret sign,
knocking on the door of the old king's cave.
Wordless presences, manifestations

SUMMER

Soft summer sounds and sparrow chirp
murmuration of a voice and fleeting cloud,
unfathomed blue, space upon distant space,
so moves the afternoon apace.

Insistent tapping, harsh metallic sound
reverberates, the world's at work,
siesta past, the silence cleaved
the birches are yet barely leaved.

Let silence be the way and no digression
stir the mind from higher sleeps –
contemplate upon the bracken slope
whether it's death, whether it's hope.

The silent room interweaves
creative light with solitude of sky
immeasurable, not understood at all

I sit and beat upon a wall.

But is it hope or desolation's end
that waits when passage past is done?
The wake astern my craft is streaked with sodden straws.
Do I weep or laugh?

LIGHTENMENT

Pausing at the front door
turning back into the garden
for another look
in the gaze of the moon.

December twilight
cloudless
beyond silhouetted twigs
grandly she rises.

Black light empowers
the onset of frost
fading sunlight filtering
a line of dark oaks.

The Old lady climbs above bleak hills
presence of place
clear lights
meeting on limestone nights.

December 2002

ON PURSUING THAT WHICH LEAVES NO TRACKS

From the beginning
there is nothing to be sought. Already within
is the complete solution.

There is no sense in travelling.
No sense in seeking to get
from a learned teacher
the wisdom you already possess.

No sense in austerity
mindlessly sitting
sifting and searching
for another's insights.

No sense in adopting ceremonies,
rituals, oblations,
doing good just to feel good
trying to reach a destination hidden in the heart.

No sense in walking
to reach a goal that isn't there.
No sense in thinking
to solve a problem that doesn't exist in thought.

All you have to do
This minute is to stop –
turn the mind upon itself.

Draw your sense within
Turn yourself inside out:

Gazing into the lake of awareness
Let what is there emerge from its lair.

Let what is there
invade your breathing.
Let what is there
pulsate in your heart.

Let what is there
warm your loins, spin in your skull.
What is this anguish of seeking in the future
that which is already lying in the palms of your hands?

Right now – you have it. Hold it close.
Look directly behind your own face.
Grasping the monster firm let him be
or he'll ride you out again along the paths of time.

And let it all go!
Fall!
Gone gone altogether gone!
See within the Universe ringing in your ears.

Time and space
are simply the ring
through which the Tiger
jumps.

1975

TEISHOS

TEISHO 1: Snowfall

Snow is falling. The white flakes drift down from the sky. Coming from the north the gentle blizzard reaches the southern hills. As the snow arrives so comes the great silence. The track is filling up, no one can come, and no one can go. Stillness lies in the reflection of the cloud brightened snow, white around the bird table. The Bullfinch is stealing the whitened buds, the tits are pecking at the nuts and the Nuthatch takes the seed to a branch and hammers it. Although it is cold, the feeling is warm. Now, as the silence and stillness descend, the Chan house is isolated. Its true nature appears.

What might Dogen say of this?

Once upon a time a famous biologist and his Zen practitioner companion were travelling in the high mountains of Dolpo in Nepal searching for Snow Leopards. For the biologist it was an ecological project; for the practitioner the Snow Leopard was an enlightenment quest in remote places. Their mutual understanding was rather slight! The winter was fast approaching and they were on their way south under falling snows.

In a remote valley they found a tiny deserted village, all inhabitants gone south over the passes for the winter. Yet, there was smoke drifting from the chimney of a small Gompa. Intrigued, they knocked upon the door. An old monk, one legged and dressed in yak cloth, woollen robes, creaked it open. He was quite alone. Knowing the villagers had all moved south, they asked him.

"Why are you staying here?"

"Oh," he said "Can't you see – a one legged man cannot cross passes in snow."

"But how can you survive the winter here, alone, deep in snow and frozen in?" they asked.

"Well," he said, "I have everything"

The biologist understood him to mean he had logs and dung for heating, and supplies for simple food and drink. The practitioner understood him to mean something quite else. What was that? Perhaps only another practitioner can understand.

When the track is blocked for vehicles at Winterhead in winter, which is a rare occurrence, there can be no coming and going except by horse or on foot. With a damaged back, there can be no movement.

What does it mean to stay in minor uncertainties? Perhaps the Calor tank will soon be empty? Maybe the electricity will fail? Are there enough supplies in the freezer? Do I have everything?

Do we have 'everything' when uncertainty strikes? What is that?

The snowflakes drift softly on the Buddha room windows. The incense burns and the candle flames wander to and fro on the silent images. The sitter sits. The gentleness of the lone home floats the air. Everything is here, nothing missing. The sitter lets self-dissolve in stillness. What is to be found?

Do you know the fruits of silence? Do you know the blessing of the snow?

5 January 2010

TEISHO 2: A Little Problem Concerning Tails

Master Wuzu, he who got stuck in an inn talking too much with three monk companions so that the lights went out on them, left us several outstanding koans. One of them reads:

"It is like a Buffalo passing through a window. Head, horns and all four legs have all passed through. Why does the tail not follow?"

What a curious story! To begin with, what on earth is a buffalo doing trying to get through a window? The whole project is decidedly bizarre. Maybe it was really a door or a gate. The 'window' shows the Buffalo was really after something. Then again, if the buffalo got its bulging bits like horn, head and legs together with the bulky body through, why not the thin small tail? What is Master Wuzu on about?

Of course, this is a koan, so we are expecting something paradoxical. The issue is how to resolve the paradox, to understand it, to use it on the path to enlightenment. Here we will have a go at exploration. Koans can be used in more than one way. The primary way is through direct meditative engagement, looking and seeing, not thinking. Yet a number of masters, especially the great Dogen, also used koans as a basis for exploring the Dharma through thinking; a form of thinking that bounces around intuitive interpretations in the search for an insight that can later lead to experiential comprehension. This is an attempt at an 'understanding' beyond both knowledge and experience- a mature knowing. So enjoy this exploration but, when you tackle the koan yourself, you must travel your own way.

How many times have you been in a situation where all has been going well until at the last moment the whole endeavour is blocked? Think of trying to pass a driving test. You have managed everything yet parking by reversing is beyond you and the examiner refuses to qualify you. Maddening! Or again, you are working on a scientific problem or a mathematical investigation. You have done splendidly but some final insight, some conclusive experiment, refuses to bring the task to a satisfactory completion. Yet, in such cases as these, you can expect to reach a solution through practical means or by logical thinking, maybe going back through the whole project carefully checking all stages, all enquiries.

Then again, in meditation, all of us practitioners have the problem of repeatedly calming the mind only to lose it yet again as ramshackle thoughts, discriminations and prejudices well up from nowhere. We know we have to reset the mind and try again. Indeed, for us with often complex karmic conditioning, this is the quite usual process. It may take a lot of practice before a beginner tastes silence or bliss for first time.

Yet, this koan is not a logical matter. It is quite ridiculous. Why should the tiny tail prevent the buffalo passing through when the rest of its hulking body has done so? Even so, the koan does not say the tail will not follow –merely that it has not done so yet. This resembles many experiences in meditation. We sit and sit but the hassling mind will not release us from our worries, our preoccupations and our self-concern. Sometimes, especially when we expect too much, each sitting seems to get worse – until suddenly it may give way as a radical shift in attitude occurs. Usually it is difficult to see what has enabled this to happen.

So maybe Master Wuzu is not actually talking about Buffalos at all. He spins a challenge to us. What is the metaphor in this story concerning something that like this "tail' unexpectedly prevents a conclusion? What blocks us from Dharma insight after so much seeming success? So what is the Dharma? At the least, it requires some re-enactment of what the Buddha did.

In studying the Dharma everyone begins with some knowledge of the Buddha's ideas, one seeks to understand them - one thinks. Yet, the understanding of Dharma does not depend only on some clever thinking. Again and again in both past and present, teachers warn us that anything academic or indeed 'rational' won't do it. All such approaches are just a preliminary look at a map. Why? Because descriptions never contact reality directly – they leave us stranded – half in, half out. Language does not touch the 'thing in itself' Traditionally therefore, after following the Buddha's horns, head and legs, we have to turn to the yoga practices of his mind.

The clumsy buffalo, the hopeful practitioner, has been using his sensation, perception and memory of past events to attempt a passage through the Dharma window. Yet, one of the attributes of mind (the 'skandhas') has only been employed in a limited way. 'Awareness' is an essential aspect of all the 'skandhas' yet it is not in itself determined by them. What if we allow awareness to arise without any cognitive or perceptive discrimination? Sensation usually arises impurely as part of the other discriminatory processes and then remains a cunning barrier. The sound or sight is accompanied by name and memory. This body-dependent 'tail' inevitably accompanies the head, legs and horns. What happens if one lets the 'tail' as 'bare awareness' function by itself?

The moment the yogic practitioner lets go of the time-bound activities of thinking with past memories and hopes for the future he/she allows the horns, head and legs to simply pass beyond the barrier and out of sight. The remaining 'tail' then glows in all its unimpeded clarity -no longer bound by time. Bare Awareness, unpolluted by memory, by expectation, by time, glows in the consciousness of the present moment. Maybe this is the 'tail' one needs to uncover.

Yet not quite! You can become aware of the current presence of sensations: hi - here is the sound of distant traffic; hi – here's the sound of a buzzard's cry; but such sounds or sights may just pass by without shifting the mental state, which at once resumes its time-bound contemplations. Holding attention within that awareness does however do the trick. Sustained awareness becomes consciousness of the presence of the present moment as it runs along without thought. Out of this emerges the clarity of freedom from concern. This freedom, this clarity, can take the practitioner all the way to seeing that this simplicity alone is the root of one's nature. Yet, at first the clarity is only a preliminary glimpse. It needs continued direct investigation.

The simple 'tail' of awareness is present throughout the whole activity of the body-mind, yet may also manifest as the mere presence of being in the presence of timeless present. Heads, horns, legs, have all gone on their way. There remains only the shining lucid 'tail' in unique purity. No time, just 'now' – a flowing with situational time. If this awareness -'tail' - is to pass through the window frame of Dharma understanding it needs a total attention beyond cognitive discriminations. The path is inevitably one of letting go - not any kind of acquisition. It is this realisation that practitioners often find so difficult to apply.

Yet, heigh–ho, to walk the Bodhisattva's path even this turns out not to be enough. The "tail' itself must also be dropped lest it too becomes attachment. Between the tailing and the tailed lies the third place. What is that?

Investigate!!

7 January 2010

TEISHO 3: Empty Midnight

From the start of our training we will have been confronted by the classical definition of Chan "A special transmission outside the scriptures, No dependence on words and letters, Direct seeing into the human heart." But if words and reading are not allowed how on earth can one start and indeed continue any practice of Chan as a beginner. Furthermore, any visit to bookshops reveals a mammoth collection of books and articles describing Chan and its methods. So, why is this extraordinary contradiction?

Certainly, anyone trying to study what Buddhism is does need some systematic approach. I have described this as a four point series of stages:

Knowledge – reading something introductory about the key "formulae' of the Buddha, Chan stories.

Experience – actually experiencing difficulty and success in Zazen (Chan meditation) and realising that there are states of mind that differ from the everyday.

Integration – starting to perceive the way knowledge is confirmed by experience and experience is understood through theory.

Understanding – the comprehension of the spiritual meaning of practice and knowledge. Indeed anyone wishing to uncover the nature of Buddhist wisdom and walk the Bodhisattva path needs to develop this fundamental understanding that comes 'gradually' through time and focus.

But, as we have seen, Chan challenges all this. Indeed great masters such as Linchi and Bassui in differing centuries - have maintained that any academic study, theorising, wordy debating are all totally useless and indeed irrelevant to uncovering the essential insight that depends on direct experience. Even time is irrelevant, since the only reality is a present moment. Yet, what is that since 'now' has always just passed by?

When one has spent some time investigating the practicality of zazen one discovers that certain experiences arise within a practice in which the everyday mind of intentionality and search is sustained. One can 'achieve' certain goals by deliberate practice and these changes do occur in a series. Thus the deliberate practice of samatha (calming the mind through breath control, or other yogic methods) or intense and extended focus on a paradoxical question (a hua tou) can bring the mind into a mode of consciousness marked by tranquillity, a feeling of ease in which the everyday awareness of one's self is none the less sustained. I call this mode 'Tranquillity' or 'Self at Ease'. During such experiences further changes in awareness may arise, for example a feeling of love of life or being – a Disinterested Love without desire but very vivid, blissful or touched with gratitude and emptiness.

These experiences disappear when the mind begins to think about them with either positive or negative evaluation and in any case they gradually fade or change into one another for a while. The Japanese refer to these as "makyo" or illusions because they are not at all enlightenment. None the less, they are a sign of effective zazen practice. Sooner or later, the practitioner may perhaps have a quite different sort of experience that throws light on the mysterious "special transmission". The mind changes its state from its own side without either intentionality or egoic will being involved. Suddenly one is present in a quite different realm that is extremely difficult to describe because it is literally beyond words. In this state, the self is 'forgotten', as Shifu puts it. The mind now has a quality of mirroring - as if in a mirror, all experience is simply reflected as it is and without judgement. Yet that mirror is clearly in being as a bare awareness itself, a condition that is a delight without words Yet, immediately the mind attempts to describe it in any way it ceases and 'I' am again the central pivot rather than the mirror. I call this 'Clarity' and it is the gate opening towards enlightenment. Actually, as Linchi and Bassui both remark, anyone who has not had this direct experience cannot understand what one who has had it is talking about; hence the 'special transmission' when a Master acknowledges it in another.

Clarity is then the gate opening a path that goes 'all the way'. It may arise at any time when a mysterious silence falls on the mind, ego is forgotten in the oncoming delight and the mirror appears. There is absolutely nothing the ego - you - can do about it. As Reb Anderson once remarked, "You cannot do it!" It arises from its own side when something is ready. Certainly, meditative practice may facilitate its appearance since it often arises on or after a retreat. Often a slight shock to a one-pointed mind can initiate it and this may occur at any time. There is no possible prediction and no wanting has any effect. Much more rarely and under similar conditions one may suddenly experience a complete absence of ego intention or comment – not just 'forgotten' but, as Shifu remarks, totally 'absent' - and the experience is recognised by an awareness of that absence - afterwards. This experience is "Seeing the Nature", the fundamental basis of mind when all the activities (skandhas) that create karmic concerns based in a self has gone. It is followed, as is Clarity, by profound 'silence' and a wonder that may perhaps explode in joy.

These states cannot be attained by any motivation rooted in self-interest. Since nearly all our daily concerns are based in time-anchored karma (conditioning) the beginner may find the whole thing deeply frustrating and may indeed wish to give up Chan altogether. While this is indeed understandable, it would be a sad mistake. What can the beginner do? The answer is "Have Faith!" But what sort of faith is this. Clearly, it is not of the Christian type depending on the kindness of a deity. This is a Faith in being itself, Life itself, a confidence that one is on a path that may show you your 'true' nature at some time when it, not you, decides. This Faith is similar to the Disinterested Love we have already mentioned. It can then be found by deliberate practice with a letting go of self-judgments in the everyday. It requires an attitude framed by Shifu as 'every day is a good day' or by Shunryu Suzuki as 'Beginner's Mind'. One discovers it through good will in all circumstances (whatever), openness in practice, freshness of spirit, gratitude and kindness to others.

Sometimes a visualisation can help one along to Tranquillity. Visualisation uses mental pictures as models of yogin practice. This is quite a common practice as both Linchi and Bassui again demonstrate. One I have been using lately is the following hua tou:

> Deserted city square, midnight.
>
> Full moon shining
>
> Footsteps!

For me the 'deserted city square' is a mental place where I find myself. It is empty of others, silent, it is midnight. Only I am there. The full moon is my state of zazen - silently illuminating. The Footsteps are startling – even slightly alarming .The question arises "What is this?" or "What is it?" This is where a discipline is vital. I do not allow any answer to arise but continue one pointedly gazing into the state of enquiry itself – the "What is it?" without seeking any answer. This is what Doubt or Great Doubt means in Zen speak. After a while, I usually find a smile appearing on my face. Tranquillity is there. Clearly there is no way "I" can shift Tranquillity into Clarity as an act of ego or will. Yet, this is enough to maintain Faith in the beauty of Being and the validity of practice. Anyway, who knows what may happen next?

Now I am not suggesting that you should use this hua tou as a visualisation in this way. Although of course, you may like to try it. You may however like to seek a simple visualisation that works for you in a similar way. We are all different, so probe your own fantasy and see what elicits a one-pointed fascination that can become a basis for a practice.

If you feel this is helpful – try it.

If not – then proceed with your own most valued method.

1 March 2010

TEISHO 4: Accepting the World

"Accept the unacceptable - only then will it leave you". So said Jean-Marc Mantel, a wise psychiatrist and savant of spirituality, at the Mindfulness conference in Bristol last summer. It was in response to a question regarding the difficulty of accepting the unexpected death of a loved one.

"Accept the unacceptable- only then will it leave you"

What is the unacceptable? When you explore this, you will find it always has to do with Time. Time changes all things, all things change in Time. Nothing remains unchangeable. Whether it is the holiday on a Turkish beach, a happy Christmas with your family or the eventide falling after a walk in the wilderness, "All good things come to an end," as my Dad used to say whenever I was grumbling in a childhood discontent. But so too do the quarrels and strife of relationships, the car crash, the wars and rebellions. Whether good or bad, all things change. As the Buddha said to Ananda who was weeping over his beloved teacher's approaching death: "Do you not yet know, Ananda, that all compounded things must fall apart?" And indeed all things are 'compounded'.

While we find the relief of change from the 'bad' encouraging if not blissful, we are saddened or distraught by the ending of events that have made us happy. This is due to our attachment to things that bring us happiness, reward, status or credential. I, you, me, – we are all the same in our addictions to self-security, reputation or advancement, health and freedom from worry. When things become unacceptable, we may become lost in distress of many kinds. Only acceptance can cure this. So what is appropriate acceptance?

The word "accept" is a tricky one. It can mean a fatalistic giving up in the face of adversity. I accept, I say, with my hands in the air in surrender handing over to the will of adversity. Yet "accept" can also mean a willingness to face the 'facts' and from that basis to do something about it.

But Time? What can one do about that?

We need to understand that Time is nothing other than the flow of events endlessly moving from cause to effect in complex patterns as the Universe unfolds. As the Buddha saw, this is the first law needed for understanding. Every apparent thing is 'empty' of permanence. Furthermore, because every apparent thing is itself endlessly changing there can be no absolute thing. Things are 'empty' of any fixed 'self'. When we look into the functioning of our own minds we find that is as true inwardly as it is outwardly.

In zazen, we sit in Time but as we develop calmness we find that Time changes as we loosen attachment to the apparent events it holds within its grasp. Time becomes stilled in a vast presence within the endless present moment of being. A sort of 'eternity' is felt within which time happens. It runs along and at such moments of present stillness this seeming eternity becomes real in us. Meditators find in such stillness the relief from time-anchored anxiety that they seek. Everything is relative and in seeing the process of mutual relativity between all things there is no thing one need or indeed can attach to. Realisation in experience heals these hurts. "There is no time – so what is memory", as one hua tou asks.

This is why trivial practice needs deeper investigation on intensive retreat. The discovery of a vastness within time is subjective and does not occur either through wanting it or in hurrying. Several days of tranquillity are essential before such Clarity can arise. In my recent book (World Crisis and Buddhist Humanism), I have tried to show how these insights may be applied to the problems besetting us in the current world situation. Clearly in political strife, whether of national, cultural or racial origin, what is needed is negotiation resting in a basis of dispassion – a reliance on reflection on the whole rather than a reactive attachment to a defended half. Acceptance of other's viewpoints as negotiable and understandable is the key. But problems today take us beyond this simple solution.

Few of us have yet realised the true immensity of the triple problem besetting our entire world culture today. Dependent on an economy based in energy from fossil fuels we resist the idea of "Peak Oil" – the awareness that our supply of fossil energy is now running down, we are past the 'peak' of its exploitation and we are running out – much faster than perhaps we think. Our usage of such fuels has blown carbon clouds into the atmosphere generating planetary warming and accompanying climate change that can herald regional disasters.

These in turn will wreck our economic structure depriving us of the resources and finance to tackle the problem, without attention, these three processes will wreck our economies so that resources and money will not be available to bring about a cure. These three processes have already begun and are so frightening that many people and their views expressed in the media fall repeatedly into denial – a refusal to accept the facts and to dream on as if such change was not already underway.

All of us, and Buddhists especially because of our wisdom lineages, need to face up to these potentially impending horrors. When we come to terms with the issue of Time we can begin to see the personal mode of transition we need to follow in growing a new world of less self-addicted cultures, social groups and individuals.

My message to you today is this. Tonight, as you sit, contemplate these realities that face us all. What is your own attitude? Is it adequate? Do you see the Dharma view? How can you face up to these realities and help others to resist their tendencies to a denial that in an eventual collective panic can lead to disaster?

Sit – contemplate – regain your vision. Accept the unacceptable – only then will it leave you. And there is work to be done.

28 April 2010

TEISHO 5: Being Buddha

We all know the last line of the Heart Sutra because we chant it every day on retreat and probably from time to time on weekly meetings. The Sanskrit is Gaté Gaté Paragaté, Parasamgaté Bodhi Svaha usually translated as "Gone, gone, gone beyond, altogether gone, Wisdom All Hail" It is often taken to be a description of the enlightenment experience known as kensho in Japanese or kaiwu in Chinese. But this is not enough.

In a valuable discussion of Great Master Dogen's account of this expression, we find that Roshi Jiyu Kennet, the foundress of Throssel Hole Abbey, gives an interesting and contrasting translation. She renders it "Going, going, going on beyond and always going on beyond, always becoming Buddha, Hail". She decided on this rendering after long discussions with her own teacher Roshi Kohõ Zenji in Japan. Why should she put it this way?

Dogen's viewpoint is fascinating. He bases his view on the idea that we all have inherent within us the same nature as the Buddha. When we explore this viewpoint practically through looking into our minds we find that the initial door to understanding it lies through considering the five aspects of mind known as the 'skandhas'. These are Sensation, Perception, Cognition, Action, Awareness, which, taken together, comprise the functions of mind. We need to discover that basic Awareness alone, still present when all other mental activities are dropped is none other than the root of Buddha nature itself.

The reason is this. The first four 'skandhas' work together to give us our ideas about who we are. They function throughout our lives to build up our karma. Here lie all our problems acquired through time, especially those fearful of threats to self, worries about ones' importance, looks, intelligence, rank, credentials, being liked or not and death as the silencing of it all. Simple awareness, being no more than 'present in the presence of the present' without all these hassling activities, brings insight and clarity. This 'emptiness' of mind is entirely practical and none other than the root nature of what the Buddha uncovered.

But awareness is continuous, it moves with time; mirroring time as it is without judging it. It is never 'gone' but is evermore 'going'. The Buddha mind that lies within us runs along in every moment, every hour, but our understanding of it is obscured by our worried preoccupations with our troubles. Once we can grasp the truth in ourselves through experience, we can manifest as 'Buddha' without any sense of self-importance.

Of course, the reality of life is that we have to become aware of our fears and worries in such a way as to go beyond them. They arise inevitably because we are human but they can be set aside, let go. The Buddha too was human; he experienced the hassles of life, managing monks, interviewing puzzled people, helping Brahmins extend their minds, founding monasteries, trying to inject wisdom into politicians. We have to think of him as an active, concerned person. He knew it all but also transcended it through letting go into the simplicity of presence in the present without avoidance.

If we want to be like the Buddha, this must also be our path. It is not a matter of letting go into some cloud nine of bliss, some endless beatitude or inner peace but rather a vivid engagement with all the troubles of life while knowing how to transcend them. In our everyday practice we need to understand this 'going on'. Sometimes we sit and go as far as we can in our meditation. Sometimes we travel to retreats because training is essential if we hope to 'go far' in the Dharma, sometimes we try to help another who is suffering. We seek to limit our own selfishness and mean tendencies. We examine the Aspirational Prayer with serious intention to practice all of it.

Gradually, we move towards understanding Buddhism not as an 'ism' but as a matured way of being, a participation. It requires endless dedication, confronting difficulties, seeing the triviality and selfishness of so much of our society and ourselves. This is what learning 'to be a Buddha' means.

Investigate!

TEISHO 6: Preceptual Truth

If you were asked "What is the most important idea in Buddhism?" what would you say? I would have to answer 'Preceptual Truth'; so, what is 'Preceptual Truth'? It is an expression that I believe comes from Roshi Jiyu Kennet, the founder and first Abbess of Throssel Hole Abbey. As we know, our Chan Lay precepts are: Not to kill; Not to steal; Not to lie; Not to commit harmful sex; Not to become inebriated. Preceptual Truth means the holding of these precepts in faith, with understanding, and with contemplative investigation so that they form an integral part of one's life practice.

Perhaps some of you may be surprised at this. Maybe you think that Enlightenment should be the most important idea in Buddhism. Certainly, this is the idea that has been most emphasized in Zen since Daisetz Suzuki first came West and played such a major role in bringing Zen to Western attention. Yet, it is not always mentioned that the uncovering of an enlightenment experience, like everything else, is subject to causes and conditions. There is nothing merely technical or automatic about it. No fixed plan can produce it. The causes and conditions need to be right if the selfish ego is to let go of its hold on the mind so that such silent freedom may arise.

The prime causes and conditions in this case involve the understanding of the precepts. Why is this? The answer is simple. Most religious systems have ethical injunctions that resemble the list of Chan precepts. Certainly in Christianity, we have the Ten Commandments. The fact must be that very early in human history it was realised that peoples who endlessly indulged in fighting, killing, stealing, deception, rape and inebriation were doomed to endless uproar – even when raiding tribes could for a time perhaps enjoy the fruits of their conquests. Only stabilised people, with ethics that could control these evils, could find peace and prosperity.

At our personal, individual level too it is easy to see that those of us who indulge in such activities cannot live happy lives, at most we will be incarcerated to save the general public from our misbehaviours, at least we will have an uneasy conscience. It is obvious that anyone with an uneasy conscience will be very unlikely to calm the mind to attain the clarity needed to even consider the possibility of enlightenment.

Living by Preceptual Truth provides the causes and conditions needed if a practitioner is to make progress in the Dharma. In Buddhism, the breaking of a precept is not a sin causing some God to wrathfully subject us to punishment or excommunication. Rather, in Buddhism such behaviour is considered a mistake. Mistakes have consequences but usually these can be corrected by subsequent actions that restore the mind to peace. The precepts are thus not commandments from outside but rather principles a wise person adopts to run his or her own life.

I often regret the negative wording of the Precepts. Indeed, Simon and I have spent some time trying to find positive statements to express the same points. It turns out that precepts have many metaphorical extensions. For example, by abusing a child one may kill its faith in itself and life, by deceiving someone one can set up mistrust of oneself that lasts a long time and may generalise among others, by drinking too much at a party one may cause an accident in which one's best friend dies through one's actions. You can think out many metaphors for these terms yourself.

One approach would be to replace the negative injunctions with positive ones such as the following:

> Always enhance life
>
> Always respect others and their possessions.
>
> Always speak truth
>
> Always share loving kindness and not just sex.
>
> Sustain the balance of the mind.

In these ways, you can contemplate in greater detail what your own ethical principles may be. It is also important to remember that the five precepts are more detailed versions of the basic Great Precepts: Do no evil, Do no harm to others, Always do only good. The precepts also appear as koans. Sometimes, for example, a lie may be compassionate or shooting a murderer may stop him or her killing even more people. In such cases, although some karmic retribution may arise, the fact of compassionate intent will lead to forgiveness.

Preceptual Truth is thus sometimes a real-life hua-tou of serious concern. To move forward in the Dharma, to find peace in meditative practice, there needs to be a firm ethical basis. Without it, there will be unease, anxiety, worry, self-concern; all of which make up an uneasy conscience. After a mistake, to rediscover innocence is crucial. There are many ways. Immaculacy may not always be possible in this difficult life but it can become an aim and a theme for investigation. We all know when we have made a mistake. The first action in practice must be to restore one's self at ease. This is why Preceptual Truth is the first consideration in pursuing the Dharma.

Go to it! This is the first move to make on Taking Refuge.

4 July 2010

TEISHO 7: Deviation

Many of us beginners do not really understand the central theme of the Dharma. This is because most of us come into practice for basically therapeutic reasons, seeking freedom from alienation in life or suffering. In fact, the Buddha supplies us with a total worldview upon which to base a personal understanding of the place of our sentient lives in the Universe. This worldview replaces the need for superstitions interpreting the meaning of life through some external authority such as some God or other. Needless to say, such a view is a challenge to all dogmatists and also to materialist atheists.

What is this worldview? It is based in an intuition that the entire cosmos is one process unified through a common essence or basis. All causation happens within this system, there is no outside or magical power imposing itself from outside. We ourselves are part of this system and both our basic sensations and our knowledge based on inferences from sensation belong within it. Our task therefore is to understand this relationship as clearly as we can and to create ways of being that bring us all ease within it.

The Buddha saw that although the only knowledge we can have of our universal context is through our senses, we get highly confused in understanding this. We fail to realise the nature of 'being'. His fundamental view is called the Law of Co-dependent Arising, which states that every identifiable cause in a sequence and in all conditions is an aspect of a single process. This process is endlessly moving forward in continuous change so that everything one may see, hear or know is essentially impermanent. This means that everything exists only in the NOW. From this comes the importance of discovering how to be 'present within the presence of the present' without confusion.

Our trouble is that we fear the loss of the entity we believe we are, the "me". This fear leads us to grab onto any illusory idea of permanent security we can think up

–indeed the normal basis of religions! We lock on to the past to fix the future, we want security, and we want credentials.

The Buddha went on to discover that by allowing impermanence to simply be, he could go beyond dualities and find a oneness within the universal flow itself. While this does not allow us to escape birth and death literally, it can transcend them in direct participation within the universal mystery as it flows along. This mystery he called the Unborn, from which any interpretation may emerge through mental discrimination. Rather than discrimination, the practice of the Dharma is to return to participation in the Unborn. Why is that of personal significance? Well - because it restores self-at-ease, prevents us locking-on to things, gives us a sense of unity with all things and enables us to help others still under delusion.

Yet, our tendency to cling onto self-concern, self-righteousness and basic pride easily distorts our practice through what are called Deviations. The great Tibetan Shakya Shri, the teacher of Tipun Padma Chogyal (See Yogins of Ladakh. Crook and Low) gives us some details about what a deviation can be and how avoided.

Fundamentally, a deviation is any preference towards attachments to worldly matters on the one hand or clinging to an idea of 'emptiness' on the other. One who may have had an enlightenment experience can nevertheless become attached to the idea of it, a memory, a longing for it and suffer through that clinging. Such a person's understanding is incomplete.

There are many examples of how we deviate from the unity expressed in the Heart Sutra:

"Form is Emptiness. Emptiness is form.

Form is precisely Emptiness, Emptiness is precisely Form"

Emptiness here means an absence of discriminations in a state of openness to all. There are two movements here, from everyday life of diversified form into the freedom of unification and back again. We often get stuck on one side or the other. The task is to find the third way by which the two imply one another. Shakya Shri gives many rather sophisticated examples.

How about us WCF practitioners?

- To maintain a balance that allows us to move freely in and out of the "brambly forest" as Hongzhi beautifully calls it, we have to avoid many of the subtle and unrecognised clingings our western egotistic minds express. Here are few we do not perhaps usually consider in our busy lives:
- To think that discussion helps insight is a deviation.

- To believe one practices Dharma through institutional management is a deviation.
- To participate in argument and believe that is practice is a deviation.
- To think that the fun of group participation helps towards personal insight is a deviation.
- To believe that going to evening groups a few times a month allows one to avoid intensive retreat while advancing on the path is a deviation.
- To confuse Dharma support (chanting, visualisation, yoga, tai-chi) with Dharma practice is deviation.
- To think one can find enlightenment through calming the mind without self-confrontation is a deviation.
- To allow reaction to replace reflection is a deviation.

We all need to consider when and how we slip into deviations. It may seem odd at first that Dharma practice takes one entirely out of social and cultural concerns. Why is this? You must work it out for yourselves. Yet, are deviations totally bad? No - not at all; to discuss, even argue, to administrate, look after accounts, to take a viewpoint, to participate in social issues, may give all us one some insights into ourselves and others, our wants and needs and some sort of ideational comprehension. They may also help us to help others though good administration and considering the Precepts. Yet, these activities cannot move us out of individualism towards that timeless insight that directly contacts the Unborn, the 'essence of mind'. That will emerge 'from its own side' when we are ready, when we have let go. How can we become ready? Watch out for those time-born attachments that comprise all deviations.

Over!

20 July 2010

TEISHO 8: Scattering

I have just returned from the ceremony of scattering the Ashes of Dr Sally Masheder at the cairn above The Maenllwyd. Before the Scattering we held a brief ceremony of chants and prayers chosen in her last days by Sally herself. I gave this short Teisho:

"I have been wondering why Sally should have chosen The Maenllwyd as the location for the scattering of her ashes. Perhaps it was because:

> Stillness and Time merge in the misted valley
>
> Soft light glittering on dew-faced

Sycamores and birch
Uncultivated fields
Beset with bracken groves and sedge
Where sheep wander
And a vixen once fed cubs in a bank
Among rabbits.
Even the brook lacks music
No heavy rain this week
Yet lawn-grass pushes up
And the compost smells like wine.
The summer chill of the Welsh hills
Is warmed by Rayburn heat
In the bright kitchen,
Coffee on the hob,
Chan Hall clappers signalling
"Come for a meditation!"
Already brewing in the softened air.

I am reminded that once when a great Chan master was dying he said to his sobbing monks around him "Why are you making such a fuss. I am going nowhere!" And Geshe Damcho Yonten once told me a beautiful Sadhana that seems relevant here.

There once was a yogin hermit who lived in a cave high up above a small village. He did his practice there and sustained his enlightenment. Once a week, some villagers would come and bring him some food, grateful to him for filling the great hills with his presence.

One day he died but the villagers, seeing how he still sat in such deep repose, left him as he was. Occasionally, they returned with incense to visit him. The years passed, his body shrank and decayed, feeding the flies, gradually the skeleton appeared. Time passed, the bones fell apart lying in the cave entrance. In the end all the passing villager could see was a pile of spreading dust.

Then, one year, a flower appeared, grew and bloomed. A wandering yogin passed by and seeing the flower, stopped, explored the cave and began to sit. Once again, the villagers came once a week bringing supplies.

When Sally's ashes are scattered at the cairn, some of them will fall on the growing grass, which the rabbits will eat. The fox will take some of them and the ashes move up the food chain. The sheep will graze along the brook taking some more and, in course of time, these may end indeed in some of ourselves or in our coats. Some will end in the bodies of mice discovered by the kites that breed now next door in the big oak. Some will fall in the stream and drift down the Marteg Brook to the River Wye and on past towns and villages to the sea and thus to the ocean. So Sally merges with earth, sky and sea passing on her way.

Sally, thinking of The Maenllwyd, came here for her last journey. The Maenllwyd was in her mind. Thus it is that, whenever you come to visit, Sally will be in your mind. She has not gone anywhere. Stillness and Time merge in the softened air."

15 August 2010

TEISHO 9: The Two Ways of Working with Knowledge

The reach of the human mind becomes more extraordinary the more one contemplates it. Some recent studies have compared the two main ways by which we deal with the knowledge that accumulates in our heads during our lifetime. These two ways have not always been recognised or one has been given priority over the other. In the practice of Zen, these two ways are both employed but to rather differing purposes and outcomes. In our practice, we need to understand this to avoid making false judgements and deviation from the "Middle Way".

The two ways of thinks can be described as 'analytical' on the one hand and 'holistic' on the other. What does this mean?

Analytical or discriminative thinking follows the normal structure of language in making distinctions between ideas and words as discrete structures or meanings each one quite distinct and differentiated from others. This is the usual way in which we talk, study, and do much thinking and science. It makes words into discrete 'things' or actions. We become so used to it that it feels quite natural and obvious, seeming to express the form of the natural world and our engagement in it.

Holistic thinking links thoughts and feelings together into patterns within which more discrete ideas are closely associated as aspects of a single 'whole'. This is actually the normal way by which we become aware of circumstances but it is quickly broken up into its precise bits through the immediate and habitual intervention of the analytical mode. Holistic thinking is the way by which we appreciate poetry and feel its power. Take for example these words from Keats' Ode to autumn;

> Season of mists and mellow fruitfulness
> Close bosom-friend of the maturing sun
> Conspiring with him how to load and bless
> With fruit the vines that round the thatch-eves run

We do not experience these words as separate things but rather take the whole picture as one, vividly felt state. Of course, it is then possible for an analyst to examine the grammar or the choice of words but that is not how poetry is read or intended to be received.

The whole issue has been opened up recently by some thoughtful work on the writings of the great German author, play writer and poet Goethe. He was actually deeply involved in scientific investigation but is barely recognised as a scientist because he did not express his discoveries in the analytical way of most scientific thought. Much of his scientific work is actually quite valid when seen in the light of the interconnectedness of the natural world. The distinction has been expressed as looking at 'unity in multiplicity' (holistic) as opposed to 'multiplicity in unity' (analytical).

It so happens that this holistic way of thinking is re-emerging in contemporary sciences. For example, in evolutionary theory it is possible to analyse the links between species living in a wood but also to apperceive the wood as a holistic system – trees taking nutriment from the soil turning it into energy through photosynthesis in leaves, providing humus giving rise to bacteria and algae, plants eaten by insects eaten by birds each within its 'own niche'. Great Tits exploring twigs and ground cover, Blue Tits more focused on twigs, Wood Warblers living in tree tops, Robins low down, while foxes take voles and rabbits . The 'whole' is the wood. Scientists see this as the ecosystem. Both analytical and holistic thinking are used here, some preferring the think one way and some the other. Another example is the co-dependency of flowers and bees. They have evolved in relation to one another.

In our practice of Zen we make distinctions between, on the one hand, the hassling mind beset with detailed fusspotting over items of concern and, on the other, the awareness of total patterns. These latter can include apperceiving the relationship between worries and the total experience of a present moment in which troubles may dissolve. We then allow the worrying distinctions between past and future merge in being 'present within the presence of the present''

When we can see clearly the difference between these two ways of being here, we can understand the differing action of these modes of thought. Understanding this is very helpful when we consider our practice of meditation. Making the distinction in practice is however not so easy. We are so educated in analytical thinking that we attach to 'things' habitually, locking ourselves up in past concerns or future possibilities. To appreciate the presence of the present we need to drop that and fall into the holistic mode. With practice, this becomes a whole mode of being present. As we know this relieves us of much anxiety, calms the mind and opens us up to a perception of reality quite distinguishable from that of our worried attachments.

When we sit, we need to know where we are in our thinking, drop the analytical and see the merging of present experiences in the continuing wholeness of being. When we understand this, we are ready to look into the Middle Way that brings them together and accepts difficulties without denying them. We place them in the wider context of a continuum of passing time. Fixating neither in 'things' nor disappearing into 'emptiness', we come to the Middle Way. This is where Self at Ease begins.

After this bit of thinking, let us now return to our practice.

TEISHO 10: Summer Night

On my way to bed, I turn out the light and notice with surprise another illumination filling the room from my large window. I open it and look outside. A full moon is riding the sky above the pear trees. Its silvery light glistens delicately on the dewy lawn. Late summer yet the air is warm while the moonlight sheds a cooling touch.

I go out onto the lawn. Nothing moves. There is a perfect silence. Not a rustle of a mouse, not an owl call - just a simple, illuminating stillness. There is something mysterious about it: not only because I cannot see beyond the shadows, but something else as if a different dimension had opened itself to the senses.

And indeed it has. The moonlight reflecting dimly the brightness coming from the distant sun takes us into another world. How rarely do we venture there! We hide away indoors as the darkness falls of an evening. Or else we scuttle in from the garage having parked the car in the dark. Moonlight is rare in Britain and full moons only appear once a month. This is special.

Why do we pay so little attention to the Night? In the still nights of a windless full moon, there is a wonder beyond the windows. That's the word – wonder! So often, we flee from the wonders of our world even when they are right there before us - demanding nothing.

Wonder – the world is full of wonder and the night can be an especial case. Let us go out now and tread on the dew-dampened grass under the moon's orb. What is this wonder about? Perhaps it is the mystery of 'half-light'?

Allow the being of the still 'moment-without–thought' to be. That is a half-light too – an opening to a thoughtless moment.

Let's not ignore the night. When it glows in silver wonder, go forth and meet that mystery. It is simple enough. And we should never avoid simplicity, for that is where one can discover a secret of Zen - the half-light of no-reason.

Dogen told us the important discovery in 'Sitting' lies not in thought nor in the rejection of thought but simply in being without thought. Moonlight is sunlight as half-light. Meditation can reveal a mental half-light as one moves from Samatha into Tranquillity and then maybe into Clarity.

Have you discovered that you can also fall into 'without-thought' at any moment? This can be surprisingly revealing. Just stop thinking, sharply surprising the mind with a "PHAT"!

Turn the inner lights out and you will discover the moon beyond the window. Explore the actuality of this. There is an opening here.

21 September 2010

TEISHO 11: The Meanings in the Flower

All of us probably know the story that founded Chan. Even so, let's retell it, briefly.

The Buddha was out walking with a bunch of monks. The monks were arguing about a number of questions such as "Does the Universe have a beginning. Yes or no?", "Does it have an end?", "Do Buddhas live forever?"

The Buddha took no part in the discussion. Noticing this, Ananda said to him "World Honoured one! Have you nothing to say about such important questions?" The Buddha did not reply but instead bent down and picking a flower he held it up before the monks. They were bewildered – all except Mahakasyapa who smiled.

The Buddha must have smiled too for he gave Mahakasyapa the flower saying something like, "Here is the sign of your special transmission without dependence on words or letters and outside the scriptures". And Zen was born.

What is going on here? Why did not the Buddha participate? What was it that Mahakasyapa understood? Well, we were not there and cannot question them, yet reading the subsequent Chan teachings and the Mahayana philosophy upon which they are based gives us some clues.

There are two aspects to this. Mahakasyapa had a vivid experiential insight. It was a psychological event. Something happened. But Mahakasyapa also intuited the Buddha's meaning. His understanding rested upon the Buddha's own talks that had introduced his insights to his first followers. These initial discoveries were the Law of Co-dependent Arising and the Four Noble Truths that followed from the Law. These indeed are the roots of Mahayana thought throughout Asia.

What's the story then? The Buddha saw that there could be no answer to these questions because there was simply no way of finding out what was the case in any of them. It was rather that some monks would have the opinion that "Yes the Universe has a beginning" and others would say "No, it does not - it has always been". Opinions without conclusive evidence goes nowhere except into argument and quarrelling. Such muddles follow from this Yes-No 'dualism', which is a constant cause of trouble in the world. You can think up our own dilemmas. Is there a God? What kind of God? Whose God is right? Is there life after death? What happened before the Big Bang? And so on.

The Buddha knew that such questions arise from seeing the Universe, the World, God or Life and Death as 'things' with their own separate existence from one another. The apparent 'thingness' of nouns in language suggests this. For example, I exist and therefore must be a thing. If my body dies, do I continue? We can't know but often we invent solutions involving further abstractions - such as 'soul' or 'heaven' or the 'Absolute'. These abstractions are merely linguistic .We cannot actually find them, see them or examine them in any empirical sense. They are inferences from dualistic arguments. Since the Buddha understood this, he knew he could not say either yes or no to any such questions? Is there a way through?

The Buddha saw every apparent thing in the universe as co-dependent. Nothing had separate 'inherent' existence by itself. Nor was anything founded on nothing. There always was a context of conditions giving rise to some thing to which we give a name. This is Buddha's view of non-dualism, 'advaita' in Sanskrit. Things certainly exist but not as independent 'things' with their own properties – rather they are representations within a process of interdependence.

Think of your 'self'. You depend on air, water, food. Without these and the organs that acquire them you could not exist. Likewise your idea of your 'self' comes from inferring that something must be the basis of you being here. This is what John, Simon, Jane, Peter is. The idea emerges from our growth as beings from babyhood in a culture that names things and their actions. They are all expressions of a process. No thing in itself exists independently; yet it is there.

So he picks the flower. The flower represents soil, water, seed growth, colour attractive to bees, pollen and the fact that the Buddha happened to see it as response to the monks confused dilemmas. So, hey, here it is. Here is something we call a flower. Here it is in its suchness (tathata) arisen from hosts of determining conditions but not a thing in any way separate in itself as a 'thing' with private powers. It is empty (sunya) of all that.

Mahakasyapa must have heard the Buddha's discourses many times and he saw that the Buddha was presenting them in one momentary symbol. In experiencing that insight he had no need for words. He simply grasped the import of the Buddha's symbol. It answered the monk's questions at the level underlying them. The Buddha's flower was expressing the nature of the universe as a process immediately present to the senses in each moment. Thus it is!

Such an experience can be 'enlightening' providing an instant clarity of how things are. It is the 'being present in the presence of the present'; the flower as the universe – now. Yet time as we usually see it is likewise an illusion. The past no longer is, the future is only in the imagination and you cannot find now because it is always a goner. Yet, here we are – endlessly moving on together with everything else. How wonderful! And so he smiled. The Buddha, seeing his smile told him "Yes - you've got it". Soon it will be your turn to convey this to others.

This story is the first of many koans and hua-tous. "What is the sound of one hand clapping?" - Without dependency, no sound, no clap. "I am not it yet it is all of me" - I am not the universe but I am totally in process with it. "What is this?" - This and only THIS is this now. "Where do these wonders exist?" - Where indeed? What 'where' are we talking about here?

All the great Mahayana philosophers argued from these points. The insight is very simple yet the philosophers go into great subtlety not necessary for the beginning practitioner. The insight comes when the mind has been calmed and the attachment to this 'thing' called me dissolves. In a flowing oneness of co-dependency, the unity of all is apparent without words and for a long time the practitioner can do without them.

Yet, if we stop here some may think. "That's all very well but what's the significance of this wordy account?" The important message to practitioners is that Mahakasyapa saw the meanings in the flower instantaneously. He was not thinking about it. What was this insight?

Such moments occur when the mind drops both ego and the attachments of the ego; the hassling mind worrying about 'things', possessions, credentials, life and death and becomes aware of the oneness of all momentary experience in the flowing presence of the Universe as a whole. There it is – a total intuited presence, a feeling of oneness and wonder. In our Western Chan, we call this clarity or tranquillity, Self at Ease. It is a moment when, as Hongzhi puts it, "Silently and serenely, one forgets all words. Clearly and vividly, it appears before you. When one realises it, time has no limits. When experiencing it, your surroundings come to life."

Here the 'it' remains unstated, mysterious, a word that stands in for an essentially wordless wonder. This is all the practitioner need know and the words of the philosophers merely thresh out the meanings within it. Yet, that is not all. When one turns again to look at the world, one sees the huge amount of distress and suffering all self-related dualistic thought produces. The wonder turns to empathy for those who suffer, this is compassion. And one begins to move towards helping others as best one can. As Shi fu puts it, the ego transforms into wisdom.

If you want to tell others about it all, then you need the skill of appropriate language. The koans are the stories that undo the stories of our illusions. Where does this undoing happen?

10 November 2010

NEW YEAR TEISHO 2011

So Christmas has come and gone – and a white Christmas too. Was it splendid as a White Christmas should be? Well - that depends. If you were quietly at home with the kids, it was probably wonderful – the beauty of the scenery, the fun of the children tobogganing but if you were struggling to fly from Heathrow or Gatwick or stuck on the M5 or M25 – then it was pretty well a cold hell. Whatever it was, we now see the New Year coming – and a HAPPY NEW YEAR TO YOU TOO.

How should we in the WCF approach the New Year? Do we make New Year resolutions? It might be a good idea for we have a lot to learn. We might perhaps ask ourselves what mistakes we may be making.

Oddly enough, perhaps our greatest mistake is our Zen exaggeration of the importance of enlightenment – or rather our failure to properly understand what this requires. Although all branches of the Buddha's Dharma focus on enlightenment only in Zen is such a fuss made about having an "enlightenment experience" defined as a precise psychological event. Furthermore, it is we in the West who engage in this error most clearly. There are historical reasons for this but that no longer excuses us from making this sometimes harmful mistake.

Let us be clear about this. An "enlightenment experience" or kensho in Japanese (Chinese kaiwu) is an event that follows from the practice of a one-pointed mind in which all awareness of the ego-self disappears for a time revealing a state of extraordinary illumination, clarity and joy. The experience is quite unique, rare and marked by the wonderment of self-absence. Such a moment may sometimes occur spontaneously outside practice and outside Zen and that tells us that it is a quite natural if rare occurrence depending like everything else on certain conditions either spontaneously or acquired through practice.

So why is it so significant? The reason is that it is an experiential verification of what is otherwise known only in thought or theory. One WCF practitioner who had had a brief glimpse told me that she now had lost all doubt in a completely clear understanding of Dharma. Even so, this does not mean one is now an 'enlightened being'. Such an accolade can only be applied to those who are not only wise but also deeply compassionate and remarkably active people such as the Dalai Lama, Archbishop Tutu or Mother Teresa to name examples from a range of cultures, religions and races. None of us would, I trust, be foolish enough to think of ourselves as among them. Shi fu sometimes said, "I am not enlightened!" and none of these three names would make such a claim either. It is we who recognise the exceptional spirituality of such persons. They themselves make nothing of it.

All that kensho means is that someone has understood something deeply and personally and thus 'attained' a level of insight more clearly than most. It means no more than that.

Now – pay attention! The teaching is repeatedly made that kensho is impossible to reach by any kind of ego thought, will or intention. The reason is obvious - if the ego is active even unconsciously, no kensho - defined as egoless - can possibly arise. Yet, speaking bluntly, many of us in the WCF, and that may include long term practitioners, seem incapable of realising this and stumble on egotistically and often unconsciously trying to get to a place we are preventing ourselves from reaching. And, in our blindness, we forget that it is within the practice of egoless, compassionate kindness that lies the path to understanding Dharma.

Be careful! Examine yourselves because any one capable of even moderate mind-reading of others easily perceives the expression of such egotistic desire. Shi fu, for example, was noticeably sharp in detecting it and returning such false aspirants to the starting base. It is essential that any Dharma Heir do the same.

But you may well say – surely, an aspiration to achieve such insight is natural. Yes – indeed but it is essential to understand the paradoxical nature of this quest. Only through the dropping of the ego inclination towards self-importance and through the practice of kindness to others can you even step upon this path. Indeed, as the Tibetans tell us, it is precisely through compassion that wisdom arises.

So what should our New Year resolution be? The answer is the renewed attention by all of us to kindness. The practice of 'Metta' is crucial here. It is an everyday practice. Let thoughts of tolerance, kindness, forbearance, and love arise in the place of self-justification and criticism of others. Compared with this any meditational statistic such as the length of one's retreats, which one chooses as a Teacher or which 'school' one follows is of little or even no significance.

It is worth recalling the very first practice recommended by old Bodhidharma. If someone is angry with you contemplate what it is that you have contributed to the other's anger. So often, we react to another's anger or scorn by rejection and self-justification. Don't do that! Reflect on one's own demerits in the situation and find a way through that lacks antagonism. Not easy – but that is the Bodhisattva way. It applies to each one of us. Go to it as the New Year arises.

29 December 2010

NEW YEAR'S DAY TEISHO 2

Kuan Yin says, "Yesterday was 2010. Today is 2011. Have you yet made the transition?"

When silence flows from the loom of illumination vastness appears, right hemisphere regaining authority over the left, a moment of complete understanding arising.

For some the word "God" evokes it; for others the stillness of space simply emerges. With the fading of clouds, the sun shines in clarity, warming the heart, brightening the vision. A paradox may uncover it, sudden laughter shattering the sky.

Available from within, this teaching is never transmitted for it is always there. Yet, listen to the teacher - lest she withdraw to the high hills where only persistent seekers can find her. The paths are rocky and steps in the wilderness only traced by the sharp.

Wooded hills surround the green valley, limestone-filtered water emerging onto sand. The ravens are calling and the young buzzard mews on high. In a far distance, the motorway hums, recalling the distant, human sea.

Single steps take the long walk back to the market place of kindness.

1 January 2011

TEISHO 12: On Taking Refuge

When someone has decided to follow the path of the Buddha it is usual for him or her to make a formal commitment to that path by participating in a simple ceremony known as Taking Refuge. We have recently put together a short liturgical text enabling people to Take Refuge through the Western Chan Fellowship. This Teisho seeks to explain what is involved and to provide a source for the presentation of the ceremony by a leader asked to do so.

Taking Refuge is a serious commitment not to be undertaken lightly. It is not like joining a club; rather it is an affirmation that you intend to follow a life-defining path of great depth that has an ancient history. You should not do this simply because you want to join up with some new friends, rather, you need to understand what you are doing by some appropriate study and preliminary practice that confirms in your heart that this path is right for you. It is fundamentally a life-long commitment although not a restrictive one: to change a path may be to admit a mistake but, in the Buddha's view, it is a choice open to you.

There are, of course, other paths that define life commitments, and it would be appropriate for you to know what they are. Through having a sincere look around, you can come to a reliable decision. Undertaking to live following the principles of the Buddha's teaching is about learning to live a more useful life both for yourself and for others. This in turn helps to create a more positive society through rejecting the patterns of ignorance that often surround us. Taking Refuge defines a spiritual path enabling you to enter a world of increasing wisdom and compassion. It confirms a resolution to study, practice and understand that Path, not as a rejection of other ways that may suit others but as a simple personal choice and preference.

Many of us are unsure about how to live our lives. Some with spiritual inclinations are also confused as to which of the many paths on offer is the one to choose.

Gone are the days when each culture had a clear practice. Today, due to world-wide information technology, we may choose from the whole repertoire of the ethical history of humanity. Two thousand five hundred years ago, the Buddha had an extraordinary insight into the nature of our minds and the practice that investigating it would entail. Essentially, this insight is summarized in his initial teachings given to five friends in the famous Deer Park at Sarnath outside Benares, a place you can still visit today. We know these teachings as the Law of Dependent Co-arising and the Four Noble Truths. On considering these, you will at once recognize the originality and depth of his discovery and its implications for humanity. His teachings developed over many years and spread through India, Sri Lanka, Burma, Thailand, China, Japan and Tibet. There are contrasts between these regional paths but the essential root is the same. Today, all these teachings in their rich variety are available in the West and provide a striking contrast to other paths you may know. When you study these root teachings and are clear about them, you have the basis for deciding whether they indicate the right path for you.

Taking Refuge has three aspects. Firstly, there is the Buddha, meaning the appreciation of a great person and his insight. Secondly, there is the Dharma, which is his teachings in Sutras and commentaries and thirdly the Sangha, the community of monastics and lay people. Taking Refuge is in these Three Jewels in their completeness not in any one of the lineages through which they are expressed. None the less, it will be through a lineage that you enter the path.

In our lineage of Chinese Zen, the path of understanding has both gradual and sudden learning. By gradual study and the practice of meditation with an accomplished teacher, you develop a deep appreciation of the depth of this path. Through meditation and intensive retreat, as well as at other times of less formal reflection, you may gain sudden, intuitive insights into the meaning. Mind and heart are united in a growing depth of realisation. Naturally, you change into someone with increasing wisdom and a growing compassion for all living things. The way forward may surprise you. It is more a matter of letting go to discover the root of being rather than a seeking for some gain.

Taking Refuge requires mutual trust between the person leading the refuge ceremony and the person taking refuge. Whoever presents this ceremony needs to have taken refuge him/herself and should show signs of a degree of wisdom and kindness in their lives. If this is not apparent to you then it may be best to look elsewhere.

Taking Refuge through the Western Chan Fellowship is therefore an entry to the Dharma in its totality and it does not mean you have to remain a member of this particular lineage forever. Your dedication is to the Three Jewels wherever they are properly expressed so that participation in the practices of other Dharma lineages is quite OK. Yet, teachings do vary and you will need to consider them. Most people do choose to follow a lineage of their choice.

The Western Chan Fellowship inherits the two main schools of Chinese Zen as assembled by a great teacher who recently passed away, the Venerable Chan Master Sheng Yen. He entrusted two people to teach in his place in Britain, the first was John Crook, currently the Teacher of the Fellowship, and the second, Simon Child. Both are known as Dharma Heirs, due to the transmission to them of the Master's trust. Yet, it is now you who must decide on their reliability for you.

Our Fellowship has expanded greatly in recent years and now has some nineteen regional groups across the United Kingdom and affiliated Sanghas in Poland, Norway and France. John and Simon are vigorously engaged in transmitting the Dharma through teachings and retreats and in training other leaders of various levels.

We wish you well and welcome to the Dharma!

January 2011

TEISHO 13: On Suffering

Sooner or later we all suffer. The nature of life ensures it, yet without life not one of us would have the extraordinary experience of Being. Life remains wonderful and mysterious in spite of suffering. Yet, to cope with suffering is often far from simple. It may require great spiritual strength. Suffering comes in so many forms, psychological and physical, social or political, through a failure in health or accident, through old age and weakness and finally through the approach of death. All of us, sooner or later, must have one or other form of failure in health. Cancer is a major enemy of us all and has certainly struck a friend, a relative, a loved one, a spouse or child of each of us. As I proceed through my seventies, so many of my relatives and friends have passed on, many of them from cancer. I can assure you, growing old is not so easy and the recurrent losses of dear ones can be very depressing.

Yet suffering comes not only to those who may be ill but also to those who care for them and seek to comfort. How difficult it is sometimes to find the right words to help someone who, perhaps for the first time, suddenly faces a threat of death much sooner than expected. How often at the hospital bedside one finds the right words so difficult to find. Indeed, paradoxically, it is often the sick person who finds the words to comfort a distressed visitor. Then again, how can we be sure whether comforting is what is actually needed. Perhaps that may be quite wrong. All that may be needed is companionship for a while, a sharing of memories, humour, and even macabre humour. One wonderful old ornithologist I knew, heavily drugged to keep him going till he finished his book on bird migration in Africa - a masterpiece, used to greet me, to the laughter of his hospital room mates, with "Hi John - back again to see the old decaying corpse!"

Perhaps often it is not speaking but listening that is the clue. Just sit and listen. As the other talks, maybe confides in the visitor, one can discover what it is right to say, to investigate, and to open up. If one has not learned to listen in one's life, it can become a problem to know when to stay silent with another. Hopefully, practitioners have discovered the importance of this.

Then again there is that especial silence when two of you enter it together and the stillness itself becomes the communication. It is here that one's mutual roots in practice show themselves. At such a moment, the fear for one's 'self' fades away for both of you. There is simply the presence of the present, as maybe so often before in easier circumstances. This being-beyond-self-concern is at such a time the true refuge. Even pain may disappear or become unimportant because there is no one hurting; the vastness of the spacious mind brings a clarity, and both of you can know it. How wonderful this can be to spouses and lovers who, a moment before, were aching with the fear of loss. While such a moment may occur without training, clearly here past practice of mindful awareness and insight into the processes of the self can yield that inner peace so important to recover when it has been lost.

The sick person may have unusual clarity of insight. Indeed the sick and the caring visitor may have an especial intimacy born of a lifetime's practice and openness to compassion. In whatever way these insights may have arisen in a life, there is karma here to generate thankfulness. Even at the end, the mysterious wonder of life shines through in the selfless moment. Sometimes the seeming misfortune can bring that inner understanding one may have longed for years. So let us not immediately believe that suffering is a misfortune. It depends, as usual, on the mind, and so it is something to investigate. Again and again "Investigate!" as the masters have told us. Never stop investigating. Our "Being", when freed from attachment and open to acceptance, continues in wonder.

My love to you all.

John

Chuan deng Jing di.
Teacher, WCF.
30 July 2009

TEISHO 14: The Arriving Birds

This morning, sitting in the Buddha Room at Winterhead, I glanced out of the window. There in the holly tree flitted a small brown bird, a Phylloscopus warbler, arrived from Africa riding on the spring weather coming up from the south. Species of this genus are difficult to identify, all small brownies. There are three of them visiting Britain, the Chiffchaff, the Willow Warbler and the Wood Warbler. Unless one has very good binoculars and precise knowledge, one can tell them apart only by their songs. Since Wood Warblers only frequent the canopy of woodland, this one could only be either Chiffchaff or a Willow Warbler. It was not singing!

This is the first migrant I have seen this spring. It reminded me of the wonders of migration; the way thousands of little birds travel annually to and from Africa crossing deserts and seas to breed in food-rich Europe and then returning for the winter to warmer climes. It is extraordinary how animals adapt to their circumstances and evolve these extraordinary abilities. Yet we, who are so clever, often fail to do so.

The wonders of nature are not always friendly. Some of us live in dangerous places. The Japanese are well adjusted to the frequency of earthquakes but the horror of the recent enormous quake and its resultant, terrifying tsunami took even them by surprise. One wonders however at the seeming stupidity of placing nuclear reactors on the coast in a most vulnerable region. No doubt there were sound economic reasons for doing this some forty years ago. Yet we are beginning to appreciate that we need to take nature and the dangers it often poses far more seriously.

It is not only the positioning of reactors but also the use of atomic radiation itself that needs questioning and indeed our entire relation to nature and our physical environment. The arrogance of our cock-a-hoop understanding of economics in relation to nature has led to this against the cautionary advice of science. We need to engage our often very ignorant politicians vigorously in this matter in this time of ever increasing urgency. What to do? Write to MPs? Join protest movements? Any sound approach will do. Spread the word – urgently.

We love nature; walks in the countryside, sailing the coast or across the Channel, climbing mountains, observing birds, mammals, insects, the excitement of spotting a fox slipping across a meadow – or, these days, even down a street. Yet many of us, including some of our would-be leaders, do not always understand the need to respect it. Nature wields awesome powers before which we need to show some of the respect age-old Shamans used to do before their gods of mountain snows, avalanches, springs and sunshine.

In our practice of Zen, we have two approaches that encourage this re-orientation. The first is the Law of Dependent Co-origination that tells us that all things are parts of a whole ever changing natural process. This insight of the Buddha was amazingly exact as modern science confirms. Then we have our meditative skills allowing us to sit silently in woods or moors appreciating the wonders that glow before us. This above all should show us how we need to respect nature if we are to remain human within a civilisation we can respect. Let us all be ever mindful of these things and consider the appropriate actions we should take.

16 March 2011

TEISHO 15: The Buddha's Face

Some of us keep a Buddha image in the place where we like to meditate. Maybe we also light a candle and incense stick before entering zazen, or do some chanting. Why do we do these things?

Maybe it is simply out of respect for the memory of the Buddha or a habitual gesture of the Sangha to which we belong. Maybe the Buddha represents for us the aspiration that underlies our practice. Yet, we also may contemplate the Buddha image more directly asking "What is that?" Here comes a hua-tou. Indeed - what is that?

Our response is likely to reflect our current state of mind yet even to ask the question is to precipitate us into a deeper appreciation of the image before us. What is it that we have placed there?

Of course, in itself, the image is just a piece of metal or a block of gilded wood subject, like us, to ageing and decay. But, why use the candle and the incense? Is this mere idolatry? Do we merely project our hopes for salvation onto a block of wood imagining it to have some occult power? Do we let superstition into our practice or some memory of Christian procedures of worship?

Someone carved that body, that face. Buddhas have many faces. Mass-produced ones have little to say but a hand-made image may be a work of art carrying within it the residues of an artist's empowerment. Buddha faces may contain many possible forms of 'interiority.' In gazing into the face, one may 'read' a moment of enlightenment, an awareness of the presence of the present or deep Samadhi. Each expression is subtly different, the skill of the artist depicting his or her own understanding. Yet, these are human faces. Given our own experiences we can interpret them and read from them an insight. If you have the chance to visit the Buddha galleries in Le Musée Guimet in Paris, you will be amazed at the depth and beauty the assembled Buddha heads of many cultures depict.

When your zazen reaches a degree of 'Self at Ease', the tranquillity may allow you to see a similar state expressing itself in your Buddha's face sitting there in your private shrine. Whose interiority is that? Your wooden block in itself has no interiority, nor is the artist present. Have you not projected your own 'Self at Ease' onto the image? Have you not empowered it yourself? And now you receive it back through the insight of zazen. This is what Tibetan lamas intend when they chant mantras while writing OM AH HUM on the back of a tangka. Given insight, you are reading the mind of the guru in his empowerment of a picture.

May be this is the secret of a Buddha image? Empowered by an artist, it never the less receives your own empowering state of mind that filters out all negatives, retaining just the clarity of your inner vision. This is your own potential enlightenment you witness there. Out of respect for 'that', you light the incense, let the candle burn. Whenever the opposites have been set aside, the Buddha mind is present. The ancient Buddha faces in their varying expressions depict this well and reflect your own condition.

Sitting with a Buddha is sitting with one's self in clarity. This is a moment for gratitude, giving thanks to the originator, Shakyamuni, who discovered the insight by himself. All of us have this potential. All of us have the face of Buddha that manifests in the interview room in moments of realisation. We need to recall it as often as we can.

1 May 2011

ACKNOWLEDGEMENTS

Thank you to the Western Chan Fellowship who are the publishers of the New Chan Forum. John Crook was the founder teacher of the organisation and all these articles appeared in issues of the magazine dating back to 1993. Their website is http://www.westernchanfellowship.org and all copies of the New Chan Forum are published there.

Thank you to Simon Child, the current teacher of the WCF, for providing much guidance and electronic copies of these articles as well as day-to-day organisational help and encouragement.

Thank you to Jin-Ho Shi for creating the first draft of this document and for being very enthusiastic about bringing these writings to a wider audience. Without her help and enthusiasm this book would still be a distant future.

Thank you to the members of the WCF especially those who helped collate and proof read these articles – Alysun Jones, Clare Dobie, Dan Meron, David Valentine-Hagart, Eddy Street, Fiona Nuttall, Hilary Richards, Jane Spray, Jeremy Woodward, Pat Simmons, Simon Child, Stuart McLeod, Susan Millington.

Thank you to Olivia Sanders for permission to use the photograph she took as the front cover.

More articles and poems by John Hurrell Crook can be found at http://www.johnhurrellcrook.com.

Printed in Great Britain
by Amazon

51689907R00383